THE COUNTER-RENAISSANCE

THE

Counter-Renaissance

BY

HIRAM HAYDN

MOUNT MARY COLLEGE LIBRARY
Milwaukee, Wisconsin 53222
WITHDRAWN

66-1457

GROVE PRESS, INC. / NEW YORK

Copyright © 1950 by Charles Scribner's Sons

First Evergreen Edition 1960

Distributed in Canada by McClelland & Stewart Ltd.,
25 Hollinger Road, Toronto 16

MANUFACTURED IN THE UNITED STATES OF AMERICA

901
H32

In gratitude, this book is dedicated to those scholars who have at one time or another given me the vision of what true scholarship may be:

Howell M. Haydn, my father, who every summer destroyed all course notes of the preceding year lest he be tempted to give his classes "stale lectures"; James Holly Hanford, who first pushed back the horizons of the Renaissance for me; Jefferson Butler Fletcher, who gave unsparingly the distillation of a long lifetime of Renaissance scholarship; Marjorie Hope Nicolson, whose extraordinary creative and analytical insights into the period were of tremendous help; and Oscar James Campbell, who kicked, prodded, pleaded, cajoled, threatened and charmed, with the dexterity of a ring-master and the discrimination of a good psychiatrist.

Special acknowledgment and thanks are due the late Professor Theodore Spencer of Harvard, and Professor Robert B. Heilman of Louisiana State University, in connection with the title of this book. Shortly after the first mention in print of the projected book, each of these men wrote to me, pointing out that he had already used the phrase "the counter-renaissance." Professor Spencer, indeed, in his article "Hamlet and the Nature of Reality," had used it in a sense very like that which I have employed in this book. Professor Heilman, on the other hand, had used the exact term, but not in reference to the intellectual movement to which it refers in this book. Both of them generously waived any objection to my use of THE COUNTER-RENAISSANCE as the title of my book.

My thanks are also due to Patricia Vos and Sony Lipton for very real assistance in the preparation of the manuscript; and especially to Louise Frankenstein, for the more than generous gift of her time and ability in seeing to it that many small mistakes were removed from the text before the manuscript went to press.

H. H.

CONTENTS

INTRODUCTION xi

PROLOGUE *The Enigmatic Elizabethans* 1

1 *Renaissance Humanism*

1. The General Question of the Renaissance 27
2. The Medieval Synthesis and Christian Humanism 30
3. Reason and Faith, and the Christian Humanism of the Renaissance 36
4. The Trend Toward a Natural Religion 42
5. The Trend Toward an Independent Humanistic Ethic 51
6. Summary and Transition 64

2 *The Counter-Renaissance and the Vanity of Learning*

1. The Historical Position and the Significance of the Counter-Renaissance 76
2. The Vanity of Learning 87
3. Fideism and the Reformation 98
4. The Vanity of Learning and Fideism in Elizabethan Literature 105
5. Summary and Transition 116

3 *The Counter-Renaissance and the Repeal of Universal Law*

1. A System of Universal Law 131
2. Universal Law Repealed: Montaigne 139
3. Universal Law Repealed: Agrippa and Machiavelli 145
4. Universal Law Repealed: Bruno 154
5. The Bell Tolls for Universal Law: John Donne 160

4 *The Science of the Counter-Renaissance*

1. Magic and the Secrets of Nature 176
2. Empiricism and the Facts of Nature: the Hand-in-the-Wound School 190
3. The Science of the Particular: Men and Things "As They Are" 223
4. Toward "A True Model of the World": Francis Bacon 251

5 *The Christian-Classical Ideals of Limit: Degree, Finality and Moderation as Value and Reality*

1. Limit as Degree, Inequality and Gradation   293
2. Limit as Finality, Completeness and Finiteness   297
3. Limit as Moderation, Balance and Harmony   308

6 *The Counter-Renaissance and the Denial of Limit: The Romanticists*

1. The Renaissance Neoplatonists and the Denial of Limit   325
2. Elizabethan Romanticism and the Metaphysical Ache   358

7 *The Counter-Renaissance and the Denial of Limit: The Naturalists*

1. Naturalism and Individualism   380
2. Sedition in the Soul   387
3. Homo homini lupus   405
4. The Machiavellian World-View   424

8 *The Counter-Renaissance and the Nature of Nature*

1. World-Views of the Counter-Renaissance   461
2. The Counter-Renaissance and Nature vs. Art   468
3. The Golden Age and the State of Nature   497
4. Pessimism and the "Disappearance" or Senescence of Nature   525

9 *The Courtly Traditions of Love and Honor*

1. The Romanticists and the Naturalists on Love and Honor   555
2. The Systematization of Honor   577
3. Variations on the Theme of Honor in Shakespeare's Plays   598

10 *Shakespeare and the Counter-Renaissance*

1. Hamlet: Honor vs. Stoicism   619
2. Lear: Nature vs. Stoicism   636
3. The Counter-Renaissance and Shakespeare's Tragic Worlds   651

BIBLIOGRAPHY   672

INDEX   689

INTRODUCTION

THE exact limits of the historical period called the Renaissance have never been fixed to general satisfaction. But certainly very few have ever thought of Petrarch as a medieval poet. On the other hand, few have denied that Francis Bacon was a child of the Renaissance. If we take as terminal points the crowning of Petrarch with the laurel at Rome on April 8, 1341, and the death of Bacon on April 9, 1626, we have a stretch of almost exactly two hundred and eighty-five years that covers the transition from the medieval to the modern world.

For that much can be said without fear of effective contradiction: between 1341 and 1626 a world died and a new world was born. Yet to attempt to characterize succinctly the almost three centuries that intervened is a bewildering task. Small wonder that there has been so much disagreement about the meaning of the term Renaissance, so many variant interpretations, and as much confusion about the relation between the Renaissance and the Reformation.

Without attempting to impose an arbitrary and artificial pattern upon the period, however, I have come to believe that there are three large distinct intellectual movements discernible between the mid-fourteenth and the early seventeenth century. The first of these is the *classical renaissance* or the *humanistic revival*. The second I call the *Counter-Renaissance*, since it originated as a protest against the basic principles of the classical renaissance, as well as against those of medieval Scholasticism. (At the same time, the Counter-Renaissance constitutes, of course, a part of the historical period called the Renaissance.) The third movement, led by Galileo and Kepler, is perhaps best termed the *Scientific Reformation*.

Needless to say, these three intellectual trends of the period did not follow one another chronologically in this way. Invading as they did the whole life of Western civilization and culture, they grew slowly and "organically," overlapping and conflicting, each with the others. Yet this is the order in time of their strongest maturities.

The classical renaissance did not constitute a sharp break with the medieval outlook. Translations from classical antiquity were plentiful enough before the mid-fourteenth century, and the heritage of Greece and Rome had had its considerable part to play in the make-up of the predominantly Judæo-Christian civilization of the Middle Ages. Yet, unquestionably, first in Italy and later in France and England, there was a quickening of interest in the fourteenth, fifteenth and sixteenth centuries, that could fairly be called a classical or humanistic revival. And this interest was not merely literary or academic; it entered and animated the life of the time. Scholarly translations and commentaries abounded, but Cicero and Plato and Seneca served as models for life as well as for style and sentiments.

Yet the humanists who led the movement were for the most part sincere Christians; and, like Thomas Aquinas and his peers, they endorsed the wedding of reason and faith, of philosophy or science and religion. Erasmus phrased his proudest boast, "I have brought it about that philosophy has begun to celebrate Christ." But however sincere such a profession may have been, there is evident a new tilting of the scales—in education, in ethical and political theory, in literature and the arts, in natural science, and even in theology. When St. Thomas adopted the philosophy of Aristotle and "baptized" it, reason was made the able handmaid of faith. As the humanistic movement of the Renaissance develops, it becomes increasingly evident that reason is the dominant partner. The trend moves slowly but ultimately toward the rational or natural theology of the seventeenth century—toward Deism.

One other significant shift in emphasis is apparent. These Christian humanists of the classical revival, like the Scholastics before them, held learning in high regard. But whereas the Scholastic curriculum emphasized abstract logic and the teleological science of the Christianized "Aristotle," the later humanistic one was built around a core of humane letters. It was primarily an ethical education, intended to develop virtuous men and rounded citizens, rather than a theological education directed to the contemplation of the wonders of God's creation and the exposition of his universal laws. The ultimate ends of the two systems differed too. The abstract learning of the Scholastics was pointed finally to the intellectual contemplation of God, while the more practical learning of the Renaissance Christian humanists—whatever their protestations to the contrary—found its final good in the exercise of right reason in virtuous action on this earth.

But the very ethical preoccupation of these humanists, under the influence of Socrates and Cato, Cicero and Seneca, precluded their being much concerned with speculation about the nature of the universe and of God's ultimate universal laws for its maintenance and preservation. They accepted for the most part the traditional concepts of a qualitatively measured world, compact with purpose, meaning and rational law—a universe with the rank and destiny of each natural order fixed. They did not challenge the synthetic vision of Thomas Aquinas, however much they felt the need to open windows to clear the intellectual air of the mustiness caused by the pretentious quibbling of degenerate Scholasticism in the fourteenth and fifteenth centuries.

Hence the classical revival does not constitute an open revolt against the medieval view (as has frequently been said) nearly so much as a continuation of the medieval tradition, but with a shift in its major areas of interest. And it was as much in protest against these Christian humanists' preoccupation with the value of humane studies, against their "moralism," as against the abstract studies and intellectualism of the Scholastics, that the Counter-Renaissance developed. Throughout the sixteenth century every aspect of the inherited medieval synthesis and the fundamental principles of Christian humanism is challenged. And no characteristic of this second movement of the Renaissance is stronger than its rejection of the established exaltation of reason—whether in terms of the abstract intellectualism of the Scholastics or the humanists' "right reason" as the normative principle of human life.

The religionists of the Counter-Renaissance (the leaders of the early Reformation) turn with an exclusive enthusiasm to faith, repudiating reason as the "devil's harlot." Its scientists are radical empiricists, pursuing the natural truths they can discover through observation and experiment, and going to the extreme of almost totally neglecting the role of hypothesis in scientific calculation. In like manner, its historical, political and ethical writers largely reject the traditional concepts of "natural law" and innate justice, and give new and almost exclusive value to the evidence of "fact" and pragmatic experience.

What unites these otherwise dissimilar thinkers of the sixteenth century is that they share completely an anti-intellectualistic, anti-moralistic, anti-synthetic, anti-authoritarian bias. The central premise of the great synthesis which Thomas Aquinas bequeathed to the later Christian humanists is summarized in Cicero's statement that "True law is right reason in agreement with nature; it is of universal application, unchanging and eternal." This was the cement which had held together a comprehensive and interlocking world order; and it is only when we understand that Luther and Calvin in theology, Machiavelli in political theory, Montaigne in his ethical and psychological studies, and the new empirical scientists in physics and astronomy and anatomy and medicine were all attacking this one central principle—it is only then that we can see clearly that what I have called the Counter-Renaissance is one great ideological revolution, and not the arbitrary uniting of isolated figures. And it is only then that the Reformation falls into place as a part of an intellectual and cultural reorientation, instead of an isolated phenomenon in the history of religion.

Once the central premise of this whole movement is grasped, we can begin to see closer, more detailed, and now only superficially surprising relationships and parallels within the ranks of the Counter-Renaissance. We begin to understand that Calvin's concept of man's nature and Machiavelli's are identical, except that one omits the theological premise of original sin. We come to understand that when Luther subscribes to power politics, and backs state absolutism, he is not being inconsistent—for he no more believes in human free will and the humanistic concept of a free society than does Machiavelli. It is easier to see how close Luther and Montaigne are in their fight for the freeing of the libido—and that, although their positive programs and their underlying philosophies are infinitely far apart, they are both motivated by their aversion to the tyranny of "reason" and even by a similar disbelief in the validity of its powers.

With its profoundly anti-intellectualistic prejudice, the Counter-Renaissance assumes the vanity of learning, whether Scholastic or humanistic, and exalts the simple and humble. Nothing more clearly demonstrates that it is one movement, infecting alike theology, natural science and the social and political sciences, than the parallel phenomena of the early Reformation's premium on the faith of the lowly and humble, the empirical scientists' concern with the value of the artisans' and practitioners' work, and the emergent democratic principles apparent in the writings of the political and social thinkers of the sixteenth century who scoffed at the established hierarchy of "professions," "vocations" and traditional castes. This tendency is even apparent in the defiant and repetitive assertion of the scientists—in contradiction to medieval attitudes—that there was nothing undignified or unworthy in working with *matter;* indeed, that it was matter that must be grappled with if we were ever to come at the truths of the physical universe.

The truths, not the Truth—for these men were as profoundly relativistic and pragmatic in their way as many of the leaders in intellectual movements of the last century. Machiavelli's "ritorno al segno" might well have been a motto for all of them, in their insistence upon the importance of *first-hand experience.* The individual scientist must have direct contact with the object of his study; the political observer must rely upon that of which he has had personal and immediate experience; the individual soul must make its own peace with God, on the basis of having experienced God. Here are parallels again: the astronomer crediting only what he has seen through his telescope with his own eyes; the religionist relying, in accordance with Luther's conviction, only upon what he has experienced in his own soul; Machiavelli proclaiming his intention to limit his political observations to what he called "verità effetuale"; and Montaigne insisting upon dealing only with "that which I palpably touche." They are utterly alike in their rejection of a middleman of received authoritarian truth—whether a scientific pundit of long standing, the Roman Catholic Church, or a traditionally accepted authority on the nature of the state and the nature of man.

Finally, where the Scholastics and Christian humanists bent all their efforts toward an effectual wedding of reason and faith, reason and nature, theory and fact, the ideal and the actual, the hypothetical and the empirical—these heretics of the Counter-Renaissance wrought mightily to achieve their *separation.* And always their efforts were in the interest of depreciating the speculative intellect and the guidance of right reason. They variously place almost exclusive value in faith, in natural instinct, in "fact," in the empirically actual—in their violent and excessive rebellion against their predecessors' exaltation of intellect and reason as the ultimate normative principles of every department of life.

Obviously, then, the Counter-Renaissance represents a radical anti-intellectual revolution, with roots in various kinds of cultural, technological, psychological and religious primitivism. But, in addition, it takes on the large general significance of an advocacy of simplification and simplicity, and of decentralized, unsynthesized particular experience—whether in the sense of direct personal contact with the object of knowledge, or the concentration upon some one aspect or department of knowledge (rather than the attempt to fit all aspects and departments together into a coherent and consistent synthesis). Practice and fact, not theory; the particular, not the universal; the intuitive or instinctive or pragmatic, not the speculative or abstract or logical.

Eventually, of course, a balance is struck again. The very violence of the Counter-Renaissance insured its demise, from one-sidedness. But the return (and a jubilant one!) to confidence in reason-and-nature did not mean a return to the earlier reconciliation between theology and science. The foundations for a new model of the universe were laid on Reason and Nature in the late sixteenth and the seventeenth centuries. But this Nature was mechanical and mathematical—its Reason that of God, the master mechanic. Universal purpose and comprehensible design (in terms of man) have disappeared altogether with Spinoza's God.

This new world view was effected by the third great movement of the historical period called the Renaissance—one perhaps best described as the Scientific Reformation. For while it owed its methodological debts to Scholastic science, its purpose, conclusions and even universe were markedly different from those of Thomas Aquinas. Its adherents no longer measured qualitatively, but quantitatively. Equally unlike the leaders of the Counter-Renaissance, they distrusted any attempt at "pure" empiricism. From Galileo on, the primary and only strictly reliable means of ascertaining natural truth was through mathematical measurement. Nature had been neutralized.

Moreover, Reason was not only thoroughly relieved of her old subservience to faith (the humanists themselves had done much in this direction); she also resumed her dignified role in science, with the restoration of hypothesis and abstracting intellect to positions of basic importance in the "new science."

In other fields, Reason and Nature and Law are once more supreme, reaching an eventual apotheosis in the eighteenth century. Humanly comprehensible purpose and design, in the old sense, disappeared from this new universe of mechanical laws—yet for Newton's world machine, Divine Reason was the mechanic. Nature and Reason also resumed their all but absolute normative functions in ethical, political and social theory, while a natural theology and a confident epistemology that began with "Cogito ergo sum" further exalted reason.

It is this Scientific Reformation that finally constitutes the starting point for the era of scientific law which stretches from Galileo and Newton to our own century. Yet the importance of the Counter-Renaissance to the intellectual history of Western civilization cannot be exaggerated. Without so powerful an agent to upset the established order of things, it is probable that the more tempered and balanced view of the Scientific Reformation would have been delayed, its full development postponed for perhaps as long as a century. The leaders of the Counter-Renaissance were all too radically one-sided in their outlook to be the founders of a new order. For that matter, their militant antagonism to the concept of comprehensible universal law in itself precluded such a possibility.

Yet they are among the most colorful and challenging thinkers in history, and their story is inextricably interwoven with the story of such modern institutions as Protestantism, capitalism and psychologism. Moreover, when their impact upon our imaginations can still be as great as it is (witness Calvin, Luther, Machiavelli, Montaigne), it is not difficult to guess its effect upon contemporaries and immediate successors. And an understanding of the havoc they wrought in the ranks of orthodoxy is imperative to any real appraisal of those enigmatic and volatile individuals whom we term the Elizabethans.

HIRAM HAYDN

THE COUNTER-RENAISSANCE

PROLOGUE

THE ENIGMATIC ELIZABETHANS

IT is perhaps as foolhardy to generalize about "periods" of literature as about national characteristics. One can always remember some Frenchman who shows no sign of possessing the proverbial Gallic clarity of mind, urbanity and irony; there always comes to mind an Englishman to whom sportsmanship, reticence and the gift of understatement are alien or irrelevant. Similarly, the literary historian has frequently to deal with an occasional writer who goes his own way, refusing with an inconsiderate obstinacy to fit congenially into the intellectual pattern which seems otherwise to summarize his age so easily.

Yet those who are interested in such patterns continue to find sufficient justification in their over-all picture of any period to warrant their generalizations. Successive historians may differ considerably in their evaluations and interpretations of the Augustan Age or the Romantic period; most of them concur in finding constants which run through the work of Pope, Gay and Addison, or that of Wordsworth, Byron, Shelley and Keats. If there is no other common denominator evident, the men in each group were at least contemporaries. It is inevitable that they lived in peace with—or opposed, or tried to escape from—the identical society and the identical intellectual and cultural traditions. And to anyone comfortably at home in English literature, for example, the blindfold test will have no terrors. He will never confuse the flavor of a Southey, say, with that of a Shenstone. Minor poets they are, and there are few memorable lines to guarantee recognition. It might be difficult to say with much conviction: "That is Southey's." It would be relatively easy to say confidently, "That is the work of a Romantic."

The casual student will make the same kind of easy generalizations about the Elizabethans that he will make about any other

period in English literature. He will refer, with assurance, to their
vigor and exuberance. He will point to their lyric felicity and fa-
cility, and—if he is past the elementary stage—will probably quiet
objections by suggesting that the rich and extravagant lyricism of
Marlowe is not incompatible with the exquisite compression of
Jonson's songs, if one considers the differences in temperament
and purpose.

In a similar way, literary historians have shown little hesitancy
over listing the major characteristics of the Elizabethan intellectual
climate. An older generation of scholars was inclined somewhat to
a romanticized picture which emphasized almost exclusively an
emergent national and even imperialistic consciousness and a new
awareness of expanding horizons—astronomical, geographical, religious, economic and political. In line with estimates of the Italian
Renaissance from Burckhardt's down, they stressed the unruly
Renaissance individualism of the Elizabethans. They pointed to the
careers of men like Bacon and Ralegh, and to the sometimes almost
comical swaggering of Marlowe's and Chapman's tragic heroes.
They followed the lead of the German Romantic criticism in seeing
in Shakespeare's Iago, Richard III and Macbeth great outlaw hero-
villains, prototypes for later Byronic and Schilleresque figures. They
reveled in allusions to the Mermaid Tavern, to Marlowe's atheism
and violent death, to Robert Greene's dramatic death-bed repentance, and to Jack Donne's rakish youth. To them the age was almost
solely one of intemperance, passion and sanguine insolence.

Inevitably, as the recent fashionable tendency to debunk the
Renaissance and to exalt the Middle Ages has gained strength,
portraits of the Elizabethans have paled, their excesses have been
minimized, and those of them most amenable to "Christian-humanistic" interpretations have been accorded the most attention—as
most representative of the true spirit of their age. Such a book as
Douglas Bush's *The Renaissance and English Humanism* illustrates
this trend admirably. Why should we make so much fuss about
Kit Marlowe's wild and foolish youth, Mr. Bush asks, and consider
it typical of the period—while we ignore or belittle the sane, sturdy
Christian humanism of scholars and teachers like Ascham, Cheke
and Mulcaster, and of poets like Daniel, Davies and Chapman?

The most immediately obvious answer is that Marlowe is so
much more interesting and his talent so much more impressive. But
there is a more deliberate and comprehensive answer.

The men whom Mr. Bush cites are representative of a constant
and tenacious tradition in the English humane letters of the six-

teenth century—a tradition which had strong roots in the group
of "Oxford reformers" gathered around Erasmus and Sir Thomas
More. Its heritage was twofold, derived on the one hand from
medieval Christianity, on the other from the resurgence of interest
in classical humanistic letters and thought that marked the Renaissance.

Moreover, the dominant characteristics of this Christian-humanistic tradition are as sane and as sturdily optimistic as Mr. Bush
finds them. Christian faith and classical reason strike an impressive
balance: the devout hope for the consummation of personal immortality in a dogmatically explored heaven is matched by an
insistence upon the rational and moderate conduct of one's life
upon this earth. The cardinal virtues of classical antiquity are invoked, along with the proverbial Christian ones: the injunction to
hope and charity is no more urgently presented than the pursuit
of justice, wisdom, temperance and fortitude advocated by Plato
and Cicero. Platonic and Stoic doctrines are given Christian baptism, and serve to supplement Aristotelian logic (similarly introduced by Albert Magnus and Thomas Aquinas in the thirteenth
century) in serving as rational apologetics for the Christian concept of an intricately ordered universe ruled by God's law.

When one considers how eloquently and consistently this balanced program is set forth in the "conduct" books of this period,
from Sir Thomas Elyot's *The Boke Named the Governour* to Sir
John Eliot's *The Monarchie of Man,* how firmly entrenched the
"new curricula" of the public schools and universities, it is not
surprising to find so many articulate advocates of it among the
Elizabethans. Poets like Samuel Daniel, George Chapman, Sir John
Davies, and even Ben Jonson; prose writers like Richard Hooker,
Roger Ascham, Thomas Wright—these and a host of others provide a many-voiced testimony to the vitality of this orthodox and
confident belief in the fundamental goodness and comprehensible
sufficiency of God, God's world, man—and all the workings thereof.
More, they testify clearly to the Renaissance Englishman's participation in the great Western cultural tradition whose cultural
disintegration in our own time has been the cause of lamentation
by such diverse thinkers as Walter Lippmann, Robert Hutchins
and Jacques Maritain.

The details of this established sixteenth-century outlook can be
found, clearly and exhaustively set forth in E. M. Tillyard's *The
Elizabethan World Picture,* among other books. But the chief difficulty with such a simplification of the Elizabethan temper is that it

leaves out so many indispensable elements and individuals—indispensable to a comprehensive historical understanding. Surely it is a little naïve of Mr. Bush and Mr. Tillyard to protest that given such a sound and admirable intellectual heritage, no one in his right mind would have paid any attention to the subversive and cynical mutterings of a Montaigne or a Machiavelli, to the irreverent and ambiguous antics of a Rabelais or an Agrippa, or to the irrational excesses of a Luther or a Calvin. More than a little naïve —when Mr. Bush goes on, in his enthusiasm, to push somewhat out of shape the views of those Elizabethans who were not sensible enough to have fulfilled, three and a half centuries before him, his preconceptions of their attitudes; and finally to excoriate as a foolish boy some one like Marlowe, who cannot be so pushed, even by as able a persuader as Mr. Bush.

The dilemma is an old one. No one who approaches intellectual history (or any other kind) from an established doctrinaire point of view is ever going to give us the full picture. And this new insistence upon whitewashing the Elizabethans (in the interests of twentieth-century Christian humanism) into grave and orderly men and sober artists, most of whose work was essentially didactic and conservative, will not down—except with those who are willing to start with this conclusion *a priori* and resolutely ignore all contradictory evidence.

This is not to say that the older, romantic view of the Elizabethans is any less doctrinaire—at least, in its origin—or any more exclusively tenable. For a long time we had needed a balance to those estimates of the period. But now we need a balance again, for the new generalized verdict leaves the picture of men like Marlowe and Marston, Bacon and Donne, Gabriel Harvey and Fulke Greville, Sidney and Ralegh, and even Shakespeare (as Theodore Spencer's *Shakespeare and the Nature of Man* adequately demonstrates) either blurred and fuzzy, or forced into an unnatural and unconvincing clarity of outline. The photographer either has not held the camera steady, or in "prettying up" the subject, has removed all the distinctive character lines and irregularities of nature.

Are there, then, any generalized premises about the Elizabethans that are acceptable to that perhaps legendary animal, the impartial and objective observer? What can be said, with equal validity, about the work of Sidney and Marlowe, or Ralegh and Nashe, or Spenser and Harvey?

Not much—at least on a superficial examination. Not much beyond a certain contradictoriness or inconsistency of mood, tone, opinion, that is apparent in each in turn. The idiom, the peculiar emphasis, will vary considerably, of course, in the case of one given man or another. But the paradox is a constant.

Take Walter Ralegh, for example. If you were to read only his *History of the World*, you would probably come away with the feeling that you had been in contact with a not very original mind (actually he was one of the worst offenders in an age of wholesale and approved plagiarism), but a highly competent and assimilative one, one that synthesized with care and a most impressive eclecticism. When you closed the book, you would continue to hear the grave and sonorous organ music of that traditional English prose style that culminated in Sir Thomas Browne's. The total effect would be one of elegance touched with sadness, of muted affirmation. Ralegh surely believed (you would say) in the conservative and orthodox values of his time, yet with a certain nostalgia— so though he hoped, but without much conviction, that when he opened the door to the next chapter, there might be a wholly unexpected occasion, an enchanting and unlikely vision, awaiting him and eventually the reader.

But Walter Ralegh also wrote a poem called "The Passionate Man's Pilgrimage," one of several of his dealing with after-death. It seems the work of another man. Explicitly Christian in attitude, it yet carries an almost insolent strain of assertiveness, more appropriate to a romantic explorer nearing *terra incognita* than to a devout believer anticipating his arrival and sojourn in God's final domain. There is an almost Marlovian upsurge and cadence (although without Marlowe's excesses) to the tone and some of the imagery.

Or take "The Lie." Can this poem have been written by the grave and elegant figure who made so stately a ceremonial of his progress to the executioner's block, and left so tender and resigned a message to his wife? Yet if one remembers the somber warning that he left his son—to avoid the conjunction of "the wood, the weed, the wag"—one is hardly surprised by the disingenuousness, not to say cynicism, of lines which repudiate the very bases of the Christian-humanistic world view, in giving the lie to all the respectable institutions of orthodox society:

> Say to the court, it glows
> And shines like rotten wood;
> Say to the church, it shows
> What's good, and doth no good.
> If church and court reply,
> Then give them both the lie . . .

Tell men of high condition
That manage the estate,
Their purpose is ambition,
Their practice only hate.
    And if they once reply,
    Then give them all the lie . . .

Tell zeal it wants devotion;
Tell love it is but lust;
Tell time it meets but motion;
Tell flesh it is but dust.
    And wish them not reply,
    For thou must give the lie . . .

Tell faith it's fled the city
Tell how the country erreth;
Tell, manhood shakes off pity
Tell, virtue least preferrèd:
    And if they do reply,
    Spare not to give the lie . . .

If in "The Lie" Ralegh points out bluntly the discrepancy between principles professed and practiced, in his *Cabinet-Council* (a study of statecraft which is deeply indebted to Machiavelli, Bodin and Guicciardini, among others) he is content to limit himself almost exclusively to what is practiced and, without any evident qualms, to advocate a political ethic of pure expediency. There is no indication at all of the acceptance of traditional moral values that one finds in the *History*.

Twentieth-century psychoanalysts would probably find it easier to interpret the inconsistencies of John Marston and Gabriel Harvey. It is not unusual to find a strident, even bawling, reformer taking evident pleasure in the depiction of the very vices which he most condemns. Nor is it necessarily startling to discover, as one does in Harvey's *Marginalia*, side by side with exhortations to live boldly, dangerously, and with ruthless self-interest, passages written in complete dejection, with an almost whining despair and in a spirit of complete self-distrust.

The work of Thomas Nashe is open to an almost equally uncomplicated analysis of apparent contradictions. Yet only superficially so. For he does not present a case of black and white—two dominant and opposed moods. There is the sometimes suspiciously evangelistic note of his "repentance tracts"—as in *Christs Teares over Jerusalem*. There is, on the contrary, the healthy delight in the physical goods of the world that he displays in *The Unfortunate*

Traveller. But there is also the prudent common-sense naturalism and the gift for sharp invective apparent in the public correspondence with Gabriel Harvey.

It is true that Nashe was a competent jobber, who probably often turned out hack work for the sake of expediency. But this is not the case with the majority of his contemporaries whose work has survived. Moreover, this explanation is utterly irrelevant to the writings of the Elizabethan courtiers. Yet this strangely insistent vein of inconsistency runs all through their work too. I have cited the case of Ralegh. There are other equally conspicuous ones—notably that of Sir Philip Sidney.

We are all familiar with the accepted picture of "the presidente of Noblesse and of chivalree"—in Spenser's phrase for him. The cup of water on the battlefield, the dying request for both the Christian and the classical versions of death and after-death, the whole life modeled consciously on Castiglione's picture of the complete gentleman in *The Book of the Courtier*—all these attest to a gentle, disciplined and chivalrous knight, and to an outstanding representative of the Christian-humanistic tradition. And surely, one who reads only books about writers—not what writers wrote—will assert that Sidney's work forms a harmonious parallel to his life: witness *An Apologie for Poetrie, Astrophel and Stella,* the *Arcadia.*

If so, this is the first invalid assumption. To be sure, *Astrophel and Stella* is full of conventional "Platonic" conceits and courtly protestations. But there are also lines like

> True, that on earth we are but pilgrims made,
> And should in soul up to our country move;
> True, and yet true that I must Stella love

and

> No more, my dear, no more these counsels try;
> Oh, give my passions leave to run their race;
> Let fortune lay on me her worst disgrace

—lines in which, in abrupt and spontaneous defiance of the winged love that abjures the flesh for the spirit, Sidney seems to be heeding literally the famous advice which his "muse" gave to him at the beginning of the sequence:

> Thus, great with child to speak, and helpless in my throes,
> Biting my truant pen, beating myself for spite,
> Fool, said my muse to me, look in thy heart and write.

And when the sequence ends with the famous sonnets "Thou blind man's mark, thou fool's self-chosen snare," and "Leave me, O love

which reachest but to dust," no unbiased reader can miss the fact
that disgust and disappointment far outweigh the strength of conviction in the beatitude of heavenly love. The lesson is primarily
negative.

Nor do Sidney's works display at all consistently the reverence
for reason and moderation that form the hallmark of the Christian-
humanistic temper. In the *Apologie,* the poet is not a sober pur-
veyer of the virtues, Christian or classical, but an inspired child of
light—and heat. Unlike the other arts, sciences and professions,
poetry "hath not the works of nature for her principal object. . . .
Only the poet, disdaining to be tied to any such subjection, lifted
up with the vigor of his own invention, doth grow, in effect, into
another nature; in making things either better than nature bringeth
forth, or quite anew . . . freely ranging within the zodiac of his
own wit."

Far from rendering homage to "the moral philosophers; whom,
methinks, I see coming toward me with a sullen gravity (as though
they could not abide vice by daylight) rudely clothed, for to witness outwardly their contempt of outward things, with books in
their hands against glory, whereto they set their names; sophis-
tically speaking against subtlety, and angry with any man in whom
they see the foul fault of anger"—far from paying them conventional
homage, Sidney's whole attitude toward them in the *Apologie* is
tellingly ironic.

A similar temper is apparent in the *Arcadia,* upon which Mr.
Bush expends considerable energy in the interests of the angels.
Musidorus, who is throughout the early part of the pastoral idyll
the sage exponent of reason, which, "if we will be men . . . is to
have absolute commandement"—as against the rule of love, which
his companion Zelmane (or Pyrocles) follows—Musidorus completely recants:

> I find indeed, that all is but lip-wisdome, which wants ex-
> perience. I now (woe is me) do try what love can doo. O
> Zelmane, who will resist it, must have either no witte, or put
> out his eyes?

Zelmane will not let him forget his earlier lectures, and drives him
on to a final admission:

> Remember that love is a passion; and that a worthie mans
> reason must ever have the masterhood. I recant, I recant
> (cryed Musidorus,) and withall falling down prostrate, O thou
> celestiall, or infernall spirit of Love, or what other heavenly
> or hellish title thou list to have. . . .

The popular misconception is as drastic in terms of Sidney's life as in those of his writings. One has only to read the biography written by his devoted friend and follower, Fulke Greville, to lose forever the traditional picture of the consistently gentle, dispassionate Galahad, and to replace it with that of a ceremonious and upright gentleman, to be sure, but one who was also a semi-Hotspur, hot-headed and hot-hearted—quick to resent and quick to act.

The love of honor, the Elizabethans agreed, was a virtue. But in no sense did it, properly interpreted, conflict with the guidance of reason or with the pursuit of the cardinal virtues. We can find many Elizabethan moral tracts that substantially endorse this attitude. They are full of exhortations similar to that in Guillaume du Vair's popular little book, *The Moral Philosophy of the Stoicks:*

> Let us . . . so moderate our affections, that the luster of Honour dazle not our Reason; and plant our minds with good resolutions for a breast-work against the assaults of Ambition: Let us first satisfie our selves that there is no true honour in the world, but that of Vertue. . . .

And there is plenty of evidence from Sidney's life and writings that this definition would not have satisfied him—that his allegiance to honor was altogether a more absolute one. In the course of the transition from the medieval institution of chivalry to the Renaissance code of the gentleman, a new and elaborate courtly system of ethics developed—one which, like its predecessor, rather involved rules concerning love and honor than the niceties of the relationships among the traditional Christian and classical virtues. Thus, when Hamlet apologizes to Laertes for whatever wrong he has done him, Laertes accepts the apology—but with reservations which express only his concern that he should not unwittingly desert an established code of honor:

> I am satisfied in nature,
> Whose motive in this case should stir me most
> To my revenge. But in my terms of honour
> I stand aloof, and will no reconcilement
> Till by some elder masters of known honour
> I have a voice and precedent of peace
> To keep my name ungor'd.

If there is no evidence that Sidney would go to such a dialectic extreme in his devotion to honor, Greville's biography at least affords several instances where he did place his personal honor above all other considerations. A Christian gentleman, surely. But not an entirely predictable one.

It would be tedious to trace these contradictory tendencies through individual after individual, but it would not be difficult. The moral allegorical niceties of the *Faerie Queene* have occupied the pedantic attention of innumerable lesser "Spenserians": it requires the critical and human stature of a scholar like Sir Herbert Grierson to perceive that for all of Spenser's avowed ethical purposes in composing the cantos, he is never so much the poet, never so passionate and compelling an artist as when—in the Bower of Bliss or Garden of Adonis passages, for example—he is dealing with sensuous and even voluptuous material.

The inconsistencies of Donne's and Bacon's lives and works are familiar to all. It is sufficiently surprising to most that the poet of the flippant early lyrics on the inconstancy of women and of the erotic *Elegies* should have become the revered Dean of Saint Paul's, who thundered damnation at the very Inns of Court where he had squandered his youth. But to limit Donne's story to these contrasting pictures is to distort it sadly by oversimplification. To do justice to his complexity, we must also remember the fantastic story of his elopement and his constant devotion to his wife; his apparent willingness to sell his poetic talents to the highest bidder, and yet his steadfast refusal over many years to take Anglican orders—despite even the king's insistence. We must add to this paradoxical mixture his intellectual virtuosity, his radical skepticism and his passionate desire for certainty, his piety and his sensualism, and his obsession with death. And finally, we must not forget that the same intensity, the same athletic intellectualism, and the same extravagance of imagery and statement mark the sermons as they do the love poems.

By comparison, the story of Francis Bacon seems consistent. Yet if its colors do not clash so blatantly, a close investigation proves that they are far from completely harmonious. No one has ever conclusively reconciled the expedient careerist and the "impresario of the new science." No one has ever reconciled, except facilely and superficially, the discrepancy between the conventional portrait of Bacon as a brilliant but cold and mean man and his passionate dedicated search for truth, together with his almost missionary fervor for presenting it convincingly to others. Only a few have understood the relation between his devotion to pragmatism and such a passage as, "The more discordant therefore and incredible any Divine mystery is, the more honour is shown to God in believing it; and the nobler is the victory of faith"—or have realized that the same man who declared that "those foolish and apish images of worlds which the fancies of men have created in philosophical systems, must be utterly scattered to the winds," and poked scornful fun at "the race of chemists," owed specific debts in his scientific methodology to the alchemists.

Even Shakespeare and Jonson do not escape entirely. The "dark" periods in their work—the apparent cynicism and misanthropy of many of their satires, and even of some of the tragedies—have incited endless speculation and conflicting interpretations. The only consistent strain in the commentaries on these plays has been the attempt to explain away the paradox implicit in their relation to the affirmation of the body of the playwrights' work.

With the lesser Elizabethans, similar paradoxes are equally obvious—if not equally interesting. Even when one turns to those whose writings are most consistent in thought and attitude, the same violent discrepancies are apt to appear. Consider Sir John Davies, who is a favorite of all the Christian-humanistic apologists. *Nosce Teipsum, Orchestra,* and his other poems seem to make him an admirable point in hand—a didactic poet who, if frequently pedestrian, at least is always predictable as representative of the orthodox and traditional values. Yet *Nosce Teipsum,* the most famous of them all, was composed as a penance for one of those exhibitions of ungovernable temper that make Elizabethan literary lore so much more lively than that of most other periods. The same unruly streak is there, however carefully painted over in the official record.

What can explain this extraordinary and epidemic dichotomy which infected the lives and work of these gifted yet dissimilar men? In no other period in any literature with which I am familiar is there such a schizophrenic tendency. Nowhere else will one find such a strange mingling—in the same men, even in single passages—of affirmation and rebellion, idealism and cynicism, aspiration and pessimism, delicacy and grossness, exuberance and despair.

Numerous historians have offered numerous explanations—explanations which have always satisfied themselves, and usually a few others. Some of these explanations have concentrated upon social and economic causes, some upon political and religious; some have dismissed the whole business as merely the popularity of certain established and traditional literary forms.

The latter, have, for example, discounted the excessive violence of Elizabethan tragedy as the result of a strict adherence to the model of Seneca, rendered grotesque by men who portrayed on the stage what was intended to be read aloud or declaimed. They have

found in the love sonnets of Shakespeare, Sidney, Spenser, merely
the facile pursuance of a literary convention; in the ideological
poetry of Donne and Greville nothing more than intellectual gym-
nastics; in the esoteric verses of George Chapman simply a somewhat precious infatuation with neo-platonic mysteries; in the excitement of Gabriel Harvey over the intellectual trade winds of the
time, the specious gossiping of a Walter Winchell.

There is, to be sure, some basis for almost all these points of
view. The "literary convention" theory, as applied by O. J. Campbell to the satires of Shakespeare, Marston and Jonson, is a healthy
antidote to a lot of transcendental nonsense that has been written
on the subject. But if one accepts all, or even most of these "literary
convention" interpretations, then the Elizabethans produced a literature so artificial that in comparison Alexander Pope is the most
naïve and spontaneous of writers.

Similarly, those who find the origin of Elizabethan inconsistency
in the economic and social problems of the individual have considerable historical justification for their claims. Sheer survival was
sufficient motive for many of the specific inconsistencies of the
playwrights, for example—a survival that depended upon keeping
abreast of transitory and ephemeral popular and aristocratic fashions. Marlowe, Greene, Nashe, Kyd and others literally lived by
their wits—in the scramble to meet the demands of the theatre
market. On a smaller scale, their dilemma was that of the men who
try today to make a living on Broadway. Again, on the other hand,
many of their poet-contemporaries relied entirely upon the patron-
age system, and produced for the most part what their sponsors
demanded, or what they hoped possible patrons might like. Shakespeare tried his hand at both of these systems, and there is perhaps
no better indication of his genius than the fact that he was expe-
diently successful and still left to us the magnificent plays and
poetry that he did.

Yet there are too many notable exceptions for this explanation
to be any more exclusively satisfactory than the "literary convention" theory. Francis Bacon and Edmund Spenser, to choose as
dissimilar examples as possible, had non-literary careers which made
it largely unnecessary for them to produce for a "timely" market.
The courtier-poets certainly did not feel the pinch of economic
necessity, and some of them even helped to make it possible for
other literary men to do really congenial work. Ralegh's "School of
Night" is a notable example.

Moreover, a man with the ingenuity of Donne was able to comply outwardly with the requirements of the patron system, and still satisfy his own craving for elaborate intellectual patterns and philosophical and metaphysical intricacies. Surely the parents of the lamented Mistress Elizabeth Drury would have been better pleased with a simple and recognizable eulogy of their daughter than with the extravagances of *An Anatomie of the World*. Surely, if Donne had been concerned only with the winning of further commissions, he would have chosen to write something of this more conventional sort.

Nor do the other specialized explanations of Elizabethan inconsistency cover the subject any better. Its feet, or a shoulder, or a hip, always emerge from the sheet, bare and unsatisfied. Other all-sufficient explanations have been presented—each with some sound evidence, but too many convenient omissions. The rise of capitalism, the schism in religion, the emergence of a strident nationalism, the new concepts of the physical universe and the nature of man—all these certainly played their parts to a greater or lesser extent in contributing to the contradictoriness and uncertainty of particular individuals. Gabriel Harvey has summarized in his characteristic style the extent to which his contemporaries were living in a bewildering and transitional world.

The Gospel taughte, not learned: Charitie Key colde: nothing good, but by Imputation: the Ceremonial Lawe, in worde abrogated: the Judiciall in effecte disannulled: the Morall indeede abandoned. . . . All inquisitive after Newes, newe Bookes, newe Fashions, newe Lawes, newe Officers, and some after newe Elementes, some after newe Heavens, and Helles to . . . as of olde Bookes, so of aunciente Vertue, Honestie, Fidelitie, Equitie, newe Abridgementes: every day, freshe span newe Opinions: Heresie in Divinitee, in Philosophie, in Humanitie, in Manners, grounded much upon hearsay: Doctors contemned: the Text knowen of moste, understood of fewe: magnified of all: practiced of none: the Divell not so hated, as the Pope: many Invectives, small amendment.

It has been customary to discount most of this testimony of Harvey's as a sophomoric excitement over intellectual fashions at the universities. But a careful analysis proves this an accurate catalogue of the most significant heresies of the period. Moreover, the way in which he links together all these "newe" trends emphasizes what we have tended to forget (or never knew): that they are related parts of the transition from the stable but senile world picture of the Middle Ages to the yet inchoate one of the post-Renaissance period.

The story of the Elizabethans is in a peculiar sense similar to our own. They, like us, were born and lived in an age when the old universal faiths were no longer tenable in their traditional forms, and yet before new ones had been fully formulated and established to take their place—before there were adequate symbols to express and compass the new horizons that men were beginning to perceive.

A vast ideological conflict, latent since the thirteenth century, had shaken the continent throughout the sixteenth. Such superficially disparate figures as Machiavelli, Luther, Montaigne, Calvin, Giordano Bruno, Rabelais, Paracelsus, Copernicus, Vesalius and Cornelius Agrippa—all these were leaders and (however unintentionally) collaborators in the greatest intellectual revolution the Western world had ever seen. Scornful as each of them was of many of the others, they were all attacking—and in surprisingly parallel or complementary ways—the great central orthodox fortress of Christian humanism, which had stood, only occasionally challenged, since the twelfth century. If the Renaissance was primarily a classical revival, nevertheless modern scholarship has conclusively shown that it did not constitute so sharp a break with the medieval civilization and synthesis as we used to think. The humanism of the Renaissance (except in fifteenth-century Italy) was basically Christian, not pagan, and it adhered faithfully in the main to that beautifully ordered world predicated by Thomas Aquinas and other Scholastic philosophers, and imaginatively depicted by Dante: a cosmos ruled by the comprehensible laws of God and nature, one in which every unit had its purpose and rank eternally fixed, its limits established.

But if the Renaissance, as described above, was essentially a continuation of the medieval tradition and outlook, then we can only describe the intellectual revolution of the sixteenth century as the Counter-Renaissance. Theology, ethics, politics, economics, natural science, psychology—not one of these interrelated parts of the comprehensive and consistent world-system of the Christian humanists escaped the challenge of one or more of the rebels of the Counter-Renaissance. And the Elizabethans found themselves trapped in a transition period of intellectual conflicts which made a consistent and positive philosophy a luxury. The literature of the age in which Hamlet asked his questions and Lear was reduced to a state of madness and moral confusion matching the political disorder of his realm and the threatening physical disintegration of the universe—such a literature was bound to be at once introspective and passionate, self-probing and self-assertive.

Yet the same age that entertained seriously a theory of the "Decay of Nature" and the imminent dissolution of the world—a theory that gained visible force with the appearance of the Nova of 1572 in the supposedly eternal Crystalline Heavens—the same age held out exciting new horizons before men's eyes, many more than the trans-Atlantic ones. The same age that prompted John Donne to say

'Tis all in peeces, all cohærence gone;
All just supply, and all Relation . . .

produced the sonorous voice of Francis Bacon, with his prophetic "I am now therefore to speak touching Hope," and Doctor Faustus' dream of power. . . .

It is tempting to say that in the paradox of the enigmatic Elizabethans lies the whole contrast between Classical and Romantic tempers, in all their conflicting colors. The only definition of the Classicist that I have found possible to apply with equal validity to Plato and Pope, to Racine and Dante, to Addison and Æschylus, is that the Classicist is a man and artist who finds it possible to accept without misgivings the authority and discipline of a fixed order and rules because he believes in the essential congruence and relatedness of the ideal and the empirically actual—that which should be and that which is. Whether the actual is but an imperfect extension of the ideal, as with Plato; whether it is an ordained and limited part of the creation effected by the ideal (in Christian terminology, God), as in Pope's and Addison's versions of the Great Chain of Being; whether, as in the concept of "immattered form" of Aristotle's mature philosophy, which recognizes the usefulness and relatedness of intellectual concept and empirical observation, it is a question of rooting the ideal in the actual, and motivating the actual by the ideal—in any case, the classicist recognizes the relation as a direct and certain one, and fixes upon that recognition his æsthetic as well as his moral, philosophical or religious creed.

The Romanticist, on the other hand, is that man or artist who, moved by the discrepancy he finds between the ideal and the empirically actual, cannot reconcile the two. As a result, he may, like Keats, yearn more and more nostalgically for an escape to, and a complete immersion in, the world of the ideal—which becomes increasingly, and perhaps even exclusively, real to him. Or, like Byron's heroes, he may actively revolt, and withdraw to a self-imposed exile in haughty isolation. Whether he turn to metaphysics, like Manfred, or to outlaw warfare, like the corsair and Lara—he occupies himself exclusively with the ideal, or fights against the established order in the name of the ideal.

On the other hand, like Shelley, the Romantic may dream of effecting a reconciliation between the two by the ultimate imposition of the ideal upon the empirical actuality in the distant and improbable future—or, in the manner variously employed by Scott, Carlyle and Morris, reach into the ideal past for the same purpose, or for an escape comparable to that envisioned otherwise by Keats. Still again, with Wordsworth, he may find the ideal in simple and primitive nature, and in those closest to her, and dream of once again imposing such an ideal upon the all too unsatisfactory actuality he finds around him.

But whether the particular Romantic's form of rebellion is escape or reform, passive or active, he is always a rebel against the established order and skeptical about the validity of the value of fixed laws. It may be the reality of the particular established ideal which he challenges—as do all agnostic or atheistic Romantics. On the other hand, it may be the reality of the empirical actuality which he challenges, holding to the fallibility of our sensory equipment; this is the stand of most mystical Romantics. Still again, it may be rather the meaning or value of the ideal or actual which he rejects, particularly if he is a "reformer" Romantic. At any rate, he does not accept the established relatedness of the ideal and the actual, and he refuses to abide by rules derived from this central premise, whether æsthetic ones or ones pertaining to the conduct of life.

If this concept of the Romanticist is acceptable, it is only a step to the definition of a Naturalist as a completely disenchanted or disillusioned Romanticist—who holds to the latter's conviction of the fundamental dichotomy of the ideal and the actual, but carries the idea of the split to its extreme logical conclusion: if there is no evidence that the empirical world of actuality is modeled on or by the ideal, then there is no evidence at all that the ideal exists. Hence the Naturalist concentrates exclusively on the empirical world as the only actuality. He cannot accept any of the Classicist's concepts of law and order and motivation, since they originated in a act of faith which he cannot share. Morally and politically, the Naturalist is consistently a pragmatist; æsthetically an empiricist, who, if he follows any models, must follow those he observes in life itself—whether in terms of nature, man or society.

Finally—to risk one more generalization—in accordance with the temper of an age, literature tends, ideologically and æsthetically, in one of two directions. In an optimistic period, one dominated by a single world-view, literature is apt to embody this largely consistent orthodoxy in a Classicist defense or exposition of the status quo—a justification of the ways of God or nature or society as they are—and hence to identify the way things should be with the way they are. The literature of such an age is usually content to employ accepted æsthetic forms, and to work within established and measured artistic disciplines.

Conversely, in an age of intellectual unrest and discovery, there is likely to be a corresponding Romanticist and Naturalist literature, emphasizing the wide gap between the ideal and the actual—until a new and satisfying relation between the two is established. Just as such a period is full of new speculation, new scientific or political or economic or religious thought, so its literature is apt to be experimental, impatient of the restraint of old forms, and inventive.

The Counter-Renaissance, coming as it did between two highly confident and secure world-views (the Scholastic and Christian-humanistic, and the Newtonian Age of Reason), is such a transition period; and its literature reveals the characteristics which one would expect. As for the Renaissance in general, it must be immediately apparent that the Christian humanists whom recent historians have so extolled are genuine Classicists. The line of Christian humanism which extends from Thomas Aquinas and his peers to John Milton is not a straight and undeviating one, by any means. There are shifts in emphasis and variations in direction. But as one reviews the dogma and practice of the major Scholastics, of Florentine Platonists like Marsilio Ficino and his group, of north European humanists like Budé and Erasmus and Justus Lipsius, of such moderate reformers as Philip Melanchthon, the Oxford group and their Anglican and Elizabethan successors, notably Richard Hooker—the basic similarities outweigh the discrepancies.

And those similarities find their origin and guiding star in the optimistic and essentially Classicist faith in the comprehensible relation between the ideal and the actual. The Christian-humanistic tradition, in whatever hands, has represented a belief in both the reality and the value of the ideals of reason, purpose, law, order, limit. This belief predicates a conviction of guidance and meaning in the very nature of the universe, and also a conviction of the relevance of that guidance and that meaning to the living of human life on earth.

Among the Elizabethans, then, it is not surprising to find that those who are least shaken by that turmoil which marks the dispositions of their contemporaries, are those who are most recognizably and truly Classicist in temper. Ben Jonson, for example, has long and justly been considered the most genuine Classicist of the period—primarily because of his considerable classical learning and his careful allegiance to Greek and Roman models in all the literary forms in which he wrote. Yet Jonson is equally a Classicist in the sense in which we have just been using the term.

His love of balance, moderation, limit, order (so beautifully rendered, for example, in the lines

> In small proportions we just beauties see;
> And in short measures, life may perfect be

and

> But all so clear, and led by reason's flame,
> As but to stumble in her sight were shame)

are an unmistakable sign of the Classicist—and are rooted in his faith in the conservative and traditional values of the humanistic tradition. When one examines the "philosophy" explicit or implicit in his plays, criticism, and verse, one finds him as devoted to the concepts of limit and balance in the conduct of life as in the craftsmanship of art. He assumes the absolute reality of the ideal, and its legitimate motivation of the empirical actuality, as confidently in terms of living as in those of writing.

Many of the Elizabethans accorded like credence or disbelief to magic, astrology and the occult, on the one hand, and to the incipient empirical science of contemporary pioneers, on the other. We are therefore unjust to Jonson if we find him sometimes incredibly blind to the significance of the great intellectual revolution already stirring around him. We lack the proper historical perspective to see our own fallacy when we approve the sturdy common sense that led him to satirize unmercifully the alchemists, astrologers and occult quacks of his time, yet berate him for being equally scornful of the astronomers who were deserting the Ptolemaic-Aristotelian explanation of the physical universe. It is we who are inconsistent, not he. The formlessness of a world in gestation held no temperamental appeal and no intellectual conviction for him. In philosophy, as in art, he rejected the confusion and uncertainty of the new in favor of the order and certainty of the old.

Perhaps the other greatest exemplar of the Classicist temper among the Elizabethans was Richard Hooker. His *Of the Laws of Ecclesiastical Polity* is a more compact if a less comprehensive *Summa Theologica*. It is an Anglican apology, to be sure, but one which extends far beyond its immediate and official capacity (it was "ordered" by Archbishop Whitgift to silence Cartwright and the Puritans) to express for his whole time the Christian-humanistic world-view. And—to reverse the order in which we approached Jonson—we discover that Hooker's prose style is as truly Classicist as his thought, as rich in conservative values, as lucid and ordered and economical, and as balanced in architectonics.

These two, major Elizabethan Classicists, are of their generations the least affected by the malaise of their time. They are, as More, Elyot and Cheke variously were before them, representative of the traditionalist sixteenth-century point of view. If the classical element far outweighs the Christian in Jonson, the balance is almost perfect in Hooker.

On the other hand, as might be expected, the leaders of the Counter-Renaissance on the continent, and those Elizabethans most affected by them, are Romanticists and Naturalists. Martin Luther's exclusive reliance on faith for man's salvation, and John Calvin's insistence upon God's inscrutable will and omnipotence and man's wretched helplessness—these dominant principles of the early Reformation make of it a Romantic movement as surely as that initiated by Rousseau and Herder and Wordsworth. The early Reformation's split between the ideal and the actual is wholly theological in premise and concern, but Calvin's dictum (in defiance of the Christian-humanistic concept of man as a humble but active and voluntary participant in the effecting of God's will) that man is utterly corrupted by original sin and can do nothing to effect his own salvation, which rests entirely upon his being arbitrarily chosen as one of the elect by God's capricious decision—this dictum as surely splits the whole working principle of the relatedness of the ideal and the actual as does the defiant nihilism of some nineteenth-century Romantics.

This is just as true of Luther's position. To assert that man has no moral worth and no freedom of choice, and hence through his own efforts can do nothing to realize the ideal (save through faith, which engenders that "imputed righteousness" that is not really his, but Christ's-in-him) is to split the ideal and the actual, and to remove meaning and value from all the humanistic virtues which the Classicist point of view endorsed. Says Luther, "Bear in mind that to be a pious man and accomplish many great works and lead an honorable and virtuous life is one thing: to be a Christian is something quite different." This is in effect what Calvin meant when he asserted the provincial character of all natural morality. Both

MOUNT MARY COLLEGE LIBRARY
Milwaukee, Wisconsin 53222

of them ask of the Christian man only faith—a faith equivalent to the acknowledgment of God's exclusive righteousness. Both of them, then, placed all value in the realm of the ideal, and severed the cord of comprehension which would at least have given some significance and direction to ethics.

To complement and balance this Romantic movement in theology, there evolved in the sixteenth century a Naturalistic movement in science, politics and ethics, perhaps most notably epitomized in Giordano Bruno, Machiavelli and Montaigne. In Machiavelli's contemptuous ignoring of the established and universal theory that behind the personal aims of any earthly ruler lay the moral imperative to pursue the laws of God and nature to the certain advantage of that ruler's subjects, and in his writing of a pragmatic handbook for the successful prince, are evident the Naturalist's conviction that the only reality is that of empirical actuality. He is quite explicit about it:

> I shall depart from the methods of other people. But, it being my intention to write a thing which shall be useful to him who apprehends it, it appears to me more appropriate to follow up the real truth of a matter than the imagination of it; for many have pictured the republics and principalities which in fact have never been known or seen; because how one lives is so far distant from how one ought to live, that he who neglects what is done for what ought to be done, sooner effects his ruin than his preservation; for a man who wishes to act entirely up to his professions of virtue soon meets with what destroys him among so much that is evil.

In the mature Montaigne's insistence upon man the animal, child of a fertile but amoral nature, and his dismissal of any possible understanding of God's design with his scornful assertion that what we foolishly consider the universal laws of God and Nature are only "municipall lawes," we have a different and cautiously qualified, but equally strong and influential Naturalist's point of view. So, too, Montaigne deserts the long-accepted medieval treatment of man the type—one form of belief in the reality of the ideal, stemming from what was called the "realist" position in the Middle Ages —and is concerned only with depicting one individual man—himself. He makes the distinction in favor of the empirical actuality as the only reality:

> Others fashion man, I repeat him, and represent a particular one, but ill made; and whom were I to forme a new, he should be far other than he is; but he is now made. And though the

lines of my picture change and vary, yet loose they not themselves.

Finally, in Bruno's theory of the identity of matter throughout a limitless universe (a theory logically developed from a point which Copernicus left half-finished in *De Revolutionibus Orbium Celestium*), and hence his implicit denial of the division of the universe, Aristotelian-wise, into up-and-down, incorruptible and corruptible, ideal and material portions, the Naturalistic view invades the hitherto theologically controlled realm of physics.

One could add to Bruno's primarily speculative discovery the radical Naturalistic movement in science that discarded theological theory and logic-law altogether, and accepted only empirical evidence—a movement led by Vesalius in anatomy; by Paracelsus (with certain qualifications) in medicine; by Tycho Brahe and those recently rediscovered Englishmen, Thomas Hariot and Thomas Digges, in astronomy; and by Vives and Telesio in biology and physics—and which culminated in the inductive method of Francis Bacon. One could recount the way in which the Naturalistic technique and approach invaded the field of history and historical method with Cornelius Agrippa, Jean Bodin and Louis LeRoy. One could relate in detail how Rabelais in a hundred ways satirized the concept of universal and established laws of God and nature and the absolutism of the ideal; one could trace at length the way in which Francisco Guicciardini developed and exceeded Machiavelli's pragmatism. But for the present these examples must suffice to demonstrate how tremendous the impact of the combined Romantic-Naturalistic rebellion of the Counter-Renaissance must have been upon the most sensitive, skeptical and undogmatic of the Elizabethans.

At the same time, a student of the period must be extremely wary to avoid becoming too entranced with this vision of a transition age and its tortured and bewildered children, lest he find genuine skepticism and philosophical uncertainty in passages which are primarily rhetoric or even bombast. With this distinction in mind, compare the following speech of Byron's in Chapman's *Tragedy of Byron* with some famous lines from Donne's *Anatomie of the World*. Byron declares:

> The world is quite inverted, Virtue thrown
> At Vice's feet, and sensual Peace confounds
> Valour and cowardice, fame and infamy;
> The rude and terrible age is turn'd again,

MOUNT MARY COLLEGE LIBRARY
Milwaukee, Wisconsin 53222

When the thick air hid heaven, and all the stars
Were drown'd in humour, tough and hard to pierce;
When the red sun held not his fixed place,
Kept not his certain course, his rise and set,
Nor yet distinguish'd with his definite bounds,
Nor in his firm conversions were discern'd
The fruitful distances of time and place
In the well-varied seasons of the year;
When th' incompos'd incursions of floods
Wasted and eat the earth, and all things show'd
Wild and disorder'd: nought was worse than now.
We must reform and have a new creation
Of state and government, and on our Chaos
Will I sit brooding up another world.

In this passage Chapman has utilized the favorite Elizabethan image of a world in chaotic dissolution primarily as effective background for the expression of his hero's *hybris*. He gives the traditional exposition and description of the return of the Iron Age, or the approach of Judgment Day (depending on whether one prefers to use the classical or Judæo-Christian version), but he uses it only for a comparison with the condition of the kingdom (according to Byron).

One can find similar passages, describing the visible and prophetic alterations in man, in the products of the earth, in the actions of the elements, and in the phenomena of the heavens, in the writings of many Elizabethans. Walter Ralegh has one in the *History of the World*. Richard Hooker presents the picture in Book I of the *Laws*, in order to refute its veracity. John Norden's *Vicissitudo Rerum* plays a hundred variations on the theme. In fact, when one becomes acquainted with all the different ways in which the general theory was treated in the last decade of the sixteenth century —the theological, philosophical, astrological, political and even scientific versions—one discovers that there is almost no one among the Elizabethans who did not at one time or another take up the question of the decay of nature and the imminent disintegration of the universe.

But all this is beside the point in considering Byron's speech. Senecan hero that he is, Byron is so swollen with self that, to express adequately his ego, he must find cosmic images as vast and pretentious as those used by Tamburlaine himself. The image of universal dissolution, chaos and rebirth serves its purpose as a literary device in setting forth both the extent of Byron's *hybris* and the violent and heroic mold of his temper.

Donne, too, uses the theory of the Decay of Nature as a literary device. Yet he leaves no doubt in the reader's mind that it is the end of a world order that he is actually describing under cover of a lament for Elizabeth Drury. In one short passage, there are unmistakable references to the new astronomy and the speculation it inspires, to Machiavelli's ruthless world of power politics, and to Montaigne's substitution of man the individual for man the type:

And new Philosophy calls all in doubt,
The Element of fire is quite put out;
The Sun is lost, and th' earth, and no mans wit
Can well direct him where to looke for it.
And freely men confesse that this world's spent,
When in the Planets, and the Firmament
They seeke so many new; they see that this
Is crumbled out again to his Atomies.
'Tis all in peeces, all cohærence gone;
All just supply, and all Relation:
Prince, Subject, Father, Sonne, are things forgot,
For every man alone thinkes he hath got
To be a Phœnix, and that there can bee
None of that kinde, of which he is, but hee.
This is the world's condition now. . . .

Here are the major heresies and subversive doctrines of the Counter-Renaissance, packed tightly, in Donne's elliptical style, into fifteen lines. One may still question (although one is less likely to if he examines the substance of these lines against the body of Donne's thought in all his verse) the extent to which the poet is seriously concerned, and the extent to which he is merely indulging in characteristic intellectual virtuosity. What one cannot question is the exact nature of his allusions; unmistakably he is referring to the passing of the medieval world-view.

King Lear affords an excellent example of still a third treatment of the general theme of the decay of the world. With his customary dramatic instinct, Shakespeare focuses the whole theme of disintegration and chaos upon the moral dilemma of Lear. Reference after familiar reference to strange portents in the heavens, to the breaking of traditional personal and social ties, to a vicious tooth-and-claw animal world, to the ultimate dissolution of the very universe, occurs. Yet the various protagonists adopt such diverse attitudes toward all these phenomena, some supporting and some discrediting the theories related to them, that the strongest impression one carries away is the shaded, ambiguous one of a perfect atmospheric background for the chaos within Lear himself. One's appreciation of this background is heightened by a familiarity with the pertinent Elizabethan theories, but the dramatic interest is centered upon the moral conflict, to which the political and physical ones play a muted counterpoint. As usual, one can be more certain about Shakespeare's artistic intentions and achievement than about his philosophical position.

In much the same way that one must learn to discriminate between consciously literary allusions to the decay of nature theme and serious philosophical considerations of the "actual" phenomena, one must learn to differentiate among the various passages which seem to deal with new and disturbing Counter-Renaissance concepts of the nature of man. The traditional Christian-humanistic evaluation of man reminds us that his nature partakes of both the divine and the animal. With a love of analogy inherited from medieval thought, the Elizabethans describe again and again how the soul of man is compounded of all the ranks of the graded hierarchy of the creation. Yet man was most himself, the favorite child of the creation, when the rational part of his soul guided and controlled the lower parts, composed of the passions and the appetites. Despite the contrary verdict of Luther and Calvin, the main line of Christian humanism upheld the view that man, redeemed by Christ, was not hopelessly damned by original sin, and could find his own way to righteousness. Still, in any single case, the battle might go either way, of course.

With all this in mind, when one reads Sir John Davies' declaration:

> I know my Soule hath power to know all things,
> Yet she is blind and ignorant in all;
> I know I am one of Natures little kings,
> Yet to the least and vilest things am thrall.
>
> I know my life's paine, and but a span,
> I know my Sense is mockt with every thing;
> And to conclude, I know my selfe a Man,
> Which is a proud and yet a wretched thing . . .

one realizes that he is not encountering the tortured confusion of a man whose traditional faith in the divine origin and destination of the human soul has been shaken by new and naturalistic concepts of man's nature, but rather the perfectly orthodox account of the twofold human condition—the spiritual and the animal.

Epernon's speech in the fourth act of *The Tragedy of Byron* gives another expression of this attitude:

> Oh of what contraries consists a man!
> Of what impossible mixtures! Vice and virtue,

Corruption, and eternesse, at one time,
And in one subject, let together loose!
We have not any strength but weakens us,
No greatness but doth crush us into air.
Our knowledges do light us but to err,
Our ornaments are burthens, our delights
Are our tormenters, fiends that, rais'd in fears,
At parting shake our roofs about our ears.

But it is also possible to miss the real thing when it comes along—
to dismiss as a traditional expression of man's constitution what
is really the statement of skepticism about that orthodox belief.
This is exactly the trap into which some scholars have fallen in
interpreting Hamlet's great speech about the nature of man. But
unlike the others quoted above, Hamlet does not set the "contraries"
in balanced array against each other. He is not concerned with
"impossible mixtures"; he does not alternate or intertwine the enumeration of virtues and beauties with those of vices and deformi-
ties. After one unbroken lyric discourse on "What a piece of work
is a man," he abruptly and expressly repudiates the whole picture,
heavily underlining the discrepancy between the traditional ideal
and the actuality that he has himself experienced, with the words,
"And yet to me what is this quintessence of dust? Man delights
me not—no, nor woman neither, though by your smiling you seem
to say so."

In fact, Hamlet is the most unmistakable child of his tumultuous
times that Shakespeare ever portrayed. Shakespeare gives Hamlet
more philosophical latitude than most of his other tragic heroes; he
permits him to generalize in a way of which Othello and Macbeth
are incapable—thus relating his personal dilemma to the general
Elizabethan intellectual one. Yet Shakespeare's ultimate emphasis
is what it always is: if the philosophical resolution that Hamlet
seeks broadens and makes universal the certainty and decisiveness
he is searching for in his personal problem, it is still more true that
the focusing on the personal problem greatly intensifies and increases the impact of the philosophical dilemma. . . .

Hamlet finds that "the readiness is all," but the dilemma remains—the dilemma of the man who walks the insecure line between the safe but no longer satisfying terrain of his fathers, and
the unexplored, ambiguous plot which will eventually be home to
his children. "There are more things in heaven and earth, Horatio,
than are dreamt of in your philosophy," and after Hamlet has been
sung to his rest by flights of angels, there are ghosts who remain

to haunt the figures wandering the stormy wastelands of *Lear* and *Macbeth*. And to haunt all the Elizabethans who did not make fast the shutters of orthodoxy and tradition against them.

The stouter spirits faced the weather of transition, but seldom with unwavering resolution. And so we find in them the paradox that we have come to think of as peculiarly Elizabethan—the paradox of lustiness and piety, of doubt and affirmation, of confidence and despair. We find Francis Bacon, for example, saying (and not entirely out of the experience of his own unhappy public career)

> The world's a bubble, and the life of a man
> Less than a span;
> In his conception wretched, and from the womb
> So to the tomb;
> Curst from the cradle, and brought up to yearn
> With cares and fears.
> Who then to frail mortality shall trust
> But limns the water, or but writes in dust . . .

and closing with the lines

> What then remains, but that we still should cry
> Not to be born, or being born, to die?

Yet the very man who intoned with apparent sincerity this dirge could also say

> I am now therefore to speak touching Hope. . . . And therefore it is fit that I publish and set forth those conjectures of mine which make hope in this matter reasonable; just as Columbus did, before that wonderful voyage of his across the Atlantic, when he gave the reasons for his conviction that new lands and continents might be discovered besides those which were known before; which reasons, though rejected at first, were afterwards made good by experience, and were the causes and beginnings of great events . . .

and

> I am building in the human understanding a true model of the world, such as it is in fact, not such as a man's own reason would have it to be; a thing which cannot be done without a very diligent dissection and anatomy of the world.

Not only could the identical man entertain these contrarieties, but apparently love them perversely as well—as Elizabethan after Elizabethan demonstrated. Infinite aspiration, infinite despair. Hamlet, as usual, is the spokesman for his generation: "O God, I could be bounded in a nutshell and count myself a king of infinite space, were it not that I have bad dreams."

CHAPTER
1

RENAISSANCE HUMANISM

I. THE GENERAL QUESTION OF THE RENAISSANCE

THE four centuries between the *Summa Theologica* of St. Thomas Aquinas and Isaac Newton's *Principia Mathematica* have become one vast arena for embattled historians of ideas. It is on this proving ground that some of the most bitter combats about the course of European intellectual history have been fought. One can seldom find any corner of it in which some pair of individuals or groups is not exchanging thrusts or blows. No matter what the hour of the scholarly day at which one strolls into the stadium; no matter how formidable the champion one has come to watch—he has been challenged, and is under attack.

It is literally impossible to cite a single generalization about the period that has escaped challenge or censure. Even the generally accepted term "Renaissance," used to designate the larger part of this era, has been protested vociferously. Some denounce the use of the word in this context as ridiculously pretentious, and contrast the achievements of the fifteenth and sixteenth centuries most unfavorably with those of the twelfth and thirteenth. Others maintain that the so-called "Renaissance" is at best merely an annex to the medieval mansion, at worst its outhouse. And even among those who stoutly maintain that there was a Renaissance, and that it was a crucial period in Western civilization—one which marked the advent of "modern" times—there is a wide difference of opinion about its outstanding characteristics. Worst of all, much of the conflict has been attended by doctrinaire and even chauvinistic evaluations.

It must be either a brave or a perverse man, then, who shakes his little sword and rushes into this particular battle. Yet the incentive to one whom the virus of intellectual, cultural or literary history has infected, is considerable, and the assault upon the objective in itself richly rewarding. For the ground to be covered is no ordinary terrain; its very dust is marked with the footprints of the great—in religion and literature and art and science and speculation—footprints which no amount of Lilliputian scuffling can erase. . . .

At either end of these four centuries stands an impressive citadel of thought. One is the work of the Scholastic philosophers, and was completed in the thirteenth century. The other was built by the late sixteenth- and the seventeenth-century scientists and philosophers, and dominates the early eighteenth-century intellectual scene. Each is massive and yet delicately precise; each inclusive, symmetrical, harmonious. The architects of the more recent of the two (which may, for easy reference, be called the Newtonian synthesis) owe, indeed, a debt to the Scholastics (notably, among them, Thomas Aquinas) who built the first—a debt, especially in scientific method, which has not been adequately recognized until fairly recently.[1]

Yet, despite this indebtedness of one to the other, and despite many similarities of structure—such as their common ebullient optimism, their common faith in the power of the abstracting intellect to find out truth, and above all their common certainty of living in a law-governed universe—these two edifices of thought present drastic differences as well.

The world system of Thomas Aquinas and his colleagues is pre-eminently concerned with the rational and theological Science of God; that blueprinted by Galileo and Descartes and Spinoza and Newton and Locke, with the rational and mathematical Science of Nature. The scientific aim of the Scholastics, unlike that of the later group, was not to discover the mechanical laws of operation of the universe, but rather to achieve "a comprehension of the meaning and significance of things, above all the chief end of man, the meaning of human life and of all creation related to it. . . ."[2] They sought answers to the questions "what?" and "why?" as well as "how?"

Starting from accepted principles about the nature of God and God's universe, and employing a great linked and interlinked chain of reasoning, the Scholastics found their ultimate goal in the contemplation of what alone gave meaning and purpose to existence, of what alone constituted final truth for them—God. On the other hand, the seventeenth-century philosophers and scientists, also beginning with hypotheses, but with mathematical ones, and checking their findings by experiment, concentrated upon ascertaining the character of natural operations, which they considered mechanical. The one group measured a "purposeful" nature qualitatively, the other a mechanical nature quantitatively. Hence, while one strove to reconcile its natural philosophy with fundamental theological premises, the other's most characteristic religious expression was radically rationalistic, in accordance with its scientific philosophy. Both systems are highly intellectualistic, but the older employed reason in the interests of the Christian religion; the more recent was inclined to exalt reason above the claims of any particular institutionalized religion—or at least to free its skirts of the clinging and hampering hands of creed and dogma.

Perhaps no clearer comparison and contrast of the two systems can be found than in a study of the similarities and dissimilarities of outlook in Dante's *Divine Comedy* and Pope's *Essay on Man*. Each is in its own way a justification of the "ways of God to man"; each presents and summarizes the world view of the age. Indeed, each is written from a summarizing vantage-point, in the twilight of the age represented. And while it is true that the two poems are not of equal literary and imaginative merit—true that Dante's great spirit dwarfs Pope—it is at least a defensible stand to maintain that these differences, too, partake of the character of their respective ages.

Probably the most significant and summarizing shift in outlook, as a result of these differences, is that from the position of Aquinas and Dante, who saw the ultimate end (or good) of man as his angelification, to that of Bolingbroke or Pope, who saw it in man's proper participation in and conformity to the rational laws of the perfectly functioning Newtonian world-machine. Those who object (and I suspect quite justifiably) to the employment of Pope's shallow optimism about "this best of all possible worlds" to represent the temper of the Newtonian Age, might prefer to substitute the sort of optimism subscribed to by members of the Royal Society and their French contemporaries, the "Moderns" of the seventeenth-century Ancients-Moderns controversy.

In opposition to the medieval idea of the return to God and the contemplation of his Truth as man's final good, these men would find that good primarily in man's increasing capacity to harness nature and thus enrich substantially the quality of his life on earth —in progress, in something like our modern sense. Such an opposition of values implies, finally, a parallel shift in outlook from the philosophy of history which sees the historical process as a single and unique progression toward a fixed and permanent supra-terrestrial state in eternity, to that which sees it as a continuous progression toward a more enlightened and more comfortable existence in time and space. . . .

Inevitably, confronted by discrepancies between the Thomist and the Newtonian views of the universe, of man's relation to it, and of his destiny, one must concede that the centuries intervening between Aquinas and Newton witnessed a period of intellectual transition and reorientation. As might be expected, the constituents of the transition are many and various, and are not to be catalogued with facile neatness. Yet a close analysis reveals three major trends or movements within the limits of the period generally called the Renaissance, extending from Petrarch's heyday in the mid-fourteenth century to the publication of Francis Bacon's *Novum Organum* (1620) and Galileo's *Dialogue of the Two Chief Systems* (1632). The first of these three movements is that of Renaissance Humanism.

2. THE MEDIEVAL SYNTHESIS AND CHRISTIAN HUMANISM

One of the principal contentions of those who minimize the originality of the Renaissance is that its famous classical humanism "was fundamentally medieval and fundamentally Christian," hence largely a continuation and elaboration of an earlier emphasis.[3] This point of view, of course, is diametrically opposed to that of those scholars who, following (with whatever modifications) the lead of Burckhardt and Michelet, have seen Renaissance humanism as a real revival of classical letters and as an individualistic or even pagan exaltation of natural man and his life on this earth.

It is difficult for any one except a specialist to keep pace with the scholars who discover, or claim to discover, hitherto unknown medieval translations from classical literature and philosophy. Therefore, it is equally difficult to appraise accurately the extent to which the "revival" of classical learning and letters in the Renaissance *was* a revival. I am inclined to accept Professor Randall's verdict that "the thirteenth century merged almost imperceptibly into what we call the humanistic revival in its narrower sense."[4] Yet, at the same time, it is unlikely that any one will deny an acceleration of interest in the literature and moral philosophy of Greek and Roman antiquity, and of productivity in the fields of translations and commentaries, in fourteenth- and fifteenth-century Italy, and elsewhere on the continent and in England during the sixteenth century.

The larger question, that of whether or not the humanism of the

Renaissance was "fundamentally medieval and fundamentally Christian" in spirit, requires more elaboration. Any just estimate must begin with an analysis of medieval Christian humanism, and thus further necessitates an understanding of the relationship of the classical heritage to that of Christianity in the thought of the Middle Ages.

As a great medievalist, Etienne Gilson, points out, one may find in a writing in the second century "the perpetual charter of Christian humanism," with Justin's assertion that "whatever has been well said is ours" and that "all truth is as by definition, Christian."[5] Indeed, from the very first, M. Gilson declares, the medieval thinkers

> found themselves faced with a double responsibility, that, namely, of maintaining on the one hand a philosophy of nature while at the same time building up a theology of supernature, and of integrating the first with the second in a coherent system.[6]

For it must be remembered that medieval Christianity was not primarily or characteristically an other-worldly religion in the sense of denying the goodness of nature and the relevance to salvation of life on this earth. Grace, to the medieval thinkers, was there, after restoring nature, to improve it. How, then, could "the science of grace . . . obstruct that of nature?" And since no science of nature was available in the New or Old Testament, they turned inevitably to Greek philosophy.[7]

On the other hand, it is immediately obvious that they could not stop with the conclusions of Plato and Aristotle, conclusions and philosophical positions which necessarily had nothing to do with the Christian revelation. So began the long process of assimilation which culminated—with the Scholastics of the thirteenth century —in an impressively comprehensive consolidation of Christian dogma with classical philosophy and science.

From Anselm, with his echo of Justin, "Omne verum a quocumque dicatur, a Spirito Sancto est,"[8] on, the principal task of the medieval philosopher was to effect the alliance of reason and faith, philosophy and theology, nature and grace—to effect it and to articulate it. The primacy of faith over reason in this synthesis is incontestable, but to the medieval philosopher such a subordination of reason in no sense belittled or degraded it. The most representative position, from Anselm and Augustine to Thomas Aquinas, is that the Christian philosopher "does not seek to understand in order to believe, but to believe in order to understand. . . ."[9]

Again, while there are realms of being and knowledge to which reason may not gain access, the efficacy of reason is not thereby denied. For Aquinas, "when reason bows before a mystery, it does not disclaim all competence, for it shows that the supra-rational is not the anti-rational."[10] There is evident, moreover, an increasingly strong preoccupation with rational and logical argument, culminating in the highly intellectualistic system of Aquinas.[11]

With varying emphases, recent medieval scholars have discussed these tendencies in tones very different from those employed by earlier historians of the thought of the Middle Ages. Christopher Dawson has written, for example,

> The great intellectual synthesis of the thirteenth century has been regarded as the triumph of theological dogmatism. It was in reality the assertion of the rights of the human reason and the foundation of European science.[12]

Carl Becker defends the thesis that the attitude of the thirteenth-century philosophers was primarily "rationalistic," explaining that

> Since eighteenth-century writers employed reason to discredit Christian dogma, a "rationalist" in common parlance came to mean an "unbeliever," one who denied the truth of Christianity. . . . But this use of the word is unfortunate, since it obscures the fact that reason may be employed to support faith as well as to destroy it.[13]

This is the exact sense in which the medieval Christian philosophers may be spoken of as "rationalistic" or "intellectualistic." For them, the basic function of intelligence was to demonstrate the truth of the body of revealed Christian dogma, and this task gave it a position of dignity. Nor did they find any anomaly in their attitude. Their primary assumption was, on the contrary, the complete compatibility and accord of the premises of reason and faith. As Thomas Aquinas' syllogism goes:

> The natural dictates of reason must certainly be true: it is impossible to think of their being otherwise. Nor again is it permissible to believe that the tenets of faith are false, being so evidently confirmed by God. Since therefore falsehood alone is contrary to truth, it is impossible for the truth of faith to be contrary to principles known by natural reason.[14]

The high rank which he accorded the cognitive faculties is everywhere evident in his writings. Not only is intelligence the noblest of all the divine perfections;[15] the final end or good of man lies in the intellectual contemplation of God, his mediate good in the moral realm in a life of virtuous activity in accordance with the dictates of reason. Or, as Dante phrases it, with a slightly different accent:

> The proper function of the human race, taken in the aggregate, is to actualize continually the entire capacity possible to the intellect, primarily in speculation, then through its extension and for its sake, secondarily in action.[16]

In the Thomist system, the supremacy of reason is apparent in the fields of ethics, psychology, metaphysics, political theory, science, logic and æsthetics.[17] To be sure, there are definite limits to intellectual knowledge. Supra-sensible reality it may not grasp, save as the purified understanding attains eventually to the intuitive cognition of the angels. Theology remains at the pinnacle of the hierarchy of medieval studies, and at the apex of the Christian dogma are the mysteries of the Trinity and Incarnation, and the Redemption. Nor is the intellect even capable of a complete knowledge of sensible reality. Nevertheless, the large spheres of life and thought which are left to reason and intellect to rule, suffice to make Scholasticism a thoroughly intellectualistic philosophy, one in which the "act of knowing" is of ultimately greater nobility than that of will or emotion or pragmatic efficiency.[18]

Finally, the Scholastics, with their confidence in the powers of reason, were optimistic philosophers. They had a dogmatic assurance that the human intelligence had been created to know truth, and their epistemology, although affected by the doctrine of original sin, was not radically altered by it.

For they did not believe that the Fall of Adam had caused the complete corruption of man, or of nature in general. Free will, they almost all agreed, remained whole; and even that *true liberty*, "the will to do right," which most of them distinguished from morally indifferent choice, had been restored through the efficacy of grace.[19] Man had been mutilated, perhaps, but "nothing can efface from conscience the fundamental tendency toward goodness. . . ."[20]

M. Gilson presents an unanswerable case:

> If in fact we suppose that the Middle Ages denied the stable persistence of nature beneath the wounds inflicted by sin, how could we possibly imagine that its philosophers would concern themselves seriously with the achievement of a physics, an ethics, and finally a metaphysics based on this physics and this ethics?[21]

No, "the work of creation is shattered, but the fragments remain good, and, with the grace of God, they may be reconstituted and restored."[22]

This attitude is clearly a humanistic one, in its implication that human life is worth while, possesses dignity and true significance. Yet it is not humanism in the sense of an "attitude of thought or action *centering* upon distinctively human interest or ideals."[23] Scholastic ethics, for example, are concerned with the value of man as a rational animal, conducting his life according to his will under the supervision of his reason. Thus man is a free agent. But to be truly free is "to will the thing known by intelligence," in agreement with the will of God:

> The Christian conscience, as an expression of the divine legislative reason, always prescribes the act to be done a *moral obligation*. . . . It is God himself Who turns our will towards Himself, and in consequence makes it good; in freely turning ourselves away we can but make it bad.[24]

True Christian liberty, then, lies not in the freedom to do anything, but in the freedom to do good. God's providence and human free will are not antithetical, but complementary; man's moral activity is directed by God, yet man cooperates with God, since God's law which directs that activity expresses itself through the immediate agency of man's reason. Man is free to turn away from the controlling supervision, but if he does he will not be acting in accordance with his distinctive rational nature, and he will not find true liberty, which is liberty implicit in doing good, and issuing from having done good.

Moreover, the final good of man is to know God. Hence the ethical ideal is inseparable from and subordinate to the metaphysical one. Herein is the essential difference between Christian ethics and most Greek ethics. In the characteristic Greek point of view, the moral life assumed a value of its own—whether happiness or virtue or pleasure, or a combination of these, was the end sought. But for the medieval Christian there was a reality that transcended the moral life.[25]

Thus Christian humanism differs from non-Christian humanism in its relating of man's activities on this earth to a supra-terrestrial end. That it is humanism is apparent in its finding such activities good and valuable. That it is Christian humanism is apparent in its *not* appraising them good *for their own sake*. And this attitude is a consistent one. It is applied not only to ethical activity, but to the whole realm of knowledge as well. Whatever knowledge furthers man's understanding of his eternal destiny and of God's universal rule is good; all other knowledge is superfluous and irrelevant.

Hence medieval philosophy is much more concerned with science, as it interprets science, than with the humanities—with Cicero's *Studia humanitatis ac litterarum.*

A John of Salisbury collected and rejoiced in the Latin poets. But it is surely significant that most of the proponents of the theory that there was a flourishing and extensive classical humanism of this sort in the Middle Ages find it necessary to make so much of him. Occasionally, Lactantius and Jerome of the fourth century are invoked, and Bernard of Chartres is cited with John·in the twelfth, but most often he alone is held triumphantly aloft as proof of the existence of a "literary humanism" in the Middle Ages. "Omne verum a quocumque dicatur, a Spirito Sancto est"—yes. But it has not been sufficiently recognized by the "medieval humanism" enthusiasts that the classical "truth" which the medievalists wanted to claim and "baptize" was not that to be gathered from the "study of humanity and letters," but that to be found in the Creation story in the *Timaeus* and in the natural philosophy and logic of Aristotle.

Again, the later Middle Ages knew a lively and virile literature extolling the pleasure of life on earth—in the songs of the "Wandering Clerks" and of the troubadours, in the *fabliaux* and romances, and in the writings of Jean de Meung and Geoffrey Chaucer. But with the possible exception of the last two, and perhaps even in them, these were not preponderantly concerned with the tradition of classical humanism. They represented rather the humanism which is humanistic largely in the sense of preoccupation with human beings, with their impulses and passions, their dreams and appetites, their laughter and grief—their *lives* in and for themselves. And orthodoxy did its best to make most of them disreputable.

Perhaps, indeed, the finest medieval humanism is to be found in Dante Alighieri. Dante is consistently and properly thought of as the very epitome of all that is medieval—as the imaginative expositor *par excellence* of the Scholastic world vision. Yet the nature of his veneration for Vergil and Cicero, and of his depiction and development of the ideal of Cicero's "gentle-man," as Professor Rand has named it (the ideal of *humanus* meaning "humanized," "civilized," in contrast to *homo ferus*), is prophetic of the literary and cultivated humanism of the Italian Renaissance.[26]

Holding the common doctrine of his age that

> False guidance is the cause, as thou canst see
> Which makes the world to be so full of guilt,
> And not your nature's own depravity . . .[27]

Dante finds Vergil his "model of perfected humanity," the representative of that *humanitas* which he defines in the abstract in the *Convivio*. Vergil is far more than a guide through the infernal regions and the lower regions of purgatory; he is Dante's teacher and exemplar of the virtuous life.

Yet eventually Vergil must yield place to Beatrice. If Dante's "study of the classics was leading him toward humanism, his more insistent absorption was in divinity."[28] In the *Convivio, divinitas* supersedes *humanitas* as the preoccupation of the ideal gentleman in his latter years. In the *Divine Comedy*, Vergil leads Dante as far as "intellect and art" may, but this is not so far as Paradise.

If Dante differs from most medieval writers in the degree of confidence he places in the unbaptized Vergil, he does not run counter to their central premise. And although there are new features (or newly revived and celebrated ones) to his humanism, it is incontestably Christian in the limitations it places on what may be attained by the exclusively human without the intervention of divine grace. Throughout medieval humanism, the Christian halo shines above the classical head and transfigures it.

3. REASON AND FAITH, AND THE CHRISTIAN HUMANISM OF THE RENAISSANCE

Although the thought of the early Middle Ages had been predominantly influenced by Platonism, or Neoplatonism, and although this strain was still evident in Scholastic thinkers, Thomas Aquinas and his followers had based their philosophy primarily on Aristotle's. As early as the mid-fourteenth century, however, the pendulum had begun its swing back. Cicero's great popularity with the Italian humanists, a revival of enthusiasm for Augustine, the Neoplatonic elements in the thought of Nicholas of Cusa, the influence of the Greek philosophers (notably Gemisthus Pletho and Bessarion) who came to Italy during the first half of the fifteenth century—all these forces strengthened the trend toward Plato, and toward Platonism of various kinds. With the advent of the Florentine Academy, Renaissance Neoplatonism burst into full flower.

The leader of the Academy, Marsilio Ficino, and his most brilliant associate, Pico della Mirandola, in at least one respect were true heirs of the Scholastic philosophers. For they devoted themselves to systematic attempts to reconcile their ardent love of philosophy with their allegiance to Christianity. Ficino believed that the truth of Plato and Plotinus was very close to the Christian truth, and capable, moreover, of making Christianity a *docta religio.* On the first page of his *De Christiana Religione* he writes,

> Let us, I pray, whensoever we are able, deliver God's sacred gift, Philosophy, from ungodliness, for indeed we can do so, if we will; let us redeem our holy religion from accursed ignorance.[29]

Ficino's self-appointed task was to re-establish and disseminate the main Platonic (or Neoplatonic) concepts, to display their harmonious accord with Christian doctrine, and "to exhibit them as the foundation of every true philosophic and religious system."[30] Pico's dream was an even more expansive one. At once a disciple of Ficino and an admirer of Aquinas, he proposed to establish a *pax philosophica* between Platonism and Aristotelianism, and to demonstrate the consistency of both philosophies, or of the one-in-two, with Christian theology. It is this attempt which Poliziano recognizes in a letter to him:

> In your treatise *De Uno et Ente,* you recall the streams that flow through the Lyceum and the Academy to their true source, and with philosophy, which is not twofold, but one and un-varying, you combine our theology.[31]

Nor does even this project represent the full scope of Pico's ambition. The philosophico-religious heritage of the ages, for him, also includes Arabian and Jewish thought—particularly that of the Cabala. "It is as though he had made it his goal," Ernst Cassirer writes, "to render vocal at the same time *all* the intellectual forces which had hitherto cooperated in establishing religious, philosophical, and scientific knowledge."[32]

It was a somewhat different kind of Platonism from that of the Florentine Academy which the northern humanists endorsed as wholly compatible with the Christian ideal. Whether their Platonism derived directly from Plato, or from the Platonism to be found in Cicero's derivative philosophical treatises, it was not a systematic philosophy. The temper of men like Erasmus, More, Colet, Grocyn and Linacre was antagonistic to speculative subtleties and to philosophical syntheses.

Erasmus is altogether too complex and supple a thinker to admit of neat labeling, but surely his major work emerges as an effort to form "the philosophy of Christ" from a blending of Cicero's *humanitas* and the loftiness of mind and simplicity of "Saint Socrates," with a return to the gospel of "Christ, that good Samaritan."[33] The fusion takes place on a different level from that of Ficino and Pico;

the rational emphasis is upon reasonableness of conduct, rather than upon logic or metaphysics.[34]

Erasmus' Christianity, then, is primarily ethical, concerned largely with men's living upon the earth the way Christ would have them live, rather than with the contemplation of the truth of God; with good works as central to salvation, rather than disputations, ritual, or the preoccupation with a Christian ontology. "The true way to worship the saints," he writes, "is to imitate their virtues. . . ."[35]

The union of classical moral philosophy and Christian ethics which is fundamental to Erasmus' thought is also evident in that of Sir Thomas More. In the *Utopia*, reason plays a major part in religious matters. Referring to the Utopians' convictions about the immortality of the soul and about rewards and punishments after death, More explains, "Though these be pertaining to religion, yet they think it meet that they should be believed and granted by proofs of reason." Again, like Erasmus, he displays a preoccupation with the good life on earth:

> They define virtue to be a life ordered according to nature; and we be hereunto ordained of God; and that he doth follow the course of nature, which in desiring and refusing things is ruled by reason. Furthermore, that reason doth chiefly and principally kindle in men the love and veneration of the divine Majesty; of whose goodness it is that we be, and we be in possibility to attain felicity.[36]

Despite the antagonistic attitudes of Luther and Calvin toward philosophy and reason, the Protestant Reformation did inherit this sort of Christian humanism. Philip Melanchthon, in particular, can best be summarized as a moral theologian and a moral philosopher.[37] From 1535 on, he deserted the doctrines of predestination and of justification by faith alone, and developed a rational Lutheranism which brought him closer in many respects to the position of Erasmus than to that of Luther. Reconciling Cicero's adaptation of the Stoic concept of the Law of Nature with Paul's saying that the law is written in the human heart, he maintained that the natural light in man had been darkened, but not destroyed by the Fall. An Aristotelian who admired Plato and Cicero, he evinced confidence in the best in classical literature and philosophy, and perpetuated through his own work and that of his students a liberal humanistic Protestantism.[38]

A similar attitude is to be found in the Elizabethan Anglican church, which carried on, during the closing years of the sixteenth century, an incessant doctrinal warfare with the champions of Puritanism. The earlier English humanists' reconciliation of reason with faith, of classical learning and culture with Christian dogma, had been innocent of any extensive systematization. But the first book of Richard Hooker's *Of the Laws of Ecclesiastical Polity* (1594) propounds in a highly systematic way a Christian and philosophic body of universal laws.

In this treatise Hooker does not pretend to attain to the originality or the immense comprehensiveness of the *Summa Theologica* (after the exposition of Book I, he is chiefly occupied with refuting the Puritans' claim to an exclusive and infallible discipline, and with a defense of the Anglican position in general). Yet in its lucidity and thoroughness his work is certainly the outstanding document of this sort in the sixteenth century. And it achieves an integral correlation of the medieval heritage with the newer classical humanism. With a certain indebtedness to Aquinas,[39] Hooker builds his system of universal laws upon the Christian dogma, the Aristotelian teleological physics, and the Stoic idea of a rational law of nature; yet there are obvious contributions from Renaissance Platonism. With the scope he allots to reason, purpose, law and design, he devises as intellectualistic a synthesis as that of Aquinas.

"God . . . is a law both to himself, and to all other things besides. . . ." The angels themselves are bound by "a law Celestial and heavenly. . . ." Natural agents, void of reason, must have a guide. "Who the guide of nature, but only the God of nature?" Hooker asks. "The natural generation of all things receiveth order of proceeding from the settled stability of divine understanding." In "the purity of God's knowledge and will" this disposition of their working to appointed ends is properly called "Providence," although "the ancients," referring to "the things themselves here disposed by it," called it "natural Destiny." Nature is really nothing but "God's instrument"; the Law of Nature "is as it were an authenticall or an original draught written in the bosom of God himself. . . ."

There is "the law of Reason, that which bindeth creatures reasonable in this world, and with which by reason they most plainly perceive themselves bound. . . ." Although, since the Fall, man's natural reason has been impaired, and requires the assistance of special revelation from God, "Divine Law," it still functions. "Human law," man-made, is "that which out of the law either of reason or of God men probably gathering to be expedient, they make it a law."[40]

Moreover, Hooker asserts outright that there is a "natural path of everlasting life," obscured, but not obliterated, by the Fall. After a qualifying warning that "the light of nature" must be understood in this connection to be identical with "performing exactly the duties and works of righteousness," he continues:

> In the natural path of everlasting life the first beginning is that ability of doing good, which God in the day of man's creation endued him with; from hence obedience unto the will of his Creator, absolute righteousness and integrity in all his actions; and last of all the justice of God rewarding the worthiness of his deserts with the crown of eternal glory.[41]

It is a forthright claim for the value of natural reason and good works, a direct inheritance from the earlier humanists of the century. Even when dealing with the ultimate definition of happiness ("salvation" . . . "blessedness" . . . "communion with God"), Hooker does not desert his confidence in nature, reason and virtue. To be sure, the way of God's "Donative" is the only completely sure way, but there is no cause for forsaking the "duties and works of righteousness." For

> when supernatural duties are necessarily exacted, natural are not rejected as needless. The law of God therefore is, though principally delivered for instruction in the one, yet fraught with precepts of the other also. The Scripture is fraught even with laws of Nature. . . .[42]

The latitude allowed reason and the moral life by Hooker is increased by his contemporaries, the two formal Stoic apologists, Justus Lipsius and Guillaume du Vair. In his *Manuductio,* expounding the Stoic idea that the innate spark of reason within man is a part of the Divine Reason, Lipsius proceeds to define the true formula of the moral law as "to live in accordance with Reason," since this really means "to imitate God."[43] In his *Two Bookes of Constancie* he declares, "Therefore we define RIGHT REASON to be, *A true sense and judgment of things human and divine.*"[44] For Du Vair,

> There is nothing in the world that tends not to some End. . . . Now the End of Man, and all his thoughts and Inclinations, is Good. . . . I think, that, properly to define Good, a man may say that it is nothing but the Essence and operation according to Nature; who is so wise a Mistress, as that she has disposed all things to their best Estate; hath given them their first inclination to Good, and the End they ought to seek; so that who will follow, cannot fail to obtain it. . . . The Good, then,

of Man consists in his healthfull Reason, that is to say, his Virtue. . . .[45]

These examples may suffice for a brief cross-section study of various Renaissance attempts to ally harmoniously the doctrines of classical humanism and philosophy with the body of Christian truth, their rational allegiances with their Christian faith. They are representative of the men and points of view invoked by those scholars to whom "the tradition of Christian humanism seems a broad and central road,"[46] from Thomas Aquinas to John Milton.

That there is such a continuity, in the general sense of an un-abated effort to effect the reconciliation of faith and reason, religion and philosophy, grace and nature, seems clear on the face of the evidence. But that in the course of this tradition (as some of these scholars further claim) the fundamental Christian solution absorbs the classical and humanistic elements, seems much more doubtful.

One's verdict, I suspect, is partly a result of the preconceptions and predilections which one brings to the examination. Moreover, whether one finds—to choose at random—the humanistic or Christian element the stronger in Petrarch or in Thomas More, the Platonic or Christian in Ficino, and the Stoic or Christian in Du Vair, depends somewhat upon one's definition of Christianity.

Who has the right to be sure that he has put exactly the right interpretation upon the reception which More's Utopians accord the Christian gospel? Again, consider Erasmus. He declared with some satisfaction, "I brought it about that humanism, which among the Italians and especially among the Romans savored of nothing but pure paganism, began nobly to celebrate Christ."[47] Yet Luther felt (as some modern scholars feel) that what Erasmus actually effected was the very reverse of this program.

The debate brings to mind the story which Fulke Greville tells of the death of Sir Philip Sidney. He reports that Sidney, lying on that memorable battlefield in Flanders, requested that he be read two accounts of the immortality of the soul—that of classical philosophy and that of the New Testament.[48]

This story at least suggests an almost perfect state of equipoise between the claims of philosophy and religion, reason and faith—and a balance so delicate that a heavy hand might disturb it un-warrantably. But in the very delicacy of balance there is an essential difference from the medieval point of view. Surely the perfect feudal knight would have asked for only one version. Nor do I believe that the Thomas Aquinas who scribbled "ave, ave Maria" in the margins of his manuscripts would have understood the compulsion

Erasmus had to speak of "Saint Socrates." Unquestionably, the "reconciliation" tradition underwent a transformation in the Renaissance; the road of Christian humanism had indeed become a broad road.

There are, I believe, two main features to this change: first, an increasing tendency to obliterate the sharp medieval line of demarcation between the realm of theology and that of philosophy, with a consequent trend toward a natural religion, or deism, which finds in man's reason a sufficient instrument for the establishment of religion; secondly, a growing preoccupation with good works and the pursuit of virtue, with a resulting inclination toward an independent humanistic ethic.

Neither of these features constitutes a sudden or wholly new departure; each is present, at least in solution, in some medieval thinkers. But each is much more persistent and emphatic in the Renaissance humanists. Finally, each suggests that in the phrase "Christian humanism," the italics are being shifted from the first to the second word.

4. THE TREND TOWARD A NATURAL RELIGION

The medieval distinction between the domain of philosophy and that of theology was fairly consistent from the time of Anselm on. To be sure, the earlier medieval thinkers had adopted the Neoplatonic and Augustinian attitude of the complete identification of philosophy with theology. This attitude is explicit in Scotus Eriugena, for example. But in the later Middle Ages, only the extreme reactionary theologians or the mystics, on the one hand, and the extreme rationalists, on the other, held to this point of view.[49]

The Scholastic philosophers, almost to a man, maintained the distinction. But their attitude is perfectly consistent with their central attempt to work out a system in which philosophy and theology are harmonious allies. "Nothing," says Thomas Aquinas,

> prevents the questions of the philosophical sciences, so far as they are known by the light of natural reason, from being studied at the same time by another science, in the measure that they are known by revelation.[50]

His whole work, in fact, is controlled by the desire to demonstrate "the concordance in difference of the two orders"[51]—the natural and supernatural orders.

Yet at the same time the Scholastics held that there was one way in which philosophy might be applied properly to theology. This was in the method of apologetics, by which philosophic argument penetrated speculative theology. Now speculative theology, at its height in the thirteenth century, aimed at the coordination of Catholic dogma; hence its chief method was founded on the authority of the sacred books. But its secondary method was this of apologetics, the attempt to show the reasonableness of dogma.[52]

Abelard, one of the founders of this apologetic method, carried it to so extensive a reliance on reason that he aroused the wrath of Bernard of Clairvaux. But most of the Scholastics pursued the method with moderation: they defined its limits and explained its value. Thomas Aquinas denies the philosophical demonstration of mystery; philosophy, he maintains, may prove only that mystery contains nothing irrational. He declares,

> If the theology borrows from philosophy, it is not because it needs its help, but in order to make more obvious the truths which it teaches.[53]

Finally, then, Aquinas divides the knowledge which man requires for his eternal salvation into two kinds: (1) that revealed, yet attainable by reason; and (2) that surpassing the range of reason—including the mysteries of the Trinity, the Incarnation, the Redemption and the supernatural end of man.[54]

It is a very different attitude which we find in most of the Renaissance reconcilers of theology and philosophy. The goal which Ficino set the Florentine Academy was "the philosophic proof of the *fundamental* truths of Christianity."[55] In his treatises on the Platonic theology and on the Christian religion, his natural theology includes the complete dogma of the Church. In one chapter he sets out to prove that the Incarnation was both reasonable and to be expected; and he attempts the formal demonstration of the rationality of the Trinity, which he supports by the "Platonic epistles."[56]

At first blush this might seem no more heretical a position than that of Aquinas, proving that mystery contains nothing irrational. But Ficino defends his procedure with an argument based on the premise, borrowed from Gemisthus Pletho, that "the primitive theology of the Gentiles, in which Zoroaster, Mercury, Orpheus, Aglaophemus, and Pythagoras are at one is to be found entire in the books of our Plato." He then goes on to establish an "historical" argument that this "primitive theology" was really identical with that of the Christian faith, but had retained its exclusively esoteric character until the Christian revelation:

In his letters Plato prophesies that these mysteries can be made plain to mankind only after many centuries. And that is what happened. For it was first in the time of Philo and Numenius that the thought of the primitive theologians, embodied in Plato's writings, began to be understood. That is to say, it was directly after the preachings of the apostles and of the disciples of the apostles, and their writings. For the Platonists used the divine light of Christians for the interpretation of the divine Plato.[57]

Another canonization has taken place; the word "divine" is used in speaking of St. Plato in the very same sentence in which it is used to refer to the "light of Christians." Moreover, Ficino maintains in one of his *Epistles*, it was Plotinus who "first and alone stripped theology of these veils"[58]—*i.e.*, those of esotericism. Surely no special pleading is required to predicate the disapproval of Aquinas, Bonaventura and Duns Scotus.

Paul Oskar Kristeller, in his recent definitive study of Ficino's thought, has summarized succinctly the new element in the Florentine's association of philosophy with religion:

Ficino obviously abandons the subordination and dependency of philosophy as it was upheld throughout the Middle Ages. Philosophy stands free and equal beside religion, but it neither can nor may conflict with religion, because their agreement is guaranteed by a common origin and content.[59]

Finally Ficino himself, in his *Laus philosophiæ*, asserts the identity of philosophy and religion.

If philosophy is defined by all as the love and study of truth and wisdom, and if truth and wisdom itself is God alone, consequently legitimate philosophy is nothing else than true religion, and legitimate religion is nothing else than true philosophy.[60]

An enthusiasm for esotericism and eclecticism, and an attempt to fuse religious and philosophical truths into a single theology, are also central to the thought of Pico della Mirandola. In his famous oration, *De Hominis Dignitate*, he speaks of his intention of bringing before the public

the opinions, not of a single school alone (which satisfied some I could name) but rather of every school, to the end that that light of truth which Plato mentions in his letters, through this comparison of several sects and this discussion of manifold philosophies, might dawn more brightly on our minds, like the sun rising from the deep.[61]

For "what were the gain," he demands,

> if only the philosophy of the Latins were investigated, *i.e.*, that of Albertus, Scotus, Ægidius, Franciscus, and Henry, if the Greek and Arabian philosophers were left out—*since all wisdom has flowed from the East to the Greeks, and from the Greeks to us?*[62]

With the Peripatetic philosophers he wishes to combine those of the Platonic Academy, whose "teaching in regard to things divine has always (as Augustine witnesses) been thought most hallowed of all philosophies. . . ." Again, he desires to add "to the tenets held in common much concerning the ancient theology of Hermes Trismegistus, much from the teachings of the Chaldeans and the Pythagoreans, and much from the more recondite mysteries of the Hebrews," as well as "theorems dealing with magic . . ."[63]

Pico uses an appositive construction in speaking of "all wise men, all peoples devoted to the study of heavenly and divine things," and he asserts,

> If you see a philosopher determining *all things* by means of right reason, him you shall reverence: he is a heavenly and not an earthly being. . . .[64]

Whatever justifications the Florentines employed to defend their orthodoxy (many of Pico's propositions got him into trouble), these passages indicate that they made little or no distinction between religious and rational activity, between the province of theology and that of philosophy—and furthermore, that they were endeavoring to make of Eastern esoteric religion and Christianity one theology.

The second of these tendencies—despite enthusiastic adherents like Reuchlin, the great Hebrew scholar, and Symphorien Champier —played a less spectacular role in the sixteenth-century Renaissance of the northern countries. Yet, although relatively few of the northern humanists display metaphysical and mystical preoccupations, they too exemplify the first tendency—to fuse completely religion and philosophy.

There is an echo of Ficino's and Pico's "certain devout philosophy" in the title of Guillaume Budé's last and largest book: *De Transitu Hellenismi ad Christianismum* (1534), which is "an exposition of Greek philosophy as a preparation for Christianity."[65] But while this purpose might also be said to be consonant with that of Erasmus and other northern humanists, we have only to turn to them to find out how different their temper is.

One may say with a wide margin of safety, I think, that Erasmus considers the purified doctrine of the "philosophy of Christ" almost identical with the religion of Plato, Cicero and Seneca.[66] In *The Education of a Christian Prince* he makes as forthright an identification of philosophy and religion as Ficino before him—but in a characteristically simpler and more generalized statement.

> To be a philosopher and to be a Christian is synonymous in fact. The only difference is in the nomenclature.[67]

But Ficino's and Pico's "Plotinian" and mystical Plato, and the Neoplatonists, have little attraction for him; it is the moral philosophers he means when he speaks of the Greeks, and he declares,

> When I read certain passages of these great men, I can hardly refrain from saying, "Saint Socrates, pray for me."[68]

For Erasmus, the gospel and the writings of the classical moral philosophers merge to form a "single undogmatic religion of simple morality."[69] And this tendency to think of Socrates and Seneca and Cicero and Cato as precursors of Christianity, an inclination foreshadowed in Dante and Petrarch, is characteristic of most of Erasmus' circle.

The conviction—so variously displayed by the Italian and by the Northern humanists of the Renaissance—that all religions have a common ground of basic truths concerning God,[70] constitutes at least a rudimentary Deism. No other book of the English Renaissance so clearly reflects this attitude as Sir Thomas More's *Utopia*. There are, in every town of the island he describes, several sorts of religion:

> yet the greater and wiser sort of them worship none of these, but adore one eternal, invisible, infinite, and incomprehensible Deity; as a Being that is far above all our apprehensions, that is spread over the whole Universe, not by His bulk, but by His power and virtue. . . . And indeed, though they differ concerning all other things, yet all agree in this, that there is one supreme Being that made and governs the world, whom they call in the language of their country Mithras.[71]

Furthermore, most of the Utopians come eventually "to agree together in that religion which seemeth to pass and excel the residue."[72] More makes the concession to Christianity that, after the Utopians heard the travelers' account of it, "it is not to be imagined how inclined they were to receive it."[73] Yet he is not sure whether this came about through the inspiration of God, or through the accord the Utopians found between their own communistic principles and those of primitive Christianity.

At any rate, all the basic elements of seventeenth-century Deism, from that of Herbert of Cherbury on, are present in the Utopians' attitude. They believe in the existence of God and in the duty of worshiping Him. They define that worship as the obligation to morality, and finally they all believe in the immortality of the soul. These common primary truths they hold to be accessible to every one, and to precede all revelations of organized religions.[74]

There are many other manifestations of this trend toward Deism, or natural religion, in the sixteenth century. That independent reformer, Zwingli, found a way to conciliate humanism and Protestanism through the idea of the unity of divine revelation in various religions; Reuchlin, in the interests of Judaism, was the advocate of "a primitive and integral Christianity" of a Deistic sort.[75] Coornhert, a leader of the extreme Protestant sect called the "Libertins Spirituels" (at least by their enemies; Calvin, for one, detested them), claimed that one could follow the laws of Christ without knowing him by name; while his colleague, Sebastian Franck, united humanism with mysticism by asserting the identification of the invisible Christ with the spark of natural light to be found in every human spirit, and hence capable of being kindled even in the heathen.[76]

Unquestionably two major influences upon this growth of natural religion in the sixteenth century were the extensive interest in the Orient (and particularly in Turkey), and the increasing number of accounts of the New World in the West.[77] The threat which the Saracen Empire offered to Europe remained mostly unabated until the battle of Lepanto in 1571, and inevitably the continued successes of the Turk in military affairs, as well as an increasingly detailed knowledge of his religion, led to some at least elementary ponderings in the direction of comparative religion. Again, while the reports of the attitudes of the inhabitants of the New World toward religion varied considerably (even more, one suspects, in accordance with the reporter's own convictions than with local customs), there were many testimonials which strengthened the position of the Deist.

Jean Bodin's *Colloquium heptaplomeres*, written in 1593, but not published until the nineteenth century, approaches in more nearly the modern sense a study in comparative religion. This work is a discussion with seven participants—a Catholic, a Lutheran, a Calvinist, a Jew, a Mohammedan, and two other men, each of whom represents one kind of Deism (or Theism, if, with the specialists, one prefers to reserve the term for the more pronounced and explicit movement of the seventeenth and eighteenth centuries).[78] While Bodin professes no final solution, and tell us that each of these men continues to worship in his own way after the debate, he is clearly most sympathetic to the position of Toralba, the "dogmatic" Deist, and that of Senamus, the "undogmatic" Deist, who differs from Toralba particularly in his refusal to oppose natural religion to the positive institutionalized religions. Indeed, an extant letter of Bodin's shows how clearly he belongs to the tradition we have been following. In this private statement, he goes, in his bold simplicity, well beyond most of his predecessors:

> Do not let thyself be led away by different views on religion. Hold fast in thy spirit to this only that true religion is nothing else than the turning of a purified soul to God. That is my, or rather Christ's, religion.[79]

The whole trend constitutes, indeed, a continuing process from the Middle Ages to the seventeenth-century Deism of Herbert of Cherbury, and beyond. But it seems clear that in the course of the journey, the Christian solution has not absorbed the humanistic. What begins as Christian humanism proceeds through the various naturalizing processes of the Renaissance to emerge eventually considerably transformed in the extremely liberal theology of the Cambridge Platonists, in Thomas Sprat's declaration that "The Universal Disposition of this Age is bent upon a rational Religion,"[80] and in the outright Deism so extensive in the Newtonian Age. The progress is a gradual but persistent one, away from the mere buttressing of faith with reason, through a fairly even balancing of faith and reason, to the domination of faith by reason. The rational humanistic element steadily gains in strength, until the universal tenets of the existence of God, the duty of worship, the pursuit of man's natural inclination to virtue, and the immortality of the soul, are held a sufficient religion, and capable of rational proof without benefit of Christian revelation.

The Middle Ages had their Abelard, with his tendency to seek purely rational solutions, and to refer all ethical problems to the subjective conscience.[81] They had their Raymond of Sabunde (or Sebond), who sought like Ficino and Pico to explain by natural reason all "the providential mysteries of Christianity,"[82] and their Raymond Lully, who wanted to support the whole body of revelation by the syllogism. But their rationalism was in the service of dogma; the rationalism which we have been tracing through the Renaissance has slowly moved from this position to its opposite —the dispensing with the necessity of dogma. In the course of this journey, we have left the world created, sustained and directed by the exclusively Christian God of the noble closing lines of the *Divine Comedy*—the God of "l'amor che move il sole e l'altre stelle." We have left that world far behind; encamped before the walls of Babylon, we are listening to Tamburlaine thunder out,

> Seeke out another Godhead to adore
> The God that sits in heaven, if any God,
> For he is God alone, and none but he.[83]

And we are aware that this is the world of the Utopians' God—"one eternal, invisible, infinite and incomprehensible Deity"—that God whom Tamburlaine describes as

> he that sits on high and never sleeps,
> Nor in one place is circumscriptible,
> But every where fils every Continent,
> With strange infusion of his sacred vigor. . . .[84]

The earlier kind of rationalism (that in support of dogma) is still evident in the sixteenth century: in Melanchthon among the early Protestants, in Suarez among the Jesuits, in Richard Hooker among the Anglicans. But even Hooker has pushed Nature and Reason to a perilous eminence:

> It sufficeth therefore that Nature and Scripture do serve in such full sort, that they *both jointly* and *not severally either of them* be so complete that unto everlasting felicity we need not the knowledge of anything more than *these two* may easily furnish our minds with on all sides. . . .[85]

And when we reach Book III, where he is in the heat of battle with the Puritans, he demands,

> The whole drift of the Scripture of God, what is it but only to teach theology? Theology, what is it but the science of things divine? What science can be attained unto without the help of natural discourses and reason? "Judge you that which I speak," saith the Apostle. In vain it were to speak anything of God but that by Reason men are able somewhat to judge of that they hear, and by discourse to discern how consonant it is to truth. Scripture indeed teacheth things above Nature, things which our Reason by itself could not reach unto. Yet those things also we believe knowing by Reason that Scripture is the Word of God.[86]

Yet even Hooker's strong vindication of the rights and efficacy of reason is orthodox almost to the point of conservatism, besides the growing line of the advocates of natural theology. Despite the opposition of Calvin and Luther, the Reformation joins and merges with this line. But the spirit and direction are evident long before. More than a hundred years before Hooker wrote the paragraph just quoted, Marsilio Ficino had anticipated his argument with the statement that "All speech, and even all action in life and all consideration is nothing but a process of reasoning."[87]

Indeed, for the learned age in which he lived, he felt it necessary to go a good deal further, if men were to be led to Christianity. He wrote to Johannes Pannonius:

> We must not think that the subtle and philosophical minds of men can ever be gradually enticed and led to the perfect religion by any lure other than a philosophical one. For subtle minds trust themselves only to reason, and if they receive religion from a religious philosopher, at once and of their own volition they recognize religion in general and from there pass more readily to the best species of religion included in that genus.[88]

One may say, then, that with Ficino reason comes to the rescue of faith. And such is certainly the case, for the remainder of the letter is devoted to explaining that "the simple preaching of faith" will hardly suffice to convert an age almost wholly given over to irreligious "Alexandrists and Averroists." Stronger measures are needed: "either divine miracles manifested on all sides or at least a philosophical religion to which philosophers will listen more readily and which will some day succeed in convincing them." And so Ficino concludes, "But in these times it pleases divine Providence to confirm *religion in general* by philosophical authority and reason until, on a day already predestined, it will confirm the true religion, as in other times, by miracles wrought among all peoples."[89]

Reason comes to the rescue of faith. . . . It is fruitless to impugn Ficino's sincerity, and, in view of his other writings, I do not propose to do so, even with regard to the "day already predestined." Perhaps the disingenuous ring which the passage has to modern ears is wholly to be accounted for by the disingenuousness of most modern ears. However that may be, reason's service in the interests of faith is a different matter in 1484 from what it was in the days of Thomas Aquinas and Dante Alighieri. And from the Florentine Academy's "certain devout philosophy" to the utter reliance of Herbert of Cherbury upon the light of nature implanted in man by

God, there is within the "reconciliation" tradition an increasing humanistic accent upon natural reason, upon the individual conscience, and away from the revealed body of truth exclusively the property of the Roman Catholic Church. As Professor Shorey dryly put it, you are at liberty to consider the change enlightenment or to consider it heresy. But deny the change you cannot.

5. THE TREND TOWARD AN INDEPENDENT HUMANISTIC ETHIC

The increasing emphasis laid by the Renaissance humanists upon the moral life, the relevance of good works to salvation, and their increasing preoccupation with the active life rather than the contemplative, with ethics rather than metaphysics, is a development complementary and parallel to the gradually increasing priority of reason and nature over faith and revelation in religion. This re-estimate of man's true good is for many individual thinkers and writers a change in emphasis, not an altering of the goal. Salvation in a Christian heaven remains the ultimate destination, but the moral life of virtuous activity supplants (at least in the interest indicated by the number of pages devoted to it) the intellectual contemplation of God or truth, as the most urgently recommended exercise leading to that destination.

Other humanists turn back to the various Greek ideals of happiness or virtue or pleasure, or a combination of these, as the true end of man's journey through life, omitting all (or all but the most perfunctory) mention of the after-life and reward in heaven. A few even attack the "reward system" as no proper basis for the attainment of true virtue. But for the authentic Christian humanists of the Renaissance, as for those of the Middle Ages,

> everything, both in the life of individuals and in the life of societies of which individuals form a part, is ordered to this supra-terrestrial end.[90]

Thus the "continuation theory" about Renaissance humanism holds good in part. Moreover, most of the Scholastics, following Aristotle, had conceded considerable importance to the ethical life. Aquinas treats extensively of happiness as a cooperative social affair.[91] Yet it remains true for Aquinas that the "last beatitude of happiness of any intelligent substance is to know God"; at the top of his hierarchical ladder of activities is the rung assigned to the theologian and the contemplative life. If the proposition is carried to its logical conclusion, the subordinate activities of men pursuing lesser ends in society are constructive and lead to happiness only when they contribute to the contemplative's realization of that "last beatitude" by relieving him of more menial tasks.[92]

In the literature of the fourteenth century, there is already evident a reaction, a trend toward more of a balance. Such English works, for example, as *Piers Plowman* and Hylton's *Of Mixed Life* find the highest life in the combination of the contemplative and active ideals.[93]

Again, although Dante maintains to a large extent the proportions endorsed by Aquinas, with Petrarch we come to a man for whom the relative merits of the contemplative and active courses of life constitute a conflict, and a major one. In his dialogue with "St. Augustine" in the *Secretum*, Petrarch says outright,

> I do not think to become as God, or to inhabit eternity, or to embrace heaven and earth. Such glory as belongs to men is enough for me. That is all I sigh after. Mortal myself, it is but mortal blessings I desire.[94]

When Augustine, horrified, rebukes him, he explains,

> I intended to say—that my wish was to use mortal things for what they are worth, to do no violence to nature by bringing to its good things a limitless and immoderate desire, and so to follow after human fame as knowing that both myself and it will perish.[95]

Augustine, who may safely be considered Petrarch's *alter ego* in the dialogue, is only partly mollified, but the immoderate seeker after human fame never really recants.

Still, whatever we may be justified in suspecting about their secret convictions (surely, it is significant that Petrarch, the exhibitionist, did not allow the *Secretum* to be published during his lifetime), few of the Italian humanists openly and formally opposed "fame," as an ideal, to the contemplative life. Much more characteristic of their public attitude are their moral treatises on happiness and the good life, modeled on the classical moral philosophers and expounding the Platonic, Aristotelian, Stoic and Epicurean ethical systems.[96] These tracts on the *summum bonum* disclose a wide divergence of opinion, or rather, argument—for it is a temptation to dismiss as a rhetorical afflatus much of the pessimism and other-worldliness which some of their authors cultivate.

At any rate, two major tendencies emerge from this somewhat controversial material: first, the widespread interest in classical systems of ethics; second, a related and new preoccupation with the search for happiness on this earth, with either very little reference to a supra-terrestrial end, or none at all. And surely it is significant that the more sober and moderate of these treatises—for example, Leonardo Bruni's *Isagogicon of Moral Discipline*—discover happiness in the practice of virtue, through a life carried on in accordance with reason and the Aristotelian golden mean.[97]

Both of these major trends discernible in the Italian humanists of the fifteenth century develop and extend their influence over the thought of sixteenth-century Europe. Above all, it is the ethical writings of Plato and Aristotle, of Cicero and Plutarch, of Seneca and even of Epicurus, that are quoted, elaborated and extolled by the sixteenth-century humanists. Translations flourished, citations abounded, imitations were legion.

In particular, the eclectic moralists like Cicero and Plutarch and Seneca achieved a great popularity. It was inevitable that the eclecticism of a man like Cicero should appeal widely. He had admitted his debt to Plato and Aristotle at the outset of *De Officiis*, and the fifth book of *De Finibus* is devoted to an exposition of the similarities of Academic, Peripatetic and Stoic ethics. Such a tolerant and "reconciling" philosophical position was very close to that held by Erasmus, among others. Moreover, since the days of the church fathers, Cicero had been accepted by many as a sort of forerunner of Christianity, and a large number of the classical concepts and ideas which had found their way into the medieval synthesis had been channeled through his writings.

Indeed, Cicero's interpretation of the Stoic Law of Nature, and of various corollaries of it, was most influential in the Renaissance movements toward a natural religion and an independent humanistic ethic. His *Tusculan Disputations* provides the *locus classicus* for the identification of the Law of Nature (*ipsa naturae ratio, quae est lex divina et humana*)[98] with the "universally accepted" or *consensus gentium:*

> omni autem in re consensio omnium gentium lex naturae putanda est (But on every matter the consensus of all peoples is to be regarded as the law of nature).[99]

This is to say that that which all men everywhere accept must be acknowledged as true. Moreover, since for Cicero reason is a universal and equal capacity of learning implanted in men by Nature,[100] it would follow that the wide belief from the earliest times in the immortality of man's soul, and in the assumption of the existence of the gods, was sufficient proof of the validity of these premises. They could be defended by rational argument alone, on the basis of *consensus gentium*.[101] Or so, at least, argued many sixteenth- and seventeenth-century writers with Deistic tendencies.

Cicero's interpretation of the famous Stoic injunction "sequere naturam" or "vivere secundum naturam" is equally crucial to the Renaissance humanists' preoccupation with ethics. In the *De Officiis* he writes,

> When the Stoics speak of the supreme good as "living conformably to nature," they mean, as I take it, something like this: that we are always to be in accord with virtue, and from all other things that may be in harmony with nature to choose only such as are not incompatible with virtue.[102]

It would be difficult to find a statement more completely in accord with the ethical ideal of most Renaissance humanists. The good life is the life lived according to nature, which for man is distinctively his rational nature, and it leads to virtue. As Ernest Hunter Wright has so eloquently described the whole process:

> Impelled by our nature to seek the good, we are provided with our reason to find it; and thus prompted and guided, we toil up toward virtue, which will be our end if we can reach it. Nature is right, and her name at last may be virtue.[103]

The idea, of course, is not peculiarly or exclusively Stoic. It is in basic (if not inclusive) harmony with the Platonic ethic; it derives from Aristotle's most characteristic interpretation of the nature of anything as its "end," or the good toward which it tends.[104] Moreover, particularly in this latter connotation, it is an integral part of the Scholastic ethical theory, and hence, in its Christianized form, was accessible to the Renaissance through Thomas Aquinas and other medieval sources. But for the Scholastics,

> the Christian finds himself placed in an order in which natural morality itself calls for the supernatural as its necessary complement. He can appeal no longer to his own virtue, righteousness and merit, in the first place, but to those only that he acquires by grace. . . .[105]

Now for many Renaissance humanists—certainly for all of those who may properly be called Christian humanists—we may assume that this qualification remains valid; but that, since most of them were not systematic philosophers and metaphysicians, they were content to leave it implicit. Nevertheless, this very fact indicates a suggestive shift of interest. Moreover, it is not only true that many of the humanists' moral treatises omit all reference to grace, but that the form in which the familiar formula of the good life is most often put is the Stoic one, as rendered especially by Cicero.[106]

There has been much disagreement about the extent of the "Stoic revival" of the Renaissance, disagreement mostly caused, I believe, by the prevalence in the period of at least two major "kinds" of Stoicism. From the writings of the fourteenth-century humanist chancellor of Florence, Coluccio Salutati, to the largely systematic attempts of Justus Lipsius and Guillaume du Vair to achieve a formal reconciliation of dogmatic philosophical Stoicism and dogmatic theological Christianity, and to such Elizabethan plays as William Shakespeare's *King Lear*[107] and George Chapman's *Revenge of Bussy*, there was indeed much interest in doctrinal Stoicism. But by far the greater allegiance of the sixteenth century was given to the eclectic and frequently Platonizing Stoic ethics of Cicero,[108] which blended harmoniously and almost indistinguishably with the eclectic Platonic ethics of the almost equally popular Plutarch, and with the traditional Aristotelian ethics. It is to this second tradition, this second sort of "Stoicism," that the majority of the great Renaissance humanists, Christian or "Christian," belonged; to call it a Stoic tradition can be justified only by the prominence in its creed of the Stoic Law of Nature, concept of *consensus gentium* and ethical motto of *sequere naturam*.

From the very beginnings of Renaissance humanism, this eclectic ethical tradition's influence plays a large part in the gradual shift from a metaphysical and ontological attitude toward salvation and the good life, to a primarily moralistic and humanistic one:

> Salutati's ideal, according to Von Martin, was to achieve virtue by means of moral philosophy and humanistic studies instead of logic and metaphysics. Thus the ideal of the Christian Middle Ages was retained while the means were rejected.[109]

This statement, in Trinkaus' *Adversity's Noblemen*, is qualified by the reminder that "to the humanist, study meant both virtue and care for the eternal, and thus this idea united the Stoic and Christian ideals."[110] Yet it is pertinent to the question of how "Christian" the humanists felt such an ideal of virtue to be, to observe that Salutati later, in *The World and Religion*, renounced his Stoicism, and accepted the idea (so central to the Reformation) that salvation is beyond all human powers, and to be attained only through the grace of God.[111] And his change of heart is by no means unique. Under the influence of Savonarola—Ficino, Pico and Benivieni of the Florentine Academy renounced their Platonic religion in a similar way; and it is reported that Lipsius recanted from Stoicism and asked for the Cross and extreme unction on his deathbed.

But the humanist ideal of virtuous activity as the end of learning and the path to salvation persists. The first dialogue of Cristoforo Landino's *Quaestiones Camaldulenses* sets it forth in a form that reconciles the medieval and Renaissance versions. He defines the Florentine Academy's ideal in these words:

> We are brought forth by nature in order that we may act virtuously and search out truth.

This dialogue is primarily a discussion of the contemplative and the active life; in his concluding comparison of Mary and Martha, Landino concedes that Mary's virtue is of a higher sort, but insists that both are pleasing to God, both necessary. In fact, contemplation is imperfect (and perhaps even dangerous) unless it issues in right conduct—and notably in social action.[112]

There can be no question of Erasmus' preference: the Philosophy of Christ (with a program identical with that of "Greek Philosophy") "is a life more than a debate, an inspiration rather than a discipline. . . ."[113] The exclusively human problems of morality, of bringing to earth the return of Christ's kingdom of peace and tolerance, engross him utterly.

Sir Thomas More discusses at some length those Utopians who believe that "by the good things a man does he secures to himself that happiness that comes after death." Some of these "spend their whole life in hard labour," serving both the public and private individuals; yet they are, for their often servile employments, "so much the more esteemed by the whole nation." He dismisses "the contemplating God in His works" politely, as "a very acceptable piece of worship to Him."[114]

In the *Utopia* the moral life is based upon the four cardinal virtues of classical philosophy,[115] and virtue is defined in the Ciceronian manner as "a life according to nature," as "ordained by God." More adds, "He doth follow the course of nature, which in desiring and refusing things is ruled by reason."[116]

Now it is quite true that the bias toward a natural religion in the *Utopia* may be justified by the fact that the discoverers of a fabulous country must almost certainly find one unfamiliar with Christianity. It is also true that More's open praise of the Utopians' natural religion may be, and has been, interpreted as a rebuke to the lax and corrupt Christians of his day: if these heathen can do so much, how much more should we, with the benefit of Christ?

Again, it is indisputable that he argues against the Lutherans, "Reason is servant to Faith, not enemy,"[117] and that we have no just motive for doubting his sincerity.

Yet the most powerful impression is left by his description of the noble life of the Utopians. There is dignity and a restrained passion of conviction when he speaks of their religious life which remains unmatched in his other writings, including his devotional work. And to evaluate the peculiarly Christian element in his view, one has only to compare it with that of John Colet:

> By the death of Christ, therefore, which was gone through for all, men are retained in life, by the marvellous grace of God; that their sins may be blotted out by the death of Christ, even as by their own, and that in all the rest of their life they may strive after virtue and aspire unto God.[118]

Here we have the perfect orthodox statement of the true Christian humanist, marking the variation from the Scholastic view, yet at the same time scrupulously observing the doctrinal Christian terminology and position. Beside this statement, the prose of More stands, infinitely nobler in expression, generally similar in purport, yet unquestionably different in tone and emphasis. . . .

The line moves on in Tudor England, through the humanistic educators, men like Elyot, Cheke, Ascham and Mulcaster—men to whom all learning is sterile save that which incites to a virtuous life. Again, for Richard Hooker, "the natural path of everlasting life" begins in "that ability of doing good, which God in the day of man's creation endued him with"; it comprises obedience to God, "righteousness and integrity in all his actions," and is crowned by the justice of God with a life everlasting.[119] And the whole Renaissance tradition of Christian humanism—the identification of right reason and virtue, of both with Christian liberty and the good life, and of all with the will of God; the envisioning of man's relation to God and his hope of attaining to God's kingdom primarily through obeying God's moral laws on earth—this tradition culminates in John Milton. Puritan he may have been, but he was also the last great Christian humanist of the Renaissance. He builds a learned Heaven and a magnificent Hell, yet (despite the contradictory passages in his voluminous tome on Christian doctrine and in *Paradise Regained*) the primary concern of most of his prose and much of his poetry is to establish the kingdom of God on earth—more particularly, in England.

Now in this whole procession, from Landino's profession for the

Academy in Florence to Milton's for the good life in Puritan England, we have not been tracing an anti-, or even an a-Christian attitude. Even in Erasmus and More, man's final goal of angelification has not been lost sight of. But what was at least secondary to the intellectual knowledge of God and truth for the Scholastics (Dante had said, *"primarily in speculation, then through its extention and for its sake, secondarily in action"*)—the "natural path of everlasting life," in Hooker's phrase—has attained an equality with the contemplative life and even, in many individuals, takes priority over it. Salvation through works, through moral life, through the pursuit of virtue, has come into its own. *The living of human life has taken precedence over contemplating the meaning of human life.*

The idea of collaborating with and imitating God to bring about his rule on earth, already prominent although subordinate in the thought of the thirteenth century, now achieves, for the Renaissance Christian humanists, the first place. Many of them accord it that explicitly; almost all of them, after the Florentines, display this bias in their characteristic choice of subject matter and in their temper.

Such is the orthodox Elizabethan ethical position, founded upon humanistic learning. Its tone is optimistic and sturdy. Much of the poetry of George Chapman illustrates this attitude admirably. Addressing Christ, he asks,

> Didst thou not offer, to restore our fall
> Thy sacrifice, full, once, and one for all?
> If we be still downe, how then can we rise
> Againe with thee, and seeke crownes in the skies?
> But we excuse this; saying, We are but men,
> And must erre, must fail: what thou didst sustaine
> To free our beastly frailties, never can
> With all thy grace, by any powre in man
> Make good thy Rise to us: O blasphemie
> In hypocriticall humilitie!

The choice remains with men, he insists, and our salvation and relationship with God depend upon how we live.

> When casting off a good life's godlike grace,
> We fall from God; and then make good our place
> When we returne to him: and so are said
> To live: when life like his true forme we leade. . . .[120]

With his mixture of Stoic, Platonic, Peripatetic and Christian doctrines, Chapman's concept of "life like his true forme" is that in which a man is able (and chooses) to embrace, in an ordered universe,

> The course his end holds, his proper place
> Not suffering his affections to disperse,
> But fit the main sway over the universe.

Will plays a part, but a qualified part, under the guidance of reason:

> The empire of the will is ever sav'd
> Except lost by itselfe, when tis deprav'd.

It should be ruled by the "Soveraigne sway" of "Imperiall Reason." Then, and then only, do we truly "imitate God, Who gives us Lawes to Keepe. . . ."[121]

Chapman further strengthens his general thesis with Neoplatonic doctrine, probably derived from Ficino:

> as Philosophie
> Saies there is evermore proportion
> Betwixt the knowing part, and what is knowne
> So joynd, that both, are absolutely one;
> So when we know God, *in things here below,*
> And truly keepe th' abstracted good we know;
> (God being all goodnesse) *we with him combine,*
> And therein shew, the all in all, doth shine. . . .[122]

Finally,

> Arme then thy mind with these;
> I have decrees set downe twixt me and God;
> I know his precepts, I will beare his lode. . . .[123]

The majority of the Renaissance humanists we have considered advocate a vigorous ethical Christianity. They make much of what man may accomplish by his own powers, under the guiding direction of reason, and they feel sure that this attitude is consistent with the Christian life. Whether Catholic or Protestant, they follow the conciliatory Catholic stand on the question of the Fall and the freedom of the human will.[124] They believe that Christ has redeemed man and man's powers, and that one may regain God's favor and salvation through the living of a virtuous life in accordance with the wholly compatible trinity of nature, right reason and the will of God.

Yet humility, that peculiarly Christian virtue, has never found large favor in either Greek or Roman moral philosophy:[125] and in an ethic so basically classical as that of the humanists, humility might well go begging. At least, so many of their detractors be-

lieved. Long before the Reformation had become a potent force,
there were not lacking men who found these allegedly "Christian"
humanists as guilty of a moral *hybris* as they believed the Scholastics to have been of a speculative *hybris*. The chief charge was
that, in the pursuit of virtue, the humanists came so to rely upon
their own powers that they found neither place for, nor need of,
God's assistance. In short, it was claimed that they, unduly optimistic
about the potency of man's nature since the Fall, pursued virtue for
its own sake; forgot that they owed even a comparative wholeness
to grace and to Christ; and thus divorced the Christian-classical
ethic from its supranatural base, so that it ceased to be Christian.

The application of this charge to men like Richard Hooker had
little justification. His humanism was clearly balanced with traditional Christian theology. And, despite what seemed to his Puritan
detractors his much too liberal endorsement of nature and reason,
he never omitted the theological base of the Christian ethic. The
fairness of the accusation is at least an open question, however,
with many others, from the Italian humanists on. Once again, one's
verdict is apt to correspond with one's definition of Christianity.

For despite the explicit concern of Erasmus with Christ, it is
"Christ, that good Samaritan," Christ the moral philosopher of
human love and peace on earth, Christ the man, whom he cites over
and over again. So, too, despite More's reverence for Christianity
and insistence upon immortality, it is for him primarily the life of
virtue, according to nature, which God has ordained for us through
his goodness, that will make possible everlasting felicity. Or at
least, so the Utopians believe, and his account rings with conviction and approval.

With these men and others like them, there is an undeniable
quickening of appreciation of the life God has given to be lived on
earth. This is not to be interpreted as "pagan" enjoyment of life,
although both Erasmus and More believed pleasure not incompatible with virtue and true happiness; it is an essentially sober ideal.
Yet it is not that of the Middle Ages, and if the speculative pro-
fundity of Thomas Aquinas and the vertical aspiration of medieval
mystical theologians are totally missing, there has nevertheless been
a perceptible broadening of the Christian horizon. John Colet, referring to quarrels between sects, speaks for the new spirit when
he asks why men try to make so narrow what Christ had made so
broad.

There is no answer, except the human need to bring everything
down to one's own measure. And there is no one definitive answer,

but rather many variant ones, to the question of whether an all but complete absorption in a liberal Christian ethic and Christian social ideal necessarily implies a defection from the Christian theology, if the terms of the theology are not explicitly stated.

In a case like Justus Lipsius, the answer is easier. Lipsius himself admitted the all but insuperable difficulties of adjusting many Stoic doctrinal points to the requirements of dogmatic Christianity.[126] His definition of Right Reason as "A true sense and judgment of things human and divine," while far from his most serious "offense," is certainly not a Christian but a Stoic definition. And despite his protestations to the contrary, his account of the pursuit of virtue— whether for better or for worse—may justly be charged with the "crime" of virtue-for-its-own-sake.

However, long before the *Two Bookes of Constancie*, Pietro Pomponazzi, the Paduan philosopher, had quite openly endorsed just such an independent ethic. His *De Immortalitate Animae* (1516) is a treatise devoted to proving that the doctrine of personal immortality is both contrary to Aristotle (whom Pomponazzi interpreted after the fashion of Alexander of Aphrodias, rather than Averroës or Thomas Aquinas) and to the truth of reason.[127] In the course of this work he discusses, following Aristotle's division of man's faculties, the relative merits of the speculative, practical and factive intellects in terms of the good life.

It is "the practical intellect . . . which is peculiarly man's," he finds; for the practical soul is that "concerned with customs, public and private affairs," while the factive soul, shared with beasts, pertains to "things mechanical and necessary to life." As for the speculative soul, its realm is more appropriate to gods than to men: "the world would not remain if any and every one were of a speculative number." Hence, he concludes, it is "being good or wicked" which "is human and lies within our power, but being a philosopher or a builder is not, nor is it necessary to man. . . . Wherefore *the universal end of mankind* is sharing relatively in regard to the speculative and factive, perfectly, however, in regard to the practical."[128]

In what seems to be a combination of Stoic, Platonic and Aristotelian emphases,[129] he goes on to urge the thesis that virtue for its own sake is the only true virtue. That which has for its aim either reward or the escape of punishment after death is rendered ignoble by greed or fear. He admits that few men are capable of his ideal, but he remains firm in his insistence that this definition alone describes true virtue.[130]

Now it is true that Pomponazzi does not, properly speaking, belong to the tradition we have been following. With his Paduan background, he rather belongs to that band of "Alexandrists and Averroists" whom Ficino condemned as denying "any form of religion." Moreover, he was separating, not reconciling, the truths of reason and faith. Yet his open avowal of an ethic independent of Christian theology is the logical terminus of the ethical road which many of the Christian humanists followed. If few of them push on to the end of the journey, or at least do so only after dark, when the visibility is poor,[131] at least his example helps to make clear the direction in which they are traveling.

Another and related charge frequently leveled at the humanists of the "reconciliation" tradition was that in their optimism about man's natural inclination to goodness and his ability to do much to further his own salvation, they belittled the potency and dignity of the doctrine of original sin. Their attitude would have been very well for pre-lapsarian Adam, when nature, including the human variety, was good; for a man living in the sixteenth century, it amounted to the Pelagian heresy.

Here, too, the fears of the humanists' adversaries were realized, and this time within the camp of the Reformation. The earlier Christian humanists maintained chiefly that man's nature had been mutilated by the Fall, but that Christ's redeeming grace had restored his powers and enabled him once more to lead a virtuous life. Their position was a very temperate one, beside that of Zwingli—"in whom the religious sincerity of the Reformer is united with the consistency of the thinker" and "with the Humanist's love for antiquity. . . ."[132] For Zwingli held that what is called "original sin" is merely an inclination to sin, and not sin itself. Moreover, this innate inclination is not the result of the sin of Adam and Eve, but has its origin simply in the fact that man is a finite and limited being.[133]

The implications of this conviction, implications which Zwingli developed logically—in combination with his concept of revelation coming directly and immediately from God to the individual, and being sufficient for salvation—led to his advocacy of self-government in the civil as well as the ecclesiastical realm.[134] They point toward the future, far beyond the orthodox Christianity of his time.

It was also from the Reformed Countries that "the *modern* doctrine of natural law . . . drew its source."[135] The trend is already discernible in the *De lege naturae apodictica methodus* (1562) of Niels Hemmingsen, a Danish theologian and a disciple of Melanchthon.

Cicero had affirmed that

> True law is right reason in agreement with nature; it is of universal application, unchanging and eternal. . . .[136]

Upon this supposedly universal basis, all positive (or man-made) law rested. An examination of Hooker's system of laws reveals that this concept had been thoroughly Christianized and integrated with divine law. Nature being God's instrument, Hooker asserts that the law of Nature "is as it were an authenticall or an original draught written in the bosom of God himself. . . ."[137]

This reconciliation of natural and divine law had been, in fact, a commonplace (although a disputed one) in medieval legal theory and philosophy.[138] But what Hemmingsen (unlike his contemporaries, Hooker and Suarez)[139] set out to produce was "a strictly scientific enunciation of the natural law." Rejecting theological explanations, he proposed to discover "how far Reason can attain without the prophetic and apostolic writings."[140]

Since the germs of morality and righteousness are given in the nature of man, he argues, citing the familiar hypothesis that the natural light enables man to discern the difference between right and wrong, man must be guided by reason, which is the true *human* law of nature: "lex naturae seu recta ratio." Hence, although man's ultimate end is the worship of God, for which purpose his natural powers are inadequate, divine revelation is not necessary for a knowledge of natural law.[141] Here, again, there is no reference— as there is in Hooker, for example—to the difference which the Fall has made.[142]

Like Melanchthon, Hemmingsen thought of the ten commandments as a short epitome of the law of nature (*epitome legis naturae*); but only after he had established the natural law did he test its agreement with the commandments. His method, then—his whole treatment of natural law—is a parallel trend to those we have been observing, and, what is more, another step toward the declaration of independence of a humanistic ethic—because of the close dependence of contemporary ethical theory upon natural law. . . .[143]

The course from a completely Christian ethic, resting upon a theological base and primarily eschatological in character, to an independent humanistic one, resting upon a human law of nature and aiming at terrestrial happiness compatible with virtue, is not in detail an easy or wholly consistent one. Yet certain general tendencies are clearly marked; chief among these are the subordina-

tion and even elimination of the Christian dogma, the increasing
confidence in natural law and reason, and the growing inclination
to anchor virtue to the earth.

In this process, Renaissance Christian humanism undoubtedly
played a major rule. It was in a large measure its influence which
made it possible for a Catholic priest to write at the beginning of
the seventeenth century:

> I will that a man be a good man even though there be no
> Heaven and no Hell. It seems to me detestable when a man
> says: If I were not a Christian, if I did not fear damnation,
> I would do this or that. I will that thou shouldst be good be-
> cause Nature and Reason so will it—because it is demanded
> by the general order of things of which Reason is only a part
> —and because thou canst not act against *thyself, thine essence
> and thine aim*—what will may follow from this. When once
> this stands firm, religion may follow after, but the converse
> relation is ruinous.[144]

6. SUMMARY AND TRANSITION

The first great intellectual movement of the Renaissance is that
of its largely Christian, if increasingly rationalistic, humanism.[145]
These Renaissance humanists turned, gradually but surely, from the
pre-eminently intellectualistic and speculative Science of God of
the Scholastics to a preoccupation with the Science of Man. Concentrating more upon the right living of life than upon the meaning
of life, they inaugurated a reform in education which led to an
almost exclusive discipline in the humane studies. The aim of this
education was to prepare men to live lives of virtuous activity, in
accordance with right reason, which meant in accordance with the
distinguishing attribute of human nature.

Whereas the Scholastics had turned to Aristotle's scientific and
logical treatises for texts, these humanists chose rather the writings
of the classical moral philosophers—above all, Cicero and Seneca,
through whose works they absorbed much of their Platonism and
Stoicism. Yet the Aristotelian ethic of the golden mean between
excess and defect was invoked by most of them as regularly as the
Platonic cardinal virtues and the Stoic law of nature; their eclectic
ethics did not prescribe the extermination of the passions in the
interests of reason, but rather the much more tolerant and moderate ideal of their control and guidance by reason.

Reason, however, remains the watchword of the movement. Na-

ture-and-reason, synonymous or mutually supplementary, constitutes an almost magical talisman. These terms had come down to
them, to be sure, from the Middle Ages, where they had done
yeoman duty in the service of epistemology, a teleologically ordered
universe, ethical and political theory, and an optimistic interpretation of the Fall of Man. But for the medieval philosophers, nevertheless, nature-and-reason had been subordinate to, and partially
dependent upon, grace and faith. With the Christian humanists of
the Renaissance, they attain an equal footing with grace and faith,
practically if not always nominally. And in the progression toward
a natural theology and an independent humanistic ethic, the human
reason attains an ascendancy to which the Thomists would not have
subscribed.

The breaking down of the wall between theology and philosophy
(a wall frequently climbed, but seldom impaired, in the Middle
Ages), and the placing of the resulting natural theology primarily
at the disposal of the moral life, effected, not a complete break from
the medieval heritage, but rather a shift in values. Virtue and good
works became more significant factors in the angelification of man
than the "contemplation of a truth static, fixed, complete, and perfect for all eternity."[146] In terminology which both the Scholastics
and the Renaissance humanists would have understood, reason in
pursuit of moral virtue becomes more important than intellect in
pursuit of the contemplation of truth.

Thomas Aquinas had written:

> If, then, the final happiness of man does not consist in those
> exterior advantages which are called goods of fortune, nor in
> good of the body, nor in goods of the soul in its sentient
> part, *nor in the intellectual part in respect of the moral vir-*
> *tues, nor in the virtues of the practical intellect, called art and*
> *prudence,* it remains that the final happiness of man consists
> in the contemplation of truth. *This act alone in man is proper*
> *to him,* and is in no way shared by any other being in this
> world. . . . *Likewise to this act all other human activities seem*
> *to be directed as toward their end.* . . . Thus, if we look at
> things rightly, we may see that all human occupations seem
> to be ministerial to the service of the contemplators of truth.[147]

One has but to compare this statement with More's definition of
virtue, with Lipsius' definition of Right Reason, with Erasmus'
explanation of the "Philosophy of Christ," even with Hooker's emphasis upon the "natural path of everlasting life," to appraise the
difference. There is no need for the explicit contradiction of a

Pomponazzi or a Charron to establish the validity of the transformation.

But if Renaissance Christian humanism came more and more to
stress morality, rather than theology, there were other divergent
humanistic tendencies, whose proponents revolted as strongly against
this very ethic as had its champions against the abstracting intellects of the Schoolmen. Despite the contributions of the Florentine
Academy and a scattering of other Italian humanists to the tradition we have been following, its main current ran through northern
Europe, and especially Germany, the Lowlands and England. Italian humanism, and to some extent that of France, concerned itself
vastly more with other aspects of man's life on earth than with the
dutiful exercise of reason in pursuit of virtue.

Petrarch, with whatever qualifications, had asserted stoutly his
interest in "mortal blessings." And there were many others in the
Renaissance who discovered in the new classical heritage and in
the world around them, happiness and pleasure in those very goods
which Thomas Aquinas had found "not proper to man." The goods
of fortune, the goods of body, the goods of the "sentient part" of
the soul—all these seemed not only rich and rewarding to some of
these vastly different humanists, but also far more tangible and
substantial goods than "the contemplation of truth" or those involving "the moral virtues." Joy in the life of the senses as well as in
that of the mind, in the beauty of flesh and the beauty of art, in all
the pleasures which a copious Nature and an exuberant age of
artistic creation could provide, found expression in this sort of
humanism.

In its more moderate and "spiritualized" form, this force lies behind that "religion of beauty," the cult of Patonic love which had
for its prophet Cardinal Bembo and for its chief expositor Count
Baldassare Castiglione.[148] The ideals of the Renaissance courtier-
gentleman and the fair lady who initiates him into the mysteries of
this spiritual and uplifting love, as set forth in the famous *Book
of the Courtier*, are in no fundamental sense antagonistic to the
values of the Christian humanist. They are rather their specialized,
aristocratic counterparts. Yet from the art of living set forth by
Castiglione, in conjunction with other traditions of courtly love and
honor, there evolved a highly romantic and systematized code of
ethics which (at least as exemplified in French and Elizabethan
literature and court life) challenged the supremacy of the orthodox
humanistic morality.

But the most forceful and influential humanistic opposition to the ethics of the Christian humanists came from the "naturalistic" humanists, who thought of nature as something quite different from reason—who used it as a catchword and a creed proclaiming the rights of a full and uninhibited life of the passions, the senses and the instincts. Petrarch and Boccaccio are the harbingers of the opposition party in Italy, although their allegiance to it is not consistent; Lorenzo Valla openly enunciates its platform; in somewhat different ways, Lorenzo de' Medici and Ariosto and Tasso flirt with it; it attains a scurrilous decadence in Aretino. In France its creed is given lyric utterance by Ronsard, and it makes a truly great contribution to literature in the writings of its two magnificent advocates, Rabelais and Montaigne. And while its temper is definitely not Anglo-Saxon, it leaves its mark upon Marlowe and Ralegh, Chapman and Harvey, Sidney and Spenser, Shakespeare and Donne.

This naturalistic humanism, however, is but one of the many prominent but diverse manifestations of strong opposition to the "continuance" tradition which we have been studying. Renaissance Christian humanism altered the emphases of the orthodox medieval world view, but did not break with it, and its protagonists retain in their entirety many of the characteristic features of the old order. Above all, it adhered staunchly to a program which reconciled philosophy and religion, reason and faith, nature and grace. On the other hand, there were forces gathering strength in opposition to the whole reconciliation tradition, Scholastic and Renaissance humanistic alike—forces, dissimilar and even alien as they were, each to the others, which found a common focus in their anti-intellectualism and anti-moralism. These forces converge in the sixteenth century upon the common foe, that great structure of unified, ordered and symmetrical thought built under the direction of Thomas Aquinas and renovated by the Renaissance Christian humanists— converge in an attack which constitutes the second large movement of the Renaissance, for which I can find no better name than that of the Counter-Renaissance.

FOOTNOTES
CHAPTER I

I.

1. Cf., among others, John Herman Randall, Jr., *The Making of the Modern Mind* (New York, 1940), 98; Etienne Gilson, *The Spirit of Mediæval Philosophy*, translated by A. H. C. Downes (New York, 1936), 13–14, 18; Harald Höffding, *A History of Modern Philosophy*, translated from the German edition by B. E. Meyer (London, 1924), Vol. I, 6; Christopher Dawson, *Progress and Religion* (London, 1929), 171–172; Carl Becker, *The Heavenly City of the Eighteenth Century Philosophers* (New Haven, 1932), 8 and *passim*.
2. Randall, *Mod. Mind*, 98.

2.

3. Douglas Bush, *The Renaissance and English Humanism* (London, 1939), 30.
4. Randall, *Mod. Mind*, 117.
5. Justin, *Second Apology*, xiii, quoted by Gilson, *Sp. Med. Phil.*, 27.
6. Gilson, *ibid.*, 423. Cf. Jacques Maritain, "The Conflict of Methods at the End of the Middle Ages," *The Thomist*, Vol. III, No. 4 (Oct., 1941), 528.
7. Gilson, *ibid.* Cf. Höffding, *Mod. Phil.*, I, 6.
8. Quoted by Gilson, *ibid.*, 428, fn. 5.
9. *Ibid.*, 33. For Anselm's position, see also Alfred Weber, *History of Philosophy*, authorized translation by Frank Thilly (New York, 1899), 212–213.
10. Maurice de Wulf, *History of Mediæval Philosophy*, translated by Ernest C. Messinger (London, 1926), Vol. II, 31; cf. Gilson, *Sp. Med. Phil.*, 35.
11. Cf. Randall, *Mod. Mind*, 93.
12. Dawson, *Prog. and Rel.*, 171–172.
13. Becker, *Heavenly City*, 8. Cf. *ibid.*, 6, and Gilson, *Sp. Med. Phil.*, 28.
14. Thomas Aquinas, *Summa contra Gentiles*, I, ch. 7, translated by Rickaby as *Of God and His Creatures*, quoted by Randall, *Mod. Mind*, 97–98.
15. Cf. De Wulf, *Med. Phil.*, II, 17.
16. Dante, *De Monarchia*, Book I, ch. 4, quoted by Randall, *Mod. Mind*, 105.
17. Maurice de Wulf, *Philosophy and Civilization in the Middle Ages* (London and Princeton, New Jersey, 1922), 187–193. In these pages, M. De Wulf also emphasizes the intellectualism of thirteenth-century culture in general, and even of the very structure of society. For a clear, brief exposition of the philosophy of Thomas Aquinas, see De Wulf, *Med. Phil.*, II, 3–32.
18. Cf. De Wulf, *Phil and Civ.*, 179–183.
19. Cf. Gilson, *Sp. Med. Phil.*, 114–125, 314–319; and De Wulf, *Phil. and Civ.*, 135–137, 270.
20. De Wulf, *ibid.*, 137.
21. Gilson, *ibid.*, 421.
22. *Ibid.*, 127.
23. *Webster's Collegiate Dictionary*, Fifth Edition (Springfield, Mass., 1942), 484. My italics.
24. Gilson, *Sp. Med. Phil.*, 117, 354, 359.
25. Cf. *ibid.*, 356. In this respect, medieval thought is much more Platonic than Aristotelian. Cf. Gilson, *ibid.*, 330–332.
26. Cf. E. K. Rand, "The Humanism of Cicero," *Proceedings of the American*

Philosophical Society, Vol. LXXI, No. 4 (1932); and Jefferson Butler Fletcher, *Literature of the Italian Renaissance* (New York, 1934), 29–35. In these pages Professor Fletcher applies Professor Rand's concept of Cicero's humanism to Dante, and cites Dante's acquaintance with Cicero's work. See pages 50–52 for the relationship of this gospel of the "gentleman" to the philosophy of love of the *dolce stil nuovo.*

27. Dante Alighieri, *The Divine Comedy,* translated by Jefferson Butler Fletcher (New York, 1931): *Purgatory,* xvi, 103–105; cf. Fletcher, *Italian Renaissance,* 27.

28. Fletcher, *Italian Renaissance,* 42. I am indebted throughout this discussion of Dante to Professor Fletcher's chapter in this book. Its beautifully lucid and keen but unpretentious treatment is in marked contrast to much Dante scholarship.

3.

29. Marsilio Ficino, *Opera* (Basle, 1573), Vol. I, 1; quoted by Nesca Robb, *Neoplatonism of the Italian Renaissance* (London, 1935), 86. Cf. Paul Oskar Kristeller, *The Philosophy of Marsilio Ficino,* translated into English by Virginia Conant (New York, 1943), 24–25, 27, and *passim.* This recent book is an exhaustive and definitive analysis of Ficino's thought, and contains many passages from his work in English translation; I have used these passages frequently in my text, since they provide an English rendering under the supervision of an expert on Ficino.

30. Ernst Cassirer, "Giovanni Pico della Mirandola" (I), *Journal of the History of Ideas,* Vol. III, No. 2 (April, 1942), 126. Cf. Kristeller, *Marsilio Ficino,* 14–17, and *passim* for various philosophical and theological influences upon Ficino's thought. Professor Kristeller summarizes,

> Hence we may conclude that Ficino owed to humanism his literary form and his preference for certain problems; to medieval Aristotelianism his metaphysical terminology and his logical method of argumentation. (14)

Cf. also two of Professor Kristeller's articles: "Florentine Platonism and its Relation with Humanism and Scholasticism," *Church History,* VIII (1939), 201 ff.; "Augustine and the Renaissance," *International Science,* I (1941), 7 ff.

31. Quoted by W. Parr Greswell, *Memoirs of Angelus Politianus, Johannes Picus of Mirandula, Actius Sincerus Sannazarius, Petrus Bembus, Hieronymus Fracastorius, Marcus Antonius Flaminius, and the Amalthei: Translations from their Poetical Works: and Notes & Observations concerning other Literary Characters of the Fifteenth and Sixteenth Centuries,* the Second Edition, greatly augmented (London, 1805), 304.

32. Cassirer, "Mirandola" (I), 125.

33. Desiderius Erasmus, *Colloquies,* translated by N. Bailey; edited, with notes, by the Rev. E. Johnson, M.A. (London, 1878), I, 182–183, 186; *The Epistles of Erasmus,* with translation and commentary by Morgan Nichols (London, 1904), II, 190.

34. Professor Shorey dissents from this estimate of Ficino's purpose, declaring that his "essential personal religion was a liberal Platonizing and Ciceronian ethical Christianity," and tracing a direct line of succession from Ficino and Pico to the Oxford Reformation. Cf. Paul Shorey, *Platonism, Ancient and Modern* (Berkeley, Cal., 1938), 122–123. However, Professor Kristeller's book has made it abundantly clear that this interpretation of Ficino's religion is not very exact. And while there is no question but that

Ficino, directly or indirectly, influenced Colet and others of the group, and that Sir Thomas More was interested in Pico, his own kinsman, the evidence that the English kind of Platonism is not basically like the Florentine seems to me overwhelming.

35. Erasmus, *Handbook of the Christian Knight,* quoted by Randall, *Mod. Mind,* 156.

36. Sir Thomas More, *Utopia,* edited by H. Goitrin from the 1551 edition of Ralph Robinson (London, n. d.) , 121, 122.

37. Cf. Henry Osborn Taylor, *Thought and Expression in the Sixteenth Century* (New York, 1920) , Vol. I, 272.

38. Cf. *Ibid.,* 271; Höffding, *Mod. Phil.,* I, 40–42; Lucien Febvre, *Martin Luther: a Destiny,* translated by Roberts Tapley (New York, 1929) , 297–299.

39. Cf. Norman Sykes, "Richard Hooker," in *The Social and Political Ideas of Some Great Thinkers of the Sixteenth and Seventeenth Centuries,* edited by F. J. C. Hearnshaw (London, 1926) , 63–89, especially 71.

40. Richard Hooker, *Of the Laws of Ecclesiastical Polity* (Everyman edition) , I, ii, 3; I, iii, 1, 4. For Thomas Aquinas' divisions of law, cf. R. W. and A. J. Carlyle, *A History of Medieval Political Theory in the West* (London, 1928) , Vol. V, 38–44. For a diagram of Hooker's system of laws, see Ch. 3, 1, of this book.

41. Hooker, *ibid.,* I, xi, 5.

42. *Ibid.,* I, xi, 5–6; xii, 1. The last sentence, in particular, evoked protests from his Puritan opponents.

43. Justus Lipsius, *Manuductio,* quoted by Léontine Zanta, *La Renaissance du Stoïcisme au XVIᵉ Siècle* (Paris, 1914) , 196.

44. Justus Lipsius: *Two Bookes of Constancie* written in Latine by Justus Lipsius, Englished by Sir John Stradling, edited with an introduction by Rudolf Kirk, notes by Clayton Morris Hall (New Brunswick, N. J., 1939) , 79.

45. Guillaume du Vair, *The Morall Philosophy of the Stoicks,* Englished by Charles Cotton, Esq. (London, 1664) , 1, 2, 4. This book was first translated into English in 1598: cf. Lipsius, *Two Bookes of Constancie, ed. cit.,* 34.

46. Bush, *Ren. and Eng. Hum.,* 24.

47. Erasmus, *Letter to Maldonato,* quoted by Randall, *Mod. Mind,* 147.

48. Cf. Roy W. Battenhouse, *Marlowe's Tamburlaine* (Nashville, Tenn., 1941) , 22.

4.

49. Cf. De Wulf, *Phil. and Civ.,* 50–53.

50. Thomas Aquinas, *Summa Theologica,* 1ᵃ, q. I, art. i, quoted by De Wulf, *ibid.,* 152.

51. Dawson, *Prog. and Rel.,* 175. Cf. *ibid.,* 173; and Karl Vossler, *Medieval Culture, An Introduction to Dante and His Times,* translated by William Cranston Lawton (New York, 1929) , Vol. I, 91.

52. Cf. De Wulf, *Phil. and Civ.,* 162–163.

53. Quoted, *ibid.,* 163–164. Duns Scotus, of course, goes much further, withdrawing all theological questions from the investigation of reason. For various attitudes toward the apologetic method, cf. De Wulf, *Med. Phil.,* I, 198.

54. Cf. Etienne Gilson, *Reason and Revelation in the Middle Ages* (New York, 1938) , 82–83. Cf. his *Sp. Med. Phil.,* 34–37.

55. Ernst Cassirer, "Giovanni Pico della Mirandola" (II) , *Journal of the History of Ideas,* Vol. III, No. 3 (June, 1942) , 335.

56. Cf. Shorey, *Platonism*, 122. Professor Shorey maintains (quite accurately), however, that Ficino desired to retain his orthodox standing with the church.
57. Ficino, *De Christiana Religione*, quoted by Shorey, *ibid.*, 124. Cf. Kristeller, *Ficino*, 15, 25.
58. Quoted by Fletcher, *Ital. Ren.*, 103.
59. Kristeller, *Ficino*, 323.
60. *Marsilii Ficini Opera omnia* (Basel, 1561), 668; translated by Kristeller-Conant, *Ficino*, 322–323.
61. Pico della Mirandola, *Of the Dignity of Man*, selected portions translated by Elizabeth Livermore Forbes, *Journal of the History of Ideas*, Vol. III, No. 3 (June, 1942), 351–52.
62. *Ibid.*, 352. My italics.
63. *Ibid.*
64. *Ibid.*, 352, 349. My italics. Pico does go on, however, to rank "the pure contemplator" even higher than the "philosopher," calling him "a more reverend divinity vested with human flesh."
65. Taylor, *Thought and Expression*, I, 300.
66. Cf. De Wulf, *Med. Phil.*, II, 282.
67. Desiderius Erasmus, *The Education of a Christian Prince*, translated with an introduction on Erasmus and on Ancient and Medieval Political Thought, by Lester K. Born (New York, 1936), 150.
68. Erasmus, *Convivium Religiosum*, quoted by Randall, *Mod. Mind*, 134.
69. Randall, *ibid.*
70. Cf. Kristeller, *Ficino*, 317–323.
71. More, *Utopia*, 167.
72. *Ibid.*, 167–168.
73. *Ibid.*, 168.
74. *Ibid.*, 121–122. For the summary of seventeenth-century Deism, I am indebted to a course lecture by Ernest Hunter Wright at Columbia University. For a similar but not identical account of the basic points of Deism, see Höffding, *Mod. Phil.*, I, 67.
75. De Wulf, *Med. Phil.*, II, 282.
76. Cf. Höffding, *Mod. Phil.*, I, 60. For this whole discussion, see Höffding's chapter on "Natural Religion," I, 59–68.
77. Cf. Geoffrey Atkinson, *Les Nouveaux Horizons de la Renaissance Française* (Paris, 1935), and Samuel C. Chew, *The Crescent and the Rose: Islam and England during the Renaissance* (New York, 1937).
78. Cf. Höffding, *ibid.*, I, 60–61. Some scholars consider one of these two men a Zwinglian.
79. Quoted by Höffding, *ibid.*, I, 62.
80. Quoted by Basil Willey, *The Seventeenth Century Background* (London, 1934), 214.
81. De Wulf, *Med. Phil.*, I, 165; cf. Edward Maslin Hulme, *The Renaissance, the Reformation and the Catholic Reformation in Continental Europe* (New York, 1915), 65. Weber's account of Abelard in his *History of Philosophy* makes his position (although not his method and detailed interests, of course) sound very much like that of Erasmus:

> What is the Gospel but a reform of the natural moral law, *'legis naturalis reformatio'*? Shall we people hell with men 'whose lives and teachings are truly evangelical and apostolic in their perfection, and differ in nothing or very little from the Christan religon'?
> *Theologia christiana*, II: Weber, 224.

Yet Abelard admits that he knows the Greek philosophers through the works of Augustine! (Weber, *ibid.*).

82. De Wulf, *Med. Phil.*, II, 244–245.
83. Christopher Marlowe, *Tamburlaine*, Part II, V, i, 4311–4313: *The Works of Christopher Marlowe*, edited by C. F. Tucker Brooke (Oxford, 1910). Cf. *Tamburlaine*, Part I, IV, ii, 1452–1453.
84. *Tamburlaine*, Part II, II, ii, 2906–2909. Part II is full of inferences about comparative religion, as well. See Sigismund's oath sworn by Christ (I, ii, 2458–2461), and later broken. Callapine swears by Mahomet (I, iii, 2556) and keeps his oath (III, i, 3181–3182), but there are many spots in the play where characters call upon Mahomet in vain. On the other hand, Tamburlaine, who has shown sympathy throughout for Christian slaves in the Orient, defies Mahomet just before the passage about "The God who sits in heaven," and feels immediately afterward the pain that presages his final illness and death. The only definite conclusion which seems to me justifiable is that of Marlowe's interest in natural religion, and his lack of faith in Christianity and other institutionalized religions. For a further portrayal of Christian faithlessness in dealing with the Turks, see *The Jew of Malta*, II, 724–761. These lines deal with the way the Governor of Malta breaks faith.

For a somewhat different interpretation of Marlowe's religious thought, read Paul H. Kocher, *Christopher Marlowe* (Chapel Hill, 1946)—especially pp. 69 ff. But although Dr. Kocher's analysis brings much light to details, it seems to offer nothing that controverts the main tendencies noted here.
85. Hooker, *Of the Laws*, I, xiv, 5. My italics.
86. *Ibid.*, III, viii, 11–12.
87. Ficino, *Op. omm.*, 262: Kristeller, *Ficino*, 34.
88. Ficino, *ibid.*, 871 ff.: Kristeller, *ibid.*, 28.
89. Ficino, *ibid.*: Kristeller, *ibid.*, 28–29.

5.

90. Gilson, *Sp. Med. Phil.*, 385.
91. Cf. C. E. Trinkaus, *Adversity's Noblemen* (New York, 1940), 31–36.
92. Thomas Aquinas, *Summa Theologica*, lit. trans. by the Fathers of the Eng. Dom. Prov. (London, 1922), Part II (Second Part) (QQ. CLXXXI–CLXXXIX), 99–144. These pages contain the *Treatise on the Active and the Contemplative Life*. Aquinas distinctly places the contemplative life on a higher level, yet with typically subtle, if clear, qualifications. See also his *Summa contra Gentiles*, literally translated by the English Dominican Fathers from the latest Leonine edition (1924–1928), III, xxv.
93. For an interesting and plausible view on the philosophy of *Piers Plowman* which goes beyond this estimate, to find in the highest life of "Do Best" the vision of a "social prophet" concerned with "the consecration to a communal utility," see Henry Willis Wells, "The Philosophy of Piers Plowman," *PMLA*, Vol. LIII, No. 2 (June, 1938), 339–349, especially 343 and 348.
94. Francisco Petrarca, *Secretum: Petrarch's Secret*, translated by W. H. Drapper (London, 1911), 172. It is a note often struck during the Italian Renaissance. For similar statements by Cosimo de' Medici, Julius II and Leo X, see Randall, *Mod. Mind*, 124.
95. Petrarch, *ibid.*, 173.
96. Cf. Trinkaus, *Adversity's Noblemen*, passim.
97. Cf. *Ibid.*, 43, 109–112. Dr. Trinkaus takes a very different view from mine upon the general significance of these treatises, however. I am as usual indebted to informal discussions with Professor Fletcher, whose wisdom

and comprehensive knowledge of Renaissance literature helped me through many problems.

98. Cicero, *De Officiis,* translated by Walter Miller (Loeb Library) , III, v, 23.

99. Cicero, *Tusculan Disputations,* I, xiii, 30. Cf. *De Natura Deorum,* I, xvii, 44, and I, xxiii, 62.

100. Cicero, *De Legibus,* I, x, 30. Cf. *A Documentary History of Primitivism and Related Ideas,* General Editors, Arthur O. Lovejoy, Gilbert Chinard, George Boas, and Ronald S. Crane. Vol. I: *Primitivism and Related Ideas in Antiquity,* by Arthur O. Lovejoy and George Boas, with Supplementary Essays by W. T. Albright and P.-E. Dumont (Baltimore, 1935) , 257. I am indebted throughout this discussion to Prof. Lovejoy's pages on Cicero, and I have followed his translations of the classical writers, or those of Professor Boas, wherever I have not indicated particular editions.

101. Lovejoy and Boas, *ibid.,* 255-256. See the two pages from *De Natura Deorum* cited in fn. 99 *(supra)* for Cicero's presentation of conflicting opinions about proof from the *consensus gentium,* and Professor Lovejoy's comments on them, *op. cit.,* 256-257.

102. Cicero, *De Officiis,* III, iii, 13.

103. Ernest Hunter Wright, *The Meaning of Rousseau* (Oxford, 1929) , 26.

104. Lovejoy and Boas, *Prim. and Rel. Ideas,* 450 (Appendix: "Some Meanings of 'Nature,' " no. 29) ; cf. *ibid.,* 188. Cf. also A. E. Taylor, *Aristotle* (London and Edinburgh, 1919) , 59. For a passage in which Cicero combines the Stoic Law of Nature, the Platonic cardinal virtues, and the Aristotelian doctrine of ends, see *De Officiis,* I, xxviii, 100.

105. Gilson, *Sp. Med. Phil.,* 340.

106. R. C. Hicks *(Stoic and Epicurean,* New York, 1910) has a good summarizing statement about Cicero as an eclectic.

> In reviewing his opinions we have to distinguish the pupil of Carneades in the *Academica, De Natura Deorum, De Divinatione,* and *De Fato,* from the pupil of Antiochus in *De Legibus* and *De Finibus;* and from the defender of Stoic ethics in the *Tusculan Disputations* and *De Officiis.* (359)

> Since Carneades was a thorough-going relativist skeptic of the New Academy, and Antiochus an apostate skeptic with a Stoic-Platonic doctrinal blend (Hicks, *ibid.,* 357) , the various direct influences on Cicero's thought are at least simplified by this statement.

107. I am indebted to Professor Marjorie Nicolson for this interpretation of *King Lear.*

108. Professor Shorey, in *Platonism, Ancient and Modern,* holds the view that Cicero, Seneca, Epictetus, Marcus Aurelius, and other expounders of Stoic ethics are all "Platonizing Stoics."

109. Trinkaus, *Adversity's Noblemen,* 57.

110. *Ibid.,* 58.

111. *Ibid.,* 58, 43.

112. Robb, *Neoplatonism,* 97, 126. My choice of Landino, a secondary figure, to represent the Academy's point of view, is intentional, for as Professor Kristeller says, the leader of the Academy, "Ficino has no real system of morals." For him, virtue is "equivalent to the spiritual ascent of the soul." (Kristeller, *Marsilio Ficino,* 289-290)

113. Erasmus, *Paraclesis,* quoted by Randall, *Mod. Mind,* 134.

114. More, *Utopia,* 172-173.

115. Cf. R. W. Chambers, *Thomas More* (New York, 1935) , 126-127.

116. More, *ibid.,* 122.

117. Chambers, *ibid.*, 128.
118. Colet, "Lectures on Romans" [Rom. vii. 24], quoted by J. H. Lupton, *The Life of John Colet* (London, 1887), 81.
119. Hooker, *Of the Laws*, I, xi, 5.
120. *The Poems of George Chapman*, edited by Phyllis Brooks Bartlett (New York, 1941), 224 ("A Hymn to Our Saviour on the Crosse," ll. 190–199; 206–209).
121. *Ibid.*, 241 ("For stay in competence," ll. 60–62; "Of the Will," ll. 1–2); 189 ("Euthymiae Raptus," l. 749).
122. *Ibid.*, 281 ("Eugenia," ll. 414–415; 423–430). For Ficino's influence on Chapman, see Frank L. Schoell, *Etudes sur l'Humanisme Continental en Angleterre à la Fin de la Renaissance* (Paris, 1926), 4 ff., 19, and *passim*.
123. *Ibid.*, 247 ("To yong imaginaries in knowledge," ll. 96–98).
124. Cf. William Perkins, *Workes* (Printed at London by John Legatt, Printer to the Universitie of Cambridge, 1612), Vol. I, 561. Perkins, a Calvinist and "Reformed Catholic," declares "Papists teach, that Originall sinne is so farre forth taken away after baptisme, that it ceaseth to be a sinne properly: and is nothing else but a want, a defect, and weaknesse, making the heart fitte and readie to conceive sinne. . . ."
125. Cf. Gilson, *Sp. Med. Phil.*, 387.
126. Among others, the Stoic concepts of destiny, natural cause. chance, and freedom of the will were ones which Lipsius admitted as serious deterrents to his task. (*Two Bookes of Constancie*, 36)
127. It is true that Pomponazzi, employing the old device of the "double truth" (which holds that what is true for philosophy need not be true for religion, and *vice versa*), professes, at the end of his tract, his perfect willingness to submit his conclusions to the authority of the Church, and even admits that anything established by reason as truth, if contrary to the Gospel, must be erroneous. Yet both the very fact that he chose to pursue his subject in the face of this profession which nullifies the validity of his work except as a philosophical exercise *in vacuo*, and the temper of the book, make it amply apparent that his heart is with his argument and not with his retraction.
128. Petrus Pomponazzi, *Tractatus de Immortalitate Animae*, translated by William Henry Hay II (Haverford College, 1938), 44–45. My italics.
129. Despite definite Stoic and Platonic elements in his thought in general, and in this treatise in particular, I am convinced that Pomponazzi's ethics remain primarily "Aristotelian." The thesis which Werner Jaeger (*Aristotle, Fundamentals of the History of His Development*, translated with the author's corrections and additions, by Richard Robinson, Oxford, 1934) so brilliantly develops—that Aristotle's thought undergoes three fairly distinct stages—is interesting in this connection. Professor Jaeger's three periods include one in which Aristotle is primarily developing and continuing the work of Plato; one colored chiefly by an overt reformation of Plato's thought (or at least of certain basic elements of his thought); and a final one, in which he develops his own highly empirical philosophy. It is tempting to generalize, and attribute Thomas Aquinas' Aristotle to those parts of Aristotle's work which belong to the first and second periods (Aquinas, with his moderate realism, upholding certain portions of Platonic thought, and, with the Aristotle of the second period, discarding or qualifying others); and the Aristotle of Pomponazzi (and hence of Alexander) to the third period. For Aristotle's ethical theory in the three stages, see Jaeger, *Aristotle*, 231–241, 280–292, 395–397.
130. Pomponazzi, *ibid.*, 49–51.

131. Cf. Erasmus, *Christian Prince*, 149—where he unobtrusively slips in the casual assertion "Surely, virtue is its own reward," immediately after a statement bearing an obvious debt to Seneca's *Epistles*.
132. Höffding, *Mod. Phil.*, I, 43.
133. Cf. Hulme, *Ren. and Ref.*, 280. Zwingli also expected to find Socrates, Seneca and Aristotle in heaven.
134. Cf. Höffding, *ibid.*, and Hulme, *ibid.*
135. Höffding, *ibid.*, I, 44. My italics.
136. Cicero, *De re publica*, III, xxiii. This treatise, of course, was not accessible to the Renaissance, since it was lost and not recovered until the nineteenth century. But the gist of the argument was preserved by Augustine and Lactantius (*Inst. Div.*, VI, 8, 6–9)., and the point of view is a largely consistent one in Cicero, repeated in other works.
137. Hooker, *Of the Laws*, I, iii, 4.
138. For a fine brief summary of Aquinas' exposition of this reconciliation, see Becker, *Heavenly City*, 3.
139. For Suarez' indebtedness to Aquinas' theory of natural law, and for his own distinctive contribution, see A. L. Lilley, "Francisco Suarez," in *The Social and Political Ideas of Some Great Thinkers of the Sixteenth and Seventeenth Centuries*, 90–104.
140. Höffding, *Mod. Phil.*, I, 42.
141. *Ibid.*
142. In view of the "corruption of our nature," Hooker maintained "that the Law of Nature doth now require of necessity some kind of regiment." (*Of the Laws*, I, x, 4)
143. Höffding, *ibid.*, I, 42–43.
144. Pierre Charron, *De la Sagesse*, quoted by Höffding, *ibid.*, I, 34. My italics. Notice the ironic incongruity of "only" in "Reason is only a part. . . ."

6.

145. Not necessarily first in time. Other kinds of humanism manifest in the fifteenth-century Italians precede this movement chronologically, for example. But of the three movements which I am considering, this is the first to gather considerable impetus and reach a full strength. See Chapter II, 1.
146. Randall, *Mod. Mind.*, 95.
147. Aquinas, *Summa contra Gentiles*, I, xxxvii, quoted by Randall, *ibid.* My italics.
148. For an account of the progress of this cult through the Renaissance, see Professor Fletcher's delightful little book, *The Religion of Beauty in Women* (New York, 1911).

CHAPTER
2

THE COUNTER–RENAISSANCE AND THE
VANITY OF LEARNING

I. THE HISTORICAL POSITION AND SIGNIFICANCE OF THE
COUNTER-RENAISSANCE

ICHEL DE MONTAIGNE, that "casuall" and "unpremeditated" philosopher beloved of those who, in every age, oppose dogmatism and bigotry, casts a particularly large shadow over the last twenty years of the sixteenth century. He represents at once the culmination and the terminus of the second great movement of the Renaissance—a movement born of men's weariness with the pretensions of the speculative intellect and the systematizing mind. He is the culmination of this reaction because, having armed himself against dogmatism of every sort with all the skeptical arguments of antiquity and his own times, he launched in his *Apologie of Raymond Sebond* an attack upon the speculative capacity and the intellectual attainments of man which, for comprehensiveness, has never since been equaled. He is the terminus because, although he had many disciples and imitators, it was impossible to go beyond the skepticism of this essay.

Montaigne—who moved on in his later work to a positive philosophy which might be described as "Nature and Montaigne, Inc." —was fully aware of the character and extent of this skeptical revolt. He summarizes it succinctly in one of his later essays:

> The rashness of those who ascribed the capacity of all things to man's wit, through spight and simulation produced this opinion in others, that humane wit was not capable of anything.[1]

From Petrarch to Descartes,[2] one finds an abundant and abusive

76

testimony to the all but universal tendency of the age to berate the Scholastics and the classical philosophers and authorities they followed, for their pretentiousness in setting themselves up as "God's councilors" and "Nature's secretaries." Aquinas, Aristotle, Ptolemy and Galen (less often Pliny, Hippocrates, Duns Scotus and Albertus Magnus) bear the brunt. These are the men who have professed to be on intimate terms with God, to share his plans and secrets. Their sin has been a "speculative *hybris.*"[3]

There is a reference in one of Petrarch's dialogues to these philosophers who "boldly talk of nature" and discuss its mysteries "as though they had come from Heaven, and had been in Almighty God's council."[4] Lorenzo Valla contributes a description of philosophers who, in order not to appear ignorant, dispute of everything, reach up to the sky (*apponentes in coelum os suum*), and wish to scale its heights. . . .[5]

The charge is made by Paracelsus, among others:

> Nor do we care for the vain talk of those who say more about God than he has revealed to them, and pretend to understand him so thoroughly as if they had been in his counsels. . . .[6]

The term "Nature's secretaries" appears frequently in a derogatory context from *The Praise of Folly* on. Erasmus writes:

> And next there come our Philosophers. . . . How pleasantly do they dote while they frame in their heads innumerable worlds; measure out the Sun, the Moon, the Stars, nay and Heaven itself, as it were with a pair of Compasses; lay down the Causes of Lightning, Winds, Eclipses, and other the like Inexplicable Matters; and all this too without the least doubting, as if they were Nature's Secretaries, or dropt down amongst us from the Council of the Gods; while in the meantime Nature laughs at them all and their blind conjectures.[7]

Astronomers and astrologers are among the favorite victims. Cornelius Agrippa fulminates against

> Those chimericall and visionary Doctors [who], after having traversed the higher and luminous regions of the Universe in person, and as if they were newly returned from this grand tour, boldly fabricate globes. . . .[8] [etc.]

Montaigne remarks somewhat more urbanely, "Man faineth a thousand pleasant societies betweene God and Him. Nay, is he not his countrieman?" He continues,

> You would say, we have the Coach-makers, Carpenters, and

> Painters, who have gone up thither, and there have placed
> engines with diverse motions, and ranged the wheelings, the
> windings, and enterlacements of celestiall bodies diapred in
> colours, according to Plato, about the spindle of necessity. . . .[9]

One of the controversial points of the Reformation crosses paths
with this tradition, with the assertion of Rabelais' Hippothadeus
that we may know God's will without acting

> as if it were such an abstruse and mysteriously hidden secret
> that for the clear understanding thereof it were necessary to
> consult with those of his celestial privy-council, or expressly
> make a voyage into the *empyrean* chamber, where order is
> given for the effectuating of his most holy pleasures.[10]

Needless to say, the exuberant Elizabethans took this kind of
invective to their hearts. One could cite passages to the point from
Ben Jonson, Ralegh and Donne, from Nashe and Marston, from
Greville and Sidney and Harvey, and doubtless from many others.
But perhaps the most literal traditional rendering is that of Gabriel
Harvey, who nevertheless lends it the peculiar flavor of his lively
although not always happy style. He scolds,

> I cannot see, and would gladly learne, how a man on Earth,
> should be of so great authoritie, and so familiar acquaintance
> with God in Heaven (unless haply for the nonce he hath
> lately intertained some fewe choice singular ones of his privie
> Counsell) as to be able in such specialties, without any justi-
> fyable certificate, or warrant to reveale hys incomprehensible
> mysteries, and definitively to give sentence of his Maiestes
> secret and inscrutable purpose. As if they had a key for all the
> lockes in Heaven.[11]

These assaults upon "God's privy counselors" and "Nature's secretaries" represent, for the most part, a scornful reaction to the
Scholastic pursuit of "Truths of God" in speculation, logic and argument. They accompany, of course, that new trend away from purely
theoretical knowledge and toward a knowledge praticable in the
virtuous conduct of life—the goal of humanistic education. In somewhat over-simplified form, Fulke Greville summarizes the change
of attitude neatly:

> What a right line is, the learned know;
> But how availes that him, who in the right
> Of life, and manners doth desire to grow?[12]

Yet if the Christian humanists of the Renaissance would mostly

have applauded this censure of the Scholastics, they were not themselves to escape from similar attacks. Throughout the sixteenth
century, the moral *hybris* of the humanists is nearly as open to
deprecations increase in frequency and violence, of course, with
deprecation as the speculative variety of the Scholastics; and these
the Reformation. The Scholastics were considered arrogant in their
confidence in the power of their intellects to comprehend the truths
of God and Nature; the humanists, so the charge ran, were insolently
confident of the ability of their reason and will, combined with the
study of the humanities, and without much or any aid from God,
to lead them to virtue.

Ramus attacks the prevalence of this attitude in the colleges:

> There, the child will learn a host of impieties: for example,
> that the principle and ideal of happiness of man are *in him,*
> that all the virtues are *in his power,* that he acquires them by
> means of *nature, art and work,* and that for this work—great
> and sublime as it is—there is no need of God's aid, nor of his
> cooperation! Nothing about Providence, not a word on the
> divine justice; finally, since Aristotle holds that souls are mortal,
> he reduces man's happiness to terms of this mortal life. There
> is the philosophy of which we make, so to speak, the founda-
> tion of our religion.[13]

But Ramus is specifically concerned with the student of Aristotle's
ethics; his accusation, while certainly leveled at those who place
too exclusive an emphasis upon moral philosophy, is pointed specifically at Aristotle.

The charge is more general in Agrippa's earlier version. He speaks
of "those proud savants" who, in making

> great efforts to prove and confirm the laws of Jesus Christ,
> support them more by the doctrine and ethics of the philoso-
> phers, than by those of the holy prophets of God, the evan-
> gelists, and the apostles; although there is a difference be-
> tween the philosophers and the inspired authors, like that
> between day and night.[14]

In his chapter "Of Morall Philosophie," he contrasts and opposes
the teaching of philosophy with that of Christ:

> Christ teacheth that perfect vertue is not gotten but by grace
> geven from above, the Philosophers saie, that it is goten by
> our owne strength and exercise. . . .[15]

He concludes,

> Furthermore, they geven us the Pelagian Heretikes with their

free will and with the instruction and natural light of righte
reason. All morall Philosophie, as Lactantius saithe, is talse,
and vaine, not instructinge to the offices of iustice, neither
confirminge the dutie and consailes of man. Finally it is alto-
geather repugnant to Goddes lawe, and to Christe himselfe,
that the glory thereof is due to none other, than to Sathan.[16]

In like context, but with very different manner, Montaigne concludes his *Apologie of Raymond Sebond* by quoting "Oh what a
vile and abject thing is man unlesse he raise himselfe above humanity," and commenting characteristically,

> Observe here a notable speech, and a profitable desire; but
> likewise absurd. For to make the handfull greater than the
> hand; and the embraced greater than the arme; and to hope
> to straddle more than our legs length; is impossible and mon-
> strous: nor that man should mount over and above himselfe
> or humanity; for, he cannot see but with his own eyes, nor take
> hold but with his owne armes. He shall raise himselfe up, if it
> please God extraordinarily to lend him his helping hand. He
> may elevate himselfe *by forsaking and renouncing his owne
> meanes,* and suffering himselfe to be elevated and raised by
> meere heavenly meanes. *It is for our Christian faith, not for
> his Stoicke vertue* to pretend or aspire to this divine Metamor-
> phosis, or miraculous transmutation.[17]

A similar declaration is made by Parlamente in one of the lively
conversations in Marguerite of Navarre's *Heptameron.* The gallant
company has been discussing those "philosophers of past times"
who were utterly "possessed . . . with the belief that there is virtue
in vanquishing oneself," and Parlamente (whom Abel Lefranc calls
the "porte-parole de Marguerite") asserts,

> In truth, it is impossible to overcome ourselves by ourselves;
> nor can one think to do so without prodigious pride. . . .

Oiselle strikes the dominant note of the Reformation when she
reminds the company,

> Did I not read to you this morning that those who believed
> themselves wiser than others, and came *by the light of reason
> to know a God,* the creator of all things, and for having been
> vain thereof, and not having attributed this glory to Him to
> whom it belonged, and for having imagined that they had
> acquired this knowledge by their own labors, became more
> ignorant and less reasonable, I will not say than other men.
> but than the very brutes? In fact, their minds having run

astray, they ascribed to themselves what belongs to God alone. . . .[18]

But it is not simply a question of "philosophers of past times."[19] Like accusations against the Renaissance humanists' moral pride, and their confidence in the capacity of the classical discipline of ethical philosophy to lead them to virtue, are often linked with vituperations against the pretensions of the new humanistic learning. In an interesting passage, Samuel Daniel illustrates well the tendency to turn from the long-drawn-out belaboring of the Scholastics to that of the humanists and reformers:

> Erasmus, Rewcline and More, brought no more wisedome into the world with all their new revived wordes than we find was before, it bred not a profounder Divine than Saint Thomas, a greater lawyer than Bartolus, a more acute logician than Scotus. . . .[20]

And he concludes in a long sentence redolent of the flavor of Montaigne,

> I thanke God that I am none of these great Schollers, if thus their hie knowledge does give them more eyes to looke out into uncertaintie and confusion, accounting my selfe, rather beholding to my ignorance, that hath set me in so lowe an under-roome of conceipt with other men, and hath given me as much distrust, as it hath done hope, daring not adventure to goe alone, but plodding on the plaine tract I finde beaten by Custome and the Time, contenting me with what I see in use.[21]

John Marston, bearing "the scourge of Just Rhamnusia," directs a heavy assault against those who believe that they may come to virtue by nature, by training, by reason, will and good works. He insists,

> It is a sacred cure
> To salve the soules dread wounds: Omnipotent
> That Nature is, that cures the impotent,
> Even in a moment; Sure Grace is infus'd
> By divine favour, not by actions us'd.[22]

If God withdraws his sacred grace, he demands,

> Yee curious sotts, vainly by Nature led,
> Where is your vice or vertuous habite now?[23]

When Marston has disposed of Aristotle, he moves on to attack the Stoics and Cynics.

> *Then vice nor vertue have from habite place,*
> *The one from want, the other sacred grace.*
> *Infus'd, displac'd, not in our will or force,*
> *But as it please* Iehova *have remorce.*
> *I will,* cries *Zeno,* ô presumption!
> *I can,* thou maist, dogged opinion
> Of thwarting Cynicks. Today vicious,
> List to their precepts, next day vertuous.
> Peace *Seneca,* thou belchest blasphemy.
> *To live from God, but to live happily*
> (I heare thee boast,) *from thy Philosophy,*
> And from thy selfe, ô ravening lunacy![24]

The shade of Bussy d'Ambois, in Chapman's *The Revenge of
Bussy,* admonishes his brother and avenger, Clermont d'Ambois (the
perfect "Senecal man . . . rightly to virtue fram'd, in very nature"[25]) in more moderate but similar terms. He declares,

> You respect not
> (With all your holinesse of life and learning)
> More than the present, like illiterate vulgars;
> Your mind (you say) kept in your flesh's bounds,
> Shows that man's will must rul'd be by his power:
> When (by true doctrine) you are taught to live
> Rather without the body than within,
> And rather to your God still than yourself. . . .[26]

Clermont, he maintains, has deserted "the body of felicity, religion,"

> And all her laws, whose observation
> Stands upon faith, above the power of reason.[27]

This long succession of passages ranges from the traditional protests, in the works of Petrarch and Valla, against the speculative
hybris of the Scholastic philosophers, down through many Renaissance variations on this essential theme, to the excoriating of the
moral pride of "Stoicke vertue" by Montaigne and the Elizabethans.
It bears witness to the existence of an anti-intellectualistic revolt
which in time undergoes a marked change of tone. Taken up at
first by those Renaissance humanists who would see man's rational
activity "brought down to earth" by an abandoning of the speculative intellect in favor of the practical reason, teaching "virtue's lore,"
the tendency was not originally antagonistic to the traditional reconciliation of reason and faith. But from the early sixteenth century
on, this new emphasis (the shift from Scholastic intellectualism to

Renaissance humanism) was in its turn decried, and—with the advent of the Reformation—"the light of Nature," "right reason," and that humanistic learning whose end was virtuous action, were all being discredited as inimical to the doctrine of God's inscrutable grace and his exclusive power.

It is this later development against which Richard Hooker writes one of his most impassioned and magnificent protests:

> But so it is, the name of the light of Nature is made hateful with men; the star of Reason and learning, and all other such helps, beginneth no otherwise to be thought of than if it were an unlucky comet; or as if God had so accursed it, that it should never shine or give light in things concerning our duty any way towards Him, but be esteemed as that star in Revelation called Wormwood: which being fallen from Heaven maketh rivers and waters in which it falleth so bitter, that men tasting them die thereof. A number there are who think they cannot admire as they ought the power and authority of the Word of God if in things divine they should attribute any force to man's Reason: for which cause *they never use Reason so willingly as to disgrace Reason.*[28]

The burden of Hooker's complaint is just. He has in mind, of course, those followers of Calvin who, in their conviction of the complete corruption of man since the Fall, esteem Reason "as that star in Revelation called Wormwood." And Calvin himself, in the systematic theology which he built with such logical care in his *Institutes of the Christian Religion*,[29] had willingly used Reason "to disgrace Reason."

But Hooker could have made his observation cover a great deal more territory without weakening or falsifying his premise. For Reason's and Learning's low estate in the sixteenth century was for many not confined to theological controversy. Religious fideism and philosophical skepticism, occultism of various sorts and a radical empiricism, an assertive individualism and a conviction of man's utter dependence on God—these and other superficially paradoxical allies consorted in the common distrust of the efficacy of man's speculative mind to grasp truth, and of his natural reason to come by virtue. Religion, epistemology, ethical and political theory, esthetics and the philosophy of history—none of these escapes violence at the hands of some of the participants in the extensive anti-intellectualistic and anti-moralistic revolt of the sixteenth century.

Moreover, as Hooker so shrewdly suggests, reason is liberally used by those who deny her validity and force. One has only to mention the names of Montaigne and Rabelais, of Machiavelli and Guicciardini, of Ronsard and Du Bellay, of Agrippa and Vives and Calvin and Bodin, among the ranks of the rebels, to convince an impartial audience that the hallmark of this movement was not simply irrationality. The whole trend, whether in science or religion, in ethics or æsthetics or whatever, represents fundamentally a turning away from the unguarded intellectualism of medieval Scholasticism (which had so sadly degenerated to intra-mural quibbling after the thirteenth century), and from the exaltation of human reason and learning of Renaissance humanists. Whether they objected to that immense framework of logical cogitation built up by the Schoolmen; the more recent attempts of Neoplatonists, Neo-aristotelians, and Neo-stoics to squeeze the Christian truth out of shape to fit their ideas of rational theology; or simply the general speculative itch to formulate rational laws *as they ought to be* for any department of physical and metaphysical experience—these rebels, stressing the discrepancy between the ideal formulated by theory and the actuality they observed themselves, demanded a different approach to truth and certainty.

By the religionists, a new appeal was made to faith, to divine grace, to revelation; by the scientists, to observation and experiment; by the writers on ethics to the goods of pleasure and instinct; by the investigators of historical, political and social phenomena, to "fact" and pragmatic experience. And there was in the vanguard of the whole movement a group who denied the possibility of any certain knowledge at all, a group whose epistemological skepticism was complete. At any rate, they all agreed that Hypothesis had ridden naked through town too long, and now her hair was too sparse to cover her decently. . . .

This revolt against intellectualism and systematization forms the second large current in the history of ideas of the Renaissance— the one which I call the Counter-Renaissance. "Counter" it was to the main stream of the humanistic Renaissance, the revival of classical letters, moral philosophy, and the "Greek art of life"— counter both in the sense of opposition and that of reciprocality. Opposition, obviously, in its distrust of reason and the light of Nature, as well as of the speculative intellect; in its conviction of the vanity of arts and sciences; in its contempt for the artifice of the systematizing mind which found rational laws in Nature, invented ideal commonwealths, and wrote interpretative commentaries. Reciprocality, since it matched and countered humanism's return to clàssical antiquity with a "renaissance" or "rebirth" of its own, a return to *first principles.*

Quite literally, this return to first principles is manifested by various kinds of cultural, technological, chronological and religious primitivism. But in addition, it takes on the large general meanings of an advocacy of simplification and simplicity, and of decentralized, unsynthesized particular experience—whether in the sense of direct personal contact with the object of knowledge, or the concentration upon some one aspect of possible knowledge (rather than the attempts to fit all aspects together into a coherent and consistent synthesis). Thus, the religionists and mystics of the Counter-Renaissance stress active volition, love and faith—or passive grace and revelation. The scientists cultivate an empirical attitude and investigate the "brute fact." The writers on social, political, ethical and historical matters adopt the pragmatic consideration of "things as they are," whether in dealing with men or events. Practice and fact, not theory; the particular, not the universal; the intuitive or volitional or empirical, not the speculative or intellectual or logical.

In this concept of a Counter-Renaissance, the Protestant Reformation finds an integral place, rather than being (as it has often been considered) a movement independent of the whole secular Renaissance. It becomes evident, indeed, that Calvin and Luther have surprising affinities with contemporaries as superficially diverse as Machiavelli and Montaigne, and that the whole trend of the early Reformation is paralleled by other anti-intellectualistic and anti-moralistic manifestations of the period.

Eventually, of course (as I indicated in the Foreword), a balance was struck; the Counter-Renaissance gave way in turn, and another reaction set in. But the return to confidence in reason-and-nature was not really a return to the reconciliation of theology and philosophy which we have traced through the Scholastics and the Renaissance Christian humanists. The foundations for a new model of the universe were laid on Reason and Nature in the late sixteenth and in the seventeenth centuries. But its Nature was mechanical and mathematical; in its religion, Reason tended more and more to supersede Faith, and to bend her to its own dictates. Universal purpose and design comprehensible to man have disappeared altogether with Spinoza's conception of God.

This new world is effected by the third great movement of the Renaissance, perhaps most accurately called the Scientific Reformation—for while it owes methodological debts to Scholastic science, its purpose and its universe are markedly different from those of

Thomas Aquinas. The shift to Galilean and Newtonian scientific "ends" is an even more drastic change than that which we have observed taking place in human "ends," through the agency of humanism.

For while the alliance between Reason and Nature is once more effected with the Scientific Reformation, Nature has ceased now to be teleological, "meaningful" and "purposeful." Men no longer measure her qualitatively, but quantitatively. The distrust which many of the sixteenth-century skeptics felt for "knowledge" to be gained through the senses results in Galileo's distinction between primary and secondary realms of knowledge. The primary and only strictly reliable means of ascertaining truth is through mathematical measurement. Nature has been "neutralized"; there has been a "transference from the Magical View of the world to the scientific."[30]

Moreover, Reason has not only been relieved of her former subservience to the interests of faith; she has also resumed her dignified role in science, with the restoration of hypothesis and the abstracting intellect to basic importance in the "New Science." The radical empiricism of the sixteenth-century alchemists and exponents of natural magic, and that more sober sort endorsed by Bacon and Vives, have left their mark, especially in the biological sciences. But after Galileo it is mostly in conjunction with mathematical calculation, as a check for hypotheses, that experiment and observation serve in physics and astronomy.

In other fields, Reason and Nature and Law are supreme, reaching an eventual apotheosis in the eighteenth century. Humanly comprehensible purpose and design, in the old sense, finally disappear from this new universe of mechanical laws. But for Newton's world machine, Divine Reason is the mechanic; nature and reason resume their normative functions in ethics and in social and political theory; natural theology and a confident epistemology which began with "Cogito ergo sum," further exalt reason. . . .

Ironically enough, it was the Counter-Renaissance, so hostile to Reason, which finally assured its triumph. For the opening wedge, driven forcefully into the cemented compound of reason and faith by William of Ockham and the Nominalist movement in the fourteenth century, was perceptibly widened by the Counter-Renaissance. And although the adherents of its skepticism and fideism, its mysticism and empiricism, its voluntarism and determinism, were all opposed to the interests of Reason, their efforts, taken over again and assimilated by the Scientific Reformation, did effactually deepen the gap between the provinces of Faith and of Reason. In combination with the humanistic trend toward natural theology and an independent ethic, they made the space too wide for any further bridging. Hence the revolt against Christian intellectualism eventually proved a most effective factor in giving birth to a de-Christianized (or at best an a-Christian) intellectualism.

Again, it must be made clear that to speak of these three "movements" as though they were distinct and successive in time is not my intention. The scientific work done in Padua in the fifteenth and sixteenth centuries proves that the Scientific Reformation was a continuous process, and well under way long before Galileo and Kepler, and even Copernicus.[31] Conversely, as late as the time of John Milton, Renaissance Christian Humanism is vital and vigorous, although no longer the dominant force it had once been. Finally, many of the constituents of the Counter-Renaissance are evident in fourteenth-century Europe, and again, in a figure like Pascal, in the seventeenth century.

Nevertheless, despite chronological overlapping, the order in which I have set these movements down is the order in which each prospered most greatly. The Counter-Renaissance gained force not simply in reaction to Scholastic intellectualism, but also in opposition to the increasing exaltation of Nature-and-Reason by the humanists. And the Scientific Reformation, in its turn, became the most powerful intellectual factor in modern history only after the Counter-Renaissance had played its part in ridiculing and destroying the general acceptance of many of the basic positions of the old synthesis. This study is primarily concerned with the way in which the Counter-Renaissance performed this very function; and we shall turn now to a more detailed consideration of its various aspects.

2. THE VANITY OF LEARNING

The Scholastics had admitted that reality exceeded the capacity of knowledge without the aid of God. For them, ideas were derived from the content of sense perception. Consequently, the natural human intelligence was limited to the understanding of the realities of sense, save as it depended upon analogy to extend its knowledge. Yet "to abstract is the law of the intellect"; they believed abstract knowledge to be superior to sense perception, and to differ from it in kind, not simply in degree. Hence "certitude, which is nothing but a firm assent to truth, is a possession of understanding and reason."[32]

This position illuminates that which most of the Scholastics, following Thomas Aquinas, held on the famous and complicated question of "universals." The extreme *realism* of the Platonist early Middle Ages had maintained that "the class, the universal, exists by itself apart from the members, the particulars," and "preceded them in time; that it is more real, that it made them, and was the source of their being."[33] Thus it exalted Man, rather than men; the Church, the guild, the order, rather than their members. It placed only a minimum value on the individual, and "it made the end of life the release from the bonds of individuality and the return to true reality or the great all that is God."[34]

But this view also tended to merge into pantheism—to deny the distinction between a perfect God and an imperfect world, and to render the moral life almost meaningless. The Church could not, in the interests of its own effectiveness, maintain such a position; under the leadership of Aquinas, she deserted this Platonic "otherworldliness" for a compromise similar to that which Aristotle had once chosen—a compromise between the truth of the universal on the one hand, and the individual, the particular, the concrete, on the other. This *moderate realism,* or *conceptualism,* agreed that the universal exists and is of importance, but it maintained that *it exists only in the particular:*

> The group exists for its members, and is nothing apart from them, no end in itself, and yet the members are in a real sense constituted by the group of which they are a part.[35]

But already in the thirteenth century, mostly within the Franciscan order, there was an opposition party moving toward the position that *the only reality is in the individual. Nominalism* achieves its real coming of age with William of Ockham, an English Franciscan who denied that the universal can be a thing, a reality (*res*), since—despite the realists—the same thing cannot exist simultaneously in several things. Hence a universal is merely a sign serving to designate several similar things, a word or name (*nomen*) without objective reality. Nothing is real except the individual, and it may be known only by intuitive knowledge, whether sensible or supra-sensible:

> The intuitive concept arises out of a direct contact with the real experienced, [but] the abstract concept is a purely mental product which does not involve the causal intervention of sensation.[36]

It is no exaggeration to say that most of the germs of the Counter-Renaissance may be found in Ockham's epistemology, although they were not all developed by him, of course. For such a position is centered in an opposition to, and distrust of, intellect and reason. It is skeptical of all science except the purely experimental (if that may be called science); it rejects the validity of rational theology, and turns exclusively to faith for its religious conviction. It invalidates the central ethical premise of the Scholastics and the Renaissance humanists: that the true freedom of the will rests upon "the intellectual presentation of the good" (or the guidance of Right Reason). And it makes of "the ideas of law, cause, and end," upon which their political theory (as well as their physics) rests, mere "mental fabrications."[37]

Ockhamism flourished in Paris and elsewhere throughout the fourteenth century, and unquestionably paved the way for modern individualism, nationalism and Protestantism. It exerted a decentralizing influence upon the unifying and reconciling tradition of Scholasticism, much as the Counter-Renaissance did two hundred years later upon the orthodox eclectic synthesis of Renaissance Christian humanism. But it was not until the Counter-Renaissance that the various tendencies implicit in nominalism struck with full strength.

To begin with, nominalistic epistemology was combined in the sixteenth century with classical philosophical skepticism, to produce a strong anti-intellectualistic movement whose leaders proclaimed "the vanity of learning"—both the scientific learning of the Scholastics and the humanistic variety of the Renaissance. This attitude is explicit in the charges made against "God's privy councilors" and "Nature's secretaries"—or, as Montaigne phrases it in his essay "Of Education," that

> rable of men that are ordinarie interpreters and contenters of God's secret designes, presuming to finde out the causes of every accident, and to prie into the secrets of God's divine will, the incomprehensible motives of his works.[38]

But fond of invective as the leaders and cohorts of the Counter-Renaissance undoubtedly were, the tradition of the vanity of learning was not simply name-calling. The Greek skeptics had attacked the dogmatic philosophies of the ancient world, and written extensively upon the complete relativity of knowledge. Both the New Academy brand of skepticism, best represented by Carneades and most widely publicized by Cicero, and that sort generally termed "Pyrrhonic," after its initiator, Pyrrho of Elis, were familiar to the Renaissance. Diogenes Laërtius' *Lives of the Philosophers*, which contains accounts of both skeptical schools, was immensely popular, and Sextus Empiricus' *Hypotyposes,* a culminating collection of the views of earlier skeptics, had been completely translated by the thirteenth century.

It is upon this basis of philosophical skepticism, including the relatively of knowledge, of law, and of ethical values, that Cornelius Agrippa builds many of his arguments in his *Of the Vanitie and Uncertaintie of Artes and Sciences.* Erasmus shows his familiarity with these concepts in *The Praise of Folly,* as does Rabelais in his writings. But after Agrippa it is Montaigne who most enthusiastically embraces the principles of this skepticism, and exploits all their possibilities to castigate the pretensions of the adherents of Scholastic science and of humanistic "Stoick vertue."

Henri Estienne published a new Latin translation of the *Hypotyposes* in 1562, and it was through this edition that Montaigne made the acquaintance of the philosophical skeptics. It is reported that he celebrated his "discovery" of this book, in 1576, by having a medal struck in commemoration of the event, and by placing mottoes from Sextus upon his walls. At any rate, "the true Pyrrhonisme" was a gospel to him for some time, and provided him with many of the arguments which he developed with such devastating effect in the *Apologie of Raymond Sebond.*[39] There are other treatises in the sixteenth century which cut a wide skeptical swath through the fields of "good arts and sciences"—notably the *Quod Nihil Scitur* of Francisco Sanchez and Fulke Greville's *Treatie of Humane Learning*[40]—but unquestionably those of Agrippa and Montaigne were the most radical and the most influential.

Knowledge is impossible for man and belongs to God alone, they insist. Both observer and observed are in a constant flux; neither sense nor reason can really grasp truth in a world compact of mutability. As Montaigne puts it:

> In few, there is no constant existence, neither of our being, nor of the objects. And we and our judgement and all mortall things else do uncessantly rowle, turne and passe away. Thus can nothing be certainely established, nor of the one nor of the other; both the judgeing and the judged being in continuall alteration and motion. Thus, seeing all things are subject to passe from one change to another, reason, which therein seeketh a reall subsistence, findes herself deceived as unable to apprehend any thing subsistent and permanent: forsomuch as each thing either commeth to a being, and is not yet altogeather: or beginneth to dy before it be borne.[41]

This is the world in which the "Pyrrhonist" lives, refusing to make "any positive assertion regarding the external realities." The wisest course he can follow, according to Sextus, is to adhere to appearances, and "live in accordance with the normal rules of life, undogmatically, seeing that we cannot remain totally inactive." The best life is therefore "a life conformable to the customs of our country and its laws and institutions, and to our own instinctive feelings." Hence, "tranquillity [ataraxia] follows on suspension of judgement. . . ."[42] Montaigne declares:

> Whosoever shall imagine a perpetuall confession of ignorance, and a judgment upright and without staggering, to what occasion soever may chance, that man conceives the true Pyrrhonisme.[43]

The "perpetuall confession of ignorance" becomes, indeed, a point of pride with many participants in the Counter-Renaissance. It is consistent with a conviction of the vanity of learning, and in its support invokes the ghost of Socrates, that "wisest of all Mortall men," who "*Said he knew nought, but that he naught did know.* . . ."[44] However disingenuous this literal interpretation of Socrates' probably ironic attitude may have been with particular men, it had the precedent of the Greek skeptics,[45] and its vogue was tremendously widespread in the sixteenth century.

Montaigne, throughout many of the *Essayes* the advocate of an inclusive primitivism, links with the idea of the wise philosopher who pretends to no knowledge, that of the goodness and wisdom of the simple and humble of earth. He declares,

> There is a kind of Abecedarie ignorance preceding science: another doctorall following science: an ignorance which science doth beget, even as it *spoileth* the first.[46]

This statement (which should hang, framed, in the office of every Doctor of Philosophy) he enlarges upon in "Of Phisiognomy," where he refers outright to "the benefit of ignorance," and demands,

> To what purpose do we so arme and steele ourselves with these labouring-efforts of learning? Let us diligently survay the surface of the earth, and there consider so many seely-poore people as we see toyling, sweltring and drooping about their businesse, which never heard of Aristotle nor of Plato, nor ever knew what examples or precepts are. For those doth nature dayly draw and afoord us effects of constancy and patternes of patience, more faire and forcible than are those we so curiously study for in schooles.[47]

He had long since found "the customes and discourses of countrie-clownish men" better shaped to the "true prescription of Philosophie" than those "of our Philosophers."[48] This theme grows on him, as does that of Socrates, the true (because simple and natural) philosopher. In "How One Ought to Governe His Will," the two are explicitly united:

> The middle region [remember the "doctorall ignorance"] harboureth stormes; the two extreames containe Philosophers and rurall men, they concurre in tranquility and good hap.[49]

This exaltation of the humble by Montaigne is thoroughly integrated with the "philosophy of Nature" in which he takes his final stand; it is not so much democratic as primitivistic, and yet it bears democratic implications. The praise of the humble and simple is, moreover, one of the most persistent features of the Counter-Renaissance, and warrants a considerable analysis.

Sometimes it merges with the old concept of the pure "fool" under the special protection and benevolence of God. In *The Praise of Folly*, Erasmus is referring to this tradition when he writes of the special privileges that fools are everywhere accorded—extending even to the treatment they receive from "the very Beasts [who], by a kind of natural instinct of their [the fools'] innocence no doubt, pass by their injuries." And he definitely allies this concept to the more practical stress which is Montaigne's concern, when he adds, "Again, take notice of this no contemptible blessing which Nature hath giv'n fools, that they are the only plain, honest men and such as speak truth."[50]

His devoted admirer, Rabelais, has Pantagruel, in his defense of Bridlegoose, speak of God's practice of manifesting

> his own ineffable glory in blunting the perspicacy [*sic*] of the eyes of the wise, in weakening the strength of potent oppressors, in depressing the pride of the rich extortioners, and in erecting, comforting, protecting, supporting, upholding, and shoring up, the poor, feeble, humble, silly, and foolish ones of the earth.[51]

And although the "morosoph" Triboulet shares the ironic treatment accorded all the oracles whom Panurge visits, it is noteworthy that Pantagruel speaks of the "wise foolery" of "noble Triboulet."[52]

Noteworthy—because, without trying to force Rabelais into a consistent philosophical position, without trying to wrench out of shape passages which are primarily magnificent robust satire, one may still mark the gradual change, after the first two books, in many of his points of view. Among these changes is that in his treatment of Pantagruel, who is presented as a figure of increasingly grave elegance, and as an interpreter and commentator whose opinion must be treated with respect, if not wholly equated with the author's.

Moreover, there is no exaggeration in declaring that the whole prologue of the Fourth Book is devoted to the exalting of the humble. Poor Tom the woodcutter may be a comical figure as he stands, bawling to the heavens "by way of litany, 'My hatchet . . . Lord Jupiter, my hatchet! my hatchet!'" But his rough, simple honesty is contrasted with the greediness of those who hope to emulate his good fortune, and it is hardly a coincidence that Jupiter sends Mercury down to help him while the Ramus-Galland controversy is left unsettled.

The fool, in this sense of the good plain honest man of "abecedarie ignorance," has roots well established in literature long before the Renaissance, and has remained a popular "type" ever since. The age represented by *Piers Plowman* and Chaucer's Plowman and Parson was not unaware of the merits of humble, simple honesty, and it is mostly these deeper roots which are evident in Elizabethan passages like George Gascoigne's invocation of Piers Plowman in *The Steel Glass:*

> Therefore I say, stand forth *Pierce* plowman first,
> Thou winst the roome by verie worthinesse.
>
> Behold him (priests) and though he stink of sweat
> Disdaine him not: for shal I tel you what?
> Such clime to heaven before the shaven crownes.
> But how? forsooth, with true humilytie.[53]

But Gascoigne is primarily expressing an anticlerical bias, not directly attacking the vanity of learning. John Marston presents the newer point of view in his *Antonio's Revenge*. After Antonio has assumed the "disguise" of a professional fool, he says:

> Whils't studious contemplation sucks the juyce
> From wizards cheekes: who maketh curious search
> For Nature's secrets, the first innating cause
> Laughes them to scorne, as man doth busie Apes
> When they will zanie men. Had Heaven bin kinde,
> Creating me an honest senselesse dolt,
> A good poore foole, I should want sense to feele
> The stings of anguish shoot through every vaine . . .[54]

In addition to the "fool" tradition of the plain man, "beholding to his ignorance," there was another related but more specifically Chris-

tian tradition, that of the "pure fool"—or "the fool for Christ," as the
Franciscan phrasing went. The Little Brothers of Assisi, despite a
few notable exceptions, had from the first shown slight enthusiasm
for speculation and learning. P. Sabatier, in his *Life of St. Francis*,
quotes Francis as saying,

> Suppose that you have enough subtlety and science to know
> all things, that you are acquainted with all languages, the
> course of the stars and all the rest, what have you to be proud
> of? A single demon in hell knows more than all men on earth
> put together. But there is one thing of which the demon is
> incapable, and which is the glory of man: to be faithful to
> God.[55]

It was within this order, too, that Jacopone da Todi celebrated
his mystic "sacrifice to love." But already in the fourteenth century,
other than Franciscan voices were being raised in protest against
the dominance of speculative theology—mystical voices like those
of Meister Eckhart, a product of the Dominican order, and the
"Friends of God."[56] For them, as for the Franciscans, the supremacy
of love over knowledge was incontestable; and with the advent of
the Reformation, what in a medieval mystic like Bonaventura had
been simply the exposition of a "symbolic" path to God, complementary and parallel to the primarily intellectualistic one of Aquinas,
became almost an exclusive emphasis. One minor but strong manifestation of the Counter-Renaissance, into which all these and other
currents flowed, was a veritable chorus of voices hymning the love
of God.

"Surgunt indocti et rapiunt caelum. . . ." The old words take on
a new force, and the primacy of love for these "fools of God" is
articulate in many different ways. There are, for example, the "Libertins Spirituels," whose semi-erotic mysticism is best (or at least,
most gracefully) presented in the later poetry of Marguerite of
Navarre. To *la Bergère* "ravie de l'Amour de Dieu," there is nothing
in the world except love; all the rest is only appearance and vanity.
When *la Sage* declares to her that

> C'est un beau chemin de science
> Que chascun doibt tant estimer . . .

she replies,

> Je ne sçay rien, sinon aymer,

and later

> Mon ame perir et noier
> Or puisse en ceste douce mer

D'amour, où n'y a point d'amer
Je ne sens corps, ame ni vie
Sinon amour, et n'ay envie
De paradis, ni d'enfer craincte,
Mais que sans fin je sois estraincte
A mon amy, unye et joincte.[57]

This unresolved confusion of human and divine love, this erotic intoxication which makes no clear distinction between rapture and mystical ecstasy, has its contemporary Catholic parallel in Theresa's account of how, in union with God, "generally even my head, and sometimes my whole body, were raised from the ground."[58] Theresa, too, uses the "drowning" imagery:

We enjoy raptures only by intervals, and the soul often engulfs herself, or rather (to speak more correctly) our Lord engulfs the soul in Himself. . . . True it is, that souls are ordinarily, in this state, *drowned* in the praises of God. . . .[59]

But "la Bergère," in her Aucassin-like rejection of Paradise and defiance of Hell, and in her implication of the moral indifference of human conduct, goes well beyond Theresa's position and close to a pantheistic mysticism like that of Marguerite Porrette, whose book was condemned by the fourteenth-century theologians of Paris:

quod animi annihilata in amore conditoris sine reprehensione conscientiae vel remorsu potest et debet dare naturae quidquod appetit vel desiderat.[60]

Despite the amusingly different imagery, Luther's influence on the Queen of Navarre's shepherdess is apparent, too. For he had early come to the conclusion that instead of exhausting himself in repelling evil, he should seek

shelter in God as chickens seek shelter under the hen, and trust . . . God's infinity to supply what he lacked. . . [61]

It is here, then, with the Reformation, that the vanity of moral exertion is plainly and urgently cited along with that of "scientific" learning. As Longarine's beatitude in the *Heptameron* goes:

Blessed are they whose faith has so humbled them that they have no need of outward acts to make them conscious of the weakness and corruption of their natures.[62]

Such an attitude leaves the way open for a delight in the irresponsible and passive abandonment of the soul to that Sea of God's Love upon which it floats. This abandon is suggested in lyrics of the Queen of Navarre like the one containing the lines:

O bergère, ma mye,
Je ne vis que d'amours . . .
Amour est ma fiance
Repoz de conscience,
Ma force et passience
Ma foy, mon espoir, mon secours.[63]

And while in Marguerite's earlier and chiefly Neoplatonic writings, one frequently suspects the cult of love and beauty of being more courtly and sophisticated entertainment than spiritual aspiration, the undeniable beauty and intensity of these later lyrics do bespeak sincerity.

It is a long step from the "folly" of Marguerite's shepherdess, drunk with love, to the semi-reverent passage on "Christ the fool" by Erasmus in *The Praise of Folly*. The one is a mystic-erotic drowning in "ceste douce mer d'amour"; the other is a tart reminder that in essence the Christian religion is "a transformation rather than a reasoning,"[64] and that Christ's wisdom was and is folly "to the general." Yet their alliance against speculative or rational theology is patent, and they share—in however diverse and even grotesque a rendering—the fundamental Pauline concept of the transforming power of love.

Erasmus' "Moria" points out the *rapport* between Christianity and folly:

And agen, when Christ gives Him thanks that he had conceal'd the Mystery of Salvation from the wise, but revealed it to babes and sucklings, that is to say, Fools. For the Greek word Babes is Fools, which he opposeth to the word Wise men . . .[65]

The humble, the innocent, the wisely foolish—of these is the Kingdom. . . . And while Christ indeed combated many sorts of human folly, it was not with the wisdom of the "Wise men":

And Christ himself, that he might the better relieve this Folly, being the wisdome of the Father, yet in some manner became a fool, when taking upon him the nature of man, he was found in shape as a man; as in like manner was made sin, that he might heal sinners. Nor did he work this Cure any other way than by the foolishness of the Cross, and a company of fat Apostles, not much better, to whom also he carefully recommended folly, but gave 'em a caution against wisdome, and drew 'em together by the Example of little Children, Lillies, Mustard-seed and Sparrows, things senseless and inconsiderable, living only by the dictates of Nature and without either craft or care.[66]

For, as Montaigne was to say, God indeed "hath made choice of the simple, common, and ignorant to teach us His wonderfull secrets."[67]

As might be expected, it is with a much soberer accent that John Colet, good humanist though he is, expresses his distrust of learning. In a letter to Erasmus, who is busy in defense of Reuchlin against charges of heresy, Colet is suspicious of the "Pythagorean and Cabalistical ideas of Reuchlin." He goes on,

> Ah, Erasmus, of books and of knowledge there is no end; but there is nothing better for this short term of ours, than that we shall lead a pure and holy life.[68]

In conclusion, he recommends exclusively and finally "the ardent love and imitation" of Jesus "in order that, leaving all indirect courses, we may proceed by a short method to the Truth."[69]

While it has not the tone of the Lutheran Reformation, Colet's injunction to "the ardent love and imitation of Jesus" is in essence very close to at least one aspect of Luther's attitude. For while Luther, with his "justification by faith alone," rejects the efficacy of good works for salvation, he explicitly states that "where works and love do not appear, there faith is not."[70] In short, true faith "is an impulse to imitate its object, to be like Christ. . . ."[71]

Yet many of the early Protestants (and Luther himself, for that matter) seem frequently to have forgotten this emphasis. The exclusive certainty of faith for salvation, they never forgot; hence (with a few exceptions, including Melanchthon), the early Reformation contributed mightily to almost all the anti-intellectualistic aspects of the Counter-Renaissance. There is overwhelming evidence for its decisive influence on the vanity-of-science and exaltation-of-the-ignorant traditions, and even stronger testimony for its opposition to the Christian humanists' reliance on their own natural reason in the moral life.

But for a clear understanding of the significance of the Reformation to these two major aspects of the vanity-of-learning tradition of the Counter-Renaissance, it is necessary to retrace the earlier course of the appeal to faith. I say "two major aspects," for it is a double tradition, excoriating at once the "science" of the Scholastics and the "humane studies" of the humanists. The one learning leads to speculative or intellectualistic arrogance, the other to an unwonted confidence in the powers of the moral virtues (as distinct from the purely Christian ones of faith, hope and love) and of man's own will, under the guidance of reason. Such is the opinion of the

Counter-Renaissance and its precursors; and they oppose the first pretension with the simplicity of the good unlettered man, the fool with "the benefit of ignorance"; the second with the humble and innocent, and with those free from the "prodigious pride" of believing themselves capable "to overcome [them]selves by [them]-selves"—with alternate kinds of "fools" of love.

"Faith," variously interpreted, plays a role in each of the two aspects. In its pristine sense of "belief" independent of proof, it is the opponent of intellectualism; in its early Lutheran sense of "the recognition by the sinner of the [exclusive] righteousness of God,"[72] it is the adversary of "moralism."

For the Thomists, we know, the first opposition did not exist: the truths of faith and reason were parallel and complementary. Their successors, the Renaissance Christian humanists, at least nominally held the same view; when they departed from it, they did so only in the sense of placing the greater reliance upon reason. But the reconciliation held good, and it held good with equal firmness on the question of the moral life. From Aquinas to John Milton, despite various modifications, the reconciliation tradition maintained that there was no opposition between "natural acquired virtue, and the righteousness of Christ," but that grace itself had redeemed man's moral nature from original sin. Again there are vagrants within the tradition, but they wander in the direction of natural reason; if they err, it is as "Pelagian Heretickes" under the influence of "morall Philosophers."

Now the position of the Fideists (to use the term inclusively) rejects both reconciling conclusions—the confidence in intellectual knowledge and in natural morality. To the first problem, it brings the epistemological support of nominalism and philosophical skepticism. For the second, it calls upon the same allies,[73] but above all upon the Lutheran and Calvinist doctrine of the complete moral helplessness of man. Hence, for the second problem, it awaits the Reformation for a full frontal attack; and while the proposition of universal corruption naturally was applied to the first problem as well, the cause of intellectualistic science had already been seriously undermined as early as the thirteenth century.

3. FIDEISM AND THE REFORMATION

A preliminary wedge was driven between science and dogma, reason and faith, by men who for the most part adhered to the moderate realism of the Scholastic reconciliation tradition. Duns Scotus' doctrine of "accidental" creation, with its implication of the contingency of the laws of nature and the moral law, did much to open this gap, while his interpretation of the principle of individuation prepared the way for William of Ockham.[74] Disciples of Aquinas and Bonaventura widened the opening.[75] But the two greatest forces in this process were nominalism and Averroism—the one in the interests of faith, the other in those of reason.

These two movements converged upon the efforts of the Thomists to maintain the accordance and sympathy between theology and philosophy. Although attacking from different angles, they had in common their opposition to rational theology, and they eventually became closely affiliated in fourteenth-century Paris.

The school of Averroës had its roots in Eastern culture and science. Its Arabian forebears had been driven west, and eventually settled in Spain in the tenth century. By the time the medieval Christian universities arose, the Alexandrian science of the Arabians, with its compound of Aristotelian and Neoplatonic elements, had been firmly established in Spain. Much of this science was assimilated into Scholasticism in the twelfth century, and to it the Scholastics owed much of their knowledge of Ptolemy, Avicenna, Hippocrates, Galen and others.[76]

Moreover, Arabian philosophy, as developed in the Orient by Alfarabi and Avicenna, and later in Spain by Averroës (1126–1198), had produced an Aristotelianism vastly different from the Christianized Scholastic version. Averroës, a physician of eminence, was known as the Commentator, and his interpretations of Aristotle became so widely influential that Thomas Aquinas and Albertus Magnus were called upon to attack and answer them.[77] Among the anti-Christian elements in Averroistic Aristotelianism were its denial of the Creation and of individual or personal immortality, its various monistic tendencies, and its psychological and moral determinism.[78] But it was its doctrine of the "double truth"—that what was true for philosophy was not necessarily true for religion, and *vice versa*—which most harassed the continuing efforts of the Schoolmen to maintain the alliance between philosophy and theology.

So-called "Latin" Averroism appeared in Paris as early as 1256,[79] and prospered for several centuries, despite the opposition of the Church. Siger of Brabant and John of Jandun were among its leaders; the latter, who styled himself "the ape of Aristotle and Averroës," was perfectly willing to admit that Averroës' doctrines were "false in the presence of his religion," quoting Augustine to the effect that the merit of faith lay in its taking hold of propositions not susceptible to reason.[80]

Averroism also flourished in Sicily, at the court of Frederick II, but from the mid-fourteenth century on, northern Italy became its stronghold, especially the University of Padua, a great medical and scientific center.[81] Here, side by side with Averroistic Aristotelianism, there thrived the interpretation of the Stagirite attributed to Alexander of Aphrodias, whose commentary was recovered in the fifteenth century. It was this latter sort (which went beyond Averroës' conviction that immortality was impersonal, to predicate the *complete annihilation* of the human soul at death[82]) which Pomponazzi endorsed,[83] although making the same obeisance to religion as had John of Jandun.

The growth and spread of these two brands of Aristotelianism so disturbed Ficino that he declared in the letter to Johannes Pannonius,

> The whole world is now in the hands of the Peripatetics and is divided mainly into two sects, Alexandrists and Averroists. Both deny any form of religion.[84]

Perhaps this is an exorbitant statement, but the "double truth" protestations of John of Jandun and Pomponazzi reveal ironic phrases and a generally disingenuous tone that leave in the impartial reader's mind little doubt that their interests, in the "separation process," lay in the cause of reason.

It seems clear that this was not the case with Ockham. His aversion to natural theology and his assertion that even the existence of God was simply an object of faith, not of demonstration ("non potest sciri evidenter quod Deus est"[85]), were apparently quite honestly motivated by his conviction of the sterility of theological speculations and his desire to see the Church "reform and return to the simplicity, purity, and holiness of the Apostolic times."[86]

Nevertheless, despite his devotion to faith, his epistemological skepticism helped to lay the foundations for religious skepticism;[87] in the fourteenth century Ockhamism and Averroism cohabited at Paris, and the data of faith which Ockham had declared inaccessible to reason came to be condemned as contrary to reason.[88]

However, as the split widened, there were many who rallied around the standard of faith, too. The practical mystics of the fourteenth century, who were numerous and influential in England, Germany and the Low Countries, exalted love and faith above knowledge, and contributed to that depreciation of the arts and sciences which was to pave the way for the Counter-Renaissance. The injunction of John Tauler, "Children, ye shall not seek after great science,"[89] might serve as an invocation for the fideism to follow.

Very early in the sixteenth century the exponents of faith began to employ the arguments of philosophical skepticism to depreciate the powers of reason and the possibility of intellectual knowledge. This skepticism was an especially convenient tool, since it advocated no active program except "to live in accordance with the normal rules of life" or according to "probability," and hence left the way clear for the declaration of only one truth—that of revelation—and for only one road to certain salvation—faith. This was the premise, for example, of Gianfrancesco Pico della Mirandola, nephew of the famous Pico, in his assault upon human reason and learning in his *Examen Vanitatis* (1520).[90]

Similarly, Agrippa, having employed the tactics of the Greek skeptics to demonstrate the vanity of arts and sciences, demands belligerently,

> How can one perceive . . . truth? Is it by scientific specula-
> tions, by the pressing witness of sensation, by the artificial
> arguments of Logic, by evident proofs, by demonstrative syl-
> logisms, by the light and efforts of human reason? Bah! Get rid
> of all that: the only means of discovering truth is faith . . .[91]

Without prolonged study, it is difficult to distinguish with exact-ness in these sixteenth-century works an indebtedness to the skep-ticism of the New Academy from one to that of the Pyrrhonic school. But by the end of the century, they have all been cited and imitated. In the anti-intellectualistic cause, Carneades, Pyrrho and Sextus Em-piricus are conscripts along with Solomon, Paul and the patristic writers.[92]

Even the "double truth" is for once invoked *against* the pride of the intellect. The Lateran Council had condemned this device alto-gether in 1512; yet sometime after 1540, harried by the Protestant doctrine of the individual conscience, the French Catholic authori-ties employed it to teach reason its proper submissiveness to faith![93]

For despite its fundamental alignment with the reconciliation position, even the Mother Church showed marked fideistic tenden-cies in this century. The Council of Trent (1542–1547), to be sure, upheld "the essential part of good works in the process of salvation," declaring, in opposition to the spirit of the early Reformation, that man is not saved by faith alone.[94] Yet the Catechism of the Council reads,

> He who is gifted with the heavenly knowledge of faith is free from an inquisitive curiosity; for when God commands us to believe, he does not propose to have us search into his divine judgments, nor to inquire their reasons and cause, but demands an immutable faith. . . . Faith, therefore, excludes not only all doubt, but even the desire of subjecting its truth to demonstration.[95]

We have come a long way from the church of Thomas Aquinas. This position is much closer, in fact, to the Lutheran one than to the Thomist. When Luther fulminates,

> We know that reason is the Devil's harlot, and can do nothing but slander and harm all that God says and does. If, outside of Christ, you wish by your own thoughts to know your relation to God, you will break your neck. Thunder strikes him who examines. It is Satan's wisdom to tell what God is, and by doing so he will draw you into the abyss. Therefore keep to revelation and do not try to understand . . .[96]

the difference is mostly one of tone.

Yet there is another difference as well. It is true that Protestants and Catholics in the Reformation era alike condemned reason and the vanities of speculative science and the "good arts" of the humanists. But the Catechism of the Council of Trent refers, at least, to "the heavenly knowledge of faith"—that is, to *a knowledge* which has no need of reason's support. For Luther, on the other hand, faith is no longer "a human participation in the Divine knowledge, but a purely non-rational experience—the conviction of personal salvation."[97] Moreover, although both Luther and Calvin[98] condemn speculative knowledge as impossible and the delusion of Satan, it is natural morality which they attack most savagely. For Luther, "justification leaves sin untouched and affords no room for natural morality. The righteousness of man is fundamentally irreconcilable with the righteousness of God."[99] Man's corruption and moral helplessness since the Fall remain absolute:

> For the first time, with the Reformation, there appeared this conception of a grace that saves man without changing him, of a justice that redeems corrupted nature without restoring it, of a Christ who pardons the sinner for self-inflicted wounds but does not heal them.[100]

Man has no moral worth, Christ all. The only righteousness man may possess is "imputed righteousness" through Christ, and even this is not his, but *Christ's in him*. Moral exertion is totally super-fluous: salvation comes only by the grace of God, extended to those who have faith, or the conviction of God's *exclusive righteousness*.

> "Bear in mind," says Luther, "that to be a pious man and ac-complish many great works and lead an honorable and virtuous life is one thing: to be a Christian is something quite dif-ferent."[101]

It is immediately evident how such a conviction strikes quickly at the heart of that concept of Christian liberty which the Christian humanists inherited from the Middle Ages, as well as at the classical concepts of the moral life under the guidance of right reason. Noth-ing is less pertinent than to speak of man's reason or will—of his capacity for free election. Again Luther is explicit:

> Free choice can belong to the majesty of God alone, because it is his power which makes and wills everything in the sky and on the earth. If one attributes it to man one attributes to him nothing less than divinity itself; but there can be no greater sacrilege.[102]

It was on this question of the freedom of the will that he and Erasmus finally publicly debated. And it is relevant to the progress of the separation of reason and faith that some one should have said that these two papers *On Free Will* and *On Predestination* might well have been named *On Natural Religion* and *On Supernatural Religion. . . .*[103]

Calvin is in complete accord with Luther's attitude toward the irrelevance of the moral life to salvation. He declares that "any one who attempts to deny the doctrine of election [*i.e.*, God's choosing of the "elect" exclusively as he sees fit], impairs the glory of God and destroys humility in man." What is more, if we seek to find any cause for election other than the mere good will and pleasure of God, we are prying into things which should remain hidden.[104]

He suggests, to be sure, the possibility that man may participate in his own salvation—only to destroy the significance of such par-ticipation by his final qualifying clause:

> to understand predestination we must realize that justification in the sight of God comes not from good works, but from a faith alone, *a faith which is the gift of the spirit and not the achievement of the man himself.*[105]

And as his follower, Théodore de Bèze, succinctly and cheerfully puts it,

> Libertas conscientiae diabolicum dogma.[106]

Calvin's concept of a God who acts solely according to his own will is anticipated by Luther:

> It is at once necessary and salutary for the Christian to know that God does not foresee any contingent thing, but that he foresees, proposes and accomplishes all by an immovable, eternal, and infallible will.[107]

But the doctrine of predestination is not formally incorporated into a systematic theology until Calvin's *Institutes,* in which it is central and tied to the concept of man's complete corruption. Not only has God chosen certain "elect" among men, purely at his own arbitrary pleasure, and predestined them to salvation—he has also predestined others to eternal damnation. In this way he has been pleased to show his unlimited power. And hence good works and the moral life are utterly irrelevant to salvation.

But inevitably the human mind and heart will ask where divine justice is in such a world. And here is where the doctrine of original sin is brought in to provide support. To those who question God's justice, His "fairness," if we allow the doctrine of predestination, Calvin replies that the divine justice cannot be considered "unequal" —for God has no obligation to elect anyone. By strict justice all should perish; it is only by God's goodness that *any* soul is saved. If one grants man's total depravity (which one does, if a solid Calvinist), God is immediately freed from any responsibility. Yet this is putting the cart before the horse; God willed the Fall too. The final retreat is always behind the curtain which veils God's arbitrary will, and man's sole access to salvation lies in faith. Yet again that same faith is "the gift of the spirit and not the achievement of the man himself"![108]

Small wonder that Sebastian Castellio should write, in his *De arte dubitandi* (1562),

> After so splendid a dawn, we are forced back into Cimmerian darkness.[109]

In terms of the depreciation of the moral life as a means to salvation, the whole fideistic movement of the Counter-Renaissance reaches a final *cul de sac* in Calvin.

4. THE VANITY OF LEARNING AND FIDEISM IN ELIZABETHAN LITERATURE

The later and parallel lines of the Catholic (or Counter-)Reformation and the Puritan Age strengthened the inflexibility of dogma, and narrowed the concept of morality to something approaching the popular modern understanding of "Puritanism."[110] Professor Grierson has written,

> To the Puritan like Baxter or Bunyan as to the greater spirits of the Counter-Reformation, Ignatius Loyola and Francis Xavier, the world and all it has to offer, science and the arts as much as wealth and honour, are intrinsically vanities. This world has significance only as a field of battle and of discipline (*askesis*) in the great cause of the salvation of man's soul.[111]

But this *askesis* is not to be confused with the moral exertion of the pursuit of virtue in the humanist sense. It is rather an ascetic disciplining by an authority demanding a complete negation of the individual reason and will, and an unquestioning faith.[112] The language of the new period may seem moderate after Luther and Calvin, but the justification by faith alone and the doctrine of "imputed righteousness" are still present:

> The Gospel offereth salvation to him that worketh not, but beleaveth in him that justifieth the ungodly [Rom. iv. 5]: not considering faith, as a worke, but as an instrument apprehending Christ, by whome we are made righteous . . .[113]

Gabriel Harvey sums up the situation for his times in his favorite staccato manner:

> The Gospel taughte, not learned: Charitie Key colde: nothing good, but by Imputation: the Ceremoniall Lawe, in word abrogated: the Judicial in effecte disannulled: the Morall indeede abandoned. . . . Heresie in Divinitie, in Philosophie, in Humanitie, in Manners, grounded much upon hearsay: Doctors contemned: the Text knowen of moste, understood of fewe: magnified of all: practiced of none: the Divell not so hated, as the Pope: many Invectives, small amendment.[114]

And it is Harvey, too, who laconically summarizes the Elizabethan version of the vanity of learning tradition with "Ineruditi vulgo ingeniosiores habiti" ("the unlettered popularly considered cleverer than the learned").[115]

For all the elements of the vanity of learning and fideistic traditions appear in Elizabethan literature, to oppose alike Hooker's "star of Reason, and learning, and all other such helps," and Chapman's "I know his precepts and I will beare his lode." We have already listened to Harvey and Daniel, to Marston and Greville, inveighing against or satirizing intellectual or moral *hybris;* we have read Gascoigne's and Marston's version of the exaltation of the humble and unlettered. And there are many other manifestations in Elizabethan literature of the conflict which centered in the validity of speculative or humanistic learning. The issue appears over and over again in what Polonius might have called the expository-exhortatory-argumentative-polemical name-calling tracts, pamphlets and "letters" of the period—notably in the Harvey-Nashe brawl. It seems to have been an integral part of the alignment of forces in the Essex-Ralegh factions,[116] and is of course related to the various attacks upon the "School of Night," that group of intellectual enthusiasts which gathered around Walter Ralegh and Thomas Hariot.[117]

Erasmus had declared in *The Praise of Folly* that fools "are the only plain, honest men and such as speak truth." We have traced briefly this theme of the "plain, honest fool" whose wisdom is not that of learning. It seems a safe conjecture that many of the fools in Elizabethan drama share this quality. They do not "speak truth" only because of the sufferance of their royal masters; that sufferance at least partially has its origin in the whole "vanity of learning" tradition. For it was "Nature," according to Erasmus, which gave the fool the blessing of honesty and truth to accompany his innocence. Thus it is Nature's "mother wit" with which Feste and Lear's Fool lampoon the artificial wit of their victims.

An interesting and related tradition is that in which the "fool" of plain speech is linked with the Cynic or Stoic "wise man" of plain living, whose "folly" is really the wisdom of ignoring worldly goods —and both with the vanity of learning theme. Augustine developed such a combination, and Petrarch's "Augustine" implies this alignment in the *Secretum*. Again, Pantagruel instructs Panurge in this tradition.[118] But it is the Elizabethan satirists who—both in their own persons and in those of the satiric commentators in their dramatic satires—develop this combination most thoroughly.

Marston, Jonson and other satirists of the nineties (whose work was eventually censored and publicly burned) gloried in "plain-speaking." They claimed a privilege of immunity similar to that of the fools', but on different grounds—grounds which are clearly derivative from the classical tradition of Cynic and Stoic primitivism.[119]

For

> The "plain-speaking" which was one of the boasts of the Cynics
> was . . . a rejection of the refinements and courtesies which
> had become conventional and civilized social intercourse;
> though it was conceived by Epictetus as merely the expression
> of the right and duty of the truly virtuous man to rebuke evil
> in others (*Disc.* III, 22, 13).[120]

Thus Marston, one of the most abusive, refers to his "Cynick
work,"[121] and it is pertinent to note that he links the "thwarting
Cynicks" with Zeno and Seneca (Stoics) in his fourth satire.

But indeed the Cynic-Stoic identification could not have escaped
the Elizabethans. Cicero had called the Stoics before his time *"paene
Cynici";*[122] Epictetus, who considered his own ideal "Cynic," had
cited the words of Diogenes the Cynic more frequently than those
of any Stoic predecessor;[123] Seneca had believed that "the most
essential moral Truths were discovered by the Greek masters of the
Cynic and Stoic schools, and stand in no need of further investigation";[124] and Juvenal, a favorite model for Eiizabethan satirists, had
written, "the Stoics differ from the Cynics only in a tunic."[125] It
hardly seems necessary to press the point further.

It is my conviction, then, that if the "plain-speaking" tradition
of the Elizabethan satirists derives largely from the example of
Roman satire,[126] it is nevertheless conscious of its ultimate debt to
Cynic-Stoic primitivism, with the latter's antagonism to all the
artifices of civilization, culture and society. The satiric commentators, like the fools, are "Nature's children" and, although not innocents, they too excoriate the pretensions of the arts and sciences, as
well as the foibles of "refinements and courtesies."

Oscar James Campbell has ably demonstrated how the "satiric
commentator" tradition of Marston's and Jonson's plays was taken
up by Shakespeare, and developed and transformed to his own purposes—from Jaques and Thersites to Apemantus (who is, incidentally, a professional Cynic) in *Timon of Athens.*[127] The relation of
my interpretation of the satiric tradition to his is made even clearer,
I think, by his citing of two sorts of satiric commentators, the "sturdy
moral teacher" and the "buffoon" or "detractor, scurrilous railer."[128]
These two correspond very closely to the Cynic or Stoic wise man
and the fool,[129] respectively, and further confirm the relationship of
these two traditions.

Let us consider the case of *King Lear,* a Stoic play through and
through. Lear's fool is certainly a wise "buffoon"—a much wiser and
subtler one than Thersites, for example. And although it has not

been noted (to the best of my knowledge), Kent is the second kind of satirical commentator, the "sturdy wise man." He is indeed the perfect doctrinal Stoic, who endures the stocks and all fortune's buffetings with "apathy,"[130] and who marches off stage at the end of the play to commit suicide in the most approved Stoic manner.[131] But he is also the Stoic "plain man" who imitates Cynic behavior as "the expression of the right and duty of the truly virtuous man to rebuke evil in others" (Epictetus, *Disc.*, III, 22, 13).

So, when Cornwall has come to the rescue of Oswald, whom Kent has been belaboring, and demands, "Why do you call him a knave?" Kent replies:

> Sir, 'tis my occupation to be plain.

Cornwall immediately claims to recognize the clan to which Kent belongs:

> This is some fellow
> Who, having been prais'd for bluntness, doth effect
> A saucy roughness, and constrains the garb
> Quite from his nature. He cannot flatter, he!
> In honest mind and plain—he must speak truth!
> An they will take it, so; if not, he's plain . . .[132]

Although the Cynic-Stoic denounced all intellectual *hybris* (among other, more worldly kinds of pride) he was certainly guilty of the moral sort, himself. Of the efficacy of man's powers to attain virtue, not only by following nature, but by disciplining himself with reason, he had no doubt. Here his primitivism broke down:

> The Cynic ethic may be said to reduce, in its practical outcome, almost wholly to primitivism. Cynicism was the first and most vigorous philosophic revolt of the civilized against civilization in nearly all essentials—*except "philosophy" itself.*[133]

Yet this same Cynic-Stoic denied the contribution of arts and sciences to his philosophy of virtue. Seneca's position was that, while virtue must be learned, and the innocence of the primitive man who is by nature inclined to good, reinforced by the conscious discipline of the Stoic wise man, humane and liberal studies did not lead to virtue:

> "What, then," you say, "do we gain no advantage at all from liberal studies?" In other respects, much advantage; but with respect to virtue, none. For even those admittedly low manual arts are very useful as aids to mere living, but they have nothing to do with virtue. . . . It may even be said that it is possible to attain to virtue without liberal studies; for although virtue

must be learned, yet it cannot be learned through them.[134]

This is a very different kind of Stoicism from that of Cicero's modified ethical version widely adopted by the Renaissance humanists. It is the far more harsh, semi-ascetic ideal of dogmatic Stoicism, with its "apathy" and "fortitude" and "wisdom." The affinity of its almost evangelical rigor with that of Calvinism is evident: there is the same emphasis upon discipline, the same anti-intellectualism, the same preference for "those admittedly low manual arts [which] are very useful as aids to mere living." And it was a recurring temptation to Renaissance thinkers to align the Stoic *fatum* with the doctrine of predestination.

Fulke Greville, among the most eclectic of the Elizabethan dilettantes and himself at least professedly a Calvinist, wrote a passage which again illustrates this tendency. He links Stoic apathy with Christian faith and humility as alternative consolations for griefs and despairs which man must undergo:

> Then Man, endure thyselfe, those clouds will vanish;
> Life is a Top which whipping Sorrow driveth;
> *Wisdome must beare what our flesh cannot banish,*
> *The humble leade, the stubborn bootlesse striveth;*
> Or man, forsake thy selfe, to heaven turn thee
> Her flames enlighten Nature, never burne thee.[135]

This is another form of that parallelism of the wise and humble which we have been tracing—in this case, of the Stoic "wise man" and the lowly "Reformed" Christian, with his exclusive appeal to faith.

Yet there is an unquestionable pride in the alleged humility of the Stoic wise man. He professes to fit his will to that of the "main sway of the universe," to follow an all-powerful Nature. Yet, more often than not, he demonstrates an explicit confidence in the power of his own reason (and through it, his will, although the Stoics do not use the term) to lead him, unaided, to virtue. Hence his practice contains an element most repugnant to fideism in general and to Calvinism in particular. Calvin himself, who as a young man wrote a commentary on Seneca's *De Clementia,* expressly objects to the comparison. In this commentary he clearly indicates that he believes Stoic apathy to be *contrary* to nature, not according to it, and he denies that man, consulting his reason only, may find his own way to virtue.[136] Furthermore, in the *Institutes* (I, xvi), he objects strongly to equating Stoic fate with the doctrine of predestination. The one is a necessity, contained in nature and depending upon the

perpetual conjunction of all things; the other is God's determining
of how things shall occur.[137]

It is interesting to note that Greville, who played with the analogy,
later expressly rejected it, in his *Treatie of Humane Learning*, declaring that

> Thus, till Man end, his Vanities goe round,
> Is credit here, and there discredited;
> *Striving to binde, and never to be bound,*
> *To governe God, and not bee governed:*
> Which is the cause his life is thus confused,
> In his corruption, by these Arts abused.[138]

And while Marston, early in *The Scourge of Villanie*, boasts of his
"Cynick work," he later recants:

> *I will*, cries Zeno, ô presumption!
> *I can*, thou maist dogged oppinion
> Of thwarting Cynicks. Today vicious,
> List to their precepts, next day vertuous.
> Peace *Seneca*, thou belchest blasphemy,
> *To live from God, but to live happily*
> (I heare thee boast,) *from thy Philosophy*,
> And from thyselfe, ô ravening lunacy![139]

"Confounded Natures brats," he shouts, "can *will* and *Fate*, Have
both their seate, & office in your pate?"[140] On the contrary, vice and
virtue are subject only to *"sacred grace,"*

> *Infus'd, displac'd, not in our will or force,*
> *But as it please* Iehova *have remorce.*[141]

Indeed, the Calvinists and Puritans so completely take over the
vanity of learning and exaltation of the humble traditions in Elizabethan England, that when Ben Jonson's Androgyno is asked what
his latest transformation is, he can reply quite simply, with confidence in being understood:

> Like one of the reformed, a Foole, as you see,
> Counting all old doctrine heresy.[142]

There is a picture of the true humility of the reformed Christian
in Thomalin's eulogy of the lowly, meek shepherd in the July
eclogue of Spenser's *Shepheards Calendar*. As Professor Fletcher
has clearly shown, Spenser is contrasting the views of a Puritan
leader like Cartwright with those of the "worldly" Anglican
church.[143] Again, in the *Treatie of Humane Learning*, Greville explicitly links "those pure, humble creatures" with Calvin's elect, who

are "in the world, not of it"—and both with the vanity of learning theme.[144]

For, as Sir John Davies (though with a different answer in mind) had asked, "What is this *knowledge?* but the Skie-stolne fire . . ." and

> What can we know? or what can we discerne?
> When *Error* chokes the windowes of the mind;
> The diverse formes of things, how can we learne,
> That have bene ever from our birth-day blind?[145]

So, Greville maintains,

> Whence all Mans fleshly idols being built,
> As humane *Wisedome, Science, Power,* and *Arts,*
> Upon the false foundation of his Guilt;
> Confusedly doe weave within our hearts,
>   Their owne advancement, state and declination,
>   As things whose beings are but transmutation.[146]

He contrasts the intellectual pride of those whose

> *Schoolemens* sleepy speculation,
> Dreaming to comprehend the Deity
> In humane reasons finite elevation;
> While they make *Sense* seat of Eternity,
>   Must bury *Faith,* whose proper obiects are
>   God's mysteries, above our Reason farre,[147]

with the humility of Calvin's "Elect":

> With many linkes and equall glorious chaine
> Of hopes eternall those pure people frame. . . .
>   Which well-linck't chaine they fix unto the sky,
>   Not to draw heaven downe, but earth up by.[148]

John Donne was no Calvinist, but in him Elizabethan fideism finds perhaps its most impressive Anglican expression, and a worthy literary opponent to Richard Hooker. No contemporary, on the face of his writings, both secular and sacred, possessed a wider learning or a livelier intellectual curiosity and virtuosity than Donne, who confessed himself early assailed "by the worst voluptuousness, which is an hydroptic, immoderate desire of human learning and languages."[149] Yet this very inquisitiveness, and his insatiable hunger for intellectual certainty, led him into many by-ways characteristic of the Counter-Renaissance.

His early poetry gives ample evidence of his interest in philosophical skepticism, for example—whether acquired under the direct influence of Sextus Empiricus or Montaigne, or simply through the general currents of the age. And this interest is evident throughout his life.[150] A sermon preached in 1626 reveals his continued preoccupation with the problem of knowledge, and at the same time his ever-growing dissatisfaction to rest in the position of the philosophic skeptic.[151] It may well have been this combination—a distrust of the traditional body of medieval and humanistic knowledge, coupled with an unwillingness to admit the complete bankruptcy of man's mental powers—which led him to accept the "New Astronomy" before most of his fellows.

At any rate, there is no evidence that this temperamental hunger for intellectual certitude was ever satisfied, and unquestionably it was his unusually high degree of intellectual integrity which helped to prevent the realization of his search. Where to turn, then? It is characteristic of the man that, finding Reason's road blocked, he should turn to Faith's with as impetuous a determination.

There are some early evidences of a tendency toward fideism in Donne, but—notorious chameleon that he was in his secular poetry —it is not easy to distinguish the posturings and intellectual *jeux d'esprit* of a young man proud of his eclectic background, from statements of a sincere conviction. Still, in the third *Satyre*, when he has been considering the claims to authority of various religious points of view, he seems serious enough:

> Foole and wretch, wilt thou let thy Soule be tyed
> To mans lawes, by which she shall not be tryed
> At the last day? Oh, will it then boot thee
> To say a Philip, or a Gregory,
> A Harry, or a Martin taught thee this?
> Is not this excuse for mere contraries
> Equally strong? cannot both sides say so?

> So perish Soules, which more chuse mens unjust
> Power from God claym'd, then God himselfe to trust.[152]

Yet, when he has finally made his choice and taken Anglican orders, he still shows at times an almost Thomistic confidence in reason. And again and again, in the years that follow, in poetry and prose alike, he brings all the rich resources of his reading and thought to bear on the attempt to *know*. Professor Bredvold has traced in some detail Donne's wrestling with the problem of reason and faith, and he has shown clearly how, slowly and painfully, the Augustinian element in Donne won out; and how in faith he discovered, not an always constant, but at least a more satisfactory, answer to the doubts which harassed him to his grave.[153]

In the *Litanie* he had written,

> Let not my minde be blinder by more light
> Nor Faith, by Reason added, lose her sight.[154]

And in a sermon preached at the Hague, he declares the vanity of speculative and humanistic learning:

> The Scriptures will be out of thy reach, and out of thy use, if thou cast and scatter them upon reason, upon philosophy, upon morality, to try how the Scriptures will fit them, and believe them so far as they agree with thy reason; but draw the Scripture to thine own heart, and to thine own actions, and thou shall find it made for that.[155]

In another sermon, elaborating the same thesis, he "names names." To think, he says,

> That we can come to this [*i.e.*, to truth and to God] by our own strength, without God's inward working a belief, or to think that we can believe out of Plato, where we may find a God, but without a Christ, or come to be good men out of Plutarch or Seneca, without a church or sacraments, to pursue the truth itself by any other way than he hath laid open to us, this is pride, and the pride of the angels.[156]

The doctrine of the corruption of man through original sin strengthens his position, as it has that of most fideists. Only divine grace and the atonement of Christ have the power to give strength and hope:

> Though thou canst not say *ego vir, I am that moral man*, safe in my natural reason and philosophy, that is spent, yet *Ego vir*, I am that Christian man, who have seen this affliction in the cause thereof, so far off, as in my sin in Adam, and the remedy of this affliction, so far off, as in the death of Christ Jesus, I am the man that cannot repine, nor murmur, since I am the cause; I am the man that cannot despair, since Christ is the remedy.[157]

Later, he is less temperate. "Miserable man!" he thunders like the early Reformers,

> A toad is a bag of poison, and a spider is a blister of poison, and yet a toad and a spider cannot poison themselves; man hath a drachm of poison, original sin, in an invisible corner, we know not where, and he cannot choose but poison himself and all his actions with that; we are so far from being able to

begin without grace, as then when we have first grace, we cannot proceed to the use of that, without more.[158]

The old Elizabethan Donne, the insatiable and passionate seeker and doubter, never wholly disappears:

> But though I have found thee, and thou my thirst hast fed,
> A holy thirsty dropsy melts me yett.[159]

And not only thirst, but doubt and fear as well. To such a man, all too conscious of the shortcomings of his own effort to attain to God's truth; even of the shortcomings, in himself, of that very faith he preached so vigorously, there can be no surety but that which is freely *given* by the love of Christ:

> I have a sinne of feare, that when I have spunne
> My last thred, I shall perish on the shore;
> But sweare by thy selfe, that at my death thy sonne
> Shall shine as he shines now, and heretofore;
> And having done that, Thou hast done,
> I fear no more.[160]

John Donne did not invoke the Averroistic "double truth" of John of Jandun and Pomponazzi. On the contrary, for him (despite occasional contradictions in the later poetry) there seems to have come to be but a single truth, that of faith. And so it was with most of the fideists of the Counter-Renaissance. Yet just as surely as though he too were "the ape of Aristotle and Averroës," he was contributing, with his Ockhamite and fideistic Augustinianism, to the permanent separation of reason and faith.

Like John of Jandun (and yet very unlike him), he follows the tradition of Tertullian and Augustine in finding in the unreasonableness of Christianity its very glory. Can men believe easily, he demands,

that from that man, that worm, and no man, ingloriously traduced as a conjurer, ingloriously apprehended as a thief, ingloriously executed as a traitor; they should look for glory, and all glory and everlasting glory? And from that melancholic man, who was never seen to laugh in all his life, and *whose soul was heavy unto death;* they should look for joy, and all joy, and everlasting joy: and for salvation, and everlasting salvation from him, who could not save himself from ignominy, from the torment, from the death of the cross? If any state, if any convocation, if any wise man had been to make a religion, a gospel; would he not have proposed a more profitable, a more credible gospel, to man's reason, than this?[161]

"Credo quia impossibile!" As Donne presents it, there can be no doubt that he is employing this ancient creed in the interests of faith. But when, a few years later, Sir Thomas Browne makes a similar profession, one can already hear the difference of tone:

> I can answer all the Objections of Satan and my rebellious reason with that odd resolution I learned of Tertullian, *certum est quia impossibile est.*[162]

Browne, too, is speaking in the interests of faith, but the magnificent and sonorous aggressiveness of Donne's statement has changed to a defensive apologetic—tonally, at least, to a plea primarily intended to comfort himself by his fireplace. And in Browne the double truth of the separation tradition has come alive again.

But indeed it came alive before him; more properly, it had never been dead. It rode the shadowy edge of the Renaissance period, deriving mostly from Padua, and it emerges again into full light with Francis Bacon.

To be sure, Bacon is no blind enthusiast for reason; those who have so interpreted him have misread him. He has no use for the syllogists' attempts to "abstract nature"; he distrusts, and has explicitly set out to refute, the authority "of the natural human reason left to itself." For

> the human understanding is no dry light, but receives an infusion from the will and affections; whence proceed sciences which may be called "sciences as one would." For what a man had rather were true he more readily believes . . .[163]

Yet there is another sort of "reason which is elicited from facts by a just and methodical process"; "from a closer and purer league between these two faculties, the experimental and the rational (such as has never yet been made), much may be hoped."[164]

This is Bacon's inductive method, his "new science," and his considerable contribution to the separation tradition may perhaps best be summarized as the separation of the realm of science from that of religion, rather than in the old reason-faith opposition of philosophy and theology. Yet it comes to the same thing; the new philosophy and the new science are hand-in-glove, and Bacon similarly uses familiar terminology.

"To study theology," he asserts, "we must quit the small vessel of human reason." And again,

> Sacred theology ought to be derived from the word and oracles of God, and not from the light of nature, or the dictates of reason.[165]

He too declares,

> The more discordant therefore and incredible any Divine mystery is, the more honour is shown to God in believing it; and the nobler is the victory of faith.[166]

One is privileged, of course, to do what some scholars actually have done: to interpret this statement as an indication of Bacon's pure Christian faith. However, to put such an interpretation upon these words from the disingenuous Lord of St. Albans requires in its turn an application of Tertullian's formula. It was science which Bacon desired to keep "pure" from religion; any other conclusion, in the face of his life's work, is preposterous.[167]

But even if we believe because it is impossible, the arrows which indicate the seventeenth-century highway have not been repointed. The "double truth" of reason and faith, of science and religion, of philosophy and theology, of nature and grace, is once more emergent, the reconciliation tradition once more challenged. And this time it is science, or rational philosophy, which assumes the offensive, religion which is defending itself.

Moreover, there is treason within the reconciliation camp itself. The Christian-humanistic solution has become super-saturated with its humanistic and rational element. Threatened by the separatists of the "double truth," faith finds herself being "defended" by an ally who is becoming too strong to be willing to share the spoils of victory anyway.

Finally, the new science of Galileo and Kepler, which (and not Bacon's) is to dominate the Newtonian synthesis as it later developed, has maintained the Scholastic methodology, but not its subservience to the Christian faith. As intellectualistic as the science of Thomas Aquinas, it is nevertheless concerned with mathematical hypotheses, not with teleological premises.

Is it any wonder that "the Countess" observes, late in the seventeenth century, that philosophy is turning mechanical?[168] Any wonder that the eighteenth century, when all of these currents finally had flowed together into one vast comprehensive system, should be called the "Age of Reason"?

5. SUMMARY AND TRANSITION

The Counter-Renaissance matched the return of Renaissance humanism to the ideals of classical antiquity with a return of its own —to "first principles." Machiavelli's phrase, "ritorno al segno," which was indeed applicable to the scholarship of the humanists, is reversed and turned upon them, as well as upon the Scholastics, to become the battle cry of the Counter-Renaissance.[169]

Necessarily, in a movement containing such divergent tendencies as did the Counter-Renaissance, the phrase (and similar ones) was susceptible of variant interpretations. Yet, in its many manifestations, there is a constant—the revolt against complicated theory, against the isolated cerebral process, against the pretense of the intellect, against primarily rational argument and demonstration, against the sophistications of learning, of culture, of the traditional arts and sciences. From these, the scientists of the Counter-Renaissance turned to a radical empiricism; the religionists to non-rational theology; the writers on ethical, political, social and historical matters to a skeptical pragmatism; the writers on æsthetics and the devotees of the occult to the doctrines of "inspiration" and revealed truth.

One of the most persistent corollaries of the ideal of a return to first principles was an emphasis upon simplicity. This is particularly marked in the aspects of the Counter-Renaissance which we have just been reviewing. The propounders of the vanity of learning, for example, advocate simplicity in two senses: (1) simplification, and (2) humble, plain "unlearnedness." The first meaning is implicit in the movement from its very inception in nominalism, which is preeminently concerned with the simplification of metaphysics.[170] Moreover, it is patent throughout the Counter-Renaissance, in the outcries against "God's counselors" and "Nature's secretaries"; in the disgust with the quibbling of decadent Scholasticism; in protests like that of Daniel's against the "delicate learning" of the Ciceronian humanists; above all, in the steadily increasing conviction of the irrelevance of much speculation and learning either to the practical living of life or to salvation.

With the admixture of philosophical skepticism, the tradition takes up the theme of simplifying life to an undogmatic course, seeing that certain knowledge is impossible. So Montaigne in his "old age" declares,

> Of ignorance I speake sumptuously and plentiously, and of learning meagerly and pitiously: This accessorily and accidentally: That expressly and principally. And purposely I treate of nothing, but of nothing: nor of any one science but of unscience.[171]

It is "unscience" which equips a man to live, and living is man's only genuine province. Commenting on the old dictum that the philosopher's sole concern is to have death ever before his eyes, and the consequent opinion of many that a peasant, who never thinks on death till he is about to encounter it, is therefore a dull and blockish sort of man, Montaigne cries in reply,

> In God's name, if it be so, let us henceforth keepe a school of brutality. . . . We shall not want good teachers, interpreters of natural simplicity. Socrates shall be one.[172]

The vanity of learning tradition, then, is both impatient of the pretensions of learning, and convinced of its futility and even wrong-headedness. And so it turns to the "poor, feeble, humble, silly, and foolish ones of the earth"—to Montaigne's "countrie-clownish" men, to Rabelais' woodcutter, to Erasmus' sly Folly, praising fools, to "Pierce plowman," to Marston's "honest senselesse dolt," and to Walter Ralegh's "cheese-wife" who "knoweth it as well as the philosopher, that sour runnet doth coagulate her milk into a curd."[173] But it also turns to Socrates, whose simplicity and profession of ignorance are at the other end of life's road from this "abecedarie" ignorance, and to the harsh and primitivistic denunciations of learning and the arts and sciences made by the Cynics and Stoics. In short, it turns both to the naturally simple and humble, and to those who have achieved simplicity through discipline—to the truly ignorant and to the disingenuous philosophical ignorant.

It is here that the fideist movement differs from its ally, the secular tradition. For the Cynics' and Stoics' primitivism does not include a disavowal of "philosophy," in their peculiar sense of man's capacity to discipline himself to virtue, and hence is equally open to the charge of moral *hybris*—is capable only of artificial simplicity and a proud humility. To the fideists, the vanity of learning lies primarily in God's displeasure with pride, and above all, with the intellectual pride of man in trying to ascertain God's secrets, and his moral pride in assuming that he may find his way to virtue through his own efforts.

Speaking of the moral philosophers, Agrippa declares

> These doubtlesse havinge don the dutie of the Serpent have given us that fruite by eating wherof we may learne to know good and ill. This is the firste pestilente opinion of them, whiche holde that the good and the ill should be knowne, and by this meanes they say that men maye the better seeke vertue and shune vice. But howe muche more sure and profitable, and also how much more happie should it bee, not onely not to doe evils, but altogether to be ignoraunt of them also.[174]

"Who is he that knoweth not," he asks, "that thorowe this alone all wee were made miserable, when the first parentes of mankinde learned what was good and what was evill. . . ."[175]

It might be necessary to pardon these classical philosophers, who had not this knowledge, he continues, were it not for the vices they taught "under the name of vertue and goodnesse."[176] And when he has finished slandering Aristotle and others, and recounting their false doctrines of the sovereign good, he concludes,

> But let us now see how these do agree with Christe, and so it shal be seene that we do not gette felicitie, blessednesse by the Stoicke vertue, neither by the Academicke purginge, neither by the Peripateticke speculation, but by faithe and grace in the worde of God.[177]

This is the attitude of the fideists of the Reformation, with their conviction of man's utter corruption through original sin. The vanity of both speculative and humanistic learning rests finally upon man's incapability, since the Fall, of either intellectual or moral knowledge —save through grace alone.

Hence fideism's interpretation of a return to first principles, and its emphasis upon simplicity, alike have a special Christian significance missing in the secular tradition. They summon skepticism in the interests of faith, not *vice versa*. While, at the end of the *Apologie*, Montaigne turns to faith as the only certain knowledge, it is not faith which has concerned him primarily through the essay. The reverse is true of the genuine fideist. For Montaigne, faith is *ex post facto;* for the true fideist, it is the beginning hypothesis. The plain, blunt man of the secular tradition may be Montaigne's simple man living close to nature, or he may be a philosopher related to Cynic or Stoic primitivism. But the good simple man of the fideist tradition and the Reformation derives from Christian primitivism.

"To return to the condition of primitive Christianity," writes E. M. Hulme of the Peasants' Revolt in Germany.

> to establish a new order based on social justice and fashioned after the will of God—that was the central demand of the peasants. . . .[178]

And this rebellion, this historical demonstration of "surgunt indocti," although eventually opposed and denied by Luther, was nevertheless at the heart of his revolution. For, inheriting the anti-intellectualistic and fideistic tendencies of Ockham and Wycliffe and Hus, Luther based his justification on faith alone on the Pauline creed, stripped of Paul's Hellenism, and the Augustinian position, bereft of Augustine's Platonism.[179]

"The Lutheran Reformation," wrote Nietzsche,

> in all its length and breadth was the indignation of the simple against something complicated. [It was] a spiritual Peasant Revolt.[180]

Such a double emphasis upon a return to first principles of Christianity and to a simplicity which repudiates the medieval intellectualized interpretations of the gospel, is evident already in Agrippa's opposition of the Christianity of the Canonical Law to the primitive Christianity of the Gospel:

> The same Christian Religion, at the beginninge wherof Christe took awaie ceremonies, hath nowe more than ever the Jewes had, the [paise?] of which being put thereto, the light and sweete yoke of Christe is become much more greavous than all the reste, and the Christians are enforced to live rather after the order of the Canons, than after the Gospel![181]

It is basic to Luther's opposition of "unum simplicem, germanum et certum sensum literalem" to the medieval fourfold interpretation of scripture.[182]

So Pantagruel prays before his battle with Loupgarou, promising God that if victory is granted him, wherever it is within his power he

> . . . "will cause the holy gospel to be purely, simply and entirely preached; so that the abuses of the rabble of hypocrites and false prophets, who by human constitutions and depraved inventions have impoisoned all the world, shall be exterminated from about me." The vow was no sooner made, but there was heard a voice from heaven, saying, "Hoc fac, & vinces"; that is to say, "Do this and thou shall overcome."[183]

And similarly the "fools" of love and faith reject all knowledge save that of love and faith. "The only means of discovering truth is faith," says Agrippa. "Je ne sçay rien, sinon aymer," chants la Bergère of Marguerite. Thus, and thus only, in the words of Colet, "leaving all indirect courses, we may proceed by a short method to the Truth." For, as Montaigne declares, God "hath made choice of the simple, common, and ignorant to teach us His wonderful secrets."

All these tendencies are inherited by Calvinism. The height of Calvin's argument for his assured reliance upon Scripture rests upon "the testimony of the Holy Spirit in our hearts," and his avowed purpose is to "bring all men back to the sure foundation of the Gospel truly and simply understood. . . ."[184]

Again, in the Puritan movement led by Cartwright in Elizabethan England, we find this creed enunciated. Spenser's May eclogue illustrates well the combination of the return to the first principles of the Apostolic Church and to the true simplicity of Christ's undistorted gospel. Employing Christianized versions of the favorite Renaissance primitivistic image of the Golden Age, and the idea of a cyclical regeneration, Spenser declares:

> The time was once, and may again retorne,
> (For ought may happen, that hath bene before)

when shepherds were happy, having only "Pan" (Christ) for "their inheritaunce. . . ."[185]

The whole trend of the religious aspects of the Counter-Renaissance, then, may be fairly summarized as characterized basically by a desire to return to first principles and to simplicity. It was a looking and harking backward, historically, to the purity of the early church; for the individual, it was a turning to the simplified and direct approach of the human heart to God, through faith.

This second tendency gave rise inevitably to an individualizing of salvation, to an increased emphasis upon the direct and unique relationship of each individual human soul to God, and hence eventually to the famous Protestant doctrine of the individual conscience.[186] Obviously, this tendency was opposed to the unity and authority of the Roman Catholic Church. It was a decentralizing process, a turning from the more or less standardized contemplation of, and acquiescence in, a largely static and permanent truth, to the assertion of the rights of the individual soul to make direct and simple contact with God through faith and love, and without the necessity for the traditional sacraments and interpretative intermediaries of the Mother Church.

This process was not confined to the religious aspects of the Counter-Renaissance. The return to first principles and to simplicity and directness of approach, interpreted in terms of such a decentralizing tendency, was also basic to its scientific attitude. For the religionists, this process meant anti-intellectualism, anti-moralism, and a return to faith. For the scientifically-minded, it also meant anti-intellectualism and anti-moralism—but in the sense of a return to fact, to empirical investigation and the pragmatic method, to the study of things as they are, not as they should be.[187]

Fundamental to this decentralizing influence of the Counter-Renaissance was its repeal of universal law.

FOOTNOTES
CHAPTER 2

I.

1. Michel, Lord of Montaigne, *Essayes,* translated by John Florio (pub. 1603), "The World's Classics" (Oxford University Press, New York, 1920–24), Vol. III, 328.

2. Petrarch, *Secretum,* 29–30, 50; for Descartes, see Gilson, *Sp. Med. Phil.,* 79.

3. Cf. Willey, *Seventeenth Century,* 261. I do not mean that this particular kind of name-calling originated with the Renaissance. Arpad Steiner in his article, "The Faust Legend and the Christian Tradition," *PMLA,* LIV (1931), 391–404, quotes and cites many similar medieval attacks—from Augustine on—on men who pretend to a place in God's inner circle. (Indeed, classical antiquity offers earlier, non-Christian charges of a like sort.) However, Professor Steiner points out,

   > The progress of Scholasticism went hand in hand with the growth of intellectualism; so it is natural that, from the tenth century, these admonitions made themselves heard more frequently, and more and more energetically. (396)

   They reached a crescendo during the Renaissance, and particularly in the sixteenth century.

4. *De Remediis Utriusque Fortunae,* chap. 46, quoted by Steiner, *ibid.,* 399. For the probable influence of Senecan primitivism, see Willard Farnham, *The Medieval Heritage of Elizabethan Tragedy* (Berkeley, California, 1936), 52. (Professor Farnham does not use the term "primitivism.")

5. *De Libero Arbitrio,* quoted by Steiner, *ibid.,* 402–403.

6. *The Hermetic and Alchemical Writings of Aureolus Philippus Theophrastus Bombast of Hohenheim, called Paracelsus the Great,* now for the first time faithfully translated into English, edited by Arthur Edward Waite, in two volumes (London, 1894), Vol. II, 5.

7. Erasmus, *The Praise of Folly.* Written by Erasmus in 1509 and translated by John Wilson in 1668. Edited with an introduction by Mrs. P. S. Allen (Oxford, 1913), 112.

8. Henry Cornelius Agrippa von Nettesheim, *De incertitudine & Vanitate scientiarum* (1537), II, 430–431. Since no English translation was accessible during much of my work, and this Latin edition has no pagination, I have made volume and page references (for the convenience of the reader) to the French edition of 1726. This edition, translated by Sr. M. de Guendeville, is in three volumes, containing also Agrippa's treatise *On the Nobility of Woman.* For my own English translation, I have deviated from the text of M. de Guendeville only when its departure from the Latin original indicated an inaccurate rendition of the thought.

9. Montaigne, *Essayes,* II, 272, 274–275.

10. François Rabelais, *Works,* completely translated into English by Urquhart and Motteux (Aldus Classics, London, 1903), III, Chap. 30. The probable *double entendre* merely changes the *spirit* in which Rabelais pays tribute to the tradition.

11. Gabriel Harvey, *Works,* edited by A. B. Grosart (London, 1884–1885), I, 56–57.

12. Fulke Greville, "Treatie of Humane Learning," st. 34: *Poems and Dramas of Fulke Greville,* edited by Geoffrey Bullough (Edinburgh, 1938), I, 162.

13. Ramus, *Collectaneae praefationes, epistolae, orationes,* quoted by Zanta, *Ren. du Stoïc.,* 23. My italics.

14. Agrippa, *De incertitudine,* I, 21.

15. Henry Cornelius Agrippa, *Of the Vanitie and Uncertaintie of Artes and Sciences,* Englished by Ja[mes] San[ford], Gent. Imprinted at London by Henry Wykes, dwelling in Fleet Street at the Sign of the Black Elephant, 1569 (British Museum, 58 b7), sig. W2ᵛ. Thanks to the generosity of Professor Marc Friedlaender of the Woman's College of the University of North Carolina, I have read and taken notes on several chapters of Sanford's translation, in photostat reproduction. Wherever possible, I have used these—otherwise my collation and translation of the Latin and French texts indicated above.

16. Agrippa, *ibid.,* sig. W3ᵛ.

17. Montaigne, *Essayes,* II, 367–368. My italics.

18. Marguerite, *Heptameron,* xxxiv (Fourth Day) : *The Heptameron of Marguerite of Navarre,* newly translated from the authentic text, with an essay upon the *Heptameron* by George Saintsbury (two volumes, privately printed for members of the Aldus Society, London, 1903) , II, 58–60. My italics.

19. The Stoics, with their doctrinal advocacy of the complete repression, not merely the control, of the passions by reason, naturally are the philosophers most often accused of moral *hybris*—in terms of what they claim to be able to accomplish by their own efforts. Yet the charge is by no means limited to the proponents of rigid dogmatic Stoicism.

20. Samuel Daniel, *A Defence of Ryme Against a Pamphlet entituled: Observations in the Art of English Poesie* (1603) : in *Elizabethan Prose,* Selected and Prefaced by Michael Roberts (London, 1933) , 114. It is, however, the "Ciceronianism" of men who "study words and not matter" which Daniel is primarily attacking. Cf. Geoffrey Bullough, "Bacon and the Defense of Learning": *Seventeenth Century Studies,* presented to Sir Herbert Grierson (Oxford, 1938) , 13.

21. *Elizabethan Prose,* 115. Yet Daniel is usually to be found on the side of learning. Geoffrey Bullough, who has been more sensitive than most scholars to the considerable battle for and against learning which preceded the work of Francis Bacon, has pointed out how *"Musophilus* worthily anticipates *The Advancement of Learning."* Cf. Bullough, *ibid.*

22. John Marston, *The Scourge of Villanie* (1599) : The Bodley Head Quartos, edited by G. B. Harrison, M.A. (London and New York, 1925) , Satyre IIII, 43.

23. *Ibid.,* 44.

24. *Ibid.,* 45.

25. George Chapman, *Revenge of Bussy,* IV, iv, 42: *The Plays and Poems of George Chapman,* edited by Thomas Marc Parrott (London, 1914) , *The Tragedies.*

26. *Ibid.,* V, i, 74–81.

27. *Ibid.,* V, i, 18, 22–23.

28. Hooker, *Of the Laws,* III, viii, 4. My italics.

29. For a good recent analysis of this aspect of Calvin's work, see Gustav E. Mueller, "Calvin's Institutes of the Christian Religion as an Illustration of Christian Thinking," *Journal of the History of Ideas,* Vol. IV, No. 1 (January, 1943) , 287–300. Cf. also Norman Sykes, "Richard Hooker," 65–66.

30. I. A. Richards, *Science and Poetry* (London, 1935) , 52.

31. Cf. John Herman Randall, Jr., "The Development of the Scientific Method in the School of Padua," *Journal of the History of Ideas,* Vol. I, No. 2 (April, 1940) , 177–206.

2.

32. De Wulf, *Phil. and Civ.*, 180–183.

33. Randall, *Mod. Mind*, 101. Professor Randall's explanation of the whole problem of universals is the clearest summary I have read anywhere. Time and again in this remarkable and comprehensive book, for that matter, Professor Randall has lucidly analyzed the problems of all sorts which remain fuzzy and complicated in books specifically and exclusively dealing with them.

34. *Ibid.*

35. *Ibid.*, 102. In this connection, see Jaeger, *Aristotle*, on Aristotle's concept of "embodied form," as it is called on pp. 3, 4; or "immattered form" (340–341; 382–385). The reason the moderate realists' position on universals parallels their attitude toward sense perception and intellectual knowledge is that in both cases they endorse the validity of universal abstract concepts, but root them in the particular and concrete.

36. De Wulf, *Med. Phil.*, II, 182; cf. Weber, *Hist. of Phil.*, 253, and De Wulf, *ibid.*, II, 167–180.

37. De Wulf, *ibid.*, II, 182, 180.

38. Montaigne, I, 257.

39. Cf. Pierre Villet, *Les Essaies de Michel de Montaigne* (Paris, 1932), 57–62; and Louis I. Bredvold, *The Intellectual Milieu of John Dryden* (Ann Arbor, Michigan, 1934), 27, 32–33. There are many books on Greek skepticism available. Most histories of classical philosophy provide adequate accounts; I have found Hicks's analysis in his *Stoics and Epicureans* particularly helpful. Mary Mills Patrick's *The Greek Skeptics* (New York, 1929), although somewhat pedestrian, is thorough and fairly comprehensive.

40. Walter Ralegh's fragmentary essay *The Sceptic* is almost a literal translation of part of the *Hypotyposes*.

41. Montaigne, II, 364.

42. Sextus Empiricus, *Hypotyposes*, with an English translation by the Rev. R. G. Bury (Loeb Library, 1933), I, 15, 23, 17, 25.

43. Montaigne, II, 232.

44. Sir John Davies, *Nosce Teipsum*, Part I: *The Poems of Sir John Davies*, with an introduction and notes by Clare Howard (New York, 1941), 116.

45. Cf. Patrick, *Greek Skeptics*, 25 and *passim*.

46. Montaigne, I, 408. My italics.

47. *Ibid.*, III, 332, 334.

48. *Ibid.*, II, 441.

49. *Ibid.*, III, 308.

50. Erasmus, *Praise of Folly*, 70, 71.

51. Rabelais, III, Chap. 43.

52. *Ibid.*, III, Chap. 46.

53. George Gascoigne, *The Steel Glass: In English Belles Lettres*, edited by Oliver H. G. Leigh (London, 1901), 106–107. In one form or another, this tradition of the exaltation of the humble is very old, of course. Of particular interest to a study of the peculiarly unqualified form which it took in the Renaissance, is the milder form in which it may be found in the writings of Thomas à Kempis, for example (if it was he who wrote the *Imitation of Christ*):

> All men by nature dearly love to know,
> But knowledge without fear of God—what is it worth?
> Better indeed a humble peasant, fearing God,
> Than the proud thinker who neglects himself in
> musing on the courses of the stars. . . .

(Thomas Kempis, *The Imitation of Christ*, Now for the First Time Set
Forth in Rhythmic Sentences, according to the original intention of the
Author, with a preface by H. P. Liddon, D.D., D.C.L. (New York, 1889),
5: Chapter II, ll. 1–4.)

In Chapter I all the vanities of the world are condemned in traditional
contemptus mundi style, before this particular warning to the speculative
philosopher opens the second chapter. But although Kempis reproaches
those guilty of speculative *hybris*, he is not concerned with the moral
hybris which was an object of equal condemnation for the later fideists.
Cf. *ibid.*, 4, Chapter I, ii, ll. 3–4:

> Deep words make no man just and holy,
> But lives of virtue make men dear to God.

54. John Marston, *Antonio's Revenge*, IV, i: *The Plays of John Marston*,
edited by H. Harvey Wood (London, 1934), I, 110. Marston's *What You
Will*, Dr. Henry W. Wells of Columbia University tells me, contains even
better material of this sort. I have chosen the present example chiefly for
its illustration of the "good, plain man" tradition. "Wizards" and "Nature's secrets" suggest, on the other hand, that Marston is employing the
"Nature's secretaries" language to attack the "magicians and scientists" (see
Chapter IV, 1, *infra*) rather than the usual Scholastic victims.

55. Quoted by Randall, *Mod. Mind*, 100–101.

56. Cf. Gilson, *Reason and Revelation*, 90. Anna Seesholtz' *The Friends of
God* (New York, 1934) contains a very complete study of the Friends of
God and similar sects.

57. Marguerite, *Comédie jouée au Mont-de-Marsan: Les dernières poésies
de Marguerite de Navarre*, edited by A. Lefranc (Paris, 1896), 108 ff. Cf.
Abel Lefranc, *Grande Ecrivains Français de la Renaissance* (Paris, 1914),
217–218.

58. *Life of Saint Theresa*, written by Herself and translated by the Reverend
John Dalton: in *Explorations in Living*, second edition, edited by Winfield H. Rogers, Ruby V. Redinger, and Hiram C. Haydn (New York,
1942), II, 524.

59. *Ibid.*, II, 527.

60. Quoted by De Wulf, *Med. Phil.*, II, 256.

61. Quoted by Febvre, *Martin Luther*, 52–53.

62. Marguerite, *Heptameron*, II, xxxiv (Fourth Day), 60.

63. Quoted by Lefranc, *Grands Ecrivains*, 224.

64. Erasmus, *Paraclesis*, quoted by Randall, *Mod. Mind*, 134.

65. Erasmus, *Praise of Folly*, 172–173.

66. *Ibid.*, 174. My interpretation of *The Praise of Folly* in general, and of
Erasmus' use of a two-edged irony in particular, is that he was far more
interested in driving home particular truths in incisive and even shocking
language, than in maintaining any serious and consistent philosophical
or theological position.

67. Montaigne, II, 225.

68. Erasmus, *Letters: The Epistles of Erasmus, ed. cit.*, II, 596.

69. *Ibid.*, II, 597.

70. Luther, quoted by Randall, *Mod. Mind*, 139.

71. *Ibid.*

72. Febvre, *Martin Luther*, 55–56.

73. In a somewhat more subtle way, since their subjectivistic and relativistic
attitudes invalidate the laws of nature and the moral law itself. Hence,
they force morality to depend upon experience or mere custom, and

promote (or at least make way for) various kinds of individualism and unconditioned voluntarism, or a negative pursuit of "tranquillity." For the influence of nominalism upon ethics, see De Wulf, *Med. Phil.*, II, 182, 185.

3.

74. Cf. Weber, *Hist. Phil.*, 252, and Gilson, *Sp. Med. Phil.*, 195–197. M. De Wulf (*Med. Phil.*, II, 79–87) argues heroically that Duns Scotus has been misinterpreted—that he and Thomas "hold in common those principles which underlie the whole of Scholasticism" (87). But while M. De Wulf is probably right in his general thesis, the course of his argument reveals that the historical significance of Scotus' thought leads away from Thomism, and particularly on the issue in question.

75. William Durand and Matthew of Aquasparta. Cf. Weber, *Hist. Phil.*, 253, and Gilson, *Sp. Med. Phil.*, 231–235.

76. Cf. Randall, *Mod. Mind*, 208–209, and Francis R. Johnson, *Astronomical Thought in Renaissance England* (Baltimore, 1937), 53.

77. Cf. De Wulf, *Med. Phil.*, II, 96.

78. For Arabian Aristotelianism and Averroism, see De Wulf, *ibid.*, I, 225 ff.; Gilson, *Sp. Med. Phil.*, 177–181; Vossler, *Med. Cult.*, I, 108–109; and Höffding, *Mod. Phil.*, I, 13.

79. De Wulf, *Med. Phil.*, II, 97.

80. *Ibid.*, II, 232–233. For Latin Averroism, cf. De Wulf, *ibid.*, II, 96–107, and his *Phil. and Civ.*, 285–289. It is probably the Latin Averroistic quality of the Aristotelianism taught in the colleges to which Ramus objects.

81. Cf. *ibid.*, II, 234.

82. *Ibid.*, II, 272.

83. *Ibid.* Cf. Höffding, *Mod. Phil.*, I, 13.

84. Kristeller (*Marsilio Ficino*, 29, fn. 47) makes it quite clear that Pomponazzi did not *introduce* the Alexandrist variety to Padua.

85. Quoted by Kristeller, *ibid.*, 28.

86. Quoted by De Wulf, *Med. Phil.*, II, 184.

87. Weber, *Hist. Phil.*, 254.

88. Cf. De Wulf, *Med. Phil.*, II, 185.

89. Quoted by Randall, *Mod. Mind*, 204.

90. Cf. Bredvold, *Int. Mil. of Dryden*, 28. Gianfrancesco displayed both a shamefaced admiration for, and a disapproval of, the vast intellectual pretensions of his uncle as a youth. Cf. More's translation of his *Life of Pico:* Sir Thomas More, *The English Works*, edited by W. E. Campbell (London, 1931), I, Facsimile Text of the 1557 Edition, 3 (modernized text, 351).

91. Agrippa, *De incertitudine*, I, 222. It is interesting to observe how much more sober a style Sanford's translation adopts than does the French text which I have mostly used. Agrippa's own Latin version (so far as I am competent to judge) is more lively and semi-Rabelaisian than the one, less bombastic than the other.

92. Cf. Bredvold, *Int. Mil. of Dryden*, 27.

93. Cf. *ibid.*, 22–24.

94. Hulme, *Ren. and Ref.*, 433–434.

95. *Catechism of the Council of Trent*, quoted by Randall, *Mod. Mind*, 166.

96. Quoted by Randall, *ibid.*, 167.

97. Dawson, *Prog. and Rel.*, 181.

98. For Calvin's explicit rejection of both "intellectual and moral culture" as pertinent to "true religion," see Mueller, "Calvin's Christian Thinking," 289–290, 296.

99. Febvre, *Martin Luther*, 54–55.

100. Gilson, *Sp. Med. Phil.*, 421.

101. Quoted by Febvre, *ibid.*, 181.

102. Quoted by Zanta, *Ren. du Stoïc.*, 48. My translation.

103. Cf. Febvre, *ibid.*, 271.

104. John Calvin, *Institutes of the Christian Religion*, translated by John Allen (Philadelphia, 1928), III, xxi, xxii.

105. *Ibid.*, III, xxi. My italics.

106. Quoted by Stefan Zweig, *The Right to Heresy: Castellio against Calvin*, translated by Eden and Cedar Paul (New York, 1936), 168.

107. Quoted by Zanta, *Ren. du Stoïc.*, 48. My translation. It is hardly to the point here to enter the discussion, often so heated, as to whether or not this same concept of a purely volitional and arbitrary God is to be found in Augustine, Duns Scotus, and other medieval thinkers. For Duns Scotus, compare Arthur O. Lovejoy's position, that Scotus held "the arbitrary and inscrutable will of the deity to be the sole ground of all distinctions of value" (*The Great Chain of Being*, Cambridge, Mass., 1936, p. 70), with M. De Wulf's opposite contention in his *History of Mediæval Philosophy* (II, 79–87). Cf. also Weber, *Hist. Phil.*, 250–251.

108. Calvin, *Institutes*, III, xxi, xxiii.

109. Quoted on flyleaf of Zweig, *Right to Heresy*.

4.

110. Cf. Randall, *Mod. Mind*, 155.

111. H. J. C. Grierson, *Cross-Currents in English Literature of the Seventeenth Century* (London, 1929), 274. My italics.

112. See, for example, Hulme, *Ren. and Ref.*, 416–417, for the spiritual exercises prescribed by Loyola. The "infallible discipline" of Puritan theocracy came of course from the Calvinistic literal interpretation of the Scriptures. Cf. Randall, *Mod. Mind*, 139, and Sykes, "Richard Hooker," 65–66. See also Erich Fromm, *Escape from Freedom* (New York, 1941), Chapter III, "Freedom in the Age of Reformation." In this remarkable chapter of his excellent book, Dr. Fromm develops in fascinating detail the psychological elements which led the Calvinists paradoxically to an ideal of a life involving moral effort. He explains plausibly how the very ability to make such an effort came to be taken *as a sign of belonging to the Elect*, since it was agreed that a virtuous life could not change the outcome in connection with the salvation of any individual. His explanation of the part this Protestant ethic played in the rise of capitalism (after Weber, Tawney and others) describes the subtle shift that occurs from such an attitude toward moral effort to one stressing simply effort in one's occupation—with the resultant position that *success* was a sign of God's grace, and *failure* one of damnation.

113. Perkins, *Workes*, III, 33.

114. Gabriel Harvey, *Letter Book*, edited by E. J. L. Scott (Camden Society's Series, no. 33, 1884), 69–71.

115. Gabriel Harvey, *Marginalia*, collected and edited by G. C. Moore Smith (Stratford-upon-Avon, 1913), 97. Cf. Chapman's version in line 94 of "A Hymne to our Saviour on the Crosse": "Impostors most, and slightest learnings please."

116. Cf. Bullough, "Bacon and the Defence of Learning," 15–20.

117. *Ibid.*, 15–17, and Campbell, *Shakespeare's Satire* (New York and London, 1943), 30–32. For full-length studies of the School of Night, see Frances

A. Yates, *A Study of Love's Labour's Lost* (Cambridge, 1936), and M. C. Bradbrook, *The School of Night* (Cambridge, 1936).

118. Rabelais, II, Chap. 37. A common source is most likely Seneca's *Epistles,* where the incompatibility of rigorous Stoic primitivism and the pursuit of the liberal arts and sciences is discussed. See especially Epistles lxxix and lxxxviii.

119. Cf. Lovejoy and Boas, *Prim. and Rel. Ideas,* 117–154, and 260–286.

120. *Ibid.,* 121.

121. Marston, *Scourge of Villanie,* 6.

122. *De Officiis,* I, xxv, 128; cf. Lovejoy and Boas, *ibid.,* 118, fn. 4.

123. Cf. Lovejoy and Boas, *ibid.*

124. *Ibid.,* 264.

125. *Satires,* XIII, quoted by Lovejoy and Boas, *ibid.,* 118, fn. 4.

126. Cf. Campbell, *Shakes.'s Sat.,* 143, for an explanation that the satirists felt that their work ought to have a certain awkward roughness to it because "their art was a development and an imitation of the scornful cries of satyrs." Professor Campbell develops this thesis at greater length in his *Comicall Satyre and Shakespeare's Troilus and Cressida* (San Marino, California, 1938). The two explanations—Professor Campbell's and mine—seem to me complementary, rather than mutually exclusive.

127. Cf. Campbell, *Shakes.'s Sat., passim.*

128. *Ibid.,* 94.

129. Cf. *ibid.,* 105–106, for the statement that "Thersites is . . . like a court fool. . . ."

130. I am indebted to Professor Marjorie Nicolson of Columbia University for this part of my interpretation.

131. For a detailed examination of Stoicism in the play, see Chapter X, 2 (*infra*).

132. *King Lear,* II, ii, 98, 102–106. Cornwall charges Kent with hypocrisy (ll. 107–110), but since he is himself corrupt, his opinion, of course, is not intended to be a just evaluation. Kent answers him roundly, too, in lines 115–120. . . . For other evidence of Kent's place in the "plain man" tradition, see Act I, i, 122–190, and especially lines 150–151:

> To plainness honour's bound
> When majesty falls to folly.

Cordelia's refusal to "heave [her] heart into [her] mouth" is of course a related theme; here, as so often, Shakespeare produces a theme with variations.

(All Shakespeare quotations are from *The Complete Works of Shakespeare,* edited by George Lyman Kittredge, Boston and New York, 1936.)

133. Lovejoy and Boas, *Prim. and Rel. Ideas,* 118. My italics.

134. Seneca, *Epistles,* lxxxviii, 20, 32: Lovejoy and Boas, *ibid.,* 278–79; cf. 285.

135. Greville, *Caelica,* LXXXVI.

136. Cf. Zanta, *Ren. du Stoïc.,* 62–63.

137. Cf. *ibid.,* 65.

138. Greville, *Treatie,* st. 59. My italics.

139. Marston, *Scourge of Villanie,* 45. Compare the speech which Bussy's ghost makes to Clermont in Chapman's *Revenge of Bussy.*

140. *Ibid.*

141. *Ibid.,* 44–45.

142. Ben Jonson, *Volpone,* I, ii, 31–32: *The Works of Ben Jonson,* edited by C. H. Herford and Percy Simpson (Oxford, 1937), Vol. V.

143. Jefferson Butler Fletcher, "Spenser the Puritan," an unpublished article.

144. Greville, *Treatie,* especially st. 128–129.

145. Davies, *Poems*, 114, 115. Anti-primitivists always tended to cite the legend of Prometheus (who brought "arts" to man) favorably; primitivists, unfavorably. Cf. Lovejoy and Boas, *Prim. and Rel. Ideas*, 24–25, 120, 132.
146. Greville, *Treatie*, st. 55.
147. *Ibid.*, st. 82.
148. *Ibid.*, st. 130.
149. Quoted by Louis I. Bredvold, "The Religious Thought of Donne in Relation to Medieval and Later Traditions," 197: in *Studies in Shakespeare, Milton and Donne*, by Members of the English Department of the University of Michigan (New York, 1925), 192–232. I am much indebted (as are most students of Donne's thought) in the following discussions to Professor Bredvold's study.
150. *Ibid.*, 198–199, 203. Cf. Bredvold, "The Naturalism of Donne in Relation to Some Renaissance Traditions," *Journal of English and Germanic Philology*, Vol. 22 (1923), 471–502.
151. Cf. *The Works of John Donne, D.D., with a Memoir of His Life*, by Henry Alford (6 vols., London, 1839), III, 472. For representative passages in Donne's poetry containing some of the arguments of philosophical skepticism and the conviction of the unceasing mutability of all things on earth, see the *Second Anniversary*, ll. 254–300, 387–434; *Progresse of the Soule*, LII, 518–520: *The Poems of John Donne*, edited by H. J. C. Grierson (London, 1929), 234 ff., 238 ff., 287.
152. Donne, *Satyre* III, 93–99, 109–110: *Poems*, 139–140.
153. Cf. Bredvold, "Religious Thought of Donne," 214–218, 221–222. In the latter two pages, Professor Bredvold explains that Donne's Augustinianism was the anti-Catholic variety of the sixteenth and seventeenth centuries. Augustine, like Aristotle, has come close to being all things to all men.
154. Donne, "The Litanie," VII, 62–63: *Poems*, 310.
155. Donne, *Works*, III, 302; cf. John Donne, *Essays in Divinity*, edited by Augustus Jessop (London, 1855), 37, 48–49.
156. *Works*, III, 47.
157. *Ibid.*, V, 320; cf. *Essays in Divinity*, 96.
158. *Works*, V, 577.
159. *Holy Sonnets*, XVII, 7–8: *Poems*, 301.
160. "A Hymne to God the Father," iii, 13–18; *Poems*, 338.
161. *Works*, V, 430–431.
162. Sir Thomas Browne, *Religio Medici*, I, ix (Boston, n. d.), 20.
163. Francis Bacon, *Novum Organum*, translated by Ellis and Spedding (New University Library, London, n. d.), lxvii, cxiii, xlix.
164. *Ibid.*, xxvi, xcv.
165. Francis Bacon, *De Augmentis*, IX, i: *The Philosophical Works of Francis Bacon*, reprinted from the texts and translations with the notes and prefaces, of Ellis and Spedding, edited with an introduction by John M. Robertson (London, 1905), 631. See also *Novum Organum*, I, LXXXIX. Cf. Willey, *Seventeenth Century*, 27–28 and *passim*, for this discussion of Bacon, and of Browne.
166. *De Augmentis*, IX, i: *Works*, 631.
167. Cf. Willey, *Seventeenth Century*, 29, 57, 59.
168. Fontenelle, *Plurality of Worlds* (1686); cf. Willey, *ibid.*, 1.

5.

169. Cf. Hulme, *Ren. and Ref.*, 221, and Höffding, *Mod. Phil.*, I, 23.
170. Cf. De Wulf, *Med. Phil.*, II, 170.
171. Montaigne, III, 357.

172. *Ibid.*, III, 353.
173. Walter Ralegh, *Works,* edited by Oldys and Birch (Oxford, 1829), II, xlv: *History of the World,* Preface.
174. Agrippa, *Vanitie and Uncertaintie,* sig. W1ᵛ. Various interpretations have been made of Agrippa's passages of this sort. His tone is frequently as ironic as that of Erasmus, yet the body of his work suggests a genuine adherence to fideism—although a variety supplemented by many unorthodox tendencies and allegiances, one not dissimilar to that of Paracelsus.
175. *Ibid.*
176. *Ibid.*
177. *Ibid.*, sig. W3ʳ. That he should cite "Peripateticke" *speculation* suggests the extent to which Aristotle had become Aquinas' Aristotle.
178. Hulme, *Ren. and Ref.,* 246.
179. Cf. Dawson, *Prog. and Rel.,* 180–181.
180. Quoted by Dawson, *ibid.,* 180.
181. Agrippa, *Van. and Uncer.,* sigs. Tt3ᵛ–Tt4.
182. Cf. Willey, *Seventeenth Century,* 65.
183. Rabelais, II, Chap. 29.
184. Taylor, *Thought and Expression,* I, 410. As Professor Taylor justly adds, however: "truly and simply understood, as by Calvin."
185. This interpretation is developed by Jefferson Butler Fletcher in the first of his two brilliant and comprehensive lectures on "The Continental Background of Edmund Spenser," given in the fall of 1942 at Columbia University (Comparative Literature 201).
186. Such a concept is Lutheran in one sense. What M. Gilson has written about Augustine is equally true of Luther:

> From the deepest roots of its inspiration down to the detail of its technical structure, the whole doctrine of St. Augustine is dominated by one fact: the religious experience of his own conversion. . . . His philosophy is essentially a "metaphysic of conversion." (*Sp. Med. Phil.,* 132).

True, that is, except for the fact that one cannot speak of Luther's "philosophy" or "metaphysic." It is the spirit, not the detail, of the passage that holds true for Luther. In just this sense, his religion was a profoundly personal one. On the other hand, Zwingli's conviction that revelation

> comes immediately from God to the individual; and it has been present and can still be found where no syllable of the Scriptures has ever penetrated . . . (Hulme, *Ren. and Ref.,* 280)

outraged Luther, who demanded,

> What else is this then but to teach that each man can be saved by his own religion and belief? (*Ibid.,* 281)

187. Cf. Alfred North Whitehead, *Science and the Modern World* (New York, 1925), 12.

CHAPTER
3

THE COUNTER–RENAISSANCE AND THE
REPEAL OF UNIVERSAL LAW

I. A SYSTEM OF UNIVERSAL LAW

> The quest of man for unity and order is the mainspring of all
> that is history. . . . Order requires a certain unity, and unity
> derives from a principle—a common source, a radical oneness.[1]

NO WORLD VISION has ever more completely realized these
ideals than that of the Scholastic philosophers. It found its starting
point in a God who was the "common source, a radical oneness"
who had created the universe:

> I asked the earth, and it answered me, "I am not He"; and
> whatsoever are in it confessed the same. I asked the sea and
> the deeps, and the living creeping things, and they answered,
> "We are not thy God, seek above us." I asked the moving air;
> and the whole air with his inhabitants answered, "Anaximines
> was deceived, I am not God." I asked the heavens, sun, moon,
> stars, "Nor," say they, "are we the God whom thou seekest."
> And I replied unto all the things which encompass the door
> of my flesh, "Ye have told me of my God, that ye are not He,
> tell me something of Him." And they cried out with a loud
> voice, "He made us."[2]

Nor had God made the universe capriciously, through any arbitrary whim of his will, but according to his wisdom. In the act
of Creation God's will had acted under the guidance of his intellect.
To Thomas Aquinas, no other of God's attributes is so noble as his
intellect: "The first author and mover of the universe is an intellect,"[3] and the *lex aeterna* is the eternal plan by which God acts.[4]
Not only does God prescribe a law to himself to follow, but he
governs the entire universe by law. "Intellectus solius est ordinare,"

says Aquinas,[5] and the universe is law-abiding throughout, with a fundamental order which rests upon the Divine Reason.

> God . . . the first unmoved mover . . . moves each thing to its end. Moreover he moves them by his intellect . . . not by natural necessity. . . . He is the governor of the whole universe by his providence. . . . To rule and govern by providence is nothing else but to move certain things to their end by one's intellect.[6]

Hence, in turn, "every work of nature," from the heavenly bodies to the lowest order of created things, is moved by some "intelligent substance," whether its own or a superior one, and

> For this reason the operations of nature are seen to proceed in an orderly manner even as the operations of a wise man.[7]

Natural law is immutable, and God could not change it "without contradicting Eternal Reason, that is to say, without destroying himself."[8]

In such a universe, saturated with reason, unity, order and design, purpose too is basic. To each of the orders of nature God has assigned a particular goal or end for it to seek, and it is in the pursuit of its particular end that everything finds its function in the universal scheme. The orders of nature below man, the subrational orders, strive to attain their ends blindly, through appetite or through the direction and influence of heavenly bodies. But man, being gifted with intelligence, seeks the good of the intellect. His ultimate good is to know God or truth by an act of his intellect, his mediate good to pursue the moral and social life according to his rational nature.

Moreover, the *lex naturalis*, based on man's detection by natural human reason of God's divine plan, constitutes man's participation in that plan.[9] Natural law is the underlying basis for all moral, political and legal principles and institutions, and is complementary and supplementary to the *lex divina*, revealed in the Scriptures. The Law of Nature, variously interpreted as it was throughout the earlier Middle Ages, becomes pre-eminently for Aquinas the regulative principle of reason in man, the operation of the Divine Reason within him. Hence all positive (man-made) law must agree with natural law and justice. For law in all its forms is the expression of reason, built upon the foundations of natural law, and its purpose is justice.[10]

Similarly, for Aquinas, the state and its institutions were not, as earlier medieval theorists had largely held, simply coercive measures made necessary by the Fall of Man.[11] Following Aristotle's *Politics*, he maintained with his customary optimism that man is a social animal, naturally directed to society, and that the state is natural since it is the proper development of the family and village and hence accords with "Aristotle's principle that the nature of a thing lies in its end or perfection."[12] In like manner, institutions such as private property are not contrary to natural law, but added to it by human reason, and therefore wholly congruous with it.[13]

For Aquinas, then, the state has its origin in nature, in accordance with God's divine plan. Furthermore, its end and purpose, like that of law, is moral—

> the maintenance of justice, or, in the terms derived from Aristotle, the setting forward of the life according to virtue. . . .[14]

Finally and sequentially, the authority of the state is limited by this end. Laws contrary to natural law are unjust, and have no force; the king, or government of whatever sort, is not the supreme authority, but rather the law of the state, and it is subordinate to the law of Nature and of God.[15]

The elements which contribute to this unified and harmonious concept come largely from classical antiquity and Christianity. Greek and Roman Stoicism, Platonism, and certain aspects of Roman law had been fused by medieval theorists with Christian ideology; and Aquinas gives the whole system a strong Aristotelian cast.

The result is a model universe of exquisite precision. Rooted in order and law, it displays design and purpose in every part, and hence proclaims the unqualified rule of Mind, which has produced unity. To confirm his belief in "a static divine order in all spheres of life," man has only to lift "up his eyes to the changeless movements of the stars—signs of divine perfection and eternal laws. . . ."[16] And to suggest the possibility of mankind's achieving a similar although necessarily less permanently perfect order on earth, he had before him the ideal of a united Christendom. A universal church, a universal language, relatively uniform and universal institutions, and common aspirations—these contributed to the social ideal of the Middle Ages, and to that dream of Dante's that the *Pax Romana* might come again, under the universal spiritual jurisdiction of the Pope and the universal temporal one of the Holy Roman Emperor:

> It is of the intention of God that all things should represent the divine likeness in so far as their peculiar nature is able to

receive it. . . . The human race, therefore, is ordered well, nay is ordered for the best, when according to the utmost of its power it becomes like unto God. But the human race is most like unto God when it is most one, for the principle of unity dwells in him alone. Wherefore it is written, "Hear, O Israel, the Lord our God is one." But the human race is most one when all are united together.[17]

Such an ideal, and indeed the whole system of thought which produced it, is noble and impressive. But it implies "a radical renunciation of the empirical world of actual fact."[18] It was in his very devotion to perfect order, unity, law, design, that Aquinas (as, to a lesser extent, Dante) was guilty of that "unguarded rationalism" which Professor Whitehead finds characteristic of the Middle Ages.[19] Thomistic Scholasticism's emphasis upon the dignity of the abstracting intellect was characteristic of its "scientific" and synthetic vision; and while it had its virtues, it led to too exclusive a reliance, in its methods, upon dialectic and analogy.

Nowhere is this more evident than in its natural science. There are three prominent features of Scholastic science which are hostile to the attitudes of modern science. All of them are bound up in some way with the primary medieval assumption that the truths of God revealed in Christian dogma are unassailably valid, although open to manifold interpretation.

The first of these is the system's basic concern with purpose. It was not the knowledge of natural operation which the Scholastics sought, but that of the purpose of everything in nature. They inquired primarily what a thing was "good for"—not how it originated or functioned.

In this respect, their major sources concurred harmoniously. Plato's cosmic scheme had included a hierarchy of "goods," culminating in the supreme Good toward which the whole creation moved. Aristotle's doctrine of "ends" had established "a universal purposiveness in organic nature," with its conviction that everything comes into being for the sake of an end "which always appears as the final result of a development, in accordance with natural law and by a continuous process, and in which the process attains its completion."[20] And there is an allied concept in the Stoic Law of Nature, with its premise that the good for any species lies in living according to its distinctive nature, and in harmony with universal Nature. Finally, it is obvious how these ideas, incorporated into a formal body of Christian doctrine, could and would be blended with that of a God who is a loving creator, purposefully directing the universe through his providence.

In short, to the Scholastics, the created universe is a work of the Divine Reason, and hence to be interpreted by its motives. And the result was that they inevitably "read into the cause and goal of the universe that which alone justifies it for man, its service of the good."[21] Their explanations are teleological.

But it is not the effort to discover what use all things in nature are to man—a perfectly legitimate *aim*—that made Scholastic physics so weak; it is rather

> in reading these uses, so complex and so human, into a simple scheme objective and absolute for the whole world . . . in interpreting the causes that actually produce change in the world on the analogy of human aspiration, and seeing all moving and living things as drawn onward by what may be said to be love for the unrealized ideals.[22]

For this interpretation leads us to the second insufficient feature of Scholastic science. Since it sees all of existence as a collection of an infinite number of types, each of which is trying to realize its particular end, it is chiefly occupied with

> the classification of all things into classes and sub-classes, the enumeration of their qualities, and the distinction between essential and non-essential qualities.[23]

As a scientist, Aristotle had been primarily a biologist and inclined to a qualitative system of measurement. It is again obvious how such a system would come conveniently to the hand of a man like Aquinas, equally Christian and philosophic, and striving to shape a philosophical model of a Christian world.

Thirdly, in harmony with a radical subordination of quantitative to qualitative measurement, the Scholastic scientists chiefly sought out physical truth by the instrument of syllogistic logic, or deductive reasoning. Aristotle's thought had revolved around logic, and his logic had been the first of his works accessible to the medieval philosophers. Moreover, in a system where the test of any single hypothesis is not experiment, but its congruity with a body of basic accepted principles, it is inevitable that a dialectical method should be adopted. Hence we have, in the synthesis of Aquinas and his colleagues, "a great chain of reasoning ultimately dependent upon its axioms."[24]

They applied similar methods to the "sciences" of ethics and politics and law. For in such a comprehensively unified world scheme, these too are exact sciences, with rules established and fixed by reason. We have seen how central the "analogy of human aspiration" is to the purposive nature of Scholastic physics, and how important analogy is to Dante's dream of a united Christendom. Indeed, with their concentration upon ordering and unifying all the component parts of the world and the various disciplines of knowledge, the Scholastics were bound to find analogy a useful tool, and its employment is everywhere apparent. To cite a prominent example, monarchy may be defended on the analogies of God's rule of the universe, the sun's of the heavens, the head's of the body, the understanding's of the human soul, the queen's of a beehive. Again, man is a little world or *microcosm,* corresponding in constitution and government to the great world or *macrocosm* —possessing, like it, four elements, and matching its rule of mind over body.

These applications are endless, and somewhat wearying. But they constitute one more significant testimonial to the fundamental preoccupation of the Scholastics with inter-relation and harmony, with centralization and unification. Their synthesis is indeed one of universal law. . . .

"The Middle Ages," Professor Whitehead wrote, "formed one long training of the intellect of Western Europe in the sense of order." And in that "long domination of scholastic logic and scholastic divinity"[25] lay the heritage of the Renaissance Christian humanists.

It is quite true, as we have seen, that they lacked and for the most part condemned the speculative enthusiasms of the Scholastics, and turned from the Science of God to that of Man. Yet their neglect of theological and natural science meant, for one thing, that they opposed no conflicting theories to the medieval synthesis; they may have had their doubts about Scholastic physics, metaphysics and theology, but their interests and talents did not lead them to the substitution of a new cosmology for the medieval Aristotelian-Ptolemaic one, or to that of a new world view for Thomas Aquinas'.[26]

Moreover, concentrating as they did upon man's pursuit of virtue and peace on earth, they mostly endorsed Aquinas' conclusions on the nature of the state and the significance of natural law to ethical and political theory. The influence of the eclectic classical moralists gave a new accent to some of their treatises, and increased in some cases the Platonic or Stoic elements already inherent in the medieval solution. But this was not to change the fundamentals

—rather the details, and mostly details of tone.

Indeed, in books like the *Utopia* and the *Education of a Christian Prince,* many of the basic medieval points of view are retained. Again, such favorite medieval arguments as those derived from analogy are as frequent as ever. One has only to examine Sir Thomas Elyot's *Boke of the Governour* to see how little they have changed. All of the fundamentals remain: the purposeful organization of the universe, and within it, of human society and individuals; the primacy of God and natural law in nature, the state and the individual man. Order, law, unity; purpose, design, centralization.

Moreover, that tendency of some of those humanists which we have observed—a growing inclination toward an exclusive reliance upon nature-and-reason, and a desertion of the revelation of a particular institutionalized religion—did little to abrogate the fundamental concept of a body of universal law. There were always Cicero and Seneca to turn to:

> Law is transcendent reason, implanted in nature, commanding what should be done, and forbidding what should not be done . . .[27]

and

> Ratio scilicet faciens, id est deus. . . .[28]

Nor could knowledge of the Natural Law be gained otherwise than through the light of man's reason, whether that reason be supplemented by divine grace or not.

Finally those Christian humanists who actually expounded a system of universal law in the sixteenth century—Suarez, Melanchthon, Hooker—were strongly influenced by the work of Aquinas. Melanchthon shows some tendencies directly attributable to the Reformation; Suarez interprets the *jus gentium* differently from Aquinas.[29] Hooker takes a middle position between the earlier medieval attitude and that of Aquinas on the question of the origin of the state and its institutions and laws;[30] they all display other small deviations from the great master. Yet these discrepancies serve mostly to throw into relief the overall similarity, and suffice to demonstrate that the widely orthodox body of universal law in the sixteenth century—whether compiled by Lutheran-humanist, Jesuit or Anglican—is a medieval product.[31] The resulting picture is still that of a beautifully coherent structure of thought and faith, builded upon the authority of God, disclosed by revelation and reason, and sustained by the dominant principles of order and unity, deriving from "a radical oneness." Possessing a common origin in God, the laws of the universe are constant and immutable, so long as "that which gave them their first institution remaineth for ever one and the same."[32]

Wherefore that here we may briefly end; of law there can be no less acknowledged, than that her seat is the bosom of God, her voice the harmony of the world; all things in heaven and earth do her homage, the very least as feeling her care, and the greatest as not exempted from her power: both Angels and men and creatures of what condition soever, though each in different sort and manner, yet all with uniform consent, admiring her as the mother of their peace and joy.[33]

A SYSTEM OF UNIVERSAL LAWS

Compiled from *Of the Laws of Ecclesiastical Polity,* Book I, by Richard Hooker (1594)

(1)   First "law eternal" (God's law to himself)

(2)   Second "law eternal" (God's law for all his creatures)

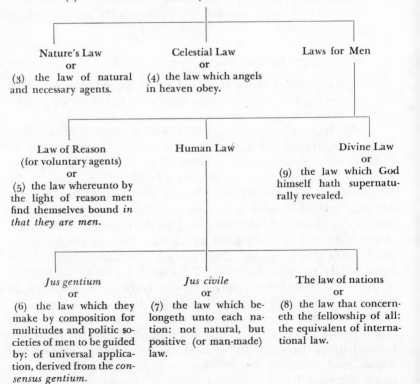

Nature's Law
or
(3) the law of natural and necessary agents.

Celestial Law
or
(4) the law which angels in heaven obey.

Laws for Men

Law of Reason
(for voluntary agents)
or
(5) the law whereunto by the light of reason men find themselves bound *in that they are men.*

Human Law

Divine Law
or
(9) the law which God himself hath supernaturally revealed.

Jus gentium
or
(6) the law which they make by composition for multitudes and politic societies of men to be guided by: of universal application, derived from the *consensus gentium.*

Jus civile
or
(7) the law which belongeth unto each nation: not natural, but positive (or man-made) law.

The law of nations
or
(8) the law that concerneth the fellowship of all: the equivalent of international law.

2. UNIVERSAL LAW REPEALED: MONTAIGNE

The Thomist and later derivative systems of universal law rest upon the basic assumption of ascertainable norms of conduct for every entity in the world—norms universally valid and, as operative in the individuals comprising each species, possessing objective reality. Hence, when Ockham asserted that the universal was merely a word (*nomen*), and that nothing was real except the individual,[34] he dealt a blow directly at the heart of this systemization. If only the individual is real, the whole fundamental unifying, centralizing tendency of the Thomistic system is artificial and unreal, and the "ideas of law, cause, and end are mental fabrications."[35] For the ultimate significance of a synthetic body of universal law is a comprehensive system of inter-related "sciences," tied together in their common origin and sharing mutually compatible, although functionally graduated, goals:

> Science has for its object the general, the universal, the necessary. The science of man, let us say in the spirit of Plato, does not deal with Peter for the sake of Peter, or with Paul for the sake of Paul; it studies Peter and Paul in order to know what man is. *It is the universal man, the species man, whom it seeks in the individual.*[36] *The same is true of all sciences.* Now, if the universal is a mere word having no objective reality, and if the individual alone is real, then there can be no anthropology, or any science. We can know and tell what both Peter and Paul are; we can study each particular plant and animal; but the universal man, plant, and animal can never become objects of science, because they nowhere exist. Hence nominalism is skeptical of science; its method agrees with that of Protagoras: *The individual is the measure of all things.*[37]

In short, nominalism begets a scientific skepticism which prohibits the knowledge and validity of law, since law cannot be applied successfully in a universe where each individual unit is considered unique. Category and abstract concept, essential for science, are dismissed as unreal.

Philosophical skepticism goes beyond nominalism, in denying the certainty of any knowledge, even that of the individual. Whereas Ockham would admit that any individual object may be known through sense percept and intuitive concept,[38] Sextus Empiricus, denying any certain objective validity to whatever is grasped by sense and intuition, as well as by intellect, would insist upon the complete relativity of all knowledge.

These two streams, nominalism and philosophical skepticism, as well as their tributaries, swelled the broad river of the Counter-Renaissance. It is not difficult to surmise the consequence to the surrounding country, that beautifully surveyed, fenced-in and marked-off land of universal law. The cartography of Aquinas and his successors has no counterpart in reality after the inundation, and the resulting wasteland is redeemed and newly developed only with the full advent of the Scientific Reformation. ·

The factors contributing to the flood are numerous; for the sake of clarity and brevity, we must confine ourselves to reviewing a few of the most significant.

Montaigne, for example, has new proofs at hand, which he employs to support his skeptical arguments. In the *Apologie,* having discussed the implications of the voyages of discovery, he blandly desires to know what conclusions we may infer, if so many of our dearest customs and beliefs and opinions are unknown or held in bad repute elsewhere in the world? What shall we think of the universal laws of God and nature?

> But let us go on: if Nature encloses within the limits of her ordinary progresse, as all other things, so the beliefes, the judgments and the opinions of men; if they have their revolutions, their seasons, their birth, and their death, even as cabbages: if heaven doth move, agitate, and rowle them at his pleasure, *what powerfull and permanent authority doe we ascribe unto them?* If by uncontrolled experience we palpably touch that the forms of our being depends of the aire, of the climate and of the soile wherein we are borne, and not onely, the hew, the stature, the complexion and the countenance, but also the soules faculties; . . . if sometime we see one art to flourish, or a beliefe, and sometimes another, by some heavenly influence: some ages to produce this or that nature, and so to encline mankind to this or that biase: mens spirits one while flourishing, another while barren, even as fields are seen to be; what become of all those goodly prerogatives wherewith we still flatter ourselves?[39]

The conviction that "the beliefes, the judgments and the opinions of men" have their cycles and seasons, "even as cabbages," was not new of course; and in the sixteenth century, Agrippa had already given it notable expression in his chapter "Of Morall Philosophie":

Moreover then this, if there be any Philosophie or Doctrine

of manners, as some will, I suppose that this doth not so muche consiste of weake reasons of Philosophers, as of divers use, custome, observation, & practise of common life, and that it is *mutable, according to the opinions of times, places, and menne, whiche with threateninges, and flatteries they teache to children, and to the elder sorte with lawes and punishment,* natural industrie hath given some things to menne, whiche they cannot be taught: *but thei take place by right or wrong, accordinge to the use of time and agreemente of menne:* whereof it commeth to passe, that, that which at one time was vice, an other time is accompted vertue: and that which in one place is vertue, in an other is vice: that whiche to one is honeste, to an other is dishoneste: that whiche to us iust, to other is uniuste, *according to the opinion, or lawes of time, of place, of estate, and of men.*[40]

Having cited numerous examples from ancient and from modern European countries, to illustrate the diversity dependent upon time and place and the difference in men, Agrippa concludes,

And every nation what soever it be either civill or barbarous hath his peculiare manners and customs geven to them from the influence of the heavens, *divers from the other.* . . .[41]

Here is a world, like Montaigne's, ruled not by the known, unchanging and universal laws of a purposeful, God-guided nature, but a mutability dependent upon the undecipherable influence of the heavens—a world in which man's standards and customs and laws and institutions do not derive from fixed and permanent and venerable norms taking form from the nature and meaning of the universe, but rather from the peculiarities of time and locality and the shifting *mores* of men.

Indeed, Montaigne goes so far as to say:

I am of opinion, that no fantasie so mad can fall into human imagination, that meetes not with the example of some publicke custome, and by consequence that our reason doth not ground and bring to a stay. . . .[42]

He continues,

The barbarous heathen are nothing more strange to us than we are to them. . . . Human reason is a tincture in like weight and measure, infused into all our opinions and customs, what form soever they be of *infinite in matter: infinite in diversitie.*[43]

For it is not that light of natural reason, common and equal in all men, to which he is referring. It he rejects, as well as the Law of Nature. As he says in the *Apologie:*

Mens opinions are received after ancient beliefs by authority and upon credit; *as if it were a religion and a law.* . . . This trueth, with all her framing of arguments and proporcioning of proofes, is received as a firme and solid body, which is no more shaken, which is no more judged. On the other side, every one the best he can patcheth up and comforteth this received beliefe with all the meanes his *reason* can afford him, which is *an instrument very supple, pliable, and yeelding to all shapes.* "Thus is the world filled with toyes, and overwhelmed in lies and leasings."[44]

In short, "when all is done, whatsoever is not as we are, is not of any worth."[45] Or as John Donne puts it,

> Ther's nothing simply good, nor ill alone
> Of every quality Comparison
> The onely measure is, and judge, Opinion.[46]

With such a conviction about the "science of man," Montaigne goes the limit in denying the fruitfulness of a search for "the universal man, the species man," and in dealing with "Peter for the sake of Peter":

> Others fashion man, I repeat him; and represent a particular one. . . .[47]

In his quest of the particular, as the only truth discernible in a world where opinions and customs are "infinite in matter: infinite in diversitie," he carries the decentralizing individuation of the nominalist to its logical extremity. More, he goes beyond it, for since "The world runnes all on wheels" and "All things therein move without intermission . . ." he admits,

> I cannot settle my object; it goeth so unquietly and staggeringly, with a naturall drunkennesse. . . .

The flux and mutability of all things on earth are too much for the Pyrrhonist really to know his object, yet he is undismayed:

> I take it in this plight, as it is at the instant I ammuse my selfe about it, I describe not th' essence but the passage. . . .[48]

Montaigne's particular man, with whose "passage" he "ammuses" himself, is of course himself. To the particularizing tendency of the nominalist and to the skeptic's conviction of the relativistic and subjectivistic nature of all knowledge, he weds the individualism of his "peinture de son Moi."[49] And with the approximate truth of "moi-même" we reach the opposite intellectual pole from the medieval absolute "truth of God," and the ultimate desertion of the universal for the particular.

Moreover, Montaigne is perfectly aware of the extent of his subversion of the orthodox centralized world of universal law, comprehensible to man's natural reason:

> Those which we call monsters are not so with God, who in the immensitie of his work seeth *the infinite of formes therein contained.* . . . From out his all-seeing wisdome proceedeth nothing but good, common, regular, and orderly; *but we neither see the sorting, nor conceive the relation.* . . . We call that against nature which cometh against custome. *There is nothing, whatsoever it be, that is not according to him.*[50]

Here is an infinite Nature, but one whose order and wisdom are not to be comprehended by man. The "universal-lawists" did indeed predicate diversity, but a *diversity in unity*—a diversity whose parts were inter-related, even inter-linked in a great chain of being, and so ordered that the whole and the inter-relations were largely comprehensible to man's reason.

Not so Montaigne. He continues ironically and scornfully,

> Let therefore this universall and naturall reason chase from us the error, and expell the astonishment, which noveltie breedeth and strangeness causeth in us.[51]

It is not uniform law and centralized order that he finds in Nature, with a common knowledge of them situated in men's common natural intelligence, but infinite diversity, and an equal diversity in men's judgments:

> I am so far from vexing my selfe to see my judgement differ from other mens, or to grow incompatible of the society or conversation of men, to be of any other faction or opinion then mine owne; that contrariwise (as variety is the most generall fashion that nature hath followed, and more in the mindes then in the bodies: forsomuch as they are of a more supple and yielding substance, and susceptible or admitting of formes) I finde it more rare to see our humor or desseignes agree in one. *And never were there two opinions in the world alike, no more than two haires or two graines. Diversity is the most universall quality.*[52]

In such a world, man's proud pretensions to a knowledge of the laws of the universe are ridiculous. Montaigne says so flatly:

> Thou seest but the order and policie of this little cell wherein thou art placed. *The question is, whether thou seest it.* His

[God's] divinitie hath an infinit jurisdiction far beyond that. This peace is nothing in respect of the whole. . . . *The law thou aleagest is but a municipall law, and thou knowest not what the universall is. . . .*[53]

"Truth," he agrees,

ought to have a like and universall visage throughout the world. Law and justice, if man know any, that had a body and true essence, he would not fasten it to the condition of this or that countries custom.[54]

"What truth is that," he demands, "which these Mountaines bound, and is a lie in the world beyond them?"[55] Yet man knows none beyond this "municipall" sort of truth, and

they are pleasant, when to allow the lawes some certaintie, they say that there be some firme, perpetuall and immoveable which they call naturall, and by the condition of their proper essence, are imprinted in mankind: of which some make three in number, some foure, some more, some lesse: an evident token that it is a marke as doubtfull as the rest. . . . [For] of these three or four choice-selected lawes there is not one alone that is not impugned or disallowed, not by one nation, but by many. . . . It is credible that there be naturall lawes, as may be seene in other creatures, but in us they are lost: this goodly humane reason engrafting it self among all men, to sway and command, confounding and topsiturving the visage of all things according to her inconstant vanitie and vaine inconstancy.[56]

The Law of Nature, the "natural" human reason, the proof from the *consensus gentium,* the objective and permanent outlines of justice and law in nature and man and state—what of them? Fables and inventions, "to allow the lawes some certaintie . . ." And "thus is the world filled with toyes, and overwhelmed in lies and leasings."

"Lawes," Montaigne asserts outright, "take their authoritie from possession and custome."[57] And the moral law is no exception:

The laws of conscience, which we say to proceed from nature, rise and proceed of custome; every man holding in speciall regard and inward veneration the opinions approved and received about him, cannot without remorse leave them, nor without applause applie himselfe unto them. . . .[58]

For, with his conviction that man's reason is "an instrument very supple, pliable, and yielding to all shapes," he believes it impossible to establish useful rules of conduct around a central rational Law of Nature.

> For us to go according to Nature [men say] is but to follow according to our understanding, as far as it can follow, and as much as we can perceive in it. Whatsoever is beyond it, is monstrous and disordered. By this accompt all shall then be monstrous, to the wisest and most sufficient, for even to such humane reason hath perswaded that she hath neither ground nor footing, no not so much as to warrant snow to be white. . . .[59]

Of all the detractors of the potency of man's reason and universal law that the Counter-Renaissance produced, Montaigne is at once the most incisive and most comprehensive. To follow in some detail his arguments and ironies, as set forth in the *Apologie* and in his later essays, constitutes an ultimate lesson in the vanity of dogmatizing. And however different may be many of the particular terms in which we of the twentieth century ask our questions and posit our hesitating answers, it is no exaggeration to say that he who will build a positive philosophy must still first answer the sly, bland, unruffled questions and the blunt and uncompromising assertions of the Lord of Montaigne.

Yet however comprehensive and influential his contributions to the repeal of universal law by the Counter-Renaissance, there are certain aspects and approaches to the subject which Montaigne does not represent in their most characteristic form. These alternative angles of attack are made clear by turning to the work of Cornelius Agrippa, Niccolò Machiavelli and Giordano Bruno.

3. UNIVERSAL LAW REPEALED: AGRIPPA AND MACHIAVELLI

Agrippa, as does Montaigne after him, assails the divine origin of law and its universal application. He refers to the determination of "aunciente Lawe makers" to bolster the authority of their laws by persuading ignorant people "that they did as they were taught by the Gods."[60] This same device has served Emperor and Pope alike:

> For this cause Leo the Pope straightly commaunded all Christian people, that noman in the Church of God should presume to iudge any thinge, nor any man, to iustifie nor to discusse any matter: but by the Authoritee of the holy Counsailes, Canons, and Decretals, whose heade is the Pope. . . .[61]

Similarly,

> The like lawe the Emperoure pretendeth to have in Philoso-
> phie, Phisicke, and other Sciences, graunting no authoritee to
> any knowledge, but so much as is geven them by the Skilfulnes
> of the Lawe. . . .[62]

"Beholde nowe," he declares,

> Yee perceive howe this knowledge of the Lawe presumeth to
> beare swaye over all other Artes, and exerciseth tyrannie, and
> howe preferringe it selfe before all other disciplines as it were
> the firste begotten of the Gods doth despise them as vile and
> vaine, *although it be altogeather made of nothinge els but of
> fraile and very weake inventions and opinions of men, which
> things be of all other the weakest.* . . .[63]

Thus far, Agrippa's and Montaigne's versions tally substantially,
except that Montaigne, a loyal if not devout Catholic, forbears,
for the most part, from attacking the Mother Church and does not
discuss the Canon Law.[64] But at this point in his argument, Agrippa,
with the fideistic accent which runs so strongly through the *Vanitie
and Uncertaintie*, relates the Law of Nature to the Fall of Man.
This "Lawe," he continues, actually

> is altered at every chaunge of time, of the state, and of the
> Prince, whiche tooke the firste beginninge of the sinne of our
> firste parent, whiche was cause of all our miseries, from whence
> *the first Lawe of corrupt nature* proceeded which they tearme
> the Lawe of nature. . . .[65]

Thus he, and the leaders of the Reformation after him, invalidate
not only man's reason and knowledge on the premise of original
sin, but also that Law of Nature which is at the heart of man's
moral and political life, of all goodness and justice. Listing the
"notable decrees" of the "first Lawe of corrupt Nature," he scornfully sets forth a category of the "tooth for a tooth" rights of man,
and concludes,

> Finally the Lawe of Nature is that wee shoulde not dye for
> thirste, for hunger, for colde, and not to hurt our selves with
> watchinges, and laboure. Whiche abandoning all the repent-
> aunce of Religion, and the workes of repentaunce, dothe ap-
> pointe the pleasure of the *Epicure* for the chiefest felicitie.[66]

In short, the true Law of Nature which Agrippa (and many others
of the Counter-Renaissance with him) recognizes is that of an individualistic, indolent and hedonistic state of nature, wholly remote
from the concepts of Thomas Aquinas and the Renaissance Chris-

tian humanists.[67] Nor does he spare those other laws, traditionally derived from the Law of Nature:

> Afterwarde the Lawe of Nations arose from whence warre, murder, bondage were derived, & dominions separated. After this came the Civill or Populare Lawe, whiche any people maketh peculiare to himselfe: from whence have growen so many debates among menne, that as the lawes doo witnes, there have ben made more businesses, then there be names of things.[68]

Yet, adopting the early medieval attitude of the Fathers and the Canon Lawyers, that the establishment of civil institutions was necessary, both as a result of, and the remedy for, the vicious desires of corrupt man,[69] Agrippa continues,

> For whereas men were prone and enclined to discorde, the publishinge of iustice whiche was to be observed by meanes of the Lawes was a necessarie thinge: to the end that the boldness of naughty men might in suche wise be bridled: and emong the wicked innocencie might be salfe, and the honest might live quietly emonge the dishoneste.[70]

"And," he comments, "these be that so notable beginninges of the Lawe, wherin have benne almost innumerable Lawemakers. . . ."[71]

Yet it must be noted that although Agrippa adopts the patristic and Canonist attitude about the need for coercive government and civil laws to restrain the corrupt natures of men, he omits the one most important emphasis of that attitude. He does not, as did the medievalists, see the establishment of civil society as a measure taken by God. He retains the theological premise of original sin, but he does not attribute the origin of the state and laws to God. On the contrary, he concludes,

> Hereof then we know that al the knowledge of the Civill Lawe dependeth upon the onely opinion and will of menne, *without any other reason urginge and enforcinge to be so,* then either the honestie of manners, or commoditie of livinge, or the authoritie of the Prince or the force of armes, whiche if it be the preserveresse of good menne, and the revengeresse of wicked men, it is good discipline, finally it is a most wicked thinge for the naughtinesse which is done when the Magistrate or the Prince neglecteth it, suffereth it, or alloweth it.[72]

With the state and its laws stripped of their divine origin, it is but a step to the denial of the universal interdependence of law and justice. Whereas the "universal-lawists" saw justice as the purpose

and the child of civil law, in its turn ultimately dependent upon
the great objective verities of natural law and God, Agrippa writes,

> It is not then sufficiently declared by this alone, that all the
> force of the Law & Justice doth not so much depend upon
> the Lawes as upon the honestie and equitie of the Judge.[73]

Here, in the "science" of natural and political law, is a position
parallel to that held by Montaigne in the "science" of man. Just as
Montaigne deserts and denies the efficacy of the study of universal
man, so Agrippa deserts and denies that of universal law. Just as
Montaigne rests his "wavering" knowledge of man upon the study
of a particular one, so Agrippa finds that "the force of Law & Justice" depends upon the honesty and fairness of any particular given
judge. The same completely decentralizing, individuating and relativizing process has taken place.

There is one more aspect of the repeal of universal law in which
an analysis of Agrippa's work supplements that of Montaigne's—
with regard to the Canon Law. "From the Civill Lawe," he explains,

> proceeded the Canon of the Popes Law, which to many may
> appear most holy, so wittily it doth shadow the precepts of
> covetousnes, and manners of robbinge under the coulour of
> godlines.[74]

He devotes many of his most scorching pronouncements to the
task of excoriating the Canon Law, the Pope, and the church's pretensions to temporal authority. And in conclusion he makes the
forthright assertion which we have been awaiting, that

> these Lawes and Canons come not from God, not be ad-
> dressed to God: but are derived from the corrupt nature and
> witte of men and are invented for gaine and covetousnesse.[75]

Agrippa includes among his alternative sanctions, "urginge and
enforcinge" the Civil Law, "the authoritee of the Prince" and "the
force of armes." His notable, not to say (however unfairly) notorious contemporary, Niccolò Machiavelli, goes well beyond him
in this respect. Says Machiavelli:

> The chief foundation of all states are good lawes and good
> armes: and as there cannot be good lawes where the state
> is not well armed, it follows that where they are well armed
> they have good laws. I shall leave the laws out of the discus-
> sion and shall speak of the arms.[76]

A simple, clear paragraph of plain expository style—yet deceptively
simple. For we have been transported to another world—out of

the world of Utopias and Christian commonwealths, and into the pragmatically functioning world of the late *quattrocento* and the early *cinquecento:* "where they are well armed they have good laws." So he dismisses the laws and turns to speak of the arms.

But this is *The Prince,* that handbook designed (for all of Machiavelli's alleged dispassionate hard-headedness) by a patriot dreaming of a re-united Italy, to be achieved by "arms and the man." If we turn to a more measured and deliberate judgment of his *Discourses on the First Ten Books of Titus Livius,* we find considerable material upon laws.

At the very outset of this treatise, Machiavelli remarks that, considering men's "general respect for antiquity," it is surprising how little imitation there is of the "ancient virtue." He continues,

> The more so as in the differences which arise between citizens, or in the maladies to which they are subjected, we see these same people have recourse to the judgments and the remedies prescribed by the ancients. *The civil laws are in fact nothing but decisions given by their jurisconsults, and which reduced to a system, direct our modern jurists in their decisions.*[77]

He is referring, of course, to that European body of practical law, derived from Roman *jus civile* and developed in the Middle Ages by the Bolognese jurists and the Civilians, which came to be practiced so universally that it was considered the equivalent of Natural Law, a *ratio scripta* which paralleled the divine Scripture of the church.[78] And, like Agrippa, he is implicitly divorcing this body of law from any normative validity ultimately derived from nature. Moreover, his account of the origin of justice is a totally disenchanted report of preventive measures taken by men who were living in a tooth-and-claw world:

> For at the beginning of the world the inhabitants were few in number, and lived for a time dispersed, like beasts. As the human race increased, the necessity for uniting themselves for defence made itself felt; the better to attain this object, they chose the strongest and most courageous from amongst themselves and placed him at their head, promising to obey him. Thence they began to know the good and the honest, and to distinguish them from the bad and the vicious; for seeing a man injure his benefactor aroused at once two sentiments in every heart, hatred against the ingrate and love for the benefactor. They blamed the first, and on the contrary honored those the more who showed themselves grateful, *for each felt*

> *that he in turn might be subject to a like wrong; and to pre-*
> *vent similar evils, they set to work to make laws, and to in-*
> *stitute punishments for those who contravened them. Such*
> *was the origin of justice.* This caused them, when they had
> afterwards to choose a prince, neither to look to the strongest
> nor bravest, but to the wisest and most just.[79]

In short, for Machiavelli, the origin of justice lies in fear and
self-interest, not in God's universal and purposeful laws of nature
and man's natural inclination to society. The first and only laws
are positive, man-made laws, and he gives as disingenuous an account as Agrippa's of how these have traditionally come to be
associated with religion.

> In truth, there never was any remarkable lawgiver amongst
> any people who did not resort to divine authority, as other-
> wise his laws would not have been accepted by the people;
> for there are many good laws, the importance of which is
> known to the sagacious lawgiver, but the reasons for which
> are not sufficiently evident to enable him to persuade others
> to submit to them; and therefore wise men, for the purpose
> of removing this difficulty, resort to divine authority.[80]

But not only does Machiavelli "explain away" the tradition of
the divine origin of laws; he also furthers the process of decentralization by considering the several and various ways in which individual states have received their laws:

> Some have had at the very beginning, or soon after, a legis-
> lator, who, like Lycurgus with the Lacedaemonians, gave them
> by a single act all the laws they needed. Others have owed
> theirs to chance and to events, and have received their laws
> at different times, as Rome did.[81]

In any case, he maintains, there is one central premise to be observed by the lawgiver, for,

> All those who have written upon civil institutions demonstrate
> (and history is full of examples to support them) that whoever
> desires to found a state and give it laws, must start with as-
> suming that all men are bad and ever ready to display their
> vicious nature, whenever they may find occasion for it. If their
> evil disposition remains concealed for a time, it must be at-
> tributed to some unknown reason; and we must assume that
> it lacked occasion to show itself, but time, which has been
> said to be the father of all truth, does not fail to bring it to
> light.[82]

Agrippa, to be sure, starts with the assumption "that all men are

bad and ever ready to display their vicious nature," and therefore
endorses the coercive and remedial nature of laws. But Agrippa
bases his premise upon Adam's sin. Machiavelli does not. He asserts
that "human events ever resemble those of preceding times," and
explains that

> This arises from the fact that they are produced by men who
> have been, and ever will be, animated by the same passions,
> and thus they must necessarily have the same results.[83]

Thus we have come still another step in that decentralizing
process of the repeal of universal law, order and unity. Agrippa
removes the main theological premise of the patristic and canonist
writers who have viewed the state, its laws and institutions as God's
remedy for original sin—removes it by omitting any mention of
God. Yet he retains original sin (or the non-theological equivalent
of man's corruption) as the cause of men's needing this restraint.
But Machiavelli merely asserts that men tend to be bad, always
have and always will. Hence, while for Agrippa pre-lapsarian Adam
might have known and obeyed God's laws, for Machiavelli there
never was a time when mankind was largely inclined to good. To
be sure, "human affairs" are "in a state of perpetual movement,
always either ascending or declining." But he concludes,

> Reflecting now upon the course of human affairs, I think
> that, as a whole, the world remains very much in the same
> condition, and the good in it always balances the evil; but the
> good and the evil change from one country to another, as we
> learn from the history of those ancient kingdoms that differed
> from each other in manners, whilst the world at large remained
> the same.[84]

The good in men anywhere is most likely to be evidenced at the
beginning of states, "by means of which they obtain their first
growth and reputation," but inevitably "in the progress of time,
this goodness becomes corrupted. . . ."[85] Hence, there is another
obstacle to any general unifying principle of law. For

> the constitution and laws established in a republic at its very
> origin, when men were still pure, no longer suit when men
> have become corrupt and bad. And although the laws may be
> changed according to circumstances and events, yet it is seldom
> or never that the constitution itself is changed; and for this
> reason the new laws do not suffice, for they are not in harmony
> with the constitution, that has remained intact.[86]

In time, then, the disintegration of the state is inevitable, "unless something intervenes to bring it back to its normal condition," to its "original principles." This purging may be accomplished by either "external or internal occurrences." Obviously the latter, "due either to the excellence of some one man, or to some law," is better—and since Machiavelli maintains that such laws, introduced "to repress the insolence and ambition of men," possess "life and vigor" only in the hands of a man who can see to their execution, this whole process depends ultimately upon some one man.[87]

Herein we return to Machiavelli's cardinal principle, variously developed in the *Prince* and the *Discourses,* that

> To Found a New Republic, or to Reform Entirely the Old Institutions of an Existing One, Must Be the Work of One Man Only.[88]

A mixed constitution is the sort Machiavelli believes best and longest-lived, least likely to undergo the otherwise inevitable political cycle from monarchy to tyranny to aristocracy to oligarchy to democracy to anarchy—and back to monarchy, if the state survives that long.[89] But whether the renovation of a corrupt state or the founding of a new one is in question, he is convinced that the success of the project rests ultimately upon the courage and wisdom of one man, who is justified in using extraordinary measures in gaining his end.[90]

In this conviction, he parallels Montaigne's pursuit of "moi-même" and Agrippa's assertion that justice depends upon the fairness and honesty of a particular judge. Once again we are witnessing the decentralizing influence of the Counter-Renaissance, away from a unified and unifying concept of universal law and order, and toward the individuation and relativization of the "sciences" of man and society.

Indeed, this tendency is basic to Machiavelli's thought. It is not only apparent in his emphasis upon the importance of a single individual to the formation of a state; it is central to his idea of the state. For him, law is not prior to the state, nor is justice. There are no universal laws or objective standards upon which the laws of a state should be founded, and to which her government is subordinate. On the contrary, law is devised (and differently) within each state to assist in its preservation and growth, and is secondary to and dependent upon military strength. For he recognizes only two kinds of states: that which, like Rome, "desires to extend its empire," and that which "confines itself merely to its own preservation";[91] and he advocates taking the former for a model.[92]

Thus Machiavelli envisions, not a world held together by a common bond of Law and Right deriving from its creator's purpose, as expressed in the normative Law of Nature, but rather one divided against itself in a constant state of "bellum omnium contra omnia"—with Law and Right dependent upon Arms and Might. The state is an individual entity in itself, dependent for its continual existence and "success" upon Power.[93] Totally contrary to the major European tradition before him, he does not envision the state as "the organized unity of the common life," but as "a governing and military body knowing no limits save those imposed by its own weakness. . . . Its real essence is its power, and its success lies in the maintenance and expansion of this."[94]

Thus Machiavelli repeats in the *Discourses* his stand in the *Prince:*

> Although I have elsewhere maintained that the foundation of states is a good military organization, yet it seems to me not superfluous to repeat here that, without such a military organization, *there can neither be good laws nor anything else good.*[95]

And he further maintains the absolute value of the state as such:

> For where the very safety of the country depends upon the resolution to be taken, no consideration of justice or injustice, humanity or cruelty, nor of glory or of shame, should be allowed to prevail. But putting all other considerations aside, the only question should be, what course will save the life and liberty of the country.[96]

This is to make a veritable religion of the state. As Professor Randall says, "He read State for church and enemy for heretic, and founded the modern Religion of the State. . . ."[97]

Finally, this decentralizing principle of Machiavelli's work is apparent also in his treatment of history. The traditional medieval view of history was one of a single and unique procession, extending to Judgment Day, and divided into "four universal empires succeeding one another as a divinely created frame of history, with the Roman empire as the last, placed above historical flux and destined to endure to the end of history. . . ."[98] The *Discourses*, with its picture of all states "on one level of natural growth and decay,"[99] undergoing a common cyclic process in a world where human nature remains always the same, flatly contradicts this view.[100] Machiavelli divorces history—as he divorces man, the state, justice and law—from revelation and divine purpose and unity. And his contribution to the breakup of the Thomist synthesis of divine and natural law is very aptly summarized by Sir Politick Would-Bee in Ben Jonson's *Volpone*. Sir Politick may be a sycophant and a fool, but he knows his Machiavelli.

> And then for your religion, professe none;
> But wonder, at the diversitie of all;
> And for your part, protest, were there no other
> But simply the lawes o' th' land, you could content you:
> Nic: Machiavel, and monsieur BODINE, both,
> Were of this minde. . . .[101]

4. UNIVERSAL LAW REPEALED: BRUNO

Giordano Bruno completes the decentralizing, particularizing and relativizing of the medieval synthesis which was the outstanding work of the Counter-Renaissance. What Montaigne, Agrippa and Machiavelli did to the traditional concepts of man, natural and moral law, justice, the state, and history, he did to that of the physical constitution of the Aristotelian-Ptolemaic universe in particular, and to the body of physical and universal law in general.

For among the revolutionary ideas which Copernicus had introduced in his *De Revolutionibus Orbium Coelestium* (1543), was the one that all motion is relative to the position of the observer. It should be immediately apparent that here, in the realm of the physical universe, is a concept parallel to those we have already traced in the thoughts of Montaigne, Agrippa, Bodin and others about the influence of locality and time upon laws, customs, morals, opinions and religion. Here, properly developed, is the final instrument with which to effect the toppling of the basic principles of a centralized and unique Christian order and of humanly ascertainable universal law—and the establishment, instead, of a universal relativity. It was not Copernicus, however, but Giordano Bruno, who "properly" developed it, and even went beyond this position to entertain the concept of a single unifying force pervading and prevailing throughout an infinite universe.

It has become the intellectual fashion to minimize Bruno's contribution to the history of thought. As Professor Baron writes,

> Today, because of the prevailing tendency to accept the coming of the mathematical method as the decisive factor distinguishing "new" from "old," Giordano Bruno, who once seemed to represent the climax of Renaissance philosophy, has receded into the background.[102]

And with this tendency, there has crept in also an inclination to dismiss Bruno simply as a pantheistic and "Platonizing" mystic who was more charlatan than philosopher. One may find a healthy corrective, I think, in Professor's Höffding's solid and exhaustive analysis of Bruno's thought—for despite all Bruno's undeniable eccentricities, his unpleasant egotism and his bombastic pretensions, there is thought there to be analyzed, and influential thought.[103]

Out of Copernicus' arguments for the relativity of motion and place, Bruno developed, on epistemological grounds which have lasting significance,[104] a world scheme which is not totally submerged in relativity only because the idealistic and Neoplatonic elements in his thought (probably derived from Cusanus) bring to it a unifying principle which it would otherwise lack.

Bruno begins his relativistic argument with the assertion that the medieval world-view, with the earth as the central point and the fixed stars as the ultimate limits, can find no justification on the evidence of the senses. For if we consider the various sense-images which we receive as we move, we discover that the horizon unceasingly changes as we change our position. Hence sense-perception should convince us of

> the possibility of conceiving any place whatever, wherever we may be, or can convey ourselves in imagination, as the central point, and also the possibility of constantly changing and exceeding the limits of our world.[105]

To this argument Bruno appends that of the infinite capacity of our imagination and thought "to add number to number, magnitude to magnitude, form to form";[106] and from the subjective impossibility of fixing a limit and of finding an absolute central point, he advances to the assertion that there is no limit and no central point—for it is inconceivable that there should be no reality to correspond to and equal our imagination and thought.[107]

> Since the horizon forms itself anew around every place occupied by the spectator as its central point, every determination of place must be relative. The universe looks different according to whether we conceive it to be regarded from the earth, the moon, Venus, the sun, etc.[108]

Such a concept of the universal relativity of place obviously destroys any absolute significance of such terms as center, pole, zenith and nadir. The old fixed "up" and "down" of the medieval universe is completely decentralized, unorientated, and the Scholastics' body of permanent and certain universal physical laws, in which the sub-lunary corruptible world is activated and directed by the trans-lunary eternal one, ceases to have any meaning.

From this complete relativity of place, Bruno moves on to the relativity of motion. Any motion will have a different appearance in accordance with the position of the observer, who will always consider his own standpoint immovable; hence absolute certainty of a distinction between what is in motion and what is at rest is impossible.[109]

It is immediately apparent that this view is in direct opposition to that of the Aristotelian-Ptolemaic one of the Middle Ages, which, in accordance with Biblical cosmology, postulated a motionless earth, around which moved the sun and the stars. And the contribution of this theory of Bruno's to the decentralization of the universe is equally obvious. For his argument points to the arbitrariness of choosing the earth as the fixed point from which all motions are to be measured.[110] If one were to accept this argument of Bruno's, all of Aristotle's proofs for a finite universe in the first book of *De Caelo* would collapse, since they are based upon the premise of the heavens rotating around a motionless earth.[111]

Again, Bruno derives the relativity of time from that of motion. For, since we can discover no absolutely regular motion, and have no body of proof that all the stars "have taken up exactly the same position, with regard to the earth, as those they previously occupied," and since motion appears different if regarded from different stars, there may be as many times in the universe as there are stars.[112]

Here again Bruno collides with the traditional medieval point of view, which held with Aristotle that the incorruptible and perfect heavens must adopt the most perfect motion, which is circular.[113] These provided an absolute measurement of time. But if, with Bruno, one denies the certainty of their perfectly regular movement, in accordance with a place-relativity dependent upon the observer, time becomes completely relative too.[114]

Finally, the establishment of all these relativities leads Bruno to the denial, in terms of the universe as a whole, of any absolute validity of concepts of weight. Central to the Aristotelian predication of the centrality of the earth was the argument that since "heaviness was the tendency to seek out the central point of the world,"[115] and the earth was the heaviest of the four elements (fire, air, water and earth), it must be the center of the world. This was even supposed to be the physical explanation of the original formation of the earth.[116] But Bruno, consistently with his relativizing and decentralizing attitude, held that "the qualities of heaviness and lightness were predicable of the particles of every individual heavenly body in their relation to this body as a whole."[117] Hence he maintained that the concepts of heaviness and lightness had only relative meaning—in terms of a particular heavenly body or system.[118]

All these relativistic pronouncements of Bruno's were of considerable influence in hastening the final demolition of the Aristotelian-Ptolemaic world order, for they were completely subversive of its primary assumption of the difference in substance between the trans-lunary and sub-lunary worlds. Closely and logically connected with Bruno's principle of relativity is his conviction of the *indifferenza della natura,* which denies utterly the incorruptibility of the heavens.[119] Actual proof of the error of this medieval premise awaits, of course, the full Scientific Reformation and Galileo's use of the telescope. But already Bruno is aware of the importance of observation in this process, and hails Tycho Brahe's observation of comets as certain proof of the fictitiousness of the crystal spheres which were supposed to divide the different regions of the world, one from another—since the comets were observed to go directly through the spheres.[120]

The contribution of Bruno's relativism to the destruction of the Thomistic system of universal physical law is even more considerable, and more immediately apparent. His work takes its place beside that of other relativistic skeptics[121]—rather, in one sense, he sits above and beyond them. For that decentralizing of the old order to which they contributed is finally complete with his work; no smallest portion of the universe is left untouched by his relativity. Physical law and order of every kind are dependent upon the position of the observer; God's physical Law of Nature is repealed, as his other natural laws have been, and we are cast adrift in Montaigne's world, where "Diversity is the most universall quality."

World? Worlds, rather, and here is where Bruno himself recoiled from his own conclusions. For if the earth is not the center, "why the sun? A candle flame grows smaller as we recede; why may not suns do likewise?"

> Why, indeed, may not all the stars be themselves suns, and each new sun appear to itself the center of the universe? Where, then, are its limits? Has it limits? Is it not rather infinite, an infinity of worlds like our solar system? There must be hundreds of thousands of suns, and about them planets rolling, each one, perhaps, inhabited; by beings possibly better, possibly worse, than ourselves. Throughout, nature must be

the same, everywhere worlds, everywhere the center, everywhere and nowhere. . . .[122]

But what then of man, the favored child of God? Here decentralization rises to smite the fundamental Christian premise. For in
such a universe, what becomes of the "central episode of Christianity"? What of the "central figure" of man? Is the redemption repeated over and over again? Or is there no redemption at all?[123]

Bruno, I say, recoiled from the logical answers to many of these
questions. If he cannot find God anywhere, he concludes that it
must be because God is everywhere. He turns to a mystic pantheism
which finds an immanent God in infinite nature. Hence with his
final position, which restores order and meaning (although not
law in the old sense) to the universe, he deserts the relativistic
skeptics.

But he deserts them for mysticism, not for intellectualism—and
their incomprehensible universe for one only intuitively comprehensible. He remains faithful to the anti-intellectualistic tendencies
of the Counter-Renaissance—and to its decentralizing and particularizing ones, too, although not so consistently. For, as Professor
Höffding points out,

> Bruno oscillates, without himself being aware of it, between
> mystical contemplation of the unity, and enthusiastic sur-
> render to the manifold.[124]

Both aspects of his thought are of significance to the decentralizing
process of the Counter-Renaissance—the first to its denial of limit,[125]
the second to its emphasis upon diversity and particularization.

The latter aspect (which is the concern of the present and succeeding chapter) is closely tied up with Bruno's relativism, and is
most marked in the works of his last period—the Frankfurt writings:

> He is here still further than in his London works from ap-
> pealing, with the Neo-Platonists, to a supernatural principle.
> And while, in the London works, it is on interconnection and
> reciprocal action that he lays most weight, here he emphasizes
> the individual elements between which the reciprocal action
> takes place. Prominence is given to the individual in his
> particularity.[126]

He goes as far as Montaigne in affirming that "no two things,
nor two cases, nor two times" are identical. "The atom (or the
minimum, or the monad) is that which has no parts, and which is
itself a primary part of a phenomenon." Even here his relativism
enters, and he does not claim that atoms are absolute, but rather

(with a semi-nominalist emphasis) that they are the first constituents we need to explain a sensuous phenomenon; the atom may itself possess parts. And finally, since he makes of it "not only a particle of matter," but "also active force, soul, and will," he calls God "the monad of monads," and so returns to his earlier basic premise of "a single substance which moves in all things."[127]

Yet, despite these ambiguities, which Bruno resolves always in his universal application of the old Neoplatonic idea of *coincidentia oppositarum*, his thought is consistently marked by his conviction that "that which is not an individual cannot be said to exist."[128] And this particularizing bent of his atomistic conception of nature, together with all the relativizing elements in his thought, effects a basic bond between his work and that of Montaigne, Agrippa and Machiavelli. The concern of these three with the particular man, the particular judge, the particular state, are all trends away from the science of the universal to the consideration of the particular; Bruno's devotion to the monad is a more philosophical application of the same general principle and tendency. . . .

So concentrated an analysis of the part these four men played in the discrediting of the traditional Christian-classical system of universal law necessitates scanting the contributions of others. We may mention in passing Lorenzo Valla's disclosure of the fraud of the Donation of Constantine,[129] which, according to Agrippa, "proceeded from this [the Canon] lawe . . .";[130] Rabelais' numerous irreverent dealings with the Law of Nature, the Law of Nations, the *consensus gentium*, the Civil and the Canon Law, and analogical arguments;[131] the works of Guicciardini, to whom "Machiavelli was a theorist, with his head wrapped in dreams of what could not come to pass"[132] and that of Jean Bodin ("monsieur BODINE") and Louis Le Roy, especially in the field of historical theory and method, political theory, and as exponents of the relativity of manners, customs, ethics and laws.[133]

Yet when all is said and done, Machiavelli, Agrippa, Bruno and Montaigne demonstrate fully and in mutually supplementary fashion the repeal of universal law by the Counter-Renaissance. The *lex aeterna*, including God's law for all of nature; the *lex divina;* the *jus naturale;* the proof from the *consensus gentium* and its derivative, the *jus gentium;* Civil and Canon Law; the laws of natural and rational agents; the very light of natural reason in man —none escapes analysis and condemnation by at least one of them. The conviction of the nominalist that only the individual is real; the assertion of the philosophical skeptic that all knowledge is relative, and all law with it; the predication of natural cycles and variations, in beliefs, opinions, morals and states, according to the circumstances of time, place, climate and men; the assertion of the complete relativity of place and motion and time; the singularizing tendency of atomism; the fideistic argument of the corruption of man from Adam's Fall, and the purely secular one based on observation and the reading of history—all these are employed to maintain that if there is a body of universal law, it is for God, not man, to understand it, and that all available evidence points to a universe, to states, and to men whose chief characteristics are diversity and singularity, rather than agreement in unity and a common working in a comprehensible and certain fashion, for a common and established purpose.

Each of the four moves on eventually toward a positive program of his own: Montaigne to the establishment of a new natural law for man, one appropriate to a universe "infinite in matter: infinite in diversitie"; Agrippa to the search for occult truth in the "secrets" of God and nature; Machiavelli to the establishment of pragmatic rules for the state to follow in a world of tooth-and-claw; and Bruno to the predication of a single substance which animates and holds together his plurality of worlds and all the atoms within them. Yet their destructive work on the old order and their repeal of its body of centralized and universal law had wide repercussions, and eventually contributed to decisive changes.

5. THE BELL TOLLS FOR UNIVERSAL LAW: JOHN DONNE

In "The First Anniversary" John Donne describes the whole decentralizing and particularizing process of the Counter-Renaissance, and in so doing makes use of many of the arguments employed by the four men we have been studying. God's Law of Nature (that "authenticall or . . . originall draught written in the bosom of God himself," according to Hooker) has been repealed, and with its disappearance all semblance of order and unity is gone too:

> She that should all parts to reunion bow,
> She that had all Magnetique force alone,
> To draw, and fasten sundred parts in one;
> She whom wise nature had invented then
> When she observed that every sort of men
> Did in their voyage in this worlds Sea stray
> And needed a new compasse for their way;
> She that was best, and first originall

> Of all faire copies, and the generall
> Steward to Fate   .   .   .   .   .   .
> .   .   .   .
> .   .   .   .
> Shee, shee is dead; shee's dead: when thou knowst this
> Thou knowst how lame a cripple this world is.[134]

Men have been reluctant to admit it:

> So mankinde feeling now a generall thaw,
> A strong example gone, equall to law
> The Cyment which did faithfully compact,
> And glue all vertues, now resolv'd and slack'd
> Thought it some blasphemy to say sh' was dead,
> Or that our weaknesse was discovered
> In that confession   .   .   .   .   .   .[135]

For with "her" death, of course, man's "natural path of everlasting life" is obliterated. Donne (unlike Hooker) argues with Agrippa and the leaders of the Reformation that the Fall finally corrupted man and destroyed the efficacy of natural moral law:

> For that first marriage was our funerall:
> One woman at one blow, that kill'd us all . . .[136]

Like Agrippa, he admits since the Fall the existence of a "Lawe of corrupt nature . . . which they terme the Lawe of Nature":

> For there's a kind of World remaining still,
> Though shee which did inanimate and fill
> The world, be gone, yet in this last long night
> Her Ghost doth walke. . . .[137]

But

> Shee, shee is dead; shee's dead: when thou knowst this,
> Thou knowst how poore a trifling thing man is.[138]

It is the voice of the Reformation, telling man that he can no longer say

> I am that moral man, safe in my natural reason and philosophy . . .

for "that is spent."[139] Hence Donne advises

> . . . that except thou feed (not banquet) on
> The supernatural food, Religion,
> Thy better Growth grows withered, and scant. . . .[140]

In short, faith and grace alone avail man now.

But it is at this point that the poet begins to employ the argu-

ments of relativism and decentralization. To Bruno, "Man is no
more than an ant in the presence of the infinite. And a star is no
more than a man,"[141] and Donne echoes him:

> Be more then man, or thou'rt less then an ant.[142]

For

> . . . as mankinde, so is the worlds whole frame
> Quite out of joynt, almost created lame. . . .[143]

Corruption entered it early, with the rebellion of the Angels; then
followed the fall of Adam, from which the seeds of decay possessed not only man but the rest of nature, "curst in the curse
of man."[144] And now, at last, with the decentralizing tendencies of
the Counter-Renaissance, all order, unity and law are torn apart,
for there is evidence that God's supposedly permanent and universal Law of Nature for all his creatures has been repealed.

Richard Hooker has envisioned such a universal catastrophe:

> Now if nature should intermit her course, and leave altogether
> though it were but for a while the observation of her own
> laws; if those principal and mother elements of the world,
> whereof all things in this lower world are made, should lose
> the qualities which now they have; if the frame of that heav-
> enly arch erected over our heads should loosen and dissolve
> itself; if celestial spheres should forget their wonted motions,
> and by irregular volubility turn themselves any way as it might
> happen; if the prince of the lights of heaven, which now as
> a giant doth run his unwearied course, should as it were
> through a languishing faintness begin to stand and to rest him-
> self; if the moon should wander from her beaten way, the
> times and seasons of the year blend themselves by disordered
> and confused mixture, the winds breathe out their last gasp,
> the clouds yield no rain, the earth be defeated of heavenly
> influence, the fruits of the earth pine away as children at the
> withered breasts of their mother no longer able to yield them
> relief: What would become of man himself, whom these things
> now do serve? *See we not plainly that the obedience of crea-*
> *tures unto the law of nature is the stay of the whole world?*[145]

But Hooker, with his optimistic view of the redemption, denies
that such a disaster has come to pass. To be sure, observed "swerv-
ings are now and then incident into the course of nature"; they
are caused by "divine malediction, laid for the sin of man upon
those creatures which God had made for the use of man. . . ." But

> nevertheless so constantly the laws of nature are by natural
> agents observed, that no man denieth but those things which

nature worketh are wrought either always or for the most part, after one and the same manner.[146]

"No man denieth . . ." But in less than twenty years John Donne "denieth" it, and vigorously. . . .

Professor Marjorie Nicolson has very strongly argued that it was the publication of Galileo's *Siderius Nuncius* in 1610, with its report of *what actually had been seen*, through a telescope, in the supposedly indestructible and immaterial heavens above the moon, which acted as a catalytic agent on the literary and philosophical imagination of England and Italy, and notably upon Donne's.[147] The date of "The First Anniversary" (1611) and Donne's unquestionable interest in and access to current astronomical news make a very strong case for her thesis.

Yet Professor Nicolson points out that Galileo's proof simply provides the spark which sets off a fire for which Donne had been heaping fagots up for years. And one particular passage in "The First Anniversary" offers indisputable evidence of his acquaintance with almost all of the relativistic and decentralizing arguments of the leaders of the Counter-Renaissance:

> And new Philosophy calls all in doubt,
> The Element of fire is quite put out;
> The Sun is lost, and th' earth, and no mans wit
> Can well direct him where to looke for it.
> And freely men confesse that this world's spent,
> When in the Planets, and the Firmament
> They seek so many new; they see that this
> Is crumbled out again to his Atomies.
> 'Tis all in peeces, all cohærence gone;
> All just supply, and all Relation:
> Prince, Subject, Father, Sonne, are things forgot,
> For every man alone thinkes he hath got
> To be a Phœnix, and that there can bee
> None of that kinde, of which he is, but hee.
> This is the worlds condition now. . . .[148]

Here Donne records, as evidence of "the decay of this whole World," the conclusions of "new Philosophy"—which has usually been taken to mean simply the new astronomy,[149] but which (it seems clear to me) is used in the larger, looser sense of the thought of men like Montaigne and Bruno. Among the ravages the world has suffered are the loss of the "element of fire," with the discovery of the corporeal nature of the worlds beyond the moon; the denial of the centrality of the earth; and the consequent "displacement" and "loss" of the sun and the earth, which suggest Bruno's totally decentralized and relativized world, rather than only the fundamental heliocentric premise of the new astronomers.[150]

Again, Donne emphasizes a plurality of new worlds, which men "seeke" out "in the Planets, and the Firmament". . . . "This world" (*i.e.*, the Aristotelian-Ptolemaic universe, under the rule and guidance of God's Law of Nature) must indeed therefore be "spent"; men "see that this is crumbled out againe to his Atomies," he declares, with almost certain reference to Bruno's atomistic universe.[151] And with the consequent destruction of order and unity, he again lays a particularizing emphasis:

> *'Tis all in peeces,* all cohærence gone;
> All just supply, and all Relation. . . ."

As Professor Nicolson has remarked,

> Here is "Copernicanism" to be sure, but it is less the position of this world than the awareness of new worlds which troubles the poet; less even the description of this little world of man, than the realization of how slight a part that one world plays in an enlarged and enlarging universe . . .[152]

that disheartens Donne. In other words, it is primarily the change in men's ideas of the nature of the entire universe, with the resultant implications of the falsity of the whole Scholastic synthesis, which most troubles him—rather than the postulated particular change of position of the earth.[153]

Yet he goes on to consider the infinite diversity to be found in the world of men as well as in the universe, and here he leaves Bruno's field for those of Machiavelli and Montaigne. In the state, in personal relations, in knowledge itself, there is no common body of accepted and certain law:

> Prince, Subject, Father, Sonne, are things forgot,
> For every man alone thinkes he hath got
> To be a Phœnix, and that there can bee
> None of that kinde, of which he is, but hee.

Here is Montaigne's wholly particularized and relativized world, in which no two opinions are ever alike, and in which only the science of "Peter for Peter's sake" may be studied. Gone is the binding and universal imperative of the rational Law of Nature, and gone the common certainty to be found in the *consensus gentium*. And in such a world the sanctions of the old order and relationships of the state are as lost as those governing private ethics and epistemology. Donne's reference to "Prince" and "Subject" is best understood if one is familiar with his presentation of Machiavelli in *Ignatius, his Conclave,* written the year before. For he there made his Machiavelli boast,

> I did not onely teach those wayes, by which, through *perfidi-ousnesse* and *dissembling of Religion,* a man might possesse, and usurpe upon the liberty of free Commonwealths; but also did arme and furnish the people with my instructions, how when they were under this oppression, they might safeliest conspire, and remove a *tyrant,* or revenge themselves of their *Prince,* and redeeme their former losses; so that from both sides, both from *Prince* and *People,* I brought an abundant harvest, and a noble encrease to this Kingdom [of Hell].[154]

With the repeal of universal law, one finds oneself in the jungle world of *Il Principe.* . . .

It is the death of a world order which Donne is celebrating, under the cover of a lament for the "untimely death of Mistris Elizabeth Drury." And since the new world is not yet born, he is filled with a passionate concern which not even his frequently extravagant imagery and metaphysical wit can hide. It seems to me unquestionable that the two *Anniversaries* mark a decisive turning point in his intellectual career. For in "The Second Anniversary" he finds his answer to being cast adrift in an infinite and unknown universe —the answer of fideism, to which he clung, more or less consistently, throughout the remainder of his life. Faith, and faith alone, could answer the profound questions which troubled him.

But I am also convinced that the *Anniversaries* serve as a decisive symbol for more than his personal career. Trapped in the transitional period between two confident and optimistic world orders, Donne peculiarly summarizes and symbolizes the dilemma bequeathed by the Counter-Renaissance. Montaigne, Agrippa, Machiavelli, Rabelais, Bodin, Le Roy, Bruno and others had done their work well—too well—and many of the Elizabethans found themselves caught in an intellectual chaos which seemed to offer no way out. The literature of the age in which Hamlet asked his questions and Lear was reduced to a state of internal disintegration matching the moral disorder of his realm and the threatening physical disintegration of the universe, is marked by a combination of aspiration and pessimism which loses its paradoxical quality when one recognizes its peculiar causes. Pessimism—since men saw their universe "crumbled out againe to his Atomies," saw "the decay of this whole world." Aspiration—since this break-up of a world order inevitably meant to certain temperaments the opportunity for a new freedom.

Nor was this opportunity solely the exultation of brigands who find in disorder the chance to pillage and win spoils for themselves. For the Counter-Renaissance was not only an age of death, but one of birth as well. The gestation period seemed endless to many; yet already, before John Donne was ringing the death knell of the Scholastic world, there were prophetic voices raised in hope. We have seen that the most subversive among the skeptics of the Counter-Renaissance turned eventually to positive programs, and in the sixteenth century there was on foot a scientific movement which, while it awaited the Scientific Reformation for a full consummation, nevertheless, with its insistence upon free individual inquiry, pointed the way for the new science of the seventeenth century. It was this preliminary movement which culminated in Francis Bacon's stirring words, "I am now therefore to speak touching Hope. . . ."

FOOTNOTES
CHAPTER 3
I.

1. Louis A. Ryan, O.P., "Of Charity and the Social Order," *The Thomist,* Vol. III, No. 4 (Oct., 1941), 539–540.
2. Augustine, *Confessions* (Everyman Edition), 208–209.
3. Aquinas, *Sum. con. Gen.,* I, i. Cf. De Wulf, *Med. Phil.,* II, 17. This is not the only Scholastic view, of course. Duns Scotus dissents—or, at least, lays a very different emphasis. See Chapter II, fn. 107 *(supra)*.
4. Cf. Otto Gierke, *Natural Law and the Theory of Society: 1500 to 1800,* with a lecture on "The Ideas of Natural Law and Humanity," by Ernst Troeltsch, translated with an introduction by Ernest Barker (Cambridge, 1934), Vol. I, 98.
5. In *Ethic. ad. Nicomach.,* Lect. 1, 7, quoted by DeWulf, *Phil. and Civ.,* 193.
6. Aquinas, *Sum. con. Gen.,* III, I, lxiv.
7. *Ibid.,* III, I, xxiii, xxiv.
8. De Wulf, *Phil. and Civ.,* 189.
9. Cf. Aquinas, *Summa Theologica,* Part II (Second Part), Q. XCI, art. ii–iii: A rational creature

    has a share of the Eternal Reason, whereby it has a natural inclination to its proper act and end: and this participation of the eternal law in the rational creature is called the natural law.

    Cf. Gierke, *Nat. Law,* I, 98; Carlyle and Carlyle, *Med. Polit. Theory,* V, 38–39; Becker, *Heavenly City,* 3.
10. Cf. Carlyle and Carlyle, *ibid.,* V, 39–44.
11. *Ibid.,* V, 10.
12. *Ibid.,* V, 12–13.
13. *Ibid.,* V, 17–18.
14. *Ibid.,* V, 35.
15. *Ibid.,* V, 43, 36. Cf. *ibid.,* 86–111, and Gilson, *Sp. Med. Phil.,* 475.
16. Hans Baron, "Towards a More Positive Evaluation of the Fifteenth Century Renaissance," *J H I,* Vol. IV, No. 1 (Jan., 1943), 34.
17. Dante, *De Monarchia,* Bk. I, Ch. 8. Cf. Randall, *Mod. Mind,* 102–106.
18. Ernst Troeltsch, "The Ideas of Natural Law and Humanity in World Politics," 2: Gierke, *Natural Law,* I, 205.
19. Cf. Whitehead, *Science and the Modern World,* 14.
20. Jaeger, *Aristotle,* 75.
21. Randall, *Mod. Mind,* 100. For this whole discussion, cf. *ibid.,* 96–101.
22. *Ibid.,* 100.
23. A. J. Wolf, *A History of Science, Technology, and Philosophy in the 16th and 17th Centuries* (London, 1935), 4.
24. Randall, *ibid.,* 98.
25. Whitehead, *Sci. and Mod. World,* 16, 17.
26. This statement requires some modification. There is a wide variance of opinion on the extent of the humanistic component in the Renaissance advancement of science. Professor Randall finds very little, maintaining that humanism contributed almost nothing to the trends leading to the development of modern science ("The Development of Scientific Methods," 177–206). Professors Baron and Kristeller, on the other hand—among others

—dissent. The former finds a "mediate but essential contribution" in Quattrocento humanism ("Towards a More Positive Evaluation," 32, fn. 21); and Professor Kristeller ("The Place of Classical Humanism in Renaissance Thought," *JHI*, Vol, IV, No. 1, January, 1943, 59–63) believes that "the influence of humanism on science as well as on philosophy was indirect, but powerful" in the Renaissance, and especially in fifteenth-century Italy (*Ibid.*, 60). Again, as regards English humanism, Professor Johnson has devoted many pages to tracing the influence of humanists like those in Sir Thomas More's circle (notably Linacre and Tunstall) upon the growth of scientific learning in the early sixteenth century (*Astron. Thought*, 80–92).

Yet all available evidence seems to me to indicate that whatever contributions humanism made were in the realm of "scientific *learning*"—further translations and commentaries on ancient scientific treatises, especially in the Neoplatonic and Neopythagorean traditions—rather than in creative accomplishments in what we would now call science. The theses of Professor Strong in *Procedures and Metaphysics* . . . (Berkeley, California, 1936), and Randall (*op. cit.*): that the growth of modern science came chiefly from "those solid operational techniques which were being developed by practical men through the study of Euclid" (Dana B. Durand, "Tradition and Innovation in Fifteenth Century Italy: 'Il Primato dell' Italia' in the Field of Science," *JHI*, Vol. IV, No. 1, January, 1943, 14), and from the School of Padua's work "within the Aristotelian framework, and by means of a critical reflection on the Aristotelian texts . . ." (Randall, "Scientific Method," 203) seem to me most plausible. Moreover, Professor Johnson's book confirms this judgment; for, while paying full tribute to humanism's contributions (especially in terms of translations and texts in the vernacular) to scientific learning in the first half of the sixteenth century, he hails the shift of English scientific activity, after 1550, from the universities to London, and from theory to a greater concern with practice, as a salutary one (*Astron. Thought*, 137–138).

Professor Johnson's most characteristic emphasis is upon the way the two forces collaborated, and upon their continuation of a scientific tradition established in England during the Middle Ages by men like Roger Bacon and Grosseteste. Professor Durand holds a similar position in terms of the continent; he is convinced that both traditions contributed, and that both owe something to medieval mathematics ("Trad. and Innov.," 14). But even if one accepts these moderate and balanced verdicts, the statement in my text which has precipitated this monstrous footnote still holds good. For while the cosmology of many late Scholastics, and of most of the Renaissance humanists, has more basic Neoplatonic elements than Aristotelian (with a resultant inclination toward quantitative measurement), its Neoplatonism is largely the medieval sort. That is, any "new" and "humanistic" cosmology which appears is chiefly derivative from the body of mathematical material (largely mystical or magical) which was elaborated in the thirteenth and fourteenth century schools of Oxford and Paris, and which has always ridden the edge of Scholasticism as a complementary feature of its cosmology—seldom one antagonistic to the main outlines of the official Aristotelian world-view. For that matter, even in Aquinas' writings, there are marked Neoplatonic elements which have been assimilated into the Aristotelian-Ptolemaic cosmology. (For the elaboration of other aspects of the whole problem, see Chapters IV and V, *infra*.)

27. Cicero, *De Legibus*, I, 6.

28. Seneca, *Epistulae Morales,* translated by R. M. Gummere (Loeb Library), I, xlv.
29. Lilley, "Francisco Suarez," 97.
30. Hooker, *Of the Laws,* I, x, 1–4. That is, Hooker gives a more affirmative attention to the thesis that men must frame their laws with post-lapsarian corruption in mind, although, like Aquinas, he sees original society as fundamentally "natural."
31. Compare the résumé of Aquinas' system with the diagram of Hooker's at the end of this section. The most significant difference lies in Hooker's interest in the "law of nations," a sort of rudimentary international law. This law suggests (1) the inevitable distinction between the concept of all Christendom as one nation (Aquinas) and the *fact* of developed and conscious nationalism which has occurred before Hooker writes; (2) Hooker's Anglicanism—the independence from Rome of the church he belongs to.
32. Hooker, *ibid.,* I, xv, 3.
33. *Ibid.,* I, xvi, 8.

2.

34. Cf. Weber, *Hist. Phil.,* 253.
35. De Wulf, *Med. Phil.,* II, 180.
36. This sentence suggests even more clearly the Aristotelian temper of Scholastic moderate realism, with its finding of the universal *in* the particular, than it does that of Platonic extreme realism, with its emphasis upon the exclusive reality of the universal. Hence I have chosen this paragraph to quote, as remarkably pertinent to the opposition of Ockham's nominalism to Aquinas' moderate realism, despite Professor Weber's selection of Plato as an illustration.
37. Weber, *Hist. Phil.,* 253–254. My italics, except for the quotation from Protagoras. For a modified interpretation of Protagoras' position, see John Burnet, *Greek Philosophy,* Part I, Thales to Plato (London, 1924), 114–118.
38. Cf. De Wulf, *Med. Phil.,* II, 182.
39. Montaigne, II, 329–330. My italics.
40. Agrippa, *Van. and Uncer.,* sigs. T3ᵛ–T4. My italics.
41. *Ibid.,* sig W1. My italics.
42. Montaigne, I, 114.
43. *Ibid.,* I, 115. My italics.
44. *Ibid.,* II, 279. My italics.
45. *Ibid.,* II, 205.
46. Donne, "Progresse of the Soule," LII, 518–520: *Poems,* 287.
47. Montaigne, III, 20.
48. *Ibid.*
49. Cf. Villey, *Essais de Montaigne,* 10.
50. Montaigne, II, 506. My italics.
51. *Ibid.*
52. *Ibid.,* II, 604–605. My italics.
53. *Ibid.,* II, 257. My italics.
54. *Ibid.,* II, 334.
55. *Ibid.,* II, 334–335.
56. *Ibid.,* II, 335–336.
57. *Ibid.,* II, 339.
58. *Ibid.,* I, 120.
59. *Ibid.,* II, 260.

3.

60. Agrippa, *Van. and Uncer.*, sig. Ss4.
61. *Ibid.*, sigs. Ss3v–Ss4.
62. *Ibid.*, sig. Ss3v.
63. *Ibid.*, sig. Ss4. My italics.
64. It is not my intention here to go into the intricacies of the relationship in the Middle Ages of natural law to Canon Law or to that European body of practical law, developed by the Bolognese jurists, called "Civil" law. For a clear brief account, see Professor Barker's introduction to Gierke's *Natural Law*, I, xxxix f. For detailed accounts, see Carlyle and Carlyle, *Med. Polit. Theory, passim.*
65. Agrippa, *ibid.*, sig. Ss4. My italics.
66. *Ibid.*, sig. Ss4v.
67. For a full explanation of this alternative interpretation of the Law of Nature, see Chapters VII, 1, and VIII, 2 *(infra)*.
68. Agrippa, *ibid.* Compare the diagram of Hooker's system of laws.
69. Cf. Carlyle and Carlyle, *Med. Polit. Theory,* Vols. I, II, III; for a summary and contrast with Aquinas' interpretation, V, 4–25.
70. Agrippa, *ibid.*
71. *Ibid.*
72. *Ibid.*, sig. Tt1v. My italics.
73. *Ibid.*, sigs. Tt1v–Tt2.
74. *Ibid.*, sig. Tt2. For the derivation of the Canon Law from the Civil, see Gierke, *Natural Law,* I, xxxix.
75. *Ibid.*, sig. Tt4.
76. Niccolò Machiavelli, *The Prince,* translated by W. K. Marriott (Everyman edition), 97.
77. Niccolò Machiavelli, *Discourses on the First Ten Books of Titus Livius,* translated from the Italian by Christian E. Detmold (Modern Library, New York, 1940). Introduction, 103–104. My italics.
78. Cf. Gierke, *Natural Law,* I, xxxix–xl. The most important point for our present consideration is Roman law *in general,* come in the Middle Ages to be called *jus civile,* and to amount to *Natural Law in practice.* As Professor Barker puts it in his introduction:

> The Natural Law which was a *part* of Roman Law, and one of its conceptions, is a conception which was adopted and developed by the Church. But when the question came to be asked, "What does this conception of Natural Law actually contain or include?" the answer tends to be, during the Middle Ages generally and down to the rise of a new School of Natural Law after 1500, "It contains or includes the *whole* of Roman Law, which is, *as a whole,* both supremely reasonable and universally diffused, and is therefore natural" *(Ibid.,* xxxix).

79. Machiavelli, *Discourses,* I, ii, 112. My italics. Cf. Lucretius, *De Rerum Natura,* V, 1143–1160. Machiavelli's account of the origin of civil society is close to the Epicurean one in general, but Lucretius gives a much more detailed summary of various stages in the development of primeval man *(De Rerum Natura,* V, 925–1142).
80. Machiavelli, *ibid.*, I, xi, 147.
81. *Ibid.*, I, ii, 110. Cf. *ibid.*, I, ii, 111, and I, iv, 119–120, for an account of how the later process may take place, and especially the subversive idea that "good laws in their turn spring from those very agitations [internal

disturbances in a state] which have been so inconsiderately condemned by many" (120).

82. *Ibid.*, I, iii, 117.
83. *Ibid.*, III, xliii, 530.
84. *Ibid.*, II, Introduction, 272.
85. *Ibid.*, III, i, 397.
86. *Ibid.*, I, xviii, 168.
87. *Ibid.*, III, i, 397–398, 399.
88. *Ibid.*, I, ix, 138.
89. *Ibid.*, I, ii, 113–115.
90. Cf. *ibid.*, I, ix, 139.
91. *Ibid.*, I, v, 123. Cf. I, xxix, 190.
92. *Ibid.*, I, vi, 129–130.
93. For these two attitudes (although with no reference to Machiavelli) and their possible reconciliation, see Gierke, *Nat. Law*, I, 223–226.
94. Norman Wilde, "Machiavelli," *The International Journal of Ethics*, Vol. XXXVIII, No. 2 (Jan., 1928), 219.
95. Machiavelli, *Discourses*, III, xxxi, 503. My italics.
96. *Ibid.*, III, xli, 528.
97. Randall, *Mod. Mind*, 197.
98. Baron, "Towards a More Positive Evaluation," 36.
99. *Ibid.*
100. Yet, as usual, not explicitly. This part of the task was thoroughly handled by Jean Bodin and Louis Le Roy. Cf. fn. 133 *(infra)*.
101. Jonson, *Volpone* (*ed. cit.*), IIII, i, 22–27. "Monsieur BODINE" is Jean Bodin. For more about Bodin, see Chapters IV, 2, and V, 2 *(infra)*, and *passim*.

4.

102. Baron, *ibid.*, 35.
103. I should like to take this opportunity to mention my great indebtedness to two histories of philosophy which are old enough now to be declared outmoded by many, but which I have found of invaluable aid: Alfred Weber's *History of Philosophy* and Harald Höffding's *History of Modern Philosophy*. Although neither of these men pretended to be a specialist on the Renaissance, their sections on that period are remarkably acute, and the further I have gone in my study of it, the more I have realized their acuteness. Their works are, in lucidity and in over-all vision, vastly superior to many more recent and specialized studies.
104. Cf. Höffding, *Mod. Phil.*, I, 127.
105. *Ibid.*, I, 123–124.
106. *Ibid.*, I, 124. There is nothing new, of course, in this Platonic-Pythagorean idea.
107. *Ibid.*
108. *Ibid.*
109. Cf. *ibid.*, I, 124–125. The medieval view, was, of course, that "the earth is the fixed point from which every motion is to be measured."
110. Cf. *ibid.*, I, 125.
111. Cf. Johnson, *Astronomical Thought*, 40.
112. Höffding, *ibid.*, I, 125.
113. The astronomers, of course, had to take account of the intricate movements of the planets, which they did variously—by altering Aristotle's concept of "homocentric spheres" (which turn on their axes and enclose the various heavenly bodies, one to each), by assigning to every planet several spheres

(each with its own motion) to which the planet is bound; or by adopting Ptolemy's mathematical system of eccentric circles and epicycles. For a clear and comprehensive treatment of these alternatives, see Chapter II, "The Pre-Copernican Conception of the Universe," in Johnson's *Astronomical Thought in Renaissance England*—especially 38–40, and 45 ff.

114. Cf. Höffding, *ibid.*, I, 125.

115. *Ibid.*, I, 125–126.

116. Cf. Johnson, *ibid.*, 45.

117. Höffding, *ibid.*, I, 125.

118. Copernicus also held to this theory of weight. For the difference between his and Bruno's emphases, however, see Höffding, *ibid.*

119. Cf. *ibid.*, I, 126–127. For the most important implications involved in this point of view, see Chapter VI, I (*infra*). It is, of course, the Aristotelian part of the "Aristotelian-Ptolemaic world order" which is most seriously affected by the Copernican and Brunonian world-view. For the latter denies the most fundamental premises of Aristotle's physics, which dominated the medieval world order. Ptolemy's mathematics had, to a certain extent, been "Aristotelianized" (chiefly through changing his "abstract constructions into material spheres"), just as Aristotle's physics had been Christianized. And of the various major adherents of medieval cosmology, the Aristotelian physicists and Christian theologians had far more reason to oppose the Copernican astronomy, from its philosophical advocacy by Bruno to its scientific defense by Galileo, than the Ptolemaic mathematicians. (See Johnson, *Astronomical Thought*, 94–96.)

120. *De immenso*, I, 5; cf. Höffding, *ibid.*, I, 128, and—for similar conclusions of Tycho Brahe's—I, 507. Professor Höffding argues that "Bruno has a much keener sense of necessity of confirming theoretical and subjective considerations by the method of experience than is generally attributed to him." (*Ibid.*, I, 127)

121. Some of his conclusions are partially anticipated in the "modes" (or "arguments" or "tropes" or "positions") of the Greek skeptics: cf. Sextus Empiricus, *Hypotyposes*, I, 36–40, 135. Others may be found in Lucretius' *De Rerum Natura*.

122. Randall, *Mod. Mind.*, 242–243.

123. Cf. *ibid.*, 243.

124. Höffding, *ibid.*, I, 136. Cf. Arthur Oncken Lovejoy, "The Dialectic of Bruno and Spinoza," *University of California Publications*, Vol. I, 141–173: *Studies in Philosophy Prepared in the Commemoration of the Seventieth Birthday of Professor George Holmes Howison* (Berkeley, California, 1904)—especially 162–165.

125. See Chapter VI (*infra*).

126. Höffding, *ibid.*, I, 138.

127. *Ibid.*, I, 138–139.

128. *Ibid.*, I, 139. Cf. I, 131, for the way this caused Bruno to deviate sharply from Plato's concept of ideas as universals.

129. Cf. Lorenzo Valla, *The Treatise on the Donation of Constantine*, text and translation into English by Christopher B. Coleman (New Haven, Conn., 1922).

130. Agrippa, *Van. and Uncer.*, sig. Tt3.

131. In I, x, he explains the meaning of white and black with the help of the Law of Nature and the proof from the *consensus gentium;* in III, 44, Pantagruel invokes the Law of Nature and the Law of Nations in defense of a murder:

On the one hand, it was an execrable crime to cut off at once both her second husband and her son. On the other hand, the course of the murder seemed so natural as to be grounded upon the law of nations and the rational instinct of all the people of the world. . . .

Six chapters in Book III are devoted to the Bridlegoose episode, during which practically every aspect of the laws is ridiculed. See especially III, 39, for the way Bridlegoose "awards [his] decrees and pronounces judgment." Rabelais is forever boisterously assailing the "Canons and Decretals," and he has an hilarious time with the use of analogy, to prove that there is only one "popehawk" (V, 3).

132. Taylor, *Thought and Expression*, I, 93. Guicciardini displays this attitude in his *Considerazione* (of Machiavelli's *Discorsi*).

133. Cf. especially Jean Bodin, *Methodus ad Facilum Historiarum* (1566), and *Les six livres de la République* (1576 [The *Six Bookes of a Commonweale*, out of the French and Latin Copies, done into English, by Richard Knolles (London, Impensis G. Bishop, 1606)]; and Louis Le Roy, *Considération sur l'histoire universelle* (1567–1588), *De la Vicissitude ou variété des choses en l'univers* (1575–1583), and *Des Troubles et différends . . . entre les hommes par diversité des Religions* (1573). For analyses of their contributions, see Atkinson, *Nouveaux Horizons, passim* (for especially interesting passages on "relativity," see 405–412); and J. B. Bury, *The Idea of Progress: An Inquiry into its Origin and Growth* (New York, 1932), 37–49. Both Bodin and Le Roy are dealt with to some extent later in this book.

5.

134. Donne, *The first Anniversary*, 220–229; 237–238; *Poems*, 214.
135. *Ibid.*, 47–53: *Poems*, 209.
136. *Ibid.*, 105–106: *Poems*, 211.
137. *Ibid.*, 67–70: *Poems*, 210.
138. *Ibid.*, 183–184: *Poems*, 213.
139. Donne, *Works*, III, 47. See Chapter II, 5 *(supra)*.
140. Donne, *The first Anniversary*, 187–189: *Poems*, 213.
141. Quoted by Randall, *Mod. Mind*, 243.
142. Donne, *The first Anniversary*, 190: *Poems*, 213.
143. *Ibid.*, 191–192: *Poems, ibid.*
144. *Ibid.*, 200: *Poems, ibid.*
145. Hooker, *Of theLaws*, I, iii, 2. My italics.
146. *Ibid.*, I, iii, 3.
147. Marjorie Nicolson, " 'The New Astronomy,' and English Literary Imagination," *Studies in Philology*, XXXII (July, 1935), 428–462. For Donne's reaction, see especially 449–462. On the subject in general, see Professor Nicolson's "The Telescope and Imagination," *Modern Philology*, XXXII (1935), 233–260; and "Milton and the Telescope," *ELH*, Vol. 2, No. 1 (April, 1935), 2–3.
148. Donne, *The first Anniversary*, 205–219: *Poems*, 213–214.
149. Not just "Copernicanism" to Professor Nicolson, however. Cf. "The Telescope and Imagination," and "The New Astronomy," 428–429, but contrast the quotation from Donne on 451.
150. In support of this thesis, see *Ignatius, his Conclave* (1611), 18–19 (edition indicated below) —where Ignatius Loyola (for the "plot" of this satire, see Chapter IV, 2, *infra*) demands of Copernicus, who has claimed to have "turned the whole frame of the world":

But for you, what new thing have you invented, by which our Lucifer gets any thing? What cares hee whether the earth travell, or stand still? Hath your raising up of the earth into heaven, brought men to that confidence, that they build up new towers or threaten God againe? Or do they out of this motion of the earth conclude, that there is no hell, or deny the punishment of sin? Do not men beleeve? do not they live just as they did before?

And, on the other hand, Donne implies in *The first Anniversary*, the idea of a plurality of worlds in a possibly infinite universe may do just these things to men. At least, he knows how much it troubles one man, and many of the very questions which Ignatius asks here only rhetorically, are stated as serious considerations in the poem.

151.	Although Donne has not necessarily taken it directly from Bruno. Among well-known proponents of atomistic philosophy at the time in England was Nicholas Hill, whose book on the subject was published in Paris in 1601, and who was ridiculed by Ben Jonson. Cf. Johnson, *Astron. Thought,* 231–232.

152.	Nicolson, " 'The New Astronomy,' " 457. See *ibid.,* 458–460, for Donne's later references to an infinite universe and a plurality of worlds.

153.	Again, I must point out that this fact does not necessarily mean that Donne is directly influenced by Bruno. The idea of an infinite universe and a plurality of worlds was of course accessible to Donne from many sources, including the ancient atomists, such as Leucippus and Democritus; Lucretius; Copernicus (although he refuses to come to a definite conclusion on the subject) ; Thomas Digges (see Chapter IV, 2, *infra*) ; Montaigne (*Apologie of Raymond Sebond*) ; William Gilbert (cf. Johnson, *Astron. Thought,* 216–217) ; and followers of Digges and Gilbert in England.

For that matter, the concept of a plurality of worlds was a logical *sequitur* to the Platonic concept of plenitude (see Lovejoy, *The Great Chain of Being,* Chapter IV) , and had been "officially" accepted, as a result of ecclesiastical pronouncement, in the fourteenth century (cf. Durand, "Trad. and Innov.," 12) ; but it was only with Bruno that this concept was fused with the Copernican cosmology.

Again, the telescope had just afforded (in 1610 and 1611) an added support to the idea of an infinite number of stars in an infinite universe. Samuel Purchas suggests the effect of Galileo's discoveries on this idea in a passage written in 1613 (quoted by Johnson, *Astron. Thought,* 259) , and we know how much interest Donne took in Galileo's findings.

However, the accumulation of evidence, the combination of different ways in which Donne's lines coincide with Bruno's doctrines, seems to me to constitute at least an impressive coincidence: "ant" and "man"; relativism and the "loss" of earth and sun; atomism, and the plurality of worlds. In this connection it is pertinent to consider Professor Johnson's arguments against the theory that Bruno had any great influence in England. He points out that Bruno met only a limited circle during his stay in England from 1583 to 1585; that his works on the infinite universe, while printed in England during that period, were in Italian, and that references in English books to his cosmological speculations do not appear for several years thereafter, and then are based on his Latin works printed abroad, rather than on the Italian ones; that he had arrived at his notions only through metaphysical speculations (Johnson, *ibid.,* 168) .

None of these arguments seems to me to preclude the possibility of a man of Donne's temper and background having been influenced by Bruno's ideas, and directly. Despite Professor Johnson's assertion that

It was Digges' treatise proclaiming the idea of an infinite universe in conjunction with the Copernican system, and not Bruno's speculations on the subject, that influenced the thought of sixteenth-century England *(ibid.)*,

it seems to me that "Bruno's speculations" would more effectively have fired the imagination of Donne, with his combination of devout and skeptical tendencies, than Digges' more sober account.

Moreover, in conclusion, I must admit that it seems of little importance to me whether there is any direct influence or not. My purpose in this section is not to prove that Donne read with care and interpreted with accuracy the thought of Bruno or Montaigne or Machiavelli. On the contrary, it is rather to show that the currents which these men very inclusively represented, had become so widespread that Donne's "anatomy of the world's condition" marks the culmination of an extensive and significant intellectual movement.

154. John Donne, *Ignatius his Conclave, or, His Inthronisation in a Late Election in Hell,* published for the Facsimile Text Society by the Columbia University Press (New York, 1941), 38.

CHAPTER 4

THE SCIENCE OF THE COUNTER–RENAISSANCE

I. MAGIC AND THE SECRETS OF NATURE

THE dissatisfaction of men like Agrippa and Montaigne with Scholastic science led them to positions of extreme skepticism about the existence of any ascertainable natural laws. But this is not to say that they denied the existence of these laws. They maintained rather that the knowledge of them was proper to God but not to man—that man could not, with his reason, attain to any considerable understanding of them.

This distinction is not simply a formal or dialectical one. The scientific and philosophical skepticism of the Counter-Renaissance was profoundly anti-intellectualistic. But it did not mean the complete loss of "that faith in the ultimate rationality of the universe" upon which "the very possibility of science is dependent. . . ."[1] Even Montaigne, the arch-heretic, makes the distinction between reason and human reason, in his version of Tertullian's *credo quia impossibile.* For he hopes

> to induce Christians to believe, when they chance to meet with any incredible thing, that it is so much the more according to reason, by how much more it is against human reason.[2]

Hence it is the impotence of man's intellect to find out the truths of nature which the leaders of the Counter-Renaissance proclaim, rather than the absence of any such truths. Hypothesis, logic, the syllogism, deductive reasoning—all the favorite instruments of Scholastic science—lead only to *the invention of an imaginary nature.* As a result, the "scientists" of the Counter-Renaissance seek other methods to the understanding of nature—methods for which the Scholastic tools are useless.

Two methods emerge as basic—those of magic and of "pure" empiricism. The first adopts a passive theory of knowledge in the interests of an aggressively individualistic motive; the second employs an aggressively active empiricism in the service of a humanitarian ideal. For the magicians seek to learn the *secrets* of nature largely through illumination, revelation and initiation into a body of ancient esoteric knowledge—while the radical empiricists of the Counter-Renaissance concentrate upon the investigation of the particular *facts* of nature. The first group, holding that nature is full of the *symbols* of God, believes that it may be understood only through esoteric lore and experiment, the formulas and equations and hieroglyphs of the Pythagoreans and the Cabala, alchemy and astrology—through the correct interpretation of a body of long-established secret knowledge. The second, holding equally that a synthetic knowledge of the *laws* of nature is impossible, is concerned with discovering particular natural facts which may be of practical utility.

Again, while both have *power* as their goal, they do not interpret "power" in the same way. The magicians, believing nature to be full of miracles and mysteries, hope to be able to learn how to control these by a proper manipulation of natural sympathies and antipathies, and thus to exercise an almost godlike individualistic power. The empiricists, believing nature to be full of things useful to the practical living of life, desire to make these available to mankind, for its greater comfort, health and prosperity. Both attitudes, it is obvious, are remote from the goal of medieval scientists—a knowledge of the truths of God—and from that of the orthodox Renaissance humanists, who (showing a greater interest in the arts and humanities than in natural science) found the value of all learning in its contribution to the virtuous life.

At first glance, the methods and goals of the magicians and the empiricists seem extremely different. Yet curiously enough, many of those practicing primarily in the tradition of one of these two groups also dabble in the other—or occupy an ambiguous position, partaking of each attitude, midway between the two. Paracelsus, Jerome Cardan and John Dee illustrate this ambiguity beautifully. Each seems half bombastic charlatan, half genuine scientist—at least to a twentieth-century observer.

However, the close relationship of the magic and the empiricism of the Counter-Renaissance is not so paradoxical as it superficially seems. In the first place, medieval empiricists like Roger Bacon and Albertus Magnus had never distinguished clearly between empirical science and the practical natural magic they endorsed, and one or another kind of experimentation is integral to various occult traditions. Moreover, Lynn Thorndike's assertion that "the sixteenth century in general was not an age of scientific specialization but marked by a somewhat amateurish literary interest," is *in general* true, and particularly of many of the Counter-Renaissance scientists.[3] Hence one should expect to find superstition and real scientific insight in the same men.

Moreover, the magicians and empiricists are at one on many points. Both groups are in revolt against the logician-physicists of Scholasticism; both are seeking anti-intellectualistic approaches to nature. Each endorses a "return to nature"—to use Francis Bacon's words, an "Interpretation" rather than an "Anticipation" of nature. Each, in a different sense, advocates a return to first principles— the one to an ancient body of revealed knowledge, the other to the direct observation of nature. Each is attempting a simplification of approach—the one in its reduction of the acquisition of knowledge to the learning of an established lore, the other in its reliance upon observation and the storing away of facts. Each takes part in the endorsement of the value of the humble peculiar to the Counter-Renaissance: the magicians in their protestations of humility as being merely God's chosen vessels of truth; the empiricists in their insistence upon the significance of the brute fact and their encouragement (and reception into their own number) of unlearned artisans; both in their refusal to consider *matter* as essentially undignified or bad. Finally, each group, interestingly enough, has certain affinities with the Reformation: the magicians in their emphasis upon faith and revelation, the empiricists in theirs upon a practical science, with utility as its goal.

Yet all these similarities of purpose point to an alliance, rather than to a complete identification; and it is possible in many individual cases to distinguish sharply between the practitioners of experimental magic and those of empirical science. The former, on the whole, live in a world which may best be called that of theosophy, since "theosophy shares theology's belief in the supernatural and philosophy's faith in nature";[4] the latter in the material world of a "neutralized" nature.

Again, both groups contribute to the decentralization process of the Counter-Renaissance: to its rejection of law and reason, and its nominalistic espousal of the particular rather than the universal —but in different ways. For the magician-scientists believe that science "rests upon an inner revelation, which is superior to sensible experience and reasoning"[5]—thus at least roughly approximating that part of Ockham's epistemology which affirms the power of intuitive *supra-sensible* knowledge to make direct contact with a particular reality.[6] On the other hand, the empiricist-scientists rest their knowledge solely upon observation and experiment, thereby endorsing Ockham's insistence upon the validity of intuitive *sensible* knowledge—"for experience brings us into contact with the singular. . . ."[7]

Hence each of these two groups, denying the validity of the abstract intellectual concept, and thus the place of reason in science, makes impossible the *study* of the *universal,* and so the understanding of the *laws* of nature. It is this common attitude which at once denies to both the status of true science, as we understand it today, and makes of them two further and allied phenomena in the decentralizing course of the Counter-Renaissance. But a clear understanding of the differences, similarities, and even overlappings of the two groups will be facilitated by an examination of their particular representatives. . . .

The occult traditions of the Counter-Renaissance are highly eclectic. Mystical Pythagoreanism, astrology, alchemy, and Neoplatonic, Cabalistic and Hermetic love meet and mingle in the doctrines of many individual figures. Yet there is a surprising unity in the outlooks, the methods, the definitions and the avowed purposes of these various esoteric factions, and for the purposes of this chapter their detailed doctrinal differences may be largely ignored.

At any rate, this unity of outlook and method results in a general conviction that magic which, according to Agrippa, constitutes "the whole knowledge of nature, the perfection of all true philosophy,"[8] is composed of three realms: Divine Magic, dealing with "the mysteries of God," which is the chief domain of the Cabala; Celestial Magic,[9] dealing with the celestial bodies and their influence upon the sublunary world, hence the concern of astrology and the Pythagorean science of numbers; and Natural Magic, dealing with the hidden virtues of natural objects, which is therefore the province of alchemy, magical medicine, and that "philosophy of nature" which treats the symbolic significances of sublunary phenomena.

THE THREE WORLDS OF THE CABALA
OR
THE THREE KINDS OF MAGIC

1. *INTELLECTUAL* or *THEOLOGICAL WORLD* or *DIVINE MAGIC*	2. *CELESTIAL* or *MATHEMATICAL WORLD*	3. *NATURAL* or *ELEMENTAL WORLD* or *NATURAL MAGIC*
deals with "the mysteries of God." Includes: Ceremonial matters, necromancy, divination, sacred names, the "spiritual" lore: heroes, demons, demi-gods.	deals with "the quantity of bodies in their three dimensions, and the motion of celestial bodies," and the "influences of the stars into these lower elements." Includes: Some kinds of astrology; the science of numbers and letters; "astronomy"; arithmetic.	deals with "the occult virtues in natural objects" and "the transmutation of metals." Includes: Natural magic, or "the philosophy of nature"; alchemy.
Chief sources:		*Chief sources:*
The higher mysteries of the Cabala and the Orphic-Pythagorean-Neoplatonic line of "a certain devout philosophy," including the Hermetic *corpus*.	*Chief sources:* The Pythagorean-Neoplatonic mathematics and some branches of the Calaba and eclectic astrology (including Hermes)	The "ancient wisdom" of Zoroaster, etc. and the Hermetic *corpus* and Albertus, Bacon, Lully and the alchemical tradition.

If this diagram is compared with one which a student of Pico has recently made of the Florentine's cosmology, as exemplified in the *Heptaplus,* it becomes evident to what extent esoteric dogma could penetrate—or, at least, did parallel—Renaissance "Christian" expositions of *Genesis* (see Chapter VIII, 4, *supra*):

PICO, *HEPTAPLUS*	*THE ECLECTIC INITIATE TRADITIONS*
GOD INTELLIGENCE HEAVENS .... ELEMENTS	INTELLECTUAL OR THEOLOGICAL WORLD-- DIVINE MAGIC CELESTIAL OR MATHEMATICAL WORLD NATURAL OR ELEMENTAL WORLD—NATURAL MAGIC
MAN, as microcosm, is parallel to whole macrocosm.	A favorite esoteric concept.[10]

There are, to be sure, quite definite medieval influences perceptible in the occultism and magic of the Counter-Renaissance.

Cusanus' Pythagorizing interests, Lully's "Ars Magna," and the more practical and empirical natural magic of Roger Bacon and Albertus Magnus were all familiar to the sixteenth-century magicians. Yet Denis Saurat points out that, to the Renaissance, occultism meant chiefly the Cabala and Hermetic books;[11] and unquestionably the publication of the *Zohar* (1559-60), with the research Pico and Reuchlin expended upon it, and Ficino's new Latin translation of Hermes' *Asclepius* (1469) and *Pimander* (1471), accelerated a general interest in these esoteric traditions. Moreover, the Neoplatonic revival centering in the Florentine Academy had an extensive influence upon the course of sixteenth-century occultism.

For Neoplatonism had frequently tended to esotericism and eclecticism. The Syrian Neoplatonism of Iamblichus and Proclus (fourth and fifth centuries A.D.) was strongly mystical, drawing its inspiration from Pythagoras, the religious mysteries of the Orient and Egypt, and other initiate traditions, as well as from Plato and Plotinus. Indeed, to Proclus the practice of magic was the essence of religion.[12] And these tendencies had marked the course of Neoplatonism ever since. To mention only a few of the barnacles which adhered to it through the centuries (some almost from its inception)—it had come to have definite associations with Orphic theology, with Neopythagoreanism, and with the Cabala.[13]

Many of these interests are apparent in Ficino's "certain devout philosophy," although they do not dominate his thought. But with Pico, we come to a veritable renascence of magic and esotericism. We have already observed how, in his office of reconciler of theology and philosophy, he contributed to the effort of the Renaissance Christian humanists to balance reason and faith. But Pico is not to be confined to a single tradition—or, rather, in his conviction that there is but *a single tradition of truth,* he necessarily will appear in a study of various, even (to others) conflicting traditions. And his attitude toward philosophic truth establishes that of succeeding Renaissance magician-scientists:

> For Pico, the criterion of philosophic truth consists in its constancy, in its uniformity and sameness. He understands philosophy as *philosophia perennis*—as *the revelation of an enduring Truth, in its main features immutable. . . . He is convinced that what is true requires no "discovery," no finding out through any personal inquiry of the individual; rather has it existed from time immemorial.*[14] What is characteristic for Pico is hence not the way in which he *increased* the store of philosophic truth, but the way in which he made it manifest.[15]

Ernest Cassirer not long ago advanced the thesis that Pico's most distinctive category of thought is that of symbolic thought. He saw Pico, although primarily a speculative thinker, as coming more and more—under the growing influence of mysticism—to believe "that our thinking and conceiving, in so far as it is directed toward the Divine, can never be an adequate expression, but only an image and metaphor."[16] Thus Pico affirms that "the deepest secrets of Being can be treated in the language of numbers and figures—"[17] which amounts to an endorsement of the Cabalistic approach to Divine and to Celestial Magic.[18]

For by "numbers" he does not mean scientific mathematics and astronomy; he does not believe that there is any road leading "to a scientific mathematics and to an exact knowledge of nature."[19] On the contrary, he asserts outright, "Nihil magis nocivum theologo quam frequens et assidua in mathematicis Euclidis exercitatio."[20] The only kind of mathematics which he recognizes with approval is the sort also to be found in Reuchlin's *De arte cabalistica* and *De verbo mirifico*—magical mathematics.[21]

Pico displays a similar enthusiasm for Natural Magic—not, to be sure, the alchemical version of Paracelsus, but a "natural philosophy" which treats of the hidden virtues of natural objects as the symbols of God. Thus he tends to deviate from the most usual Neoplatonic solutions, from Plotinus down, of the problem of "the Many and the One"—of the emanating God and the transcendent God.[22] Professor Cassirer explains,

> Pico is no longer trying to exhibit the Many as the *effect* of the One, or to deduce them as such from their cause, with the aid of rational concepts. He sees the Many rather as *expressions*, as *images*, as *symbols* of the One.[23]

In Pico's own highly figurative language:

> Then Bacchus, leader of the Muses, showing forth to us philosophers in his mysteries, that is in the visible symbols of nature, the invisible things of God, shall satisfy us from the abundance of the house of God, in all of which we shall, like Moses, be found faithful.[24]

Clearly, then, Pico desires to compass the *secrets* and *mysteries* of nature. Magic abounds, he declares in his oration *Of the Dignity of Man*,

> in the loftiest mysteries, embraces the deepest contemplation of the most secret things, and at last the affinity of all nature.[25]

The glory is God's and nature's; the magician does not exhibit the power of his own mind so much as he reveals the miracles which God has sown in nature. For magic,

> in calling forth into the light as if from their hiding-places the powers scattered and sown in the world by the loving kindness of God, does not so much work wonders as diligently serve a wonder-working nature. . . . [It,] making use of the suitable and peculiar inducements . . . for *each single thing,*[26] brings forth into the open the miracles concealed in the recesses of the world, in the depths of nature, and in the storehouses and mysteries of God, just as if nature herself were their maker; and, as the farmer weds his elms to vines, even so does the *magus* wed earth and heaven, that is, he weds lower things to the endowments of higher things.[27]

Pico is here referring to the Neoplatonic principle of magic

> that the world is a hierarchy of divine forces, a system of agencies forming an ascending and descending scale, in which the higher agencies command and the lower ones obey.[28]

Pico, to be sure, does not inform us why the magus should want to "wed earth to heaven," except with the safe and pious explanation that

> nothing moves one to religion and to the worship of God more than the diligent contemplation of the wonders of God; if we thoroughly examine them by this natural magic which is my subject, we shall be compelled to sing, more ardently inspired to the worship and love of the Creator: "The heaven and all the earth are full of the majesty of thy glory."[29]

Yet he hastens to add, "And this is enough about magic"—quite appropriately, for surely the desire of the magician to be united with the "higher agencies" whom "the lower ones obey" is motivated by his hope "to govern nature and to change it according to his wishes."[30]

There was no doubt in Pico's nephew's mind that his uncle's motive was not simply "The worship and love of the Creator":

> Ful of pryde & desirous of glorie and mannes praise (for yet was he not kindled in the love of god) he went to Rome, and there (covetinge to make a show of his conning, and litel considering how great envie he should raise against himself) ix.C. questions he purposed, of diverse and sondry maters: as well in logike and Philosophie as divinitee, with great studie piked and sought out, as wel of the Laten auctours as the grekes: and partly set out of the secret misteries of the Hebrewes, Caldees & Arabies: and many things drawen out of

the olde obscure Philosophie of Pythagoras, Trismegistus, and
Orpheus, & many other thynges strange: and to all folks (except right few speciall excellent men) before that day: not
unknowen only: but also unherd.[31]

Nor did his propositions meet with much favor from the Church. . . .[32]

Finally, Pico, with his overt statement that his *Magica Theoremata* include an interpretation of the "mysterious poems of Orpheus," and his contention that Pythagoras had founded his secret
doctrine of numbers upon the model of Orphic theology,[33] could
hardly have been unaware that "the aim of Orphism and the mysteries [was] to make gods" of men.[34]

Thus we find illustrated in Pico all the basic characteristics of
the magician-scientist of the Counter-Renaissance: his concern with
the secrets or mysteries of nature; his emphasis upon the roles of
revelation and initiation and interpretation in the process, rather
than upon "personal inquiry"; and despite his denial of the importance of his own intellectual contribution (Pico explains, "I
have wished to give assurance by this contest of mine, not so much
that I know a great deal, as that I know things of which many are
ignorant"[35]), the individualistic goal of power and glory.

To be sure, this last question is wrapped up in the larger one of
the distinction between "lawful" and "black" magic. Pico makes a
particular and redundant point of emphasizing this difference, declaring that

> Magic has two forms, one of which depends entirely on the
> work and authority of devils, a thing to be abhorred, so help
> me the God of truth, and a monstrous thing. The other, when
> it is rightly pursued, is nothing else than the utter perfection
> of natural philosophy. . . . The former is the most deceitful
> of arts, the latter is a higher and more holy philosophy. The
> former is vain and empty, the latter, sure, trustworthy, and
> sound.[36]

And we have no reason, on the face of his performance, to doubt
his sincerity. Yet similar protestations are forthcoming from Paracelsus, Agrippa, John Dee, and all those other fascinating figures
of the sixteenth century who are constantly embroiled in controversies over their practice of the "black art," often fleeing from the
authorities and an outraged population, frequently accused of being
in league with Satan—and consistently protesting their innocence.

The whole somewhat complicated problem narrows down to
these alternatives: the practitioner of "lawful" magic is celebrating
the majesty of God through "the diligent contemplation of the

wonders of God"; while the "black" magician, sold "to the enemies of God," turns his back on God[37] and exercises his art in pursuit of personal power. Yet for individual cases, the problem remains unresolved. Who is to judge of the legality of the practices of a particular magician? Everyone, and therefore no one.

Consider Paracelsus. He rejects the "philosophical wisdom of the Greeks as being *a mere speculation,* utterly distinct and separate from other true arts and sciences."[38] He attacks Thomas Aquinas —with charges of blasphemy (*sic*) against the "secret fire of the philosophers"[39]—and all the rest who ignore the inner light "that is much superior to bestial reason."[40]

> For man is assuredly born in ignorance, so that he cannot know or understand anything of himself, but only that which he receives from God, and understands from Nature.[41]

But he himself has been chosen by God for a vessel of revelation:

> From the middle of this age the Monarchy of all the Arts has been at length derived and conferred on me, Theophrastus Paracelsus, Prince of Philosophy and of Medicine. For this purpose I have been chosen by God to extinguish and blot out all the phantasies of elaborate and false works, of delusive and presumptuous words, be they the words of Aristotle, Galen, Avicenna, Mesva, or the dogmas of any among their followers.[42]

"Not," he goes on shortly thereafter, with the "humility" of the magical tradition,

> that I praise myself: Nature praises me. Of her I am born; her I follow. She knows me, and I know her. The light which is in her I have beheld in her.[43]

Yet this man, this self-acknowledged chosen of God and of Nature, is the "devil's disciple" to the majority of his age. And whomever he worships, he is obviously drunk with the sense of power.

However, from Raymond Lully down, the occult philosophers and magical scientists had all cherished the legend of the "Philosopher's Stone"—had envisioned the discovery of a single formula which would "reduce man's search for knowledge to a principle of unity leading to mastery of Nature."[44] It is thus unquestionably a dream of power which motivates them. And this dream finds frequent expression like the following words of Trithemius, Agrippa's teacher and friend:

> Study generates knowledge; knowledge bears love; love, likeness; likeness, communion; communion, virtue; virtue, dignity;

dignity, power; and *power performs the miracle. This is the unique path to the goal of magic perception, divine as well as natural. . . .*[45]

Beyond this we cannot go. For it is only in a play or a story that a man permits the naïve lay world to see with what forces he is trafficking. Yet it is certainly pertinent that Marlowe's Doctor Faustus, who dips his pen into his own blood to assure us that he is really in league with Lucifer, and who travels the world with Mephistopheles, is a true son of the magician-scientists of the Counter-Renaissance. He endorses and utilizes their methods and their materials, and his imagination is fired by the same vision of godlike power. Finally, if one may believe current rumor that Marlowe's association with Ralegh, Northumberland and Hariot would give him an opportunity to watch magic and occult practices at first hand, here is important testimony to the uniformity of the magic and occultism practiced by the "seers" of the Counter-Renaissance, with that of black magic.

Faustus reveals the new spirit of the Counter-Renaissance at the outset of Marlowe's play, in his rejection of each of the Scholastic studies. He pins upon "Logicke" the definition given it by Peter Ramus, in defiance of Aristotle: "Bene disserere est finis logices."[46] He associates medicine with alchemy.[47] He employs the new belittling techniques of the scientific and legalistic skeptics to

> . . . the institute
> And universall body of the law. . . .[48]

And he sardonically applies the Reformation's doctrine of original sin and predestination to the medieval "the wages of sin is death," to argue a fatalistic necessity for universal sin and everlasting death.[49]

Thus, he depreciates the major disciplines of the Scholastic learning through the agency of those new forces of the Counter-Renaissance which were weakening and disrupting each: Aristotle's logic, through Ramus'; Galen's medicine, through Paracelsus'; Justinian's *Institutes* through arguments like those of Agrippa; theology ("Divinitie" and "Jerome's Bible") through Calvinism. In other words, Faustus establishes himself as a child of the Counter-Renaissance before he ever mentions the word "magic."

But " 'tis Magicke, Magicke that hath ravisht" him;[50] he has already made it clear that he has the magician's itch. After reviewing "Logicke," he demands

> Affoords this Art *no greater myracle?*[51]

He turns to medicine with the exultant injunction to himself,

> Be a physitian *Faustus, heape up golde,*
> And be eternizde for *some wondrous cure.*[52]

And after professing contempt for the traditional "end of physicke" as "our bodies health," he asks,

> Wouldst thou make man to live eternally?
> Or being dead, raise them to life againe?[53]

(both dreams of the alchemical physicians in connection with their search for the Philosopher's Stone), and concludes

> *Then* this profession were to be esteemed.[54]

The law he finds "too servile and illiberall for me";[55] divinity he rejects because of its denial of free will.[56]

What he wants is a knowledge of the mysteries, secrets and miracles of "nature's treasury,"[57] and he wants it for the power it will give him. "Yet art thou still but *Faustus,* and a man," he cries after reviewing his past exploits as a physician.[58] It is magic alone that can provide this godlike power, and he finds that

> These Metaphysickes of Magicians,
> And Negromanticke bookes are heavenly:
> Lines, circles, sceanes, letters and characters. . . .[59]

He exclaims,

> O what a world of profit and delight,
> Of power, of honor, of omnipotence
> Is promised to the studious Artizan?[60]

and is jubilantly convinced that

> his dominion that exceedes in this,
> Stretcheth as farre as doth the minde of man.
> A sound Magician is a mighty god:
> Heere *Faustus* trie thy braines to gain a deitie.[61]

These last lines do not imply that he expects to master the "science" of magic through his own intellectual efforts. Instead (and observe the use of "*sound* magician") they refer to the work involved in learning the revealed body of knowledge. Moreover, the very next lines indicate that he is aware of the need of an interpreter to guide him to an understanding of this body of revealed truth. Sending Wagner for Valdes and Cornelius, he tells himself,

> Their conference will be a greater help to me,
> Than all my labours, plodde I nere so fast.[62]

With the arrival of Valdes and Cornelius, he announces that he

> Will be as cunning as *Agrippa* was,
> Whose shadows made *all Europe* honor him.[63]

And the ensuing conversation follows the traditional lines of the magic of the Counter-Renaissance. Valdes declares,

> *Faustus,*
> These bookes, thy wit and our experience
> Shall make all nations to canonize us,
> As Indian Moores obey their Spanish lords,
> *So shall the subjects of every element*
> *Be alwaies serviceable to us three.*[64]

Cornelius outlines the needs of the magician:

> He that is grounded in Astrologie,
> Inricht with tongues, well seene in minerals,
> Hath all the principles Magicke doth require,[65]

and these three requirements—astrology; the use of languages, to read the Cabalistic and other occult literature, and to understand and pronounce "sacred names"; and alchemy—correspond very neatly to the generally approved three realms of magic: the Celestial, Divine and Natural, respectively.

But Faustus himself later gives an even more exact rendition of the three worlds of the Cabala, or the three divisions of magic, when he asks Mephistopheles for three books: first, one

> Wherein I might beholde al spels and incantations, that I might raise up spirits when I please;

secondly, one containing

> al characters and planets of the heavens, that I might know their motions and dispositions;   .

and thirdly, one

> wherin I might see al plants, hearbes and trees that grow upon the earth.[66]

These three correspond with scholarly exactitude to the three worlds of the Cabala and the three kinds of magic. . . .

The conversation with Valdes and Cornelius contains other references and allusions which are related to a consideration of the magical science of the Counter-Renaissance. Faustus is eager to behold "some demonstrations magicall," and Valdes requests him to bring

> wise Bacons and Albanus workes,
> The Hebrew Psalter, and new Testament. . . .[67]

This combination of the Jewish and Christian Cabala with the practical natural magic of Roger Bacon and Albertus Magnus,[68] as requisites for the practice of what we soon discover to be black magic,[69] suggest that, to Marlowe, there is no real distinction between "legitimate" and "illegitimate" magic.

Finally, Cornelius states,

> *Valdes*, first let him know the words of art,
> And then all other ceremonies learnd,
> *Faustus* may trie his cunning by himselfe,[70]

thereby asserting plainly once more the dependence of the "cunning" of the magician upon the set procedure of a revealed body of knowledge.

There are other passages in the play which suggest further similarities between Faustus' experience with magic and the professional accounts of the sixteenth century,[71] but those quoted should suffice to establish the relation beyond doubt. Like the magician-scientists of the Counter-Renaissance, Faustus seeks to investigate the secrets and mysteries of nature, which are contained in the threefold world of the Cabala; like them, he practices a magic which is a revealed body of knowledge, and to which he is introduced by "masters" or initiate interpreter-guides; like them, he seeks to control Nature and plans to change its course[72] through a union with its "higher agencies."

And so, like them, his dream is one of unlimited power. The discrepancy between his aspirations and the actual use he makes of his magical skill has often been noted. That a man with the intoxicating vision of extending his sway "as farre" as "the minde of man" might reach, and even to the condition of a "deitie," should entertain himself with the horseplay of the scenes with the Pope, the antlered Knight, and the Horse-courser, and with the stage manipulator's tricks of producing Alexander and his paramour, or a "dish of ripe grapes" in winter, is indeed ridiculous. But even a casual student of Marlowe knows that these incongruities run everywhere through the ore of his rich and extravagant but often naïve genius. *Faustus* is no exception; here, as elsewhere, most of the meaty passages which show his awareness of the intellectual currents of his time are packed into the early part of the play; it is as though he wearies of the ideas he is treating after an enthusiastic beginning, and usually he regains his intellectual and æsthetic interest and power only near the end of the play. In *Doctor Faustus* the serious interest in magic drops off sharply after the first six hundred lines; indeed, most of it is crowded into the first two hundred. But as long as Marlowe is actually concerned with this aspect of his subject, the play provides the most vivid imaginative treatment of the whole field in the literature of the sixteenth century —a treatment, moreover, as authentically faithful as it is lively.

2. EMPIRICISM AND THE FACTS OF NATURE: THE HAND-IN-THE-WOUND SCHOOL

The word "experience" is almost as popular in the sixteenth century as "reason" in the eighteenth. It is, of course, frequently used in its loosest, most general sense—the sense in which every individual in every country in every age has employed it: as a talisman to vindicate the infallibility of his own judgment. Both in this sense, and in one at least claiming a more scientific significance, the Middle Ages had also invoked "experience." But Scholastic science had radically subordinated sense perception to intellectual cognition as an agency of knowledge, and it is with a new enthusiasm and reverence (if not with a new vocabulary) that the "scientists" of the Counter-Renaissance refer to experience as "the mother of all wisdom" and "mistress of all things."

Such references are frequent among the proponents of natural magic and alchemy. Paracelsus gives characteristic expression to this vogue:

> And let no one wonder at the school of our learning. Though it be contrary to the courses and methods of the ancients, still it is firmly based on experience, which is mistress of all things, and by which all arts should be proved.[73]

But other passages in his writings make it clear that experience, or experimentation, usually means for him the alchemists' "test by fire," through which alone one attains to ultimate certainty.

> For every person may and ought to believe in another only in those matters which he has tried by fire. If anyone shall have brought forward anything contrary to this method of experimentation in the Spagyric Art or in Medicine, there is no reason for your belief in him, since, experimentally, through the agency of fire, the true is separated from the false.[74]

Yet at times he also proudly proclaims his independence of "ancient" practitioners of alchemy and natural magic. His "new operations" may "differ from the writings of ancient operators and natural philosophers, but [they] have been discovered and confirmed by full proof and experimentation."[75] Thus we find him straddling the line between the revealed science of magic and the experimental science of the empiricists of the Counter-Renaissance.

Nor is this, if one accepts any of his basic premises, really an inconsistent position. For both the "renovators" of natural science (the magicians who turned to occult means of bringing to light the virtues hidden in nature, and particularly the alchemists who dreamed of renovating and restoring to nature her pristine vigor, lost since the Fall) and the "innovators" (the empiricists who demanded the right to investigate "brute fact" for themselves) were primarily rebelling against the Scholastics' attempt to deal with nature by means of reason and logic. Not only were they allies; frequently one man belonged to both groups.

Hence, in one passage Paracelsus may berate "God's privy counsellors" and turn to the occult route to the knowledge of nature as the only corrective for their pride:

> Nor do we care for the vain talk of those who say more about God than he has revealed to them, and pretend to understand Him so thoroughly as if they had been in his counsels. . . . Yet we, by custom imitating them, easily learn, together with them, to bend the word of our Teacher and Creator to our own pride. But since this word is not exactly known to us, can only be apprehended by faith, and is founded on no human reason, however specious, let us rather cast off this yoke, and investigate the mysteries of Nature, the end whereof approves the foundation of truth. . . .[76]

In another, he may assume an exclusively practical tone and speak only in terms of "proof," "demonstration" and "experiment."

Nor should we forget that in the latter role he is not simply indulging in rhetoric. For it was his followers who gave the main impetus to the pursuit of iatro-(*i.e.*, medicinal) chemistry.[77] Galenic medicine, against which the Paracelsan Revival constituted a protest and rebellion, had become more and more preoccupied with translations and textual criticisms of the ancient Greek medical writers;[78] and many contemporaries who suspected Paracelsus himself of charlatanism endorsed his "experimentall medicine" as a healthy antidote to so exclusive an emphasis upon theory and authority.

Thus "R. B.," writing in 1585, defends "Paracelsical Phisicke" without approving of Paracelsus himself—by the simple (and largely just) expedient of pointing out that it is much older than its alleged founder. He goes on to appeal to various touchstones—"Gods worde, experience and nature"—which the Counter-Renaissance opposes to the Scholastic confidence in reason, logic and authority; and his language has the naïve vigor of sixteenth-century invective:

> As long as *Scotus* or *Thomas Aquinas,* and such other were so priviledged in the scholes, that no interpretation of Gods worde was allowed, but such as was brought out of them, or agreed with them, the cause of true Religion, and serving of God was in a desperate state, and it lay oppressed and hidden. And as long as those that noseled in such puddle, were mainteyned, defended and priviledged by princes and potentates, it was hard for truth to shewe his face abroade openly. Wheerefore if the Chymicall doctrine agreeing with Gods worde, experience and nature may come into the Schooles and Cities insteade of *Aristotle, Galen,* and other heathen and their followers. And if it were lawful and commendable [for] every honest student to labour in the Philosophicall searching out of the truth . . . then should there be no time spent in vayne, and vaine glorious bable and sophisticall disputations, without due triall by labor and worke of fire, and other requisite experiments, then should it be easily seen . . . whose writings and travailes were most available for mans health. . . .[79]

Paracelsus is but one of many, however, who may be found in either of the two new scientific camps. Jerome Cardan, the Italian physician who so modestly declared that "Among natural prodigies the first and greatest is that I was born in this age,"[80] is similar to Paracelsus in this respect. In his *Autobiography* he insists that he has "reduced the observation of things in Nature to a definite art and method, which, before him, had been attempted by no one." History, however, as Professor Höffding dryly remarks, has not confirmed this judgment.[81] To be sure, Cardan's *De Subtilitate* is full of sober empirical statements such as

> There are those whom I must avoid, as, for example, Pliny and Albertus Magnus, who cannot be trusted in this field because they clearly misrepresent the facts. . . . I have no one to follow. And yet if I do not investigate everything to the last detail, I shall waste, as the saying goes, my labor and toil . . .[82]

and

> What shall I say regarding causes? I must bring them to light, but as yet no one has touched them. It is just as if they had been received from some sort of an oracle. But to oracles cre-

dence was given without proof, while to me, if I do not furnish proof, no credence will be given. . . .[83]

And some of the diagrams and explanations of his experiments in this book suggest that he is justified in his final satisfaction: "So many, then, and so strong are the proofs in this treatise."[84]

Yet in this same book one also finds a strange and chaotic mixture of superstition and fantastic claims—for magic and for the "scientific" authenticity of dreams. Throughout his works, a weakness for palmistry, portents, natural magic and astrology is mingled with shrewd insight, a genuinely naturalistic empiricism, and a hard-headed determinism. He is truly a child of his age—this man who dismissed Leonardo da Vinci's scientific pretensions with the laconic comment, "Leonardo da Vinci also attempted to fly, but he was not successful: he was an excellent painter."[85]

A child of his age—for this paradoxical combination of attitudes is displayed over and over again by sixteenth-century scientists, making any just and inclusive estimate of their work extremely difficult. So able a scholar as Francis Johnson, for instance, has been both misled and misleading in his treatment of John Dee in his *Astronomical Thought in Renaissance England*. Professor Johnson, aroused by the tendency to emphasize Dee's

> reputation as an astrologer, alchemist and dabbler in spiritualism, at the expense of his significant work in legitimate science . . .[86]

dismisses Dee's magical interest:

> Dee's later career, during which his unrestrained optimism concerning the possibilities of natural science made him the dupe of the charlatan Edward Kelley and caused him to turn his energies to alchemy and crystal gazing . . .[87]

and concentrates, in accordance with the subject of his book, upon

> Dee's great significance in English science . . . as teacher, adviser, and friend to most of the English mathematicians, astronomers, and geographers of his day.[88]

There can be no doubt that Professor Johnson brings a balance which has been needed to the study of Dee, and that the latter's influence on the course of astronomical learning in England has gone almost unappreciated. A list of his devoted pupils, including Thomas Digges, "the first modern astronomer of note to portray an infinite, heliocentric universe, with the stars scattered at varying distances throughout infinite space,"[89] is almost sufficient proof in itself.

But Professor Johnson claims for Dee's preface to Henry Billingsley's translation of Euclid, the setting forth of "experimental science, as we understand the term" under "the name of 'Archemastrie' . . ." and further maintains that "his explanation of this term . . . shows his clear realization of the interdependence of all the sciences. . . ."[90] He then quotes the passage in question, pointing out in conclusion that "by 'experience,' Dee means both observation and experiments in the modern sense."[91]

Actually, the passage deals chiefly with the *Scientia Experimentalis* of the Neoplatonic *magus,* and with Pythagorean magical mathematics, rather than with "experimental science, as we understand the term." The very name which Dee uses, "Archemastrie," gives him away. And he begins,

> This Arte, teacheth to bryng to actuall experience sensible *all worthy conclusions by all the Artes Mathematicall purposed, & by true Naturall Philosophie concluded: & both addeth to them a farder scope,* in the terms of the same Artes, *& also by hys proper Method, and in peculiar terms,* proceedeth, with helpe of the foresayd Artes, *to the performance of complet Experiences, which of no particular Art, are liable (Formally) to be challenged. . . .* And by cause it procedeth by Experiences, and searcheth forth the causes of Conclusions by Experiences: and also putteth the Conclusions them selves, in Experience, it is named of some, *Scientia Experimentalis. The Experimentall Science.*[92]

That is, "Archemastrie" is the secret experimental method which adds a "farther scope" to "all mathematical arts" and to "true natural philosophy" (the favorite distinction of the magician-scientists; Dee in the same passage discusses the limitations of ordinary natural philosophy: see below), and more—by its "proper method," and in "peculiar terms," employs these arts *"to the performance of complet Experiences,"* which cannot be attained for any "particular Art." It is, in short, the universally applicable method which was always the goal and sometimes the proud claim of the initiate traditions: it is *"The* Experimentall Science."

And in his very next sentence Dee (who elsewhere in his preface, as Professor Johnson notes,[93] quotes the Neopythagorean explanation of Number as the original pattern in God's mind of all things in nature;[94] makes the usual threefold division of the world according to the cabalists and magicians;[95] and refers to Pico della Miran-

dola in connection with Neoplatonic mathematics[96]) explains that
this is the name which Nicholas Cusanus gave to it in his *"Experiments Statikall,"* and lauds Roger Bacon, who "did write thereof
largely. . . ."[97] Thus he identifies his "Archemastrie" on the one
hand with a treatise which "attempts to reduce a wide variety of
scientific or pseudo-scientific 'experiments' to a simple technique of
weighing,"[98] and on the other with the work of the leading medieval
exponent of experimental natural magic.[99]

Moreover, he contrasts, in the usual manner of the Counter-
Renaissance, the proof of "this Arte," which lies in "Experience
complete and absolute," with the "persuasion" of "other Artes, with
Argumentes and demonstrations." He emphasizes, in regular Counter-Renaissance accents, the point that "wordes, and Argumentes
are no sensible certifying: nor the full and finall frute of Sciences
practisable." And he concludes, clearly indicating—with his reference to "the Astronomer, and the Opticall Mechanicien"—that he
is *not* here referring to experimental science in the modern sense:

> And though some Artes, have in them, Experiences, yet they
> are not complete, and brought to the uttermost they may be
> stretched unto, and applyed sensibly. As for example: the
> Naturall Philosopher disputeth and maketh goodly shew of
> reason: And *the Astronomer, and the Opticall Mechanicien,
> put some thynges in Experience:* but neither, all, that they
> may: nor yet sufficiently, and to the utmost, those, which they
> do. There, then, the Archemaster steppeth in, and *leadeth forth
> on,* the Experiences, *by order of his doctrine Experimentall,*
> to the chief and finall *power* of Naturall and Mathematicall
> Artes.[100]

A comparison of this passage with those of Pico and Paracelsus
quoted above reveals the same temper and approach. "By order of
his doctrine Experimentall," the "Archemaster" is enabled to lead
"forth on," or reveal, that which is in nature, and thus to make
apparent the full "power" of the "Naturall and Mathematicall Artes."
I can find nothing in the passage which indicates that Dee is here
talking a purely scientific language, any more than Walter Ralegh
is when he describes

> The third kind of magic [which] containeth the whole phi-
> losophy of nature; not the brabblings of the Aristotelians, but
> that which bringeth to light the inmost virtues, and draweth
> them out of nature's hidden bosom to human use . . .[101]

or Robert Recorde, Dee's predecessor "as the guiding spirit of the

English school of mathematicians,"[102] in his preface to the *Whetstone of Witte:*

> This nomber also hath other prerogatives, *above all naturalle thynges,* for neither is there certaintie in any thyng without it, nor other good agremente where it wanteth. Whereof no man can doubte, that hath been accustomed in the Bookes of Plato, Aristotell, and other aunciente Philosophers, where he shall see, *how thei searche all secrete knowledge and hid misteries, by the aide of nomber. For not onely the constitution of the whole worlde, dooe thei referre to nomber, but also the composition of manne, yea and the verie substance of the soule.* . . . It is confessed emongste all men, that knowe what learnyng meaneth, that *besides the Mathematicalle artes, there is no unfallible knowledge, excepte it bee borrowed of them.*[103]

Even Thomas Digges, true scientific empiricist though he was, did not escape the occult Neoplatonic tradition. He inserts in the text of his translation of Copernicus' *De revolutionibus* a paragraph of his own, in which he echoes Pico's "the visible symbol of nature, the invisible things of God," declaring that God's

> unsearchable worcks invisible we may partly by these his visible coniecture;

he admits it is only "with *Geometricall eyes*" that one may

> beehoulde the secret perfection of *Copernicus Theoricke,*

which is

> auncient doctrine revived, and by *Copernicus* so demonstratively approved.[104]

This analysis of the occult element in the thought of these English astronomers is not intended to belittle their truly scientific achievements, which include Recorde's textbooks in the vernacular, Dee's teaching and general influence, and Digges's observational work and coupling of the idea of infinity with Copernicanism. Rather, it further serves to illustrate how men of considerable scientific and intellectual stature combine their study of Euclidean with that of mystical Pythagorean mathematics; their truly scientific empiricism with an occult variety, dependent upon received, "secret" and "auncient doctrine."

One final example must suffice—that of Jean Bodin. For he is truly master of a measured empiricism which he applies with conspicuously scientific results to history, to politics, to economics,[105] and to nature. Moreover, a powerful, if frequently confused thinker, he was not simply a "loose" empiricist of the sort Francis Bacon condemned; his work in historical method proves this conclusively. As early as 1560 to 1561, Bodin had in mind a plan for a "synthetic philosophy of the universe," which he finally expounded in *Le Théâtre de la Nature Universelle,* published some thirty-five years later.[106]

Yet this very book is almost as strange a combination of disparate elements as the work of Cardan. It illustrates Bodin's predilection for solid fact, for original thought, and for a careful induction which collects hundreds of examples before coming to a conclusion. It also demonstrates his apparently equal enthusiasm for eclectic Neoplatonism, for astrology and the Pythagorean science of numbers, and for the world of spirits which natural magic explores.

He goes even farther in his *Démonomanie des Sorciers,* where he reduces the "argument from experience" to absurdity:

> As a magistrate, he had conducted trials, and knew the facts, which had been judicially proved! He would stand by the decisions of tribunals, which condemned witch or sorcerer upon the facts![107]

Bodin, in a fashion similar to that of the English astronomers, stands

> à mi-chemin entre la mysticisme hérité de ses devanciers, et la méthode scientifique et expérimentale qu'il légua, surtout dans le domaine politique, à ses successeurs.[108]

Yet at the same time the Counter-Renaissance produced in the sixteenth century a group of men who were for the most part "pure" empiricists—who, if they were "tainted" with natural magic or astrology or one of various contemporary mystical or occult influences, nevertheless followed with considerable fidelity, in some one department of knowledge, the pragmatic path of naturalistic empiricism. This group notably includes Vives and Telesio in natural science; Vesalius in anatomy; Machiavelli and Guicciardini in history and political theory; Bodin (with reservations) and Le Roy in historical method and social, political and economic theory; and Montaigne here, there and everywhere, but especially in the study of man, his constitution and his motives.

In addition to the work of this basic group, other factors contributed to the widespread appeal to experience, which eventually culminated in the observational aspects of the new astronomy, the empirical science of William Gilbert, and the inductive method of Francis Bacon. Among these factors were the nominalistic and philosophical skepticism about intellectual science and philosophy; the experimental portions of the occult philosophies of men like Paracelsus, Cardan and Dee; the fideistic movement, which belittled the efficacy of reason in finding out truth, and encouraged the practical and utilitarian ethics and science endorsed by the Reformation; and the voyages of discovery, which disclosed the existence of realms, standards, customs and facts hitherto unguessed at.

The "pure" or "naturalistic" empiricists of the sixteenth century advocated investigation, observation and direct experience, as the only sure tests of truth. Go to Nature itself, to the state, to man, they insisted; do not simply read books about them or hunt for them "in the narrow cells of the human understanding."[109] Thus Vesalius, whose *De humani corporis fabrica* (1543) revolutionized the science of anatomy, speaks of "that true bible as we count it of the human body and of the nature of man";[110] and Paracelsus asserts that "The sick should be the doctor's books."[111]

These new appeals in anatomy and medicine to observation and practice, to experience and contact with the concrete and particular, are well illustrated in the writings of Juan Luis Vives, the Spanish humanistic educator and empirical psychologist, whose stay in England was abruptly terminated by Henry VIII's displeasure at his loyalty to Catherine of Aragon. Vives, writing about medicine, combines in one passage the emphases of Vesalius and Paracelsus:

> Students should follow, frequently and assiduously, the dissection of the body, to study whence the veins, the nerves, the bones originate, whither they proceed and whence, what is the size of them, what is their purpose in a living body and what relation there is between them. In the second place, there will be practical training of such a kind that students may visit with some experienced physician, and diligently observe, sick folk, and note how the physician applies the precepts of his art to his practice.[112]

There have been, indeed, few more radical empiricists than Vives. He insists, in his *De Anima et Vita* (1538), that we must adopt an approach based upon observation and experience, if we hope to find out what the soul *does*. For this, he points out, is all that we can hope to know: what the soul *is* is beyond our reach and the subject simply of fruitless speculation.[113]

Again, writing on elementary studies in the natural sciences, he says, "In these studies there is no disputation necessary; there is nothing needed but the silent contemplation of Nature." And even when he turns to the more advanced aspects of natural science, he clings (in the violence of his antipathy to the Scholastic "babblement which has corrupted every branch of knowledge in the name of Logic"[114]) to what amounts to "nature study"—only on a vast scale.

> He who would advance still further must study outward nature by close observation. . . . *All that is wanted is a certain power of observation.* So will he observe the nature of things in the heavens, in cloudy and clear weather, in the plains, on the mountains, in the woods. Hence he will seek out, and get to know, many things about those who inhabit those spots. Let him have recourse, for instance, to gardeners, husbandmen, shepherds, and hunters. . . . For no one man can possibly make all observations without help in such a multitude and variety of directions.[115]

Here is an ultimate faith in a "storehouse of facts" which only Francis Bacon's surpasses. What Vives says of medicine—"Out of how many practical experiences on all sides has the art of medicine to be built up, like rain-water composed of drops!"[116]—might serve as a peculiarly apt summary of his general attitude toward natural science. To him, as to Montaigne, that which "by uncontrolled experience we palpably touch"[117] gives as good warrant of truth as we may have; like Montaigne, he scorns the scientist or physician who is content to guide and teach

> as one who, sitting in his chaire, paints seas, rockes, shelves and havens upon a board, and makes the modell of a tall ship to sail in all safety; But put him to it in earnest, he knowes not what to doe nor where to begin.[118]

If there is a palpable weakness in such loose empiricism, in the almost infinite gathering of "facts," it is rather in the fallibility of observation and sense perception than in the accumulation of data itself. The Scholastic "world-scheme was open to attack on two sides":

> Firstly, when observations and calculations should be brought forward conflicting with it or, at least, making another conception possible or probable. Secondly . . . whenever the naïve confidence in the absolute validity of sensuous space should be disputed. When it has become evident that every determination of place is dependent on the place of the ob-

server, there is no longer any absolute distinction between the
heavenly and the earthly regions, nor between the natural
places within the earthly region.[119]

These two influences upon the breakup of the medieval synthesis
unquestionably gain impetus from the Counter-Renaissance, although they attain to a certain and final confirmation only with
the full advent of the Scientific Reformation. We have already
traced the course of the second of these approaches, that of the
relativistic arguments—especially in the discussion on Bruno. The
Counter-Renaissance was equally influential in furthering the first.
For the attention to the collecting of natural facts and observations
which empiricists like Vives sponsored, helped unquestionably to
produce an intellectual climate favorable to the accumulation of
a vast store of accurate observation. If this "storehouse" awaited the
work of Tycho Brahe, Digges, Kepler and Galileo for any appre-
ciable realization in terms of accuracy, it was because the earlier
"pure" empiricists failed to see that experience and observation
were wholly dependable and accurate measuring rods only when
supported by a scientific mathematical method.

While it is not the particular province of this study to trace the
development of this true Scientific Reformation, a brief account of
it will facilitate greatly an understanding of the particular merits
and shortcomings of those radical empiricists of the Counter-Renaissance who also contributed (although not decisively) to the scientific and intellectual revolution which effected the inclusive change
from the medieval teleological physics to the later mechanical
variety.

Such an account must mention the development, during the later
Middle Ages, of "a positive science of physics," at both Paris and
Oxford, by followers of Ockham who moved on from his skeptical
position to a scientific empiricism which concerned itself with a
"constructive criticism of the natural philosophy of Aristotle."[120] It
must take notice of Leonardo da Vinci, who predicted almost all
the elements of Galileo's method (although there is not much evidence that he applied them consistently and thoroughly)—combining the tools of experience and exact thought with a rigidly mathematical method.[121] And it must include a reference to those sixteenth-century Italians, including Tartaglia and Benedetti, whose
work in dynamics paved the way for Galileo's.[122]

Yet, in so brief an account, we may pause only over the most
strategic contributions. These, for the sixteenth century, were made
by the School of Padua. Professor Randall has made out an im-

pressive case for Galileo's inheritance from this school, a group of
natural philosophers who, without being radical empiricists in the
sense of the scientists of the Counter-Renaissance, upheld "the basic
idea of an experimentally grounded science."[123]

Primarily concerned with methodological problems, and influenced by their close association with the Paduan medical faculty
to a consistently careful analysis of experience, the school of Padua
was largely responsible for the fact that "the most daring departures
from Aristotelian science were carried on within the Aristotelian
framework, and by means of a critical reflection on the Aristotelian
texts. . . ."[124] Through the influence of the Paduans' single greatest
figure, Zabarella, and through his own residence at the University
(1592–1610), Galileo owed much to this school. "In method and
philosophy if not in physics he remained a typical Paduan Aristotelian"; and, in turn, his wedding of Paduan method with quantitative or mathematical measurement played a large part in determining the character of modern science.[125] For, as we have seen,
it was their neglect of mathematics, their failure to recognize the
necessity for the formulation of scientific natural *laws,* and their
lack of method which recognized the importance of hypothesis and
deduction, which proved fatal to the efforts of the Counter-Renaissance empiricists.

Professor Randall has defined "Science" as "a body of mathematical demonstrations, the principles of which are discovered by
the resolution of selected instances in experience." This is the
method, he continues,

> called by Euclid and Archimedes a combination of "analysis"
> and "synthesis," and by the Paduans and Galileo, "resolution"
> and "composition." It is traditional and Aristotelian in regard-
> ing the structure of science as dialectical and deductive, and
> in seeing all verification and demonstration as inclusion within
> a logical system of ideas. It has altered the scheme of the medi-
> eval Aristotelians in making the principles of demonstration
> mathematical in character; and to the scholastic empiricism it
> has added the insistence that the way of discovery is not mere
> observation and generalization, not mere abstraction from com-
> mon experience, but a careful and precise mathematical anal-
> ysis of a scientific experience—what the medical tradition of
> Padua called "resolution" and what Archimedes called "anal-
> ysis." And to that experience demonstration must return, in
> a "regress," for confirmation, illustration, and the guarantee
> of the existence of the deduced consequences. *But the return
> to experience is not for the sake of certain proof: for through-*

> *out the seventeenth century it is almost impossible to find any*
> *natural scientist maintaining that a mere fact can prove any*
> *certain truth.*[126]

Herein lies the greatest single difference and the distinguishing mark between the scientists of the Counter-Renaissance and those who belong to the at once "traditional" and "critical" lines of the Scientific Reformation. There are, to be sure, many similarities, and one finds at Padua many of the attitudes characteristic of Vives, Telesio, Bacon and other radical empiricists. One finds, for example, that Zabarella opposed the use of Scholastic "value" explanation —that explanation which considered the functioning of all things in the universe in terms of what they were "good for." The Paduan medical Aristotelians in general denied the "power of *intellectus* to recognize the truth of principles."[127] Throughout the whole school there was a rejection of the loose, "abstracting" Scholastic empiricism, against which Bacon also inveighed. Even induction appears in Zabarella's exposition, although in a far more subordinate position than Bacon accords it;[128] and further parallels with the empiricists of the Counter-Renaissance could be cited and quoted.

But—and it is in this important respect that the Paduans (and the future course of science at large) most clearly differed from the school of "brute fact"—their scientific method "set forth a formulation of the structure of a science of *hypothesis* and demonstration. . . ."[129] To Zabarella, "logic and method are inter-changeable terms"; the syllogism is "the common genus of all methods and logical instruments."[130] Experience, systematic demonstration, are added to the solution—are vital to it—but they are combined with hypothesis, "within a logical system of ideas." This approach is in no sense an anti-intellectualistic one; its *temper* is much closer (for all of the other differences) to the Scholastic methodology than to that of the Counter-Renaissance.

There is, in short, a world of difference between Ramus' position (typical of the Counter-Renaissance) when he urges Rheticus to "convince us by cogent proof" that astronomy "can stand very well without any hypothesis"[131] and Galileo's method, with its Paduan roots:

> The scientist begins with a "hypothetical assumption," a mathematical hypothesis that does not come immediately from the observation and measurement of facts, but rather from an analysis of the mathematical relations involved in a given effect. The properties that follow are then deductively demonstrated. Thirdly, cases or illustrations of that effect are ana-

lysed to discover how far those properties are really exemplified in them and confirmed by them.[132]

In such a method, although there are strong empirical factors, the "structure of science" remains "dialectical and deductive"; "a logical system of ideas" is retained. Both in these features, inherited from the Paduans, and in the mathematical emphasis of his thought, Galileo finally points the way to the most characteristic qualities of the science-to-come—and away from the road traveled by most of the "appeal to fact" rebels, including Bacon. Like so many of the elements which characterized the Counter-Renaissance, its scientists' almost exclusive "appeal to fact" was not to last: "for throughout the seventeenth century it is almost impossible to find any natural scientist maintaining that a mere fact can prove any certain truth. . . ."

At the same time, it was the peculiar service of the Counter-Renaissance's faith in experience to help to convince men that calculation must be verified by observation. Thus it was Tycho's painstaking insistence upon observation which finally led Kepler "from high-flying speculations to the foundation of an exact science of experience."[133] When Kepler submitted his first work, *Mysterium cosmographicum* (1597), with its "theological and Pythagorean suppositions," to Tycho, the latter remarked "that the observations of thirty-five years did not lead him to concur in Kepler's speculations, in spite of their great ingenuity."[134]

It was Tycho's accurate records, too, which revealed to Kepler the inadequacy of Copernicus' combinations of circular movements to chart the orbits of the planets; and it was Tycho's training which taught him so thoroughly the lesson of "verification by fact" that, in searching out the laws of the planets' motions, he did not succumb to the temptation to accept one geometrical scheme he had worked out with a deviation of only 8′ from Tycho's records. Kepler writes,

> Since the divine goodness has given to us in Tycho Brahe a most careful observer, from whose observations the error of 8′ is shown in this calculation, . . . it is right that we should with gratitude recognize and make use of this gift of God. . . . For if we could have treated 8′ of longitude as negligible I should already have corrected sufficiently the hypothesis. . . . But as they could not be neglected, *these 8′ alone have led the way toward the complete reformation of astronomy*, and have been made the subject matter of a great part of this work.[135]

Similarly, Galileo declares,

Ignorance has been the best teacher I have ever had, since in order to be able to demonstrate to my opponents the truths of my conclusions, I have been forced to prove them by a variety of experiments, though to satisfy myself alone I have never felt it necessary to make many.[136]

And Tomasso Campanella, who declared the need for a philosophy based upon experience, argues,

If Galilei's conclusions are right . . . we shall have to philosophize in a new way. And since Galilei always relies on observations, he can only be refuted by other observations.[137]

Years before, for that matter, Thomas Digges had hoped that the super-nova which appeared in the constellation of Cassiopeia in November, 1572, would afford him an opportunity to verify the Copernican system of the universe "by means of accurate astronomical observations of the new star and other heavenly bodies."[138] But, being unable to detect any annual parallax for the nova, he was disappointed.[139]

Similarly, in 1563 Ramus had urged Rheticus, the friend of Copernicus, to "undertake the task . . . of freeing astronomy from the fictions of hypotheses,"[140] and—according to Kepler—later offered to surrender his professorship at the Collège de France to the man who should produce an "astronomy without hypotheses."[141]

The invocation of experience and observation by the Counter-Renaissance, then, however loosely applied by its protagonists, unquestionably had a hand in the influences which led to the break-up of the old world-order. If its contribution to astronomy and physics was not so immediately apparent as that which it made to anatomy and medicine, it was far from negligible. Galileo and Thomas Hariot did not train the telescope upon the heavens until 1609, but earlier observations had already done much to discredit the Aristotelian physics. The nova of 1572, the comet of 1577, and other comets which appeared in the last twenty years of the century had been carefully observed in England and on the continent; and these observations had

contradicted the theory of solid orbs, disproved the doctrine of the immutability of the heavens above the moon, and made it seem probable that the matter of the heavens was not essentially different from sublunary matter.[142]

We are already moving toward the new universe of mathematical law,[143] but it remains true that the science of the Counter-Renaissance did not contribute directly to its formulation. Its occult scientists were primarily concerned with mystical or magical mathematics (the secrets of mathematics, not its laws), and its radical empiricists held no traffic with mathematics at all. Yet the emphasis of both groups upon experiment, and that of the latter camp upon the observation of fact, played an important part in restoring that balance of emphases destroyed by the overly intellectualized Scholastic science, and in furthering the interests of the Copernican system. . . .

Among the most interesting features of the transitional empirical science of the Counter-Renaissance are the various ways in which it endorsed those ideals of simplicity and simplification which were representative of other aspects (such as the religious) of the general movement.

There is, first of all, an obvious (and indeed, excessive) simplification in its conviction that the mere amassing of facts, of all possible data, constitutes science. If the point of view of few of the empiricists was actually as naïve as this, at least this was the direction in which—with their impatience with Scholastic science—they tended. And it was a natural, if extreme, reaction from the opposite pole—from the tendency to ignore, or at least minimize, the world of empirical reality.

Moreover, there was at least one feature of this general attitude which made a genuine and direct contribution to scientific progress. This was the empiricists' conviction that there was nothing intrinsically "mean" about simple and "humble" facts, and, inversely, nothing essentially "lofty" about vast and generalized hypotheses.

Leonardo da Vinci, to be sure, had made this point emphatically in his *Notebooks:*

> Truth is . . . of such excellence that even when it treats of humble and lowly matters it yet immeasurably outweighs the sophistries and falsehoods which are spread out over great and high-sounding discourses. . . . But you who live in dreams, the specious reasonings, the feints which *palla* players might use, if only they treat of things vast and uncertain, please you more than do the things which are sure and natural and of no such high pretension.[144]

And this attitude was characteristic of those Paduans who nurtured the true Scientific Reformation. Yet it is also prevalent among the radical empiricists of the Counter-Renaissance, and given voice by many of their most notable members.

So Vives, discussing "well-known philosophers," confesses that

he can cite only a few in whose writings one can find "some treatment of the facts of nature." Again, he urges, "Let the keenness of
the mind descend from its height to the intimate working of Nature."[145] It is the exact parallel in the realm of science to Montaigne's plea in terms of man, his conduct, and his "proper" life.
For Montaigne's praise of Socrates is centered in the fact that

> He it is that brought humane wisdom from heaven againe,
> where for a long time it had been lost, to restore it unto man;
> where her most just and laborious worke is.[146]

"There is nothing," he maintains,

> so goodly, so faire, and so lawfull, as to play the man well
> and duely . . .[147]

and he remarks,

> Super-celestiall opinions and under-terrestrial manners are
> things amongst us I have ever seene to bee of singular accord.[148]

"Transcending humours affright" Montaigne "as much" as do
"steepy, high and inaccessible places."[149] He pleads throughout the
last book of the *Essayes* for a life which will be just and fruitful
to the senses and the body as well as to the mind and spirit. And
on the final page he writes,

> We seek for other conditions because we understand not the
> use of ours, and goe out of our selves forasmuch as we know
> not what abiding there is. Wee may long enough get upon
> stilts, for be wee upon them, yet must we goe with our owne
> legges. And sit we upon the highest throne of the World, yet
> sit we upon our own taile. The best and most commendable
> lives and best pleasing men are (in my conceit) those which
> with order are fitted, and with decorum are ranged to the
> common mould and humane model, but without wonder or
> extravagancy. . . .[150]

Vives' appeal for the descent of the mind "to the intimate workings of nature" and to a realization of the importance of "humble
fact" is apparent as well in the book which earned him the title
of "the father of empirical psychology."[151] For there, dealing with
the relationship of two associated ideas (*recordatio gemina*), he
points out that the mind often "travels more readily from the lesser
to the greater idea." He describes how the taste of cherries vividly
recalls to him, through an associative process, an early illness. And
he concludes,

Wherefore it behoves us to let the "clues" intended to stir up our memory, be quite bare of importance, lest they should destroy the significance of what they are to suggest to us.[152]

"'Clues' *intended* to stir up" and "what they *are* to suggest" seem at first glance to constitute a reversion to the teleological explanation of phenomena; yet Vives' emphasis upon the necessity of these "clues" being "quite bare of *importance,* lest they should destroy the *significance*" corrects this impression and indicates that an objective scientific ideal is intended—one which opposes the application of *a priori* concepts of value to the comprehension of phenomenal particulars. In this passage, Vives is pointing toward Bacon's induction, and laying an emphasis similar to that in Bacon's assertion that

> One method of delivery alone remains to us; which is simply this: we must lead men to particulars themselves, and their series and order; while men on their side must force themselves for awhile to lay their notions by and begin to familiarize themselves with facts. . . .[153]

And like the earlier empiricists, Bacon is contemptuous of the idea that there is something "shameful and undignified" about dealing "with experiments and particulars, subject to sense and bound in matter."[154] There is an ironic footnote to the tragi-comic history of Aristotelian interpretation in the realization that Aristotle, accused by many of the Counter-Renaissance empiricists of holding this very opinion, had himself protested against it.[155]

Another manifestation of the empiricists' endorsement of simplicity links their creed with that of those who subscribed to the vanity of learning. For, like the advocates of "unlearnedness," they call upon humble witnesses—in their case to aid in the process of observation and the accumulation of facts. Thus Vives advises the natural scientist to "have recourse . . . to gardeners, husbandmen, shepherds, and hunters. . . ."[156]

It was, of course, inevitable that a movement enamoured of experience should utilize any weapon which could make way against the dominance of speculation, theory and untested authority, and inevitable, therefore, that it should flaunt the findings of the unlettered, in contradiction of the learned, with some satisfaction. Among the many passages which Geoffroy Atkinson has collected from the writings of voyagers to the New World and the Orient, and published in his brilliant *Nouveaux Horizons de la Renaissance*

Française, there are several which place exactly this emphasis. Among these is a statement by Jacques Cartier, in his *Bref Récit et succincte narration:*

> The simple sailors of today . . . have come to know [ont connu] the opposite of the opinion of the philosophers by true experience. . . .[157]

The most entertaining of these accounts is that of Jean de Léry, who extols the ability of a sailor happily named Jean de Meun:

> I have seen one of our pilots, named Jean de Meun, of Harfleur, who, although he did not know his ABC's, had nevertheless through long experience with his charts, astrolabes, and "baton de Jacob," so well profited in the art of navigation, that he silenced at every turn a learned personage . . . who, being on our ship, nevertheless was boasting, in speaking of theory. Not that for that reason I condemn or wish to blame in any way knowledge which is acquired and learned at schools and through books. . . . But I should indeed like to ask without paying any attention to the opinion of anyone (whoever he may be) that no one ever urge me to an argument against the experience of a thing.[158]

The tradition takes on more sober and scientific tones when Robert Norman, in his *New Attractive* (which sets forth his discovery of the dip of the magnetic needle), shows that the observations of mariners prove that the variations of the compass are not regular, as had before been maintained.[159] Again, William Borough, comptroller of Elizabeth's navy, in the preface of his *Discours of the Variation of the Cumpas,* addresses himself "To the Travelers, Seamen, and Mariners of Englande," with the plea that they collect

> accurate data on the variation of the compass in different parts of the world, so that the maps and sailing charts could be improved. Profound learning, according to Borough, was not essential for this task.[160]

These passages suggest very clearly a parallel tendency, in the "appeal to fact and experience," to one displayed by the vanity of learning tradition—the tendency to assert the equality or superiority of the humble and uneducated to the speculative and learned, at least in those aspects of knowledge in which experience counts far more than theory. Vives' shepherds and Léry's Jean de Meun, who "did not know his ABC's" to some extent match Montaigne's "countrie-clownish men" and Greville's "pure, humble creatures." There is at least a corresponding, if not so inclusive, inclination to oppose their "expérience[s] vécue[s]"[161] to learned theory and pretentious speculative knowledge. . . .

Democratic allusions and implications are very rare in Renaissance political theory. Yet here, in a totally non-political context, there are apparent what seem to be at least the germs of a democratic principle. There is, to be sure, no real evidence that the attitudes of those participating in the "vanity of learning" and "appeal to fact" aspects of the Counter-Renaissance were consciously advocating what we would call democratic principles. On the contrary, it seems certain that these tendencies are primarily simply a reaction against the schoolmen's excessive emphasis upon speculation and authority, and that of the humanists upon learning. Even the voyagers' and cosmographers' very legitimate enthusiasm for experience is probably not a wholly independent movement, based solely upon what they have seen and done in the New World and in the Orient. As Professor Atkinson has concluded,

> Il faut croire qu'il y avait, et même longtemps avant 1575, une forte tradition littéraire en faveur de l'expérience et une habitude assez entendue de critiquer les arguments basés uniquement sur l'autorité.[162]

Walter Ralegh offers an excellent example of how dangerous it is to predicate any conscious democratic stand from an invocation of the humble and of experience:

> That these and these be the cause of these and these effects, time hath taught us, and not reason; and so hath experience, without art. The cheese-wife knoweth it as well as the philosopher, that sour runnet doth coagulate her milk into a curd. But if we ask a reason of this cause, why the sourness doth it? whereby it doth it? and the manner how? I think there is nothing to be found in vulgar [i.e., non-Christian or non-theological] philosophy to satisfy this and many other like questions.[163]

The cheese-wife is a co-worker with the shepherds and sailors under the shingle "Experience." Yes, but Ralegh is also the man who recognized the change in temper and growing strength of the people in England under James I, watched that growth with dissatisfaction, and proposed Machiavellian tactics to meet it.[164] His confidence in the cheese-wife is hardly extravagant; his basic concern is to demonstrate that God has not "shut up all light of learning within the lantern of Aristotle's brains" (or any one else's), and that what may be known about nature is discovered through "experience, without art." He, too, has something to say about the vanity and uncertainty of the arts and sciences:

> Tell wit how much it wrangles
> In tickle points of niceness;
> Tell wisdom she entangles
> Herself in over-wiseness:
>   And when they do reply,
>   Straight give them both the lie. . . .
>
> Tell arts they have no soundness,
> But vary by esteeming;
> Tell schools they want profoundness,
> And stand too much on seeming:
>   If arts and schools reply,
>   Give arts and schools the lie.[165]

On the other hand, there are real democratic implications in another aspect of the growing empirical science of the Counter-Renaissance, especially in the England of the last half of the sixteenth century. The "experience" in which the shepherds and husbandmen, sailors and cheese-wife may participate is apt to remain a loose empiricism, with relatively little strict accuracy of observation. But that progressively closer contact between scholars and the artisan classes which had already been established in Italy and elsewhere,[166] was conceived and born in the democratic impulses of men like Recorde, Dee, Digges and Gilbert. As Professor Johnson summarizes the trend:

> A closer liaison between the systematized learning of the scholarly scientist and the technological skill of the artisan was fostered by men like Recorde, Digges, Dee, and Gilbert. The merchant companies, such as the Muscovy Company, became patrons and promoters of practical science, and employed some of the ablest scientists as expert advisers. Before the end of the century Thomas Hood, and later the Gresham College professors, were delivering public lectures on science, in English, to the tradesmen and artisans of London.[167]

"Democratic impulses"—for Recorde's textbooks on mathematics and astronomy in the vernacular,[168] and various passages in the writings of Digges and Dee,[169] demonstrate clearly a conscious purpose to add, to the largely practical knowledge of technological artisans, the basic mathematical principles of sound scientific theory. The result was a veritable "surgunt indocti" movement made by men without university educations:

Such men were William Bourne, the writer of many able and popular books on navigation; Robert Norman, who, in his book *The New Attractive,* first demonstrated the dip of the magnetic needle; William Borough, comptroller of Queen Elizabeth's navy and the author of a valuable book, *A Discours of the Variation of the Cumpas;* and John Blagrave, the most famous designer of astronomical instruments in Elizabethan England.[170]

This advance into prominence of "unlearned" but technically experienced scientists came with the "full rise of capitalism in the mining, metal and related industries" and "the new urban society."[171] Thus its democratic roots are twofold—technological as well as humanitarian—and it constitutes an historical phenomenon which parallels in events the process we have been tracing ideologically, just as the Peasants' Revolt parallels the ideological growth of fideism and the exaltation of the humble. Moreover, like the Peasants' Revolt (if not in so extreme a way) it displays an aggressive consciousness of its anti-intellectualistic and anti-erudite nature. For example, Robert Norman writes in the preface to his *New Attractive:*

But I doe verilie thinke, that notwithstanding the learned in those sciences beeing in their studies amongst their bookes, can imagine great matters, and set downe their farre fetcht conceits, in faire shew, and with plausible wordes, wishing that all Mechaniciens, were such as for want of utterance might be forced to deliver unto them their knowledge and conceits, that they might flourish uppon them, & applie them at their pleasures: yet there are in this land diverse Mechaniciens, that in their severall faculties and professions, *have the use of those arts at their fingers ends, and can applie them to their severall purposes, as effectuallie, and more readilie,* then those that would most condemne them.[172]

After referring to the mathematical works available in English, "*Euclides* Elements" and "*Records* workes," which

are sufficient to ye industrious Mechanicien, to make him perfect and readie in those sciences, but especiallie to apply the same to the art or facultie which he chieflie professeth,

Norman concludes,

And therefore I would wish the learned to use modestie in publishing their conceits, & not disdainfullie to condemne men that will search out the secrets of their artes and professions, and publish the same to the behoofe & use of others, no more

then they would that others should iudge of them, for promising much and performing little or nothing at al.[173]

It is not surprising to find that Gabriel Harvey, with his nose for
news, is the literary Elizabethan who takes fullest cognizance of
this movement. In his usual pithy manner, he writes in *Pierces
Supererogation:*

> He that remembereth Humfrey Cole, a Mathematicall Mech-
> anician, Mathew Baker a ship-wright, Iohn Shute, an Archi-
> tect, Robert Norman a Navigator, William Bourne a Gunner,
> Iohn Hester a Chimist, *or any like cunning and subtile Em-
> pirique* (Cole, Baker, Shute, Norman, Bourne, Hester, will be
> remembred, when greater Clarkes shalbe forgotten) is a prowd
> man, if he contemne *expert artisans, or any sensible industrious
> Practitioner, howsoever Unlectured in Schooles, or Unlettered
> in Bookes. . . .*[174]

The parallel between the religious and scientific endorsements
of simplicity in the Counter-Renaissance extends even beyond the
aspects just set forth—to include the basic preoccupation of each
trend with a return to first principles. The two senses in which this
emphasis was characteristic of the fideists in general and the thinkers of the Reformation in particular were (1) in their insistence
upon a return to the purity of primitive Christianity or the early
church, and (2) in their desire to establish a direct contact between
the individual Christian conscience and God. In the twofold scientific movement of the Counter-Renaissance, with its occult and
empirical schools (so often intermingled), the two senses in which
a return to first principles is advocated are amazingly similar. For
the renovators (the magician-scientists) wish to return to an ancient doctrine, a body of revealed knowledge; while the innovators
(the radical empiricists) invoke the imperative need for a direct
contact with Nature herself.

The ancient revealed body of knowledge to whose authority the
magician-scientists consistently appealed was susceptible to variant
expositions and interpretations—depending upon the occult line of
succession to which the particular practitioner owed his loyalty. Yet
almost all of the magician-scientists stress *continuity* and *uniformity:*
"Knowledge (or truth) is one." The variations, the differences, are
most often terminological, rather than actual. Illustrative of this
concept of a permanent body of esoteric truth, admitting of variant
interpretations and emphases, yet universal enough to absorb them
all, is Marsilio Ficino's view of "Platonism . . . as the culminating
point in a philosophical tradition that had its origin in Zoroaster

and Orpheus and Hermes Trismegistus and the obscure beginnings of human wisdom":[175]

> Once among the Persians under Zoroaster, and among the Egyptians under Mercury, a certain devout philosophy was born, the one consonant with the other. Then among the Thracians under Orpheus and Aglaophemus this philosophy was nursed. Under Pythagoras among the Greeks and Italians it attained its youth. Finally by the divine Plato at Athens it reached full maturity. . . . Plotinus, however, first and alone stripped theology of these veils. . . .[176]

The last sentence points the way for Ficino's reconciliation of "philosophy" and "theology." So, too, the chart that shows the close parallels in concepts of the three worlds of the Cabala, the traditional three kinds of magic, and the Christian cosmology as developed in Pico's *Heptaplus*,[177] is suggestive of the way in which many of these magician-scientists sought to combine, or at least ally, various occult traditions with Christian dogma.

Pico was a notable offender in this respect. In his oration *On the Dignity of Man,* which was drawn up in the form of an address to the learned audience he anticipated for his projected public disputations, he asserts that the "institutions" of Moses shadow forth the "sublime course of progressive discipline" necessary for the initiate into esoteric mysteries. This course of discipline is also to be found, he says, in the three celebrated Delphic sentences, in the precepts of Pythagoras, the parables of Zoroaster and the Chaldees, and in the *dogmata* of Moorish and Cabalistic philosophers.

Finally, he was ready, in his "Conclusiones," to illustrate and confirm the principal truths of the Christian faith and doctrine from the Jewish Cabala. Pico's explanation of the validity of this project was that when God had given the written law to Moses on the Mount, he had also favored him with its secret interpretation. This interpretative wisdom had been handed down by oral tradition only, until Esdras had persuaded the Jewish wise men to let him commit it to writing.[178]

As Ernst Cassirer has said, "What is characteristic of Pico is . . . not the way in which he *increased* the store of philosophic truth, but the way in which he made it *manifest*."[179]

"Interpretation" is the *art* of the initiate, who is rarely concerned with *science* in our sense of the word. For example, Cornelius Agrippa begins a passage in *De Incertitudine* in sufficiently orthodox fashion: "All the secrets of God and Nature, all instructions in morals and laws, all knowledge of past, present, future, all that is shut up in the body of the Bible." Yes, "in uno sacro bibliorum volumine omnia continentur, & traduntur." But observe the magician's regular use of "secrets" and "instructions." And he concludes, thus changing the whole texture of the passage, that "these things may not be understood, except by the 'illuminated.'"[180] The way in which a man may become one of the illuminated is more fully treated in a definition of the Cabala written by the Abbé Tenaud of Mellynays at the request of Francis I. Tenaud, who professes a thoroughgoing skepticism about the doctrine he expounds, presents a definition which—with the exception of its peculiar emphasis upon free will—develops interesting parallels between the tenets of the occult tradition and the emphases of the early Reformation:

> The Cabala is defined as science and knowledge of God and of the separate substances of the spiritual world and its secrets which cannot be known by the external senses, experience, reason, demonstration, syllogism, study or other human and rational method, but *only by faith, illumination and celestial revelation which moves the free will to believe that which is inspired* and know the aforesaid secrets by the holy written law of God and also by figures, names, numbers, symbols and other ways revealed to the patriarchs, prophets and doctors of the Hebrews.[181]

One factor of great importance in most accounts, however, is omitted in this definition—the role of the initiate guide, the magus who "turns over" to the neophyte or apprentice his share of the traditional revealed knowledge. Faustus may not *absolutely* need the help of Valdes and Cornelius, but he knows that "their conference will be a greater help to me, than all my labours, plodde I nere so fast," and Valdes declares explicitly that their contribution will be "our experience."

And just so, behind all the particular initiate-guides, stands the shadow of the great original initiate-guide, the inspired prophet, the original vessel of truth, the peculiarly and divinely gifted son of God, if you will—by whatever name he is known. M. Brunschvicq, in his study of the role Pythagoreanism has played in the history of ideas, illuminates this concept of the great original in a passage in which he distinguishes between two sorts of Pythagoreans:

> qui l'un en face de l'autre se définissent par les dénominations les plus caractéristiques qu'on puisse trouver, d'un côté les *mathématiciens,* ceux qui cultivent la science pour eux-mêmes et par eux-mêmes, de l'autre les *acousmatiques,* ceux qui écoutent et répètent ce qu'ils ont entendu, récitant des caté-

chismes dont plus d'un fragment est venu jusqu'a nous avec la consécration de la parole révélée: "c'est Lui qui l'a dit."[182]

The description of this second group would apply equally well to the other occult traditions of the Renaissance. For all of them professed "la consécration de la parole révélée." All of them repeated ceremoniously—whether of golden-thighed Pythagoras himself, of "thrice great Hermes," of "the great mocking Maister," or of "the attic Moses"—"c'est Lui qui l'a dit." Even with such an assertion as the one to be found in the preface to the *Book Concerning the Tincture of the Philosophers:*

> From the middle of this age the Monarchy of all Arts has been at length derived and conferred on me, Theophrastus Paracelsus, Prince of Philosophy and of Medicine . . .[183]

we are treating the same material. It is simply the substitution of "Moi" for "Lui." For the passage continues, "For this purpose *I have been chosen by God* to extinguish and blot out all phantasies of elaborate and false works, of delusive and presumptuous words. . . .[184] The truth "I" speak (Paracelsus would reply) is that of revelation; far from being consumed by megalomania, "I" fulfill the purpose of God and expressly extinguish the "presumptuous."

However superb an act of rationalization is here involved, the tradition of the anointed vessel of truth and of the consecration of the revealed word, remains a constant throughout the ranks of the *renovators.* . . .

With the *innovators,* the radical empiricists of the Counter-Renaissance, we encounter a very different constant. Rebelling strenuously against the Scholastic reliance on logic as an instrument of finding out natural and physical truth, they carry their drastic skepticism about hypotheses to the point of trusting as truth only that fact which they can demonstrably experience themselves. They swing full circle from the discipleship of Thomas Aquinas to that of another Thomas—the skeptical "doubting Thomas" who needed to thrust his hand into the wound before he could believe. It is no fanciful exaggeration to term them the *Hand-in-the-Wound School* —for there is no authority they will accept, no faith they will avow, save that of *their own experience.*

Montaigne, of course, is in the vanguard. He asserts scornfully,

> The God of scholasticall learning is Aristotle: It is religion to debate of his ordinances. . . . His doctrine is to us as a canon law, which peradventure is as false as another.[185]

Why, he demands, should we permit "his authoritie" to be "the marke beyond which it is not lawfull to enquire?" There is a hint of the removal of the "ne" from "Ne plus ultra" in the question, but Montaigne's refutation of this "authoritie" points no alternative path to truth, except that of turning to ordinary experience; he does not believe in *any* "scientific" method. The "philosophers" are to blame if we refuse to accept their answers to the question, "Is ice cold?" For we can put some in our bosom and find out.[186]

As for the schoolmen and their like, he advocates anatomizing one, stripped of his learned accessories:

> Let him pull of his two-faced hoode, his gowne and his latine, let him not fill our eares with meerely beleeved Aristotle, you will discover and take him for one of us, and worse if may be.[187]

From the early essay in which he demands,

> Wee can talke and prate, Cicero saith thus, These are Platoes customes, These are the verie words of Aristotle; but what say we our selves? what doe we? what judge we?[188]

to the final essay's (*Of Experience*) "I had rather understand my selfe well in my selfe then in Cicero,"[189] he denies the validity of any authority except personal *experience*. The whole significance of that "peinture de son Moi" of which Pierre Villey speaks[190] lies in Montaigne's conviction of the exclusive certainty of what the individual can investigate for himself. That the truth of "moi-même" should be for him the object of the investigation is the result of his belief that no other truth is even approximately ascertainable.

This is not to say that sober and respectful attention is due to every one in the period who invoked experience as his mistress. There is a wide gap between most of such advocates of "experience" and those who not only professed the ideal, but demonstrably fulfilled it.

When Machiavelli declares at the end of the *Discourses*, "Herein I have expressed what I know, and what I have learned by a long experience, and continual reading of the affairs of the world,"[191] the reader has already gone through some five hundred pages which convincingly justify the statement. When Guicciardini reiterates over and over again a phrase like "experience shows," one feels no impatience. For this is not merely another "appeal to experience"; however cynical he may be, he satisfies us in the body of his book that experience has really been his mistress. When Vives asserts in *De Anima et Vita* (1538) that we must adopt the method of observation and experience, not to find out what the soul *is*, but what it *does*, he proves by example that he is pursuing this method himself.[192] When Montaigne changes his early statement, "Je fais les essais de mon jugement," to the later one, "Je fais les essais de ma vie," we listen with respect and conviction. He has provided us with clear evidence of the validity of one of his last statements: "Out of the experience I have of my selfe I find sufficient ground to make my selfe wise were I but a good proficient scholler."[193] Indeed, we do not want the qualification.

For these men, only the *lived experience*, the personally viewed or interpreted event, that which they have seen, felt, entertained, themselves, has certain validity. As we have seen, it was inevitable that none of them—not even Montaigne—could maintain without "blemish" so radical an empiricism. Yet all of those in this group carried their profession sufficiently into practice to warrant a careful and respectful hearing. . . .

But perhaps no single practitioner of the "Hand-in-the-Wound" school so graphically illustrates its creed as Sir Thomas Smith, Secretary of State under Edward VI and Elizabeth, and ardent advocate of practical statecraft, in the conclusion to his *De Republica Anglorum*. He has not, Smith points out, been dealing with such imaginary "common wealths" as those which occupied Plato, Xenophon and Sir Thomas More (a favorite point with all the empirical political writers of the time)——

> such as never was nor ever shall be, vaine imaginations, phantasies of Philosophers to occupie the time and to exercise their wittes: but so as Englande standeth and is governed at this day the xxviij of March *Anno* 1565, in the vij yeare of the raigne and administration thereof by the most vertuous and noble Queene *Elizabeth*. . . . *So that whether I writ true or not, it is easie to be seene with eyes (as a man would say) and felt with hands.*[194]

"Seene with eyes" and "felt with hands." It is a creed for which one would expect to find even more adherents than one does—in a hundred-year span which saw theories of ancient prestige and authority shaken by voyages of discovery and the remapping of the heavens; which witnessed the production of a treatise of anatomy not derived from Galen, but based upon actual dissection and observation; which greeted the completion of the first tour of the globe, and the invention and use of the telescope.

Yet Sir Thomas' invitation—or challenge—is accepted, or utilized, by many. What one may do or see for oneself—eventually establishes for the innovators a reverence for "C'est moi qui l'ai fait," equal to that of the renovators for their "C'est Lui qui l'a dit."

To choose an example at random, consider the correspondence of Sir William Lower with Thomas Hariot in 1610. (Hariot had promised to send to him further "perspective cylinders" or telescopes.) Lower writes,

> We both with wonder and delighte fell a consideringe your letter, we are here so on fire with thes thinges that I must renew my request and your promise to send mee of all sortes of thes Cylinders.[195]

Once again that power and wonder of *the observed fact* is testified to, as Sir William describes his own observation of three stars in Orion.

> Asking some that had better eyes than my selfe they told me, they were three starres lying close together in a right line. Thes starres with my cylinder this last winter I often observed, and it was longe er I believed that I saw them, they appearinge through the Cylinder so farre and distinctlie asunder that without I can not yet dissever.[196]

"I often observed. . . . I saw. . . ." It is the magic of the first person pronoun that does as much as any other single factor to promote the doctrine of experience and fact in the sixteenth century. Long before the advent of the telescope, this device was employed in attacks against authority, theory and the powers of the human mind unaided by experience. Geoffroy Atkinson, in his *Nouveaux Horizons de la Renaissance Française*, has disclosed and quoted scores of such statements—sentences, paragraphs and whole passages from voyagers to the New World and the Orient, who oppose to the theoretical conclusions of the "philosophers" (ancients, church fathers, and schoolmen alike) the truths of "une expérience vécue."[197]

The changes are rung over and over again on this single tune, whether about the existence of the Antipodes, the inhabitation of the Torrid Zone, or the authenticity of certain "traditional" animals. To cite only a few representative ones:

> But this opinion is false and entirely contrary to truth . . . because in these southerly parts I have found the country more thickly populated than is our Europe, or Asia, or Africa.

> I shall relate . . . that which I have seen and experienced. . . .

> Present experience demonstrates and permits this truth to be known by those of this time.

And I shall base my arguments [m'asseoir] on experience alone. . . .

I [Vespucci] saw there . . . the fixed stars of the eighth sphere, of which there is no memory in our sphere, and which have never been known [connues], up to today, by the most learned and wise of all the Ancients.

Now it is time to reply to those who say that there are no Antipodes, and that this region *where we are living* cannot be inhabited.[198]

If the phrase "C'est Lui qui l'a dit," with its consecrated authority, lent a sense of authority to the occult traditions in their war against the Scholastics and orthodox humanists, that of "C'est moi qui l'ai vu" or "C'est moi qui l'ai fait" was equally conclusive to these men in their similar cause. For they were participating in the same battle; however tolerant of the blunders of "the Ancients" some of them are, they oppose, over and over again, experience, proof and fact to "opinion," "conjecture," "theory," "reasoning" and "philosophy."

But this opinion is untrue [nulle], as I have said, and experience has made us realize it.

. . . not so much for the reasons that the Philosophers give for it in their [books on] Meteors, as for the certain proof that one has been able to make of it.

But the route is already so frequented and familiar, that every day Spaniards go there very easily. And thus experience is contrary to philosophy.[199]

"C'est Lui" . . . "C'est moi . . ." Revelation *vs.* radical empiricism, the renovators *vs.* the innovators. Yet, interestingly enough, and with the paradoxical quality so often characteristic of the "scientific" leaders of the Counter-Renaissance, we sometimes find a man straddling the line of division, a foot in each camp, paying tribute to both concepts, uttering both war cries.

It was not, for example, exclusively through a charlatan's delusion of grandeur that Paracelsus, a magus of the initiate tradition, substituted "Moi" for "Lui." He could at once proceed according to the ritual of an ancient and secret tradition of knowledge, and test by direct experience, when he set about to "investigate the mysteries of Nature." One can find like assertions in terms of the revival of ancient knowledge combined with demonstration by "ex

perience" or "experiment" in the writings of Pico, Agrippa and John
Dee. Similarly, Thomas Digges speaks of *"Copernicus Theoricke"* as

> auncient doctrine revived, and by Copernicus so demonstra-
> tively approved.[200]

There may, then, be several combinations. A man may profess
revelation, and yet need to "find out" the revealed body of knowledge. He may adhere to magic, and yet do genuine scientific experimentation in one or another field. He may "return" to ancient
doctrine, but bolster it by "demonstrations" of an empirical sort.
And finally, he may profess to be, or may be recognized as, an in-
novator, while all the time he is more accurately a renovator.

Moreover, "R. B." goes a step further in his book on Paracel-
sian medicine and chemistry, and links the "renovation," or return
to first principles, of the Reformation with those of the new "phisicke" and the new astronomy, in a passage which explicitly compares these three aspects of the Counter-Renaissance, thus demonstrating their phenomenal or ideological parallelism in the mind
of at least one contemporary witness. Speaking of Paracelsus, he
declares,

> He was not the author and inventour of this arte as the fol-
> lowers of the Ethnickes phisicke doe imagine, as by the former
> writers may appeare, no more than *Wickliffe, Luther, Oecolan-*
> *padius, Swinglius, Calvin, &c.* were the Author and inventours
> of the Gospell and religion in Christes Church, when they
> restored it to his puritie, according to Gods word, . . . And
> no more then *Nicholaus Copernicus,* which lived at the time
> of this *Paracelsus,* and restored to us the place of the starres
> according to the truth, as experience & true observation doth
> teach is to be called the author and inventor of the motions
> of the starres, which long before were taught by *Ptolomeus*
> Rules Astronomicall, and Tables for motions and Places of the
> starres. . . .[201]

In the passage quoted from him earlier, "R. B." affirms the agreement of the "Chymicall doctrine . . . with Gods worde, experience
and nature"; these two passages, taken together, reveal clearly an
awareness of the alliance of fideism, empiricism and occultism
against Scholastic science and speculative theology, and they invoke
a return to first principles in the two senses of the Counter-Renaissance: the return to the purity of "ancient doctrine" and the turning to the direct contact to be established only by particular experience.

A similar, although not identical, alignment of the forces of the Counter-Renaissance, with a like emphasis upon the "renovating" qualities of its "innovators," is presented by John Donne, twenty-five years later, in his pamphlet against the Jesuits, *Ignatius, his Conclave.* Copernicus, Paracelsus and Machiavelli are the major pretenders to "the principall place, next to *Lucifer's* owne Throne,"[202] now occupied by Ignatius Loyola, the "hero" of the piece. The right to the select group of Lucifer's initiates is limited to those

> which had so attempted any innovation in this life, that they gave an affront to all antiquitie, and induced doubts, and anxieties, and scruples, and after, a libertie of beleeving what they would; at length established opinions, directly contrary to all established before.[203]

The claims of Copernicus, Paracelsus and Machiavelli to this coveted honor are pretentious. Copernicus believes that he has "turned the whole frame of the world," and is "thereby almost a new Creator."[204] Paracelsus has worked to discredit "all *Methodicall Phisitians,* and the`art it selfe"; his chief purpose has been to make sure

> that no certaine new Art, nor fixed rules might be established, but that al remedies might be dangerously drawne from my uncertaine, ragged, and imperfect experiments in triall whereof, how many men have been made carkases?[205]

And Machiavelli introduces many arguments to prove that he has completely undermined the order of the state.[206]

Yet each, through the machinations of Ignatius Loyola, is rejected. And each of Loyola's ingenious rebuttals to the arguments of his rivals makes much of the fact that their "innovations" are not really new, but have been anticipated long before. Thus he points out to Copernicus that ancient astronomers had held his views; he has merely revived their doctrine.[207] As for Paracelsus, his own followers refer his whole doctrine "to the most ancient times."[208] Nor are Machiavelli's ideas new: Plato "and other fashioners of Common-wealths," as well as Fathers of the Church like Origen, Chrysostom and Jerome, had advocated, long before, "the liberty of dissembling and lying" for the "good" of the state. Moreover, so far as Machiavelli's general practices go,

> In all times in the *Romane* Church there have bene *Friers* which have far exceeded *Machiavel.*[209]

Finally, Machiavelli, who gave the strongest opposition to Loyola,

the eventual victor, manages to apply this same device to the
Jesuit's claim of unequaled innovation. For, having ironically con-
gratulated him and the Pope on their success in bringing "into the
world a new art of *Equivocation*," Machiavelli immediately goes
on to point out that what they have really done is not new. Rather,
they

> have raised to life againe the language of the Tower of Babel,
> so long concealed, and brought us againe from understanding
> one an other.[210]

In this witty and delightful satire, Donne fires here, there, and
everywhere; his treatment of particular individuals, although largely
consistent with the opinions which he expresses elsewhere, should
not necessarily be taken as measured judgments. But his conviction
that these various leaders of the Counter-Renaissance, who claim
to be innovators, have actually returned to various old doctrines
and convictions, is incontestable. . . .

The appeal to fact and experience, to experiment and observation, of the radical empiricists of the Counter-Renaissance, we have
discovered, bears a striking resemblance to other aspects of the
whole movement, in many particulars. It is anti-intellectualistic
and anti-speculative; it affirms its belief in the simplification of
science, and in the importance of the "humble," both in nature and
among men, to the promotion of scientific progress; it appeals to
a return to first principles, both in the historical sense of a revival
of ancient "natural philosophies" and "secret traditions," and in
the literal one of leaving speculation and theory, and turning to the
observation of nature itself. Some of these tendencies are more
marked among the practitioners of the occult empiricists, some
among the naturalistic empiricists.

But the latter sort of empiricism was not confined to natural science. Once again the interrelation of attitudes in separate fields is
immediately apparent. For that "science of the particular" which
followed inevitably the nominalistic and skeptical attitudes of those
who participated in the relativizing and decentralizing of law,
overspread all realms of thought and action in the Counter-Renaissance. Thus a study of the growing "appeal to fact" and the invocation of experience in natural science leads directly to a consideration
of the empirical and pragmatic thinkers and writers in other fields.
"We are much beholden to Machiavel and to others, that write
what men do and not what they ought to do," says Francis Bacon;[211]

and no account of the empiricism of the Counter-Renaissance would be complete without a consideration of these men.

3. THE SCIENCE OF THE PARTICULAR: MEN AND THINGS "AS THEY ARE"

Machiavelli begins the famous fifteenth chapter of the *Prince* with a forthright statement of his intention to break with the precedents set by traditional idealistic handbooks on the proper conduct of princes.[212] He declares

> I shall depart from the methods of other people. But, it being my intention to write a thing which shall be useful to him who apprehends it, it appears to me more appropriate to follow up *the real truth of the matter* than the imagination of it; for many have pictured republics and principalities which *in fact* have never been known or seen; because how one lives is so far distant from how one ought to live, that he who neglects *what is done* for *what ought to be done,* sooner effects his ruin than his preservation; for a man who wishes to act entirely up to his professions of virtue soon meets with what destroys him among so much that is evil.[213]

There is no doubt in his mind that one *can* perceive "the real truth of a matter"; he does not question the objectivity of "fact." All about him lies a world of men which he may observe, and the reading of history confirms his conviction of the over-all sameness of human nature. From these two sources, empirical reality and history, through observation and research, he has established to his own satisfaction the existence of a completely real world of concrete facts about human nature upon which one may build wise and sure rules of public conduct. So, in the foreword to the *Discourses,* he opens his dedication to Zanobi Buondelmonte and Cosimo Rucellai:

> With this I send you a gift which, if it bears no proportion to the extent of the obligations which I owe you, is nevertheless the best that I am able to offer to you; for I have endeavored to embody in it all that long experience and assiduous research have taught me of the affairs of the world.[214]

After Machiavelli, one reads more often in books on statecraft the expression of the author's purpose to deal with things "as they are," and not simply with Utopias and ideal conduct impossible or futile in the actual world in which men live. Jean Bodin, whose attitude toward Machiavelli undergoes a considerable shift between the publication of the *Methodus* and that of the *Republic* (from that of a sometimes sympathetic *critique* to a Gentillet-like vitupera-tive one),[215] declares such a determination in the latter work—al-though without drawing Machiavelli's conclusions:

> It is not our intent or purpose to figure out the only imaginary forme and idea of a commonwealth without effect, or sub-stance, as have Plato, and Sir Thomas More, Chancellor of England, vainly imagined; but so nere as we possibly can pre-cisely to follow the best laws and rules of the most flourishing cities and commonweales.[216]

Later, in the fifth book of the *Republic,* he combines in a single short passage the emphasis of the Counter-Renaissance upon the science of the particular and the appeal to fact, with its decentral-izing, relativistic attitude and its conviction that one will distort and "force" the nature of things as they are if one concentrates upon the theoretical, *a priori* approach of "universal" science. Having stated, "So far, we have taken up what concerned the universal state of commonwealths" (for contrary to his preliminary remarks, and with characteristic inconsistency, this is what he has been doing), he continues:

> Let us speak now of what may be peculiar to some of them as a result of diversity of peoples, in order to adapt the form of the state to the nature of the place, and human decrees to natural laws. Having failed to take heed of this, and by try-ing to force nature to serve their edicts, a number [plusieurs] have disturbed and often ruined great states. And yet those who have written of the commonwealth have not treated this question. Now, just as we see in all kinds of animals a very great variety, and in each species certain notable differences, so can we say that there are almost as many variations in the nature of men as there are regions; even in the same climates we find that the Oriental is very different from the Occidental: and in the same latitude and at the same distance from the equator the people of the north differ from the people of the south. And, what is more, in the same climate, latitude and longitude, and at the same degree, one can see the difference between hilly country and the plain. . . . The difference be-tween high places and valleys brings about a variety of tem-peraments [humeurs], and also of customs [mœurs], which causes towns built in rough places to be more subject to sedi-tion and to changes than those which are situated in very flat country.[217]

This reaction from ideal political treatises is but one manifestation of the empirical side of Bodin's thought;[218] in the foreword to
his *Théâtre de la Nature Universelle,* he expresses his intention of
discussing "les causes de chacune chose avec son hystoire," and he
goes on to make it clear that he is distinguishing *efficient* causes
from *final* ones, turning from the medieval teleological explanations
of physical phenomena to empirical ones:

> There is nothing . . . which is more properly the function of
> the Physicist than to seek out the efficient causes of all things,
> & to refute the false opinions of others by very certain & evi-
> dent demonstrations.[219]

However, it is in his political and historical writings that he fur-
nishes us with the best evidence that he believes, with Machiavelli,
that "what is needed is an understanding of things as they are, not
dreams of what they might be."[220] Both Bodin and Louis Le Roy
did much to purge the study of history of the "imaginary," and to
change it from an art to at least an incipient science.

In this respect, however, the trail blazer of the Counter-Renaissance was Agrippa, who had made very flat and unpleasant statements about "Historiographers," who

> doo so mutche disagree amonge themselves, and doo write so
> variable and divers thinges of one matter, that it is impossible,
> but that a number of them shoulde be verie Liers. . . .[221]

After listing and describing various sorts of lying, flattering and
corrupt historians, Agrippa goes on to develop the Machiavellian
emphasis:

> There be moreover many, whiche write Histories, not so mutche
> to tell the Truthe, as to delite that thei maie expresse, and
> depainte, the Image of a noble Prince, in whom they please.
> Whiche if any shal reprove for liynge, they saie, that *they*
> *have not so greate a regarde, to things done, as to the profite*
> *of the posteritee, and to the fame of witte,* and therefore they
> have not declared *all things, as they have benne donne, but*
> *how they ought to be declared.* . . .[222]

Of all the figures of the Counter-Renaissance who based their
thought upon this central distinction, however, perhaps Francisco
Guicciardini was the most ruthlessly consistent. After writing, "We
are much beholden to Machiavel," Bacon adds—"and to others, that
write what men do and not what they ought to do. . . ." Of those
"others," it is doubtful if he is more "beholden" to any one than to

Guicciardini, whom he paraphrases in his essay, "Of Simulation and Dissimulation."[223]

Whether one summarizes Guicciardini's disillusioned observation of events and men "as they are" in the way Montaigne (hardly an ingénu himself) did:

> Of all actions how glorious soever in appearance they be of themselves, he doth ever impute the cause of them to some vicious and blame-worthie occasion, or to some commoditie and profit,[224]

or in terms of Geffray Fenton, who translated Guicciardini's *History of Italy* into English in 1578:

> Onely the man for his integritie and roundness was such one, as whose vertues were farre from all suspicion of parcialitie, favour, hatred, love, reward, or any other propertie of humaine affection, which might have force to corrupt or turne from the truth the minds of a writer . . .[225]

one must admit that his objectivity exceeds that of Machiavelli. This man who could describe with cold precision the imminent dissolution of Italy as a nation, and then advise "his compatriots to forget it and look to their private interests—as he was doing—"[226] possessed a cynicism of outlook far more extensive than that of the man who wrote the last chapter of *The Prince*. And while, as Professor Taylor has said, Guicciardini was "a matchless observer of the concrete human fact," far less likely than Machiavelli to allow his observations "to be deflected to the constructive uses of his thought," and hence quick to observe the flaws in some of his older friend's arguments[227]—this very "superiority" makes him a much colder, more cynical, and less appealing man than Machiavelli, who, during his retirement at his farm, would ceremoniously dress in his best clothes to read his favorite classical authors.[228]

At any rate, Guicciardini's writings display, over and over again, an unwavering insistence upon the need to distinguish between the way things, men and the world ought to be, and the way they really are. He warns that

> In that which concerns affairs of state one must not so much consider what is according to reason, the duty of the prince, as his probable conduct in the light of his nature or his habits, for it often happens that princes do not do their duty, but rather what appears to them good; and he who chooses to make a decision by other rules exposes himself to enormous blunders.[229]

Here we have the now familiar rejection of the traditional concept of a prince who acts in accordance with the dictates of natural reason in the pursuit of justice. And Guicciardini makes his advice more general, to include all men:

> Have always in mind . . . not so much that which men ought to do rationally as that which, considering well their nature and their customs, you can believe that they will do.[230]

"What men do and not what they ought to do. . . ." Guicciardini goes so far as to assert that a man who wants to live as God would have him, must leave society together. And he explains that it is not wise to be overheard talking as honestly as he is now, for here he is speaking

> as the true nature of things demands.[231]

Finally, his belief that this "true nature of things" may be discovered only through "experience" and the "observation of facts"— that knowledge and reality exist exclusively through and in the world of empirical actuality—becomes apparent when he is explaining the similarity of the proverbs of various nations:

> The proverbs of all nations are almost all either identical or similar. The reason for this is that the proverbs are born of experience—that is to say, from the observations of facts, which are everywhere identical or similar.[232]

Perhaps no other single characteristic of the Counter-Renaissance has so extensive an elaboration in the sixteenth- and early seventeenth-century literature as the pragmatic emphasis of its empiricists upon the discrepancy between the ideal and the actual. And in this observation is to be found one key to the importance of this movement to the disintegration of the medieval world-view.

For there are three major philosophical (or semi-philosophical) attitudes toward the relationship between the ideal and the actual —that which ought to be and that which is.[233] The first, which ignores or belittles empiricism, maintains the identity of that which ought to be and that which is, endorses the objective validity of normative laws and principles in the very nature of the universe. Any discrepancy between these standards and observed reality is to the discredit of the latter, which is most often depreciated as unreliable, either because the constant flux of the sensible world makes certain knowledge through experience impossible, or because of the unreliability of the never constant or accurate observer. The philosopher holding such a position relies upon the intellect to find out the permanent truth and law.

The second attitude neither denies the discrepancy between the ideal and the actual, nor believes it irremediable. It at once subscribes to the over-all validity of what ought to be, and admits the failure of the empirical world to achieve that perfection. It roots the ideal in the actual, and it motivates the actual by the ideal. It holds a middle ground, recognizing the usefulness to knowledge of both intellectual concept and the observation of the empirical world, and asserting their mutually supplementary characters.

The third attitude rejects altogether the possibility of any realization of the ideal, which it completely divorces from the actual. On the one hand, it sees what ought to be, compounded of theory, hypothesis and fancy; and on the other, what is, consisting of practice, observation and fact. It either denies any reality to the former, or at least any value relevant to the living of life; it acknowledges the world of experience alone as real. Hence it distrusts intellectual knowledge and relies upon a radical empiricism—that of Machiavelli's "verità effetuale" and Montaigne's advocacy of what "by uncontrolled experience we palpably touch. . . ."

For the third attitude is, of course, that of the men we have been studying, and the violence of their reaction leads them to accuse all the Scholastics of holding to the first. In so far as the accusation is just, its validity rests upon the presence of Platonic elements in the Scholastics' thought, or in their Platonizing and Christianizing interpretation of Aristotle—for Aristotle's own mature philosophy is centered in the concept of "immattered form" which is one of the clearest statements of the second position ever made. And a very good case, for that matter, may also be made for many of the Scholastics having held to the second attitude.

At all events, the basic distinction, for men like Machiavelli, Guicciardini, Agrippa, Montaigne and Bacon, between men and things as they ought to be and as they are, is reflected countless times in Italian, French, Spanish and English literature from the early sixteenth century to the early seventeenth. It is no exaggeration to say that this theme, together with its sister one, the discrepancy between appearance and reality, appears in most of the major imaginative literature of the period. Ariosto's *Orlando Furioso* and Cervantes' *Don Quixote* turn these themes to the service of "debunking" various aspects of chivalry. In other connotations, they are central to Rabelais' satire and to Montaigne's *Essayes*. And they literally saturate Elizabethan literature. To take Shakespeare alone—

if one were to remove the variations on these themes from *Much Ado about Nothing, Measure for Measure, Troilus and Cressida, All's Well That Ends Well, King Lear, Hamlet, Macbeth, Othello, Timon of Athens,* and *The Tempest,* there would be little left of the ideological structure of these plays.[234]

To be sure, these themes are not peculiar to the period. They are the food of satire, in particular, in all ages. The Middle Ages, for that matter, had produced a Chaucer and a Jean de Meun. Moreover, when one considers all the conceivable variations of two such sweeping generalizations, one comes close to having a catalogue of all possible literary themes.

But not quite, for—to risk one more generalization—in accordance with the temper of an age, literature tends ideologically in one of two directions. In an optimistic period, one dominated by a single world-view, literature is apt to embody this largely consistent orthodoxy in a defense of the *status quo,* a justification of the ways of God or nature or the state of things as they are—hence to identify, or at least relate, the way they should be with the way they are. Conversely, in an age of intellectual unrest and disenchantment, there is likely to be a corresponding literature, emphasizing the wide gap between the ideal and the actual. And such a preponderance of the second kind of theme in the Counter-Renaissance is one of the clearest indications of its transitional nature, its wasteland character of skepticism and uncertainty, coming as it does between two highly confident and secure world-views.

Finally, much of this dichotomy of the ideal and the actual, the apparent and the real, in the sixteenth-century literature does seem to me derivative from its forthright exposition in the thought of the empiricists and pragmatists we have been studying, from Machiavelli to Bacon. Machiavelli states, in advocating retaining at least "the semblance of the old forms" of a state. that

> the great majority of mankind are satisfied with appearances, as though they were realities, and are often even more influenced by the things that seem than by those that are.[235]

And Bacon asks:

> Doth any man doubt, that if there were taken out of Mens Mindes, Vaine Opinions, Flattering Hopes, False valuations, Imaginations as one would, and the like; but it would leave the Mindes, of a Number of Men, poore shrunken Things; full of Melancholy, and Indisposition, and unpleasing to themselves?[236]

But while both of these men suggest the ways in which this gullibility of mankind may be turned to the advantage of "les esprits avisés," they themselves do much to make "the great majority of mankind" less reliant upon "appearances," "Imaginations as one would," etc. And their contributions to the scientific attitude and method of thousands of men who violently condemned their ethic of expediency is incontestable.

There is no greater influence in the growth of the science of the particular in the Counter-Renaissance than that of these men whose fundamental premise was the incompatibility of the ideal and the actual. For this assumption was for them another way of saying that the universal has no reality, and that only the individual or particular has.

Montaigne illustrates the identity or strong similarity of these two positions particularly clearly. "Others fashion man, I repeat him," he declares,

> and represent *a particular one*, but ill made; and whom were I to forme a new, he should be far other than he is; *but he is now made*. And though the lines of my picture change and vary, *yet loose they not themselves.*[237]

Herein Montaigne identifies the science of the particular with that of man "as he is," and expresses his confidence in the truth of empirical reality. This is the essay "Of Repenting," and he has moved on from the inclusive skepticism of the "Apologie" to the affirmation of that knowledge to be gained through observation; his picture from life may have wavering lines, but those lines are never really "lost." The actual may be recorded, the ideal only feigned; so he describes "not th' essence but the passage," and

> not a passage from age to age, or as the people reckon, from seaven yeares to seaven, but from day to day, from minute to minute.[238]

Here he becomes the first man (to the best of my knowledge) to express in literature an awareness of the modern consciousness of time (not, to be sure, time-space)—to divorce time from its theological and cyclic connotations and present it "as it is" (still arbitrarily recorded, of course) to the average man. Surely it is not extravagant to see in this specification of "from minute to minute" an idea which parallels, in terms of time, the enthusiasm demonstrated in other aspects of the Counter-Renaissance for the particular, for the empirically "actual," and even for the "humble."

This whole passage is pregnant with Montaigne's realization that he is breaking new ground. He goes on to say that most writers on man have discussed the ideal, the universal, the *genus* man. He, on the contrary, is content to deal with a particular one—and not an exalted one, at that:

> I propose a meane life and without luster; 'Tis all one. They fasten all morall Philosophy as well to a popular and private life as to one of richer stuffe. Every man beareth the whole stampe of humane condition. Authors communicate themselves unto the world by some speciall and strange marke; *I the first, by my generall disposition; as Michael de Montaigne, not as a Grammarian, or a Poet, or a Lawyer.* If the world complaine I speake too much of my selfe, I complaine it thinkes no more of itselfe.[239]

It is the first statement in literature of a conscious attempt to depict at length a single and particular man, with his peculiarities, his unique characteristics, his own and unmatched idiosyncracies.[240] It is Michel de Montaigne, not the representative ·of a trade, a guild or a profession, who is the subject of this study—an individual, not the *genus* man. It is, moreover, an actual man, in the sense of one who is living upon earth at this time, and not an idealized portrait of man as he should be.

Nor does the author doubt his ability to come at the truth of himself. "Nosce teipsum," the humanist watchword of the ages, takes on new force here; its traditional meanings[241] are thrown to the winds, and it acquires a new psychological, semi-scientific significance—and a wholly particularized one. He declares expressly that he has no use for those who

> alledge Plato and Saint Thomas for things, which the first man they meete would decide as well, and stand for as good a witnesse. . . .

Such men, he maintains,

> are buried and entombed under the Arte of CAPSULA TOTAE. It is because they do not sufficiently know themselves. . . .[242]

"Looke a little into the course of our experience," he advises:

> There is no man (*if he listen to himselfe*) that doth not discover in himselfe a *peculiar* forme of his, a swaying forme, which wrestleth against the institution, and against the tempests of passions, *which are contrary unto him*.[243]

This is his famous *patron dedans,* and it is clearly not, as usually interpreted, simply another version of the idea of the light of natural reason.[244] On the contrary, in *each* man, it assumes a form peculiar to him. So Montaigne explains,

> The world lookes ever for right, I turne my sight inward, there I fix it, there I ammuse it. Every man lookes before himselfe, I looke within my selfe: I have no business but with my selfe. I uncessantly consider, controle and taste my selfe: other men go ever else where if they thinke well on it: they go ever foreward.[245]

From the very outset, the reader is to understand this clearly: "Thus gentle Reader my selfe am the groundworke of my booke: It is then no reason thou shouldest employ thy time about so frivolous and vaine a Subject."[246] He repeats over and over again the identification of book and author:

> Else-where one may commend or condemme the worke without the worke-man, heere not; who toucheth one toucheth the other . . .[247]

and his almost exclusive concern with the study of himself:

> I study my selfe more than any other subject. It is my supernatural Metaphysike, it is my naturall Philosophy.[248]

True to the Hand-in-the-Wound school, he has no patience with those who prefer classical texts to the testimony of their own experience:

> We can talk and prate, Cicero saith thus, These are Platoes customes, These are the verie words of Aristotle; but what say we ourselves? What doe we? What judge we?[249]

and:

> I had rather understand my selfe well in my selfe then in Cicero. Out of the experience I have of my selfe I find sufficient ground to make my selfe wise were I but a good proficient scholler. Whosoever shall commit to memory the excesse or inconvenience of his rage or anger past, and how farre that fit transported him, may see the deformity of that passion better than in Aristotle, and conceive a more just hatred against it.[250]

Thus he explicitly carries to its logical conclusion the divorcing of the ideal and the actual propounded by men like Machiavelli, Guicciardini and Bacon. His *Essayes* constitute an inclusive testimonial to the superior certainty of one's own particular experience over that of universal theory. And he further links this conviction to his preference for "unscience" and his distrust of man's learning and capacity for knowledge:

> It is by my experience I accuse human ignorance, which (in mine opinion) is the surest part of the Worlds schoole.[251]

To be sure, in his pursuit of "Moi-même" and his recounting of his experience, he has not had a totally free course:

> I speake truth, not my belly-full, but as much as I dare; and I dare the more the more I grow into yeares, for it seemeth, custome alloweth old age more liberty to babble, and indiscretion to talke of it selfe.[252]

In short, he admits to his reader that "publicke reverence" hampers somewhat the exactness of his portrait. Yet, he points out,

> Had my intention beene to forstal and purchase the worlds opinion and favour, I would surely have adorned my selfe more quaintly, or kept a more grave and solemne march. *I desire therein to be delineated in mine owne genuine, simple, and ordinarie fashion, without contention, art or study; for it is my selfe I pourtray.* My imperfections shall therein be read to the life, and my naturall forme discerned, so farre-forth as publike reverence hath permitted me. For if my fortune had beene to have lived among those nations, which yet are said to live under the sweet liberty of Natures first and uncorrupted lawes, I assure thee, I would most willingly have pourtrayed my selfe fully and naked.[253]

But even as it is, he is convinced

> that never man handled subject he understood or knew better then I doe this I have undertaken, being therein the cunningst man alive,

and, secondly,

> .that never man waded further into his matter, nor more distinctly sifted the parts and dependences of it, nor arrived more exactly and fully to the end he proposed unto himselfe. . . .[254]

Lest it seem that this account of Montaigne's original contribution to the history of thought be simply one of those willful or unintentional intellectual anachronisms which takes no account of "semantic change" or the "historical 'meaning' of a given 'idea'";[255] and that therefore the Elizabethans, for example, would not have attributed this significance to Montaigne's work, let me quote from Samuel Daniel's poem, written "To my deere friend M, *John Florio*, concerning his *translation* of Montaigne":

> . . . this great Potentate,
> This Prince *Montaigne* (if he be not more)
> Hath more adventur'd of his own estate
> Then ever man did of himselfe before . . .
>
> .   .   .   .
>
> .   .   .   .
>
> .   .   .   .
>
> And let the *Critic* say the worst he can,
> He cannot say but that *Montaigne* yet,
> Yeeldes most rich pieces and extracts of man;
> Though in a troubled frame confus'dly set. . . .[256]

In Montaigne's "culte de moi" the science of the particular is carried as far as it may be. Careful as is Machiavelli, for example, to appeal to particularized historical events (and, in the *Prince* especially, to recent ones[257]), he does not go so far as Montaigne. For he is not content simply to present the fact. Thus in the chapter, "Of the Value of Artillery to Modern Armies . . ." (in the *Discourses*), he writes, noting place, date, and protagonists very exactly,

> All this cannot be gainsaid, for we have seen how the Swiss at Novara, in 1513, without cavalry or artillery, went to encounter the French, who were well provided in their entrenchments with artillery, and routed them without suffering much from the effect of the guns.

But he does not stop there; he gives the reason, and draws general conclusions concerning the use of artillery:

> And the reason of this is, that, beside the other things mentioned above, the artillery, to be well served, needs to be protected by walls, ditches, or earthworks; and if it lacks this protection it is either captured or becomes useless. . . .

He even asserts dogmatically,

> And whoever employs artillery differently does not understand the matter well. . . .[258]

In the words of Professor Taylor,

> His furthest intellectual end and practical object all in one, was validity, pragmatic truth, *verità effetuele*, the rule that may be acted on successfully.[259]

Hence, while Machiavelli continually depreciates the conclusions reached by those who discuss things "as they should be," he eventually is guilty of the very sort of rationalizing of which he accuses the idealists. This is nowhere more apparent than in his sweeping conclusions about the nature of man.

It is especially clear in *The Prince* that one weakness of Machiavelli's reasoning lies in itself—that it is sheer reasoning, and will not fit the unexpected turns of human life. A writer who sets forth, not what men should do, but how they will necessarily act, may fool himself as readily as one who takes into account the irrational and generous conduct of men struggling for ideals or uplifted by a situation.[260]

This is a sound observation. Professor Fletcher has said well, "The pure objectivity of Machiavelli's historical judgments, and of his political policies too, was affected by a theoretic philosophy as *a prioristic* as it is pessimistic";[261] and a careful reading of Machiavelli's text inevitably leads one to the conviction that if he did go to the *facts* first, his lantern-lighted search for an honest man was wholly unsuccessful.

It is, then, Montaigne (who never professes a cynicism so extensive as Machiavelli's), who is actually the greater realist, in our modern sense of the word. For, even if we accept the Florentine's assertion of his observation of things as they are, and his more enlightened employment of the axiom which he applies with conviction to the generality of men—that they "only judge of matters by the result"[262]—yet, even upon that basis he sets down pragmatic rules with as basically naïve a certainty as any of the idealists whom he condemns for being unrealistic. On the other hand, Montaigne, mostly content to fasten upon one subject, himself, and to confine generalizations drawn from that study to an almost irreducible minimum, is much more faithful to the ideal of the science of the particular.

It is quite true, of course, that objectivity is tremendously difficult of attainment in such a limiting of one's focus to oneself. Francisco Sanchez recognizes this in his . . . *Quod Nihil Scitur:*

No external knowledge, he says, can be more certain than that which I possess of my own states and my own actions; the latter is immediate as the former can never be. I have greater certainty that a thought, a desire, a will, stirs within me than I can have that I perceive a certain object or a certain person without me. *On the other hand, inner experience is inferior to outer in clearness and exactitude.*[263]

Yet this is largely to return to the position of a philosophical skepticism which contradicts the possibility of any certain knowledge. Montaigne never formally rejects this position, but in the third book of the *Essayes* he moves consistently toward a greater and greater trust in that which "by uncontrolled experience we palpably touch. . . ." And this tendency is apparent in most of the skeptics of the Counter-Renaissance. Unwilling to rest in an attitude which denies validity alike to sensitive and to rational knowledge, they prefer, for a positive program, to trust practice rather than theory, empiricism rather than logic, sense rather than reason, the particular rather than the universal. None of their characteristics more clearly marks their disagreement with the thinkers of the Scientific Reformation, with their emphasis upon the quantitative measurement of reality, culminating in Galileo's distinction between primary and secondary knowledge, with its disparagement of the accuracy of sense perception.[264]

Montaigne is representative of the opposite trend, followed by the Counter-Renaissance. He tells us that he has been told

> that in Geometry (which supposeth to have gained the high point of certainty among all sciences) there are found unavoidable Demonstrations, and which subvert the truth of all experience. . . .[265]

He recognizes that the mathematical truth of reason and the pragmatic truth of experience "are things that often shock together"; but he is content with his reply to "one of those professours of novelties, and Physicall reformations":

> I had rather follow the effects, then his reason. . . .[266]

This is in the *Apologie*, where he denies any certain knowledge to the senses. Yet even here he declares,

> There is no greater absurditie in our judgment, then to maintaine that fire heateth not. . . . Nor beliefe or science in man, that may be compared unto that, in certaintie.[267]

If we don't accept the answers of the philosophers to such questions as "is ice cold?" it is the philosophers who are to blame, he argues—for one can always apply a piece of ice to one's bosom, for a more forceful answer than theirs. If they had been content to leave us in the happy "state of nature," judging by our "senses, and had suffered us to follow our naturall appetites" and experience, all would have been well. But since they taught us to believe "that man's reason is the generall controuler . . . by meanes whereof all things are knowne and discerned," they must produce better evidence if they would be believed.[268]

A comparison of Louis Le Roy's description of man's intellectual progress with that of Jean Bodin illustrates admirably this attitude of the Counter-Renaissance, and its almost exclusive emphasis upon the part the senses play in knowledge. Bodin's account (in the *Republic*) follows the traditional, largely Platonic theory of knowledge:

> Puis, se tournant à la beauté de la nature, l'homme prend plaisir à la variété des animaux, des plantes, des minéraux . . . puis laissant la région élémentaire, il dresse son vol jusqu'au ciel avec les ailes de contemplation, pour voir la splendeur, la beauté, la force des lumières célestes . . . alors il est ravi d'un plaisir admirable, accompagné d'un désir perpétuel de trouver là la première cause et celui qui fut auteur d'un si beau chef-d'œuvre: auquel, étant parvenu, il arrête là le cours de ses contemplations, voyant qu'il est infini et incompréhensible, en essence, en grandeur, en puissance, en sagesse, en bonté.[269]

Here Bodin, manifesting the conservative side of his thought, simply follows orthodoxy's traditional concept of successive stages of knowledge—from that of the sublunary world, mostly perceived through the senses, to the intellectual contemplation of the translunary world, and finally to the fulfillment of the "proper" human end, the contemplation of God.[270]

Le Roy, on the other hand, sees the story of man's intellectual progress as a particular *historical* transformation in time and space —not as a universal progression toward the final good of God.[271] He describes how men, after learning through experience the way to provide themselves with necessary commodities, apply themselves "à l'étude des lettres."

> Parce que tous, naturellement, désirent savoir les choses nouvelles, étranges, admirables, belles, et en entendre les causes: chérissant entre les sens principalement la vue et l'ouïe, qui leur aident à en avoir connaisance.[272]

In the course of his long description of the various kinds of knowledge sought, he dutifully records that

> Ils [les hommes] ont appelé cette partie inférieure du monde . . . la région de fausseté et d'opinion: et l'autre [partie] supérieure . . . où sont les formes et exemples des choses, le siège de vérité.

Yet he goes on directly to the statement that

> *En ce progrès de savoir, ils ont connu quelques choses par*

> *instinct naturel sans doctrine, les autres choses avec observa-*
> *tions, usage, et expérience.* . . .[273]

The attitude of Sanchez well sums up the ultimate relationship between the skepticism and the radical empiricism of the Counter-Renaissance—sums it up in a fashion which convincingly parallels its manifestation in Montaigne. For Sanchez is not simply a skeptic:

> Doubt is for him not an end but a means. His skeptical work only forms the introduction to *a series of empirical works on particular subjects.* It was his intention also to write a special treatise on method. He commends *observation and experiment,* in conjunction with the exercise of the judgment, as the best way to knowledge. His motto is: *Go to things themselves!* . . . [Yet] *he regards a complete knowledge of things as an unattainable ideal.*[274]

This summary of his stand on knowledge and science includes almost all of the characteristic features of the Counter-Renaissance science of the particular. Beginning in skepticism, he moves on to "a *series* of *empirical* works on *particular* subjects." Approving "observation and experiment," he advocates going "to things themselves" for knowledge, but without any conviction of the possibility of "a complete knowledge of things." It is clearly the nominalistic science of the particular to which Sanchez turns from his philosophical skepticism.[275]

Yet this statement must be qualified, for Sanchez approves "observation and experiment, *in conjunction with the exercise of the judgment,* as the best way to knowledge." This position, together with his quoted motto and his emphasis upon *method,* mark him as one of the middle figures of the Counter-Renaissance, halfway between the radical "loose" empiricists and Francis Bacon.

Indeed, perhaps it would be more accurate to admit that there never were any empiricists who were capable of totally divorcing experience from reason. For all their protestations, their almost exclusive verbal *emphasis* upon experience, Vives, Machiavelli, Guicciardini, Sanchez, Ramus, even Montaigne—all of the radical empiricists—eventually found it impossible to isolate raw experience, the mere act of observing, from the "contamination" of reason. That they should desire to do so—and to believe that it was possible to do away with hypothesis—is understandable and excusable in the face of the Scholastics' largely unguarded rationalism; what they actually accomplished was to bring home forcibly to men's minds that the world of empirical reality could not be ignored without disastrous results to knowledge and science. Their appeal for a return to Nature—to the observation and interpretation of her, rather than the "anticipation" of her by pure hypothesis—had an eventual salutary effect; although, particularly in physics, the Scientific Reformation was once more to turn to "anticipating" nature before testing her.

Salutary—for while Galileo and other representatives of the science-to-come returned to the traditional Aristotelian view of science as dialectical and deductive,[276] they did not return to a teleological physics, but turned instead to a mathematical one. And the contribution which the empiricists of the Counter-Renaissance made toward this scientific progress was considerable. For despite their indifference to mathematics, their emphasis upon the world of matter resulted in the neutralizing of nature, in the replacing of the Aristotelian "form" as the cardinal unit in nature by that of physical force.

Here, in other words, is another (and perhaps the last) of those parallel interpretations of the defenders of "things as they are." To the dichotomy of the ideal and the actual, of appearance and reality, of the universal and the particular, may be added that of form and matter. The Aristotelian concept of "immattered form" had united mental concept and sensitive knowledge, had bridged "the contrast between pure thought and the empirical study of individuals."[277] But the scientists of the Counter-Renaissance strove to separate them, to destroy the bridge which maintained a purpose in nature, and one of these scientists, Bernardino Telesio, to this end replaced the idea of "form" with that of "force." This meant that

> explanation must not be sought in quality, in the complete form of the phenomenon, as is the case with the work of an artist, which we understand as soon as we discover the ideal he has sought to realise,[278]

but that instead it must be confined to material, physical explanation.

Professor De Wulf's summary of Telesio's *De natura rerum juxta propria principia*[279]—that it is the

> work of a naif but logical physicist, in which he endeavours to explain nature by a restricted number of physical forces[280]

—is largely just. What Telesio's explanations lack is "an insight into the regular interconnection of phenomena"[281]—the concept of mathematical law provided by the Scientific Reformation. And it is this very midway position between the espousers of the laws of teleological nature and those of a mathematical nature which makes him so satisfactory an example of the physical science of the Counter-Renaissance. His physics, based on the primary principles of matter and force, is the scientific twin to Machiavelli's politics. Each denies purposive and normative law in his respective realm; each is convinced that *nothing* strives after any goal *except self-preservation.*[282]

In almost every aspect of his thought, Telesio (who greatly influenced Bacon and Bruno) illustrates those features of the Counter-Renaissance which we have been considering. He attacks "Nature's secretaries" in the usual way, and expresses his intention of being satisfied with human wisdom, which is limited to sensuous experience: "Non ratione, sed sensu!"[283] He anticipates Bruno's *indifferenza della natura,* maintaining that the expanding and contracting principles of force which he postulates work upon a matter universally uniform.[284] His devotion to his motto is so inclusive that he attributes consciousness to matter, and strives to reduce all thought to feeling, denying the distinction between the two.[285]

When Francisco Patrizzi reproaches him for his contempt for reason (*ratio*), his definition of reason clearly anticipates that of Bacon in *Novum Organum.* For he says,

> I in no way despite reason, *i.e. that knowledge of things which is given to us,* not through sensation, but *through the resemblance of things which are perceived by sensation,* and I could never believe that it is to be despised. But I shall always maintain that sensation is more to be trusted than reason.[286]

Even when Telesio leaves purely naturalistic explanations to predicate a second soul, besides the material one in man—a second soul which is "non-corporeal form . . . super-added from above (*forma superaddita*)"[287]—like Bruno, and true to the "double" nominalistic tradition, he deserts the empirical only for the mystical. His doctrine of "forma superaddita" may have been simply a concession to theology; at any rate, Telesio never clearly explains its relation to the rest of his philosophy, makes no attempt to fit it into any intellectual synthesis. . . .

If the neutralizing of nature, the denial of its functioning by *purposive* law, was the most significant contribution made by the empirical scientists and philosophers of the Counter-Renaissance to scientific progress, it was not the only one. The *goal* which these empiricists found most appropriate and legitimate for scientific knowledge also marked a radical departure from the Scholastic and humanistic traditions, and established the direction which the later Scientific Reformation was to follow. The Scholastic scientists had found their goal in the contemplation of God's truth, the Renaissance humanists (inclined to emphasize the arts more than the sciences) found theirs in the virtuous conduct of life. But the empiricists of the Counter-Renaissance conceive of knowledge in general, and of scientific knowledge in particular, as valuable in proportion to their practical usefulness to men—not so much in terms of helping them to lead virtuous lives, as comfortable, secure and healthy ones. If, with their increasing concern with ethical activity, the orthodox humanists took the first step toward the establishment of an "attitude of thought or action centering upon distinctively human interests or ideals,"[288] these empirical scientists complete the shift in emphasis from the angelification of man to the furthering of "progress," in the modern sense.

Vives, who was an orthodox humanist in many respects, nevertheless exemplifies well the emergence of this new ideal in the early sixteenth century. Adopting a typical yet modified (since it is not *all* learning which he condemns) "vanity" attitude, he finds a "useful" inquiry, one pointed towards man's *needs*, far more "worthy" and "suitable" than "an investigation as to the measure or material of the heavens. . . ."[289] If asked, what arts and sciences should we study? his reply is,

> What other than those which are necessary for the aims of either this or the eternal life. They will either advance piety or be of service to the necessities, or at least the uses of life, *for the latter are not greatly different from the necessities.*[290]

This is a quite different concept of "the uses of life" from that of the average Christian humanist, and various attitudes characteristic of the Counter-Renaissance are implicit in this and other passages in his *De Tradendis Disciplinis*. Here he presents the alternative goals of knowledge as those of devout Catholicism and of the new utilitarianism. He is clearly of the "separatist," not the "reconciliation" party; although he does not consistently believe, with the fideists, in the complete corruption of man's intellectual powers by original sin, he entertains a qualified "corruption theory," and is thoroughly skeptical of the capacity of those powers to attain certain knowledge—which is rather "the function of religion."[291] Hence he advises turning either to the sciences of the particular (and with a practical emphasis, to supplying the *needs* of life), or to the devout and reverent contemplation of God and his works:

The first precept in the contemplation and discussion of nature, is that since we cannot gain any certain knowledge from it, we must not indulge ourselves too much in examining and inquiring into those things which we can never attain, but that all our studies should be applied to the necessities of life, to some bodily or mental gain, to the cultivation and increase of reverence.[292]

If the second of his three alternative aims in this passage suggests the humanistic ideal, and the third the Scholastic, a further consideration of his thought reveals the distinctive difference of his emphasis. For it is clear that he endorses no intellectualistic science. He asserts that "even the contemplation of God . . . should be turned to some use," and he has already denied the possibility of any certain knowledge of nature. Nor does he relate scientific study to an ethical ideal. His tone is forthright and practical:

Before everything, we must remember that the needs of life are varied and numerous, since they pass by in single moments, one need arising out of another, so that if we rightly spend our time, there is no moment remains over for trifling, and all branches of knowledge must be applied, not to any empty dilettantism but to the practice of life.[293]

It has been customary to think of such passages in Vives as expositions of the humanist ideal of virtuous activity, the "good life"; but an analysis of this paragraph, for example, shows clearly that it is the empiricists' program which he sponsors. There is a suggestion of that new fluid, dynamic concept of time which Montaigne is to develop in Vives' "they pass by in single moments, one need arising out of another"; and his businesslike emphasis upon "use," "need" and "practice" strikes a very different chord from that sounded by the proponents of Right Reason in pursuit of virtue.

Indeed, when Vives called "practical wisdom, the directress of the whole of life,"[294] he sums up the whole tone of his De Tradendis —more, of the empiricist movement of the Counter-Renaissance. The orthodox Christian humanists, too, espouse an ideal which is practical, in its concern with the living of life on earth. But the latter invoke an *a priori* moral principle and purpose; knowledge is acquired in the service of a rational ideal which leads to virtue. The empiricists are moving instead toward a wholly utilitarian ideal; it is not the ethical art of life, but the converting of nature's resources to the uses and needs of life which interests them. And although Vives is at one with the humanists on many points, his scientific ideal is of this other, utilitarian order.

Yet he is not fully representative of it. In his writings it is an emergent ideal, germinating slowly from the ground prepared by the protest against Scholastic intellectualism. As developed later, by thoroughly naturalistic empiricists of the Machiavelli-Montaigne-Bacon cast, it becomes the inevitable logical sequitur to their "neutralizing" of nature, to their recognition of the all but exclusive reality of matter, to their basic distinction between things as they are and as they should be.

"Now who doth not enter into distrust of sciences," Montaigne demands,

> And who is not in doubt, whether in any necessity of life he may reape solid fruit of them, if he consider the use we have of them?[295]

It is *utility* which Machiavelli stresses in both the *Prince* and the *Discourses*—stresses as the very purpose of his writing at all, and as the mainspring of his departure from traditional attitudes:

> It being my intention to write a thing which shall be useful to him who apprehends it, it appears to me more appropriate to follow up the real truth of a matter than the imagination of it . . .[296]

and

> If my poor talents, my little experience of the present and insufficient study of the past, should make the result of my labors defective and *of little utility*, I shall at least have shown the way to others. . . .[297]

But it is Bacon who is, of course, the great publicizer of the movement for a purely utilitarian scientific ideal. Men, he declares, tend to ask too much "wherefrom," when they should be asking "whereby things are produced";

> Their labor is spent in investigating and handling the first principles of things and the highest generalities of nature; whereas *utility and the means of working* result entirely from things intermediate. Hence it is that men cease not from abstracting nature till they come to potential and uninformed matter, nor on the other hand from dissecting nature till they reach the atom; *things which, even if true, can do but little for the welfare of man.* . . .[298]

And in his *Author's Preface to the Great Instauration*, he proclaims:

> Lastly, I would address one general admonition to all; that they consider what are the true ends of knowledge, and that they seek it not either for pleasure of the mind, or for con-

tention or for superiority to others, or for profit, or fame, or power, or any of these inferior things; *but for the benefit and use of life;* and that they perfect and govern it in charity.[299]

Whether in negative or in positive, in critical or in expository terms, this is his plea everywhere. What he has to say in his essay "Of Building" might be taken as a motto for his outlook:

> Houses are built to live in, and not to Looke on: Therefore let Use bee preferred before Uniformitie; Except where both may be had.[300]

The utilitarian scientific ideal, with its appeal to common sense, inevitably attracted those technical artisans, the "unlearned" scientists of the Renaissance who contributed so much to the advancement of empirical science. Robert Norman speaks for them when he writes,

> To conclude, the chiefest & onely marke whereat I lay levell, was the benefiting of my Countriemen, in whom I wish continuall increase of knowledge and cunning, as in all other commendable professions, *so chieflie in those that are most necessary and profitable.*[301]

To these utilitarian empiricists, the goal of the sciences is, in short, the promotion of the comfort and happiness of men, in very concrete terms—terms which forecast the ultimate modern ideal of technological progress. Man, harnessing nature, achieves a new power to develop his material civilization. Bacon speaks for this whole movement of the Counter-Renaissance when he says definitively:

> Now the true and lawful goal of the sciences is none other than this: that human life be endowed with new discoveries and powers.[302]

We have come as far as we may from the Scholastic scientific ideal, when we reach this one of power. And with this sentence, the comparison and contrast of the goals of the magician-scientist and the pure empiricist of the Counter-Renaissance which I made at the beginning of this chapter should be illuminated. For power was also the goal of the magician—that power which might turn a man into a god. The power which empiricists invoke, however, is not an individualistic goal (we have seen that Bacon expressly repudiates "power" in that sense), but the power to enrich the material life of mankind: "the use we have of them" . . . "of little utility" . . . "the welfare of man" . . . "the benefit and use of life"

. . . "the benefiting of my Countriemen" . . . "that human life be
endowed with new discoveries and powers. . . ."

The ubiquitous Gabriel Harvey agreeably links the two concepts
of power in a short passage which explicitly contrasts (without
passing judgment) the public ideal of the empiricist with the individualistic one of the esotericist:

> Let every man in his degree enioy his due: and let the brave
> enginer, fine Daedalist, skilfull Neptunist, marvelous Vulcanist,
> and every Mercurial occupationer, that is, *every Master of his
> craft,* and every *Doctour of his mystery,* be respected accord-
> ing to the uttermost extent of *his publique service,* or *private
> industry.*[303]

The "Master" of a "craft" with "his publique service"; the "Doc-
tour" of a "mystery" with his "private industry." . . .

Vives had propounded the goal of knowledge as twofold, to
contribute either to "reverence" and "the eternal life," or to the
"necessities" and "uses" of this life. A passage in his *De Tradendis*
indicates clearly how these two concepts blended in his mind, and
—in its emphasis upon original sin and a return to the simplicity
of pure primitive Christianity—anticipates the attitude of the Reformation towards science:

> Let me give a warning, now at the threshold, [that] since
> human sinfulness has matured all over the world, and the de-
> praved affections of the soul have become so strong, it has
> become necessary that the sciences should be handed on more
> purely, more simply, and that they should be less infected and
> imbued with craft and impostures. For it is only by this means
> (as far as this may be possible) that Christian people may be
> taken back to the true and native simplicity, and thus all
> branches of knowledge may scatter fewer sparks by which
> minds are inflamed wrongly. . . .[304]

The attitude of the Reformation—for no study of the utilitarian
ideal of Counter-Renaissance science would be complete without
mention of the interesting way in which the Reformation contributed to this ideal.

It is quite true that neither Luther nor Calvin had much use for
the arts and sciences. To them and their followers, the vanity of
learning was undeniable. Yet, laying as they did an almost exclusive emphasis upon the means of salvation, and denying, in terms
of salvation, any efficacy to knowledge and to morality, they (especially Luther) left almost completely open to variant individual
interpretations the course of daily practical life. Whatever recom-

mendations they did make were, in the spirit of Vives, in favor of the simplifying of the sciences and arts alike (as a preventive measure against over-emphasizing them)—and hence largely in favor of those most practical, empirical and utilitarian.

Out of this attitude, despite the rigor of early Protestant convictions about salvation, there emerged "a thoroughly worldly social ideal of labor and commercial gain"[305] which replaced the Christian-classical ethical ideal with one best described as an "ethic of industry and thrift."[306] Even Calvinism, because of its basic antagonism to moralism, contributed to this trend, in its conviction that

> Christian freedom consists in this realization of the provisional, not to say provincial character of moral values and values of gifts, talents, skills and perfections.[307]

The relationship of this tendency to the scientific ideal of utilitarianism is immediately apparent. The new scientific emphasis of the empiricists upon the material welfare of man grows out of the rise of the artisan class and the increasing complexity and wealth of economic life.[308] The Lutheran endorsement of the holiness of work, and the Calvinistic support of capitalism as increasing one's "activity" and "responsibility,"[309] contribute to and swell the current. Thus the early Reformation, in its eagerness to divorce the moral life from salvation, accelerates the age's preoccupation with the practical and utilitarian. And, while in no direct way concerned with scientific progress, it lends its support to the empiricists' program of utility, to further its own ends of depreciating the importance of the moral and intellectual life.

Hence, we become aware of another of those parallel phenomena which characterize the Counter-Renaissance. Just as in the vanity of learning movement, two traditions—the secular and the fideistic —met and became allied, so in the rise of the utilitarian ideal, the secular and pragmatic empiricists gain at least the negative support of the Reformation. And again the alliance is a part of the revolt against moralism and intellectualism—the naturalistic empiricists contributing in the interests of material welfare, the religionists in those of the exclusive pertinence to salvation of faith and grace.

Among the Elizabethans, Fulke Greville illustrates particularly well this alliance of the Reformation with the empiricists. After sixty stanzas (in *A Treatie of Humane Learning*) in which he has brought the weapons of skepticism to bear upon the question of the vanity of learning, he asks outright:

> Yet shall we straight resolve that by neglect

> Of Science, Nature doth the richer grow?
> > That *Ignorance is the mother of Devotion,*
> > *Since Schooles give them that teach this*
> > > *such promotion?*[310]

He will not go all the way with Montaigne, from whom "Nature doth the richer grow" through "unscience"; for "Ignorance," he maintains, is "Nurse, and Mother unto every lust,"[311] and he concludes,

> > Men must not therefore rashly Science scorne,
> > But choose, and read with care; since *Learning* is
> > A bunch of grapes sprung up among the thornes,
> > Where, but by caution, none the harme can misse. . . .[312]

> The corrupt world
> > > still more declines,
> > Both from the truth, and wisedome of Creation:
> > So at the truth she more and more repines,
> > As making host to her last declination.[313]

It is too late to "cure" her completely, and to salvage most of mankind:

> > We must divide God's Children from the rest. . . .[314]

They alone, the "elect," will profit from instruction in discriminating among the sciences, and he sets about their education with the statement:

> > I wish all curious Sciences let blood. . . .[315]

The faithful, in short, will have no intercourse with speculative or occult studies,

> > For man being finite both in wit, time, might,
> > His dayes in vanities may be misspent;
> > Use therefore must stand higher than delight;
> > *The active hate a fruitlesse instrument:*
> > > So must the World those busie idle fooles,
> > > That serve no other market than the Schooles.[316]

Vives' emphasis upon the shortness of man's alloted time, Calvin's and Luther's endorsement of work and activity, the empiricists' ideal of utility—all these are crowded into a single stanza.

And as with the sciences, so with the arts:

> > Again the active, necessarie Arts,
> > Ought to be briefe in bookes, in practise long. . . .

.　.　.　.　.　.　.　.　.　.　.
　　For if these two be in one ballance weigh'd,
　　The artlesse Use beares down the uselesse Arts. . . .[317]

Again the emphasis on the practical—on the "need" and "uses" of
life—and in conjunction with an anti-intellectual bias. So Greville
concludes,

　　Forme Art directly under Natures Lawes;
　　And all effects so in their causes mould . . .
and
　　For Sciences from Nature should be drawne,
　　As Arts from practise, never out of Bookes . . .[318]

thereby completing his affiliation with the empiricists of the Counter-Renaissance, by advocating their rejection of hypothesis, theory,
and *a priori* logic, in favor of a return to direct contact with nature
herself and with efficient causes. . . .

　Together, the traditions of the magician-scientists and the radical
empiricists present the scientific attitudes characteristic of the Counter-Renaissance. In open and extreme revolt against the intellectualistic science of the Scholastics, these two schools opposed the
application of hypothesis and logic to the workings of nature, denied
the possibility of formulating universal laws about these workings,
and turned their backs on all attempts to synthesize scientific knowledge through the employment of dialectic and deduction. The one
group turned from an investigation of the laws of nature to that
of its secrets; the other made an appeal for a return to the observation of the "brute facts" of nature.

　Many prominent individuals figured in both movements; indeed,
some of them dabbled in both occult and naturalistic empiricism.
But the second sort was the hardier growth, and made by far the
more significant contribution to scientific progress. Aside from its
wholly negative contribution (its assistance in the destruction of
Scholastic science), the occult scientists' influence upon the eventual course of the Scientific Reformation was largely indirect and
perhaps even coincidental. For it lies in the fact that Copernicus,
Kepler, Recorde, Dee, Digges and others who played considerable
roles in the development of mathematics and astronomy were (at
least during parts of their careers) strongly affected by the doctrines of Neoplatonic magic or Pythagorean mystical mathematics.
The consequent assertion has been made by E. A. Burtt and others
that the roots of modern physical science are sunk in Platonic meta-

physics, but the convincing evidence presented by John Herman Randall, Jr., E. W. Strong and others, that this influence was minor, and that the real impetus to Galilean and later science came through the Aristotelian tradition sustained throughout the sixteenth century by the School of Padua and through the wedding of artisan and technological empiricism with the mathematics of Euclid and Archimedes, has greatly detracted from the favorable reception of this view.[319]

On the other hand, I believe that the radical empiricists of the Counter-Renaissance, whose significance has of late—chiefly because of their lack of interest in mathematics—been widely depreciated by historians of Renaissance science and philosophy, did make some lasting contributions. Their emphasis upon experiment, observation, and the importance of a return to "particulars," if one-sided and naïvely extreme, certainly helped to induce an intellectual atmosphere favorable to that close consideration of empirical reality which had been largely neglected by Scholastic science. It is true that the Paduan Aristotelians, with a method composed of "resolution" and "composition," had not only not neglected the world of empirical reality, but with scientific insight superior to that of the "pure" empiricists, had seen "all verification and demonstration as inclusion within a logical system of ideas," and had subjected "scientific experience" to "a careful and precise mathematical analysis."[320] Yet the very one-sidedness of the Counter-Renaissance empiricists' emphasis upon "fact," "observation," and "experience" must have been a strong, if secondary, factor in undermining the earlier and equally one-sided Scholastic emphasis upon speculative science.

Again, the radical empiricists' insistence upon a respect for matter, and their establishment of utility as a legitimate criterion of the value of scientific knowledge, may not have been *essential* to the future development of science in these directions; for these views were also held by such sixteenth-century representatives of the critical Aristotelian tradition at Padua as Zabarella. He deserts the medieval teleological science; he demonstrates a healthy concern for "neutralized" matter; he makes "the end of knowledge and inquiry a human thing" and directs "the sciences toward human goals and aims."[321] And in addition, he foreshadows Galileo and the eventual course of science by recognizing the importance of combining hypothesis and principle with empiricism; he does not make the mistake of deserting "universal" science. Yet, once more, the widespread and redundant emphasis of the radical empiricists upon matter and utility must have made its contribution, as well.

It is probably impossible to trace with complete exactitude the eventual influence of the science of the Counter-Renaissance. At all events, both of its important movements died in the seventeenth century, and whatever their influences, they lost their distinctive characteristics and became merged with the new science.

Two distinguished scholars have written their obituaries, which might be headed, "For Want of Mathematics." Of the occult traditions, Lynn Thorndike has written,

> As the later [sixteenth] century wore on, the turning away from Aristotle's natural philosophy and the rise of Paracelsanism encouraged the development of occult philosophy and a favoring attitude toward natural magic.
>
> This tendency continued briskly into the seventeenth century until by its excesses it exhausted and killed itself, and was replaced by the skeptical rationalism and enlightenment of the eighteenth century.[322]

Professor Randall, writing of the Paduan School, disposes of the radical empiricist with a succinct epitaph:

> But the return to experience is not for the sake of certain proof: for throughout the seventeenth century it is almost impossible to find any natural scientist maintaining that a mere fact can prove any certain truth.[323]

In short, the science of the Counter-Renaissance suffered the same fate as did the movement's other particular manifestations. It acted as a buffer between two scientific philosophies, and as a buffer made its contribution to the changes finally introduced by the second of these world-views. Like the other manifestations of the whole movement, it provided a healthful corrective to the extravagances against which it protested; but it was itself too violent an antidote to remain satisfactory for continued use. The Scientific Reformation drained it for those ingredients which it found useful; the others were discarded.

Yet it served its purpose, and it produced one culminating figure who has always merited attention on his own account and deserves it here as the inheritor and final expositor of Counter-Renaissance science. Francis Bacon, like other Elizabethans, and like the Counter-Renaissance itself, stands between two worlds. Especially in his optimism and his concern for methodical systematization, he belongs to the new order of the Scientific Reformation. Yet, "for want of mathematics," he is a true and important son of the Counter-

Renaissance—and in other ways too. For he went to school under Machiavelli, Montaigne, Guicciardini, Vives, Telesio and even (I am inclined to believe) the alchemists, and he has many of their insights and many of their shortcomings. But since he has something more, which is his own, he warrants our particular attention.

4. TOWARD "A TRUE MODEL OF THE WORLD": FRANCIS BACON

Throughout the sixteenth century, there were men aware of standing on the brink of a new order. The vast expanse of *terra incognita* discovered in the last decade of the previous century and the first years of the new one fired their imaginations and gave wings to their words as they spoke, in their turns, of a conviction that in their various fields of knowledge, they, too, were setting out upon "unpathed waters."

When one considers the discoveries made from 1492 to 1610, this is not surprising. What is surprising is that these statements are not more frequent than they are—surprising, at least, until one realizes the hold that various theories concerning the degeneration and decay of man, of nature, of the entire universe, had upon the popular (and even, often, the enlightened) outlook of the time. For all of the period's violent protests against the constricting influence of authority, the conviction that in "this old age of the world" man's capacities were dwindling even as his physical stature had, was too strong and widespread to be shaken off easily. As George Hakewill expresses it early in the seventeenth century, man had too long believed the ancients "to be *Gyants,* and ourselves *Dwarfes. . . .*"[324]

This lack of confidence in the merits of the age, and particularly in the possibility of attaining to any certain scientific knowledge, is especially characteristic of the more sober empiricists of the Counter-Renaissance. The skeptical vein in their thought, their emphasis upon the science of the particular, and their very subversion of the old order—all contribute to give their statements a somber cast. Thus Vives follows the assertion that "truth stands open to all" with the admission that "I do not profess myself the equal of the ancients . . ."[325] and Tycho Brahe leaves his observations of the New Star of 1572, which seem to contradict the Aristotelian doctrine of the immutable heavens, with the expressed conviction that the world is hastening to its end.[326]

Again, many statements which carry a superficial impression of exhilaration in participating in a "springtime of the world" actually speak more for personal arrogance and the conviction of possessing an infallible method or unique pathway to knowledge than of belonging to a period rich in significant discoveries. The bombastic pretensions of Paracelsus and Cardan and Bruno illustrate this tendency.

Yet at the same time, there is a scattering of men in whom the idea of progress is stirring, and who are conscious that the century in which they live is no ordinary one. Cardan gives voice to this conviction too; and it is variously but clearly enunciated by Ramus, Le Roy and Bodin, among others. If their tone is seldom as jubilant as that of Rabelais, dismissing "that Gothic night" of the Middle Ages, or those of the earlier humanists, hymning the praises of learning, still it is steady and sensible and justly proud. And to a man, combating the pessimistic utterances of their time, they point to the many new phenomena disclosed recently.

Typical of these statements is that written by Louis Le Roy in 1567, when he expresses his conviction that the sixteenth is probably the most advanced of all centuries. He buttresses his assertion with this very argument, listing recent discoveries:

> Nouvelles mers, nouvelles terres, nouvelles façons d'hommes, mœurs, lois, coutumes, nouvelles herbes . . . arbres . . . minéraux . . . nouvelles inventions . . .: l'imprimerie . . . l'artillerie . . . l'usage de l'aiguille et de l'aimant pour les navigations . . .[327]

—the catalogue goes on and on.

And it may well be supplemented by Gabriel Harvey's, which vouches for a similar trend in intellectual fashions:

> All inquisitive after Newes, newe Bookes, newe Fashions, newe Lawes, newe Officers, and some after newe Elementes, some after newe Heavens, and Helles to . . . as of olde Bookes, so of aunciente Vertue, Honestie, Fidelitie, Equitie, newe Abridgementes: every day freshe span newe Opinions: Heresie in Divinitie, in Philosophie, in Humanitie, in Manners. . . .[328]

Yet there were many, too, intent upon disproving the authentic novelty of these innovations, as the passages about "renovators" from "R. B." and Donne's *Ignatius* indicate. And if one sets aside the obviously spurious claims of the charlatans of the age who profess the discovery of new methods and short-cuts to universal knowledge, the company of those who assert the newness of their own accomplishment is narrowed to a small and distinguished group.

The leaders of the Counter-Rennaissance and of the Scientific

Reformation are prominent in this group. Montaigne asserts flatly that he is

> a new figure: an unpremeditated philosopher and a casuall . . .[329]

and declares,

> Authors communicate themselves unto the world by some speciall and strange marke; I the first, by my generall disposition; as Michael de Montaigne, not as a Grammarian, or a Poet, or a Lawyer. . . .[330]

We know his study of "moi-même," and we cannot dispute his claim. Nor are we disposed to contest the truth of Galileo's statement (in his *Discorsi e Demonstrazioni*) that he is presenting "a very new science about a very old subject."[331] Similarly, for all of the "mystical" and "magical" elements in Kepler's early thought, the justice of his title, *Astronomia Nova*, is surely established.[332]

But perhaps Francis Bacon's proclamation of the newness of his contribution to the furtherance of science is the most famous of these statements. Certainly, at least, it is he who makes the most dramatic use of the imagery of discovery, when he compares himself and his venture of a new scientific method to Columbus and "that wonderful voyage of his across the Atlantic,"[333] and when he chooses for the frontispiece to his *Instauratio Magna* the picture of a ship sailing between the Pillars of Hercules, the uttermost limits of the old world, and for the inscription below it "Multi pertransibunt & augebitur scientia." Hence it is particularly interesting to discover that Machiavelli had employed this (or, at least, very similar) imagery before him. For the introduction to the first book of the *Discourses* begins,

> Although the envious nature of man, so prompt to blame and so slow to praise, makes the discovery and introduction of any new principles and systems as dangerous almost as the exploration of unknown seas and continents, yet, animated by the desire which impels me to do what may prove for the common benefit of all, I have resolved to open a new route, which has not yet been followed by any one, and may prove difficult and troublesome. . . .[334]

The tone and substance are almost exactly those of Bacon: the recognition of the obstacles to free inquiry and the pursuit of knowledge, the use of the "discovery" imagery, the expression of a determination to persist at all costs, and the motivation of doing "what may prove for the common benefit of all"—anticipating

Bacon's emphasis upon "the welfare of man" and "for the benefit and use of life." Surely the man whose vision is set forth in the words

> Now the true and lawful goal of the sciences is none other than this: that human life be endowed with new discoveries and powers[335]

went to school in Florence.

Moreover, for all of Bacon's assertion that he is treading a new path, his antecedents are not hard to trace. Other leaders of the Counter-Renaissance were his teachers, too. Tendency after tendency, position after position in his thought reveals their influence.

We have already seen that he shares their general enthusiasm for a utilitarian scientific ideal—is, indeed, perhaps its most notable expounder. He is completely convinced, with King Solamona, that "the finding out of the true nature of all things" brings not only to God "the more glory in the workmanship of them," but also to men "the more fruit in the use of them"; and that "the noblest foundation . . . that ever was upon the earth" is that "dedicated to the study of the works and creatures of God."[336] The end of the "foundation" of Salomon's House is that of Bacon's greatest and most characteristic dream:

> The knowledge of causes, and secret notions of things; and the enlarging of the bounds of human empire, to the effecting of all things possible.[337]

Again, his voice is among those raised most loudly in protest against men who find something "shameful and undignified" about dealing "with experiments and particulars, subject to sense and bound in matter."[338] Like Telesio, he places more faith in the evidence of sense than in that of reason. Describing his inductive method, he declares,

> I propose to establish progressive stages of certainty. The evidence of the senses, helped and guided by a certain process of correction, I retain. But the mental operation which follows the act of sense I for the most part reject; and instead of it I open and lay out a new and certain path for the mind to proceed in, starting directly from the simple sensuous perception. . . .[339]

His emphasis upon matter is exactly that of the Counter-Renaissance empiricists—one related to the conviction that the world of empirical reality contains "things as they are":

Matter rather than forms should be the objects of our attention, its configurations and changes of configuration, and simple
action, and law of action or motion; for forms are figments of
the human mind, unless you call those laws of action forms.[340]

Thus he follows Telesio's lead in replacing medieval "form" with
naturalistic "force."

This attitude toward nature is wholly congruous with his con-
gratulatory recognition of "Machiavel and . . . others, that write
what men do and not what they ought to do." Indeed, in every field
which he touches he discloses his inheritance of the Counter-Renaissance insistence upon a cleavage between the ideal and the actual.
His *History of the Reign of King Henry VII*, for example, puts into
practice the historical methods of Agrippa, Bodin and Le Roy; he
has no intention of drawing a king as he should be. On the contrary, his portrait of Henry

> is a true study from nature, and one of the most careful, curi-
> ous, and ingenious studies of the kind ever produced.[341]

Similarly, Bacon's ethical writings show a strong pragmatic bias.
Believing that

> men have preferred revelling in imaginings of the ideal to
> diligently studying how ideals may be realized[342]

—he maintains that

> Reading good Bookes of Morality, is a little Flat, and Dead.[343]

For, he objects,

> In the handling of this science, those which have written seem
> to me to have done as if a man that professeth to teach to
> write did only exhibit fair copies of alphabets and letters
> joined, without giving any precepts or directions for the car-
> riage of the hand and framing of the letters. So have they made
> good and fair exemplars and copies, carrying the draughts and
> portraitures of Good, Virtue, Duty, Felicity; propounding them
> well described as the true objects and scope of man's will and
> desires; but *how* to attain these excellent marks, and *how* to
> frame and subdue the will of man to become true and com-
> formable to these pursuits, they pass it over altogether, or
> slightly and unprofitably.[344]

He is making the same plea here as in natural philosophy—that
men should cease to chant uninspired hymns to the ideal and begin
to consider fact and utility. And the justice of his charge in this
connection is patent enough to any one who has waded through

many of the righteous but tedious and undistinguished moral treatises written in Elizabeth's reign. He has no more patience than we of the twentieth century do with these fatuous academic arguments, these set pieces laboriously copied down from the classical moral philosophers, while the practical conduct of life is largely ignored. He points out that

> it is not the disputing that moral virtues are in the mind by habit and not by nature,[345] or the distinguishing that generous spirits are won by doctrines and persuasion, and the vulgar sort by reward and punishment,[346] and the like scattered glances and touches, that can excuse the absence of this part.[347]

Bacon is really arguing for the application of a psychological analysis of the motives and behavior to the studies of "morality and policy"—for an ethic rooted in a knowledge of men as they are through "what men do." And he attributes the failure of men to deal with this part of the subject to the same causes which he has found responsible for their disregard of matter and empiricism in science:

> that men have despised to be conversant in ordinary and common matters, but contrariwise they have compounded sciences chiefly of a certain resplendent or lustrous mass of matter, chosen to give glory either to the subtility of disputations, or the eloquence of discourses.[348]

It is the familiar war-cry of the Counter-Renaissance empiricists. . . .

In however elementary a form, Bacon lays down a few preliminary conclusions himself, maintaining that in everything

> we may discover a double impulse: the one moves the thing to assert itself as a whole; the other causes it to work as part of a large whole. The former has as its object the good of the individual, the latter the general good.[349]

This general theory clearly has roots in the physics of Telesio and the political theory of Machiavelli, dominated as they are by the concept of self-preservation as the universal motivating force. And Bacon's conclusion that the claims of the general good are of a higher sort (which usually has been interpreted as proof of his conservative and traditional ethical position) is set forth primarily in a spirit similar to Machiavelli's, with a wholly practical emphasis.

For, while it is customary with Bacon's editors and commentators to point out that his ethical conclusions are traditional and humanistic, it seems clear to me that this is as incomplete and misleading a conclusion as that of maintaining that he separated the realms of religion and science in the interests of faith. It is not simply which "division" of life or knowledge a man explicitly declares the "higher," that enables us to form conclusions about his intellectual enthusiasms or convictions, but the way in which he treats those divisions, and the attention he gives to them in his work.

Thus, while it is true that the section on ethics in the *Advancement of Learning*[350] differs from orthodox classical-Christian ethical theory primarily in its practical and pragmatic treatment, rather than in any obviously "evil," "Machiavellian" advice (which is the point many Baconians have made triumphantly), it is pertinent to observe how Bacon proceeds in the following section—that on "Civil Knowledge."

For here is a typical Baconian distinction and "separation." For traditionalists, the subject is all of a piece: "private" and "public" ethics are not separate matters—nor are ethical and political theory. All are related, each to the others, and all are concerned with different applications of Christian living, in accordance with Right Reason, and in pursuit of virtue.

But Bacon begins,

> Civil knowledge is conversant about a subject which of all others is most immersed in matter, and hardiest reduced to axiom.[351]

He distinguishes between "moral philosophy," which

> propoundeth to itself the framing of internal goodness . . .

and "civil knowledge," which

> requireth only an external goodness; for that as to society sufficeth.[352]

He explains,

> This knowledge hath three parts, according to the three summary actions of society; which are conversation, negotiation, and government. For man seeketh in society comfort, use, and protection: and they be three wisdoms of divers natures, which do often sever: wisdom of the behaviour, wisdom of business, and wisdom of state.[353]

There follows, in accordance with this outline, a wholly pragmatic discussion of how a man may conduct himself in society to his own advantage—a discussion which clearly and certainly owes much to "Machiavel and to others, that write what men do and not what they ought to do." And while it is true, as one of his commentators claims,[354] that he concludes this discussion with a warning against "evil and corrupt positions" by which "the pressing of a man's fortune may be more hasty and compendious," and includes in this company "principles" of "Machiavel"—while this is true, I cannot see that he does so, as claimed, "with all the weight of his most impressive eloquence."[355] What he actually says is,

> But it is in life as it is in ways, the shortest way is commonly the foulest, and surely the fair way is not much about.[356]

Laconic enough, and followed by a conventional exhortation to turn to "the divine foundation" which "is upon the rock,"[357] rather than to rely upon "the architecture of fortune."

But there is no need to quibble. Bacon's debt to Machiavelli and the other empiricists of the Counter-Renaissance is an authentic one, and could be traced, point by point, in detail. But it is not the notorious "Machiavel" of much Elizabethan melodrama in whom he is primarily interested; it is the *historical* figure, the first great conscious pragmatist of the Counter-Renaissance, to whom he owes his debt. And when in a book dedicated to his king, he makes occasional perfunctory references to the "evil arts" of Machiavelli, it does not seem far-fetched (especially in the light of his own career) to assume that he is pursuing in practice the pragmatic and diplomatic course which his master had so clearly outlined.

It remains, in connection with this aspect of Bacon's thought and work, to underline his separation of "civil knowledge" from "moral philosophy." It is a parallel intellectual distinction to that which he makes between the domains of science and faith, and thoroughly characteristic. Its significance, in terms of his relationship to the Counter-Renaissance, is analogous to that movement's favorite cleavage between the ideal and the actual. And the realization of this fact, it seems to me, illuminates both Montaigne's and Bacon's adherence to the "separatist" tradition. For while Machiavelli and Guicciardini are largely hard-boiled naturalists who, in separating the ideal from the actual, attribute to the former no reality—or at least no relevance to life as it is lived—Montaigne and Bacon separate them primarily in order to deal with a consideration of empirical actuality unhampered by embarrassing discrepancies between it and the ideal—but without ever denying the existence of the ideal. It is as though they said (and they do, too, often enough), "All that belongs to religion. Being a plain man, I do not pretend to authority on such matters."

In short, they shelve the question. Montaigne, as he grows older, becomes bolder and bolder, however, and eventually blurts out flatly that all "these goodly precepts"

> are discourses that will send us into the other world on horseback. Life is a materiall and corporal motion, an action imperfect and disordered by its own essence; I employ or apply my selfe to serve it according to it selfe.[358]

Bacon (for prudential reasons, I suspect) is never so frank. His brief section on laws in the *Advancement of Learning* is representative of his approach. He declares,

> for the more public part of government which is laws, I think good to note only one deficience; which is, that all those which have written of laws, have written either as philosophers or as lawyers, and none as statesmen. *As for the philosophers, they make imaginary laws for imaginary commonwealths,* and their discourses are as the stars, which give little light because they are so high.

He admits that

> there are in nature certain fountains of justice, whence all civil laws are derived but as streams . . .

but like waters, they "take tinctures and tastes from the soils through which they run"; and he stresses the fact that

> the wisdom of a lawmaker consisteth not only in a platform of justice, but in the application thereof; taking by what means laws may be made certain . . . by what means laws may be made apt and easy to be executed . . . [etc., etc.][359]

In short, addressing James I as he does on the same page regarding "your Majesty's laws of England," he finds it much simpler to admit in a conventional phrase the validity of the traditional concept of law without argument, and then to go happily on his way, wholly (if unobtrusively) modifying the original statement (without ever referring to it again) by concentrating upon his characteristic pragmatic angle of attack—so that when he has finished, the original statement has been divested of all real significance.

For wherever one turns in Bacon's philosophical or literary works, one does find an insistence upon the discrepancy between the ideal and the actual; and no one who reads in them carefully and extensively can fail to perceive how completely he aligns himself with the leaders of the Counter-Renaissance. . . .[360]

Like them, again, he has no patience with the Scholastics' scientific methodology. Syllogistic logic seems to him utterly incompetent for the task of finding out physical truth. "Aristotle," he declares,

> who made his natural philosophy a mere bond-servant to his
> logic, thereby rendered it contentious and well nigh use-
> less. . . .[361]

The "art of Logic . . . has had the effect of fixing errors rather
than disclosing truth."[362] As for the syllogism itself, it

> is not applied to the first principles of science, and is applied
> in vain to intermediate axioms; being no match for the subtlety
> of nature. It commands assent therefore to the *proposition*,
> but does not take hold of the *thing*.
>
> The syllogism consists of propositions, propositions consist of
> words, words are symbols of notions. Therefore, if the notions
> themselves (which is the root of the matter) are confused
> and over-hastily abstracted from the facts, there can be no
> firmness in the superstructure.[363]

It is the inability of logic to "take hold of the thing"—to deal
with matter, which is reality—that makes it an unsuitable instrument for science. For to Bacon, as to Montaigne and others of the
Counter-Renaissance, the

> human understanding is like a false mirror, which, receiving
> rays irregularly, distorts and discolours the nature of things
> by mingling its own nature with it.[364]

Bacon explicitly charges that Aristotle's science is guilty on all these
counts:

> Nor let any weight be given to the fact, that in his books on
> animals, and his problems, and other of his treatises, there is
> frequent dealing with experiments. For he had come to his
> conclusion before; he did not consult experience, as he should
> have done, in order [to proceed] to the framing of his deci-
> sions and axioms; but having first determined the question to
> his will, he then resorts to experience, and bending her unto
> conformity with his placets leads her about like a captive in
> a procession; so that even on this count he is more guilty than
> his modern followers, the schoolmen, who have abandoned
> experience altogether.[365]

Everywhere he expresses his distrust of intellectualistic science
and philosophy.

> For the Rational School of philosophers snatches from experi-
> ence a variety of common instances, neither duly ascertained
> nor diligently examined and weighed, and leaves all the rest
> to meditation and agitation of wit.[366]

Such men desert nature to search for truth in the "narrow cells of the human understanding"—a futile occupation. Hypothesis holds only a tentative and shaky position in Bacon's own system, and *a priori* rules of procedure disgust him as much as they do Montaigne:

> To make Judgement wholly by their Rules is the Humour of a Scholler. They perfect Nature, and are perfected by Experience: For Naturall Abilities, are like Naturall Plants, that need Proyning by Study: and Studies themselves, doe give forth Directions too much at Large, except they be bounded in by Experience. Crafty Men Contemne Studies; Simple Men Admire them; And Wise Men Use them; For they teach not their owne Use; But that is a Wisdome without them, and above them, won by Observation.[367]

"Truth is to be sought" only "in the light of nature and experience, which is eternal. . . ."[368] And while "the light of nature" sounds superficially like the humanists' creed, it is soon clear that Bacon has no faith that the light of natural reason may find out truth. On the contrary, his "doctrine . . . of the expurgation of the intellect" (the cleansing of it from the "Idols") includes "three refutations":

> The refutation of the Philosophies; the refutation of the Demonstrations; and the refutation of the Natural Human Reason.[369]

For, however disingenuously, he more than once describes the *Instauration* as an attempt to regain as much as possible of what man has lost through the Fall.[370] He begins his "Proemium" with the words, "Francis of Verulam reasoned thus with himself . . ."

> Being convinced that the human intellect makes its own difficulties, not using the true helps which are at man's disposal soberly and judiciously . . . he thought all trial should be made, whether the commerce between the mind of men and the nature of things, which is more precious than anything on earth, or at least than anything that is of the earth,[371] might by any means be restored to its perfect and original condition, or if that may not be, yet reduced to a better condition than that in which it now is.[372]

To be sure, if the human intellect were unimpaired, men would be capable of adhering to two simple rules and could dispense with his method of "helps." For then

> they would be able by the native and genuine force of the mind, without any art, to fall into my form of interpretation.

> For interpretation is the true and natural work of the mind when freed from impediments.[373]

And they would find these two simple rules wholly sufficient:

> the first, to lay aside received opinions and notions; and the second to refrain the mind for a time from the highest generalizations, and those next to them. . . .[374]

But such is *not* the case, and

> Our only hope therefore lies in a true induction . . .[375]

in which the mind must be "guided at every step."[376] Thus, and thus only, can men be enabled to investigate Nature *as she really is;* Bacon issues his invitation and challenge to men to join with him in the exalted tones of a high priest about to administer the sacrament:

> But if any man there be who, not content to rest in and use the knowledge which has already been discovered, aspires to penetrate further; to overcome, not an adversary in argument, but nature in action; to seek, *not pretty and probable conjectures but certain and demonstrable knowledge;* I invite all such to join themselves, as true sons of knowledge, with me, that passing by the outer courts of nature, which numbers have trodden, we may find a way at length into her inner chambers.[377]

Exaltation, perhaps, but—he would have pointed out—not arrogance. Here are echoes from other aspects of the Counter-Renaissance, now familiar overtones. Here is the appeal for a return to first principles, in Machiavelli's sense of "ritorno al segno" (Bacon uses the expression, not once, but many times, in only slightly modified language)—in the sense of going to nature itself and making direct contact with the *thing* in question. Here is also the anti-speculative cast of mind which we have encountered so often, with its profession of humility. For he accuses the "rational philosophers" expressly of intellectual *hybris*, while defending himself from the charge:

> Nor could we hope to succeed, if we arrogantly searched for the sciences in the narrow cells of the human understanding, and not submissively in the wider world.[378]

Yet if he is not "arrogant," he is ringed about with an aura of confidence hard to equal in intellectual history. He is conscious at all times (and makes us conscious, too) of his prophetic mission, and if we do not classify his proclamations of this message with

those egotistic ones of Paracelsus, Cardan and Bruno, it is only because of his superior mastery of words, his truly wonderful capacity
to keep his trumpet clean of overly brassy notes. In spirit he is not
far from "Theophrastus Paracelsus, Prince of Philosophy and of
Medicine. . . . I have been chosen by God to extinguish and blot
out all the phantasies of elaborate and false works, of delusive and
presumptuous words," etc., when he declares,

> I am building in the human understanding a true model of
> the world, such as it is in fact, not such as a man's own reason
> would have it to be; a thing which cannot be done without
> a very diligent dissection and anatomy of the world. But I
> say that those foolish and apish images of worlds which the
> fancies of men have created in philosophical systems, must be
> utterly scattered to the winds[379]

—but what a difference in tone! It is the difference between the
wind of bombast and the sonorous organ peal of genuine dignity.
We have only to go so far as the first semi-colon, and we are captured and acquiescent.

The comparison of Bacon and the "Prince" of alchemists need
not be confined to the similarity of their convictions of being voices
crying in the wilderness, however. Bacon is frequently contemptuous of the alchemists, it is true; they share with William Gilbert
the *onus* of building up "a fantastic philosophy" on the basis of "a
few experiments," to offer excellent examples of the workings of
the *Idols of the Cave:*

> The race of chemists again out of a few experiments of the
> furnace have built up a fantastic philosophy, framed with
> reference to a few things; and Gilbert also, after he had em-
> ployed himself most laboriously in the study and observation
> of the loadstone, proceeded at once to construct an entire sys-
> tem in accordance with his favorite subject.[380]

In short, he frequently indicates that he has no more respect for
them, loose experimenters as they are, than for the initiate *magi*
of the Neoplatonic tradition,

> those who out of faith and veneration mix their philosophy
> with theology and traditions; among whom the vanity of some
> has gone so far aside as to seek the origin of sciences among
> spirits and genii.[381]

Thus it seems that, if one is to claim him as a scientist of the
Counter-Renaissance, one must recognize him as belonging exclu-

sively to the group of naturalistic empiricists, and as a detractor of the occult group.

This judgment is certainly correct in the direction in which it leads, yet I believe it to be an over-statement. For this much at least can be said with assurance: he has a weakness for the terminology, the imagery and the lore of the alchemists. Sometimes he cites them specifically:

> . . . and if it be true likewise that [which] the Alchemists do so much inculcate, that Vulcan is a second nature, and imitateth that dextrously and compendiously which nature worketh by ambages and length of time . . .[382]

The idea (that of "leading out" the truths of nature, and not trying to "force" her), if not in its special alchemical significance, is a favorite one of Bacon's, and at the heart of his method—for to *master* nature and bend her to man's use, he argues again and again, we must be willing to *serve* her. So, even when he attacks the alchemists with this very charge—that they try to force nature by building a natural philosophy out of "a few experiments"—he uses their favorite myth of Erichthonius to drive home his point.[383]

He is also prone to use their phrase "tried by fire" or "proof by fire"—as in this instance, during his discussion of the *Idols of the Theatre:*

> But for that going to and fro to remote and heterogeneous instances, by which axioms are tried as in the fire, the intellect is altogether slow and unfit. . . .[384]

But there is one particular respect in which he is even willing to align himself explicitly with the alchemists. This is in the matter of the scientific investigator's need for "helps." Not for him Montaigne's "uncontrolled experience." Rather, Bacon is at one with many skeptics of the Counter-Renaissance who distrust unaided sense perception. No more than the unaided intellect is it a measure of truth:

> The Idols of the Tribe have their foundation in human nature itself, and in the tribe or race of men. For it is a false assertion that the sense of man is the measure of things. On the contrary, all perceptions as well of the sense as of the mind are according to the measure of the individual and not according to the measure of the universe. . . .[385]

Yet he refuses to rest in the skeptical position. He will not admit that he is making "a denial of the capacity of the mind to comprehend truth. . . . That which I meditate and propound is not

denial of the capacity to understand but provision for understanding truly; for I do not take away authority from the
senses, but supply them with helps; I do not slight the understanding, but govern it.[386]

He makes it clear what these "helps" are when he explains,

> For the sense by itself is a thing infirm and erring; neither
> can instruments for enlarging or sharpening the senses do
> much;[387] but all the truer kind of interpretation of nature
> is effected by instances and experiments fit and apposite;[388]
> wherein the sense decides touching the experiment only, and
> the experiment touching the point in nature and the thing
> itself.[389]

And in the *Advancement of Learning*, he—reluctant and half shamefaced though he may be—openly associates himself with the alchemists in this respect:

> Another defect I note, wherein I shall need some alchemist
> to help me, who call upon men to sell their books, and to build
> furnaces; quitting and forsaking Minerva and the Muses as
> barren Virgins, and relying upon Vulcan. But certain it is, that
> unto the deep, fruitful, and operative study of many sciences,
> specially natural philosophy and physic, books be not the only
> instrumentals. . . . In general, there will hardly be any main
> proficience in the disclosing of nature, except there be some
> allowance for expenses about experiments; whether they be
> experiments appertaining to Vulcanus or Dædalus, furnace or
> engine, or any other kind.[390]

Yet if Bacon often seems to owe a debt to the very alchemists
whom he is wont to berate, just as he shares with the Neoplatonic
magician-scientists (whom he also ridicules) their dream of the
mastery of nature through the discovery of a single universal method,
he remains primarily the son of the naturalistic empiricists. He has
lines of communication to practically all of the varied scientific
attitudes of the Counter-Renaissance, but the strongest and most
direct lead to the pragmatists—to the exponents of "brute fact" and
the "science of the particular."

For his own inductive method, he asserts, "is simply this":

> we must lead men to particulars themselves, and their series
> and order; while men on their side must force themselves for
> awhile to lay their notions by and begin to familiarize them-
> selves with facts. . . .[391]

His emphasis upon *particular* is a note sustained against "the premature hurry of the understanding to leap or fly to universals and principles of things. . . ."[392] For, he finds,

> The human understanding is of its own nature prone to suppose the existence of more order and regularity in the world than it finds. And though there be many things in nature which are singular and unmatched, yet it devises for them parallels and conjugates and relatives which do not exist.[393]

Thus, convinced that

> in nature nothing really exists besides individual bodies, performing pure individual acts according to a fixed law,[394]

he is extremely skeptical of the old science of the universal, and he preaches emphatically the new pragmatic approach:

> Although the roads to human power and to human knowledge lie close together, and are nearly the same, nevertheless on account of the pernicious and inveterate habit of dwelling on abstractions, it is safer to begin and raise the sciences from those foundations which have relation to practice, and to let the active part itself be as the seal which prints and determines the contemplative counterpart.[395]

He says it again and again. In all sorts of contexts, he preaches the science of the particular. But nowhere, perhaps, does he make his intellectual heritage more explicitly obvious than in his discussion of that part of "civil knowledge" which he calls "wisdom of business":

> And therefore the form of writing which of all others is fittest for this variable argument of negotiation and occasions is that which Machiavel chose wisely and aptly for government; namely, discourse upon histories or examples. *For knowledge drawn freshly and in our view out of particulars, knoweth the way best to particulars again. And it hath much greater life for practice when the discourse attendeth upon the example, than when the example attendeth upon the discourse. For this is no point of order, as it seemeth at first, but of substance.* For when the example is the ground, being set down in an history at large, it is set down with all the circumstances, which may sometimes control the discourse thereupon made, and sometimes supply it, as a very pattern for action; whereas the examples alleged for the discourse's sake are cited succinctly, and *without particularity,* and carry a servile aspect towards the discourse which they are brought in to make good.[396]

The evidence that Bacon is best understood through an acquaintance with and an understanding of the scientists and thinkers of the Counter-Renaissance seems to me incontrovertible. Rudolf Metz's generalization about Bacon's position in the history of ideas,

> Spiritually, he stands in much closer relationship to such Renaissance philosophers as Vives, Ramus, Paracelsus, Telesio, Bruno, and Montaigne, than to Descartes, Hobbes, Spinoza, Leibniz, and Locke, though in point of time he stands exactly midway between these two groups[397]

—is not only true; it may be supported by detailed evidence.

Yet this is not to accept the attitude which has gained more and more supporters of late: that Bacon's work was simply "specious and theatrical," that he was the "mountebank of science," and nothing more.[398] It should be sufficiently clear, I think, that whatever the shortcomings of the scientists and philosophers of the Counter-Renaissance, so sweeping a condemnation of their work would be totally unjust. And if it is unjust to them, it is still more so, applied to Francis Bacon.

For it is finally true that he marks the culmination of this scientific movement in more ways than that of chronology. Nurtured and developed in the environment they largely created, he nevertheless outgrows and surpasses them in two important respects—in his understanding of the need to go beyond that science of the particular which he inherited and developed, to a concept of *law*, and in his unwavering faith in the possibility of an indefinite expansion of the borders of knowledge, with a corollary and firm, if rudimentary, conception of the idea of progress.

The first of these two aspects of Bacon's thought and method requires some elaboration. It is rooted in his conviction of the necessity to go beyond a loose empiricism. He makes this clear throughout his writings, but nowhere more so than in his *Novum Organum:*

> Those who have handled sciences have been either men of experiment or men of dogmas. The men of experiment are like the ant; they only collect and use: the reasoners resemble spiders who make cobwebs out of their own substance.[399] But the bee takes the middle course; it gathers its material from the flowers of the garden and the field, but transforms and digests it by a power of its own. Not unlike this is the true business of philosophy; for it neither relies solely or chiefly on the powers of the mind, nor does it take the matter which it gathers from natural history and mechanical experiments and lay it up in the memory whole, as it finds it; but lays it up in the understanding altered and digested. Therefore from

a closer and purer league between these two faculties, the
experimental and the rational, (such as has never yet been
made) much may be hoped.[400]

The recognition of the need for this "closer and purer league" is
in the direction which modern science is to take. But Bacon's
account of the workings of this relationship is not, of course, for
he largely ignores mathematics, and the place he makes for "the
rational faculty" is a carefully guarded one, and one which must
for the most part follow observation and experiment, rather than
also precede them:

> The conclusions of human reason as ordinarily applied in the
> matter of nature, I call for the sake of distinction *Anticipa-
> tions of Nature* (as a thing rash or premature). That reason
> which is elicited from facts by a just and methodical process,
> I call *Interpretation of Nature*.[401]

It is true that he says, in the very accents of the Counter-Renaissance,

> Now if any one of ripe age, unimpaired senses, and well-purged
> mind, apply himself anew to *experience and particulars*, better
> hopes may be entertained of that man.[402]

It is true that he declares

> There is no hope except in a new birth of science; that is,
> in raising it regularly up from experience and building it
> afresh. . . .[403]

It is true that a great "store of particulars," "a Storehouse of Facts,"
"a greater abundance of experiments" are his constant concern.[404]
But he does not stop there; his method is not merely collection; he
makes it abundantly clear that

> after this store of particulars has been set out duly and in
> order before our eyes, we are not to pass at once to the in-
> vestigation and discovery of new particulars or works; or at
> any rate if we do so we must not stop there.

Rather, the course must be one in which "axioms,"

> having been educed from those particulars by a certain method
> and rule, shall in their turn point out the way again to new
> particulars. . . .[405]

Here is where "that reason which is elicited from facts by a just
and methodical process" enters Bacon's method. For the process is

to "hang" the understanding "with weights, to keep it from leaping and flying," and so

> by successive steps not interrupted or broken, we rise from particulars to lesser axioms; and then to middle axioms, one above the other; and last of all to the most general.[406]

Thus one moves slowly and step by step from "bare experience" to "notional and abstract" axioms, using an induction which is not the "childish" one "which proceeds by simple enumeration," but that which analyzes "nature by proper rejections and exclusions; and then, after a sufficient number of negatives, comes to a conclusion on the affirmative instances. . . ."[407]

With this picture of Bacon's inductive method before us, it is now possible to say with certainty that many of its features had been anticipated by various Counter-Renaissance scientists. Vives, for example, I have consistently called a "radical empiricist." Yet Vives, too, recognized that "experiences are casual and uncertain unless they are ruled by reason":

> Otherwise they will be risky, and the whole art will be fortuitous and not certain. This may be seen in the case of those who are led by experiences alone without a standard as to their nature and quality, and without respect to the place, time, and the remaining circumstances. . . .[408]

If this is still vague, he is more specific as he continues:

> I only call that knowledge which we receive when the senses are properly brought to observe things and in a methodical way to which clear reason leads on, reason so closely connected with the nature of our mind that there is no one who does not accept its lead. . . . [This] knowledge . . . is called science, firm and indubitable. . . .[409]

Foster Watson, building on passages of this sort, affirms Vives' anticipation of Bacon's inductive method.[410] It seems to me a very hazardous claim. For while their general statements are similar, Bacon by no means endorses Vives' confidence in the part the natural human reason may play;[411] this is why he is so insistent upon "helps." And Vives never develops such a method in detail; the justification of calling him a "radical empiricist" rests on the discrepancy between these statements and his actual performance in the body of his writings.

Similarly, one finds in the thought of men like Sanchez and Ramus anticipatory hints of the direction in which Bacon is to move

—in terms, respectively, of the combination of experiment and reason,[412] and of the insistence upon going back to nature first and "interpreting" rather than "anticipating" her.[413] Yet neither runs the whole course; their contributions remain hints, rather than real anticipations of the Baconian method.

Much the same may be said of Bacon's debt to Telesio, despite the fact that the latter was the truer physicist. His replacing of "form" with "force," his emphasis upon evolving physical laws in terms of *matter* alone, his motivating principle of *self-preservation*, his definition of reason as "that knowledge of things which is given to us . . . through the resemblance of things which are perceived by sensation"—all these suggest some of the most prominent and characteristic features of Bacon's method. But they do not add up to that method, although they come nearer to it than the principles of any other single predecessor.

Nearer—because nearest to Bacon's attempt to lead to "an insight into the regular interconnection of phenomena."[414] Telesio's explanations lack this insight, which was provided by the Scientific Reformation's concept of mathematical law; Bacon's lack it, too, because of his almost exclusive reliance upon induction and his failure to realize the importance of mathematics. It is true that he lays weight on "the formation of provisional hypotheses as a means of survey and orientation," and that "his inductive method proceeds, after the establishment of these provisional hypotheses, using them as finger-posts."[415] Yet these hypotheses are to him only a trial, what he calls the "first vintage,"[416] and despite his use of them, his method calls for a radical subordination of deduction:

> It had not dawned on him that it is a deduction which affords the real proof of the correctness of the inductive conclusion.[417]

His dilemma is clearly apparent in his discussion of that science of common principles which he calls *prima philosophia*, where he uses these common principles both as *presuppositions* and *results* of induction—"a circle which is unavoidable in all forms of pure empiricism."[418]

So, too, Bacon's subordination of quantitative determination betrayed him. For he largely ignored the fact that any exact empirical science was possible only when "by means of the exact measurement of phenomena, a foundation of mathematical deduction could be laid."[419]

Bacon failed, in short, in his attempt to build up a science of natural law, and hence a science of the universal, mostly because he built upon the foundations of the Counter-Renaissance science of the particular. But he made the attempt, and in this respect he departs from the tradition of the Counter-Renaissance empiricists.[420] Faithful to their anti-speculative bias, he deserts the parallel one implicit in their repeal of universal law, and finds himself caught halfway between their science and that of the Scientific Reformation.

And it is just this combination of elements in him which comes close to justifying at times the often expressed conviction that he was a "great amateur." In fields where technical training was not generally necessary, and where mathematics played no part, his observations are acute. Thus, following Machiavelli's approach in his desire to frame rules of useful practice for "morality and policy," he observes that while "distinctions" among many kinds of men are numerous,

> We conclude no precepts upon them; wherein our fault is the greater, because both history, poesy, and daily experience are as goodly fields where these observations grow; whereof we make a few posies to hold in our hands, but no man bringeth them to the confectionary, that receits might be made of them for use of life.[421]

He is never content with "a few posies," and thus in natural science, despite his nominalistic position that

> in nature nothing really exists beside individual bodies, performing individual acts according to a fixed law,

he is not content with the "science of Peter for the sake of Peter," for

> this very law, and the investigation, discovery, and explanation of it, is the foundation as well of knowledge as of operation.[422]

His theoretical idea of natural law is as "neutralized" and free of teleological considerations as that of the true participants in the Scientific Reformation, but he works with the wrong tools, and he never really comes to grips with the object of his search. What remains most significant about Bacon is not his interpretation of law, but his insistent search for it, his refusal to acquiesce in the Counter-Renaissance's conviction that no certain and inclusive scientific knowledge may be had, and the resultant widening of intellectual horizons that he effected.

"Those who have taken upon them to lay down the law of nature as a thing already searched out and understood," he announces, whether they have spoken in simple assurance of professional affectation, have therein done philosophy and the sciences great injury. For as they have been successful in inducing belief, so they have been effective in quenching and stopping inquiry; and have done more harm by spoiling and putting an end to other men's efforts than good by their own.[423]

But,

Those on the other hand who have taken a contrary course, and asserted that absolutely nothing can be known—whether it were from hatred of the ancient sophists, or from uncertainty and fluctuation of mind, or even from a kind of fulness of learning, that they fell upon this opinion—have certainly advanced reasons for it that are not to be despised; but yet they have neither started from true principles nor rested in the just conclusion, zeal and affectation having carried them too far.[424]

Even "the school of Democritus, which went further into nature than the rest,"[425] was guilty on an important score, for

they too, trusting entirely to the force of their understanding, applied no rule, but made everything turn upon hard thinking and perpetual working and exercising of the mind.[426]

It is not that he minimizes the difficulty of attaining to a true knowledge of nature; but men have given over to a facile despair, and erected barriers to knowledge which are wholly artificial. Bacon records these obstacles, one after another, and the list reads like a catalogue of all the points of view against which the empiricists of the Counter-Renaissance rebelled: the subordination of natural philosophy to other studies; haphazard experimentation; contempt for dealing with "particulars"; "reverence for antiquity"; charlatanism; "littleness" alike of spirit and of tasks projected; "superstition and the blind immoderate zeal of religion"; the authoritarian curricula of schools and colleges; "the speculations of those who have taken upon themselves to deduce the truth of the Christian religion from the principles of philosophers, and to confirm it by their authority"—all these, leading to the greatest obstacle of all, that "men despair and think things impossible."[427]

But whereas many of those naturalistic empiricists acquiesce in that "despair"—at least to the extent of believing that certain knowledge is impossible—Bacon does not. He goes on to make his stirring and memorable statement:

I am now therefore to speak touching Hope. . . . And therefore it is fit that I publish and set forth those conjectures of

mine which make hope in this matter reasonable; just as Columbus did, before that wonderful voyage of his across the Atlantic, when he gave the reasons for his conviction that new
lands and continents might be discovered besides those which
were known before; which reasons, though rejected at first,
were afterwards made good by experience, and were the cause
and beginnings of great events.[428]

We have come to realize that not only was Bacon on the wrong
track methodologically, but also that he was not prone to give the
credit which he might have to men who preceded him in this
expression of faith in the future, in the possibility of further knowledge and progress.[429] Yet again, I think the tendency has been to
go too far with the swing of the pendulum. It may be that Bacon
intentionally exaggerated, "for purposes of propaganda,"[430] the extent to which "men despair and think things impossible." But it
would have been very difficult, indeed, to exaggerate the extent
of popular pessimism in England during the last years of Elizabeth's reign and the first of her successors. Cite the true Scientific
Reformation working its sound course in Padua and elsewhere; point
out the confident tones of Le Roy and Bodin and Ramus and Campanella about the age in which they lived; remind us of the achievements and healthy scientific attitude of English astronomers like
Digges and Hariot: it remains true, with testimony a thousand-
fold, that the average, not unintelligent Englishman of the late
sixteenth century did despair, not only of certain knowledge, but
of the very continued existence of his world. That pessimism to
which John Donne gave elaborate and intellectualized expression
in 1611 had long permeated the articulate channels of his world.
Not only does it sound from the lines of the great writers of the
period; it screams from the pages of their multiple lesser colleagues.

And into the midst of this bedlam, this curious rioting chorus
incited by theological, astrological and astronomical sources (to cite
only the most important), comes the sound of the voice of Francis,
Lord of Verulam: "I am now therefore to speak touching Hope."
No matter how many quieter and more profound voices have
spoken before, no matter how many circus tricks he had in his
bag, no matter how clearly we now realize that he was not methodologically on the track which science was to follow—this remains
true: his voice was heard. He is the Great Impresario of modern
science.

Not of modern scientific method, but of the modern scientific
attitude—in the sense of devoting oneself to a body of physical

knowledge entirely freed of all teleological considerations, and one to be placed at the disposal of men, "for the benefit and use of life." He has something to say of both of the ideals of modern science —that of "pure knowledge" and that of utility. For he pays his respects to the part to be played in "the further advance of knowledge" by

> a variety of experiments, which are of no use in themselves, but simply serve to discover causes and axioms.

These, he explains,

> I call *"experimenta lucifera,"* experiments of light, to distinguish them from those which I call *"fructifera,"* experiments of fruit.[431]

He even goes so far as to say that

> works themselves are of greater value as pledges of truth than as contributing to the comforts of life,[432]

and to assert that

> as the uses of light are infinite, in enabling us to walk, to ply our arts, to read, to recognise one another, and nevertheless the very beholding of the light is itself a more excellent and a fairer thing than all the uses of it;—so assuredly the very contemplation of things as they are, without superstition or imposture, error or confusion, is in itself more worthy than all the fruit of inventions.[433]

With such a point of view, he leaves the Counter-Renaissance utterly behind. Raising its enthusiasm for "things as they are" to the level of a religious reverence, he transforms the meaning of that enthusiasm to a concept of the end of science as a contemplation of truth in as finally intellectualistic a way as that of Thomas Aquinas. But the truth to be contemplated is that of a neutralized nature, and so the vision is that of knowledge for its own sake, not for God's; it is the prophecy of the scientific vision to come, not a return to that which has been.

Yet Rudolf Metz says truly that

> he did not know what to make of the ideal of pure knowledge, forever turning in vacancy on its own axis and detached from every contact of life. . . .[434]

Once again the ideal which a man expressly considers the highest is not necessarily the dearest to him. In his search for a natural law and in his exaltation of pure knowledge, Bacon heralds an age which is to come, but his most characteristic and reiterated notes are those which he derived from the Counter-Renaissance—primarily his faith in a utilitarian, pragmatic and empirical science. He dreams of how the ideal may be made an actuality, and with the dream points beyond the Pillars of Hercules into the magnificent future. But his greatest single accomplishment in the actual realm of science perhaps lies in his emphasis upon a Storehouse of Facts, in his development of that science of the particular which was the contribution of the Counter-Renaissance.

"Greatest," for while modern physics took another road, and while this Counter-Renaissance science of the particular was assimilated into the larger vision of the Scientific Reformation and lost its autonomy—its emphasis and method, as finally developed by Bacon, has reappeared in the last one hundred years. That astute historian of science, who pointed out that "throughout the seventeenth century it is almost impossible to find any natural scientist maintaining that a mere fact can prove any certain truth," has stated the case for this re-emergence of the ideal of the science of the particular as well as it may be—although he does not explicitly make the connection:

> Perhaps the fundamental emphasis brought by Evolution into men's minds has been upon *the detailed causal analysis of the specific processes of change.* Instead of seeking the end or purpose of the world-process as a whole, or to discern the ultimate cause or ground of all existent things—the fundamental task of earlier science and philosophy—men have come to examine *just what the process is and just what it does in its parts.* They have rejected the ultimate goal of both Thomas and Spinoza, the contemplation of a fixed and static structure of Truth, and adopted instead *the aim of investigating all the little truths which experimentation can reveal.* Not that Truth which is the source of all truths, lifting man's soul above all human experience to the realm of the eternal, whether it be, with Aristotle and Thomas, the ultimate purpose of all things, or whether it be, with Spinoza, the universal mathematical system and structure of the world; but *the patient, tireless, and endless search after an infinity of finite truths in our experience*—this is the present-day goal of all scientific and philosophical endeavour.[435]

That is, with the rise of the biological sciences, men have returned to that position of the science of the particular which was content to pursue "an infinity of finite truths in our experience," to investigate "all the little truths which experimentation can reveal." They have returned to it only, of course, with a considerable refinement in method. Yet the spirit is surely the same; the age in which even an Einstein despairs of coming at "that Truth which is the source of all truths," is another Counter-Renaissance. And to those who are disposed to belittle the achievements of Francis Bacon, I would point out that his ultimate development of the Counter-Renaissance science of the particular grew out of his insistence upon "the detailed causal analysis of the specific processes of change," in his plea for men "to examine just what the process is and just what it does in its parts."

FOOTNOTES
CHAPTER 4

I.

1. Dawson, *Prog. and Rel.*, 183–184.
2. Montaigne, *Essayes*, II, 223–224.
3. Lynn Thorndike, *A History of Magic and Experimental Science*, Vol. V (New York, 1941), 8. This statement is certainly accurate, it seems to me, in terms of Professor Thorndike's particular interest: magic and experimental science, and with the qualification "in general." Yet it does a good deal less than justice to the School of Padua and to many astronomers of the last three decades of the century. For a passing estimate of their part in the Scientific Reformation, see the present chapter.
4. Weber, *Hist. Phil.*, 265.
5. *Ibid.*, 265–266.
6. De Wulf, *Med. Phil.*, II, 179.
7. *Ibid.*, II, 179, 171.
8. Agrippa, *De Occulta Philosophia Libri Tres, Book II.* Cf. Thorndike, *Magic and Science*, V, 134, and Henry Morley, *The Life of Cornelius Agrippa von Nettesheim* (London, 1856), I, 116. Compare Professor Thorndike's definition of magic as "a systematized and ordered *marvel-believing* and *marvel-working*, a consistent body of error." (*Ibid.*, V, 13. My italics.)
9. The term "Celestial Magic" was never used *as such,* so far as I know. But the Celestial or Mathematical World of the Cabala is always made equivalent to the second kind or department of magic, and I have found it convenient in this preliminary section to employ the term in this way.
10. Avery Dulles, *Princeps Concordiae:* Pico della Mirandola and the Scholastic Tradition (Cambridge, Mass., 1941), 82.
11. Denis Saurat, *Literature and Occult Tradition,* translated by Dorothy Bolton (New York, 1930), 65.
12. Weber, *Hist. Phil.*, 181–183.
13. Cf., respectively, Greswell, *Memoirs . . .*, 259–260 (concerning Pico della Mirandola); Leon Brunschvicq, *Le Rôle du Pythagorisme dans l'Evolution des Idées* (Paris, 1937), 17–18; and Thorndike, *Magic and Science*, VI, 444 (in connection with Reuchlin's *De arte cabalistica libri tres Leoni X, dedicati, 1517).*
14. My italics.
15. Cassirer, "Mirandola" (I), 124.
16. *Ibid.* (I), 137.
17. *Ibid.* (I), 142.
18. Pico, however, was always antagonistic to astrology, possibly because of the centrality of his concept of liberty, although in his *Disputationes adversus astrologium* he does not rest his argument upon this thesis. Cf. Don Cameron Allen, *The Star-Crossed Renaissance: The Quarrel about Astrology and Its Influence in England* (Durham, North Carolina, 1941), 19–30. This endorsement of certain occult traditions and rejection of others is not unusual, however. Like the Calvinists, each magician or esoteric master of whatever sort is likely to claim an infallible and unique discipline.
19. Cassirer, *ibid.* (I), 143.

20. *Ibid.*

21. *Ibid.* In this respect he differs from a man like John Dee, who endorsed both Euclidean and mystical Pythagorean mathematics.

22. This paradox, its origin in Plato's thought (as represented by the *Republic* and the *Timaeus*), and its resolution by Plotinus and others, are discussed by Professor Lovejoy in the early chapters of *The Great Chain of Being.*

23. Cassirer, *ibid.* (I), 138–139.

24. Pico, *De Hominis Dignitate: Opera,* I, 320, translation by Robb, *Neoplatonism,* 87.

25. Pico, *Dignity of Man, JHI,* III, 3, 353. Again, the triad in this statement corresponds to the threefold world of the Cabala, or the three kinds of magic. One can find many similar statements in the writings of Agrippa, Dee, Ralegh, *et al.*

26. My italics. Note here again the particularizing, the "science" of the singular.

27. Pico, *Dignity of Man,* 353.

28. Weber, *Hist. Phil.,* 266.

29. Pico, *ibid.,* 353–354.

30. Weber, *ibid.*

31. More, *English Works,* I, 3.

32. The proposed public disputations were never held, and many of Pico's theses were condemned. Cf. Avery Dulles, *Princeps Concordiae,* 89, 139.

33. Greswell, *Memoirs . . .,* 259–260.

34. Saurat, *Lit. and Occ. Trad.,* 42–43.

35. Pico, *Dignity of Man,* 354.

36. *Ibid.,* 352–353. Cf. 353 and 354 for further protestations of this sort.

37. Cf. *ibid.,* 353.

38. Paracelsus, *Works,* I, 51. My italics.

39. *Ibid.,* I, 69.

40. Weber, *Hist. Phil.,* 267.

41. Paracelsus, *ibid.,* I, 72. Consider this "independent" parallel to the doctrine of "imputed righteousness" in the early Reformation.

42. *Ibid.,* I, 19–20.

43. *Ibid.,* I, 39.

44. D. B. Durand, "Nicole Oresme and the Medieval Origins of Modern Science," *Speculum,* Vol. XVI, No. 2 (April, 1941), 184.

45. Quoted by Thorndike, *Magic and Science,* VI, 439. My italics.

46. Christopher Marlowe, *The tragicall Historie of Doctor Faustus (ed. cit.),* 35. Cf. Bruno Tapper, "Aristotle's 'Sweete Analutikes' in Marlowe's *Doctor Faustus,*" *Studies in Philology,* Vol. XXVII, No. 2 (April, 1930), 215–219; and De Wulf, *Med. Phil.,* II, 267. See also *The Massacre at Paris,* 390–418, for proof that Marlowe is well acquainted with Ramus, especially lines 400, 413–415, and 416–418—with which compare respectively Taylor, *Thought and Express.,* I, 379, 381; *ibid.,* 382; and the quotation from Ramus in Chapter II, Section 1 *(supra).*

47. Marlowe, *ibid.,* 42–43.

48. *Ibid.,* 55–61.

49. *Ibid.,* 65–76.

50. *Ibid.,* 138.

51. *Ibid.,* 37. My italics.

52. *Ibid.,* 42–43. My italics. He is not referring to wealth, but to alchemy, when he says, "heape up golde."

53. *Ibid.,* 52–53.

54. *Ibid.,* 54. My italics.

55. *Ibid.,* 64.

56. *Ibid.,* 75–76: "*Che sera, sera* What will be, shall be? Divinitie, adieu . . ."
For the importance of "free will" to the occult traditions, see the Abbé
Tenaud's definition of the Cabala (Thorndike, *Magic and Science,* VI,
453) .

57. Marlowe, *ibid.,* 103.

58. *Ibid.,* 51.

59. *Ibid.,* 77–79.

60. *Ibid.,* 81–83.

61. *Ibid.,* 88–91. To observe the similarity of line 89 to an idea of Bruno's
related to his doctrine of place-relativity, cf. Höffding, *Mod. Phil.,* I, 124.
Donne gives a different twist to the same fundamental concept in his
Devotions.

62. *Ibid.,* 96–97. The role of the occult interpreter-guide plays another important part in the tradition. See Rabelais, Book V, for an interesting
treatment of this—however ironic the intent may have been.

63. *Ibid.,* 145–146.

64. *Ibid.,* 147–148. My italics. Cf. lines 104–105 for the similar assertion of the
Evil Angel.

65. *Ibid.,* 167–169.

66. *Ibid.,* 599–600, 603–604, 606–607.

67. Marlowe, *ibid.,* 179, 183–184.

68. I accept the conjecture of Mitford, Dyce and others that Albanus does
mean Albertus.

69. It is possible to hold that Cornelius and Valdes were practitioners of
legitimate magic, and that Faustus alone moves from it to the black art
endorsed by the Devil, but the comment of the First Scholar, when he
hears from Wagner that Faustus is dining with Valdes and Cornelius, seems
to belie this interpretation:

> Nay then I feare, he is falne into that damned art, for which they two
> are infamous through the world (227–228) .

70. Marlowe, *ibid.,* 187–189.

71. Notably the conjuring scene (235–257) . The incantation Faustus pronounces bears a striking likeness to some of those in John Dee's record of
his occult experiences (*A True & Faithfull Relation of What Passed for
Many Yeers Betweene Dr. John Dee and some Spirits* . . . with a preface
by Meric Causabon, London, 1659) .

72. Cf. Marlowe, *ibid.,* 117, for example, and compare Weber, *Hist. Phil.,* 266.

2.

73. Paracelsus, *Works,* II, 9.

74. *Ibid.,* I, 4.

75. *Ibid.,* I, 6.

76. *Ibid.,* II, 5.

77. Cf. Wolf, *Sci., Tech., and Phil.,* 325.

78. Cf. Thorndike, *Magic and Science,* V, 620.

79. Quoted by Richard Foster Jones, *Ancients and Moderns,* Washington University Studies, New Series, Language and Literature, No. 6 (St. Louis,
1936) , 9. "R. B." is Richard Bostocke: cf. Johnson, *Astron. Thought,* 183.

80. Quoted by Thorndike, *Magic and Science,* V, 3.

81. Höffding, *Mod. Phil.,* I, 505.

82. Jerome Cardan, *De Subtilitate,* I: *The First Book of Jerome Cardan's De
Subtilitate,* translated by Myrtle Marguerite Cass (Williamsport, Pa., 1934) ,
75–76.

83. *Ibid.,* 76.
84. *Ibid.*
85. Edward MacCurdy, *The Mind of Leonardo da Vinci* (New York, 1928), 258; cf. 277 and 280.
86. Johnson, *Astron. Thought,* 136.
87. *Ibid.,* 135–136.
88. *Ibid.,* 137.
89. *Ibid.,* 164–165.
90. *Ibid.,* 153.
91. *Ibid.,* 154, fn. 77.
92. *Ibid.,* 153. My italics. For clarity, I have omitted the extensive italics of the original text preserved by Professor Johnson.
93. Although not exactly in the following terms.
94. *Ibid.,* 151; cf. Brunschvicq, *Pythagorisme,* 5, 18.
95. Johnson, *ibid.,* 152. The division is worded less technically in this textbook for general consumption, however, than in Dee's exclusively occult writings. Cf. Dee, *A True. . . . Relation,* 47.
96. Cf. Johnson, *ibid.,* 153. It is all the more surprising that Professor Johnson misses the significance of this, since he has just cited on the previous page another scholar's discussion of "the indebtedness of Renaissance writers like Dee to Proclus and the ancient neo-Platonists" (152, fn. 74), and early in his book mentioned this scholar's (Edward W. Strong, *Procedures and Metaphysics,* Berkeley, California, 1936) insistence

> upon the necessity for distinguishing between metaphysical theories of mathematics and the methodological procedures of mathematical and physical investigation. The former, he maintains, belonged to *the neo-Platonic tradition which assigned an ontological and cosmological status to numbers and forms* [note Dee's parenthetical "Formally"], and were therefore not qualified to guide and instruct the Renaissance scientists in their practical problems, which were strictly methodological. (5, fn. 3. My italics.)

Immediately thereafter, Professor Johnson makes the very point I am stressing: "It is difficult . . . to completely dissociate the true traditions in analyzing the work of a sixteenth century writer . . . [since] many of the Renaissance scientists shared in both traditions."

97. Johnson, *ibid.,* 153.
98. Durand, "Tradition and Innovation," 17, fn. 40. Cusanus' treatise is his *De Staticis Experimentis.*
99. For a good, clear treatment of Roger Bacon's empirical science, and one which illuminates this discussion, see De Wulf, *Med. Phil.,* II, 142–143.
100. Johnson, *ibid.,* 153–154. My italics. For the Pythagorean doctrine implicit in Dee's "by order of his doctrine Experimentall," see Burnet, *Greek Phil.,* I, 53. There seems to be very little doubt that Dee, like his acknowledged forebears, is mostly interested in "Metamathematics," which Professor Durand defines as

> the hunch that mathematics was key to all natural knowledge, the pattern of philosophical certitude—[which] had haunted the imagination of Grosseteste, Roger Bacon and Oresme, and the gap between Oresme and Nicholas of Cusa is very small (Durand, *ibid.,* 14–15).

101. Raleigh, *Works,* II, 384–385.
102. Johnson, *Astron. Thought,* 135.
103. Quoted, *ibid.,* 134. My italics.
104. Quoted, *ibid.,* 165–167.

105. It has been said that his *Réponse* (1568) founded political economy. Cf. J. W. Allen, "Jean Bodin," 43, in *Social and Political Ideas*, 42–61.

106. *Ibid.*, 42–43.

107. Taylor, *Thought and Express.*, I, 359. Cf. Machiavelli, *Discourses*, I, lvi: "The Occurrence of Important Events in any City or Country is Generally Preceded by Signs and Portents, or by Men who Predict Them"—where Machiavelli invokes "both ancient and modern instances" to prove that "the truth of the fact exists, that these portents are invariably followed by the most remarkable events" (*ibid.*, 257–258).

108. Atkinson, *Nouveaux Horizons*, 421; cf. *ibid.*, 324 and 420.

109. Bacon, *Novum Organum*, Preface.

110. Quoted by Edward MacCurdy, *The Notebooks of Leonardo da Vinci* (2 vols., New York, 1938), Preface, I, 29. For a good account of Vesalius' work (and a clear indication of how representative he was of what I call the "Counter-Renaissance"), see Ernst Cassirer, "The Place of Vesalius in the Culture of the Renaissance," *The Yale Journal of Biology and Medicine*, Vol. 16, No. 2 (December, 1943), 110–119.

111. Quoted by Taylor, *Thought and Express.*, II, 320.

112. Juan Luis (Ludovicus) Vives, *De Tradendis Disciplinis*, translated by Foster Watson as *Vives: on Education* (Cambridge, 1913), 221.

113. Cf. *ibid.*, xcv, cxxi–cxxii.

114. Vives, *Pseudo-dialecticos* (1519), quoted by Watson in the preface to *De Tradendis*, lxi.

115. Vives, *De Tradendis*, 169–170.

116. *Ibid.*, 233.

117. Montaigne, *Essayes*, II, 329.

118. *Ibid.*, III, 386–387.

119. Höffding, *Mod. Phil.*, I, 82.

120. Randall, *Mod. Mind*, 212, 216.

121. Cf. *ibid.*, 216, 220–221; and Höffding, *Mod. Phil.*, I, 164–166. Professor Randall's quotations on pages 220–221 of his *Making of the Modern Mind* form a particularly clear summary of Leonardo's thought and scientific position, and Leonardo's *Notebooks* (*ed. cit.*) furnish such excellent evidence of his soundly scientific attitude, that I cannot agree with Professor Thorndike, who largely denies Leonardo a truly scientific attitude (*Magic and Science*, V, 18, 19), although he does concede the excellence and accuracy of some of Leonardo's observations in geology, botany, anatomy, etc. (*ibid.*, 27–29, 33).

122. Cf. Randall, *Mod. Mind*, 216–217.

123. Randall, "Sci. Method," 177–179.

124. *Ibid.*, 177–178, 203.

125. *Ibid.*, 183, 205.

126. *Ibid.*, 205–206. As I have suggested elsewhere, I subscribe to this interpretation of the origin of modern science, although other historians of scientific thought have rather emphasized the collaboration of Renaissance empiricism and Platonic-Pythagorean metaphysics (which unquestionably did influence such notable astronomers as Copernicus, Kepler and the sixteenth-century Englishmen already dealt with) as crucial to its inception. Such a point of view is summarized briefly in Christopher Dawson's statement that

> modern science owes its birth to the union of the creative genius of the Renaissance [with its empirical emphasis upon a return to nature itself] with the mathematical idealism of Platonic metaphysics (*Rel. and Prog.*, 184).

My conviction that Professor Randall has made the more accurate analysis of the roots of Galilean (and hence, of modern) science derives particularly from the evidence he presents (in his article on Paduan scientific method) as proof that it was the mathematics of Euclid and (especially) Archimedes which influenced Galileo, not the Pythagorean variety—and that it was this mathematics which he combined with the critical Aristotelian methodology of the Paduan school. Moreover, I am convinced that the scientific value and influence of Renaissance Neopythagorean mathematics has been vastly over-estimated in such books as E. A. Burtt's *The Metaphysical Foundation of Modern Physical Science*. Yet this is not to say (as I hope the present chapter indicates) that I believe that the occult and empirical science of the Counter-Renaissance (in the former of which Platonic metaphysics and Pythagorean mystical mathematics certainly played a large part) was without its influence in effecting the transition from medieval to modern science.

In short, I would recognize as primarily Counter-Renaissance figures of the Platonic-Pythagorean scientific variety, Copernicus, Recorde and Dee. Tycho Brahe, despite other elements in his thought and scientific attitude, seems to me most characteristically the one astronomer who best represents the Counter-Renaissance empiricists, while in Thomas Digges one finds both aspects of the Counter-Renaissance represented. All of these men seem to me to stand apart, in one way or another, from the main line of scientific methodology, which leads to Galileo and beyond to seventeenth- and eighteenth-century science. Kepler, again, while influenced in his early thought by Neoplatonic metaphysics, later—and after undergoing the empirical discipline of Tycho Brahe—emerges as a true son of the Scientific Reformation and a peer of Galileo's, although he did not arrive at that position by the same route.

127. Randall, "Sci. Method," 194. Professor Randall explains,

> The *Posterior Analytics* had seemed to say that while the principles and causes in terms of which a given subject-matter might be understood were to be discovered through sense-experience, they were seen to be true through *voũs*, by sheer intellectual vision.

128. *Ibid.*, 198–200.
129. *Ibid.*, 194. My italics.
130. *Ibid.*, 196–197.
131. Edward Rosen, "The Ramus-Rheticus Correspondence," under "Notes and Documents," *JHI*, Vol. I, No. 3 (June, 1940), 363. Ramus' interest in mathematics was a late development in his career, and one in which he did not progress very far. Cf. Johnson, *Astron. Thought*, 144–145. Yet Professor Johnson points out the influence of Ramus' mathematical works on "the spread of mathematical and scientific knowledge" in England (*ibid.*, 195), and declares,

> Had it not been for the Ramist influence, mathematics and science would probably have been seriously neglected at Cambridge during the last three decades of the sixteenth century (*ibid.*, 196).

132. Randall, "Sci. Meth.," 206, fn. 41. Cf. Burtt, *Meta Found.*, 70.
133. Höffding, *Mod. Phil.*, I, 167.
134. *Ibid.*, 168–169.
135. Kepler, *Commentary on the Motions of Mars*, Part II, ch. 19; quoted by Randall, *Mod. Mind*, 231. My italics.
136. Quoted by Randall, *ibid.*, 235.

137. Quoted by Höffding, *ibid.*, I, 151.

138. Johnson, *Astron. Thought,* 159.

139. But not defeated. Cf. Johnson, *ibid.*, 174–175, for his reference in 1579 to "late Observations to ratifye and confirme" Copernicus' "Theorikes and Hypothesis," and the possibility that he may have used "a combination of lenses and mirrors corresponding to our modern telescope. . . ." See pages 174–180 for his many contributions to experimental science.

140. Rosen, "Ramus-Rheticus Corres.," 363.

141. Cf. Johnson, *Astron. Thought,* 143–144; and Bacon, *Works,* 674.

142. Johnson, *ibid.*, 214; cf. 154–155. Galileo clinched the last point with his observations of the mountains on the moon and the dark spots on the sun, and produced strong enough evidence in confirmation of Copernicus' theory that the earth moves around the sun, to change it from a mathematical truth to a physical one. Cf. Randall, *Mod. Mind,* 232–233.

143. Although a complete mechanical demonstration of the Copernican system was produced only with the publication of Newton's *Principia* in 1687. Cf. Johnson, *ibid.*, 215.

144. Da Vinci, *Notebooks,* I, 92.

145. Vives, *De Tradendis,* 213, 41.

146. Montaigne, *Essayes,* III, 331.

147. *Ibid.*, III, 432.

148. *Ibid.*, III, 438.

149. *Ibid.*, III, 439.

150. *Ibid.*, III, 440.

151. *De Anima et Vita.*

152. Quoted by Watson, *Vives: On Education,* cxxi–cxxii.

153. Bacon, *Novum Organum,* I, xxxvi.

154. *Ibid.*, lxxxiii.

155. Cf. Aristotle, *Part. An.*, I, 5, 644^b 22: quoted by Jaeger, *Aristotle,* 338–339. In fairness to Vives, it must be stated that he frequently expresses respect for Aristotle, and demonstrates an understanding of the ways in which his attitude had been distorted. Cf., for example, Vives, *De Tradendis,* 9.

156. Vives, *De Tradendis,* 169–170.

157. Jacques Cartier, *Bref Récit et succincte narration* (Paris, 1545) , 2: Atkinson, *Nouveaux Horizons,* 256. Wherever I have employed quotations collected by Profesor Atkinson from these voyagers, I have indicated, for convenience, the pages on which they appear in his book, as well as the original pagination which he records. All the translations (except where otherwise noted) into English are mine, and are translations of Professor Atkinson's modernizations of the original French texts.

158. Jean de Léry, *Histoire d'un voyage . . . Brésil* (La Rochelle, 1578) , 38–39: Atkinson, 286–287.

159. Cf. Johnson, *Astron. Thought,* 172.

160. Quoted by Johnson, *ibid.*, 173.

161. Atkinson, *Nouveaux Horizons,* 255.

162. *Ibid.*, 287.

163. Ralegh, *Works,* II, xlv–xlvi: *History of the World,* Preface.

164. *Ibid.*, VIII, 184; cf. Lawrence Stapleton, "Halifax and Ralegh," *JHI,* Vol. II, No. 2 (April, 1941) , 222.

165. Ralegh, "The Lie," (from Francis Davison's *Poetical Rhapsody,* 1608) : *Poetry of the English Renaissance* (1509–1660) , Selected from early editions and manuscripts and edited by J. William Hebel and Hoyt H. Hudson (New York, 1938) , 140.

166. Cf. Baron, "Towards a More Positive Evaluation," 40–46; and Edgar

Zilsel, "The Sociological Roots of Science," *The American Journal of Sociology*, 47 (1942), 544–560.

167. Francis R. Johnson, "Preparation and Innovation in the Progress of Science," *JHI*, Vol. IV, No. 1 (January, 1943), 57.

168. Cf. Johnson, *Astron. Thought*, 120–133.

169. Cf. *ibid.*, 170–171.

170. *Ibid.*, 171.

171. Baron, "Positive Evaluation," 43.

172. Quoted by Johnson, *Astron. Thought*, 171–172.

173. *Ibid.*, 172.

174. Harvey, *Works*, II, 289. My italics.

175. Robb, *Neoplatonism*, 48.

176. Quoted by Fletcher, *Italian Renaissance*, 103.

177. See chart on p. 180 (*supra*).

178. Cf. Greswell, *Memoirs* . . ., 245, 250, 260.

179. Cassirer, "Mirandola," 124.

180. Agrippa, *De incertitudine*, III, 1344, 1348.

181. Thorndike, *Magic and Science*, VI, 453. This is Professor Thorndike's summary of Tenaud's statement. My italics.

182. Léon Brunschvicq, *Le Rôle du Pythagorisme*, 17–18.

183. Paracelsus, *Alchemical Writings*, I, 19.

184. *Ibid.*, I, 19–20. My italics.

185. Montaigne, II, 279.

186. *Ibid.*, 280–281.

187. *Ibid.*, III, 182–183.

188. *Ibid.*, I, 149.

189. *Ibid.*, III, 379.

190. Villey, *Essais de Montaigne*, 10.

191. Machiavelli, *Discourses*, III, 506.

192. Cf. Watson, *Vives: On Education*, xcv, cxxi–cxxii.

193. Villey, *Essais de Montaigne*, 9; Montaigne, III, 379.

194. Sir Thomas Smith, *De Republica Anglorum: A Discourse on the Commonwealth of England*, edited by L. Alston (Cambridge, 1906), 142 (III, 9). My italics.

195. Henry Stevens of Vermont, *Thomas Hariot* (London, 1900), 117–118.

196. *Ibid.*, 116–117.

197. Cf. Atkinson, *Nouveaux Horizons*, 255.

198. Amerigo Vespucci (?) *Sensuit le Nouveau Monde*, Paris, 1516–1517 (?), 72: Atkinson, *Nouveaux Horizons*, 255. *Ibid.*, 73: Atkinson, 256. Hernando Cortez, *Des Marches, iles et terre ferme*, Anvers, 1523, 2: Atkinson, 256. J. Léon, *Historiale description de l'Afrique*. Lyon, 1556, I, 469: Atkinson, 258. François de Belleforest, *L'Histoire universelle du Monde*, Paris, 1570, 246: Atkinson, 258. Joseph Acosta, *Histoire Naturelle et morale des Indes*, Paris, 1598, 31: Atkinson, 260; my italics.

199. L. Du Voisin (De la Popelinière), *Les Trois Mondes*, Paris, 1582, I, 7: Atkinson, 259. Acosta, *Histoire . . . des Indes*, 101: Atkinson, 287. F. Lopez de Gómara, *Histoire générale des Indes*, Paris, 1568, Chapter VI: Atkinson, 257.

200. See fn. 104, *supra*.

201. Quoted by Johnson, *Ast. Thought*, 183.

202. Donne, *Ignatius*, 140.

203. *Ibid.*, 6.

204. *Ibid.*, 14.

205. *Ibid.*, 23–24. Donne's attitude toward Paracelsus and his "philosophy" is

not wholly consistent, but he is thoroughly interested in him. See Don Cameron Allen, "John Donne's Knowledge of Renaissance Medicine," *Journal of English and Germanic Philology*, XLII, 3 (July, 1943), 323–326, for the conviction that Donne was on the whole favorably impressed with Paracelsianism. Professor Allen, however, makes no reference to *Ignatius*.

206. *Ibid.*, 30–35, 38. See quotation in Chapter III, 5 (*supra*).
207. *Ibid.*, 20–21.
208. *Ibid.*, 29.
209. For the long passage devoted to Machiavelli, see *ibid.*, 40–90.
210. *Ibid.*, 32.
211. Bacon, *Works*, 140: *Advancement of Learning*, Book II.

3.

212. For this tradition of books "de Regimine Principium," in relation to Machiavelli, see Allen H. Gilbert, *Machiavelli's Prince and Its Forerunners: The Prince as a Typical book de Regimine Principium* (Durham, North Carolina, 1938). For another summary of the classical and medieval roots of the tradition, see Lester K. Born's introduction to his translation of Erasmus' *The Education of a Christian Prince*, 94–130.
213. Machiavelli, *Prince*, 121. My italics.
214. Machiavelli, *Discourses*, "Greeting," 101.
215. Cf. Brown, *The Methodus . . . of Jean Bodin*, xix.
216. Bodin, *Republic* (Knolles' translation), 3. Bodin, who seems to have followed Aristotle faithfully through the first three books of this work (cf. Allen, "Jean Bodin," 44), is here speaking in the spirit of Books IV and V of Aristotle's *Politics* (especially IV, i, $1288^{b}21-1289^{a}7$), where the ideal state of Plato is deserted for one to be derived empirically from existing constitutions, etc. See Jaeger, *Aristotle*, 261. It is interesting to note that Professor Jaeger affirms (doubtless to the horror of many Aristotelians and Neo-Thomists) that "Machiavelli got his rules from the *Politics*" (*ibid.*, 5–6), and that "Aristotle did indeed formulate the problem of power clearly" in terms of politics (*ibid.*, 399).
217. Bodin, *Republic*, V, i, 461–462: Atkinson, 406–407. Here, as in some other passages below which I have translated from Professor Atkinson's modernized version of Bodin and Le Roy, I am indebted to Professor Malcolm K. Hooke of the department of Romance Languages at the Woman's College of the University of North Carolina, for his help in a consideration of various constructions and words susceptible to semantic change. While the responsibility for all these translations remains finally mine, Professor Hooke's assistance has been very valuable.
218. It is necessary to make this distinction, for, as J. W. Allen points out, Bodin's thought, however original and powerful, is far from consistent. Cf. Allen, "Jean Bodin," 42–61.
219. Bodin, *Théâtre*, n.p. It must be added, however, that, like others of his age, his promise here is more impressive than his performance in the body of his text.
220. Allen, "Jean Bodin," 43.
221. Agrippa, *Van. and Uncer.*, sig. E2.
222. *Ibid.*, sig. E4. My italics.
223. Cf. *Guichardin: Pensées et Portraits*, translated by Juliette Bertrand, with an introductory study by Jacques Bainville (Les Éditions Denöel et Steele, Paris, 1933), 30–31. Quotations from Guicciardini below are my translations of passages in this book.

224. Montaigne, *Essayes,* II, 116–117.
225. The Epistle Dedicatorie, iiij^v.
226. Fletcher, *Ital. Ren.,* 19.
227. Taylor, *Thought and Express.,* I, 83, 93.
228. Fletcher, *Ital. Ren.,* 188.
229. Guicciardini, *Pensées,* 18.
230. *Ibid.,* 53.
231. *Ibid.,* 65.
232. *Ibid.,* 90. "Everywhere identical or similar"—for, like Machiavelli, Guicciardini sees history as a cyclical process, with human nature and the course of events ever the same, under outward appearances of difference, according to time and place. He declares,

> All which has been in the past and all which is at present will be again in the future; but things so change their names and appearances that those who do not possess good eyes do not recognize this at all and neither know how to guide themselves by them [the recurring phenomena] nor how to arrive at a judgment from the observation of them *(ibid., 29)* .

233. These three, as developed here, are of course related to the definitions of Classicism, Romanticism and Naturalism in the Prologue. The first position cited in the present chapter, *roughly* corresponds to that of some Romanticists; the second to that of the Classicist; the third to that of the Naturalist—as set forth in the Prologue. The reason that there is no place in the present discussion for the other sort of Romanticists is that theirs is not, exactly speaking, a *philosophical* position at all.

234. This is not to say, obviously, that all of these plays are actually treating the same, or even closely related aspects of the discrepancies between the ideal and the actual, and between the apparent and the real. Many and diverse intellectual currents flow into the particular and different angles of these two generalized themes, with which, otherwise, it would seem that Shakespeare had been obsessed. And the failure to distinguish sufficiently the dissimilarities of these various angles, and their separate intellectual antecedents, seems to me the great weakness of Theodore Spencer's *Shakespeare and the Nature of Man* (New York, 1942) , a study which is effectively pointed in a direction largely neglected hitherto by Shakespearian scholars.

　　Professor Spencer, after a brief preliminary description of the ideological clash between the medieval world-view and that of what I call the Counter-Renaissance, lumps Shakespeare's presentation of the various aspects of this conflict under one heading: appearance *vs.* reality. This comes close to asserting the identity (to choose examples at random) of the source of Hamlet's brooding, of Angelo's "double standard," of Iago's dissimulation, and of Lear's divesting himself of his "lendings"—obviously a simplification which is somewhat too facile. If I am guilty here of the very offense with which I charge Professor Spencer, and hence (in so short an account) am unjust to his development of his theme, the reader will have ample opportunity to compare what I have to say about some of these plays, in the body of this book, with Professor Spencer's account.

　　Again, compare the discussion of Classicism, Romanticism and Naturalism in the Prologue.

235. Machiavelli, *Discourses,* I, xxv, 182.
236. Francis Bacon, "Of Truth": *The Essayes or Counsels, Civill and Morall,* of Francis Lo. Verulam, Viscount St. Alban, Newly enlarged (London, 1625) :

The Essays of Francis Bacon, with an introduction by William H. Hudson (New York, 1901), 2.

237. Montaigne, Essayes, III, 20. My italics.

238. Ibid.

239. Ibid., 20–21. My italics.

240. Cf. Ernst Cassirer, "Some Remarks on the Question of the Originality of the Renaissance," JHI, Vol. IV, No. 1 (January, 1943), 54. I have read the late Professor Cassirer's exposition of this idea, which he attributes in substance (not about Montaigne in particular) to Burckhardt, since working out my own interpretation of Montaigne's meaning, and am happy to have my view substantiated by that of so distinguished a scholar.

241. For its most persistent meaning in the Medieval period and in the early Renaissance, see Chapter V, 1 (infra). For some of the innumerable variations in interpretation which this phrase has undergone throughout the centuries, see Eliza Gregory Wilkins, The Delphic Maxims in Literature (Chicago, 1929).

242. Montaigne, Essays, III, 42.

243. Ibid., III, 23. My italics.

244. As Pierre Villey points out, it is significant that Montaigne later changes his early assertion, "Je fais les essais de mon jugement" to "Je fais les essais de ma vie" (Villey, Essais de . . . Montaigne, 9).

245. Ibid., III, 437. My italics.

246. Ibid., "The Author to the Reader."

247. Ibid., III, 21.

248. Ibid., III, 377.

249. Ibid., I, 149.

250. Ibid., III, 379.

251. Ibid., III, 380.

252. Ibid., III, 21.

253. Ibid., "The Author to the Reader." My italics.

254. Ibid., III, 21.

255. Cassirer, "Orig. of Ren.," 50.

256. Preface to the Modern Library edition of The Essayes of Montaigne (Florio's translation), xxv–xxvi. As for Montaigne's popularity with the Elizabethans, it is pertinent to note that when Ben Jonson wanted a measuring rod by which to indicate the current popularity of Guarini's Pastor Fido, he declared that contemporary writers would soon be stealing as much from it as they already did from "Montagnie" (Volpone, III, iii).

257. See also Discourses, II, xviii, 342, and II, xxiv, 365.

258. Machiavelli, Discourses, II, xvii, 337–338.

259. Taylor, Thought and Express., I, 85.

260. Ibid., I, 89.

261. Fletcher, Ital. Ren., 189.

262. Machiavelli, Discourses, III, xxxv, 513.

263. Höffding, Mod. Phil., I, 188. My italics.

264. In this connection, it is interesting to observe the different use which Galileo makes of Bruno's argument for the epistemological principle of relativity from the evidence of the senses. Bruno maintains that

> If we examine the different sense-images which we receive when we move, we see that the horizon continually changes as we change our place. (Höffding, Mod. Phil., I, 124)

Bruno uses this argument in the service of his thesis that there is no limit or central point to the universe. But Galileo's representative in the

Dialogues, stressing rather the subjectivity of the sense-qualities, says of sunrise and sunset:

> All these are only changes from the standpoint of the earth. Think away the earth and there is neither sunrise nor sunset, no horizon, no meridian, no day, and no night! (Quoted, *ibid.,* I, 183)

In perfect agreement regarding the principle of relativity involved, nevertheless one employs evidence from the senses to further his point; the other makes the unreliability of sense evidence his point.

265. Montaigne, *Essayes,* II, 323.
266. *Ibid.*
267. *Ibid.,* II, 345.
268. *Ibid.,* II, 281–282. Thus he extends the depreciation of reason characteristic of the Counter-Renaissance even to reason as used by the thinkers of the Scientific Reformation.
269. Bodin, *Republic,* 5: Atkinson, *Nouv. Hor.,* 394.
270. Since Bodin is following the Neoplatonic rather than the Aristotelian pattern, he stresses the "incomprehensibility" and "infiniteness" of God—but for our present purposes, this is beside the point.
271. Cf. Atkinson, *ibid.,* 393–394.
272. Le Roy, *Vicissitudes . . .* (1575), 25: Atkinson, 348.
273. Le Roy, *ibid.,* 25–27: Atkinson, *ibid.,* 393, 348. My italics. See also, however, Atkinson, *ibid.,* 393–394, where the passage in question reads the same through "les autres choses avec . . ."; then, omitting "observations, usage, et expérience," substitutes "discours raisonnable . . . les autres par inspiration divine." I have been unable to discover whether this difference is due to the use of different editions, but it is at any rate a very suggestive point for this discussion that some one (presumably Le Roy himself) somewhere, sometime during the sixteenth century found it necessary to make this change—and equally suggestive in the alignment of the two conflicting forces we have been following, whether the appeal to experience was the first version or the later one.
274. Höffding, *Mod. Phil.,* I, 188. My italics.
275. Cf. Chapter III, 2 *(supra).*
276. Cf. Randall, "Scientific Method," 205–206.
277. Jaeger, *Aristotle,* 340.
278. Höffding, *Mod. Phil.,* I, 162.
279. Compare the title with the preceding paragraph.
280. De Wulf, *Med. Phil.,* II, 275.
281. Höffding, *ibid.,* I, 162.
282. For Telesio, see *ibid.,* I, 100–101.
283. *Ibid.,* I, 94.
284. *Ibid.*
285. *Ibid.,* 98–99.
286. Quoted, *ibid.,* 100. My italics.
287. *Ibid.,* 101–102.
288. Cf. p. 34 *supra* (Chapter I).
289. Vives, *De Tradendis,* 17.
290. *Ibid.,* 35. My italics.
291. *Ibid.,* 18.
292. *Ibid.,* 166.
293. *Ibid.,* 46–47.
294. *Ibid.,* 56.

295. Montaigne, *Essayes*, III, 182.
296. Machiavelli, *Prince*, 121.
297. Machiavelli, *Discourses*, I, Introduction, 103. My italics.
298. Bacon, *Novum Organum*, I, lxvi. My italics.
299. Bacon, *Works*, 247. My italics.
300. Bacon, *Essayes*, 183.
301. Quoted by Johnson, *Ast. Thought*, 172. My italics. Cf. *ibid.*, 196.
302. Bacon, *Nov. Org.*, I, lxxxi.
303. Harvey, *Works*, II, 290. My italics.
304. Vives, *De Tradendis*, 47.
305. Randall, *Mod. Mind*, 139.
306. *Ibid.*, 136.
307. Mueller, "Calvin's . . . Christian Thinking," 297.
308. Cf. Randall, *ibid.*, 137.
309. Cf. Mueller, *ibid.* See also Erich Fromm's discussion and interpretation in *Escape from Freedom*.
310. Greville, *Treatie*, st. 60.
311. *Ibid.*, st. 61.
312. *Ibid.*, st. 62.
313. *Ibid.*, st. 63.
314. *Ibid.*, st. 64.
315. *Ibid.*, st. 66.
316. *Ibid.*, st. 67. My italics.
317. *Ibid.*, st's 68–69.
318. *Ibid.*, st's 74–75.
319. Yet this is not to say that the other point of view, that most notably sponsored by Burtt, has no longer any adherents. The most recent article I have seen on the subject [Alexander Koyré, "Galileo and Plato," *JHI*, Vol. IV, No. 3 (October, 1943), 400–428] defends the thesis that Galileo was a Platonist, and that the roots of modern science rest in the soil of Neoplatonic metaphysics. However, Professor Koyré's article does not seem to me to present any conclusive evidence for this position. He makes Galileo a Platonist chiefly by the expedient of insisting that Archimedes, "the *divus*" was a "*philosophus platonicus*" despite the contradictory testimony of the "doxographic tradition." ("Galileo and Plato," 423). However satisfying this approach may be to Professor Koyré, it seems to me tenuous and unconvincing; and the further evidence which he shows to present Galileo's direct indebtedness to traditional Platonism (*ibid.*, 424–428) is not impressive. The quotations on p. 427 indicate nothing more than Galileo's general sympathy with the Platonic epistemology and emphasis upon mathematics, if that. I cannot agree with Professor Koyré's assertion that Galileo's belief that he had demonstrated factually the truth of Platonism (if that *is* what Galileo meant) has any greater significance than that of a general conviction that he had proved factually the over-all validity of quantitative measurement; and certainly Galileo's attitude toward the "numerical speculations of the Pythagoreans," cited by Professor Koyré (*ibid.*, 425), indicates clearly that he had no faith in the Platonic-Pythagorean metamathematics. The best part of the article is the lucid and detailed treatment of Scholastic physics.
320. Randall, "Sci. Method," 205.
321. *Ibid.*, 203.
322. Thorndike, *Magic and Science*, V, 14.
323. Randall, *ibid.*, 206.

4.

324. George Hakewill, *An Apologie or Declaration of the Power and Providence of God in the Government of the World* (3d ed., London, 1635), Epistle Dedicatory, a3. Cf. Watson, *Vives: On Education*, cv–cvi.
325. Vives, *De Tradendis*, 9.
326. Cf. Thorndike, *Magic and Science*, VI, 69.
327. Le Roy, *Considérations sur l'histoire universelle*: Atkinson, 404–405. Compare the passage from Le Roy's *De la Vicissitude* (Ashley's translation), quoted by Johnson, *Ast. Thought*, 298–299, for a variant version.
328. Harvey, *Letter Book*, 69–71.
329. Montaigne, *Essayes*, II, 577.
330. *Ibid.*, III, 20–21.
331. Quoted by Cassirer, "Orig. of the Ren.," 50–51.
332. Cf. *ibid.*, 53.
333. Bacon, *Nov. Org.*, I, xcii.
334. Machiavelli, *Discourses*, I, Introduction, 103.
335. Bacon, *Nov. Org.*, I, lxxxi.
336. Bacon, *New Atlantis: The Advancement of Learning and New Atlantis*, with a preface by Thomas Case (World's Classics, Oxford University Press, London, n.d.), 255.
337. *Ibid.*, 265.
338. Bacon, *Nov. Org.*, I, lxxxiii.
339. *Ibid.*, Preface.
340. *Ibid.*, I, li.
341. Spedding, Preface to the *History of the Reign of King Henry VII: Works* (2 vol. ed.), II, 28.
342. Höffding, *Mod. Phil.*, I, 206.
343. Bacon, *Essayes*, 113 ("Of Friendship").
344. Bacon, *Adv. of Learning*, II, xx, 1, p. 163. My italics.
345. For one of the least pedantic of these ubiquitous discussions, see Book IV of Castiglione's *Book of the Courtier*. Cf. Albert D. Menut, "Castiglione and the Nichomachean Ethics," *PLMA*, Vol. LVIII, No. 2 (June, 1943), 309–321.
346. Another favorite topic. Pomponazzi's elaboration of it is as satisfactory as any: *De Immortalitate Animae*, 50–56.
347. Bacon, *Adv. of Learn.*, II, xx, 1, p. 163.
348. *Ibid.*, II, xx, 2, p. 163.
349. Höffding, *Mod. Phil.*, I, 206.
350. Bacon, *Adv. of Learn.*, II, xx–xxii.
351. *Ibid.*, II, xxiii, 1, p. 190.
352. *Ibid.*
353. *Ibid.*, II, xxiii, 2, pp. 190–191.
354. Thomas Case, *ed. cit.*, Preface, xiv.
355. *Ibid.*
356. *Adv. of Learn.*, II, xxiii, 45, p. 215.
357. *Ibid.*, II, xxiii, 46, p. 217.
358. Montaigne, *Essayes*, III, 267.
359. Bacon, *Adv. of Learn.*, II, xxiii, 49, pp. 218–219.
360. Among other apposite passages, see the first paragraph in *Novum Organum*, I, lx, on the *Idols of the Market-Place*.
361. Bacon, *Nov. Org.*, I, liv.
362. *Ibid.*, Author's Preface.
363. *Ibid.*, I, xiii–xiv. My italics.

364. *Ibid.,* xli.
365. *Ibid.,* lxiii.
366. *Ibid.,* lxii. Cf. lxi.
367. *Essayes,* 208 ("Of Studies").
368. *Nov. Org.,* I, lvi.
369. *Works,* 251 ("The Plan of the Work"). He expressly repudiates the rational Law of Nature in the Author's Preface to *Novum Organum.*
370. See, for example, *Works,* 33.
371. Observe the typical, formally cautious phrasing of which I have spoken.
372. And again here.
373. *Nov. Org.,* I, cxxx.
374. *Ibid.*
375. *Ibid.,* xiv.
376. *Ibid.,* Author's Preface.
377. *Ibid.* My italics.
378. Bacon, *De Augmentis,* 10; quoted by Willey, *Seventeenth Century,* 36.
379. Bacon, *Nov. Org.,* I, cxxiv.
380. *Ibid.,* liv. Cf. *ibid.,* lxii–lxiv. It is interesting in this connection to note Professor Johnson's point that Gilbert's brilliant work could be justly criticized on the score of "insufficient evidence," since it needed more experimental confirmation (*Ast. Thought,* 239); and that Gilbert (true child of the Counter-Renaissance) failed to evolve laws of dynamics to strengthen and complete the assurance of his discovery (*ibid.,* 217).
381. *Nov. Org.,* I, lxii. Cf. *ibid.,* lxiii and lxxxv.
382. *Works,* 92.
383. Bacon, *De sapientia veterum,* "Erichthonius," quoted by Charles W. Lemmi, *The Classical Deities in Bacon* (Baltimore, 1933), 102–103. See this book, *passim,* for a study of Bacon's interest in and indebtedness to the alchemists and Neoplatonists.
384. *Nov. Org.,* I, xlvii.
385. *Ibid.,* xli.
386. *Ibid.,* cxxvi.
387. Here he misses the path, as he almost always does in connection with astronomy. Galileo's "Tuscan glass" he will always underestimate.
388. Very nearly John Dee's language, incidentally.
389. *Nov. Org.,* I, 1.
390. *Adv. of Learn.,* II, To the King, 10, pp. 71–72.
391. *Nov. Org.,* I, xxxvi.
392. *Ibid.,* lxiv.
393. *Ibid.,* xlv. He illustrates this point with the "fictions" that "all celestial bodies move in perfect circles" and that there is an "element of Fire . . . brought in to make up the square with the other three which the sense perceives," among others.
394. *Ibid.,* II, ii. From the context, it is clear that Bacon is here referring to a "neutralized" law of natural necessity, not to natural law in the traditional teleological sense. He has just remarked that "the final cause rather corrupts than advances the sciences, except such as have to do with human action" (for example, ethics).
395. *Ibid.,* II, iv.
396. *Adv. of Learn.,* II, xxiii, 8, p. 197. My italics.
397. Rudolf Metz, "Bacon's Part in the Intellectual Movement of His Time," translated by Joan Drever, *Seventeenth Century Studies,* 29.
398. Cf. *ibid.,* 22–24. This is not Professor Metz's opinion.
399. Once again—the actual and the ideal.

400. Bacon, *Nov. Org.*, I, xcv. See *ibid.*, xcviii–ciii, for the elaboration of this theme, particularly in terms of his strictures against loose and aimless experimentation.

401. *Ibid.*, I, xxvi. Cf. Author's Preface.

402. *Ibid.*, xcvii. My italics.

403. *Ibid.*

404. *Ibid.*, ciii, c.

405. *Ibid.*, ciii.

406. *Ibid.*, civ.

407. *Ibid.*, civ, cv.

408. Vives, *De Tradendis*, 21.

409. *Ibid.*, 22.

410. For this comparison of Vives and Bacon, see his *Vives: On Education,* cvi–cxi.

411. An inconsistent confidence, since Vives, as we have seen, elsewhere expresses his conviction that man's understanding has been at least corrupted since the Fall. See pp. 241 and 245 in this chapter.

412. See this chapter, 3.

413. Ramus' insistence upon an astronomy without hypothesis.

414. Höffding, *Mod. Phil.*, I, 162.

415. *Ibid.*, 198.

416. Cf. *Nov. Org.*, II, xx.

417. Höffding, *ibid.*, I, 200.

418. *Ibid.*, 203.

419. *Ibid.*, 199.

420. Telesio alone foreshadows him in this respect. But Telesio's attempt is marked by an excessive simplification, far more drastic than Bacon's.

421. Bacon, *Works*, 143.

422. Bacon, *Nov. Org.*, II, ii.

423. *Ibid.*, Preface.

424. *Ibid.*

425. *Ibid.*, I, li.

426. *Ibid.*, Preface.

427. *Ibid.*, I, lxxxix–xcii.

428. *Ibid.*, xcii.

429. See, for example, Professor Johnson's quotations from Louis Le Roy, and his comparison of the earlier statement with Bacon's position (*Ast. Thought,* 298–299). The early pages of J. B. Bury's *Idea of Progress* trace in some detail the extent to which Le Roy, Bodin and others had endorsed the general point of view which Bacon publicized, before him.

430. Johnson, *ibid.*, 299.

431. Bacon, *Nov. Org.*, I, xcix.

432. *Ibid.*, cxxiv.

433. *Ibid.*, cxxix.

434. Metz, "Bacon's Part," 31.

435. Randall, *Mod. Mind,* 490–491. My italics.

CHAPTER
5

THE CHRISTIAN–CLASSICAL IDEALS OF LIMIT:

DEGREE, FINALITY AND MODERATION AS VALUE AND REALITY

I. LIMIT AS DEGREE, INEQUALITY AND GRADATION

THE preoccupation of the Scholastics and—to a lesser extent—the Renaissance Christian humanists with universal law and order, with design and purpose and unity, necessarily also implies a preoccupation with the idea of limit. For, in the first place, it is obviously impossible to predicate with any confidence a body of universal law unless one knows the whole, including the boundaries, of that for which these laws function. Hence the medieval world-view, influenced alike by Greek and by Christian predilections for finites, is thoroughly convinced of the truth of limit in the very nature of things: limit, or finiteness, is an attribute of all reality save God.

Secondly, since these thinkers maintained the essential congruity of the actual with the ideal (no matter how far short of what it ought to be any *particular* actuality might fall), it follows that what they found true or real must possess excellence. Limit is characteristic not only of reality, but also of value. This statement—in view of the Greek and Roman tendency to attribute permanent norms to Nature, and of the Christian conviction that the created universe was the work of a rational and loving God—might be reversed, of course. Indeed, one of the favorite criticisms directed at the medieval and traditional Renaissance thinkers has been that they first formulated their ideal and then strove to explain the actual in terms of that ideal. Those who believe this charge might, therefore, hold that because limit had value for the Scholastics, they postulated limit as an attribute of reality. It is the reversal of the traditional view that one must first have faith, before one can hope to understand.

But whichever view one holds, the importance to this line of thinkers of the concept of limit, in terms both of reality and of value, is indisputable.[1] It is integral to their convictions about the constitution of the universe, the course of history, the nature of man and of society, and it even involves them in embarrassing theological paradoxes about the nature of God. It is characteristic of their thought not only in all its departments, but also in many different contexts—too many for a complete exposition here.

Yet among the various ways in which "limit" is central to the thinking of the medieval and Renaissance Christian-classical traditionalists, three stand out as crucial and decisive. There are three basic concepts implying, or related to, "limit," which color almost all of their thought about reality and value: that of "degree" or inequality or gradation; that of finality or completeness or finiteness; and that of harmony or moderation or balance. And despite the inter-relations and inter-penetrations of these three concepts, despite their various applications to different realms of thought and life, it is possible to distinguish and describe them with some conclusiveness and clarity.

The first of these concepts—that of "degree" or inequality or gradation—is fundamental to medieval thought, and in many of its aspects inherited and approved by the Renaissance Christian humanists. It is, first of all, inherent in the very nature of things: the whole creation is an immense "chain of being," arranged in hierarchical order from the lowliest to the highest possible kind of creature.[2] Ultimately derivative from the thought of Plato and Aristotle, this idea was first fully developed into an integral part of a general system by the Neoplatonists,[3] and taken over and "baptized" by Christian thinkers (notably Augustine and the pseudo-Dionysius),[4] to become the dominant European picture of the structure of the world until the late eighteenth century.[5] As Plotinus phrases it,

> The world is a sort of Life stretched out to an immense span, in which each of the parts has its own place in the series, all of them different and yet the whole continuous, and that which precedes never wholly absorbed in that which comes after.[6]

Moreover, throughout the long life of this concept—from Plotinus to Pope, one might say—this difference of kind is almost always treated as equal to difference of excellence, "diversity of rank in a hierarchy,"[7] or difference in degree of perfection. As medieval thought develops this idea, man, for example, is a "little lower than the angels," and superior to animal and plant life. He is most characteristically the central link in the chain, partaking of the angelic and the bestial, yet knowing his proper sphere when he so conducts himself that his higher nature, the rational, rules and guides his lower, the sensitive or appetitive. Yet to aspire to be "more than man," in any sense other than the hope of beatitude after death, is to be guilty of overweening and evil ambition—more, is to threaten to disrupt the universal order of things. Centuries before Pope's warning,

> On superior pow'rs
> Were we to press, inferior might on ours;
> Or in the full creation leave a void,
> Where, one step broken, the great scale's destroy'd;
> From Nature's chain whatever link you strike,
> Tenth, or ten thousandth, breaks the chain alike,[8]

the good Christian and the good classical humanist alike had adopted this ontological argument to support basic theological and philosophical premises.

Or again, one may reverse the argument, and, as did the pseudo-Dionysius among others, justify the nature of things by an appeal to the "goodness" of God—which, being infinite, must make all possible things, and therefore all possible *kinds* of things. For, in Augustine's words, *non essent omnia, si essent aequalia.*[9] But, from whichever bias one approaches the matter, this conviction remains unchanged: the nature of the universe is hierarchical, a graded scale of being with ascending degrees of perfection (or, if you prefer, with descending degrees of "privation," to use Aristotle's terminology), in which each created and living entity has its own place. Moreover, not only is this principle of "degree," of gradation, inherent in reality; it also implies excellence of value in two senses: (1) it is indispensable to the perfection of the universe, for God could not have manifested and fulfilled his infinite goodness and love in creating all things, save through the use of inequality; (2) without "degree" there could be no meaning to "good" or "better" or "best," and hence no value.

Thomas Aquinas develops both of these interpretations. He summarizes the first one with these statements:

> The best thing in creation is the perfection of the universe, which consists in *the orderly variety of things.* . . . The perfection of the universe . . . requires not only a multitude of individuals, but also *diverse kinds, and therefore diverse grades of things.* . . . If there were a dead level of equality in things,

only one kind of created good would exist, which would be a manifest derogation from the perfection of the creation.[10]

And of the second he declares,

Although an angel, considered absolutely, is better than a stone, nevertheless two natures are better than one only; and therefore a universe containing angels and other things is better than one containing angels only; since the perfection of the universe is attained essentially in proportion to the diversity of natures in it, *whereby the divers grades of goodness are filled,* and not in proportion to the multiplication of individuals of a single nature.[11]

How closely these concepts of "degree" and gradation and inequality are linked to the principles of limit, both in terms of reality and value, should be immediately apparent. In such a universe, it is the requirement both of the very continuance of existence and of the moral order of things that each grade of creation should keep its appointed place. Let but a single link of nature "intermit its course," as Richard Hooker puts it, and the result is inevitable chaos. For there is no order without degree, as Sir Thomas Elyot reminds us:

In every thyng is ordre, and without ordre may be nothing stable or permanent; and it may not be called ordre, excepte it do contayne in it degrees, high and base, accordynge to the merite or estimation of the thyng that is ordred.[12]

And as to each other order of creation, so to man. Down from classical times through the Renaissance, the most traditional (though frequently unrecognized and unacknowledged) meaning of "Nosce teipsum" is "Know thy place, man"—its privileges, but also its limitations. The full weight of the Greek concept of *moira* (with its antithesis of *hybris*), of the Aristotelian theory of "ends," of the Stoic injunction to man to find his good in the fulfillment of his own distinctive nature, and of the Christian insistence upon humility and obedience to the will of God—the full weight of all these powerfully influential identifications of the nature of life with the purpose of life, was thrown into the balance to favor this interpretation.

Inevitably, therefore, the idea of limit as both *real* and *good,* and embodied in concepts of degree—of gradation and inequality—invaded the traditional Christian-classical view of all fields of theory and life. To the Scholastic and to the Renaissance Christian humanist, all social, political and religious institutions maintained order through the exercise of degree. To the church, the state, the court, as to the universe, hierarchical order was integral.[13] And to the workings of man, the microcosm (whether in terms of the proper functioning of body or soul, or the two together),[14] as to those of the macrocosm and all human institutions, this recognition of degree is essential. All ethical theory, as well as political and physical, is rooted in it; and it is no exaggeration to say that Shakespeare's Ulysses is spokesman not only for the world but for the ages as well, when he declares:

> Degree being vizarded,
> Th' unworthiest shows as fairly in the mask.
> The heavens themselves, the planets, and this centre
> Observe *degree*, priority and place,
> Insisture, course, proportion, season form,
> Office and custom, in all line of order. . . .
> . . . .
> . . . .
> . . . . O, when *degree* is shak'd,
> Which is the ladder to all high designs,
> Then enterprise is sick! How could communities,
> *Degrees* in schools and brotherhoods in cities,
> Peaceful commerce from dividable shores,
> The primogenity and due of birth,
> Prerogative of age, crowns, sceptres, laurels,
> But by *degree*, stand in authentic place?
> Take but *degree* away, untune that string,
> And mark what discord follows! . . .
> . . . .
> . . . .
> . . . . Great Agamemnon,
> This chaos, when *degree* is suffocate,
> Follows the choking.
> And this neglection of *degree* it is
> That by a pace goes backward with a purpose
> It hath to climb. The general's disdain'd
> By him one step below, he by the next;
> That next by him beneath. So every step,
> Exampled by the first pace that is sick
> Of his superior, grows to an envious fever
> Of pale and bloodless emulation.[15]

2. LIMIT AS FINALITY, COMPLETENESS AND FINITENESS

Closely related to the basic concept of limit as degree or gradation is that of limit in the sense of finality, or completeness, or finiteness. Something of the distaste of Greek thought for the infinite, as too much akin to the indefinite,[16] and of the Christian view of the historic process "as a finite thing, having a beginning, a middle and an end"[17] under the supervision of a loving and prescient God, is combined by the most distinguished medieval minds, to produce a world-picture in which the appointed end or goal of every species is known (or at least knowable). To each of the orders of nature, God has assigned its end or good, and he directs it to that end through his providence.

Thus

> the Scholastic physicist sees all moving and living things as drawn onward by what may be said to be love for their un-realized ideals,[18]

and consequently concerns himself primarily with discovering the nature of the particular good or end or motive of each part of the creation. His greater interest in final causes than in efficient ones, is one manifestation of the Christian-classical mind's preoccupation with finality or completeness. For him, as for his master Aristotle, the most satisfying definition of the nature of a thing is that which it tends to *become*. Hence the importance of the concepts of "actuality" and "potentiality" to Scholastic physics.

Qualifications are necessary. In the lowest orders of nature, the "love" which draws all life toward its appointed end is, of course, simply blind obedience to Providence. Sublunary life of the sub-rational classes is ruled by the movements of the stars, according to the dispensation of God. While Aquinas, for example, admits the apparent existence of chance in nature (only "apparent," because although we may not understand some given end, "the world is God's work and nothing it contains is withdrawn from his providence"[19]), his ultimate conclusion is *Nihil igitur casu fit in mundo;*[20] he, like his peers,

> tightens the bonds of natural determinism by reducing the apparent disorder of nature to the laws of higher reason. . . . In the act of bringing chance under law it frees nature from Fate; for everything has a sufficient reason, but this can be none other than Reason itself.[21]

This is not to say that everything reaches its end. But when some one type or individual fails to do so, there exists evil:

> It is no part of divine providence wholly to exclude from things the possibility of their falling short of good; but what *can* thus fall short, sometimes *will* do so; and the lack of good is evil.[22]

And it contributes at once to the glory and shame of man that God has given to him the widest scope in this respect. For man is the sole earthly representative of the creation who *knows* his end.[23] And knowing it, he is free (unlike the rest of earthly creation) to reject it consciously. He alone on the earth is a *rational* animal; this is his distinctive and characteristic or "proper" nature, and, as such, he possesses free will. For to the Scholastic and the Renaissance Christian humanist alike, there is no incompatibility between providence and free will:

> Human foresight is to the providence of God what human causality is to divine creation. God, therefore, not only controls man by His providence, but also associates him with his providence; while all the rest is simply ruled by providence, man is ruled by it and rules himself; and not only himself but also all the rest. To say everything in one word, each human being is a *person;* his acts are *personal* acts, because they arise from the free decision of a reasonable being, and depend only on his own initiative. It is therefore precisely as such that divine providence has to bear upon them. God, who directs all according to His will, has bestowed on each of us an unique privilege, a signal honour, that of association with his own divine government.[24]

Man, that is to say, alone participates in the functioning of providence, associates with God in the government of the world—so long as he acts in accordance with reason, his highest nature. For man alone among all creatures is capable of knowing final ends, including his own—which is to know God. He alone is not subject to that natural determinism extending through the rest of the creation under God's or Reason's laws.

At the same time, limit (finality) is just as applicable to the concept of man's Christian liberty as to any other concept of the great Christian-humanist tradition. For true liberty is not "wild liberty," in Emerson's sense; on the contrary, "to will the thing known by intelligence is to be free. . . ."[25] True freedom, to the Christian as to the Stoic,[26] is liberty-under-law. Man attains to virtue through his own free will under the direction of Right Reason, in harmony with the will of God, and thus achieves his *end* or *good*—at least so far as he may on this earth. Hence characteristic Christian freedom is the freedom to achieve the highest of the hierarchy of goods on this earth (second only, for the Thomists, at least, to the direct contemplation of God). Free to choose man may be, but there is finality in this whole relationship all the same—the *end* is known by the intelligence or reason, and to attain his proper end, his will must pursue the course directed by intelligence. In short, true Christian liberty is not freedom *from* anything, but freedom *to become* something—specifically, freedom to grow to the full stature of a Christian man in the likeness of God, and thus to come to the knowledge of God:

> We have nothing that we have not received. In the universal circulation of love spoken of by St. Thomas and Dionysius, it is God Himself Who turns our will towards Himself, and in consequence makes it good; in freely turning ourselves away we can but make it bad. *In this sense all our moral activity is therefore ruled, directed; its measure lies in God, and nevertheless it remains true to say that its source is altogether interior, since the divine law that rules us, expresses itself in us by the organ of our reason.*[27]

Thus freedom, as the medieval and Renaissance Christian-humanistic tradition conceives it, is limited and bounded, just as is the rest of creation, by the basic concept of known *ends*. The path is marked, the gait prescribed, the goal established. The difference betwen man's position and that of the sub-rational creatures lies in the fact that although man is naturally impelled toward his goal, as are the rest, he is not *obliged* to follow it. Yet if he does not, he cannot retain his true and characteristic freedom as a man, a person, and he cannot grow to the full stature of a man—for if he deserts the end prescribed by reason, he loses his rational standing. Evil is for him, too, the privation of good, and falling short of his established and distinctive end, he drops to the level of sub-rational life.

Indeed, "to be capable of the greatest of goods is also to be capable of losing it,"[28] and the great prototype for this truth was of course Adam. Yet it is characteristic of the Christian-humanist tradition's optimism to maintain that while the subsequent tendency to sin has weakened man's natural inclination toward good, it has not effaced it, or even impaired man's basic metaphysical status. "Primum igitur bonum naturae, nec tollitur, nec diminuitur per peccatum," says Aquinas.[29] And he further insists that nothing can take away from man his "natural" freedom—[30] although his natural inclination to virtue has been diminished by Adam's fault.

To be sure, moreover, original sin did deprive free will of "all moral qualification":

> All choice, precisely as choice, is at once both psychologically indetermined and morally indifferent.[31]

Hence freedom, in its original inclusive sense, will no longer be possible. But grace has intervened, and it is representative of the whole tradition, from the twelfth century through the Renaissance, to unify the meanings of the word "liberty" by reducing "psychological freedom to its liberation by grace"—and so to arrive at that conclusion, already set forth, that

the only liberty is true liberty, that is to say, liberty to do right.[32]

This only superficially paradoxical concept of liberty as inseparable from limit in the sense of finality, fits harmoniously into the medieval world-view which sponsored and developed it by mingling classical and Christian elements. For while the metaphysical premise in this concept (as in others of this world-view) is peculiarly Christian, the roots of the theory of liberty-under-law are sunk in Greek ethical soil—a soil compounded of Platonic, Aristotelian and Stoic ingredients. And liberty-under-law, even without the specific Christian metaphysical premise, implies limit and finality. But the Christian idea of a God who is a loving Creator willing that all which He has made shall return to Him, increases the "finality" element of the solution far beyond that possible when dealing with Plato's creative Goodness of the *Timaeus*, Aristotle's Unmoved Mover, or the pantheistic Divine Reason of the Stoics.[33] As Etienne Gilson writes, in terms of the Christian tradition,

Born of a final cause, the universe is necessarily saturated with finality, that is to say, we can never in any case disassociate the explanation of things from the consideration of their *raison d'être*. That is the reason why, in spite of all the resistance, and occasionally even violent opposition, of modern science and philosophy to the idea of finality, Christian thought has never yet renounced it, and never will.[34]

Everything, in short, has its known *place*, its *final* appropriate and predetermined *end* to reach: "omnia in mensura, et numero, et pondere disposuisti."[35] One may consider this concept in terms of Aristotelian-Scholastic teleological physics, in which "each thing has, according to its nature, a determined 'place' in the Universe, which is in some sense its own,"[36] and which it seeks by the very law of its nature, or in the symbolic and more specifically Christian terms so beautifully summarized by Professor Randall:

The power that moved all things was Love; that love of God which kept all things eternally aspiring to be themselves, the love of the flame for fire that caused it to strain upward, the love of the stone that is its hardness, of the grass that is its

greenness, of the beasts that is their bestiality, of the bad man
for evil that is his nature, and of the good man for God that
is his home. From the highest heaven to the lowest clod, aspiration to fulfill the will of God, to blend with the divine purpose, was the cosmic force that made the world go round. And
highest and lowest could truly say, "In his will is our peace."[37]

In either case, the same principle is invoked: that of limit in the
sense of finality or end, of the completeness and finiteness which
surrounds aspiration or activity—although not so much in an in-
hibiting sense as in a directive one. Even man, who is filled with
an infinite longing which no finite good may satisfy, proves by this
very tendency that his end is God, who is infinite.[38] And although
the end or good here is infinite, it may be attained, and the principle of completion again holds good. . . .

With its characteristic allegiance to synthesis and analogy, the
Christian-classical tradition applies this second class of concepts
of limit (finality—completeness—finiteness), as it does the first (degree—inequality—gradation), to political and social theory. To begin
with, the state has its origin in nature, by divine appointment. One
of the two great commandments, that to love one's fellow-man, is
often equated with the thesis (after Aristotle) that man is by nature
a social or political animal; as Richard Hooker puts it,

> [My desire to be loved] by *my equals in nature* as much as
> possible may be, imposeth upon me *a natural duty* of bearing
> to them-ward fully the like affection.[39]

Theoretically, at least, then, human society is a natural institution,
composed of free and equal individuals—free and equal as *human
beings,* as *persons,* since "the reality that constitutes the human
person admits of no degrees."[40] The state is the natural or proper
development of the family and the village, and it, like any other
entity in the Christian-classical world view, has its known *end* or
good:

> the maintenance of justice, or, in the terms derived from Aris-
> totle, the setting forward of the life according to virtue. . . .[41]

Finality is basic to this interpretation of society and the state.
Society is, in Aristotle's terminology, the *final cause* or *end* of man's
gregarious instinct; the state, society's most highly *developed* and
organized form, and hence its highest and best, in turn has its
end in promoting the welfare of the individuals which comprise it
through "the maintenance of justice" or the "setting forward of the

life according to virtue." All social and political theory is based upon these fundamental premises, and hence is soaked, as are they, in the solution of finality. The ends or purposes of both social and political individuals and institutions are known and established.

This concept of *finality* provides one sense in which *limit* is *basic* to social and political theory. An allied one is that of *finiteness*. For in such a scheme there are established bounds to the authority and proper activity of all its constituents. The state's end of justice, for example, limits its authority. Since natural law, in its capacity of a permanent norm established by a good and loving creator, promotes justice, all laws contrary to natural law are unjust, and have no force. Valid man-made law is *limited* by the necessity of its agreement with the eternal law of God and Nature. Justice, then, while open to interpretation in particular instances (especially, and practically, to interpretations based on custom), rests finally upon, and is ultimately bounded by, the established moral nature of the universe.

Hence, again, the king, or government of whatever sort, is clearly not the supreme authority—but instead, law, rooted in nature, expressing reason, and pointing to justice. George Chapman's King Henry, like Shakespeare's Ulysses, speaks for a strongly established tradition when he declares to Biron,

> I have no power, more than yourself, in things
> That are beyond my reason,[42]

and avows his intention to remain within "religious confines" as ordained by "justice and our true laws."[43]

"No power, *more than yourself*," Henry says, and brings to mind the essential premise that all men, *as men*, are equals. As Maurice De Wulf says,

> The human perfection which constitutes *human reality* is of the same kind in each person—king or subject, seigneur or vassal, master or servant, rich or poor, these all have a similar essence.[44]

And another King Henry—Shakespeare's Hal in his maturity—explicitly agrees, although characteristically in less exalted and less traditional language:

> I think the King is but a man, as I am. The violet smells to him as it doth to me; the element shows to him as it doth to me; all his senses have but human conditions. His ceremonies laid by, in his nakedness he appears but a man; and though

his affections are higher mounted than ours, yet when they stoop, they stoop with the like wing. Therefore, when he sees reason of fears, as we do, his fears, out of doubt, be of the same relish as ours are.[45]

Yet it must be remembered that the king and his subject are "equals in nature," in Hooker's words, and in *nature*, as *persons*, only. This is not a politically democratic speech of King Hal's; what he is expounding is the traditional Christian humanist view of the metaphysical status of man. And neither he, nor any other representative of the tradition we have been studying, believes that the king and his subject are *social* and *political* equals, or that the nature of their respective duties to the state are the same. As Hal goes on to say,

> Every subject's duty, is the King's, but every subject's soul is his own.[46]

All men, are, in short, "equals in nature"—equals in that they share "human conditions." They are not, however, all equals as social animals, any more than they are equal in abilities.

We have observed that all social, political and religious institutions are traditionally arranged (as, analogically, are the orders of nature) in graded hierarchies, in degrees, estates and ranks as "closed" and rigid as Victorian class distinctions. And just as limit operates in this aspect of social theory—in terms of gradation and equality—so it does in another sense, that of finality and finiteness. Not only is it the duty of every member of society to observe the laws of *degree;* he must also observe those of *vocation.*

For, Hooker points out,

> We see the whole world and each part thereof so compacted, that as long as each thing performeth *only that work which is natural unto it*, it thereby preserveth both other things and also itself.[47]

And the same principle, by analogical argument, applies to society, which is divided—and should be divided—into groups to which individuals are "called" or ordained by God and nature.[48]

As always for the great European humanistic tradition, this concept of "vocation" has both Christian and classical roots. Consider the Pauline teaching that, while "we have many members in one body . . . all members have not the same office," and the exhortation to exercise those "gifts differing according to the grace that is given to us";[49] Plato's threefold division of society into the guardian, warrior and worker classes; the Aristotelian doctrine that to function properly everything must seek the particular good for which it is made; and Cicero's Stoic distinction between the universal and individual nature of man:

> We must realize that we are invested by Nature with two characters, as it were; one of these is universal, arising from the fact of our being all alike endowed with reason and with that superiority which lifts us above the brute. . . . The other character is the one that is assigned to individuals in particular. . . . [And] we must so act as not to oppose the universal laws of human nature, but, while safeguarding these, to follow the bent of our own particular nature; and even if other careers should be better and nobler, we may still regulate our own pursuits by the standard of our own nature.[50]

Sixteenth-century social theory inherited the principle of vocation ultimately from these sources, directly from medieval theory, and adapted it to its own needs. While handbooks on the subject vary in details, the principal vocations listed by sixteenth-century theory are those of the ruling nobility, learned scholars and priests, military forces, merchants, craftsmen and agricultural workers.[51] Yet these distinctions obviously have not only a theoretical origin and justification; just as in medieval times similar vocations grew out of the very conditions of life,[52] so these specific ones grew out of the needs and organic development of sixteenth-century society. Theory and practice are here, as elsewhere in the Christian-humanistic outlook, complementary and interdependent, however far short of theory particular practice may sometimes fall.

At the heart of this whole "vocational" system is that same principle of "finality" or "finiteness" which we have already recognized in other contexts. For the conviction that every man's duty, both to himself and to society, is fixed and established by God and nature, and that on his recognition of and obedience to that duty depend order in the state and his own happiness, is the very epitome of the principles of limit in these senses. Medieval and Renaissance life and literature are stocked with examples of those who attempted to defy the limitations imposed by "vocation." "Horrible examples," too, accompanied by grave warnings—for while we may laugh a Malvolio out of countenance for his aspirations beyond his "natural" place, we have no choice but to take an Achilles or a Macbeth seriously.

That is, the higher we climb the ladder of degree, the more important becomes the principle of vocation, since more individuals are involved in the consequence of disobedience to it. Hence, of all vocations, that of the "specialty of rule" bears the heaviest responsibilities. For if "every subject's duty is the King's," the relationship is reciprocal:

> The king is to command, the subject to obey: both with like readines in their places, & like affection to each other.[53]

A proper ruler, according to Sir Thomas Elyot, will not forget his obligation to "imploye" all his powers to help and preserve his "inferiours."[54] And not only has he this obligation; he has also no right to give up that calling to which he has been summoned by God and Nature. The chaos which Lear precipitates when he lays by his crown that he may "unburthen'd crawl toward death" is specifically occasioned by his defiance of the divine and natural imperative implied in the principle of vocation.

Vocation, then, like degree, makes for the continuance of order and law in all things—is essential to life, if life is to have any meaning:

> More over take away ordre from all thynges what shulde then remayne? Certes nothynge finally, except some man wolde imagine eftsones *Chaos:* whiche of some is expounde a confuse mixture.[55]

And vocation demonstrates once more the ultimate significance of limit, as finality and as finiteness, to the Christian-humanistic tradition. Finality, in terms of value—since the particular task or purpose of every entity in such a world-view is known, and the good or end of that entity rests in its fulfilling this peculiar function. Finiteness, in terms of reality—since the knowledge of function and goal sets a limit to the proper activity of every entity. Finally, finiteness as value, since any final good is to be found in the entity's *reaching* its goal; and finality as reality, since reaching its good means that any given entity thereby becomes its most characteristic and significant self.

Such views of both value and reality make, of course, for an eminently picturable universe—a universe that is a completed and perfect work of art (in the mind of God), even though the imperfect copy which is being worked out by those engaged in the world of empirical reality at any given time remains unfinished until Judgment Day. Limit is ultimately established; picturability, finiteness and completeness are apparent in every feature:

The men of the fifteenth century still lived in a walled universe as well as in walled towns. And—unlike medieval towns and other medieval things—this cosmical scheme had the essential qualities of a work of classical art; indeed, the most classical thing in the Middle Ages may be said to have been the universe. . . . The world had a clear intelligible unity of structure, and not only definite shape, but what was deemed at once the simplest and most perfect shape, as had all the bodies composing it. It had no loose ends, no irregularities of outline.[56]

So integral to the medieval and traditionalist-Renaissance way of thinking is this over-all concept of "limit" that its apologists almost always draw back from the full logical development of the basic principles of their hierarchical universal order: those of "plenitude" and of "continuity."[57] For these principles should logically have led to the conclusion that the number of links of the great chain of being, or the number of temporal beings, is infinite—since the creative goodness of God is incapable of not fulfilling its infinite capacity. Yet the medieval theologians and philosophers, like Plotinus and other Greek thinkers (not all), shrank from this logical conclusion, preferring to involve themselves in all sorts of theological paradoxes, rather than entertain the "vague" and "formless" concept of infinity.[58]

To the great Christian-classical tradition, then, the universe is complete and finite, limited and bounded—"a tiny bubble in the illimitable realm of spirit that is God's mind."[59] And static, too— hence completely measurable and comprehensible—throughout the "moment in eternity" which is "its whole duration." For

> During this brief period there was no growth, no development, no change outside human affairs; the world had been created for the one purpose of furnishing the background for the drama of Man's salvation, and as such it was fixed and immutable till the last trump.[60]

In time, then, as in space, it is a limited universe: its philosophy of history rests, as does its physics, upon principles of degree, finality and finitude. Human history, as well as nature, is arranged in hierarchic order:

> The famous doctrines of four universal empires succeeding one another as a divinely created frame of history, with the Roman empire as the last, placed above historical flux and destined to endure to the end of history, was the exact equivalent in his-

torical outlook of the gradation of the crystal spheres in the
Ptolemaic system.[61]

Moreover, since the "frame of history" is "divinely created" by
a provident and loving creator to furnish "the background for the
drama of Man's salvation," it is pregnant with purpose, with finality
(its end or goal is fixed), and even the extent of its duration and
the nature of its destruction are established (its end or limit is
known).[62] In Professor Lovejoy's words

> The historic process, too, in the Christian tradition—in spite
> of opposing Aristotelian and other influences—was conceived
> as a finite thing, having a beginning, a middle and an end
> —neither an interminable undulation, nor an endless recur-
> rence of similar cycles, nor even a perpetual movement towards
> an infinitely distant and therefore unattainable goal.[63]

Etienne Gilson summarizes the whole attitude succinctly:

> Following St. Augustine's lead, the Middle Ages therefore
> represented the history of the world as a great poem, which
> takes on a complete and intelligible meaning as soon as we
> know the beginning and the end.[64]

3. LIMIT AS MODERATION, BALANCE AND HARMONY

To whatever aspect of the thought of this great central intellectual
tradition of Europe the student may turn, he is almost certain to
find an attitude steeped in one or both of these fundamental principles of limit—"degree—gradation—inequality" and "finality—finiteness—completeness." A third principle of limit, that of moderation
or balance or harmony, is equally basic to the tradition's thinking,
whether in terms of relativity or of value. The classical aversion to
extremes, the Greek ideal of moderation and harmony, decisively
influenced Christian thinking about the nature of the universe, the
meaning of life, the nature and purpose of society, and the nature
and end of man.

In the first place, central to Greek thought about the nature of
the universe is the concept of four primary and disparate elements,
out of which the universe is compounded, and whose otherwise
chaotic strife is held in check by a divine directive agency. From
Anaximander on, the idea that "the world presents us with a series
of opposites, of which the most primary are hot and cold, wet and

dry,"[65] dominates Greek physical theory; and his conception of natural "justice and injustice"—that is to say, of "the encroachment of one opposite or 'element' upon another," with a resultant reabsorption of both into their common ground—often recurs in Ionic natural philosophy. In Anaximander's phraseology, things

> give satisfaction and reparation to one another for their injustice, as is appointed according to the ordering of time.[66]

The scientific conception of four primary elements—fire, air, earth and water—does not appear until the system of Empedocles, and is developed in its decisive form by Aristotle. But the primitive and popular theory of the four elements can be traced back to a fourfold or threefold division of this kind in Homer and Hesiod;[67] and certainly the basic and traditional problem of Milesian cosmology is this one of "the opposites."[68]

As we advance in the history of Greek thought, we sometimes find the view held that the "Mean" which holds the warring elements or opposites together, and thus sustains the universe, is to be found in a "blend" of these opposites (Pythagoras and the Plato of the *Timaeus*);[69] sometimes the contradictory view that the world's stability depends upon this very strife, upon the tension between the elements—which constitutes natural justice, rather than injustice (Heraclitus);[70] sometimes a combination of and balance between the two (Empedocles' "Love" and "Strife").[71]

But whatever particular form the general concept takes, one constant is discernible—that of the crucial centrality of the principle of balance or harmony or moderation to the preservation of life. The symbol employed may be one of the Greek favorites, the "well-tuned lyre" or the "mixing bowl"—but whichever, nature's norm and preservation lie in this realization of equilibrium or "justice." And as theism is added to the cosmological picture (in at least one sense, with Anaxagoras[72]), and hence the concept of Mind or deity, directing or limiting all motion, this central principle of harmony or balance becomes purposeful: the "tuner" or "mixer" emerges.

Among the various ways in which these concepts develop, to dominate Western physical theory until the advent of the Counter-Renaissance, two stand out. Ultimately derivative from Plato and Aristotle, and perhaps most characteristically developed by the Neoplatonists and the Scholastics, respectively, both adaptations underwent Christian baptism without substantial alteration. They are not contradictory, but parallel; each views the universe as orderly and planned, each predicates the conservation of the universe as dependent upon a harmonizing force which reconciles the elements. But the Neoplatonists, the more poetic and mystical tradition, speak of a world held together by *love;* the Aristotelian-Scholastics, the more scientific and intellectualistic tradition, of one governed by *law.*

To be sure, these two interpretations may be employed interchangeably; sometimes both systems of terminology will be found in the writings of one man. Again, and conversely, since the Neoplatonist concept tends far more than the other toward the concept of a single conserving force running through and penetrating all nature, its idea of *love* is much more apt to merge into pantheism than is the other tradition's idea of *law.*[73] Yet through the Middle Ages, and among the Renaissance Christian humanists with a Neoplatonic bias, *love* as the harmonizer and reconciler of the elements is most often the poetic or mystical counterpart of *law.*

Hence, when Boethius writes,

> Love, ruling heaven and earth, and seas, them in this
>   course doth bind.
> And if it once let loose their reins, their friend-
>   ship turns to war,
> Tearing the world whose ordered form their quiet
>   motions bear . . .[74]

and Richard Hooker tells us that

> if nature should intermit her course, and leave altogether
> though it were but for a while the observation of her own laws,

dire catastrophes would result, and concludes,

> See we not plainly that the obedience of creatures unto the
> law of nature is the stay of the whole world?[75]

—it is only the tone and the terminology which differ.

Again, if one compares Walter Ralegh's reference to

> God, who hath formed this nature, and whose divine love was
> the beginning, and is the bond of the universal . . .[76]

with Hooker's assertion that the "World's first creation," and "preservation" since, constitute a manifestation by execution of the "eternal law of God . . . concerning things natural," and his declaration that

> heaven and earth have hearkened unto his voice, and their

labour hath been to do his will: He "made a law for the rain";
He gave his "decree unto the sea, that the waters should not
pass his commandment"[77]

—one discovers that the two passages contain the same parallelism,
each rendering the specifically Christian adaptation of one of the
two traditions. They are in perfect accord (although with the theological qualification) with Spenser's version of the old Greek story,
which relates how the four elements conspired against each other,

> Threatening their owne confusion and decay:
> Ayre hated earth, and water hated fire
> Till Love relented their rebellious yre . . .

and how Love further, "tempering goodly well their contrary dis-
likes with loved meanes,"

> Did place them all in order, and compell
> To keepe them selves within their sundrie raines . . .

with the result that ever since

> .   .   . they firmely have remained,
> And duly well observed his beheast. . . .[78]

The supreme cosmic force which conserves the universe, then,
may be law or love; in either case it is a regulative and restrain-
ing and equilibrizing power which has divine origin. Within the
great Christian-classical tradition, the choice of terms is more often
an indication of temperamental bias than anything else—for the
natural *law* referred to is the disposition of a *loving* God's Providence to natural phenomena:

> That law, the performance whereof we behold in things natural,
> is as it were an authentical or an original draught written in
> the bosom of God himself; whose Spirit being to execute the
> same useth every particular nature, every mere natural agent,
> only as an instrument created at the beginning, and ever since
> the beginning used, to work his own will and pleasure withal.
> Nature therefore is nothing else but God's instrument.[79]

So Hooker; and conversely, Benivieni, in his *Ode of Love*, expressly
considers cosmic *love* as a divine *law*-giving agency:

> I tell how Love from its celestial source
> In Primal Good flows to the world of sense;
> When it had birth; and whence;
> How moves the heavens, refines the soul, gives lawe
> To all. . . .[80]

Whatever the terminology, this basically consistent view of divine justice or love maintaining order throughout the universe implies two related concepts about the nature of things. First, it predicates a harmonious interaction between the higher and lower elements. "Midway between the two natures, love completes a whole, which gathers all the Universe into one," Diotima had told Socrates, and this conviction persists. It finds expression, for example, in the words of Castiglione's Bembo, apostrophizing Love: "Thou the most sweete bond of the world, a meane betwixt heavenly and earthly thinges"[81]; it is implicit negatively in Richard Hooker's picture of the disasters which would overtake the earth "if those principal and mother elements of the world, whereof all things in this lower world are made, should lose the qualities which now they have"[82]—a picture fully developed by John Donne in "The First Anniversary":

> Nor in ought this worlds decay appeares,
> Then that her influence the heav'n forbeares,
> Or that the Elements do not feele this,
> The father, or the mother barren is.
> The cloudes conceive not raine, or doe not powre,
> In the due birth time, downe the balmy showre;
> Th' Ayre doth not motherly sit on the earth,
> To hatch her seasons, and give all things birth

—in short, the harmony which keeps the elements in check and balance is lost,

> and correspondence too.
> For heaven gives little, and the earth takes lesse;

the "commerce twixt heaven and earth" is "embarr'd, and all this traffique quite forgot."[83] Hence

> 'Tis all in peeces, all cohærence gone;
> All just supply, and all Relation.[84]

The principle of limit in the sense of harmony, balance and moderation, then, not only involves keeping the elements which constitute the world from infringing upon each other's proper sphere of activity, but also establishing and maintaining the relationship between the translunary world (the element of fire, and the fifth element—after Aristotle—of the heavens) and the sublunary one (the other elements). Whether the directive power of the higher elements is thought of philosophically or theologically or simply in that astrological tradition which deals with "skyey influences" upon human and sub-human life on the earth, and is the popular counterpart of the other traditions—it is all one; these are but different ways of describing this one aspect of the limited, harmonious, interlocked, up-and-down Christian-classical universe: "this huge stage . . . Whereon the stars in secret influence comment."

A second important principle related to the concept of limit as harmony and balance is that of the functioning of the part, or individual entity, and the whole, for mutual good. "For we see the whole world and each part thereof so compacted," says Richard Hooker,

> that as long as each thing performeth only that work that is natural unto it, it thereby preserveth both other things and also itself. Contrariwise, let any principal thing, as the sun, the moon, anyone of the heavens or elements, but once cease or fail, or swerve, and who doth not easily conceive that the sequel therefore would be ruin both to itself and whatsoever dependeth on it?[85]

Not only, moreover, does the ultimate conservation of other things depend upon each one's doing its appointed and natural work; the whole hierarchy of nature is built upon the principle that the "best" grades of creatures are thus most capable of effecting good for others through pursuing their own good. Thus a planet[86] may influence any number of sub-lunary organic processes, and a man may direct himself, other men and animals. But vegetation, on the other hand, can effect even its own good only as a "necessary agent," through a superior and external influence. Thomas Aquinas declares that

> the creature approaches more nearly to God's likeness if it is not only good but can also act for the goodness of other things, than if it is merely good in itself.

Hence it is well that "there is in the creatures plurality and inequality"; if all were in all respects equal, none could "act for the advantage of another."[87] Thus the concept of limit as degree and that of limit as harmony, involving a balance of interaction and interrelations, merge and supplement each other, both in terms of reality and value.

Finally, not only do the various components of the world lend aid to each other; they also thereby sustain and fulfill the whole. Crack one link in the great chain of being, and you impair the whole. Break a sufficiently large one, and you destroy the whole. . . .

Such is the nature of things to the traditional Christian-classical world-view. It is a world containing great diversity, but diversity-

in-unity. In it, order and equilibrium are maintained above all
through the agency of the principle of limit. And just as inequality
and finiteness are integral to it, so are moderation, balance and
harmony. By their being held in check and restrained to their separate and particular realms, or blended—when they must be—peace-
ably, the elements observe moderation. Through their cooperative
influence upon each other and working toward a common goal—
the furthering of the glory of God and the conservation of his universe—they achieve harmony. And in recognition of the individual
good being attained only in agreement with the universal good, and
of the universal good as resting in the attainment of all the individual goods, this world-view approximates at once a delicacy and
equity of balance which is difficult to match.

Such is God's world, and such is the world he would have. It is
steeped in the element of limit, which is another way of saying that
it is immersed in law or love. Whether we use the poets' words or
the theologians', we must say that

> of law there can be no less acknowledged, than that her seat
> is in the bosom of God, *her voice the harmony of the world;*
> all things in heaven and earth do her homage, the very least
> as feeling her care, and the greatest as not exempted from her
> power: both Angels and men and creatures of what condition
> soever, *though each in different sort and manner, yet all with
> uniform consent, admiring her as the mother of their peace
> and joy. . . .*[88]

Once one has grasped the consistent analogical approach of the
Christian-classical outlook, it will be immediately apparent that
these same principles of balance, harmony and moderation will be
of equal force to its social, political, psychological and ethical views.
They are at once evident, for example, in the traditional view of
the nature of the state. Professor Randall summarizes clearly the
way in which the mutual obligations and privileges of the individual and of society function in medieval civilization:

> Each man is a member of some state or group, and each estate
> is an essential organ of the whole, discharging a function at
> once *peculiar to itself and necessary to the full life of Christen-
> dom.* Only through his participation in this group life can the
> individual attain his own ends, and conversely, only with the
> aid of every individual and every group can society afford the
> appropriate setting for the fullest life of its individual mem-
> bers.[89]

This social idea of balance and harmony, adapted to the specific needs of medieval society and Christendom, is set forth fully by Thomas Aquinas.[90] It is in essence a blending of the Aristotelian concepts of man's natural inclination to group life and of the importance of civil society to the preservation of man's life and to the furtherance of the good life; of Cicero's harmonizing of the universal and the individual laws of nature,[91] and of Paul's teaching:

> For as we have many members in one body, and all members have not the same office, so we, being many, are one body in Christ, and every one members one of another. . . . And whether one member suffer, all the members suffer with it; or one member be honored, all the members rejoice with it. . . .[92]

And however altered, to fit the needs of the increasing tendency towards nationalism and away from a unified and centralized Christendom, the traditionalist Renaissance view of the state is clearly derivative. "A publike weale," declares Sir Thomas Elyot,

> is the body lyving, compacte or made of sondry astates and degrees of men, whiche is disposed by the order of equite and governed by the rule and moderation of reason. . . .[93]

Equity, not equality. As Shakespeare's Exeter puts it:

> For government, though high, and low, and lower,
> Put into parts, doth keep in one consent,
> Congreeing to a full and natural close,
> Like music;

and the Archbishop of Canterbury agrees,

> True! Therefore doth heaven divide
> The state of man in divers functions,
> Setting endeavour in continual motion;
> To which is fixed as an aim or butt
> Obedience;

and concludes, after drawing the popular analogy between a beehive and a state,

> I this infer,
> That many things having full reference
> To one consent may work contrariously,
> As many arrows loosed several ways
> Come to one mark, as many ways meet in one town,
> As many fresh streams meet in one salt sea,
> As many lines close in the dial's centre;
> So may a thousand actions, once afoot,

> End in one purpose, and be all well borne
> Without defeat.[94]

In short, whatever modification time and place may require, the basic social and political ideal of the Christian-classical tradition remains pre-eminently unchanged; its concept of the functional nature of society and the state continues to stress the *balance* of interdependence and mutual assistance; the *moderation* of the reasonable apportioning of duties and a consideration of each other's rights and duties, established formally by metes and bounds; and the *harmony* fundamental to a society in which, from king to apprentice, every one performs his task in relation to the common duty of all:

> the conservation of the whole, the publike utilitie and good. . . .[95]

Hence there is no other social sin so heinous as that of excessive individualism and ambition, of the insubordination of the common good to one's selfish ends. As John Higgins puts it in his edition of the *Mirror for Magistrates:*

> For to covet without consideration: to passe the measure of his degree: and to lette will run at random, is the only destruction of all estates. Else howe were it possible, so many learned, politike, wise, renouned, valiaunt, and victorious personages, might ever have come to such utter decaye.[96]

The analogical tendencies of the Christian-classical tradition are nowhere more apparent than in the application to the microcosm, man, of the same principles of limit which hold true of the macrocosm. The psychological and physiological doctrines of four humours and complexions of man, corresponding to the four elements of the universe, and ultimately derivative from Greek medicine, are basic to characterization in both medieval and Renaissance literature, as they are to medicine and psychology. And the mentally or physically sick man is he who suffers from the "o'ergrowth of some complexion"—in Ben Jonson's words,

> As when some one peculiar qualitie
> Doth so possesse a man, that it doth draw
> All his affects, his spirits, and his powers
> In their confluctions all to runne one way—[97]

the man in whom some one humour has overflowed its proper limits and destroyed in him, temporarily or permanently, balance and moderation. Conversely, when Antony says of the dead Brutus,

> His life was gentle, and the elements
> So mix'd in him that Nature might stand up
> And say to all the world, "This was a man!"[98]

he is expressing eloquently and precisely the Christian-humanistic ideal of a man—one within whom all is in harmony, in balance, and in moderation.[99]

The same ideals are applied to the proper cooperative function-ing of the parts of the body and those of the soul. Once again we may turn to Shakespeare for a summarizing passage. When Menenius (in *Coriolanus*) harangues the aroused Roman rabble, seeking to point out to them the injustice of their charges against the Senate, he turns for forceful analogy to the functioning of the body. For he relates the fable of the rebellion of "all the body's members . . . against the belly," whom they accuse of "never bearing like labour with the rest"; and he recounts the belly's rejoinder:

> "True is it, my incorporate friends," quoth he,
> "That I receive the general food at first
> Which you do live upon, and fit it is,
> Because I am the storehouse and the shop
> Of the whole body. But, if you do remember,
> I send it through the rivers of your blood
> Even to the court, the heart, to th' seat of th' brain,
> And, through the cranks and offices of man,
> The strongest nerves and small inferior veins
> From me receive that natural competency
> Whereby they live. . . ."[100]

Similarly, medieval and Renaissance psychologists, following for the most part a modification of the Platonic tri-partite division of the powers of the soul, stress the congruent and harmonious work-ing of the various appetites or affections (which make up the sensi-tive part of the soul) with the cognitive faculties. A healthy and virtuous soul, like a healthy and virtuous body or state or universe, finds use for all of its constituent parts. None, when functioning properly, is bad or even superfluous; all the units of the vegetative soul (the soul of growth), the sensitive soul (the soul of sense), and the rational soul, have their parts to play in furthering the well-being of the whole.[101] Yet, as in the universe, the state and the human body, the ruling principles of harmony, moderation and bal-ance do not imply equality. The will, directed by "sov'ran Reason," makes the choices of the soul:

AN ANATOMY OF THE SOUL

SOUL[S] OF MAN

1. VEGETATIVE
Soul of Growth, concerned with "engendering nourishing, waxing and growing."

(man shares with plants, trees, etc.—and with beasts)

Hooker: Realm of simple natural agents. The goodness sought is that of "continuance of their being."

2. SENSIBLE
Soul of Sense, concerned with "the judgment of common sense or fancy."

(man shares with beasts only)

Hooker: Realm of second kind of natural agents, who work "after a sort of their own kind." The goodness sought is "the sensible goodness of those objects wherewith they are moved."

3. RATIONAL
Soul of Reason, concerned with "the sentence that Reason giveth."

(unique property of man)

Hooker: Realm of voluntary agents. The goodness sought is "the goodness of things which they are to do."

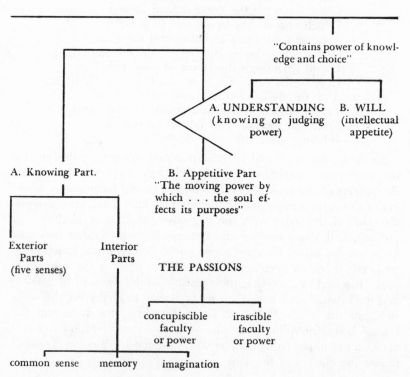

"Contains power of knowledge and choice"

A. UNDERSTANDING
(knowing or judging power)

B. WILL
(intellectual appetite)

A. Knowing Part.

B. Appetitive Part
"The moving power by which . . . the soul effects its purposes"

Exterior Parts (five senses)

Interior Parts

THE PASSIONS

concupiscible faculty or power

irascible faculty or power

common sense   memory   imagination

To choose is to will one thing before another. And to will is to bend our souls to the having or doing of that which they see to be good. Goodness is seen with the eye of the understanding. And the light of that eye is reason. So that two principal fountains there are of human action, Knowledge and Will; which Will in things tending towards any end, is termed Choice.[102]

Hence volition, while making the soul's decisions, is typically checked and limited by understanding: nothing is more alien to the Christian-humanistic tradition than the concept of a life directed by the autonomous and unlimited will. Indeed, if the will revolts from the guidance of reason, it is simply to fall victim to "inferior," irrational powers, and hence to lose all true freedom. So Milton describes the condition of Adam and Eve after they have eaten of the forbidden fruit:

> For Understanding rul'd not, and the will
> Heard not her lore; both in subjection now
> To sensuall Appetite, who from beneath
> Usurping over sov'ran Reason claim'd
> Superior sway. . . .[103]

It is the psychological application of the humanistic idea of liberty-under-law; and just as the soul, considered as a unit, directs the body, so the two great powers of the rational soul, working in harmony, direct the other faculties of the soul. Says Richard Hooker,

> This is therefore the first Law, whereby the highest power of the mind requireth general obedience at the hands of all the rest concurring with it unto action.[104]

And the analogy between the smoothly and peacefully functioning state and "the Kingdom of the mind" or soul appears over and over again in medieval and Renaissance literature:

> But as that land or nation best doth thrive,
> Which to smooth-fronted peace is most proclive,
> So doth that mind whose faire affections rang'd
> By reasons rules, stand constant and unchanged. . . .[105]

In full agreement with these physiological and psychological principles, and in analogical concordance with the similar concepts involved in its interpretation of the nature and ideals of the universe and of human society, the classical-Christian tradition evolves its great central ethical doctrines. The ideals of Christian liberty and the Golden Rule; of the Aristotelian mean between the excess and the defect of qualities; of the Platonic cardinal virtue of Temperance; of Cicero's adaptation of this Platonic concept and his peculiar relating of it to the idea of *decorum;*[106] of his subordinating the law of individual nature to that of universal nature;[107] and of his modification of the old ascetic Stoic ethic[108]—all these merge to form the ethical corpus of the Christian-humanistic tradition, and to make of it a way of life that is dominated by concepts of moderation, of balance, of harmony. As Professor Lovejoy says, speaking of this great intellectual tradition of Western Europe,

> There were important opposing strains in this older tradition, but the most prevalent and orthodox tendency had been to think in terms of finites, and to regard limitation as an essential element of excellence, at least for mortals.[109]

Clearly, there is no concept more basic to the classical mind— and to the medieval and traditionalist Renaissance mind, largely concerned with adapting the classical heritage to the specifics of Christianity—than this principle of limit. Variously applied to all the interrelated departments of life and thought—now as degree, inequality, gradation; now as finality, completeness, finiteness; now as harmony, moderation, balance—it dominates the whole classical-Christian tradition's outlook, both in terms of its explanation of reality and of its interpretation of value.

FOOTNOTES
CHAPTER 5

I.

1. Cf. Arthur O. Lovejoy, "The Meaning of Romanticism for the Historian of Ideas," *JHI*, Vol. II, No. 3 (June, 1941), 262–278, and especially 263.
2. Cf. Lovejoy, *Great Chain of Being*, 59. See also the relation of the Chain to the hierarchies of value and of being in Ernst Cassirer, "The Place of Vesalius," 110–111.
3. Cf. *ibid.*, 59–61.
4. *Ibid.*, 67.
5. *Ibid.*, 59.
6. *Enneads*, V, 2, 1–2; quoted by Lovejoy, *ibid.*, 63.
7. Lovejoy, *ibid.*, 64.
8. Pope, *Essay on Man*, I, 241–246.
9. Quoted by Lovejoy, *Chain of Being*, 67. As Professor Lovejoy points out, if the idea of the "Great Chain of Being" were developed with vigorous logical consistency, it would extend to an *infinite* number of links. But it seldom was (*ibid.*, 59).
10. Aquinas, *Summa contra Gentiles* (tr. Rickaby), II, 45; III, 71: quoted by Lovejoy, *ibid.*, 75, 76, 77. My italics.
11. Aquinas, I *Sent. dist.* XLIV, q. 1, a.2, in *Opera Omnia*, Pavia (1855), V, 355: quoted by Lovejoy, *ibid.*, 77. My italics.
12. Sir Thomas Elyot, *The Boke Named the Governour*, edited by Foster Watson (Everyman edition), 4.
13. Cf. De Wulf, *Phil and Civ.*, 192–193.
14. See diagram on page 318.
15. Shakespeare, *Works* (*ed. cit.*): *Troilus and Cressida*, I, iii, 83–88, 101–110, 124–134. My italics. Compare the last few lines on the process involved in the "neglection of degree" with the lines quoted above from Pope's *Essay on Man*.

2.

16. Cf. Lovejoy, *Chain of Being*, 66.
17. Lovejoy, "Meaning of Romanticism," 263.
18. Randall, *Mod. Mind*, 100.
19. Gilson, *Sp. Med. Phil.*, 369.
20. *Ibid.*, 369.
21. *Ibid.*, 370.
22. Aquinas, *Sum. con. Gen.*, III, 71: Lovejoy, *Chain of Being*, 77. My italics. Cf. Randall, *Mod. Mind*, 99.
23. As distinguished from animals, which "perceive" their ends through the senses only (cf., among others, Gilson, *Sp. Med. Phil.*, 106).
24. Gilson, *ibid.*, 168.
25. *Ibid.*, 117.
26. This is not to say that their concepts are identical; it would be difficult to identify completely the relation of the Stoic law of nature and concept of necessity to the Stoic idea of freedom with the relation of Christian providence to Christian freedom (see Gilson, *ibid.*, 153, 314–315, 359, and elsewhere); yet as *Christian stoicism* is developed—from the Christian appropriation of Cicero's eclectic sort of Stoicism to the formal reconciliation of Christianity and Stoicism attempted in the Renaissance by men like

Salutati and Lipsius—we find at least a rough approximation of this equation. See the discussion on Renaissance Christian humanists in Chapter I (*supra*).

27. Gilson, *ibid.*, 359. My italics.
28. *Ibid.*, 117.
29. Quoted by Gilson, *ibid.*, 125.
30. Cf. Gilson, *ibid.*, 314.
31. *Ibid.*
32. *Ibid.*, 316.
33. Cf. *ibid.*, 153.
34. *Ibid.*, 104.
35. *Book of Wisdom*, xi, 21; quoted, *ibid.*, 101.
36. Koyré, "Galileo and Plato," 408.
37. Randall, *Mod. Mind*, 36. Professor Randall's one misinterpretation here. it seems to me, concerns the love of the bad man "for evil that is his nature."
38. Cf. Gilson, *Sp. Med. Phil.*, 271–273, and De Wulf, *Phil. and Civ.*, 185.
39. Hooker, *Of the Laws of Eccles. Pol.*, I, viii, 7. My italics.
40. De Wulf, *Phil. and Civ.*, 58.
41. Carlyle and Carlyle, *Med. Pol. Theory*, V, 12–13.
42. Chapman, *Conspiracy of Biron* (ed. cit.) , V, i, 83–84.
43. See this whole speech (V, i, 49–65) for a clear and traditional statement of the duties and established limits of scope of the good Christian Prince. Cf. *ibid.*, IV, ii, 63–85.
44. De Wulf, *Phil. and Civ.*, 58.
45. Shakespeare, *The Life of King Henry the Fifth* (ed. cit.) , IV, i, 104–115.
46. *Ibid.*, IV, i, 185–186.
47. Hooker, *Of the Laws*, I, ix, i.
48. Cf. James Emerson Phillips, Jr., *The State in Shakespeare's Greek and Roman Plays* (New York, 1940) , 81.
49. *Romans*, XII, 4, 5, 6.
50. Cicero, *De Officiis*, I, xxx, 107; xxxi, 110. Observe Sir Thomas Elyot's application of this principle to education in *The Boke Named the Governour*, 28.
51. Phillips, *Shakespeare's State*, 81.
52. Cf. Randall, *Mod. Mind*, 59.
53. Sir John Eliot, *The Monarchie of Man*, edited by Alexander B. Grosart (London, 1879) , II, 13.
54. Elyot, *Governour*, 6.
55. *Ibid.*, 3.
56. Lovejoy, *Great Chain*, 101.
57. Cf. *ibid.*, Chapter II, especially 59 and 66.
58. Nor was this the only prominent inconsistency in their dealings with the basic principles of the great chain of being. See Lovejoy, *ibid.*, 70–79, for the way in which they tried to avoid the heresy of the "necessitarian optimism."
59. Randall, *Mod. Mind*, 33.
60. *Ibid.*
61. Baron, "Towards a More Positive Evaluation," 36.
62. Cf. Randall, *ibid.*, for Dante's computation of the age of the world.
63. Lovejoy, "The Meaning of Romanticism," 263. Cf. the first chapter in Lovejoy and Boas, *Prim. and Rel. Ideas*, for an inclusive summary of ancient and modern views of the historic process.
64. Gilson, *Sp. Med. Phil.*, 391.

3.

65. Burnet, *Greek Phil.*, I, 22.
66. Fragment of Anaximander, quoted by Burnet, *ibid.*
67. Cf. Burnet, *ibid.*, 26.
68. *Ibid.*, 26, 60.
69. *Ibid.*, 48–49.
70. *Ibid.*, 61–62.
71. *Ibid.*, 72–74.
72. Cf. *ibid.*, 79–81.
73. Stoic pantheism constitutes one exception to this generalization.
74. Boethius, *De Consolatione* (Loeb Library edition), II, viii.
75. Hooker, *Of the Laws*, I, iii, 2. James Holly Hanford has compared these two passages to one in Shakespeare's *Troilus and Cressida* (I, iii, 85 ff.; cf. fn. 15 *supra*) in his article, "A Platonic Passage in Troilus and Cressida," *Studies in Philology*, Vol. XIII (1916).
76. Ralegh, *Works*, II, 36 (*History of the World*, I, 1, xiii). Cf. Marcellus Palingenius Stellatus, *The Zodiake of life*, translated out of Latine into English by Barnaby Googe (London, 1588), 62 (mistaken pagination for 51).
77. Hooker, *Of the Laws*, ibid.
78. Edmund Spenser, *The Fowre Hymnes*, edited by Lilian Winstanley (Cambridge, 1930): "An Hymne in Honour of Love," ll. 78–88, 92–95. Compare the peculiar twist Sir John Davies gives the concept in his *Orchestra, or a poem of dancing*, ll. 113–119, 125–126, 137–140: Hebel and Hudson, *Poetry of the Eng. Ren.*, 337. Cf. also Chaucer's *Knight's Tale*, ll. 2987–2993. This passage is another illustration of the "Great Chain of Being" idea, too.
79. Hooker, *Of the Laws*, I, iii, 4.
80. Girolamo Benivieni, *Ode of Love*, st. ii, translated by Fletcher, *Ital. Ren.*, 337.
81. Count Baldassare Castiglione, *The Book of the Courtier*, Done into English by Sir Thomas Hoby, 1561: Everyman edition, 321.
82. Hooker, *Of the Laws*, I, iii, 4.
83. Donne, "The first Anniversary," ll. 377–384, 396–397, 399–400: *Poems*, 218–219.
84. Donne, *ibid.*, ll. 213–214: *Poems*, 214.
85. Hooker, *Of the Laws*, I, ix, 1.
86. Or the angelic intellects and spirits which direct each of the nine spheres containing the heavenly bodies.
87. Aquinas, *Sum. con. Gen.*, II, 45, quoted by Lovejoy, *Chain of Being*, 86.
88. Hooker, *Of the Laws*, I, xiv, 8. My italics.
89. Randall, *Mod. Mind*, 58–59. My italics.
90. See, for example, his *Commentary on Nicomachean Ethics*, Lib. I; cf. Randall, *ibid.*, 59.
91. Cicero, *De Officiis*, I, xxxi, 110.
92. *Romans*, XII, 4, 5; *I Corinthians*, xii, 26.
93. Elyot, *Governour*, 1.
94. Shakespeare, *Henry V*, I, ii, 180–184, 184–187, 204–213.
95. Eliot, *The Monarchie of Man*, II, 12.
96. Edition of 1574, sig *3 *verso;* quoted by Farnham, *Medieval Heritage of Elizabethan Tragedy*, 295.
97. Jonson, *Every Man Out of his Humour*, Induction.
98. Shakespeare, *Julius Caesar*, V, v, 73–75.

99. For a brief, lucid discussion of this whole topic of the mixture of elements or humours in man, see Lowes, *Geoffrey Chaucer*, 29–38.

100. Shakespeare, *Coriolanus*, I, i, 99–100, 103–104, 134–144.

101. See diagram on page 318.

102. Hooker, *Of the Laws*, I, vii, 2. Cf. Aristotle, *Nic. Eth.*, III, 1, 3; VI, 2.

103. John Milton, *Paradise Lost*, IX, 1123 ff.

104. Hooker, *ibid.*, I, viii, 6. Cf. Aristotle, *Politics*, I, v, 5–6.

105. Ben Jonson, *Every Man in his Humour* (First Quarto, *ed. cit.*), II, ii, 27–30. This speech is omitted in the Folio.

106. Cf. *De Officiis*, I, xxvii–xxviii.

107. Cf. *ibid.*, I, xxx, 107.

108. Cf. *ibid.*, I, xxx, 106.

109. Lovejoy, "Meaning of Romanticism," 263.

CHAPTER
6

THE COUNTER–RENAISSANCE AND THE DENIAL
OF LIMIT: THE ROMANTICISTS

I. THE RENAISSANCE NEOPLATONISTS AND THE DENIAL OF LIMIT

THERE are few interwoven threads in the history of thought more difficult to disentangle than those of the various kinds of Platonism and Neoplatonism. Perhaps, as Professor Whitehead has said, "The safest general characterization of the European philosophical tradition is that it consists in a series of footnotes to Plato."[1] But if this is true, the footnotes have frequently been made by the kind of scholars who find the gloss more important than the text.

To be sure, the starting point, the basic concept involved, has usually been truly Platonic. Often the letter has been followed conscientiously throughout. But the original temper of the dialogues —that almost indefinable blending of idealism, sanity and irony— has been retained less frequently. Nor is this surprising, for the man who finds satisfaction in the dialectic of Socrates is rarely the sort to revel in the myths and in the Pythagorean elements of Plato's thought. And few of us, endorsing the one and rejecting the other, are able to resist the temptation to "make over" Plato according to our own predilection.

Montaigne follows this road in his last essay, recognizing the Platonic element which is not congenial to him, but brushing it arbitrarily aside as unrepresentative:

> Pythagoras (say they) hath followed a Philosophie all in contemplation; Socrates altogether in manners and in action; Plato hath found a mediocrity between both. *But they say so by way of discourse.* For *the true temperature* is found in Socrates, and Plato is more Socratical than Pythagorical, and *it becomes him best.*[2]

Moreover, there are, of course, contradictory elements in Plato's thought itself. For example, Arthur O. Lovejoy, in his monumental *Great Chain of Being*, has shown conclusively how central to the history of Western thought has been the struggle between (and the attempt to reconcile) Plato's two concepts of God.

Finally and inevitably, each restatement of "Platonism" has involved the addition of extraneous and yet often similar concepts. The combining of Christian, Judaic and occult thought with Platonism has greatly increased the confusion attending the attempt to determine the extent of the original deposit in particular "Platonists" and "Neoplatonists."

Seldom has the mixture been more confusing than in the Renaissance. Throughout the Middle Ages, even during the supremacy of Aquinas' Aristotle, there had been a strong undercurrent of Neoplatonism, chiefly derivatory from the Church Fathers. In addition to this medieval heritage, the revival of interest in Augustine (one of the most "Platonic" of the patristic writers) among the Italian humanists from Petrarch on provided a considerable impetus to Renaissance Neoplatonism. Cicero, too, from whom Augustine had inherited much of his Platonism, was a darling of the day; and one can observe, in the frequent linking of his name with that of Plato or Socrates, by Erasmus and others, that he was as important a source for Renaissance Platonism as he was for its eclectic Stoicism. In a characteristic passage, Sir Thomas Elyot exclaims, "Lorde god, what incomparable swetnesse of wordes and mater shall he [the reader] finde in the said workes of Plato and Cicero!"[3]

But however much the influx of Platonism through these channels affected Renaissance thought, the visit to Italy of such Greek scholars as Pletho and Bessarion (who, among others, remained in Italy) occasioned by the Councils of Ferrara (1438–39) and of Florence (1439–42), and the ensuing prominence of the Platonic-Aristotelian controversy, gave a final decisive impetus to the trend.

More particularly, Pletho's enthusiasm for the mysticism of the Alexandrians, and his concept of Platonism as the high point of a secret philosophic tradition stemming from the hidden "wisdom of the ancients," from Zoroaster and Orpheus and Hermes Trismegistus—together with Bessarion's emphasis upon Pythagorean number mysticism—pointed the way for such occult Platonists as Pico. Again, Pletho's friendship with Cosmo de' Medici seems to have been instrumental in the founding of the Florentine Academy and thus, indirectly, influential in Cosmo's training of Ficino as the translator and interpreter of Platonism.[4]

These were the chief Platonic and Neoplatonic sources available to Ficino when he began his translations of Plato. His major work, the dissemination of Platonism and the effecting of a Platonic-Christian synthesis, was done between 1463 and 1491. It included his translations of Plato, of Plotinus' *Enneads,* and of the principal works of lesser Neoplatonists; commentaries on Plato and Plotinus; and the *Theologica Platonica de Immortalite Animae* and the *De Christiana Religione.*[5]

Ficino's work, together with that of Pico, Benivieni, Christoforo Landino (whose most notable contribution was a commentary on Dante's *Divine Comedy*—a Neoplatonic interpretation), and other members of the Academy, constituted the real fountainhead of Renaissance Neoplatonism. Their Plotinian emphasis upon love as "the supreme force, cosmic, moral, religious,"[6] mingles with other traditions to receive a new interpretation at the hands of Pietro Bembo, arch-priest of the "Platonic cult of love," and to emerge as the religion of Castiglione's courtier. A new interpretation—since, although Bembo's exposition of "Platonic" love in the fourth book of *The Courtier* follows Benivieni's account of the progress of the soul up the "ladder of love" to a final union with God, it is nevertheless, in tone as in setting, a mixture of metaphysics and gallantry. Bembo (as, later, Castiglione) is at least equally concerned with a detailed account of the perfecting influence of women, who "by their beauty, of body and mind conjoined . . . lead upward and onward" those men who are capable of this refinement of love.[7]

This Platonic "religion" of love and beauty extended a wide sway over Renaissance courtly society, from the circles of Isabella d'Este, Vittoria Colonna, and Elizabetta Gonzaga in Italy, to those of Marguerite of Navarre in France and Henrietta Maria and Lady Carlisle in Caroline England—with varying degrees of sincerity involved. And there were varying degrees of sincerity, of course (although frequently unascertainable), in its celebration by the poets: by Marguerite of Navarre, Maurice Scève, and Joachim du Bellay, for example, in France, or by Spenser and Sidney in England. Moreover, the poets' treatments of the standard themes are by no means uniform: an essentially Christian ideal of love is sometimes apparent, sometimes absent; frequently Petrarchan elements are interwoven with Platonic. But it is safe to say that all these differing versions are either directly or indirectly indebted to Ficino and, more particularly, to Benivieni's *Canzona dello Amore celeste e divino.*[8]

Yet if this Platonic cult of love was the most popular and widely publicized variety of Renaissance Platonism, it was far from being the only influential one. From 1540 on, the philosophical and learned tradition of Platonism, which had largely engaged Ficino's and Pico's efforts, flourished in France, side by side with the "secular-ized" version we have just been describing.[9] Indeed, with the ap-pearance in 1543 of Ramus' *Animadversiones Aristotelicae,* the Pla-tonic "threat" to Aristotelian supremacy in France became overt.

Ramus' book might be called a negative profession of faith in Plato and the Platonic dialectic—negative, because its explicit pur-pose was simply the undermining of Aristotle's authority and Aris-totelian logic. But, as Abel Lefranc has pointed out, both the *Animadversiones* and Ramus' later work (in his editions of *Somnium Scipionis* and Plato's *Epistles*) show unmistakable evidence of his Platonic discipleship.[10] On a somewhat different level (being much more interested in the Socratic dialectic than in Platonic-Plotinian metaphysics), Ramus, like Ficino and Pico, attempted a Christian-Platonic synthesis.

French Platonism has frequently been identified with the Ref-ormation, most particularly as a hallmark of the Huguenots. As a generalization, this statement may be justified. But any generaliza-tion about Renaissance Platonism is dangerous. The taste of the times was for eclecticism, and most of the Platonists or Neopla-tonists drew extensively from other sources as well. As we have seen, various occult traditions were heavily tapped. Then, too, with all the riches of recent humanist translations and commentaries at their disposal, the temptation for synthesizing minds to skim the cream from Aristotle, Plato and the Stoics alike was strong. Pref-erences are clear enough in individual writers, but they are seldom exclusive preferences. For example, Chapman is often pointed to as a man who expounds a more or less systematic Christian Pla-tonism in his poetry. So he does, yet to stop there is misleading. For he was a devoted admirer of Epictetus, and there are major Stoic elements in both his plays and poems.

Again, when a divine like Richard Hooker, the defender of "Reason's star," works out his system of universal laws, he draws from Aristotle, from Plato, and from the Stoics, to bolster his Chris-tian theology. It is a mistake to consider Aristotle as "dead and buried" in the Renaissance; aside from those who used his name indiscriminately to cover the sins of degenerate scholasticism, only the anti-intellectualists and the leaders of the Reformation attacked him with vehement invectives. As late as 1573, the Roman Catholic Church of the Counter-Reformation proclaimed solemnly, "Doctrina Aristoteli sequenda est" (in logic and metaphysics); the majority,

of whatever faith, accepted his account of the physical universe up
to the time of Galileo; the orthodox moral tracts and the literature
itself of the Renaissance featured Aristotelian ethics as often as
Platonic and Stoic; the naturalists of the Counter-Renaissance, following the "Aristotle" of the Averroistic-Paduan schools rather than
the "Aristotle" of Thomas Aquinas, developed an Aristotelian "real-
politik" and an ethic totally divorced from metaphysical premises.

Finally, the Renaissance humanists' favorite sources were Cicero,
Seneca and Plutarch. I would call these three *eclectic Stoic moralists*.
Yet if one word should be stressed, it is *eclectic*.[11] Neither Cicero
nor Plutarch can be called a Stoic in any rigorous sense. Both attacked the more extreme types of dogmatic Stoicism; both gave
numerous expositions of Aristotle's and Plato's positions; both probably preferred Plato to any other single philosopher. Inevitably,
therefore, the solid middle-road group of Christian humanists of
the Renaissance drew as they chose, for the most part, from Peripateticism, Academicism and Stoicism.

It is evident, then, as the parallel references to "love" and "law"
(developed in the previous chapter's discussion of the principle of
limit as balance and harmony) have suggested, that there is nothing *necessarily* antagonistic between many features of Renaissance
Platonism and of Renaissance Aristotelianism. Indeed, the two could
be explicitly reconciled with each other, and both with Christianity
—such was an important part of the comprehensive task which the
young Pico della Mirandola set forth for himself. Yet there are
many other features of certain varieties of Renaissance Platonism
or Neoplatonism that were manifestly opposed to the various concepts of limit so integral to the medieval Christian-Aristotelian
world-view. These not only, in themselves, sharply challenged the
several interpretations of limit as value and as reality—they also
fostered other more radical departures from established theories of
limit, departures not expressly Platonic or Neoplatonic at all. . . .

I have referred to the way Professor Lovejoy has traced through
the centuries the course of the two often conflicting Platonic concepts of God. From the concept in the *Republic* of deity as transcendent, self-sufficient, completely "other" from all created existence, we turn in the *Timaeus* to deity as the dynamic "World-
Ground" which produced the universe from itself.[12]

To understand the contrast in its full force and lucidity, we cannot
do better than quote Professor Lovejoy:

> It was a conflict between two irreconcilable conceptions of the
> good . . . the Idea of the Good . . . [and] the Idea of Good-

ness; and though the second attribute was nominally deduced from the first, no two notions could be more antithetic. The one was an apotheosis of unity, self-sufficiency, and quietude, the other of diversity, self-transcendence, and fecundity. . . .

The one God was the goal of the "way up," of that ascending process by which the finite soul, turning from all created things, took its way back to the immutable Perfection in which alone it could find rest. The other God was the source and the informing energy of that descending process by which being flows through all the levels of possibility down to the very lowest. . . .[13]

The greatest difficulty in reconciling these two concepts, however, was not in terms of the contradiction implied in the nature of deity. Professor Lovejoy points out that it has never been difficult for theologians, metaphysicians and mystics to postulate a "coincidentia oppositorum," a "meeting of extremes in the Absolute."[14] Indeed, Plotinus is able to make the double concept appear superbly logical:

The One is perfect because it seeks for nothing; and being perfect, it overflows, and thus its superabundance produces an Other. . . . Whenever anything reaches its own perfection, we see that it cannot endure to remain in itself, but generates and produces something else. . . . How then should the Most Perfect Being and the First Good remain shut up in itself, as though it were jealous or impotent—itself the potency of all things?[15]

But, as Professor Lovejoy argues, while "it might appear easy to affirm of the divine nature what to us must seem incompatible metaphysical predicates," it is quite another matter to try "to reconcile *in human practice* what to us must seem incompatible notions of value."

There was [he continues] no way in which the flight from the Many to the One, the quest of a perfection defined wholly in terms of contrast with the created world, could be effectually harmonized with the imitation of a Goodness that delights in diversity and manifests itself in the emanation of the Many out of the One. The one program demanded a withdrawal from all "attachment to creatures" and culminated in the ecstatic contemplation of the indivisible Divine Essence; the other, if it had been formulated, would have summoned man to participate, in some finite measure, in the creative passion of God, to collaborate consciously in the processes by which the diversity of things, the fullness of the universe is achieved.[16]

This passage provides, I think, an excellent testing ground for the different sorts of Christian Platonism in the Renaissance. Certainly the second course, the participation and collaboration in the creative processes was not "formulated" into a conscious formal creed by Erasmus and More and Colet. Yet surely it was an "imitation of a Goodness," of God, in just this sense, which was their Christian-Platonic code of living. Surely it was in this concept that they found *their* Plato, *their* Socrates, *their* Christ, and *their* relationship to God.

But it is Chapman, again, who provides a definitive statement of this code—in *Eugenia*—and in terms very close to Professor Lovejoy's:

> . . . . as Philosophie
> Saies there is evermore proportion
> Betwixt the knowing part, and what is knowne
> So joynd, that both, are absolutely one;
> So when we know God, *in things here below*
> And truly keepe th'abstracted good we know;
> (God being all goodnesse) *we with him combine*
> And therein shew, the all in all, doth shine. . . .[17]

Sir Philip Sidney envisions a similar participation "in the creative passion of God" as the task and privilege of a poet:

> Only the poet, disdaining to be tied to any such subjection to nature, lifted up with the vigor of his own invention, doth grow, in effect, into another nature; in making things either better than nature bringeth forth, or quite anew. . . . Neither let it be deemed too saucy a comparison to balance the highest point of man's wit with the efficacy of nature; but rather give right honor to the heavenly Maker of that maker, who having made man to His own likeness, set him beyond and over all the works of *that second nature;* which in nothing he showeth so much as in poetry; when *with the force of a divine breath, he bringeth things forth surpassing her doings,* with no small arguments to the incredulous of that first accursed fall of Adam; *since our erected wit maketh us know what perfection is, and yet our infected will keepeth us from reaching unto it.*[18]

In this statement we have an equating (and constantly a Christian "toning down") of the *furor poeticus* of the *Ion* with the "divine breath" of God in man, who has been made in His image —with the full implication of that summoning to "men to participate, in some finite measure, in the creative passion of God, to collaborate consciously in the process by which the diversity of

things, the fullness of the universe is achieved," of which Professor
Lovejoy speaks. We find, moreover, that clear statement of man's
but little impaired rational capacity to *know* good (in Sidney's
case, with the shunting off of all the blame for the Fall onto "our
infected will") which is so characteristic of the optimistic middle-
path liberal humanists from Erasmus and More to Hooker and
Chapman.

A few paragraphs later, Sidney completes his alignment with this
sort of Platonism, with his application of Aristotelian "imitation"
to the three proper kinds of poetry:

> For these three be they which most properly do imitate to
> teach and delight; and to imitate, borrow nothing of what is,
> hath been, or shall be; but range only, reined with learned
> discretion, into the divine consideration of what may be, and
> should be.[19]

"The imitation of a Goodness that delights in diversity. . . ."

But while this "collaboration" and "participation" in, and "imitation" of, the creative Goodness of God which appeals to the
liberal humanist tradition, the quest of an otherworldly "perfection," the withdrawal from "attachment to creatures," the "way up,"
also elicited much of the most characteristic writing of the Renaissance Neoplatonists, from Ficino and Pico to Edmund Spenser.
Their good, the focus of their concept of man's relationship to God,
most often lies in the "ascent."

By this statement I do not mean that the other concept, the Goodness of the "descending process," does not appear, even prominently,
in their work. It was essential to the systematic nature of Ficino's
task, for instance, to deal extensively with the Creation, the qualities of the "creative God," the way in which the government of
the universe is conducted. To a certain extent, the same is true of
Pico. Aside from the fundamental contradiction which we have
considered, this was not inconsistent. In fact, it was almost unavoidable, for the central thesis of the Neoplatonists, derived especially
from Plotinus, is that love is the supreme cosmic force, dominant
in the Creation and in the regulation of the world,[20] as it is in the
ascent of the soul. Hence, one can only understand fully its importance to the "way up" when one realizes that—in the words of
Professor Fletcher—"the course of love is a circle beginning and
ending in God."[21] As Benivieni puts it in his *Ode of Love:*

> I tell how Love from its celestial source
> In Primal Good flows to the world of sense;

When it had birth; and whence;
How moves the heavens, refines the soul, gives laws
To all; in men's hearts taking residence,
With what arms keen and ready in resource,
It is the gracious force
Which mortal minds from earth to heaven draws. . . .[22]

Or, as Bembo says in the fourth book of the *Courtier,* addressing sacred Love: "Thou, fairest, best, wisest, from the divine union of Beauty, Goodness and Wisdom derivest, and in that abidest, and to that through that as in a circle returnest."[23]

I say that, to the Neoplatonists, love is the supreme cosmic force. By this I do not mean to suggest any vague, emotional, or arbitrary anti-intellectualism. "Wisdom" participates in "the divine union" from which Love "derivest." Indeed, it would be very difficult to attribute to Plato a purposeless, designless world scheme, functioning without law. And Plotinus, whose interpretation of Plato the Renaissance Neoplatonists followed almost unanimously, explicitly denies such a charge.[24] Moreover, the second of the eternal hypostases, the "Other" produced by the perfect "One" or "Absolute," is the Divine or Universal Reason.[25] As Pico puts it:

No Creature, but this first Mind, proceeds immediately from God. . . . This by Plato, Hermes, and Zoroaster, is called the Daughter of God, the Mind, Wisdom, Divine Reason, by some interpreted the Word; not meaning (with our Divines) the Son of God, he not being a Creature, but one Essence, co-equal with the Creator. . . .

[In this first Mind] God . . . produced the Ideas and Forms of all, and that in their most perfect Being, that is, the Idea, for which Reason, they call this the Mind, the Intelligible World. . . .

And finally, "After the Pattern of that Mind, they affirm this sensible World was made. . . ."[26]

In this conception, we find a first challenge to the Christian-humanistic concept of limit. For the concept of this secondary deity (expressly not "the Son of God") contradicts (despite the Neoplatonic evasion of a "coincidentia oppositorum") the theological concept of a transcendent God who, according to the main tradition from Aquinas to Hooker, makes a law of operation for himself and for the universe, from which he stands totally apart. Limit, in the sense of God's own purposeful direction of the universe by law, and the concept of God as Intellect, "moving" all creation to its

several ends, was integral to this tradition.[27] It is totally missing
in the Neoplatonists' picture. Pico declares, "It is more improperly
said of God that he is intellect or intelligence than of a rational
soul that it is an angel."[28] Or again, more inclusively:

> Platonists assert . . . that in God is nothing, but from him
> all things; that Intellect is not in him, but that he is the orig-
> inal Spring of every Intellect. Such is Plotinus's Meaning, when
> he affirms God neither understands nor knows; that is to say,
> after a formal Way, as Dionysius Areopagita, God is neither
> an intellectual nor intelligent Nature, but unspeakably exalted
> above all Intellect and Knowledge. . . .[29]

At the risk of brash irreverence, one might say that God has, in
such a concept, been "kicked upstairs." In the process of being
"unspeakably exalted," he loses the most salient characteristic of
the traditional Christian humanist's God, that of being a purposeful and law-giving creator, and becomes, however "unspeakably
exalted," the *ground* of creation only—purposeless and unknowing
and uncaring. Exit limit as the defining of purpose.

It is interesting to compare this Neoplatonic concept of God the
Creator with that of Luther and Calvin, who stress God's inscrutable will. Both concepts emphasize God's unknowability; both,
although with different accents, place value on God as unbridled
creative energy and power. But the one removes him from our comprehension by attributing purposelessness to him (of course placing
him *above*, rather than below or to one side of purpose), the other
by asserting that he does not choose to disclose his purpose. Both
deny "limit" to him—the one by making him only the matrix of
creation, the other by making him an arbitrary dictator. . . .[30]

There is another sense in which the Neoplatonists denied traditional "limit" to God. Plotinus' central thesis about God is that He
is the "One"; and to show how God can at once be "perfect" and
"other," and yet the "All" which he must become in the multiplicity
of the Creation which is "of Him," he is forced to turn to the argument of "coincidentia oppositorum"—to say that the One and the
All are at once the same thing and not the same thing, in effect
that God is at once, and yet differently, transcendent and immanent.

This was the *tour de force* to which most Neoplatonists thereafter resorted. Thus any "definition" of God as at once "perfect"
(and hence by implication transcendent) and "loving" (the God
of the Creation still manifest in the multiplicity of the Creation—
hence immanent) must be made by means of a symbolism which
holds for the two concepts.

Let us consider, for an example, the way Marguerite of Navarre handles the contradiction. She uses a formula variously traced back to Empedocles, the Plato of the *Symposium* and the *Phaedrus*, Plotinus, and Hermes Trismegistus; employed by medieval mystics like Bonaventura and Nicholas Cusanus (the latter was probably the direct source, through Ficino, of its popularity in the Renaissance); and repeated, with only slight changes of phrasing, by many Renaissance eclectic Platonists from Ficino to Ralegh.[31]

This formula is simply that God is a circle or sphere, whose center is everywhere, whose circumference nowhere. Cusanus' words in *De docta ignorantia* are: "Illi vero qui actualissimam Dei existentiam considerarunt, *Deum quasi sphaeram infinitum* affirmarunt." In *De Ludo globi*, he uses the expression, "Deum circulum, cujus centrum est ubique." Ficino's version is "Deus est . . . circulus spiritalis, cujus centrum est ubique, circumferentia nusquam."[32]

Rabelais employs the formula twice. In Book III, Pantagruel speaks of the "contemplation of that infinite and intellectual sphere, whereof the centre is everywhere, and the circumference in no place of the universal world, to wit, God, according to the doctrine of Hermes Trismegistus. . . ." And in the final chapter of Book V, the priestess begins her farewell speech to the departing pilgrims with the prayer:

> Now, my friends, you may depart, and may that intellectual sphere, whose centre is everywhere, and circumference nowhere, whom we call GOD, keep you in his almighty protection.[33]

Marguerite of Navarre completes our excursion in her definition, by identifying this abstract mathematical God of the Pythagorizing Platonists with the God of Love from whom all things flow and by whom they are preserved:

> Celluy qui est fait . . .
> Du sercle rond sans la circunference,
> Par tous costez egal sans difference;
> Commancement ne fin ne s'y retrouve,
> Et n'y a chose, estant ou vieille ou neufve,
> Qui, de ce rond, n'ayt pris creation
> Et nourriture et conservation.[34]

It is as though the Neoplatonist finds in the agency of Love the only sufficient explanation of how the transcendent Good was persuaded to "come down." As the strange words of the Pseudo-Dionysius have it, God had been "cozened by goodness and affec-

tion and love, and led down from his eminence above all and surpassing all, to being in all."[35]

Moreover, Marguerite postulates in this God of Love not only
the "creation" of everything, but the "nourriture" and "conservation" as well. The third concept of the Neoplatonic cosmology in
which law does not play the dominant part concerns the government of the world. "Midway between the two natures [divine and
human], Love completes a whole, which gathers all the Universe
into one," Diotima had told Socrates, and to all doctrinal Neoplatonists it was Love that held the world together.

This does not, I have already explained, *necessarily* imply any
deviation from the traditional medieval concept of *law* as the sustaining force of the universe; it may rather be only the expression
of a concept that is the poetic counterpart of the concept of universal law. Yet there is a subtle difference between the climate of
this Neoplatonic love, and that of the similar Christian concept of
the circulation of love which is expounded, for example, by Etienne
Gilson:

> Born of love, the whole universe is penetrated, moved, vivified
> from within by love that circulates through it like the life-
> giving blood through the body. There is therefore a circulation
> of love that starts from God and finds him again.[36]

This sounds like the Neoplatonic version, but Gilson expressly
repudiates any pantheistic significance. Love, here, like law, *comes
from* God, and God gives its universal circulation the initial impetus. But this does not make God immanent, and the circulation
does not contradict the ordering by law of each entity in the great
chain of being. The difference is well expressed in a paragraph
of E. M. Hulme's:

> [The Aristotelians of the time] regarded the universe as being
> limited in extent and as being created by God who stands apart
> from his work, transcending it, and regarding it as a potter re-
> gards the vessel he has turned upon his wheel. The Platonists
> of the time held that God is immanent in the universe; that
> nature is but the vesture of its creator. The former were legal-
> ists; the latter were mystics.[37]

And the Neoplatonists' use of love as a binding force further
demonstrates this difference. If it is sometimes implicit that Love,
the "most dear bond of the world," is literally and specifically God's
love in the Christian sense, it is rarely explicit. Walter Ralegh seems
to make it so, when he speaks of "God, who hath formed this nature,

and whose divine love was the beginning, and is the bond of the universal," and goes on to drive home the point that "God therefore, who could only be the cause of all, can only provide for all, and sustain all. . . ."[38]

But for most of the Renaissance Neoplatonists, what M. Lefranc says of Marguerite of Navarre's concern with Love as a world force —"Elle lui assigne un rôle universel tant dans la nature physique que dans le monde moral"[39]—holds good. Either expressly or by implication, they predicate an immanent God and a pantheistic nature.

For while doctrinal Neoplatonism has not been so characteristically pantheistic as monistic, the latter position is always close to the former. Moreover, the Renaissance version of the "devout philosophy" is so permeated with occult doctrines that it inevitably contains many pantheistic or animistic concepts.

M. Saurat has said, speaking of those philosophical poets who have been most influenced by Neoplatonism and occult tradition, that

> they are all pantheists, starting out generally from the same conception of an inaccessible god with no perceptible relations with the world, acknowledging a demiurge or secondary deity whose business it is to look after the world and who is himself the entirety of the world.[40]

This concept of the secondary deity is of course a convenient way to resolve the difficulties of a Being which "should include all the *esse* of all things without possessing the attributes of any of those things"—a Being which must embrace all the diversity of the universe within itself, although itself without parts, one within which all things may live and move and have a being, although it itself is immutable.[41] The demiurge is not only a protagonist in the Renaissance Neoplatonists' account of the Creation; he figures in the lore of most of the occult traditions. Hence the initiate traditions, stressing the immanence of God as much as (perhaps more than) God's inaccessibility, also display pantheistic tendencies at almost every turn. And this tendency is manifest in single figures who do not fit neatly into either a Neoplatonic or occult category.

Bruno, for instance, despite the emphasis of one side of his thought upon the absolute, unknowable, and indefinable God, made "the monistic side of Neoplatonism, its doctrine of immanence, far more conspicuous and vivid" than its medieval expounders had. He found in this doctrine, Professor Lovejoy says, "a source of pantheistic 'cosmic emotion' that earlier Platonists never felt in any such intensity. He corrected Neoplatonism, moreover, at a point where it was unnecessarily at variance with itself, by merging the conception of 'matter' (the potential) in that of God, or the Infinite."[42]

The importance of this "correction," in terms of the occult Neoplatonists' idea of nature, is that it means that nature, permeated throughout with the divine, is good. Matter, M. Saurat points out, has always been "good" to the occult traditions, but "bad" to Neoplatonism—until the Renaissance variety, which was "contaminated" by the esoteric doctrines.[43]

Moreover, Nature is not only good; it is animated with spiritual presences, the very "breath" of God. Obviously, therefore, any investigation of Nature must be the investigation of her mysteries or secrets; it can follow only upon revelation; she must be accosted with reverence.

This is the world of which Bruno writes, "We delight in one Being which embraces all, and most of all in that one which is the whole itself."[44] And Campanella declares:

> The world's a living creature, whole and great,
> God's image, praising God whose type it is.[45]

Pico includes among his *Conclusiones* the following statements, which he attributes to Hermetic sources:

> Nothing in the world is devoid of life. . . . Wherever there is life, there is a soul; Wherever there is a soul, there is a mind. . . . Nothing in the universe is subject to death or corruption. Wherever there is life, there is Providence and immortality.[46]

The alchemists considered the "metalline soul," or pure metalline spirit common to all metals, an emanation or metalline manifestation of the "anima mundi" which informed all matter; the "anima mundi," in turn, emanated from the "spirit of the universe," and hence ultimately from God.[47] And interestingly enough, the animistic tendency is nowhere stronger than among those scientists, beginning with Copernicus, whom we think of as the founders of modern astronomy. Thus William Gilbert writes in *De Magnete*:

> We consider that the whole universe is animated, and that all the globes, all the stars, and also the noble earth have been governed since the beginnings by their own appointed souls and have the motives of self-conservation.[48]

He even specifically includes the magnetic force in this version of the universe. One of the chapter headings in *De Magnete* reads:

"The magnetic force is animated or is similar to soul; it by far surpasses the human soul as long as that is bound to an organic body."[49]

Copernicus himself had been eager to find a mystical as well as a scientific sanction for the place he allotted to the sun:

> Then in the middle of all stands the sun. For who, in our most beautiful temple, could set this light in another or better place, than that from which it can at once illuminate the whole? Not to speak of the fact that not unfittingly do some call it the light of the world, others the soul, still others the governor. Trismegistus calls it the visible God; Sophocles' Electra, the All-Seer. And in fact does the sun, seated on his royal throne, guide his family of planets as they circle round him.[50]

"Who . . . could set this light in another or better place. . . ?" This is very close to being the question which the "Theoricien" asks Jean Bodin's Neo-Platonic "Mystagogue" in the *Théâtre de la Nature Universelle*—and the Mystagogue's description of the sun, with "son siege au milieu des Planetes, comme un Prince parmy ses subiects," is very close to that of Copernicus.[51] Undoubtedly the latter's six years of study with Novara (who participated in the Platonic-Pythagorean revival centering in the Florentine Academy) at the University of Bologna (1496–1502) influenced the development of his thought.

Kepler also finds the Sun the proper dwelling place for God, if He desires a material one. One form which Kepler's animism takes is to equate the Sun with God the Father, the sphere of fixed stars with the Son, and the ethereal medium with the Holy Ghost.[52] Moreover, one could include appropriate quotations from leading early English astronomers, such as Recorde, Dee and Digges; but they would simply add parallel evidence.

It is unmistakably clear that among these scientists there is a frequent inclination toward that mystical Pythagoreanism, stemming from the Orphic sects, which finds "in sensible beauty . . . the reflection, the presentiment of a spiritual order."[53] Almost all of them showed an interest in this Pythagorean tradition of the "acousmatiques" who listen to the harmony of the spheres—rather than an exclusive preoccupation with the tradition of the pure "mathématiciens." Descartes could still write in 1635:

> On voit bien plus de gens capables d'introduire dans les mathématiques les conjectures des philosophes que de ceux qui peuvent introduire la certitude et l'évidence des démonstra-

tions mathématiques dans les matières de philosophie, telles que sont les sons et la lumière.[54]

But if the scientific astronomers showed an "inclination" toward Neoplatonic and Pythagorean mysticism, there were many other Renaissance thinkers to whom the whole field of astronomy was nothing but astrology and the science of numbers, or to whom no mathematics except the magical kind possessed any real value in the search for the truths of God and nature. A John Dee might "balance" his experimental and practical astronomy with the drawing up of his mystical number charts;[55] a Pico della Mirandola could and did assert, "Nihil magis nocivum theologo quam frequens et assidua in mathematicis Euclidis exercitatio."[56]

Pico believed, indeed, that "the deepest secrets of Being can be treated in the language of numbers and figures." But he did not believe that there was any road leading "to a *scientific* mathematics and to an *exact* knowledge of nature"; the kind of mathematics he recognized and approved is the kind which is also to be found in Reuchlin's *De arte cabalistica* and *De verbo mirifico*—magical mathematics.[57]

The late Ernst Cassirer advanced the theory that Pico's most distinctive category of thought is that of symbolic thought. He sees Pico, although primarily a speculative thinker, as a man who—under the growing influence of mysticism—came more and more to believe "that our thinking and conceiving, in so far as it is directed toward the Divine, can never be an adequate expression, but only an image and a metaphor." Thus Pico tends to deviate from the most usual Neoplatonic solutions of the problem of "the Many and the One"—of the emanating God and the transcendent God. As Professor Cassirer puts it:

> Pico is no longer trying to exhibit the Many as the *effect* of the One, or to deduce them as such from their cause, with the aid of rational concepts. He sees the Many rather as *expressions*, as *images*, as *symbols* of the One. And what he is trying to show is that only in this mediate and symbolic way can the absolutely One and absolutely unconditioned Being manifest itself to human knowledge.[58]

Indeed, Professor Cassirer has argued convincingly that Pico's conception of nature is out and out pan-psychism or a "universal vitalism"—that is, that it contains a much more sophisticated philosophical position than a crudely pantheistic one. Moreover, he asserts that it flatly contradicts the traditional hierarchical division of nature, hence (though he does not, of course, use this terminology) denying the application of limit as degree and gradation in nature:

> Nature itself is not composed of parts, and does not fall into different classes of entities, that are distinct in substance from each other. It forms a single great interconnected Life; and this Life is of such a kind that the whole is to be detected in each part. There is here not only a continuous chain of effects continuing spatially from one point to the next; there rules an original and thoroughgoing "sympathy" by virtue of which each individual occurrence is bound up with the whole system of occurrences.[59]

And the understanding of the "immanent vital interconnection of nature" is magic, as Pico defines the term.[60] It should be clear that what Professor Cassirer is describing is not the traditional concept of the Great Chain of Being, which—for all of the specific connection of the links—is not concerned with such "interconnection" and "sympathy."

A similar pan-vitalism or pan-psychism is perceptible in the thought of Agrippa and Paracelsus (who were probably directly influenced by Pico[61]) and of Jerome Cardan and Bruno. Parcelsus[62] and Cardan[63] stretched this principle to a final explicit denial of gradation in nature when they asserted that sublunary phenomena did not differ from translunary.[64] Bruno, we have already seen, took a similar position; moreover, although he balances on a tightrope to avoid heretical pantheism, he proclaims outright this sort of pan-vitalism:

> For spirit is found in all things, those which are not living creatures are still vitalized, if not according to the perceptible presence of animation and life, yet they are animate according to the principle and, as it were, primal being of animation and life.[65]

In our discussion of Renaissance pantheism, one further important distinction remains to be made. That is the one between the sort of animism, vitalism or pantheism, primarily Neoplatonic, which we have been studying—and Stoic pantheism. The distinction is important because of the resurgence of doctrinal Stoicism (as well as the eclectic, semi-Platonic, loose variety) in the Renaissance.

The Stoic conceives of a universe permeated with thought or "pronoia" (the Stoic world-mind), "the one world as a united commonwealth or state."[66] As Seneca puts it, "What is nature if not God and the Divine Reason inherent in the entire world and in all its parts?"[67] (The Christian apologists tended to equate "pronoia" with God's providence, while retaining the purposeful "legal" organization of nature: "a Nature of wisdome, goodnes, & providence."[68]) This sort of pantheism does not invalidate the concept of degree, gradation, vocation, etc., in nature. On the contrary, in addition to the Stoic universal law of nature, there is a "particular" law of nature for each individual entity.

Among the Neoplatonists and occult pantheists, there are concepts of radiant intelligences such as Gilbert's "magnetic force," which "far surpasses the human soul," yet what is pre-eminent about most of the souls which make up Nature is again their being visible *manifestations* of God's "invisible things." Their nature is not permeated in *law*. Copernicus quotes Trismegistus on the Sun's being "the visible God"; Pico finds in the Many the "images . . . of the One"; Paracelsus advocates the doctrine of "signatures" in plants; Agrippa finds one way to know God in the mystical union of the soul with nature.[69] Whereas Stoic pantheism deals basically with a universe directed by a world-mind or Providence which makes for regulation by law, occult or Neoplatonic pantheism's chief concern is having the mysteries of an otherwise incomprehensible God revealed through the secrets of Nature which symbolize these mysteries. It is the difference between an idea of nature as offering precepts and examples for right living, and an idea of nature as opening vistas of mysterious and eternal truth. Finally, it is roughly the difference between an ideal of doing and one of being; it is significant that most of the occult currents derived from the East. . . .[70]

It is now time to return to, and to complete, that trip which Jefferson Fletcher has described in the words, "The course of love is a circle beginning and ending in God." For the "way up," or—to avoid mixed metaphors—the last part of the circumference to be traced, was the special province of Renaissance Neoplatonists. Once more, with Benivieni, just as Love

> from its celestial source
> In Primal Good flows to the world of sense . . .

and thereafter is the conserving force of the world—since it "moves the heavens, refines the soul, gives laws to all"—so too, finally, it completes the circle, since

> It is the gracious force
> Which mortal minds from earth to heaven draws. . . .

And Benivieni develops, in his *Ode of Love,* the six steps that make up that ladder of love by which the soul ascends from the contemplation of earthly beauty to that of heavenly beauty—and beyond, to the often not described final consummation with God. As Pietro Bembo puts it to the company assembled at Urbino:

> For like as through the particular beautie of one bodie hee [love] guideth her [the soul] to the universall beautie of all bodies: Even so in the least [last] degree of perfection through particular understanding hee guideth her to the universall understanding.

> Thus the soule kindled in the most holy fire of true heavenly love, fleeth to couple her selfe with the nature of Angels, and not onely cleane forsaketh sense, but hath no more neede of the discourse of reason, for being changed into an Angell, she understandeth all things that may be understood; and without any veil or cloud, she seeth the maine sea of the pure heavenly beautie and receiveth it unto her, and enjoyeth the soveraigne happiness, that cannot be comprehended of the senses.[71]

It is the doctrine of the *Symposium* and the *Phaedrus,* yet within the Christian mystical tradition St. Augustine had propounded six steps of progressive ascent to God, and Bonaventura had conceived of the spiritual ascension in terms of six grades.[72] A learned writer on the Christian mysticism of the Elizabethan period has demonstrated "the community of idea between the Christian mystics and the Neoplatonists" in the Renaissance.[73]

But Professor Lovejoy's phrase, "the flight from the Many to the One," used to describe the "way up"—that "quest of a perfection defined wholly in terms of contrast with the created world . . ." marks one important difference between the primarily orthodox Christian (though Platonized) account of the ascent, and the most characteristic version of the Italian Neoplatonists from Benivieni on. In such a book as Cardinal Bellarmino's *De ascensione mentis in Deum per scalas creaturarum,* for example, the ascent is achieved in the progress from the contemplation of "the various goods which are found distributed among created things" to the final unity and transformation of all these "goods" in God.[74]

In his *Republic,* Jean Bodin describes this progress in terms of man's successive contemplations of the material, celestial and intelligible worlds, and—at the last—of God:

> Then, turning to the beauty of nature, man takes pleasure in the variety of animals, plants, minerals. . . . Then, leaving the elementary region, he addresses his flight to heaven, on

the wings of contemplation, in order to see the splendor, the
beauty, the power of celestial lights. . . . Then he is ravished
by an admirable pleasure, accompanied by a perpetual desire
to find the First Cause, Him who was author of so beautiful
a masterpiece: when he has attained this purpose, he stops
there the course of his contemplations, seeing that He is infinite and incomprehensible—in essence, in grandeur, in power,
in wisdom, in goodness. . . .[75]

But the Florentine Neoplatonists found their most characteristic
point of departure for the ascending soul, not in the sight of the
goodness in a variety of created things, but in that of a beautiful
woman. This concept, hinted at in Benivieni's exposition, was so
developed by Bembo and Castiglione that it became the cardinal
feature of that Renaissance courtly religion of love and beauty to
which I have referred. Bembo's brief summary in *Gli Asolani*, "Love
is one, and from particular love we pass to love that is ideal, and
from the ideal to love that is divine,"[76] when read in its context,
expounds this idea; in his role of the prophet of this religion in
Castiglione's *Courtier,* he develops his theme in details which were
destined to enchant court society in Italy, France and England.

Although the participation of a beautiful woman is properly lacking in Ficino's and Pico's theologico-philosophical accounts of the
ascent of the soul, and barely implied in Benivieni's relatively austere version, there is clearly, in all other respects, a direct line of
succession from these to the versions of Bembo and Castiglione,
and to Michelangelo's lyrics to Vittoria Colonna. There are other
contributory factors, of course, in the later writers' cult of beauty
and love. Moreover, the exact terms that describe the process that
the soul undergoes may vary from individual to individual; most
of the important details remain similar.

Basic among these details are the ideas that love is a desire of
the beautiful, that nothing can be loved which is not known, and
nothing known attained except through the exercise of the will.
All the way from the first particular object loved to the final union
with God, love seeks the beautiful; mind seeks knowledge; will
seeks the good. The accounts of Pico and Bembo should be sufficient
to illustrate these terms clearly. Pico's version reads:

As Desire generally follows Knowledge, so several Knowings
are annexed to several desiring Powers. We distinguish the
Knowing into three Degrees, Sense, Reason, Intellect, attended
by three desiderative Virtues; Appetite, Election, Will. Appetite is in Brutes, Election in Men, Will in Angels. . . . Thus

it appears, that corporeal Objects are desired, either by Sensual Appetite, or Election of Reason inclining to Sense; Incorporeal by Angelick Will, or the Election of Reason, elevated to intellectual Heights.[77]

And Bembo (in the *Courtier*):

Love is nothing else but a certaine coveting to enjoy beautie: and for so much as coveting longeth for nothing, but for things known, it is requisite that knowledge goe evermore before coveting, which of his owne nature willeth the good, but of himselfe is blind, and knoweth it not. Therefore hath nature so ordained that to every vertue of knowledge there is annexed a vertue of longing. And because in our soule there be three manner waies to know, namely by sense, reason, and understanding: of sense ariseth appetite or longing, which is common to us with brute beastes: of reason ariseth election or choice, which is proper to man: of understanding by the which man may partner with Angels, ariseth will.[78]

But, it may be complained, in what way does such a concept of the soul's pursuit of God differ from that of Aquinas? In him, too, we will find that the understanding seeks the truth of God as the final object of contemplation and the will His goodness as the final object of love. Or, in the words of Hooker:

Capable we are of God both by understanding and will: by understanding, as He is that sovereign Truth which comprehendeth the rich treasures of all wisdom; by will, as He is that sea of Goodness whereof whoso tasteth shall thirst no more. As the will doth now work upon that object by desire, which is as it were a motion towards the end as yet unobtained; so likewise upon the same hereafter received it shall work also by love.[79]

The apparent identity of the concepts of Aquinas, Hooker, Pico, and Bembo holds good in general. That parallelism of the contributions of will and intellect in the approach to God, dramatically presented by Dante in the speeches of Aquinas and Bonaventura in the eleventh and twelfth cantos of the *Paradiso*, and summarized in the thirteenth, is explicitly set forth by the major figures of Italian Neoplatonism: Ficino, Pico and Benivieni (especially in their early work); Bembo and Castiglione. Pico and Benivieni, in particular, stress the guiding and superior role of the intellect, both in the ascent and the final union with God.

Yet there is another side to the picture. Even as early as his commentary on Benivieni's *Ode*, Pico suggests that there is a last mystic step—or rather a final spring completely away from the ladder —which bears no similarity to Aquinas' insistence upon the intellectual, the contemplative nature of the final act of knowledge of, or union with, God.[80]

The relative roles of "intellectus" and "voluntas" in the medieval Christian version of the ascent of the soul to God have constituted the ground for an almost literally unending debate, both then and —for scholars—ever since. The two major positions, whether considered as opposing ones, or merely complementary ones, are most often attributed to Thomas Aquinas and Duns Scotus. Aquinas is usually considered to have given priority, in the ascent and in the final act, to the role of *intellectus* or knowing; Scotus is usually alleged rather to have emphasized *voluntas* in the ascent and love in the final act. Regardless of the merits of this particular argument, it is a safe generalization to say that those whom Hulme has termed "the legalists" defended the first position; "the mystics," the second.[81]

And despite other tendencies in their early writings, the Renaissance Neoplatonists increasingly leaned toward the second view. Ficino, Pico and Benivieni all eventually turned, partly under the influence of Savonarola, to a more intensely personal religion. Pico's letters to his nephew, for example, show a fideistic mysticism which undoubtedly influenced that of Gianfrancesco. Indeed, much earlier, addressing Poliziano in *De Ente et Uno*, Pico had recognized the superiority of the path of love to that of the intellect in approaching God, but as yet had felt himself incapable of pursuing it:

> But see, my Angelo, what madness possesses us. Love God while we are in the body we rather may than either define or know him. By loving Him we more profit ourselves, have less trouble, please Him better. Yet had we rather ever seeking Him by the way of speculation never find Him than by loving Him possess that which without loving were in vain found.[82]

And by 1492 he writes to Gianfrancesco, exhorting him, in an exclusive emphasis, to "exhibit ye whynges of the love of God whyle thou laborest to hevenwarde. . . ."[83]

Again, Benivieni's *Advice of Man to his Soul*, is in the strict Christian mystical tradition, and although it contains echoes of his earlier work, there is a new emphasis in such expressions as "without ravishment it [the visible creation] cannot be contemplated," and "He is that blessed Spouse who is in thee, and outside of thee; for Him thou dost ever burn ardently, and when thou wilt, mayst enjoy Him—O unheard of Love!"[84]

This is very close to the tone of Augustine in his final period, when he turned almost exclusively to the love of God—a tone and an attitude which declared substantially, "Love and do what you will."[85] And it is precisely this source which P. O. Kristeller points to as influential on Ficino: "The parallelism of intellect and will and the insistence on the superiority of will and love over intellect and knowledge, which is so characteristic of Ficino's later period in particular, goes back to Augustine. . . ."[86]

However, influential as Augustine and the Christian mystical tradition, with their stress upon love and will, were on the later work of Ficino, Pico and Benivieni, one need not wait for this development to find an emphasis upon love and will in their writings. If any final proof is needed to show that these concepts were inherent in their doctrinal Neoplatonism *per se*, it is available in the even more marked concern with will and love in the writings of other members of the Florentine group—such men as Landino and Lorenzo de' Medici.

One particularly significant way in which the whole group broke away from traditional Christian mysticism has been cited by Joseph B. Collins: "The formula of the Christian mystic: Man—Christ—God gives way to the Platonic 'ladder of love.' There is an idealized human, not divine, love; and the charity of Christ, repentance for sin, and the contemplation of a *personal* God are entirely lacking."[87]

These differences from Christian mysticism may be summarized as follows: (1) The Neoplatonists rejected the need for an intermediary between man and God; (2) they emphasized the dignity of man, not his frailty; (3) they gave a prominent place to the efficacy of individual effort; (4) they looked to a final absorption into a transcendent Absolute, rather than a final contemplation of a personal God. The first three points emphasize a dynamic ideal, the fourth a superficially paradoxical concept of ultimate rest.

In the first place, to Ficino, the divine principle is within man; God's purpose in becoming man was that man might become God:

> Therefore, because God has joined Himself unto man without intermediary, it behoves us to remember that our felicity consists in being turned to Him, so that without intermediary we may cleave unto God.[88]

This rejection of an intermediary is also to be found in Pico.[89]

Hence the soul of man seeks God always, and in everything, and cannot be satisfied until it finds him. Yet God has left him free; he may exercise his own will to turn either to things below or above him. In Ficino, this concept of freedom at times threatens to break the traditional bonds of man the microcosm, who has in him all the constituent elements of the macrocosm, and hence is free to develop the godlike in him or the bestial (in which case, paradoxically, he loses his freedom)—and to become the expression of an autonomous freedom of the will. He declares that man "strives to be everywhere as God is. He strives also to be like God in being forever"—says that no bounds can restrain him, and that he seeks always to bear rule and to be honored. He resents any form of servitude and degradation, however slight the shame.[90] This concept of the God-in-man has a very different tone from Chapman's "a good lifes godlike grace."

There is an almost unique combination of dignified exaltation and vigorous athleticism in the imagery in which Ficino expresses this central thesis in one of his letters:

> Know thyself, O divine race, clothed in mortal raiment; strip thyself, I beseech thee, in so far as thou canst; nay more, I say, with thine utmost endeavour separate the soul from the body, and reason from the affections of the senses. Then straightway thou shalt see the pure gold freed from the defilements of earth, thou shalt see the clean air when the clouds are dispersed; then, believe me, thou shalt reflect thyself as a sempiternal ray of the divine sun. . . . Yet thou believest thyself to be in the lowest part of the world, because thou seest not thyself soaring above the heavens, but only thy shadow, the body, in a lowly place. It is as if . . . a bird, flying through the air, should think itself on earth while it sees its shadow flying on the ground. Therefore, forsaking these shadows, return unto thyself, for thus shalt thou return unto greatness.[91]

Yet a considered study of Ficino's work leaves the conviction that the God-in-man element in his thought is not so daring as the imagery and the emotional overtones. Professor Kristeller's definitive book-length study indicates an increasing emphasis in the later years on the volitional element, the roles of will and love, but there is no overt final statement of the autonomy of the will.

This we find rather in Pico—if one accepts Ernst Cassirer's persuasive interpretation of his ideas. Professor Cassirer insists that Pico did not accept the conventional "mixtum compositum" sense of man the microcosm when he uttered the famous words he attributed to God: "I have given thee neither a fixed abode nor a form that is thine alone nor any function peculiar to thyself, Adam, to the end that, according to thy longing and according to thy judgment, thou mayest have and possess that abode, that form, and those functions which thou thyself shalt desire."[92]

It is not man's *similarity* to the world (microcosm-macrocosm), Cassirer points out, that Pico is expounding—but his *difference*. No longer are we confronted with the idea that God has created man in His own image, but that man's resemblance to God must be attained entirely by his own creative capacity and efforts.[93] The limiting principle of the Christian humanist's concept of the only true liberty being the liberty to do good, which is both God's will for man and man's distinctive good, is broken down and replaced by a really autonomous conception of the will, an *unlimited* freedom of choice.

Man, Cassirer believes Pico to have thought, really stands higher than "the angels and the heavenly intelligences"—in the sense that he is not enclosed from the beginning *within the limits of a determinate being*. Man possesses his perfection only as he achieves it for himself *independently*, and on the basis of a *free* decision.[94] Despite the other obvious discrepancies, this concept of freedom makes the will as autonomous as in Sartre's Existentialism.

Finally, Cassirer stresses the fact that Pico says God "accorded to Man the function of a form not set apart," and declared to Adam, " '*The nature of all other things is limited and constrained within the bounds of laws prescribed by me:* thou, coerced by no necessity, *shalt ordain for thyself* the limits of thy nature in accordance with *thine own free will, in whose hand I have placed thee.*' "[95] Man is *really free* to sin or do any of many goods, as free as the Pelagian heresy would have him; and Pico rejects *totally* the traditional theologian's view that Adam's fall has lost man his complete freedom of choice. Cassirer finds in his position a concept of man's "almost unlimited power of self-transformation."[96]

Pico's own words make a strong case for this interpretation. In his oration "Of the Dignity of Man," he does not follow any established pattern of what is man's *peculiar* good, but offers a variety of goods, with the implication that one is not necessarily better than another. And then he concludes this passage with the words: "If, happy in the lot of no created thing, he [man] withdraws *into the center of his own unity*, his spirit made one with God in the solitary darkness of God who is set above all things, he shall surpass them all."[97] What is this, if not a statement of the identification of man with God, of man *as* God?

Appealing to various occult sources, Pico repeats again and again such phrases about man as that "he himself moulds, fashions and changes himself,"[98] or "Who will not admire this our chameleon? And who could more greatly admire *aught else whatever?*"[99] And again, "Man has no semblance that is inborn and his very own. . . ."[100] No wonder that the authorities, shocked at his proposition, did not allow him to hold the proposed disputation.

As for the "ascent," he describes it in terms that break all precedents for the expression of will that knows no restraint in its determination almost literally to storm the ultimate citadel:

> Let a certain holy ambition invade our souls, so that, not content with the mediocre, we shall pant after the highest, and (since we may if we wish) toil with all our strength to follow it. Let us disdain earthly things, strive for heavenly things, and finally, esteeming less whatever is of the world, hasten to that court which is beyond the world and nearest to the Godhead. There, as the sacred mysteries relate, Seraphim, Cherubim, and Thrones hold the first place; let us, incapable of yielding to them and intolerant of a lower place, emulate both their dignity and their glory. Since we have willed it, we shall be second to them in nothing.[101]

The arrogance of Pico's denial of limit, as applied to man, is indisputable. He goes far beyond the other Florentine Neoplatonists[102] in his refutation of the principle of limit—both in terms of value and reality—in all three of its major meanings for the Christian-classical tradition: finality and finiteness, harmony and moderation (since the individual is not working for the good of the whole, but for himself), degree and gradation. Man's nature (and hence "good") is not established, but indeterminate, roving and almost infinite; he need not limit his liberty to a specified kind of liberty, under the guidance of God's demonstrated will and right reason; he does not have to accept a determined position in the hierarchy of being. He may turn where he will, in accordance with the autonomy of his will. He is literally a god-man.

With Pico, we find ourselves at the opposite pole from Luther and Calvin. If one attributes free choice to man, Luther has solemnly warned us, "one attributes to him nothing less than divinity itself." Pico has anticipated his logic impeccably, although with diametrically opposed conclusions—for where Luther finds the greatest sacrilege, he finds the greatest privilege, and the true nature of man.

Nor, I think, does the point that the spirit of this exaltation of man differs from that of the middle-path Christian humanists require laboring. From Erasmus to Justus Lipsius, the middle-path humanists, concentrating upon a horizontal ethical ideal, a way of living, invariably exalt Reason's role and accede to the principles of limit. On the other hand, the Neoplatonists—and especially Pico —accenting rather a vertical metaphysical ideal, a way of returning to true being in God, show clearly a greater imaginative sympathy for the Will, and sometimes lay an exclusive emphasis upon it. . . .

There are a few members of the Medici circle who state outright the supremacy of will and love, in the ascent to God, more consistently, if less boldly, than Pico. Landino, in the second book of his *Quaestiones Camaldulenses*, suggests that God is to be known through the will, rather than the intellect. He remarks:

> But since in truth we will not attain to the divine essence by knowing alone, but also will desire it and love it and will enjoy it by loving—all of which are founded in the will—it is rightly questioned among the theologians, whether so great a matter should not be entrusted to the will, rather than to the understanding itself.[103]

Lorenzo de' Medici, in his *Altercazione,* which owed much to the second book of the *Quaestiones*, says that the approach to God may be made either through the intellect or the will, which are the two wings of the soul. However, the will (which he equates with desire or love), is the more perfect and will receive a richer reward, for true knowledge of God is impossible.

> As he who hateth God commits more great
> And certain fault than who discerns him not,
> So who most loves Him wins the loftiest state.[104]

Love makes no mistakes, but pride may attend speculation and blind the seeker. Moreover, we desire to know the good that we may possess and enjoy it. While knowledge does not necessarily imply joy, joy does imply sight and understanding. It alone is desired for its own sake, and our minds will become divine "amando Deo, non sol vedendo."

Indeed, for Lorenzo, any intellectual contemplation to which man is able to rise is bound to be dulled and bound by the soul's own limitations. He makes absolute the attitude which Pico propounded in *De Ente et Uno*, but confessed he could not follow:

> Thus fares the soul when God it strives to know;
> In its own bounds it cribs His amplitude
> And God into itself contracteth so. . . .

> Even as through a cloud we contemplate

> The chasm of His divine infinity,
> Though hard the mind's eye strive to penetrate.
> But let us love Him well and perfectly;
> Who knows God, God into himself doth draw,
> Loving, we soar to His high majesty.[105]

It is such an emphasis as that of the last line which we almost invariably identify as the very keynote of Florentine Neoplatonism. Its peculiar quality is nowhere more beautifully communicated than in some of Michelangelo's lines:

> Oh, Love, not mortal is thy loveliness!
> There's not a face among us to come nigh
> The image in the heart which thou dost high
> Lift on strange wings, and with strange fire possess

and:

> Though mortal that first blow to me, it brings
> A message, sent me on behalf of Love,
> That bids "Love on, flame on! For none can move
> From earth to heaven save upon such wings."[106]

The deepening of understanding (the rational element) is of course implicit in each step of the ascent. Yet it is inevitably the "strange wings" of love that dominate the concept of the ascent. And it is love again—love and rapture— which dominates the Neoplatonic imagery in the treatment of the higher reaches of the approach to God. While Benivieni invokes the priority of "knowing," it is love that is central to his description of the mingling with other blessed spirits in the eternal world of ideas, a domain

> Where every thought without disguise is known
> As hearts do each the other penetrate,
> In each one love, one mind, one will alone
> One love that lives in love by love create.
> One love that loves rejoicing in its own;
> Loving, enjoys, of love insatiate.[107]

And Bembo prays, in the quaint wording of Sir Thomas Hoby's translation of the *Courtier*:

> Make us dronken with the bottomlesse fountaine of contentation, that alwaies doth delight, and never giveth fill, and that giveth a smacke [taste] of the right blisse unto who so drinketh of the renuing and clene water thereof.[108]

There is a tendency (manifest, for example, in Benivieni's and Castiglione's most famous passages) either to draw a reticent silence

over the final union with God, or to speak of it in mystical symbols. Bembo speaks of "the great fire in the which . . . Hercules
was buried on the toppe of the mountain Œta," and of "the fiery
bush of Moses."[109] Benivieni tells how

> the secret fire
> Which is the abysm of Thine infinite
> Darkness burns on, hid from our eyes' desire.[110]

Yet when the Neoplatonists do come closer to a definition, two
conclusions are clear: first, that the union is a compete absorption
in or assimilation to God, and secondly, that it is depicted primarily
as an act of love that brings a final peace—"a voluntary death."
For Ficino, "beatitude is that supreme act of love by which the
human soul gives itself to God and so becomes assimilated to
Him."[111] He declares,

> It is indeed possible now to know Him perfectly. For truly
> it is possible and easy to love what is known in any way. Those
> who know God please him not unless knowing Him they love
> Him; and this is not because they know but because whoso
> loveth is loved of God.[112]

And the reference made by Bembo to those "fathers of older time,
whose soules . . . thou [Love] didst hale from the bodie, and
coupledst them with God"[113] is reminiscent of those other words
of Ficino's—"so that without intermediary we may cleave unto God."
    The debt of these passages to the Plotinian concept of the union
as complete contact with, and a final haven in, the Absolute is
obvious. He, too, had conceived of the final experience as a mystical ecstasy which completes the "deification" of the soul:

> He who has seen It, knows whereof I speak. . . . The soul
> is anxious to be free, so that we may attach ourselves to It by
> the whole of our being; no part of it not touching God. Then
> it will be possible for the soul to see both God and herself
> divinely, and she will see herself illumined, full of intelligible
> light; *or rather, she will be light itself*—pure, unfettered, agile,
> become a God *or rather being a God,* and wholly aflame.[114]

Ficino speaks of this final *touch* of the soul with God, just as
Pico echoes Plotinus' non-Platonic concept of a special "gift" needed
by the soul—"a presence better than knowledge," better even than
"intellectual perception. . . ."[115]
    Once again the principle of limit is involved. For these descrip-
tions of the final act, couched in terms of a "supernatural erot-

icism," are characteristic of monistic mysticism, and heretical in the degree to which the soul is identified with God Himself.[116] Orthodox Christian (or pluralistic) mysticism always keeps the soul "distinct from the Divine Being in its substantial entity,"[117] and thus—by this distinction or separation, even in union—preserves the principle of limit in man, and in his soul's relation with God. . . .

Yet if most of the Neoplatonists find at once an ecstasy and a peace in the final absorption in God at their end of their strenuous ascent, there is one Counter-Renaissance figure who, although imbued with many of their ideas, conceives of the search as endless —comes close to making the activity the end in itself. Miss Robb has said that "the peculiar character of Florentine Neoplatonism appears in nothing more than in its insistence on man's power to seize reality by his own efforts; in its endeavour, one might almost say, to take the kingdom of heaven by force."[118] This statement seems to me to render much more exactly the flavor of Giordano Bruno's thought and imagery.

Yet for him, the storming of "heaven" continues indefinitely. His concepts of an infinite God and an infinite universe are matched by his conviction that it is right that the infinite should be infinitely sought. The concept of limit—as finality, completeness or finiteness —is utterly foreign to him.

Thus, in Gl'Eroici Furori (1585), he asserts that man's true good lies in the mastery of nature. Mind is immanent in all things, and beyond the knowledge of this Mind, or nature, human science cannot go. No doubt a Transcendent Mind lies beyond, but it is unknowable by men except though faith.

There are, Bruno maintains, two kinds of truth. The one is supernatural, and may be revealed by prophets, who are passive vessels of truth. The other is that pursued by men of science—active seekers after truth. In their "heroic madness" lies their superiority to other men.

Bruno's appropriation of a series of Neoplatonic love sonnets (of Tansillo's and others) for his own purposes suggests the way in which he transforms the traditional Neoplatonic doctrine into a pattern of his own. These sonnets he makes into allegories of the search for truth. The lady represents knowledge, which (since infinite) may not be fully possessed. The seeker seeks an end where there is none; he finds joy in the quest, despite no possibility of fulfillment.[119]

To be sure, Bruno thinks of the everlasting quest of the men of science as the speculative life. Its goal is truth, or the knowledge of nature. Yet it is hardly a scientific ideal. One is tempted to describe his "heroic madness" in the words of Guido Cavalcanti about love:

> Its essence is whenas the passionate will
> Beyond the measure of natural pleasure goes;
> Then with repose forever is unblest.
> .   .   .   Yet chiefly manifest
> Thou shalt observe it in the nobly wise. . . .[120]

An equally interesting deviation is observable in the writings of a much more traditional Neoplatonist, Marguerite of Navarre. Consider, for example, that exposition of "perfect love" by Parlamente (whom M. Lefranc calls the "porte-parole de Marguerite") in the nineteenth tale of the *Heptameron.*

> "I call perfect lovers," replied Parlamente, "those who seek in what they love some perfection, be it goodness, beauty, or charming demeanor; who aim always at virtue, and whose hearts are so noble and so spotless that they would rather lose their lives than devote them to low things forbidden by honor and conscience; for the soul which is created only to return to its sovereign good, so long as it is imprisoned in the body, does but long to arrive at that high destination."[121]

So far, this is good, if somewhat naïve, Bemboism. But at this point, Marguerite's Calvinism enters, with her use of the dogma of the Fall. For Parlamente continues,

> "But because the senses, which can give it views thereof, are obscured and carnal since the sin of our first parents, they can only present to it those visible objects which approach nearest to perfection."[122]

And the main outlines, while similar, from the time when "the soul rushes forth, and thinks to find in outward beauty, in visible graces, and in mortal virtues, the supreme beauty, grace and virtue," to its eventual discovery "that there is neither perfection nor felicity in the things of this earth," and its subsequent turning to "the true felicity, and Him who is its source and principle"[123]— introduce a Calvinistic note in the rejection of "the things of this earth" as bad, rather than "steps" toward the ultimate Good.

But it is at this point that Marguerite in effect denies that central tenet of the Neoplatonic creed—the dynamic concept of man raising himself to God by his own efforts. For she concludes,

> "Still, if God did not open the eyes of its faith, it would be in danger of passing from ignorance to infidel philosophy; *for*

> *it is faith alone that demonstrates and makes the soul receive*
> *that good which the carnal and animal man cannot know.*"[124]

M. Lefranc, who has established Marguerite's acquaintance with
the writings of Cusanus, points out the similarity to his doctrine that
faith is the condition of any final and intimate *rapport* with God.[125]
Yet although Calvin was no mystic, and unconcerned with any
"ascent of the soul" in the sense we have been considering, surely
it is partially Marguerite the Huguenot who is speaking here.

This supposition becomes a certainty in a later conversation in
the *Heptameron*—a conversation which focuses upon the pride of
reason. After a discussion of those "philosophers of past times" who
were utterly "possessed . . . with the belief that there is virtue
in vanquishing oneself," Parlamente declares,

> In truth, it is impossible to overcome ourselves by ourselves;
> nor can one think to do so without prodigious pride. . . .[126]

Oiselle strikes a completely Calvinistic note when she reminds
the company,

> Did I not read to you this morning that those who believed
> themselves wiser than others, and came *by the light of reason*
> *to know a God,* the creator of all things, and for having been
> vain thereof, and not having attributed this glory to Him to
> whom it belonged, and for having imagined that they had
> acquired this knowledge by their own labors, became more
> ignorant and less reasonable, I will not say than other men,
> but than the very brutes? In fact, their minds having run
> astray, they ascribed to themselves what belongs to God
> alone. . . .[127]

And Longarine completes the picture with a Calvinistic beatitude:

> Blessed are they whom faith has so humbled that they have
> no need of outward acts to make them conscious of the weak-
> ness and corruption of their natures.[128]

But Oiselle and Longarine are not Parlamente; in her (and Marguerite) the Platonist and Protestant are mostly harmoniously
merged. The effort of the soul is through willing and loving; yet
the process depends, too, upon the soul having "the eyes of its
faith" opened by God. Thus will (or love) and grace combine to
reach

> la perfection
> De ce sçavoir qui n'est par l'homme acquis
> Et qui seul est à l'homme bien requis.[129]

Moreover, Marguerite's last work reasserts the primacy of love almost exclusively. La Bergère "ravie de l'Amour de Dieu," indeed, goes well beyond Neoplatonism—to speak in the accents of the "Libertins Spirituels," that extreme Protestant sect which brought down upon itself the wrath of Calvin. To her, as to them, there is nothing in the world except Love; all the rest is only appearance and vanity. Thus to the declaration of "la Sage,"

> C'est un beau chemin de science,
> Que chascun doibt tant estimer . . .

la Bergère replies,

> Je ne sçay rien, sinon aymer,

and later

> Mon ame perir et noier
> Or puisse en ceste douce mer
> D'amour, où n'y a point d'amer;
> Je ne sens corps, ame ni vie,
> Sinon amour, et n'ay envie
> De paradis, ni d'enfer craincte,
> Mais que sans fin je sois estraincte
> A mon amy, unye et joincte.[130]

The unresolved confusion of human and divine love, peculiar to the "Libertins," is suggested as well in such lyrics as the one containing the lines:

> O bergère, ma mye,
> Je ne vis que d'amours. . . .
> Amour est ma fiance,
> Repoz de conscience,
> Ma force et passience,
> Ma foy, mon espoir, mon secours.

Yet the other, earlier, clearer note reappears, as when she writes,

> En Dieu tout seul, ma sœur, ton amour jecte . . .
> Et prens ton vol à la vie éternelle.[131]

What is perhaps most interesting about the currents which meet in Marguerite's work, and to a certain extent in a poem like Spenser's *Hymne of Heavenly Love,* is that they represent the converging of the "left and right wings" of the Counter-Renaissance.

With the exception of Pico, who at least for a while hoped for an ultimate reconciliation of Platonism and Aristotelianism, the Neoplatonists (or left wing) strove to replace the intellectualist synthesis of Thomas Aquinas with one which gave a larger place to concepts of love and will—culminating in their emphasis upon man's free will, upon the prominent roles of will and desire or love in the ascent to God, and upon that of love in a final intimate assimilation to God. The extreme Reformers (or right wing), on the other hand, denied completely the efficacy of man's own efforts as a means of salvation, and centered their attacks upon the Christian or classical humanists who exalted man's reason.

Both repudiated any intermediary between God and man—but with differing emphases. The left wing stressed man's capacity to attain a final union with God through his own efforts; the right wing denied any such powers at all, and granted him salvation only through God's grace and Christ's intercession. Yet, again, both of them turned with equal decisiveness from a vision which saw man's final happiness as the purely intellectual contemplation of God, or his mediate one as the obedience to God's laws, in accordance with Right Reason, on this earth. Both rejected the Christian-classical principle of limit—whether as value or reality—in terms of defined concepts of God's nature, and in terms of man's acknowledgment of his established limitations of degree, moderation, and ascertainable "end."

And still, just as the primarily opposed currents of skepticism and fideism eventually met, even in a single writer, in their common anti-Scholastic and -humanistic cause, so the equally divergent ideals of Neoplatonism and Calvinism finally converged, in the same common cause, in a figure like Marguerite of Navarre.[132]

2. ELIZABETHAN ROMANTICISM AND THE METAPHYSICAL ACHE

Certain prominent Renaissance Neoplatonists—particularly those of a synthesizing turn of mind—can properly be considered as belonging within the great European tradition of Christian humanism. Marsilio Ficino, for example, despite occasional divergent tendencies which we have noted, follows the tradition's consistent tendency to balance reason and faith, philosophy and theology. His thought is substantially Neoplatonic, just as that of Justus Lipsius and Guillaume Du Vair is Stoic—but within the eclectic ranks of the great tradition, this is no basic deterrent. In his cosmology, his concept of the nature of man, his treatment of ethics and politics, he reveals a fundamentally classicist mind, however romantic his idiom may sometimes be. And throughout his writings one finds the concept of limit, in most of its traditional meanings, developed and upheld.

But this, we have seen, was not the case with Pico, nor with other as widely differing Neoplatonists (or independent thinkers with a large admixture of Neoplatonism) as Giordano Bruno and Marguerite of Navarre. There are, in fact, a good many such figures who can quite properly be considered to have participated in the Counter-Renaissance. Whether such a participation is to be based on the particular figure's anti-intellectualism (revolt against the Scholastic mind), anti-moralism (revolt against the Christian humanist's ethical position), anti-legalism (revolt against the established system of universal law), or a combination of all these—the whole Renaissance Neoplatonic tendency was subversive to the Christian-classical principle of limit. The naturalistic empiricist, the mystic, the fideist, the advocate of volitionalism, the occult practitioner, the hedonist—all these, however dissimilar in other respects, contributed to the Counter-Renaissance's denial of limit; and among these were many individuals with Neoplatonic interests of one sort or another.

If we revert to the definitions in the prologue about the Elizabethans, we shall throw fresh light on this whole matter. The classicist was there defined as one who finds a congruence and established relation between the ideal and the empirically actual, between what should be and what is—both in terms of reality and value. Hence it should be clear that the classicist accepts and expounds the principle of limit in all of the three major meanings that we have explored.[133]

The romanticist, on the other hand, concentrates upon the discrepancy between the ideal and the empirical actuality, that which should be and that which is. It is almost always his distaste for the empirical actuality that he finds around him which causes him to retreat to one or another world of the ideal, although his repugnance may also extend to a particular established and accepted ideal. Therefore, failing to accept the relatedness and congruence of the ideal and the empirically actual, the Renaissance romanticist tended to repudiate the various status quo concepts of limits, which were all intimately tied in with that relatedness and congruence. Hence it is characteristic of Renaissance romanticists to espouse one or another of the attitudes and positions of the Counter-Renaissance —just as it is of the Counter-Renaissance naturalists (the pragmatists and radical empiricists) to whom, however, that relatedness and congruence are fictitious for the opposite reason, their total distrust of the ideal as either reality or value.

We have discussed the various ways in which the Neoplatonists, or Neoplatonist-tinged thinkers, of the Counter-Renaissance denied the concept of limit—in some cases, defied it—especially in its meanings of degree, moderation and finiteness. We have observed that one important half of Neoplatonism's province is that of the "ascent" —and this concept is in itself, of course, one form that the flight to the ideal from the empirically actual may take. Moreover, the *vertical* imagery of the ascent, the emphasis upon volition and longing, Pico's concept of man as a roving free agent, possessed of an autonomous will, and Bruno's heroic spirit pursuing infinitely the infinite—all these transcend the letter of Neoplatonic doctrine to imply a boldness, an assertiveness, a rebellious, aggressive spirit, that gives the lie to any sort of limitation.

Finally, since the Neoplatonism of the Counter-Renaissance variety was highly eclectic and not meticulously traditional in many of its attitudes, its endorsement of one or another kind of pantheism meant that it gave a value to nature (and matter) that was not characteristic of traditional Neoplatonism. This tendency, of course, was not concerned with the "ascent" side of Neoplatonic doctrine, but with that other side, of the "descent" and the Creative Goodness that overflowed itself to make of itself the universe.

We have seen how these conflicting sides of Neoplatonic doctrine were most characteristically resolved in the concept of a "coincidentia oppositorum." An extension of these conflicting values haunted many of the Elizabethans. By "extension" I do not mean to imply that these Elizabethans consciously and literally placed in opposition the two Neoplatonic "goods." I do not even mean that this conflict of theirs was in any way directly inherited from the Neoplatonism of the Counter-Renaissance. I mean only that the intellectual air some of the Elizabethans breathed was saturated with two concepts which must have grown largely, however deviously, from the two Neoplatonic emphases.

Those two concepts were that of the insatiable, roving, infinitely seeking spirit of man, and that of the goodness, the value, of the natural and material. Both denied limit: the first in its senses of degree, moderation, finiteness and finality for man, the second in its implication that the supra-sensible was not *necessarily* superior to the sensible—hence subverting established concepts of degree and gradation in the hierarchy of goods.

Moreover, they were incompatible. If the first set up a new ideal of man's nature, and especially his freedom, as *unlimited*, the second established a *finite* good in his life on earth that was inexorably ended for him, at least as an individual, by death. The obedient classicist (here the Christian humanist), accepting the rules of limit, could find moderate and mediate goods in life on earth, but at the same time knew that his ultimate good, his final end, lay in heaven. The romanticist whom I have been describing had no such consolation. It was the discrepancy between the ideal and actuality that dominated his thinking.[134] On the one hand, an assertive ideal of unlimited freedom, on the other the sense of transiency. And since most of these thinkers and writers among the Elizabethans applied the ideal of unlimited freedom to the limited goods of mortal life—especially the goods of sensuous love and beauty—they were really treating a naturalistic position with a romanticist attitude. The resultant conflict is everywhere apparent in Elizabethan literature.

Let us examine first the constantly recurring theme of the transiency of human life, and the mortality of beauty and love, together with the revelation of the degree to which the Elizabethans prized them.

This is the favorite burden of most Elizabethan sonnets: the mutability and decay of all things under the sun, and the ravages inflicted upon beauty and love by time. Spenser, Shakespeare, Sidney, Donne and all the rest celebrated it. But even at its most formal and exquisite, there is an underlying passion of grief or defiance or incredulousness that pricks the imagination and haunts the memory. Nor is the theme limited to the sonneteers; it appears and reappears throughout the whole of their literature; it finds its way into the most unexpected places.

When, for example, Chapman has Bussy d'Ambois, the most flamboyant and ebullient of all his swaggering heroes, declaim

> Man is a torch, borne in the wind; a dream
> But of a shadow, summ'd with all his substance . . .[135]

it is not in character. Besides, we are aware that this is only a paraphrase of a favorite classical image, one popular throughout the sixteenth century—Erasmus, to mention only one, used it before Chapman. On any score, here is an artificial moment. Yet the lines still haunt us; we are sure that the poet himself must have been moved when he wrote them.

Again, when Nashe, in one of his reformatory-polemical tracts, suddenly exclaims, "O, what is beauty more than a wind-blowne bladder, that it should forget whereto it is borne?"[136] we can remind ourselves as much as we choose that this is a conventional Elizabethan protest—this repudiation of transient earthly beauty.

Yet again it is the strength and passion of the voice and the image, rather than its formal meaning, that impresses us. And this impression is confirmed, not contradicted, when one remembers Nashe's description of the magnifico's wife in *The Unfortunate Traveller:* "A skin as slike and soft as the backe of a swan, it doth me good when I remember her."[137]

There is in fact no stronger single impression that one carries away from an imaginatively sympathetic rereading of the Elizabethans than this conviction of their immoderate and unregenerate love of the transitory world of sensuous beauty. Reject it, rail against it, abjure it as they will; make love to it, and then disclose its cruel fate at the hands of time, as Ralegh does in "Nature, that washed her hands in milk"—no matter, they cannot conceal its fascination for them. And they record that fascination with a gusto and freshness that suggest the proud and naïve belief that this world is their peculiar discovery.

Faustus repents, but Helen's lips have "sucke[d] forth [his] soule," and the reader's as well: the pious old man's injunctions to Faustus to repent do not remain with us as do Mephostopheles' words,

> Thinkst thou heaven is such a glorious thing?
> I tel thee tis not halfe so faire as thou
> Or any man that breathes on earth,[138]

Sidney has learned from "virtue . . . this better lesson":

> Within myself to seek my only hire,
> Desiring nought but how to kill desire.

Yet what we remember is the passion of the first lines of this sonnet:

> Thou blind man's mark, thou fool's self-chosen snare,
> Fond fancy's scum, and dregs of scattered thought;
> Band of all evils, cradle of causeless care;
> Thou web of will, whose end is never wrought;
> Desire, Desire! I have too dearly bought,
> With price of mangled mind, thy worthless ware. . . .[139]

As in the case of Nashe, the feeling breaks through and destroys the intent of the literal and reasoned meaning. Stella is formally renounced, yet her power over Astrophel was never greater; beauty may be "a wind-blowne bladder" when it forgets "whereto it is borne," yet the very force of the image convinces us of its hold upon the writer.

So, too, Spenser dutifully destroys the Bower of Bliss, but only after having expended on it all the inspired resources of his gift for sensuous imagery. The song which he adapted from Tasso's *Jerusalem Delivered* develops in all its nostalgic beauty the recurrent Elizabethan story of mutability and mortality:

> So passeth, in the passing of a day,
> Of mortall life the leafe, the bud, the flowre;
> Ne more doth flourish after first decay,
> That earst was sought to decke both bed and bowre,
> Of many a ladie, and many a paramowre.
> Gather therefore the rose, whilest yet is prime,
> For soone comes age that will her pride deflowre:
> Gather the rose of love, whilest yet is time
> Whilest loving thou mayst loved be with equall crime.[140]

And when he writes hymns to "Heavenly Beauty" and "Heavenly Love," replete with Christian-Platonic lore, because he has repented of his profane hymns to "Beauty" and "Love," he is betrayed in much the same fashion. We cannot forget that in the earlier "Hymne to Love" he declares outright, "For all that fair is, is by nature good."[141]

Or consider that sweetest singer of all the Elizabethans, Thomas Campion. He may extol "the man of life upright," who makes

> Good thoughts his only friends,
> His wealth a well-spent age,
> The earth his sober inn
> And quiet pilgrimage[142]

—and what haunts even the most felicitous of his verses is the realization that

> Fortune, honor, beauty, youth
> Are but blossoms dying;
> Wanton pleasures, doting love
> Are but shadows flying.[143]

"Earth," he admits, is

> but a point to the world, and a man
> Is but a point to world's comparëd centure;

and he asks,

> Shall then the point of a point be so vain
> As to triumph in a seely point's adventure?[144]

Campion's general answer to the question will surprise only those to whom the Elizabethans are unfamiliar:

> My sweetest Lesbia, let us live and love,
> And though the sager sort our deeds reprove,
> Let us not weigh them.

He reminds her that

> soon as once set is our little light
> Then must we sleep one ever-during night.

Only

> fools do live, and waste their little light,
> And seek with pain their ever-during night.[145]

And so, in "Hark, all you ladies that do sleep!" he brings Proserpina's message:

> All you that love, or loved before,
>   The fairy queen Proserpina
> Bids you increase that loving humor more;
>   They that yet have not fed
>   On delight amorous,
>   She vows that they shall lead
>   Apes in Avernus.[146]

When to her lute Corinna sings of sadness, the poet's heart may break, but the dying blossoms and the flying shadows are of the world he loves and celebrates most convincingly. As in the sonnets of Shakespeare and Spenser and Sidney, so in these delicate lyrics the transiency of earthly beauty and love but increases their power and heightens their value.

In more forthright and prosaic terms, this devotion to the sensuous values of a mortal world may be explicitly naturalistic—as in Harvey's famous letter to Spenser, in which he discusses fashions in moral philosophy, and advocates right out the indulgence of appetite:

> To be shorte . . . your greatist and most erronious suppose is that Reason should be mistrisse and Appetite attend on her ladiships person as a pore servante and hand mayden of hers. Nowe that had bene a probable defence and plausible speache a thousande yeares since. There is a variable course and revolution of all things. Summer gettith the upperhande of wynter, and wynter agayne of summer. . . .[147]

But more often the Elizabethan recognizes formally the principle of limit and the authority of traditional classical values—the governance of reason and the subservience of passion and appetite—while at the same time admitting his susceptibility to their reversal, and frequently exalting romantically that which has traditionally been suspect or—unless held in check—even evil. So Greville's chorus of priests in *Mustapha* describes the conflict between the accepted rational law of nature and that other law of nature which they feel

within themselves—a law rooted in no dogma, but in the unruly
human constitution:

> Oh, wearisome condition of humanity,
> Born under one law, to another bound;
> Vainly begot, and yet forbidden vanity,
> Created sick, commanded to be sound.
> What meaneth nature by these diverse laws?
> Passion and reason self-division cause.
> It is the mark or majesty of power
> To make offences that it may forgive.
> Nature herself doth her own self deflower,
> To hate those errors she herself doth give.[148]

And the priests conclude, applying to their special condition the
general romantic principle of the discrepancy between the ideal
and the actual:

> We that are bound by vows and by promotion,
> With pomp of holy sacrifice and rites,
> To teach belief in God and still devotion,
> To preach of heaven's wonders and delights,—
> Yet when each of us in his own heart looks
> He finds the God there far unlike his books.[149]

But whether the individual poet's allegiance to sensuous beauty
and human love is explicit or only implied in tone and quality of
feeling, whether it is primarily romantic, or naturalistic with romantic overtones—one thing is certain. The whole intellectual climate stirred these men to a fresh and exuberant passion for the
material world, and to an uneasy skepticism about the orthodox
values that subordinated it to spiritual good, or even condemned
it outright. In the brassy and over-insistent scolding of a Marston,
the thunderous denunciation of the later Donne, the undisciplined
and willful aspiration of a Marlowe, and the sweet sensuousness of a
Spenser—in all these alike, this quality appears, however differently
expressed. Indeed, with many of the Elizabethans it seems as though
they felt a defiant need to deny the very truth that so often over-
shadowed their delight in the world of physical experience—the
knowledge that it must end, that the blossoms had to die and the
shadows slip away.

But this particular form of the general Elizabethan susceptibility
to the denial of limit is but one of many. Their literature is filled
with bold metaphysical imagery, hyperbole and exaggeration that
insist upon the impossibility of satiety. And it is here that the other
element—the bold and questing concept of man and his infinite

longing, in terms directly reminiscent of Pico and Bruno—enters the situation.

Thus the old Elizabethan Jack Donne, the insatiable seeker after certainty and yet an unanswerable skeptic, never wholly disappears in the Dean of Saint Paul's. His pursuit is of God now—

> But though I have found thee, and thou my thirst hast fed,
> A holy thirsty dropsy melts mee yett.[150]

Such a statement is in direct contradiction of the traditional Christian-humanistic view, which—from Thomas Aquinas to Richard Hooker—uses the idea of infinite longing in the human soul as proof of man's divine destiny, since such an infinite hunger can be satisfied only with an infinite object, which must be that God "which is our home."[151]

The boldness of Donne's assertion not only contradicts this orthodox attitude, but partakes of the flavor of Bruno's theme of heroic and infinite striving, never to be satisfied in man's experience and tending to become the goal-in-itself. The almost drunken ardor of Donne's search extends *beyond* God, and so can have no goal, no final satisfaction.[152] It is a very different expression of the spirit of Ralegh's passionate man's pilgrimage; and allowing for the utterly dissimilar temperaments of the two writers, it has much of the quality of aspiration to be found in those great lines which Marlowe gives to Tamburlaine:

> Nature that fram'd us of foure Elements,
> Warring within our breasts for regiment,
> Doth teach us all to have aspyring minds:
> Our soules, whose faculties can comprehend
> The wondrous Architecture of the world;
> And measure every wandring plannets course,
> Still climing after knowledge infinite,
> And alwaies mooving as the restles Spheares,
> Wils us to weare our selves and never rest . . .[153]

and in the vertical imagery of Faustus' defiant cry, "O Ile leap up to my God."[154]

The aspiration expressed in these passages articulates a *metaphysical ache* that spurns the ordinary goods of human life and the human soul, or extends them to extraordinary and excessive value. What is in Donne a never-to-be-satisfied longing of the soul; in Marlowe a delight in the infinite possibilities of the human mind (in the Tamburlaine speech), and an expression of repentance as passionate and willful as the most unregenerate sinner's defiance

(Faustus' line); in Ralegh an assertive exploration of the hills and plains of Heaven; and in a speech like Harry Hotspur's "pluck bright honour from the pale-fac'd moon," a deification of honor—all these, different as they are, have in common the expression of will and longing, the denial of limit in the nature of man, and an excessive insatiate emphasis upon some one value—variously certainty, knowledge, power, honor—that constitutes quite literally a revolt of the ego. And worthy to stand beside them in their extravagant ambitiousness are Francis Bacon's avowed purpose of taking all knowledge to be his province, and his proposal to build a new model of the universe.

Thus far we have investigated separately these two recurrent themes in the literature of Elizabethan romanticism—(1) the fascination of earthly love and beauty, the goodness of physical values, and the regret over their frailty and transiency, producing various reactions ranging from rage and disgust to the *carpe diem* theme; (2) the exalted or exultant expression of man's longing, vertical aspiration, autonomous free will—his metaphysical ache. While some expression of one or both of these points of view can be found (approvingly or disapprovingly stated) in the work of almost every Elizabethan, the pronounced romanticists (of one sort or the other) are Spenser, Campion, Sidney, Ralegh, Chapman, Donne, Bacon, Marlowe and—in one aspect of his nature—Shakespeare. There are other elements as strong in some of them—for example, in Bacon. As a philosopher of science, he is a naturalist. As a man and an impresario of science, he is a thoroughgoing romanticist. But they all, even when expressing classical or Christian-humanistic concepts, display the feeling, and speak in the idiom, of the romanticist.

Yet it is only in Marlowe and Shakespeare that we find the conflict between these two romantic themes or concepts treated extensively and explicitly. Marlowe's *romantic humanism* sets up the issue squarely in *Doctor Faustus:* on the one hand, Mephistopheles' declaration that heaven is "not halfe so faire as thou or any man that breathes on earth," and on the other, Faustus' despairing cry,

Yet are thou still but *Faustus*, and a man.[155]

The splendor of the ideal of the man-god is contrasted with the limitations of the actuality, the tribute to the beauty of man on earth with its and his transiency. One good asserts the value of natural man, the other of a supernatural urge within him.[156]

This conflict, this split, throws some light on the long-debated passage in *Tamburlaine*, beginning "Nature that fram'd us of foure

Elements. . . ." Why, scholar after scholar has asked, should Marlowe have written nine lines (quoted above) of matchless cosmic imagery, expressing an ideal of man's infinite search for knowledge, only to end them with the flattest anti-climax in literature?

> Untill we reach the ripest fruit of all,
> That perfect blisse and sole felicitie,
> The sweet fruition of an earthly crowne.[157]

One answer is, of course, that this is, to Tamburlaine the peasant, the most "perfect blisse" and "sole felicitie." But Marlowe is rarely so careful about psychological realism, and, moreover, Tamburlaine is not ultimately satisfied with an earthly crown. His defiant dismissal of limit (in the sense, first, of the social and political hierarchy that would forbid his becoming a ruler) finally extends even to threats against God. What is pertinent to our inquiry, at any rate, is that here again Marlowe combines the heroic fury and the vertical aspiration with a flat (in both senses) avowal of the primacy of *human* interests *on earth.* The spiraling search *upward* should end in God (by Neoplatonic standards, for example); instead it ends in the assertion of power on earth. The combination used in *Faustus* to produce defeat and despair is here given a different twist, to pronounce defiance.[158]

The metaphysical ache of the man-god to achieve infinite knowledge (Faustus), infinite power (Tamburlaine), infinite riches (Barabas in *The Jew of Malta*), is apparent in almost all Marlowe's plays. One can trace it as well in the characters and speeches of Mortimer in *Edward II,* Guise in *The Massacre at Paris,* and Dido in *The Tragedy of Dido.* In most cases, the protagonist comes eventually to grief, in obedient accordance to the demands of the *De Casibus* tradition, although only after it has been abundantly established that all Marlowe's sympathy and creative delight have been lavished upon him.

But this is not the case with Tamburlaine. He rages through Part I and most of Part II without a vestige of defeat—even his loss of Zenocrate and his disappointment in his son do not curb his arrogance or unlimited ambition. True, he is finally stricken down by death, but even in death his defiance and egotism are unabated. He maintains that God wants him for himself:

> In vaine I strive and raile against those powers
> That meane t'invest me in a higher throne,
> As much too high for this disdainfull earth.[159]

At the very moment he is making plans for his sons to complete his conquest of the world,[160] and he enjoins his son-successor, Amyras, "So, rayne my sonne, scourge and controlle these slaves."[161] As for himself, he goes to "glut" his "longings with a heaven of joy."[162] He denies and defies all the concepts of limit implicit in traditional ideas of the nature of the state, of man's political status, of ethics and true religion, and he is never really punished. He dies unrepentant and defiant, waiting to print the extension of his wholly materialistic ambition upon the very walls of Heaven.

To be sure, other Elizabethans seemed to share this defiance, but their expression of it was not so extravagant as Marlowe's. Most of them expressed it by applying the metaphysical ache to the most physical of subjects; in this way they tried to deny and "disprove" the very truth they so frequently and nostalgically celebrated: the transitoriness of physical beauty and love. The most obvious and formalized way in which they did this is well exemplified by those of Shakespeare's sonnets that develop the thesis that the poet will defeat "envious Time" by making this love and beauty immortal through his verse. But such a conceit is hardly satisfying to a lover of Elizabethan intensity, and it is in *Antony and Cleopatra* that Shakespeare provides the most convincing poetic expression of this longing to immortalize what is most mortal.

Worthy to stand beside Faustus' dream of infinite knowledge and Tamburlaine's dream of an infinite power that threatens to

> march against the powers of heaven,
> And set black streamers in the firmament,
> To signifie the slaughter of the Gods[163]

—is this tremendous love between the most generous but faulty of men and the woman who is called every synonym of whore that the English language then provided, by nearly every character in the play, including her lover.

The scholars who pedantically hold that *Antony and Cleopatra* is the old Aristotelian tragedy of a man betrayed and overcome through his "tragic flaw" are displaying only their own limitations of literal-mindedness. They have missed the whole imaginative *timbre* of the play, and have ignored the imagery that recurs again and again to insist upon the stature of these two most frailly human lovers. From the moment the play opens and Antony answers Cleopatra's

> I'll set a bourn how far to be belov'd

with

> Then must thou needs find out new heaven, new earth[164]

—they defy the traditional limitations of such a love.
  She says of Antony,

>   For his bounty,
>   There was no winter in't; an autumn 'twas
>   That grew the more by reaping. His delights
>   Were dolphin-like: they show'd his back above
>   The element they liv'd in[165]

—and Enobarbus of her:

>   Age cannot wither her nor custom stale
>   Her infinite variety. Other women cloy
>   The appetites they feed, but she makes hungry
>   Where most she satisfies; for vile things
>   Become themselves in her, that the holy priests
>   Bless her when she is riggish.[166]

  When Antony dies, Cleopatra declares,

>   Young boys and girls
>   Are level now with men. The odds is gone,
>   And there is nothing left remarkable
>   Beneath the visiting moon[167]

—and when both of them are dead, we are inclined to agree with
her.

  Images of vastness, superhuman images, are used again and
again, with no sense of incongruity on our part, to refer to one or
the other of them, or to their love.

>   Eternity was in our lips and eyes. . . .[168]

>   None our parts so poor but was a race of heaven. . . .[169]

>   Thy beck might from the bidding of the gods command
>   me. . . .[170]

>   O thou day o' th' world. . . .[171]

>   His face was as the heav'ns, and therein stuck
>   A sun and moon, which kept their course and lighted
>   The little O, the earth.[172]

>   His legs bestrid the ocean: his rear'd arm
>   Crested the world. . . .[173]

And when Antony believes Cleopatra dead, after their quarrel and
the defeat of their forces, he will not admit that even death can
keep him from her:

>   I will o'ertake thee, Cleopatra, and weep for my pardon
and

> I will be
> A bridegroom in my death and run into't
> As to a lover's bed.[174]

So she, when Antony actually has died, expresses her decision to join him in similar terms—

> Show me, my women, like a queen. Go fetch
> My best attires. I am again for Cydnus,
> To meet Mark Antony[175]

—and that unforgettable speech,

> Give me my robe, put on my crown. I have
> Immortal longings in me . . . . .
>
> . . . .
>
> . . . . . Methinks I hear
> Antony call. I see him rouse himself
> To praise my noble act, I hear him mock
> The luck of Cæsar, which the gods give men
> To excuse their after wrath. Husband, I come!
> Now to that name my courage prove my title!
> I am fire and air; my other elements
> I give to baser life.[176]

Even Octavius, that coldest and least poetic and imaginative of men, pronounces the benediction as he looks at the dead Cleopatra:

> But she looks like sleep, as she would catch another Antony
> in her strong toil of grace.[177]

In a play shot through with such a situation, such characters, and such lines, to find only the prudent and moral injunction to subject passion and appetite to the reins of reason, if you would not go the way of all erring flesh, is to reveal a pitiful poverty of imaginative insight. Antony may be guilty of the worst kind of *hybris*, when he declares, embracing Cleopatra early in the play,

> Let Rome in Tiber melt and the wide arch
> Of the rang'd empire fall! Here is my space.
> Kingdoms are clay; our dungy earth alike
> Feeds beast as man. The nobleness of life
> Is to do thus; when such a mutual pair
> And such a twain can do't, in which I bind,
> On pain of punishment, the world to weet
> We stand up peerless.[178]

But by the end of the play he has in action proved his right to the conviction. Their love recalls that of Aucassin and Nicolette, of

Paolo and Francesca, of Launcelot and Guinevere, and of Tristan and Iseult. When Octavius says his final words over Cleopatra, it requires little "willing suspension of disbelief" to believe Antony's assertion,

> Where souls do couch on flowers, we'll hand in hand
> And with our sprightly port make the ghosts gaze.
> Dido and her Æneas shall want troops,
> And all the haunt be ours—[179]

That reunion in heaven of which Petrarch dreamed, and of which Ronsard had written to his Cassandre in a picture of the Elysian Fields which Shakespeare has Antony echo—

> Parmy le grand espace
> De ce verger heureux,
> Nous aurons tous deux place
> Entre les amouroux,
> Et comme eux sans soucy
> Nous aimerons aussi[180]

—has never been pictured more compellingly, with a stronger assertion of the absolute primacy of human love, than with these two. We can almost see them walking the meadows of their pagan heaven.

Yet there is also one element which sets them apart from the other great lovers of legend and literature. For we are constantly being reminded of their faults, their all too earthy humanness, their displays of jealousy and bad temper, their lack of faith in each other. Even when Cleopatra is preparing to die, and discovers that her waiting-woman, Iras, had already applied the asp, she thinks in terms of Antony's possible infidelity:

> If she first meet the curled Antony,
> He'll make demand of her, and spend that kiss
> Which is my heaven to have.[181]

But in their end they transcend these limitations, and their love is a genuine love of personalities—even of great ones. It too is transcendent—over the exclusively physical. Yet it is formidably bedded in the physical, and we are not allowed to forget it. For all of the eminence on which they live and move, they would be more at home—especially Cleopatra—in the company of Falstaff and Juliet's nurse than in that of the great legendary lovers. For like Falstaff and the nurse, they are of the earth earthy. And it is perhaps the greatest imaginative triumph of Shakespeare's genius that he can at once permit us to listen to the just accusation (but only half-truth) that Cleopatra is a whore and a bitch, and let us watch Antony lose his temper in disgraceful and childish irrationality—and at the same time convince us that they are magnificent human beings.

Again, while they belong unmistakably to the company of Elizabethan characters who transcend the feelings and characteristics of most human beings in their possession of a metaphysical ache that exceeds the bounds of ordinary aspiration and experience (characters like Hamlet, Hotspur, Tamburlaine, Bussy d'Ambois, Faustus), they alone among these find (in each other) a full resolution of the longing—and that in distinctively and exclusively human love. The Shakespeare who wrote "Love's not Time's fool, though rosy lips and cheeks within his bending sickle's compass come," satisfied with the grave and prudent envisioning of the poet's way to immortalize love, has changed to a man who can describe in action and dialogue a love that literally defies time, death and all other limiting obstacles. In *Antony and Cleopatra* the Elizabethan nostalgia over the transiency of physical beauty and human love is finally epitomized, given a defiant metaphysical value, and transformed from a finite to an unlimited good by the implication that it will continue forever in "le grand espace de ce verger heureux." It is the ultimate statement of Elizabethan romantic humanism.

Willard Farnham has said that the power of Elizabethan tragedy lies in its revelation "that the same mankind which has capacity for spiritual nobility must live and die in a physical world productive of grossness and horror. . . ."[182] The statement holds well enough, whether applied to plays involving the traditional god-beast alternatives in man's nature, or to Hamlet's dilemma. But the terms are altered in the literature we have just been studying to "the same mankind which has infinite dreams must live and die in a physical world that imposes set limitations upon him." The denial of these bonds of limit captured the imagination of the Elizabethan romanticists. But only Marlowe and Shakespeare took the conflicting elements of the predicament and drew them together, to comment on them with originality. Only Marlowe and Shakespeare harnessed man's infinite longing and restlessness to the earth-bound chariot of his nature. And only Marlowe and Shakespeare drove this strange vehicle through the heavens.

CHAPTER 6
FOOTNOTES

I.

1. Quoted by Lovejoy, *The Great Chain of Being*, 24.
2. Montaigne, III, 427–428. My italics.
3. Sir Thomas Elyot, *The Boke Named the Governour* (Everyman edition), 48.
4. For details on the sojourn of these Greeks, and for an account of their colleagues, cf. Nesca Robb, *Neoplatonism of the Italian Renaissance* (London, 1935), 46–54.
5. Cf. Robb, *Neoplatonism*, 59.
6. Jefferson Butler Fletcher, *The Religion of Beauty in Woman* (New York, 1911), 7. Cf. Gilson, *Sp. Med. Phil.*, 269, for confirmation of the fact that this concept of love really had its inception in the Renaissance.
7. Fletcher, *ibid.*, 23.
8. For a definitive and beautifully lucid treatment of the whole subject, see Prof. Fletcher's *The Religion of Beauty*.
9. Cf. Abel Lefranc, *Grands Écrivains Français de la Renaissance* (Paris, 1914), 84–85.
10. *Ibid.*, 105–106.
11. Cf. Léontine Zanta, *La Renaissance du Stoïcisme au XVIᵉ Siècle* (Paris, 1914), especially 72, 88.
12. Lovejoy, *Great Chain*, Chapter II, "The Genesis of the Idea."
13. *Ibid.*, 82–83.
14. *Ibid.*, 83.
15. *Enneads*, V, 2, 1; V, 4, 1: quoted by Lovejoy, *ibid.*, 62.
16. Lovejoy, *ibid.*, 83–84.
17. Chapman, *Poems*, 281 ("Eugenia," ll. 423–430). My italics.
18. Sir Philip Sidney, *An Apologie for Poetrie*, in *English Belles Lettres*, ed. by Oliver H. G. Leigh (London, 1901), 118–119. My italics.
19. *Ibid.*, 120–121.
20. See Chapter V (*supra*) for "love" in this sense as the poetic counterpart of "law"—as the regulative principle and sustaining force of the universe.
21. Fletcher, *Italian Renaissance*, 109.
22. Girolamo Benivieni, *Ode of Love*, translated by J. B. Fletcher, *ibid.*, 337.
23. Quoted by Fletcher, *ibid.*, 109.
24. *Enneads*, III, 3, 3: quoted by Lovejoy, *Great Chain*, 64.
25. Cf. Lovejoy, *ibid.*, 62, 64.
26. John Picus, Earl of Mirandula, *A Platonick Discourse, in Explication of a Sonnet*, by Hieronimo Benivieni, I, iv, v, vi, in Thomas Stanley, *The History of Philosophy* (London, 1743), 207.
27. Cf. Aquinas, *Sum. con. Gent.*, Book III, Part I, Chap. lxiv.
28. *Concl. nov.*, 49, quoted by Dulles, *Princeps Concordiae*, 74.
29. Pico della Mirandola, *A Platonick Discourse*, I, i: Stanley, *History of Philosophy*, 206.
30. Of course the God of Aquinas or Hooker was not limited, in the sense of not being omniscient or omnipotent. But he "worked" by intellect, law and established purpose; he "limited" himself voluntarily, in the interests of order. Cf. Hooker, *Of the Laws*, I, ii, 5, for a relevant account of the Creation.
31. For a discussion of the origin of this formula and exact references for, or

quotations from, many of the writers who have used it, see Lefranc, *Grands Écrivains*, 160 ff. For Plotinus' use of circle imagery, see particularly *Enneads*, VI, 9, 8. One of the most famous uses of the formula is, of course, Pascal's.

32. Quoted by Lefranc, *ibid.*, 178, 180, 181. My italics.
33. Rabelais, III, 13; V, 47. He is the only one in this tradition who uses the word "intellectual" ("intellectuelle").
34. Quoted by Lefranc, *Grands Écrivains*, 170.
35. Quoted by Lovejoy, *Great Chain*, 84. The Pseudo-Dionysius provides one of the best of the "circle of love" statements—one which contains almost all of the points of the discussion:

> For in all things, from the beginning and forever, Divine Love desires itself, moving as in an eternal circle, from goodness to goodness; proceeding in unchanging change, ever the same, ever according to the same, proceeding ever, and ever remaining (*De Divinis Nominibus*, IV, 14).

Cf. Charles W. Lemmi, *The Classic Deities in Bacon* (Baltimore, 1933), 71.
36. Gilson, *Sp. Med. Phil.*, 276.
37. Hulme, *Ren. and Ref.*, 525.
38. Ralegh, *Works*, II, 36 (*History of the World* I, 1, xiii). Cf. Marcellus Palingenius Stellatus, *The Zodiake of life*, translated out of Latine into English by Barnaby Googe (London, 1588), 62 (mistaken pagination for 51).
39. Lefranc, *Grands Écrivains*, 226.
40. Saurat, *Literature and Occult Tradition*, 8.
41. Cf. Arthur O. Lovejoy, "The Dialectic of Bruno and Spinoza," University of California Publications (Berkeley, 1904), Vol. I, 152.
42. *Ibid.*, 160.
43. Saurat, *ibid.*, 64.
44. Bruno, *De la Causa*, V, 290. Quoted by Lovejoy, *ibid.*, 162.
45. Tommaso Campanella, *Sonnets*, III: *The Sonnets of Michelangelo Buonarroti and Tommaso Campanella*, translated into English by John Addington Symonds (London, 1878), 121.
46. Quoted by Dulles, *Princeps Concordiae*, 89.
47. Lemmi, *Classical Deities*, 78, 79–80.
48. William Gilbert, *On the Magnet* (The Gilbert Club, London, 1900), 209. Quoted by A. J. Wolf, *A History of Science, Technology, and Philosophy in the 16th and 17th Centuries* (London, 1935), 668.
49. *De Magnete*, V, 12. Quoted by Edgar Zilsel, "The Origins of William Gilbert's Scientific Method," *JHI*, January, 1941, Vol. II, No. 1, 4.
50. Copernicus, *De Revolutionibus*, I, 10, quoted by Burtt, *Metaphysical Foundations*, 45.
51. Jean Bodin, *Le Théâtre de la Nature Universelle*, Traduict du Latin par M. François de Fougerolles Bourbonnais Docteur aux Arts & en Médecine (A. Lyon, par Jean Pillehotte, à l'enseigne du nom de Jesus, 1597), 830 ff. In the *Théâtre*, Bodin's Mystagogue does not accept Copernicus' theory, but he devotes a great deal of time to it, and treats it with some sympathy.
52. Burtt, *ibid.*, 47–48.
53. Brunschvicq, *Pythagorisme*, 9.
54. Quoted, *ibid.*, 18–19 (Letter to Constantin Huyghens).
55. See the full-page chart in John Dee, *A True . . . Relation*.
56. Quoted by Cassirer, "Mirandola" (I), 143.
57. Cassirer, *ibid.*, 142–143. My italics.

58. *Ibid.*, 137–138. While using very different terminology, Bruno, it seems to me, made similar distinctions. See *Concerning the Cause, the Principle, and the One*, translated by Josiah Royce and Katherine Royce, II, 1–23 (especially 14) : *Modern Classical Philosophers*, selections compiled by Benjamin Rand (Boston, 1908).

59. Cassirer, "Mirandola" (II) , 338.

60. *Ibid.*, 339.

61. *Ibid.*, 338.

62. Höffding, I, 92.

63. *Ibid.*, and Hulme, *Ren. and Ref.*, 526.

64. Cassirer claims a similar extension of this principle for Pico. Cf. "Mirandola" (II) , 336.

65. Bruno, *Concerning the Cause*, II, 14.

66. Cicero, *De Natura Deorum* (Loeb Library) , II, xxii, xxxi.

67. Seneca, *Of Benefits*, IV, vii.

68. Sir Philip Sidney, *The Countesse of Pembrokes Arcadia* (published 1590) , edited by Albert Feuillerat (Cambridge, 1912) , III, 10, 5.

69. Cf. Morley, *Agrippa*, I, 296.

70. For an illuminating discussion of these differences, see W. E. H. Lecky, *A History of European Morals* (New York, 1897) , I, 325–334.

71. Castiglione, *Courtier*, 319.

72. Collins, *Elizabethan Mysticism*, 116.

73. *Ibid.*, 112–118.

74. Lovejoy, *Great Chain*, 91–92.

75. Jean Bodin, *Republic*, 5; Atkinson, *Les Nouveaux Horizons*, 394.

76. Pietro Bembo, *Gli Asolani*, Book III. Quoted by Collins, *Elizabethan Mysticism*, 113.

77. Pico, *A Platonick Discourse*, II, iv: Stanley, *History of Philosophy*, 209.

78. Castiglione, *Courtier*, 303.

79. Hooker, *Of the Laws*, I, xi, 3.

80. Ernst Cassirer holds that "the true *Amor Dei* is for Pico *amor Dei intellectualis*," yet he also points out that Pico's final "suprasensible knowledge" of God is the "scientia abdita" of the Cabala (hence not "intellectual contemplation" in the sense of Aquinas) . [Cassirer, "Mirandola" (I) , 138, 144.]

81. Extensive discussions of the niceties of this argument may be found in De Wulf, *Phil. and Civ.*, and Gilson, *Sp. Med. Phil.*

82. *Giovanni Pico della Mirandola*, translated from the Latin by Sir Thomas More, edited with introduction and notes by J. M. Rigg, Esq. (London, 1890) , xxiv.

83. *Ibid.*, 44.

84. Girolamo Benivieni, *The Advice of Man to his Soul*, reprinted by Frederick M. Padelford in "Spenser's *Fowre Hymnes, A Resurvey*," *Studies in Philology*, XXIX (1932) 225–230. Cf. Collins, *Elizabethan Mysticism*, 118–120.

85. Zanta, *Renaissance du Stoïcisme*, 337. Cf. Bredvold, "The Religious Thought of Donne," 220–221.

86. Kristeller, "Augustine and the Renaissance," *International Science* (May, 1941) , 7 (reprint pagination) . See also Kristeller, *Phil. Mar. Ficino*, 256–258; 262–266; 269–274.

87. Collins, *Elizabethan Mysticism*, 113. My italics.

88. Quoted by Robb, *Neoplatonism*, 87. (See also *ibid.*, 67.)

89. Cf. Cassirer, "Mirandola" (II) , 344.

90. Cf. Robb, *Neoplatonism*, 73, 88.

91. *Ibid.*, 87.

92. Pico, *Of the Dignity of Man*, 348. Cf. Cassirer, "Mirandola" (II) , 320.

93. Cassirer, *ibid.*, 320–321.
94. *Ibid.*, 323.
95. Pico, *Of the Dignity*, 3: *JHI*, III, 3, 348. My italics.
96. Cassirer, *ibid.*, 328–329, 331.
97. Pico, *Of the Dignity*, 4: *JHI*, III, 3, 349. My italics.
98. *Ibid.*, 6: *JHI*, III, 3, 349.
99. *Ibid.*, 4: *JHI, ibid.* My italics.
100. *Ibid.*, 6: *JHI, ibid.*
101. *Ibid.*, 6–7: *JHI, ibid.*, 350.
102. For a comparison with Ficino's position, see Kristeller, *Phil. Mar. Ficino,* 388, 396, 398, 407 ff., and Don Cameron Allen, *The Star-Crossed Renaissance:* The Quarrel about Astrology and its Influence in England (Durham, N. C., 1941) , 20.
103. Robb, *Neoplatonism,* 98, 101. My translation from the Latin.
104. *Ibid.*, 101.
105. *Ibid.*, 127. I am wholly indebted to Miss Robb for her summary of Lorenzo's poem, as I am for all these translations from the Italian.
106. *Ibid.*, 269.
107. *Ibid.*, 134.
108. Castiglione, *Courtier,* 322.
109. *Ibid.*, 320.
110. Robb, *Neoplatonism,* 134.
111. *Ibid.*, 68.
112. *Ibid.*, 89.
113. Castiglione, *Courtier,* 322.
114. *Enneads*, vi, 9, 9. Quoted by Collins, *Elizabethan Mysticism,* 13–14. My italics. Cf. *Ennéades*, Vol. III, 559–560.
115. Collins, *ibid.*, 116. Cf. *Ennéades*, Vol. III, 542–543.
116. De Wulf, *Hist. Med. Phil.*, I, 211.
117. *Ibid.*
118. Robb, *Neoplatonism,* 69.
119. For a suggestion of the same sense of joy in the seeking for its own sake, see several of the passages quoted from Pico (*supra*) and—for Ficino— Kristeller, *Phil. Mar. Ficino,* 211–213. The concept is never explicit in their thought, however, in the way it is in Bruno's.
120. Guido Cavalcanti, *Ode of Love,* translated by J. B. Fletcher, *Italian Renaissance,* 335.
121. Marguerite, *Heptameron,* I, xix (Second Day) , 142.
122. *Ibid.*
123. *Ibid.*
124. *Ibid.* My italics.
125. Lefranc, *Grands Écrivains,* 154, 157. Observe, however, that Pico, too, spoke of a special "gift" needed by the soul, and there had been many mystics who had made the point.
126. Marguerite, *Heptameron,* II, xxxiv (Fourth Day) , 58.
127. *Ibid.*, 59. My italics.
128. *Ibid.*, 60.
129. Marguerite, *Les dernières poésies,* 208.
130. Marguerite, *ibid.*, 108 ff. (Comédie jouée au Mont-de Marsan) . Cf. Lefranc, *Grands Écrivains,* 217–218.
131. Quoted by Lefranc, *ibid.*, 224.
132. Some of these elements were actually anticipated, in combination, in the thought of Ockham. Moreover, as indicated earlier, the Florentine Neoplatonists who fell under the spell of Savonarola provide a partial parallel.

2.

133. Although almost all of the particulars in my treatment of classicism and romanticism are my own, the starting point for my exploration of these definitions was my reading of Arthur O. Lovejoy's "The Meaning of Romanticism in the History of Ideas," Vol. II, No. 3 (June, 1941), 262–278, in which he contrasts the one tradition's concern with finites with the other's emphasis upon the "infinite" or "unlimited." In the latter connection, he deals mostly with the 18th–19th-century romantic movement.

134. See the definitions and discussion in the Prologue to this book.

135. Chapman, *Bussy D'Ambois*, I, i, 18–19.

136. Nashe, *Works*, edited by R. B. McKerrow (London, 1904), I, 139.

137. Nashe, *The Unfortunate Traveller or the Life of Jack Wilton*, edited by H. F. B. Brett Smith (The Percy Reprints, No. 1, Oxford, 1920), 57.

138. Marlowe, *Doctor Faustus*, ll. 616–618: *Works*, 165.

139. Sidney, *Astrophel and Stella: Poetry of Eng. Ren.*, 120.

140. Spenser, *Faerie Queene*, II, xii, 75.

141. Spenser, "Hymne to Love," l. 139: *The Fowre Hymnes*, edited by Lilian Winstanley (Cambridge, 1930).

142. Campion, "The Man of Life Upright": *The Portable Elizabethan Reader*, edited by Hiram Haydn (New York, 1946), 661.

143. Campion, "What If a Day": *Eliz. Reader*, 657.

144. Campion, *ibid.: Eliz. Reader*, 657–658.

145. Campion, "My Sweetest Lesbia": *Eliz. Reader*, 658.

146. Campion, "Hark, All You Ladies": *Eliz. Reader*, 661.

147. Harvey, *Letter Book*, 213.

148. Greville, "Chorus from Mustapha": *Poetry Eng. Ren.*, 126–127.

149. *Ibid.*, 127.

150. Donne, "Holy Sonnets," XVII, 7–8: *Poems*, 301.

151. Cf. Gilson, *Sp. Med. Phil.*, 271–272.

152. Cf. Randall, *Mod. Mind*, 129–130.

153. Marlowe, *Tamburlaine* (Part I), II, vi, 869–877: *Works*, 32.

154. Marlowe, *Faustus*, l. 1432: *Works*, 192.

155. Marlowe, *Faustus*, l. 51: *Works*, 147.

156. I realize that it will be thought by many reprehensible to attribute to Marlowe sentiments expressed by Mephistopheles. Yet the lines ring with the author's most sonorous voice: it is impossible for an imaginative reader not to catch the delight in them.

157. Marlowe, *Tamburlaine* (Part I), II, vi, 878–880: *Works*, 32.

158. As indication that Marlowe was familiar with the Neoplatonic concepts and imagery, read the passage beginning, "What is beauty saith my sufferings then?" (*Tamburlaine*, Part I, V, ii, 1941–1971: *Works*, 60–61.) See also Roy Battenhouse's *Marlowe's Tamburlaine* (already cited).

159. *Tamburlaine* (Part II), V, iii, 4513–4515: *Works*, 135.

160. *Ibid.*, 4516–4518: *ibid.*

161. *Ibid.*, 4621: *Works*, 137.

162. *Ibid.*, 4620: *ibid.*

163. *Ibid.*, 4440–4442: *Works*, 133.

164. Shakespeare, *Antony and Cleopatra*, I, i, 16–17.

165. *Ibid.*, V, ii, 86–90.

166. *Ibid.*, II, ii, 240–245.

167. *Ibid.*, IV, xv, 65–68.

168. *Ibid.*, I, iii, 35.

169. *Ibid.*, I, iii, 36–37.
170. *Ibid.*, III, xi, 60–61.
171. *Ibid.*, IV, viii, 13.
172. *Ibid.*, V, ii, 79–81.
173. *Ibid.*, 82–83.
174. *Ibid.*, IV, xiv, 44–45; *ibid.*, 99–101.
175. *Ibid.*, V, ii, 227–229.
176. *Ibid.*, 283–284; 286–293.
177. *Ibid.*, 349–351.
178. *Ibid.*, I, i, 33–40.
179. *Ibid.*, IV, xiv, 51–54.
180. Pierre Ronsard, "Le Recueil des Odes," A Cassandre (1550) : George Wyndham, *Ronsard and La Pléiade*, with Selections from their Poetry (London, 1906), 120.
181. Shakespeare, *Antony and Cleopatra*, V, ii, 304–306.
182. Farnham, *Med. Her. Eliz. Trag.*, 424.

CHAPTER
7

THE COUNTER–RENAISSANCE AND THE DENIAL
OF LIMIT: THE NATURALISTS

I. NATURALISM AND INDIVIDUALISM

THE romanticists of the Counter-Renaissance denied, or at the least challenged, the Christian-classical concept of limit (in various of its meanings in relation to reality and value) in its traditional definitions of God, of nature, of man's status, goods or ends, and of his distinctive nature. Developing the discrepancy and split between the ideal and the empirical actuality—in a number of particulars —they characteristically concentrated upon the ideal, which they extended "upward" beyond its traditional defined significance. That is, their God was indefinable because "all" (in the Neoplatonists' sense of "le cercle rond") or all-powerful (in the Reformers' sense of the exclusive righteousness and inscrutable, incomprehensible will of God); their Nature was either "spiritualized" (the Neoplatonists and pantheists) or worthless, with all value removed to another, non-natural world (the Reformers); their concept of man contradicted or ignored the well-defined position, the peculiar good, and the established metes and bounds accorded to him by the Scholastics and the Christian humanists: they either recognized in him an autonomous free will which he would most representatively exercise to "scale the shining walls of heaven" (the Neoplatonists and their derivants), or found in him no strength at all to achieve his own salvation save that of faith (the presence of Jesus Christ in him, according to the Reformers). And while (unlike the former, which enhanced the dignity of man to a godlike role) the latter of these two attitudes seemingly debased man, it had an "upward" tendency, too—since it placed all man's good in salvation and another world. Moreover, it broke the "chains" of his traditional re-

sponsibilities to right reason and virtue. Although Luther denied
the human soul any private initiative, he too gave force to the conviction that it had no laws to follow:

> Nothing binds the human soul. To this view Martin Luther
> had repeatedly given utterance . . .

and while theologians could dwell upon the qualifications in his
position,

> Those who were avidly drinking the intoxicating wine of re-
> volt from the very lips of the embattled monk cared little for
> this.[1]

The denial of limit by the more philosophical *naturalists* of the
Counter-Renaissance is of a much soberer variety. The naturalist's
position, like that of the romanticist, finds a discrepancy, not a
congruence, between the ideal and the empirical actuality. But the
agreement ends at this point, for the naturalist, disbelieving in both
the reality and value of the ideal, which seem to him largely fictitious, will deal only with the empirically actual. Hence that very
repudiation of, or disbelief in, or indifference to, matter and un-
adorned nature which is characteristic of the romanticist, is matched
by an opposite strain in the naturalist, who is exclusively concerned
with matter and neutralized (non-spiritualized) nature. Yet he too
rejects the traditional and hypothetical "laws of nature," to find
out for himself its truths or facts.

To be sure, with the welter of cross-currents one finds in the
Counter-Renaissance, there are individual figures who demonstrate
both romantic and naturalistic tendencies: Bruno, Bodin, Agrippa,
Paracelsus, Cardan—to name only a few. But one trend or the other
is usually stronger, even in these; and such figures as Machiavelli,
Montaigne, Guicciardini, are almost exclusively naturalistic, with
a "downward" emphasis in their refutations of Christian-classical
concepts of limit. By "downward" I do not necessarily mean a
belittling tendency or an acceptance of "evil," but only that they
find truth and fact in nature and matter, which, according to the
traditional view, involved things corruptible and "changeable"—and
hence "lower" or "inferior."

For example—Bruno's "indifferenza della natura," in denying the
old up-and-down graded universe, predicated matter throughout the
universe, and hence "dropped down" to the level of the "inferior"
sub-lunar world, the eternal and unchanging trans-lunar world. Because the temper of his thought was split, and he also, on the

romantic side, held an animistic position, only one aspect of his thought illustrates the naturalistic attitude. With Montaigne and Machiavelli, the tendency is less complicated. Emphasizing man's origin in nature as an animal, they demonstrate the "downward" direction almost exclusively. Let us examine man, they say—whether as an individual, a political animal, or an entity in the entire scheme of things—solely on the merits of what we can *observe* him to be, without paying homage to any preconceived idea of what he should be, or to the rules and precepts of any established metaphysical or supernatural premise.

"Downward," then, I said, without any intention of belittling or predicating "evil." Yet, necessarily, when centuries of tradition had mostly endorsed the idea of man the established microcosm, the reaction of many who accepted, and of many who rejected, this new approach, was that this *did* mean a degrading of man. Their theological conditioning was too strong for them not to feel that the naturalistic position involved a debasing of the image of man. Hence, among those influenced, pro or con, by the naturalistic trend in the Counter-Renaissance, we will find many who, lacking the philosophic detachment of the innovators, did so interpret this shift in the attitude toward the nature of man—his origin, history, society and functioning.

The discussion of the "repeal" of universal law and the "decentralizing" influence of some of the leading thinkers of the Counter-Renaissance (in Chapter III) in itself constitutes, at least by implication, a large body of material illustrating the ways in which the naturalists denied the traditional concept of limit. But there remain a good many particulars to be examined, and none is more in need of clarification than a consideration of the relation of "individualism" to naturalism, which relation in turn directly concerns the "upward" and "downward" treatments of the nature of man.

The Christian humanists of the Renaissance inherited and held the most commonly accepted medieval attitude toward the individual—that "it is the individual soul which is to be saved, and each soul is different from all others."[2] In accordance with the medieval conviction that true liberty is the freedom to do good—a "restricted" liberty—they upheld a restricted individualism, which recognizes the "separateness" of each man or human soul within the generality of mankind or souls. "But even this restricted individualism is further hedged about by the fact that each individual must strive toward a perfection implicit in human nature and fully revealed in Christ's incarnation."[3]

Hence the Christian-humanistic philosophy of individualism, which might be called *personalism,* is concerned with the individual as a value.[4] This is quite a different matter from the meaning that Burckhardt, for example, gives to individualism when he speaks of it as a Renaissance point of view—and the arguments between those supporting his approach and such Thomist apologists as MM. De Wulf, Gilson and Maritain are largely fruitless.[5]

The Burckhardtian concept is best represented, for our purposes, by Cassirer's portrait of Pico.

> We are to distinguish, then, between the development, within an absolute standard, of special talents to fit into the highly specialized organization of a world institution, and, on the other hand, the moral autonomy which allows every man to work out his own life-pattern according to the law of his own singular nature.[6]

Complete moral *autonomy* enters the picture with Pico's concept of man and his dignity. Yet this "upward" concept of the nature of man—as opposed to the "fixed" Christian-humanistic one—while emphasizing a sort of man-god concept, partakes in no sense of any meaning of aggressive lawless individualism. For that—for the sense of individualism as *self-assertiveness,* we must wait for Machiavelli, who propounds as *fact* the idea that men's desires are insatiable, and that men act primarily upon amoral motives of self-preservation.[7]

Here is the philosophical naturalist's position on individualism—a "downward" estimate of man's nature, presented as true, without a moral judgment. In terms of man, it is the equivalent of Telesio's philosophy of nature as governed by laws of self-preservation. But when Tamburlaine, for example, illustrates this principle in action, he (or Marlowe) also glorifies and morally (or immorally) justifies such an attitude in a typical romanticist denial of limit. Machiavelli's "scientific" concept of individualism as *self-assertiveness* also denies traditional limit, since the Christian-classical view would hold that there is finality and even finiteness in such an apparently infinite longing or desire—since its end is in God; and moreover, the motive is not the naturalistic one of self-preservation, but the directed turning of love or longing to that which is man's final haven. Yet Machiavelli never deserts the naturalists' objective search through empirical actuality, nor a course of action based on it without moral judgment, beyond the criteria of success. Tamburlaine (like Byron and most other superman or brigand Elizabethan heroes) *makes a romantic ideal* of this *self-assertiveness.*

In addition to these concepts of individualism as recognition of value (medieval and Christian humanistic), the sanction for moral autonomy (Pico and the lawfully "upward" romanticists), the recognition of *self-assertiveness* (Machiavelli and the "downward" naturalistic view), and the glorification of *self-assertiveness* (Tamburlaine and the unlawfully "upward" romanticists), there remains another interpretation of individualism as the recognition of *singularity,* and even, again, a sanction for singularity.[8]

This interpretation is characteristic of Montaigne. The medievalists and Christian humanists had upheld the idea of diversity *in unity:* such a concept runs through their whole world picture. But Montaigne, as we have seen, expounds diversity *without* the unity. Nothing, he says often, is so universal as diversity. From this starting point develops his "science of the particular," and his lifelong study of himself. For "Moi-même" is all that he can know. And thus singularity and subjectivity are closely united.

In one sense, Montaigne is also concerned with the *sanction* of singularity—for he revels in his study of singularity and diversity until he develops it into a *philosophy.* But his emphasis is always "downward"; with his conviction that "supercelestial" opinions consort with "subterrestrial" manners, he finds nothing so goodly as to play the man—natural man—here on earth.

Once again, however, others find in singularity a romantic philosophy that takes its stand in defiantly following the peculiar *law of its own nature,* rather than any general law of nature—thus tending to merge with the self-assertive romantic who interprets liberty as license and makes laws in accordance with his own desires, stressing the ultimate *value* of the expression of his own peculiarities—a swollen romantic attitude utterly foreign to Montaigne's naturalism.

There is the case of Pietro Aretino, and what he represents to his Elizabethan admirers. Aretino had called himself "per la grazia di Dio uomo libero,"[9] and although it is difficult to see just where the grace of God enters, he was indeed "uomo libero"—in a not very respectable sense.

Yet he was taken seriously as a representative of true liberty by Thomas Nashe and Gabriel Harvey—perhaps the only point on which they ever agreed. Nashe declares,

> He was no timorous servile flatterer of the commonwealth wherein he lived, his tongue & his invention were foreborne, what they thought they would confidently utter. . . . His lyfe he contemned in comparison of the libertie of speech.[10]

Harvey's tribute is directly in the "follow one's own nature" tradition of singularity:

> Aretines glory, to be himself: to speake, & write like himself; to imitate none, but him selfe & ever to maintaine *his owne singularity.*[11]

"Ever to maintaine his owne singularity . . ." We are close here to Ben Jonson's "humours," and indeed it seems probable that he drew his new satiric version of this famous concept from current individualistic philosophies. To be sure, "humour" comes to take on a special Jonsonian significance in time, but a comparison of the first quarto and folio versions of the definition in *Every Man in his Humour* seems to conform this theory of its origin. The early variant (1601) reads:

> Piso: Marrie ile tell thee what it is (as tis generally received in these daies) it is a monster bred in a man by selfe love, and affection, and fed by folly.[12]

And the folio (1616):

> Cash: Mary, Ile tell thee, COB: It is a gentleman-like monster, bred, in the speciall gallantrie of our time, by affectation; and fed by folly.[13]

In short, "humour" later comes to take on the special coinage of "style," "whim," "fancy" or "idiosyncrasy"—usually with a foppish implication. But as Jonson first uses it, it refers to the pursuit of one's own inclinations—those dictated by "selfe love, and affection." As confirmation of this distinction, we may consider Clement's speech in the first version:

> I Lorenzo, but election is now governed altogether by the influence of humor—[14]

a rejection of the traditional supremacy—in the act of choice—of reason, in favor of the variant reading of following one's own inclination. The speech is missing from the folio text.

Again, Asper makes this very distinction in *Every Man Out of his Humour* (1599). Having defined "humour" as the pursuit of one's inclinations or peculiar nature, he goes on:

> This may be truly said to be a Humour.
> But that a rooke, in wearing a pyed feather,
> The cable hat-band, or the three-pild ruffe,
> A yard of shovetye, or the *Switzers* knot
> On his *French* garters, should affect a Humour!
> O, 'tis more then most ridiculous.[15]

And in *Cynthia's Revels*, "humour" is again used in its pristine sense of egoistic individualism, and associated with a frank hedonism:

> Humour is now the test we try things in:
> All power is just; nought that delights is sin.[16]

But it is in *Volpone* that Jonson's phrasing comes closest to the individualistic "singularity" tradition. Cicero had said, "Nothing is proper . . . if it is in direct opposition to one's natural genius," and Volpone, omitting the qualification "not to oppose the *universal* laws of human nature," demands,

> What should I doe,
> But cocker up my genius, and live free
> To all delights, my fortune calls me to?[17]

"Humour" is used in both the Jonsonian meanings by other Elizabethans, but most frequently in the sense of following instinct, or appetite, or "inclination," instead of reason. Thus the Friar in Chapman's *Bussy*, discussing Tamara's passion for Bussy, declares:

> You know besides, that our affections' storm,
> Rais'd in our blood, no reason can reform—

and continues,

> This frailty sticks in them beyond their sex,
> Which to reform, reason is too perplex:
> Urge reason to them, it will do no good;
> Humour (that is the chariot of our food
> In everybody) must in them be fed,
> To carry their affections by it bred.[18]

And Fulke Greville writes,

> Humours are mans religion, Power his lawes,
> His Wit confusion, and his Will the cause.[19]

That is, man follows his inclination, and makes the "affections" (or "powers" or "appetites") his law, instead of reason. Reason is in confusion because the will, obeying "humour" or "appetite," ignores reason's counsel.

"Humour," in the sense of following one's own inclination, was not coined by Jonson, of course. Florio's use of it in his translation from Montaigne, for instance, is an exact translation of Montaigne's "humeur."[20]

> I have a minde free and altogether her owne; accustomed to follow her owne humor.[21]

And therefore (according to my humour) . . .[22]

> This free humour I have, not very easily to subject my beliefe,
> I owe especially unto my selfe, for the most constant and gen-
> erall imaginations I have are those which (as one would say)
> were borne with me: *they are naturall unto me, and wholy
> mine.*[23]

Here, one might say, is the *locus classicus* for this development
of the Counter-Renaissance naturalistic individualism that finds firm
reality and ultimate value in singularity. And in these passages are
also to be found the probable bridge to the Elizabethan—as distinct from the traditional—use of the term "humour." As far as Ben
Jonson, classicist to the core, goes, it is amply evident that he does
not give the sanction of his approval to this point of view, but uses
it for satirical purposes. Yet it is all the more significant that he
was one of those who made overt reference to Montaigne's popularity among the Elizabethans.

For that matter, while there are Elizabethan romanticists who
treat the individualism of singularity and self-assertiveness sympathetically, the majority are sufficiently antipathetic or discreet
to put such opinions into the mouths of characters established as
villains. And there is little enough outward similarity between the
usually violent espousal of "humours" by the protagonists of Elizabethan plays, and Montaigne's urbane and subtle cultivation of
"son Moi." But as Montaigne grows older, he finds that

> it seemeth custome alloweth old age more liberty to babble,
> and indiscretion to talke of it selfe.[24]

And not of "selfe" only—for in the same essay he says deliberately,
"Will and desires are a lawe to themselves . . ." adding in a magnificent understatement, "All these proceedings of mine are somewhat dissonant from our formes. . . ."[25]

2. SEDITION IN THE SOUL

It should be immediately apparent that these various Counter-
Renaissance applications of the principle of individualism—romantic
and naturalistic alike—directly contradicted the concept of limit as
it applied to the orthodox Renaissance anatomies of the soul (or
souls) of man. (See chart on page 318, *supra.*) They contradicted this central concept as it pertained to the workings within
the soul of degree and gradation, moderation and harmony, finality

and finiteness. For they challenged reason's supremacy, and gave undue authority to the appetites, the passions and will, thereby completely upsetting the established hierarchical applecart.

Orthodox Renaissance anatomies (or analyses) of man's soul describe it either as made up of two or three "souls" or "parts of the soul" or "powers of the soul." If the tripartite division is followed, these are the vegetative soul, or that of growth; the sensitive soul, or that of sense and appetite; and the rational soul, or that of reason and will. John Donne follows this division when he says:

> First, in a naturall man wee conceive there is a soule of vegetation and of growth; and secondly, a soule of motion and of sense; and then thirdly, a soule of reason and understanding, an immortal soule.[26]

Even with those who favor the two-way division, the basic organization is really the same. Walter Ralegh, for instance, opens his *Treatise of the Soul* with this statement:

> There are two kinds of souls, one void of reason, another endued with reason; and of those without reason there are two sorts, one which feedeth and nourisheth the body, the other which giveth sense and feeling.[27]

In other words, the vegetative and sensitive souls, separate in Donne's description, are made the two "sorts" of Ralegh's soul "void of reason."

In either case, the vegetative soul (or part) is concerned only with generation, nourishment and growth. The sensitive soul, however, has significant sub-divisions: it is divided into the knowing and desiring parts, both of which are needed if the ends prescribed by nature are to be obtained.[28] Each of these parts, again, contains further sub-divisions. The knowing part includes the five senses (its exterior parts).[29] The desiring or appetitive part has two "faculties" or "powers": the concupiscible or desiring power and the irascible power, "that part where[by] the Soul seeks the means she hath to obtain, or shun what appears good or evil to her. . . ." As the concupiscible power moves "according to the appearance of a Good or Ill," so the irascible stirs up "Hope or Despair," and "Fear or Anger."[30]

The highest or rational soul, in its turn, is composed of two great powers—the knowing or judging or understanding power (reason), and the desiring power or intellectual appetite (will). That is, as Hooker puts it:

To choose is to will one thing before another. And to will is to bend our souls to the having or doing of that which they see to be good. Goodness is seen with the eye of the understanding. And the light of that eye is reason. So that two principal fountains there are of human action, Knowledge and Will; which Will in things tending towards any end, is termed Choice.[31]

Such are the constituents of man's soul, and since the best things, if not hindered, "do still produce the best operations," the best things in the soul should guide the others, just as the soul itself should guide the body. "This is therefore the first law," says Hooker,

> whereby the highest power of the mind requireth general obedience at the hands of all the rest concurring with it unto action.[32]

This highest power in the soul is of course understanding or reason, whose "mandates" must "be obeyed by the will of Man." For "the object of Will is that good which Reason doth lead us to seek."[33]

Analogy is constantly invoked to substantiate these premises. In such a manner God directs the universe; in such a way the sun, sometimes designated as the light of God, stands chief among the planets; in a similar fashion a monarch conducts the affairs of a commonwealth. As in all these other "worlds," so in man the microcosm, the principles of order, degree and cooperation are observed.

It would seem, then, with Reason directing and Will obeying, that man would be certain to achieve his goal of virtue. But the appetitive part of the sensitive soul (which we share with beasts) houses the "passions," "affections" or "perturbations"—"the forms of Appetite," as Hooker calls them—and these may be stirred, whether we wish them to be or not. Before the Fall, they were infallibly under the control of Will, guided by Reason:

> Finally, Appetite is the Will's solicitor, and the Will is the Appetite's controller; what we covet according to the one by the other we often reject; neither is any other desire termed properly Will, but that where Reason and Understanding, or the show of Reason, prescribeth the thing desired. Reason is the director of man's Will by discovering in action what is good. For the Laws of well-doing are the dictates of right Reason.[34]

But Hooker qualifies his statement with "the show of Reason," for this beautifully worked out schematization is not infallible since the Fall. "Option" and "custom" have crept in to corrupt man's "natural reason" since Adam's sin, and it may become so infected that it is no longer capable of judging rightly. Again, often "Reason . . . may rightly discern the thing which is good, and yet the will of man not incline itself thereunto, as oft as the prejudice of sensible experience doth oversway."[35] So John Milton describes Adam's and Eve's condition after the Fall:

> For Understanding rul'd not, and the Will
> Heard not her lore; both in subjection now
> To sensuall Appetite, who from beneath
> Usurping over sov'ran Reason claim'd
> Superior sway. . . .[36]

The Will, functioning properly, obeys Reason; corrupted or perverted by the excessive power of the passions, it asserts its independence of Reason. The basic opposition, then (whatever the variant details and terminology), is between Reason and the Passions —and since the Fall, not an uneven one:

> Ill they desir'd to know, and Ill they did;
> And to give *Passion* eyes, made *Reason* blind.[37]

It will perhaps be wise to follow Guillaume du Vair's representative summary of how "rebellious Passions . . . by their smoak obnubilate the eye of Reason. . . ."[38]

Definition of Passion	1. We call that Passion, which is a violent motion of the Soul in her sensitive part, and makes her either apply her self to what she thinks is good, or recede from what she takes to be ill. . . .
The process begins with the senses' instinctive reaction toward or away from a perceived object.	2. Now Nature has given this force and power . . . to the senses, to apply themselves to things, to extract their forms, and as they are fit or unfit, to embrace or reject them. . . .
The senses should be obedient sentinels, but often they are deceived, and take an "enemy disguised, for a friend"—or vice versa.	3. The Senses . . . are oft abused by appearance, and take for advantageous, what is wholly against us: When upon this judgment, and without expecting the command of Reason,

they come to disturb the Irascible and Concupiscible powers, they raise a sedition, and tumult in the Soul, during which, Reason is no more heard nor the understanding obeyed, than is the Law of Magistrate in a troubled estate of civil discord.

Revolt of the Passions in the Concupiscible part: "This is the first body of Mutineers that disturb the peace of the Soul."

4. Now in this Commotion, the Passions which disturb the peace of the mind, and mutiny against the soul, make their first insurrection in the Concupiscible part, that is to say, in the place where the Soul exerciseth this faculty of desiring, or rejecting things offered to her, as they are proper, or contrary to her delight, or conservation. They move then according to the appearance of a Good or Ill.

Advance into the irascible part.

5. Those first motions, formed in that part by the presented object, immediately shift into the irascible part, that is to say, into that part where the Soul seeks the means she hath to obtain, or shun what appears good or evil to her; and there . . . falls into a prompter speed; so the Soul, already stirred with the first apprehension, and adding a second effort to the first, is hurried with more violence than before, and raises up Passions more powerful, and more difficult to tame. . . .

Distinction and conclusion.

6. For the first Passions, that are formed to the object of a seeming Good, falling into consideration of the means to

atchieve it, either stir up in us
Hope or Despair; and such as
are formed to the object of
Ill, give birth to Fear and Anger: which four Passions are
strangely strong and violent,
and wholly subvert that Reason they find already shaken.
These (in my opinion) are the
winds that create the tempests
of the Soul. . . .[39]

So sedition in the soul . . . But it must always be borne in mind
that, while they admitted the occurrence of such mutinies, the
middle-path humanists did not admit the total impairment of man's
rational faculties. They continued to exhort man to the pursuit of
virtue through the proper government of the soul by the will acting under reason's direction—with the conviction that he might
attain his goal. In conclusion, then, let us balance Du Vair's account
of a mutinous soul with Hooker's presentation of the working of
a virtuous one.

(1) The knowing part of the Sensitive Soul makes contact with
some object. (2) The appetitive part of the same soul (through
its concupiscible faculty) solicits the Will. (3) The Will consults
the Understanding, and makes its choice on the basis of the Understanding's decision. (4) The choice made known to the appetitive
part, it acts (through its irascible faculty) in accordance with the
election of the Will, under reason's (or Understanding's) guidance:
for the appetitive part of the Sensitive Soul is the moving power
by which the soul effects its purposes. . . .

The basic opposition, I said, is recognized as one between Reason
and the Passions—and if the traditionalists, the classicists, interpret
the warfare always as a lawless revolt of the passions against their
rightful ruler, reason, there are others who see the whole issue quite
differently.

Petrarch, in his *De Remediis Utriusque Fortuna,* writes a dialogue between these two opponents. Reason tries to prove by argument the unreality of all pains and pleasures, while the passions
(significantly) simply repeat the same phrases over and over again,
without arguing.[40]

In the Second Eclogues of Sidney's *Arcadia* there is held "a
daunce, which they called the skirmish betwixt Reason and Passion." A sung dialogue follows, which presents the main arguments

of the humanists and their opponents of the Counter-Renaissance in a lively fashion. Reason calls Passion, "Thou Rebell vile." Passion retaliates with "Tyrant," qualifying the charge with "If Reason will, that Passions be not free."

Reason maintains, "By nature you to Reason faith have sworne." Passion denies it: "Not so, but fellowlike together borne." They exchange further epithets; Reason calls Passion, "O foolish thing, which glory doth destroye," and Passion replies, "O glorious title of a foolish toye." At the end they admit that the contest ends in a tie (certainly at least a moral victory for Passion), and, embracing each other, chant together:

> Then let us both to heavenly rules give place,
> Which Passions skill, and Reason do deface.[41]

There is no such final reconciliation in Greville's sober *Chorus sacerdotum*, from his *Mustapha*. The priests begin by contrasting nature's two laws, and identifying them—despite a Calvinistic glance at original sin—with the claims of passion and reason:

> Oh, wearisome condition of humanity,
> *Born* under one law, to another *bound;*
> Vainly begot, and yet forbidden vanity,
> Created sick, commanded to be sound.
> What meaneth nature by these diverse laws?
> Passion and reason self division cause.

It is not *natural* for Nature to make a rational Law of Nature:

> Nature herself doth her own self deflower,
> To hate those errors she herself doth give.

She is a "tyrant," commanding only "things difficult and hard," and making "easy pains, unpossible reward."

> If nature did not take delight in blood,[42]
> She would have made more easy ways to good.

In the somber conclusion, the opponents take on religious nomenclature; they remain the same:

> We that are bound by vows and by promotion,
> With pomp of holy sacrifice and rites
> To teach belief in God and still devotion,
> To preach of heaven's wonders and delights,—
> Yet when each of us in his own heart looks
> He finds the God there far unlike his books.[43]

In these passages—and they could be trebled—we find chiefly a romantic rebellion against the traditional view of the supremacy of reason. Erasmus' chipper jester in the *Praise of Folly* takes a shrewder, more matter-of-fact tone, in saying more incisively what amounts to the same thing:

> Of how much more Passion than Reason has Jupiter compos'd us . . . putting in, as one would say, "scarce half an ounce to a pound." Besides, he has confin'd Reason to a narrow corner of the brain, and left all the rest of the body to our Passions; has also set up, against this one, two as it were, masterless Tyrants—Anger, that possesseth the region of the heart, and consequently the very Fountain of Life, the Heart it self; and Lust, that stretcheth its Empire every where. Against which double force how powerful Reason is, let common experience declare, inasmuch as she [Reason] which yet is all she can do, may call out to us till she be hoarse again, and tell us the Rules of Honesty and Virtue; while they give up the Reins to their Governour, and make a hideous clamour, till at last being wearied, he suffer himself to be carried whither they please to hurry him.[44]

Then there is the forthright espousal of the appetites' priority of claim in Harvey's famous letter to Spenser:

> Affections are infectious; and appetite must sometime have his swinge. Were Appetite a loyall subject to Reason, and Will an affectionate servant to Wisdom; as Labour is a dutifull vassal to Commodity, and Travail a flying post to Honour; O heavens, what exploites of worth, or rather what miracles of excellency, might be atcheeved in an age of Pollicy, & a world of Industry. . . .[45]

But all such protests—romantic, naturalistic, or whatever—predicate spadework by thinkers who had challenged orthodoxy more "scientifically." A small but redoubtable group of men kept hammering away at the hard, compact shell of orthodox humanistic ethical and psychological theory; sometimes they cracked it, and sometimes they chipped off at least a small piece.

Thus Jean Bodin evinces his disgust with "cette absurdité" of three parts of the soul:

> Ce qu'on appelle partie en l'ame vegetante, ou sensuelle, ou intellectuelle, soit sa puissance ou faculté, & leurs effects soyent compris soubs le nom d'action ou de function.

His (or his Mystagogue's) reply to the question, "But isn't the soul divided?" is

Ouy certes, comme le genre en ses especes: mais pas comme le tout in ses parties. . . .[46]

But this distinction was soon to be incorporated into orthodox anatomies; at most only a very small chip flies off. Leonardo (although the Renaissance-at-large was certainly not aware of it) hewed out a bigger piece when he wrote: "Similarity does not imply equality."[47] For this statement from the man who wrote that "no human investigation can call itself science unless it passes through mathematical demonstrations" is a direct rap at the whole system of analogical argument, upon which the Christian humanists depended so greatly for justification and substantiation of their theories.

Rabelais is having sport with that same use of analogy when he explains why there is only one "pope-hawk." For the favorite defense of monarchy, not only as the best, but as the only *natural* form of government, was to point out an analogy to bees, to the human body, to the planets, etc.: i.e., there was only one queen-bee, one head, one sun, etc. Thus, after "the clerg-hawks begot the priest-hawks and monk-hawks, . . .

> the priest-hawks begat the bish-hawks, the bish-hawks the stately cardin-hawks, and the stately cardin-hawks, if they live long enough, at last come to be pope-hawk.
>
> Of this last kind, there never is more than one at a time; as in a beehive there is but one king, and in the world is but one sun.[48]

Indeed, in one of the early chapters of *Gargantua* (I, x), Rabelais has a delightful time with the most sacred institutions of the traditionalists, invoking boisterously and irreverently the Law of Nature and *consensus gentium* to explain the meaning of white and black.

But, as usual, Montaigne deals the most telling blow:

> There is no more retrogradation, trepidation, augmentation, recoyling, and violence in the starres and celestiall bodies than they [the moral philosophers] have fained and devised in this poor seely little body of man. Verily they have thence had reason to name it Microcosmus, or little world, so many several parts and visages have they imploied to fashion and frame the same.

The "divisions of the soul" do not escape.

> To accommodate the motions which they see in man, the divers functions and faculties that we feel in our selves. Into how many severall parts have they divided our soule? Into how many seats have they placed her? Into how many orders, stages,

and stations have they divided this wretched man, beside the
naturall and perceptible?

Nor does he forget the sacred principles of man's function in society—the limiting principles of degree and vocation:

and to how many distinct offices and vocations? They make a
publike imaginarie thing of it. It is a subject which they hold
and handle: they have all power granted them to rip him, to
sever him, to range him, to join and reunite him together
againe, and to stuffe him every one according to his fantasie;
and yet they neither have nor possess him.

For, finally, their theorizing cannot compass Nature:

They cannot so order or rule him, not in truth onely, but in
imagination, but still some cadence or sound is discovered
which escapeth their architecture, bad as it is, and botched
together with a thousand false patches and fantasticall peeces.[49]

The appeal to experience, in judging what man's nature is, and
how he "works," is implicit through all these criticisms of the "man-
ufacturers" and "architects" of man. It is explicit in Sidney's *Arcadia*,
when Musidorus, who had earlier harangued Pyrocles (who was
lovesick) with a rigidly orthodox account of how to overcome the
passions with reason,[50] himself falls in love. For he admits woefully,

I find indeed, that all is but lip-wisdome, which wants experience.[51]

Indeed, a personal letter of Lorenzo de' Medicis reveals clearly
that there were men who thought in practical terms of these strug-
gles in the soul, without even making a formal bow to "anatomies."
Poliziano has been afraid to write to Lorenzo and tell him of his
children's illness, and Lorenzo, annoyed, appeals to experience much
as one would today:

And do you then really think me of a temper so imbecile, as
to be discomposed by such an event?—But admitting myself
to be naturally so constituted, as to be the sport of my own
passions,—yet I have surely learned constancy by long experience.

He reminds Poliziano that he has witnessed not only the illness,
but the death of his own children—and, at only twenty-one, his
father's death, which had left him

exposed to the assaults of fortune. You ought therefore to conclude that experience has given me that fortitude, which nature
denied.[52]

Here, in the very context where an orthodox Stoic appeal to reason is most appropriate—the need for constancy in the face of fortune's buffetings—Lorenzo turns to experience. First, he admits that he is *naturally* "the sport" of his own passions; then that he has learned to correct that natural imperfection, not by reason, but by experience.

Although we know that such cannot have been the case, Lorenzo's letter is written as though he had never heard of orthodox anatomies of the soul and the innumerable moral tracts extolling the guidance of reason—those books which caused Francis Bacon to write, in a superb understatement:

> Reading good Bookes of Morality, is a little Flat, and Dead.[53]

Bacon himself helped to make them flatter and "more" dead by his keen analysis of them. Concerning the knowledge "of the Appetite and Will of Man," he writes:

> In the handling of this science, those which have written seem to me to have done as if a man that professeth to teach to write did only exhibit fair copies of alphabets and letters joined, without giving any precepts or directions for the carriage of the hand and framing of the letters. So have they made good and fair exemplars and copies, carrying the draughts and portraitures of Good, Virtue, Duty, Felicity; propounding them well described as the true objects and scopes of man's will and desires; but *how* to attain these excellent marks, and *how* to frame and subdue the will of man to become true and conformable to these pursuits, they pass it over altogether, or slightly and unprofitably.[54]

It is the same Bacon, making the same demands in the field of ethics and psychology that he does in that of natural philosophy —stressing fact and utility. For it is *useful* precepts that he wants, and he does not exonerate, from failure on this score, even the naturalists who shout "custom" and the Machiavellians who propound a "double standard" of public morality:

> For it is not the disputing that moral virtues are in the mind of man by habit and not by nature, or the distinguishing that generous spirits are won by doctrines and persuasion, and the vulgar sort by reward and punishment, and the like scattered glances and touches, that can excuse the absence of this part.[55]

He is really arguing for the application of a psychological analysis of men to the studies of "morality and policy." For "distinctions" amongst many kinds of men are numerous, but we conclude no precepts upon them; wherein our fault is the greater, because both history, poesy, and daily experience are as goodly fields where these observations grow; whereof we make a few posies to hold in our hands, but no man bringeth them to the confectionary, that receits might be made of them for use of life.[56]

He has never had any use for "loose induction"; collecting without conclusion is as foolish in "morality" as in natural philosophy. Finally, his aim, as always, is to produce conclusions for the "use of life."

Bacon is also explicit about the relative importance of reason and the affections in any study of man's nature:

And here again I find strange, as before, that Aristotle should have written divers volumes of Ethics, and never handled the affections, *which is the principal subject thereof.*[57]

An emphasis similar to Bacon's, at least in utilitarian approach, had already been laid by Pomponazzi, who had opposed the systematization and intellectualization of ethics in general. The absolutism of the Law of Nature seemed to him unjustified. Although he endorsed the use and efficacy of reason, he did not mean by reason a speculative intellect or a hypothetical monarch of the soul, but a practical wisdom that could deal with matters of right and wrong—which, in turn, were not rigid, but flexible values.[58]

Even Lorenzo Valla's hedonistic ethics, for that matter, were built upon (at least professed) utilitarian bases. For what, he demands, is more proper to living than "voluptas"?

ut in gustu, visu, auditu, odoratu, tactu, sine quibus vivere non possumus, sine honestate possumus. Ita si quis in se quod natura praescribit, violare audeat, *contra sua utilitate fecerit.* . . .[59]

This is not far from Montaigne's wedding of Pleasure and Necessity; and Montaigne's plea for temperance, we remember, is for the sake of pleasure, not virtue. Hence it is hardly surprising to find him advocating the temperate evasion of extreme passions and fancies, rather than the temperate governing of them by reason:

A sharpe conceit possesseth, and a violent imagination holdeth me; I find it a shorter course to alter and divert, than to tame and vanquish the same: if I cannot substitute a contrary unto it, at least I present another unto it. Change ever easeth, Varietie dissolveth, and shifting dissipateth. . . . Nature proceedeth thus, by the benefit of inconstancy: for the time it hath bestowed on us, as a soveraigne purpose that way. . . ."[60]

"Nature proceedeth thus . . ." And it is through experience that he has come to the realization that "substitution" or evasion is a shorter way to victory than reason. The eventual healing or calming will be done by time. This is Nature's way—not that of Nature, the mother of Reason, but Nature, the mother of Experience.

For, again by experience, he has found that man does not work the way the story books say he does:

> I say, moreover, that even wisdom and consultation for the most part followeth the conduct of hazard. My will and my discourse is sometimes moved by one ayre and sometimes by another; and there may be many of these motions that are governed without me. My reason hath dayly impulsions and casuall agitations. . . ."[61]

Implicit in many of these passages is a naturalistic treatment of man—the discovery of how he actually functions—a treatment of him as the human animal. A variant upon this sort of attack lay in the tendency to deny to him the exclusive ownership of his traditionally God-given unique property: reason, which distinguished him from the animals.[62] Following the lead of Sextus Empiricus, some of these thinkers pursue devious arguments to show that "the so-called irrational animals" possess powers equal to man's. Ralegh asks,

> Why should I presume to prefer my conceit and imagination, in affirming that a thing is thus and thus in its own nature, because it seemeth to me to be so, before the conceit of other living creatures, who may as well think it to be otherwise in its nature, because it appeareth otherwise to them than it doth to me?[63]

Pomponazzi, having given examples of animals who displayed a certain nobility in preferring death to disgrace, bounces the rational Law of Nature back at its proponents:

> Since these things, moreover, were done by nature they were done according to reason, in as much by the opinion of Themistius and Averroes [this looks suspiciously like the intentional avoidance of more orthodox authorities], nature is directed by an unerring intelligence. Therefore in man also this is not contrary to reason.[64]

Small consolation in the final qualification!

Montaigne speaks of "the discourse of beasts" and makes the same comparison with man, declaring that, whatever you may choose

to call it, "it is one same nature which still doth keepe her course."
Perhaps the crowning indignity he offers (at least in the *Apologie*)
is the statement that "elephants have some apprehension of religion!"[65] *Consensus gentium* loses not a little dignity here.

In Des Périers' *Cymbalum Mundi*, Phlegon, the talking horse,
harangues his human audience:

> But if We could speak, and tell *our Reason*, you are so Humane,
> or *at least you ought to be so*, that after hearing us speak,
> you would treat us in another manner. . . .

And he maintains,

> If Speech had been preserv'd to us, as well as it was to you,
> you shou'd not have found us such Beasts as you make us.[66]

He has his own interpretation of the Law of Nature, as well:

> You Men wou'd have one Law for yourselves, and another for
> your Neighbours. You are very well contented to take all your
> natural Pleasures, but you will not let others take them, namely
> us Beasts.[67]

Gostanzo, Chapman's parody of a Machiavellian in *All Fools*,
retains the orthodox distinction between man and beast, but twists
it, in keeping with his role, to man's disadvantage:

> Beasts utter but one sound; but men have change
> Of speech and reason, even by nature given them,
> Now to say one thing, and another now,
> As best may serve their profitable ends.[68]

It is hardly surprising that Jean Bodin should object to terming
man's distinctive property "raison." His Mystagogue says, that since
so many have undertaken to prove that beasts

> estoyent raisonnables, j'ay pris de là occasion, de substituer
> à la raison le nom d'entendement, à fin de separer par ceste
> difference les hommes des bestes brutes, lesquelles ils avoyent
> conjoinctes par le lien de la raison.[69]

His authority for the fact that animals do not possess "l'entende-
ment" is Scripture.

Yet later he declares that

> si nous voulons que l'homme aist plus d'un ame, il faudra pare
> mesme moyen juger que *les autres animaux* en ont plusieurs.[70]

This time, his authority is Averroës. . . .

Montaigne, as usual, goes further than most. There is nothing
antipathetic to the traditional point of view in his frequent asser-

tion of the inferiority of man's senses to those of animals; that is as it should be, for the senses are the animals' only guides. But Montaigne (at this period) believes that "the senses are the beginning and end of humane knowledge."[71] Hence, when he asks who knows whether the beasts do not have some sense beyond any of ours, he is indeed asking "whether some of them have by that means a fuller and more perfect life than ours."[72]

We of the twentieth century have lost the significance of many of Montaigne's allusions, but those closer to him in time had not. Bossuet speaks of those "belles sentences" (written by "Montaigne: je le nomme")

> qui préfèrent les animaux à l'homme, leur instinct à notre raison, leur nature simple, innocente et sans fard (c'est ainsi qu'on parle) à nos raffinements et à nos malices.[73]

It is time to consider further the general implications behind all these assertions. It would be tedious and superfluous to track down and explicate the way in which each of these statements (whether rejecting the traditional hierarchy of man's soul, repudiating the validity of analogical argument, denying the power of reason in human conduct, or contradicting the accepted premise that reason is man's *unique* property) constitutes one of a series of denials of the principle of limit—whether in terms of reality or value, or both. What is more to the point is to recognize the effect of such judgments upon a tenable concept of the good life for man. What, for instance, is the relation of virtue to happiness?

Throughout the writings of the naturalistic thinkers of the Counter-Renaissance, with their emphasis upon "what men are, and not what they ought to be," one finds a relatively low—if usually dispassionate—estimate of human character.

"Men know not how to be honourably mischievous, nor perfectly good," states Machiavelli, using an interesting pair of alternatives.[74] "No man," Montaigne asserts (making a point that the recent Kinsey report, in a more limited sense, treats),

> is so exquisitely honest or upright in living but brings all his actions and thoughts within compasse and danger of the lawes, and that ten times in his life might not lawfully be hanged. . . .[75]

and he speaks of the true test of a man taking place "within, and in bosome, *where all things are lawfull*, where all is concealed. . . ."[76] "A mixture of a Lie doth ever adde Pleasure," Bacon remarks.

Doth any man doubt, that if there were taken out of Mens

Mindes, Vaine Opinons, Flattering Hopes, False valuations,
Imaginations as one would, and the like; but it would leave
the Mindes of a Number of Men, poore shrunken Things; full
of Melancholy, and Indisposition, and unpleasing to themselves?[77]

And the reason lies are held in such high favor, he maintains, is
"a naturall, though corrupt Love, of the Lie it selfe."[78]

It is the nearest any of these men comes to the language of
original sin. Indeed, if they were to hang out a corporate shingle,
they could find no better words to inscribe on it than those Marston
employs in his prologue to *Antonio's Revenge*. This is not going to
be, he warns (however unjustifiably), the play for you—if you are
one of those

Who winkes, and shuts his apprehension up
From common sense of what men were, and are,
Who would not knowe what men must be. . . .[79]

Machiavelli and Montaigne distinguish sharply between the rational ideals of virtue to which men give lip-service and not only
their practices, but their actual intentions. In the preface to the
Discourses, Machiavelli writes,

. . . seeing the most vertuous actions that Histories relate
us . . . that these, I say, have been rather admired than followed, or rather by every one have been so much avoided,
that now the very footsteps of that ancient vertue is utterly
defaced . . .[80]

And there is that famous passage in the fifteenth chapter of the
Prince, in which he professes his realistic and utilitarian creed:

because how one lives is so far distant from how one ought
to live, that he who neglects what is done for what ought to
be done, sooner effects his ruin than his preservation. . . .[81]

"I willingly returne to this discourse of the fondnesse of our
institution," says Montaigne:

whose aime hath been to make us not good and wittie, but
wise and learned. She hath attained her purpose. It hath not
taught us to follow vertue and embrace wisdome: but made
an impression in us of its Etymologie and derivation. We can
decline vertue, yet can we not love it. If wee know not what
wisdome is by effect and experience, wee know it by prattling
and by rote.[82]

He does not find this pedanticism of the orthodox Christian humanists a very intelligent course for any one to pursue.

Man doth necessarily ordaine unto himself to bee in fault. Hee is not very crafty to measure his duty by the reason of another being than his owne. *To whom prescribes he that which hee expects no man will performe?* Is he unjust in not dooing that which he cannot possibly atchieve? The lawes which condemne us not to be able, condemne us for that we cannot performe.

As for himself, he refuses to separate the truth he professes from that which he lives:

I must walke with my penne as I goe with my feete. The common high way must have conference with other wayes.[83]

It is but a short logical step from the contention that man has no intention of following his rules of reason and virtue, to the statement that there is no direct relation between virtue and happiness. To the creed of the humanists, on the other hand, no hypothesis is more vital than the positing of such a direct relationship. As Du Vair writes,

the happiness of all things is their Perfection, and Perfection the fruition of the End; so the Felicity of Man shall consist in the acquisition and atchievement of that he proposes to himself, and to which all his Actions tend . . . which is Good . . .

and

The Good, then, of Man consists in his healthfull Reason, that is to say, his Virtue. . . .[84]

Now both Pomponazzi and Montaigne would admit that "the essential reward of virtue is that of virtue itself, which makes men happy."[85] They do, however, not only thus strip the ethical ideal of its Christian metaphysical premise, but also divorce it from its association with natural reason. Montaigne, we have seen, will not concede that "our institution" has aimed "to make us . . . good and wittie." It is concerned only with the "Etymologie and derivation" of "vertue"; it cannot really effect it, since it never comes to grips with the real problem.

Pomponazzi is holding a similar position when he writes that the "end which belongs to the most perfect part [of man] cannot, nor does, suit." And his identification of virtue with happiness has a different sound from that of Du Vair. Anyone, he says,

if he is moral, can be called happy, and is truly so, and goes off content with his lot. In addition, even disregarding moral happiness, he can be called a happy farmer or a happy builder, if he works prosperously in agriculture or in building, although he is not so properly called happy on this account.[86]

"Not so properly. . . ." This is considerably more latitude than orthodoxy would permit. And the whole tone is a common-sense, matter-of-fact one, of course—even in the description of "moral happiness." It is a happiness proper to men, not gods, that he is considering, he says (rejecting *homo deus* much as Montaigne does), and concludes,

it is characteristic of the temperate man to be contented with what suits him and what he can have.[87]

An eminently forthright statement, but hardly satisfactory to the traditionalists—if they were to study the context.

We have seen that Machiavelli goes a step further and wishes for his friends "that good or that evil which you your selves have desired," with the implication that happiness is amoral. Guicciardini, far from being content with denying the identification of virtue with happiness, implies unmistakably that vice at least may be so identified, rather than virtue. For he summarizes the life of Pope Alexander VI, the most infamous of all the Borgias, by saying that

he was the worst and the happiest pope that one had seen for many centuries. . . .[88]

Here is an attitude toward the problem of happiness quite different from that of the traditional Christian humanist. To the latter, man's happiness lies in the perfection of himself, which on earth consists in his pursuit of virtue under the guidance of right reason. Herein lies his *value*, his good—and also his *true nature*. As in other respects, the classicist sees a congruence between the two, and his positive definition of man's nature and goal obeys all the principles of limit.

But the romanticists of Pico's sort, predicating man's complete moral autonomy, and hence tending toward a man-god ideal, accept no limitations, no *general generic* concept of man's proper place, and hence defy the concept of limit altogether.

The naturalists of the Counter-Renaissance, on the other hand, treat man primarily as the human animal. In a thinker like Montaigne, this tendency is explicit when he considers the popular treatises on how to prepare to die well. He declares, "Such transcending humours affright me as much as steepy, high and inaccessible places," and "super-celestiall opinions and under-terrestrial manners are things amongst us I have ever seen to bee of singular accord."[89]

He flares out in the last pages that he wrote:

> We seeke for other conditions because we understand not the use of ours, and goe out of our selves foreasmuch as we know not what abiding there is. Wee long enough get upon stilts, for be wee upon them, yet must wee goe with our owne legges. And sit we upon the highest throne of the World, yet sit we upon our owne taile.[90]

Inevitably he returns to a "common feeling of Humanity," to "the common mould and humane model," fashioned "without wonder or extravagancy."[91]

His concern is not with death; death will take care of itself, and *naturally*. If there is something beyond, it is not *human life*, and he would certainly exclaim with Erasmus' *Folly*, "As if there were any difference between perishing, and being another thing!"[92]

"Life," says Montaigne, as dogmatically as he has ever spoken,

> is a materiall and corporal motion, an action imperfect and disordered by its owne essence; I employ or apply my selfe to serve it according to it selfe.[93]

3. HOMO HOMINI LUPUS

Montaigne's naturalism (certainly comprehensible and sympathetic to many twentieth-century thinkers), while rejecting any concept of the godlike and aspiring in man, does also contradict the Christian-humanistic principle of limit—in that it does not accept the guiding role of reason, the hierarchical composition of the soul, the traditional linking of happiness and virtue under right reason, etc. But it still proclaims (with qualifications) the essential goodness of man's nature (we shall have reason later to examine Montaigne's primitivism)—only under another dispensation than that of the Christian humanists.

There is yet another kind of Counter-Renaissance naturalistic position, however, one not so optimistic about man's nature. The naturalists of Machiavelli's and Guicciardini's caliber counter Pico's man-god with a man-beast. As Machiavelli puts it in a famous passage in the *Prince*,

> A prince being thus obliged to know well how to act as a beast must imitate the fox and the lion, for the lion cannot protect himself from traps, and the fox cannot defend himself from wolves. . . .[94]

In the catalogue of John Dee's unprinted books and treatises
there is an item which reads:

> 47.   Certain Considerations, and conferrings together, of these
> three sentences, (aunciently accounted as Oracles) *Nosce
> teipsum: Homo Homini Deus: Homo Homini Lupus.*

and another, listed as 49:
An. 1592

> To which compendious rehearsall, doth now belong an *Appen-
> dix,* of these two last years: In which I have had many just
> occasions, to confess, that *Homo Homini Deus* and *Homo
> Homini Lupus,* was and is an Argument worthy of the decy-
> phering, and large discussing: as may, one day, hereafter (by
> God's help) be published, in some manner very strange.[95]

We may count with confidence upon the manner being "very
strange," since John Dee was connected with it; we may admit
that he did have (if that is what he means) "many just occasions,
to confesse, that *Homo Homini Deus* and *Homo Homini Lupus,* was
and is an Argument worthy of the decyphering. . . ." Beyond these
premises, since I do not know the rest of his argument, I cannot go.

But although John Dee may have had a particular and esoteric
message to deliver on the subject of "man's being a god to man"
and "man's being a wolf to man," the age in which he lived was
quite capable of offering its own less obscure renditions of these
two phrases. Indeed, there was to the Renaissance at large no concept more familiar, none more frequently evoked—in many and
varied contexts—than this double one of "man a god to man" and
"man a wolf to man."[96]

In the sense of what man *means* to man, what man thinks man
is really compounded of, the double concept is a major Renaissance
motif. Sidney gives one account of its origin in the *Arcadia.* Before the advent of man, the beasts decided they wanted a king.
Jupiter demurred, warning them

> O beasts, take heed what you of me desire.
> Rulers will thinke all things made them to please . . .

but since they are adamant, he consents—on condition that he and
they share the making of this ruler:

> But since you will, part of my heav'nly fire
>   I will you lende; the rest your selves must give,
>   That it both seene and felte may with you live.[97]

Hence man—part god, part beast.

These alternatives are at the very heart of the orthodox Renaissance anatomies of the soul, with their divisions into rational and sensitive parts or powers—the first of which men share with the angels (since the understanding becomes angelic intellect in the contemplation of God), the second with the brutes. They are implicit again in the logical distinction between the origin of rational soul and that of the two lower ones:

> And the two first soules of vegetation, and of sense, wee conceive to arise out of the temperament, and good disposition of the substance of which that man is made, they arise out of man himselfe; But the last soule, the perfect and immortal soule, that is immediately infused by God.[98]

And it is integral to the frequently associated ideas of the native seed of natural reason (for the Stoics a "spark" of the Divine Reason) and of original sin—as it is, again, to the perennial theme of the combined fullness and briefness of man's life.

It is used in many ways. A Bodin may invoke experience when citing the god and beast alternatives:

> And who is there who does not know by the testimony of the eye, that among men there are some who have less judgment than the brute beasts? and others in whom the marks of the divine light are so clear, that they seem rather angels than men?[99]

and a Davies may imply them in a more conventional context:

> I know my soule hath power to know all things,
> Yet is she blind and ignorant in all;
> I know I am one of Natures little kings,
> Yet to the least and vilest things am thrall.
>
> I know my life's a paine, and but a span,
> I know my Sense is mockt with every thing;
> And to conclude, I know my selfe a Man,
> Which is a proud and yet a wretched thing.[100]

But it is only with the Counter-Renaissance naturalists of the Machiavellian sort that half of the concept is omitted. Pico and the Romanticists admit both halves of the proposition, but deny the traditional mixed composition and set place of man in the total picture. Moreover, *as romanticists*, they stress always the ideal, the god-in-man. Montaigne expressly denies both halves as fictitious in their traditional form, and advocates *playing the man*—indicating that man is something quite different from god or beast, or even from a set combination of them. But the *animalists* (Machiavelli, Guicciardini, etc.), as we might call them to distinguish between their sort of naturalism and Montaigne's, see primarily the beast in man—in his desires and ambitions, and in his attitude toward his fellow-men. And here is a far more serious attack upon the traditional view of man's nature than any playful or satirical conferring of reason upon animals.

Let us return for a moment to the Christian-classicist attitude. According to it, man was literally born to virtue, through his god-given natural reason and natural inclination to justice and fellowship with his brother-men. Aristotle had held that man was a political animal, and Cicero had declared,

> Nature likewise by the power of reason associates man with man in the common bonds of speech and life. . . . She also prompts men to meet in companies, to form public assemblies. . . .[101]

Moreover—

> This, then, ought to be the chief end of all men, to make the interest of each individual and of the whole body politic identical. For if the individual appropriates to selfish ends what should be devoted to the common good, all human fellowship will be destroyed. And further if nature ordains that one man shall desire to promote the interests of a fellow man, whoever he may be, just because he is a fellow man, then it follows, in accordance with that same nature, that there are interests that all men have in common. And if this is true, we are all subject to one and the same law of nature; and if this also is true, we are certainly forbidden by nature's law to wrong our neighbor.[102]

It is an argument and an ideal that we find stressed over and over again by the middle-path Christian humanists and orthodox writers of ethical and political tracts in the Renaissance. Yes, the Fall has intervened, but it is characteristic of these men to make a bow to theology (sometimes they even forget their manners) and then to continue talking about natural reason, the Law of Nature; *consensus gentium,* and *jus gentium*—just as though there had been no Fall. Or, if they are, like Richard Hooker, Christian apologists, they buttress the laws of Nature with those of God, and deal with both. The Fall is not an irremediable event: to construe it as such would make their program's goal of virtuous action meaningless.

No, the way is grown over with brambles, and one can no longer say with the old assurance,

ad honestatem nati sumus . . . ut Zenoni visum est[103]

but—since the advent of a Redeemer—the way is not impassable, and God helps those who help themselves.

Indeed, it would have been very difficult to eradicate the concepts of natural reason, natural law and justice, and a natural impulsion to virtue and a universal brotherliness—for these concepts were vital, in slightly different forms, to the whole medieval ethical and political structure, too. The legislators of the Middle Ages had inherited the larger part of their basic tenets from Roman law, and it, in its turn, was solidly founded upon what were held to be the permanent truths of natural law.[104] Thus these fundamental concepts of orthodox Stoicism had long been embedded in the body of political law endorsed by Christendom; the greater interest of the Renaissance in "Tullie" was not an interest in strange doctrines, but in his authoritative exposition of concepts which were already an integral part of men's convictions and—presumably—lives.

We will not, I repeat, find Renaissance orthodoxy holding expressly that "homo homini deus est." Yet these basic ideas: that man comes to justice naturally, that it is natural for him to do good to his fellow-man, that he naturally desires "to meet in companies, to form public assemblies"—in sum, that he is naturally impelled to virtuous and social action—these basic ideas imply that man is very good indeed to man. "Naturally impelled to virtuous action?" No, even more, for Cicero had said,

Nihil est tam contra naturam quam turpitudo. . . .[105]

Yet, long before Thomas Hobbes made it his peculiar property, men were repeating—and without qualification—that ancient phrase,

Homo homini lupus.

Montaigne says that Julian the Apostate declared, "There is no beast in the world so much of man to be feared as man" (or at least something "very neare"), when he had, "by the cruelty of some Christians," discovered the discrepancy between the ideal and the actuality. But Montaigne comes to a similar, if less dogmatic, conclusion himself, for all of his primitivism and Golden Age conceits:

Nature (I fear me) hath of her owne selfe added unto man a certaine instinct to inhumanitie.[106]

Louis Le Roy categorically denies the Law of Nature. The mere comparison of men to wolves does not suffice him. He depicts a "perpétuel combat entre les hommes"; he asserts outright that "les hommes sont enclins à contentation." And, having produced many illustrations of his thesis, he even points finally to the example of "des noises entre les enfants qui n'ont encore pas de connaissances."[107] Elsewhere, he calls upon the New World for testimony:

. . . et au Brésil, les Sauvages vont jusqu'a s'entre-manger, quand ils sont pris en guerre.[108]

There is nothing truly iconoclastic in these statements—to us. But we have lost, somewhere between Wordsworth and Freud, the conviction of the sanctity of nature's rational law—even the conviction of its existence. Such was not the case, of course, with the Renaissance, and statements like these of Montaigne and Le Roy constituted the most dangerous "innovations" of the whole anti-humanistic revolt. For if man was not naturally good—or at the least, guided by his natural reason to seek good—other basic principles upon which the whole order of society was founded were challenged too; the entire structure was threatened.

For it cannot be too often repeated that this structure was composed of interdependent parts, all derivatory from that fundamental premise of the Law of Nature: that there was a moral purpose behind the workings of the universe. God and Reason had dictated the Law of Nature, and the law of man's nature was reason, which would lead him to virtue. The defense of monarchy as the God-chosen form of government rested upon the analogy between political society and God's handiwork in visible nature; the concepts of order and degree and vocation, which held that cooperation and rank and particular purpose were universal laws, depended upon similar bases; political equity and moral responsibility derived from natural equity and the natural imperative to virtue. . . . The endorsement of "Homo homini lupus" constituted sedition in the Macrocosm.

And sedition there was. The "new" relativist concepts of the significant influence of climate and environment upon the nature of man are apparent in another passage of Le Roy's—one which makes at least some men naturally vulpine:

The Ethiopians, black, and with curly hair and beard . . . and the inhabitants of the cold and icy regions, who have a white skin and straight blond hair, are alike *naturally cruel,* from the excessive heat or excessive cold. . . .[109]

In his *Discourses,* Machiavelli had made no qualifications of any sort about man's natural acquisitiveness. The "desire of man," he says, is "insatiable"—

> because *of nature he hath it,* that he can and will desire everything, though of fortune he be so limited, that he can attain but a few[110]—

and if the corresponding statement in the *Prince* is milder, the judgment would still not meet with the approval of orthodoxy:

> The wish to acquire is in truth very natural and common, and men always do so when they can, and for this they will be praised not blamed; but when they cannot do so, yet wish to do so by any means, then there is folly and blame.[111]

To get the full force of this matter-of-fact assertion, compare it with a representative orthodox position on the same subject:

> Now let us know what gives this unruly desire of having. 'Tis a Gangrene in the soul, that with a poysonous heat consumes our natural affections to supply their roots with virulent humours. . . .[112]

This is Du Vair's, and what to Machiavelli is "natural and common," is to him "a Gangrene in the soul"—an unnatural infection that "consumes our natural affections."

The virus appears even in the supposedly solid ranks of the middle-path humanistic tradition. Justus Lipsius writes,

> For it is naturally geven to mens dispositions, to use imperial authority insolently, neither can they easily keep a meane in that thing which is above mediocritie. Even we our selves that thus complaine of tiranny, do beare in our breasts some seede thereof, and many of us doe not want wil to performe it, but ability.[113]

Strange words for the advocate of God and Right Reason. . . .

Remembering Cicero's conviction that "nature ordains that one man shall desire to promote the interests of a fellow man," the following words from Erasmus' jester would be equally surprising—if we did not already know him for a disreputable character.

> And now I consider it, Nature has planted not onely in particular men but even in every Nation, and scarce any City is there without it, a kind of common self-love.[114]

It should be increasingly apparent that remarks like these, which otherwise seem to be merely shrewd, hard-headed thrusts at man's vulnerable points, take on a new significance when one understands the background of allusion. For each of them aims at one of those corollary axioms of the central Law of Nature—whether at that of man's natural brotherliness, or that of his natural subordination of his own interests to those of the majority, or some other. And it becomes increasingly apparent that there are men who do not find their brothers (or themselves?) naturally inclined to virtue.

But so far we have witnessed only sniping. The real attack opens in the Italian sector. In discussing the various natures of men, Pomponazzi admits that

> some are men of ability and of a nature well formed by God, who are led to the virtues by the nobility of the virtues alone.

Others, he continues, require "rewards, praises, and honors"; still others may be "led" to virtuous conduct only through the "hope of some good and the fear of bodily punishment." And finally, he says, "as daily experience teaches," some, from "fierceness or perversity are moved by none of these."[115]

Indeed,

> the greater part of men, if they do good, do it more from fear of eternal punishment than hope of eternal good . . . if all men were in that class first enumerated, even granting the mortality of souls, they would be upright. *But almost none are of that nature.*

He is warming to his task:

> Nor is this inconsistent, since human nature is almost completely immersed in matter, and *the intellect participates very little;* whence man is further from the intelligences than a sick man from a healthy one, a boy from a man, and a fool from a wise man.[116]

It is quite a volley, and I would remind you that the cartridges do not bear the trademark of Geneva, but of Padua. There is no theological premise involved; the Fall of Man is not mentioned. Nor is it on the adjoining front.

For there is firing going on over in Florence:

> It is necessary for a prince to understand how to avail himself of the beast and the man. . . . If men were entirely good this precept would not hold, *but because they are bad,* and will not keep faith with you, you too are not bound to observe it with them.[117]

Like Pomponazzi, Machiavelli is interested in "men of ability." But
—unlike Pomponazzi—he does not equate these with men "who are
led to the virtues by the nobility of the virtues alone." On the
contrary:

> The mercenary captains are either capable men or they are
> not; if they are, you cannot trust them . . . [if not] you are
> ruined in the usual way.[118]

Guicciardini's machine gun, leveled in the same direction, carries the objective:

> If men were good *or* wise, whoever commands them could
> legitimately use more gentleness than severity; but the majority
> being either not good enough *or* not wise enough, it is sensible
> to count more upon severity; whoever sees things differently
> deceives himself.[119]

It is not quite such "total" war on the northern front. Yet it is
not quiet, either. We have heard already from Le Roy. Jean Bodin
is another who finds the majority of men either bad or incompetent.
In deprecating "des états populaires," he points out that

> les voix en toute assemblée sont comptées sans les peser: et
> toujours le nombre des fous, des méchants et des ignorants est
> mille fois plus grand que celui des gens de bien.[120]

Ben Jonson's account in *Timber* is equally undemocratic:

> The vulgar are commonly ill-natur'd. . . . There was not that
> variety of beasts in the Arke; as is of beastly natures in the
> multitude; especially when they come to that iniquity, to
> censure their *Soveraign's* actions.[121]

Much of Ralegh's *Cabinet-Council* is taken directly from Machiavelli, some from Bodin, Lipsius, and Sansovino.[122] He, too, denies
that men are naturally inclined to good:

> The nature of men is such, as will not endeavor any thing good,
> unless they be forced thereunto; for where liberty aboundeth,
> there confusion and disorder follow. It is therefore supposed,
> that hunger and poverty make men industrious, but good laws
> enforce them to be honest; for if men were of themselves good,
> then laws were needless.[123]

And again,

> All histories do shew, and wise politicians do hold it necessary,
> that for the well-governing of every commonweal it behoveth
> to presuppose that all men are evil, and will declare them-
> selves so to be when occasion is offered. . . .[124]

Bacon records with mild surprise the existence in some men of a natural "Disposition" to "Goodness"; he takes "Naturall Malignitie" more as a matter of course, and moves on to a sound Machiavellian conclusion:

> Neither is there only a *Habit of Goodnesse,* directed by right Reason; but there is, in some Men, even in Nature, a Disposition towards it: As on the other side, there is a Naturall Malignitie. For there be, that in their Nature, does not affect the Good of others. . . . Such Dispositions are the very Errours of Humane Nature: And yet they are the fittest Timber, to make great Politiques of: Like to knee Timber, that is good for Ships, that are ordained to be tossed; But not for Building houses, that shall stand firme.[125]

Where does it come from, this sudden series of assertions that men are "naturally bad," that they are by nature cruel, avaricious, acquisitive? The immediate and obvious answer is: from these men's own experience. And indeed such is their own claim, for they make up that group which Bacon eulogized for describing "what men do, and not what they ought to do."

Yet they had, of course, predecessors—a line stretching back into classical antiquity. We may not stop to note more than one or two of them here—and these only to show that once again "orthodoxy" itself provided ammunition for the enemy. For in the very first book of Aristotle's *Politics* is the statement:

> The man who first united people in such a partnership was the greatest of benefactors. For as man is the best of the animals when perfected, so he is the worst of all when sundered from law and justice. For unrighteousness is most pernicious when possessed of weapons, and man is born possessing weapons for the use of wisdom and virtue, which it is possible to employ entirely for the opposite ends. Hence when devoid of virtue man is the most unholy and savage of animals. . . .[126]

Yes, "man is born possessing weapons for the use of wisdom and virtue," but there is no mention of his being afforded also a natural impulse so to use them. It is one of those perfectly good statements which becomes ambiguous only in the light of warring interpretations; Aristotle himself had no way of knowing how his text was to be mauled and pulled out of shape in a battle between the Thomists and the Averroists—a battle to be renewed near the end of the sixteenth century. For we may remember that Gabriel Harvey, writing of innovations and innovators, notes "Aristotle muche named, but little read," and yet

You can not steppe into a schollars studye but (ten to one) you shall litely finde open either Bodin de Republica or Le Royes Exposition uppon Aristotles Politiques. . . .[127]

It is quite probable that the passage from the *Politics* quoted above is one upon which Le Roy elaborated in his "Exposition"—as we shall see when we come to his description of man's condition before society was organized.

One does not find much mention of Carneades in Renaissance political and ethical tracts, yet he must have been widely known, if only through the accounts given of him by Augustine and Lactantius. And this man who was the brilliant spokesman of the New Academy skeptics in the second century B.C. delivered in Rome orations which shook the foundations of the whole sacred legal systems of the Mistress of the World. Nor did Cicero, Lactantius and St. Augustine fail to record the substance of those orations. His theme was that of the relativity and mutability of justice, religion, morals, laws.

But if skepticism, relativism, empiricism and the new utilitarianism contribute to the Counter-Renaissance naturalistic attack upon the traditional interpretation of man's nature, there are of course entirely different factors involved in the early Reformation's equally exuberant opposition. In this respect, Luther and Calvin explicitly part company. Calvin, and, say, such a representative English follower of his as William Perkins, are not in fundamental disagreement with the traditionalists about the *nature* of the soul. Their divergence from the Christian humanists is in terms of the difference between what was true of the soul *naturally*, and what is true of it *since* the Fall. For Calvin declares,

> Original sin does not reside in one part of the body only, but holds its dominion over the whole man, and so occupies every part of the soul, that none remains in its integrity.[128]

As Perkins says,

> Man must bee considered in a foure-fold estate, as he was created, as he was corrupted, as hee is renewed, as hee shall be glorified.[129]

Since it is in terms of man "as he was corrupted" and "as he is renewed" that the anatomies of the soul deal, they are theologically inacceptable to Calvinists, who believe man to be "renewed" only through Grace.

Calvin thunders:

Let it stand, therefore, as an indubitable truth, which no engines can shake, that the mind of man is so entirely alienated from the righteousness of God that he cannot conceive, desire or design anything but what is wicked, distorted, foul, impure, and iniquitous; that his heart is so thoroughly envenomed by sin that it can breathe out nothing but corruption and rottenness; that if some men occasionally make a show of goodness, their mind is ever interwoven with hypocrisy and deceit; their soul inwardly bound with the fetters of wickedness.[130]

For Calvin, original sin "seizes upon the very seat of reason":

For although there is still some residue of intelligence and judgment as well as will, we cannot call a mind sound and entire which is both weak and immersed in darkness. As to the will, its depravity is but too well known. Therefore, since reason, by which man discerns between good and evil, and by which he understands and judges, is a natural gift, it could not be entirely destroyed; but being partly weakened and partly *corrupted, a shapeless ruin is all that remains.* . . . In like manner, the will, because inseparable from the nature of man, did not perish, but was so enslaved by depraved lust as to be incapable of righteous desire.[131]

Or, in Perkins' words:

Though liberty of nature remains, yet liberty of grace, that is, to will well, is lost, extinguished, abolished by the fall of Adam.[132]

Calvin, however, alarmed at the widespread tendency of the naturalists to expound the following of instinct or appetite, rather than reason, and at the consequent ambiguous use of the term "free will," even gave grudging approval to "the schoolmen" in one passage—doubtless feeling that such a course was the lesser evil. He admits that "natural law" is the same as conscience, and that man has an innate sense of justice and injustice, although this is of no use in particulars. Then he continues,

And at the outset, to guard against its being thought that the doctrine taught by philosophers, and generally received, viz., that all things by natural instinct have a desire of good, is any proof of the rectitude of the human will,—let us observe, that *the power of free will is not to be considered in any of those desires which proceed more from instinct than mental deliberation.* Even the schoolmen admit, (Thomas, Part I, Quaest. 83. art. 3), that *there is no act of free will, except when reason looks at opposites.* By this they mean, that the things desired must be such as may be made the object of choice, and that to pave the way for choice, deliberation must precede.[133]

What is more—

if you attend to *what this natural desire of good in man* is, you will find that it *is common to him with the brutes.* They, too, desire what is good; and when any semblance of good capable of moving the sense appears, they follow after it. Here, however, man does not, in accordance with the excellence of his immortal nature [!], rationally choose, and studiously pursue, what is truly for his good. He does not admit reason to his counsel, nor exert his intellect; but *without reason, without counsel, follows the bent of his nature like the lower animals.* The question of freedom, therefore, has nothing to do with the fact of man's being led by natural instinct to desire good.[134]

He concludes with a summary about this "double misnomer":

For this appetite is not properly a movement of the will, but natural inclination; and this good is not one of virtue and righteousness, but of condition, viz., that the individual may feel comfortable. . . .[135]

Luther's attitude is quite another matter. One does not need to turn to Jacques Maritain's scorching (and perhaps disastrously partisan) arraignment of him to find ample evidence that Luther, however unintentionally, heaped fuel on the fires built by the naturalists. Maritain declares that he freed "material individuality . . . the animal man";[136] that he was "wholly and systematically ruled by his affective and appetitive faculties";[137] that in him we have "the absolute predominance of Feeling and Appetite."[138] He cites Luther's approval of a rape of nuns, and claims that he poured "morbid pity" on young men and girls who were "tormented by the fire of the senses," and used "his evangelical zeal to deliver their *libido*," still declaring that

nothing can cure *libido,* not even marriage—libido nullo remedio potest curari, nequidem conjugio,—for the most part of married people live in adultery (Opp. exeg. lat., I, 212, 26–27, 29–30 [1536]. Weim. XLII, 8–10).[139]

One need not, I say, turn to M. Maritain for this judgment. The sober Hulme speaks of the early Reformation's and Luther's influence as providing

an enormous mass of testimony that would seem to show that

its immediate effect was a relaxation of the restraints of religion and an increase of immorality.[140]

And even an accomplished biographer quotes the famous passage—

> Come, accept. Be a sinner! *Esto peccator!* And don't do the
> thing by halves; sin squarely and with gusto, *pecca fortiter!*
> Not just playful sins. No, but real, substantial, tremendous
> sins![141]

commenting on "this extravagant manner of reasoning," and on
"what a chance such an impulsive excitable thinker affords . . . for
artful hands to manœuvre him, incite him, direct him!"

Pecca fortiter! It adds a thick, gusty, Germanic romanticism to
the mixture stirred more soberly by the naturalists of the Counter-
Renaissance. On the one hand as forthright a denial of limit as
Pico's nobler dream of freedom, Luther's statement was on the other
an exhortation to live shamelessly in the animal world of the naturalists—and so forthright a one that its following qualifying reservations were often not even heard. And behind it—and here in
conjunction with Calvin—lay, of course, another premise held in
common with the animalists—that of man's badness. A premise held
only with a theological reservation, but one pointing in the same
direction, nevertheless. The humanists' cartography of the nature
of man is as ruthlessly altered by the one as the other. And more
—much more, when one remembers the centrality of the principle
of analogy. All this ripping and tearing at the neatly limited, carefully graded and defined picture of man's constitution could not
leave unaffected the picture of him as a political and social being.
If the established principles of limit that governed one's understanding of his nature and value were so grossly assailed, how could
one's attitude toward his status in his society—indeed, toward very
society itself—remain unaffected?

The answer is, of course, that it couldn't. *Order?* "To conclude,"
says Montaigne, speaking of the Civil War in France,

> I see by our example that the societie of men doth hold and
> is sewed together, at what rate so-ever it be; where ever they
> be placed, in mooving and closing, they are ranged and stowed
> together, as uneven and ragged bodies, that orderlesse are
> hudled in some close place, of themselve finde the way to be
> united and joyned together one with another; and many times
> better then Art could have disposed them.[142]

Degree? "It is by the mediation of custome that every man is contented with the place where nature hath settled him." It is the irrepressible Montaigne again—and he has more to say:

> Lawes are nowe maintained in credit, not because they are essentially just, but because they are lawes. It is the mysticall foundation of their authority—they have none other—which availes them much: They are often made by fooles; more often by men who, *in hatred of equality*, have want of equity: But ever by men who are vaine and irresolute Authours. There is nothing so grossly and largely offending, nor so ordinarily wronging as the Lawes.[143]

But there are other voices, too: Ralegh's (is he brooding on his own experience?)—

> Certainly there is no other account to be made of this ridiculous world, than to resolve, that the change of fortune on the great Theatre, is but as the change of garments on the less. For when on the one and the other, *every man wears but his own skin; the players are all alike.*[144]

and a somewhat obscure, but defiant one—that of Michael Baudier:

> *Le monde a été crée en commun;* les pauvres y possèdent aussi bien le droit de bourgeoisie que les riches; puisque *la nature fait naître les hommes également nus* et dépourvus de toute sorte de commodités, et que la terre les reçoit de même, et n'enferme point dans les sépulchres la vaine possession des richesses.[145]

But Montaigne makes the definitive statement—

> Superiority and inferiority, maistry and subjection, are joyntly tied unto a naturall kind of envy and contestation; they must perpetually enter-spoile one another.[146]

Vocation?

> Into how many orders, stages, and stations have they divided this wretched man, beside the naturall and perceptible? and to how many distinct offices and vocations? They make a publike imaginarie thing of it.[147]

But if there are only scattered voices on these particulars, a full chorus can be heard on the subject of the "specialty of rule." To get its direct force, it would be wise first to review the orthodox concept of a good king—as ably and representatively presented by Jean Bodin, for example. In his earlier book, the *Methodus,* he had discussed absolutism with a freedom and—it seemed to some—a sympathy, that were casually naturalistic. But, as his translator writes,

> It is only in the light of increasingly alarming political conditions, from 1565 to 1576, that one can explain the change that took place in his political philosophy between the writing of the *Methodus* and of the *Republic*.[148]

At any rate, in the following passage from the *Republic*, he speaks exclusively the language of orthodoxy:

> The king ought to obey the lawes of nature: that is to say, ought to governe his subiects, and to guide his actions according unto naturall iustice, whose luster was brighter than the light of the sunne it selfe. It is then the true marke of a Royall Monarchie, when the prince sheweth himselfe as obedient unto the lawes of nature, as he wisheth his subiects to be unto himselfe.[149]

The stories of the apostles of "fact" and "homo lupus" are different. Writing about Alexander, Valla says,

> He had already determined to cross the ocean, and if there was any other world, to explore it and subject it to his will. He would have tried, I think, last of all to ascend the heavens. Some such wish all kings have, even though not all are so bold.[150]

Agrippa asks, with a disarming appearance of ingenuousness, whether our rulers are really "persuaded that their principal duty . . . is to procure . . . the happiness of their subjects?" But the appearance of ingenuousness does not remain for long. After discussing tyrants and their abuse of power, he continues,

> If some monarchs, more moderate, exempt or relieve their subjects of this heavy, & insupportable burden, do not believe that in that they are considering common good: no, without doubt they have no other end, no other motive, than personal interest.[151]

"Everyone," says Machiavelli,

> admits how praiseworthy it is in a prince to keep faith, and to live with integrity and not with craft. Nevertheless our experience has been that those princes who have done great things have held good faith of little account, and have known how to circumvent the intellect of men by craft, and in the end have overcome those who have relied on their word.[152]

Guicciardini openly attacks the rationalists in their stronghold:

The philosophers will have it that the government of one alone, when he is good, is the best of all, and natural reason confirms it. They call him good when, after deliberate consultation, they have put at the head of all the man most able to govern—a thing which is more simple to desire than to hope for from our time. In actuality principalities and modern grandeurs are born either of disorder, or of arms, or, yet again, of factions: one had not at all in mind the choosing of the best or the most deserving, but rather the one better favored by chance or by means. . . .[153]

Rabelais' ridicule in this matter is subtle. First he presents the good king, Grangousier, deciding that he must take up arms in defense of his people.

But now I must (I see it well) load with arms my poor, weary, and feebled shoulders, and take in my trembling hand the lance and horseman's mace to succour and protect my honest subjects. *Reason will have it so;* for by their labour am I maintained, and with their sweat am I nourished, I, my children, and my family.

But he concludes, rather ingloriously, "This notwithstanding, I will not undertake war, until I have first tried all the ways and means of peace; that I resolve upon."[154]

A few pages farther on, Picrochole, who is planning on conquering the world, has been listening to his ministers telling him how it can be done.

"Come," said Picrochole, "let us go join them quickly; for I will be emperor of Trebezonde also. Shall we not kill all these dog Turks and Mahometans?" "What a devil should we do else?" said they; "and you shall give their goods and lands to such as shall have served you honestly." *"Reason,"* said he, *"will have it so; that is but just. . . ."*[155]

Once again, however, there is a step to take from the ridiculing of the Christian-humanistic accounts of the behavior of a king, and the pointing of the discrepancy between such unlikely ideal conduct and the observed actuality—to the endorsing of power politics. And there were those, notably Machiavelli, who did endorse them.

As I have already said, one must first face the actualities of the world, and particularly the country, in which Machiavelli found himself. On the one hand, his conviction of the actuality of *homo homini lupus* as a constant factor in human life, on the other the desperate condition of Italy's national autonomy—these decisive factors led to the position he held in the *Prince,* and only modified in the *Discourses.*

Granting such conditions, then, he says that the essentially private virtues have only a subordinate claim upon a prince. In such a world, he, too—if he is to persevere and achieve any success—must use tooth and claw. Men engaged in politics and war (for Machiavelli a prince's almost exclusive concern[156]) have never been noted for observing the amenities of the moral virtues. This emphasis was not, of course, new. We may remember, for example, that Aristotle remarked, "In the case of military command one must consider experience more than virtue."[157]

Guicciardini echoes Machiavelli's views and reasons:

> Today, in order to preserve power and the State, one should use, when one can, pity and kindness; but, when one cannot do it, at other times it is necessary to employ cruelty and bad faith . . . it is impossible to maintain the Government and the State in conformity with the precepts of the Christian life, if one wishes to maintain them in the manner of today.[158]

And, the implication is, if one does not wish "to maintain them in the manner of today," one will not maintain them at all.

Again, just as Machiavelli points out that "liberality exercised in a way that does not bring you the reputation for it, injures you"[159] (implying that liberality in itself is not a virtue in a prince), so Jean Bodin declares,

> Now they that praise the goodness, bountie, and courtesie of a prince, without wisdom: are themselves unwise and ignorant in matters of state, abusing therein both their praise and leisure: for as much as such simplicitie without wisedome is most dangerous and pernitious unto a king, and much more to be feared than is the great severitie of a cruell, covetous, and inaccessible prince. So that it seemeth our auntient fathers not without cause to have used this Proverbe, *That of a craftie and subtill man is made a good king.* . . .[160]

Bodin, like Machiavelli, is aware that he may be censured for such a statement; he continues,

> which saying unto the delicate eares of such as measure all things by false opinions rather than by sound reasons, may seem right strange. . . .

Yet he knows that he is right—

> for by the too much suffrance and simplicitie of too good a

king, it cometh to passe that flatterers, extorcioners, and men
of most wicked disposition
come to power.[161]

Moreover, we discover almost instantly that (in this instance, at
least) Bodin means by "sound reasons" observed facts, by "false
opinions" reason in the orthodox sense—for he illustrates his point
with the case of Francis I, who was a wayward ruler, yet caused
France to prosper.

In short, we are dealing with a group of men (however dissimilar
in other respects) who put the good of the state first—let the private
moral virtues, often ineffective for political purposes, fall where
they may. But the orthodox political writers put the good of the
state first, too—yet insist that it rests upon those very premises
which these men discard. How may the discrepancy be explained?

The answer is, I think, that to the Christian humanists the good
of the state means the happiness of the greatest number, while to
the "animalistic" naturalists of the Counter-Renaissance, it is an
absolute in itself,[162] which (if it is identified with anyone) means
that the good of the state is the good of those who rule it. For the
traditionalist theorists, the state is built upon divine and natural
principles of order, degree and harmony, ruled by reason, and
pointed toward the twin goal of virtue and happiness for all. For
the naturalists (or at least the extreme ones: the statement would
not hold for the Bodin of the *Republic*[163]) the state is most likely
to come to mean those who control it.

Thus, while Machiavelli writes in the *Discourses,*

> Wherefore a wise founder of a Republick, who seeks not his
> own advantage, but the publick good; not to strengthen his
> own succession, but seeks his Countreys profit, ought endeavour
> to get the power wholly into his own hands, . . .[164]

in the *Prince* he says,

> And again, he need not make himself uneasy at incurring a
> reproach for these vices without which *the state* can only be
> saved with difficulty, for . . . it will be found that something
> which looks like virtue, if followed, would be *his* ruin; whilst
> something else, which looks like vice, yet followed brings *him*
> security and prosperity.[165]

And while it is certainly true that, for Machiavelli himself, the views
of the *Discourses* are his long-range ones, and he is indeed capable
of envisioning, with his enthusiasm for "l'antico valore,"[166] the state
as an ideal *per se*—for the "Machiavellians" the *Prince* tends to be

the book. And they ignore the master's primary justification of the tactics he advocates as resting in their production of political stability, to concentrate almost exclusively upon the idea of absolute sovereignty, or upon "the motives of personal ambition in the princely actions."[167]

Hence Machiavelli at least professes *political stability* as his justification of power politics, while such "Machiavellians" as Chapman portrays in the *Revenge of Bussy* make the distinction between public and private virtue solely on the basis of the king's absolute rights. Here all treachery performed for the king is "loyalty" and "grave deep policy." One character asserts that

> All acts that seem ill in particular respects are good as they respect your universal rule—

and after hesitating over the provision, "so that no man be wronged thereby," concludes,

> . . . no not though all men's reasons,
> All law, all conscience, concludes it wrong.[168]

And the king agrees—so holy is the head that wears a crown!

4. THE MACHIAVELLIAN WORLD-VIEW

Yet, despite this evidence that Machiavelli did identify the state with the man of power at its head, a deeper and more thoughtful consideration of the *Discourses* reveals that this identification is not a constant in his picture of the state, but rather a part of his theory of political cycles (which we shall take up in a moment). The single man *is* the state only at a certain point in the cyclical progression. "A city declining by corruption of matter," he says,

> if ever it chances to rise again, it is merely by the vertue of one man, who is then living, and not by the vertue of the generality, that keeps the good Laws in force . . .[169]

and the evil bogey of his *Prince* is somewhat altered as we begin to see how all his theory holds together. Let us reread a paragraph already cited:

> Wherefore a wise founder of a Republick [for this is to Machiavelli the best form of government in an established state], who seeks not his own advantage, but the publicke good; not to strengthen his own succession, but seeks his Countreys profit, ought endeavour to get the power wholly into his hands. . . .

Yes, he admits that it takes many "to maintain" a good State. Yet "many are not proper for the framing of one thing."[170]

In one passage he speaks of how "the Ordinances and Laws made in a Republick at birth thereof, when men were good, serve not to purpose afterwards, when once they are grown vicious"[171]—thus seemingly accepting the degeneration theory. And elsewhere he declares,

> all beginnings of Sects, Commonwealths and Kingdoms, must needs contain some goodness in them, by means whereof they recover their first reputation and increase: for in process of time that goodness growes corrupt, and unless something happen, that reduces it to the just mark, that body must needs be destroyed.[172]

There is indeed a return to first principles involved here, yet Machiavelli does not mean that men in general grow worse and then reform. He does not really believe that there is a "decay in men," to be rectified only by a new Golden Age—

> I think the world hath continued alwayes in one manner, and that in it hath been always as much good as evil; but that the good and evil does change from Countrey to Countrey, as it appears by that which is discover'd to us of those ancient kingdoms, which alter'd from the one to the other, by change of manners. But the world continued the same.[173]

The key words and phrases to an understanding of what Machiavelli does mean by these references to a process of decay are ones like "a city declining by corruption of matter" . . . "birth" . . . "that body must needs be destroyed." Several European students of Machiavelli have seen that in such phrases we are dealing with a new kind of analogy (one very different from the medieval sort) —in fact, with a body of biological analogy.[174] In other words, Machiavelli, apparently under the influence of the medical school at Padua, constantly refers to the state in medical terms, as though it were a biological organism. It is evident in the *Prince* that he considers his own country "a sick person,"[175] and one of the scholars just referred to, Leonardo Olschki, is convinced that Machiavelli himself considered his study of history and politics the introduction to an empirical *science*.[176]

Two passages from the *Discourses* should serve to illustrate this concept of the state as a biological entity or organism, and Machiavelli's use of biological analogy and medical terminology even when dealing with the whole human race, which he considers "a compound body." The first passage illustrates this second attitude:

> For in nature [he has been talking of floods, pestilences and famines] as in simple bodies, when there is an accumulation of superfluous matter, a spontaneous purgation takes place, which preserves the health of the body. And so it is with that compound body, the human race; when countries become over-populated and there is no longer room for all the inhabitants to live, nor any other places for them to go to, these being likewise all fully occupied,—and when human cunning and wickedness have gone as far as they can go,—then of necessity the world must relieve itself of this excess of population by one of those three causes; so that mankind, having been chastised and reduced in numbers, may become better and live with more convenience.[177]

The second passage concerns the state, considered as an organism:

> There is nothing more true than that all the things of this world have a limit to their existence; but those only run the entire course ordained for them by Heaven that do not allow their body to become disorganized, but keep it undamaged in the manner ordained, or if they change it, so do it that it shall be for their advantage, and not to their injury. And as I speak here of mixed bodies, such as republics or religious sects, I say that those changes are beneficial that bring them back to their original principles. And those are the best constituted bodies, and have the longest existence, which possess the intrinsic means of frequently renewing themselves, or such as obtain this renovation in consequence of some extrinsic accidents. And it is a truth clearer than light that, without such renovation, these bodies cannot continue to exist; and the means of renewing them is to bring them back to their original principles. For, as all religious republics and monarchies must have within themselves some goodness, by means of which they obtain their first growth and reputation, and as in the process of time this goodness becomes corrupted, it will of necessity destroy the body unless something intervenes to bring it back to its normal condition. Thus, the doctors of medicine say, in speaking of the human body, that "every day some ill humors gather which must be cured."[178]

The important thing to notice here is the way in which Machiavelli uses "goodness" (as the translator puts it). The arguments about the meaning of his famous *virtù* have been long and, frequently, unenlightening. But Olschki again has a good point to make:

> In the medieval medical terminology "virtus" designated the *potestas quaedam efficiendi* attributed—for instance—to offici-nal plants, herbs and drugs. But the first modern example of the employment of that term in a strictly scientific function is to be found in Leonardo da Vinci's notes on dynamics, where the same word *virtù* designates the motive power in a physical sense.[179]

This is an important point in connection with the passage from the *Discourses* just read. For Machiavelli says that all such bodies (religious or political) must have within themselves "some good-ness, *by means of which* they obtain their first growth and reputa-tion"; he then takes it for granted that in time that goodness will become corrupted, and the "body" will be destroyed unless it re-turns to its *normal condition*. He concludes with an analogy to the human body. Is it not clear that he is not talking about "goodness" and "corruption" in the established moral sense? His *virtù*, which Olschki points out, is "not only an individual quality but also a collective qualification for the authority, liberty, peace, stability and welfare of a political community,"[180] in this context seems clearly to mean "motive power" in a political situation—"efficiency" or "effectiveness," if you will, in a new application of Leonardo's sense.[181] So far Olschki—but I believe that this passage carries even more freight, that it establishes *virtù* as "*healthful* efficiency" in the sense of the medieval medical use of "virtus" cited by Olschki. Hence the medical reference, and the organic analogy.

In other words, Machiavelli has neatly turned the tables on the medieval teleologists. They looked for *purpose* in each plant, seek-ing the meaning with which a natural object had been endowed by a supernatural agency, and found intention and aspiration in nature. Machiavelli takes the humanly artifacted social and political institution and "reduces" it to an organic agency of uninformed nature. His *naturalism,* which we have long been considering, is never more blatant than here. It is a crude, naïve naturalism, per-haps, and—when qualified—as unwarranted as the reverse process of the medievalists. But the intention and direction of his thought are what we are after, and I think they emerge clearly. He looks at *everything* as a part of nature, of natural growth, and *virtue is health,* the process of efficient functioning in accordance with the particular object's norm of health.

Here is another crucial step in the denial of limit. It is ironic that in this passage Machiavelli is talking about "limit," saying that "all the things of this world have a limit to their existence"—for in *our* sense of "limit," this reduction of everything to natural, material forces is the apotheosis of the denial of limit. In this and similar passages, he pronounces the same principle for political and historical matters that Bruno did for cosmic ones with his concept of "indifferenza della natura." As Olschki puts it, Machiavelli's conviction that human nature was always and everywhere the same amounted to saying that "men, just as heaven, the sun and the elements, never had changed their motion, order and power,"[182] and on this premise rested his doctrine of "the eternal recurrence of typical events and of the possible renewal of culminating historical situations through voluntary imitation of typical political accomplishments."[183] Says Olschki:

> The axiom that human nature is constant has its exact scientific counterpart in Galileo's fundamental assumption that "matter is unalterable," i.e., always the same, and that because of its eternal and necessary character it is possible to produce demonstrations of it no less straight and neat than those of mathematics.[184]

It is interesting to bring confirmatory evidence to this theory of Machiavelli's "biological" concept of the growth and life of states and political institutions, from another scholar's findings about another, but later, influential leader of the Counter-Renaissance. Speaking of Louis Le Roy's philosophy of history, this scholar says, "The concomitant rise of power and arts in a nation, 'concurrence des armes et des lettres,' was advanced by him as a sort of *biological growth*. . . ."[185]

Waiving the question of Le Roy's direct indebtedness to Machiavelli, which seems probable, this at least establishes a tendency in the intellectual climate among the naturalists of the Counter-Renaissance. Le Roy also depicted the life of a state in these terms of birth, early vigor, full "manhood," relaxing and disintegration, although I have been unable to find any evidence of his having built up so sharp and exact a biological theory as that of Machiavelli.

At any rate, it is time for us to return to Machiavelli's philosophy of history, which is necessarily bound up with those propositions of his which we have been studying.

He does not see history as a single progression, a unique phenomenon in time—as Christian theology did. Nor is he one of the early prophets of progress, in the modern sense. Concerned almost exclusively with political institutions, he considers the rise and fall of states as a cyclical process. In other words, he applies the ubiquitous Greek theory of cycles to political society—as Plato and Polybius had done before him. The origin of a state invariably involves that process which we have seen him describe in his account of man's first progress from the state of nature to civil society: a strong man either takes hold or is given complete authority, and out of chaos emerges form.

But this power, utilized properly by him, is apt to become tyranny in the hands of his heirs. The nobles, eventually unwilling to endure this tyranny, take over the government themselves, and from tyranny evolves the rule of an aristocracy whose heirs, in turn, are likely to convert it into an oligarchic tyranny. And so the process goes: from monarchy to tyranny to aristocracy to oligarchic tyranny to democracy to anarchy—and then once more a single strong man emerges to make order out of chaos, if that state is to survive at all. "Such is the circle which all republics are destined to run through." [186]

It is true that, in the *Discourses*, he offers a solution:

> Sagacious legislators, knowing the vices of each of these systems of government by themselves, have chosen one that should partake of all of them, judging that to be the most stable and solid. In fact, when there is combined under the same constitution a prince, a nobility, and the power of the people, then these three powers will watch and keep each other reciprocally in check. [187]

Yet, throughout the body of his work and thought, it is the cyclical theory which most concerns him, and most frequently recurs. If the mixed state is best, it is still rare; and Machiavelli's faith is pledged to "things as they are, not as they should be."

Of course, he has not been able in a lifetime to observe the actual fulfilling of these cycles. What he has observed in his own time, he has found to agree with "that which is discover'd to us of those ancient kingdoms," and he believes, moreover, that these cycles are so clearly discernible that one can accurately predict the future course of things. For "Wise men are wont to say":

> that he who will see what shall be, let him consider what hath been: for all things in the world at all times have their encounter with the times of old. Which comes to pass, because those things are wrought by men, *who were alwayes and are subject to the same passions;* and therefore follows it of necessity, that they take the same effect. [188]

It is a sentence upon men equal to those passed by Montaigne—indeed, in its ultimate dreariness of outlook, it far exceeds the tellingness of Montaigne's blows at orthodoxy. But Machiavelli does not consider it especially dreary; what he has to say seems to hold no particular emotional connotation for him. He is telling the truth, based upon *fact* and *observation* (of various kinds) and *personal experience:* that is his story. And if incidentally, he divorces human history from revelation and purpose and progress alike; if he denies to man either the guidance of reason or the pursuit of virtue; if he omits utterly (and so, by implication, gives the lie to them) any mention of natural law, natural justice, a state founded upon these laws inherent in God's and Nature's purposes—all that is incidental.

Nor should we believe that such a picture is confined to Machiavelli. Guicciardini exploits the same ideas, and draws the same conclusions:

> All which has been in the past and which is at present will be again in the future; but things change in names and appearances in such a way that those who have not good eyes do not recognize them at all and know neither how to regulate themselves [their own lives] by them nor how to draw some judgment from their observation.[189]

A character in the *Heptameron,* surprisingly enough, speaks the same language—and although at first he seems to draw a different conclusion from the fact that man's nature is a constant, his explanation of what he means brings us to the same destination as that of the Italians:

> The wicked are always wicked, and the good always good: and as long as wickedness and goodness reign on earth, something new will always be taking place, although Solomon says that nothing new happens under the sun. As we have not been called to the privy council of God, and consequently are ignorant of first causes, *all things seem new to us,* and the more wonderful the less we could or would do them. So do not be afraid that the days to come will not be as good as the past. . . .[190]

A hint of the "cycles of government" theme is to be found in Agrippa's *De incertitudine,* with a somewhat lame attempt to fasten the blame for the deterioration of a state upon the meddling of the savants.[191] And while Bacon is far too exuberant an optimist to accept the cyclical theory in terms of man's possible knowledge, he does suggest something very like political cycles in the essay on "Returnes and Vicissitudes:"

> In the *Youth* of a *State,* Armes doe flourish; In the *Middle*

Ages of a *State, Learning;* And then both of them together
for a time: in the *Declining Age* of a *State, Mechanicall Arts*
and *Merchandize.*[192]

But perhaps the clearest restatement among the Elizabethans
(although with characteristic variations) of the Machiavellian theory
is to be found in Greville's *A Treatie of Warres:*

> Needful it therefore is, and cleerely true,
> That all great Empires, Cities, Seats of Power
> Must rise and fall, waxe old, and not renew
> Some by diseases, that from without devour,
> Others even by disorders in them bred,
> Seene onely, and discover'd in the dead.[193]

So, he continues, revolts, discords, civil wars take place—

> All have their growing, and declining states. . . .[194]

He envisions a similar return to first principles, although to him
these involve "Natures Lawes, and Truths simplicity":

> That by vicissitude of these translations,
> And change of place, corruption, and excesse,
> Craft overbuilding all degenerations,
> Might be reduced to the first addresse
> Of Natures Lawes, and Truths simplicity;
> These planting worth, and worth authority—

and he concludes the passage by connecting political cycles with
the favorite Renaissance theme of mutability in general, and by
making Machiavelli's biological analogy:

> All which best root, and spring in new foundations
> Of States, or Kingdomes; and againe in age,
> Or height of pride, and power feele declination;
> Mortality is Changes proper stage:
> States have degrees, as humane bodies have,
> Spring, Summer, Autumne, Winter and the grave.[195]

George Hakewill, a post-Elizabethan, directly calls upon Machiavelli for confirmation of his argument that there has been no progressive decay in man's nature, but rather, "as in the Arts & Sciences,
so likewise in matter of manners, there is a vicissitude, an alterna-
tion & revolution"—

> And though exceptions bee taken at Machiavell in other cases,
> yet I know no sufficient reason but wee may well enough
> admit of his testimonie in this, being a matter of civill wisedome
> & observation, wherein without doubt few of his age were
> matchable with him. . . .[196]

The interest in, and application of, the cyclical theory was not, of course, confined to politics and governments and states. As Greville's poem suggests—and as he elsewhere indicates—the general theory was widely held, and applied to all aspects of civilization. Most often it was accompanied by the related premise of four ages of descending merit—the golden, silver, bronze and iron ones (clay sometimes made a fifth)—and thus the idea of a cyclical regeneration, already implicit, was developed specifically. At least as old as Hesiod, doctrinally developed by the Stoics, mythically by Plato, prophetically—after the Sibylline writings—by Vergil in his *Fourth Eclogue*, the concept had many and diverse treatments in the Renaissance. Edmund Spenser, for example, applies it to a dream of a reformation within the Anglican church, in the February Eclogue of his *Shepheards Calendar:*

> Must not the world wend in his common course,
> From good to badd, and from badde to worse,
> From worse unto that is worst of all,
> And then returne to his former fall?[197]

—and in the May Eclogue, there are two lines reminiscent, in a different context, of Machiavelli's and Guicciardini's conviction that everything in the past and present will be repeated in the future:

> The time was once, and may againe retorne,
> (For ought may happen, that hath bene beforne).[198]

This idea of the four ages and cyclical regeneration might or might not take Christianity explicitly into account. Spenser refers to a "returne to his former fall," yet no rigidly orthodox account could hold that the whole drama of man's sin and ultimate salvation would be repeated. In this sense, as well as in the general concept of eternal or indefinite recurrence, there is a denial of limit (in the denial of the uniqueness and finiteness of the process of history, and especially the history of the Christian story).

But leaving the religious question to one side, there was a great revival of interest in applying the cyclical theory to lay history, and in the formulation of a philosophy of history. Machiavelli and Guicciardini, with their views on history, political and governmental cycles, and the basically unchanging nature of man, held an all-out position on the theory of cyclical decline and regeneration. Such a man as Louis Le Roy, with his major interest in civilizations, rather than political states, held a modified view.

Although Le Roy largely shared the others' views on the rise and fall of nations,[199] his philosophy of history was not concerned with the exposition of a simple repeated cycle, but held fast to "a more dynamic sense of continuity."[200] Moreover, he frequently seems to stand on the threshold of the outright declaration of a philosophy of progress;[201] we have already seen part of one of his catalogues of "new" things—inventions, discoveries, etc.—which lead him to exclaim over the intellectual riches and resourcefulness of his own times. Yet on the very brink of such a declaration, he hesitates. From past examples, he comes to fear that the excellence of present ideas and events may be the indication of a decline or retrogression in the near future. Perhaps a natural catastrophe or even an invasion of Europe from the East is at hand—just as pestilences and floods occurred in the past.[202] As Mr. Bates (his translator) says of him:

> His philosophy of history bears thus two faces: in the individual parts he saw a cyclic movement of rise and fall, the repetition of state destiny which made him apprehensive for his own land; but in the more extended annals of man he saw the cumulative existence of man's spiritual and material creations, which despite fluctuations outlived their original surroundings and mixed with new life in the future.[203]

Jean Bodin, while expressly repudiating the "golden age" theory, and even more flatly extolling the accomplishments of his own century,[204] does make the qualification, "since by some eternal law of nature the path of change seems to go in a circle. . . ."[205] And he is even harder on the generally accepted medieval picture of history (already mentioned in Chapter III) as the limited succession of four great Empires—with the end of the fourth (Roman, and including the Christian dispensation), dissolving and bringing the earth to an end. He declares, "A long-established, but mistaken, idea about four great empires, made famous by the prestige of great men, has sent its roots down so far that it seems difficult to eradicate."[206]

In a dryly naturalistic spirit, he observes,

> . . . the interpreters of the prophecies [of Daniel, about the four beasts, and the destruction of Babylon] have not defined it at all clearly. They suppose from this vision of four beasts and an image that an equal number of empires was signified: that is, of Assyrians, Persians, Greeks, and Romans. They augured that there will be no more. Eventually the Germans were to control the Roman Empire. Since it was explained in this way by Germans, I judged it was written for the glory of their name and empire, for it is altogether strange to the interpretation of Daniel.[207]

Several pages farther on, he continues, "There are, and have been until now, not only four, but almost an infinitude of empires greater than the Babylonian."[208] He cites the Chaldeans, the Medes, the Parthians and the Arabs among many others.[209] And he concludes with a curt dismissal of "the mistaken custom that each man should interpret the prophecies of Daniel according to his own judgment, not according to *accurate history*."[210] A similar view was held by Machiavelli and Agrippa (see Chapter III) among others. . . .

We have seen that Greville associated political cycles with mutability in general. The identification was probably inevitable, for few themes were of more general interest to the Elizabethans that those of change, mutability and decay. But in this particular context—in connection with the idea that the rise and fall of states followed a regular cyclic pattern—the concept of mutability called into question the whole meaning of life.

For if the state and justice and sovereignty did not rest upon divine and natural bases, what did? If one part—and so important a one—of the analogical framework should be proved fallacious, what of the rest? What, even, of the ultimate source?

The leaders of the Counter-Renaissance were there to answer— and they did, although often not loudly. Most of them preferred to hide behind the fortifications of Calvinism, or some other institution which would permit them to attribute most of what happened to fortune and chance—and then explain that they had meant the incomprehensible workings of the unknowable will of an inscrutable God.

Yet denials of a Divine Reason guiding the world, of purpose, knowable or unknowable, of established limit as reality and value, there were—as there always had been. The prime offenders of antiquity—according to Renaissance Christian humanists—had been the Epicureans and (in the light of certain interpretations) Aristotle. For Epicurus had "denied the universal truth of cause, and explained freedom, together with chance, as uncaused occurrence."[211] Aristotle was held guilty on two counts—his belief in the eternity of the world[212] and his disbelief in the immortality of the individual (or passive) soul.

Ralegh makes all except the last of these charges in his preface to the *History of the World*, when he declares that Epicurus denied the *Creation* and *Providence*, and Aristotle the *Creation* and the *Beginning*. The remaining accusation leveled at Aristotle—regarding the immortality of the soul—was more likely to be made in Italy, where (thanks to Padua) the interpretations of Averroës and of

Alexander of Aphrodias were more often meant, when one spoke of "Aristotle," than that of Thomas Aquinas. We find Ficino referring to both of these variant philosophical interpretations in this very context, in his introduction to his edition of the *Enneads:*

> The learned world, in which the peripatetics dominate, is generally divided into two sects: the first is that of the alexandrians, the second that of the averroists. The first hold that our understanding is mortal, the second maintain that it is *one* for all men; both oppose all religion, principally because they deny that the Providence of God exercises itself concerning men; and in these points they are equally distant from Aristotle.[213]

But in addition to this kind of Aristotelianism, and to the Epicurean concept of the gods as remote and indifferent, there were many other available sources for the idea that nature was "blind" and that fortune or chance ruled events and men—sources, as usual, which were a part of perfectly orthodox concepts.

Fortune, in particular, was a favorite word (one might almost say personality) in the Renaissance. Professor Samuel Chew's study of the iconography of the period has clearly demonstrated how effective an influence upon the popular and visual imagination the ideas of the Goddess Fortuna and of the Wheel of Fortune had.

Furthermore, the *leit-motifs* of such books as Boccaccio's *De Casibus* and the English *Mirror for Magistrates*[214] merged harmoniously the concept of Fortune and that of a retributive justice which it was easy to equate (or at least associate) with Providence—to point home the moral of "keeping one's place," and particularly the political lesson of limit in the sense of "degree." All these ideas, suggesting the part that vicissitude plays in the affairs of men (although especial reference to the Wheel of Fortune seems clear), are apparent in such lines as these of Marston's:

> He needs must rise, who can no lower fall,
> For still impetuous *Vicissitude*
> Towzeth the world. . . .[215]

To be sure, the medieval world had been vastly concerned with the question of fortune's relation to the order of things. Those who had followed the other-worldly "de contemptu mundi" tradition had been largely contented to admit the irrational control of things by fortune or chance in the sub-lunary world—like Luther and Calvin later, their eyes were fixed on another world, in which they found all value and the significant part of reality. And like the early Reformers, they attributed the evil state of matters on earth to the

Fall.[216] But Thomas, his followers, and the Christian humanists thereafter would not accept such an interpretation. Christianity brought chance under law, thus freeing nature from fortune—although it admitted an "apparent disorder of nature."[217] The Renaissance Christian humanists insisted upon not only man's free will, but law and order running throughout nature.

To be sure, there was the influence of the stars to consider. There were few men in the Renaissance who would not endorse some kind of astrology. Yet Fate (for all of its opposition to free will) was assimilated into the Christian-humanistic structure more easily than Fortune or Chance. Fate—Destiny—Providence: one can step lightly from rock to rock. Calvin might (and did) deny emphatically that predestination had anything to do with Stoic Fate; some of the humanists might (and did) explain that Fate was just the expression which the benighted ancients used for God's Providence. But the middle-path reconcilers of Christianity and classicism, and especially those systematic harmonizers of Christianity and Stoicism, Lipsius and Du Vair, even welcomed Fate into the fold. For they found the Stoic idea of man enduring and thus overcoming the buffetings of Fate irresistible. The most frequent interpretation was that Fate or Destiny (usually the influence of the heavens) was a sort of lesser disposition of Providence, and could affect only that which was primarily *sensitive*. In other words, it was admitted that the stars influenced, directed and guided sublunary life on all levels *below the rational*.[218] At any rate, if man's reason continued to guide him, he could stand firm with his free will against Fate's buffetings.

In a loose way, "Fortune" and "Chance" are sometimes used instead of "Fate" in this connection. But so long as man does stand firm against them, one may be sure that one is reading the passage of a humanist, who believes that there is a purpose in the universe, and that if man exercises his free will, under the guidance of right reason, he may not be overcome by "Fate" or "Fortune" or "Chance." Such a passage is this one from Poliziano's *Stanze*, with its Stoic flavor:

> O happy He who Fortune's frown perceives
> Undaunted, and her fiercest shock sustains
> Firm as a rock resists the assailing waves,
> Or tow'r the tempest's idle rage disdains:
> With brow serene her each assault he braves
> Prepar'd, nor ever of reverse complains:
> Still self collected, in himself confides,
> Nor by chance govern'd, even o'er chance presides.[219]

Most often, however, even the suggestion that "Fortune" or "Chance" rules over the lives of men means that an "atheist" is speaking—one who denies any rational purpose to the universe and to life. There is such an identification in the chapter heading in Sidney's *Arcadia* which reads "The Auntes Atheisme refuted by the Neeces Divinitie."[220] And although the aunt, Cecropia, doesn't use the words "Fortune" and "Chance," the "Neece," Pamela, turns them back upon her in her "refutation." After giving many other reasons why the world is not ruled by "Chaunce," she declares,

> Lastly, Chaunce is variable, or els it is not to be called Chaunce: but we see this worke is steady and permanent. If nothing but Chaunce had glewed those pieces of this All, the heavie partes would have gone indefinitely downwarde [etc., etc.][221]

And again, in a passage which clearly links together *chance, fortune* and *blind nature* as the "guiding" principles for an atheist—

> Lastly, perfect order, perfect beautie, perfect constancie, if these be the children of Chaunce, or Fortune be the efficient of these, let Wisedome be counted the roote of wickednesse, and eternitie the fruite of her inconstancie. But you will say it is so by nature, as much as if you said it is so, because it is so: if you meane of many natures conspiring together, as in a popular governement to establish this fayre estate . . . there must needes have bene a wisdome which made them concurre. . . . But you may perhaps affirme, that one universall Nature (which hath bene for ever) is the knitting together of these many partes to such an excellent unitie.[222]

"If," she continues, "you meane a Nature of wisdome, goodnesse, & providence," then there is no offense. But if you mean one "blind" Nature, then

> it is still the same absurditie subscribed with another title. For this worde, one, being attributed to that which is All, is but one mingling of many, and many ones. . . .[223]

When Pamela concludes with the statement that "this worlde therfore cannot otherwise consist but by a minde of Wisedome, whiche governes it . . ." the field is finally ready, the sides drawn up: Fortune, Chance, blind Nature vs. God's Providence or Wisdom, Purpose, Nature's law. And exactly the same opposition, with the same outcome extended to a vision of the final Judgment Day, is to be found in the conclusion to Spenser's "Mutability Cantos":

> Then gin I thinke on that which Nature sayd,
> Of that same time when no more change shall be,

> But stedfast rest of all things, firmely stayd
> Upon the pillours of eternity,
> That is contrayre to Mutabilitie:
> For all that moveth doth in change delight:
> But thenceforth all shall rest eternally
> With Him that is the God of Sabbaoth hight:
> O that Sabbaoth God grant me that Sabaoths sight.[224]

Mutability has been arguing like Cecropia, that change, diversity, lawless fortune, rules the world. But Dame Nature (representing law, "a nature of wisdom and providence") not only predicates that final rest of Eternity quoted above, but argues successfully for the existence of an order running through all nature, a constancy of purpose and operation running through all change. . . .

It is quite possible that one of the reasons Des Périers' *Cymbalum Mundi* was held to be such an "atheistical" book, is to be found in a speech of the suddenly disillusioned Mercury. He has been wondering why Jupiter hadn't read in his book containing "Fatorum praescriptum: sive, eorum quae futura sunt, certae dispositiones" that it was going to be stolen. Then, suddenly, he declares,

> I believe he is become purblind for this Accident must have been foreseen in it, as well as all others, or the Book must be false.[225]

And, "Tell fortune of her blindness," says the equally disillusioned Ralegh, distinguishing between the vaguer, more respectable use of the word and its sinister one.

Machiavelli admits in the *Prince* that he is half inclined at times to say that Fortune controls everything. "Nevertheless," he concludes briskly,

> not to extinguish our free will, I hold it to be true that fortune is the arbiter of one half of our actions, but that she still leaves us to direct the other half, or perhaps a little less.[226]

He is much more detailed in the *Discourses*—much more exact—and we begin to see the sense in which Olschki was able to write of Machiavelli's *fortuna:*

> It is . . . an abstract and secular concept which eludes and substitutes for the superstitious belief in occult forces and also the Christian faith in the unfathomable decrees of God.[227]

I should go farther. I should say even more boldly that, in most of the uses of the word in the *Discourses*, Fortune is Machiavelli's equivalent for Luther's and Calvin's inscrutable God, whose will man may not know, but whose favorite he may become, and their concept of predestination. More—I should say that although Machiavelli once refers to *Fortuna,* with grim playfulness, as a goddess, and although he once equates Fortune loosely and casually with "the will of Heaven" in the *Discourses,* all the most characteristic passages indicate that he does not think of it as any supernatural agency, but as the aggregate of all the unpredictable elements in human life.[228] At the same time, in his single longest treatment of Fortune, in Chapter XXIX of Book II of the *Discourses,* he speaks of Fortune as "she" and "her," and attributes to her "wishes," "designs" and "aims." Fortune, thus personified or deified, bears some resemblance to the Stoic *fatum*—and in one passage[229] Machiavelli even advocates typical Stoic apathy as the best remedy for "good" or "bad" fortune.

Yet his Fortune is not bleakly impersonal, operating, at least partly predictably, as justice in nature, in the tradition of the Stoic *fatum*—but capricious and unknowable. Moreover, she presents a naturalistic or pagan equivalent to the Reformation's concept of predestination, for she chooses favorites; one may become one of her "elect," whom "she select[s] for her instrument."[230] Again one may not oppose her omnipotence—"men may second Fortune, but cannot oppose her; they may develop her designs, but cannot defeat them."[231] Yet one can woo her, he asserts in the *Prince*—and here boldness is of greatest importance.[232]

But with the last allusion, we are back in the more playful mood, which considers her a woman. The tune of this peculiar lay parallel to the Reformation is again evident when Machiavelli writes of man's inability to achieve his end unless he is given Fortune's special aid. Then, even then, it is not his own effort that clinches the favorable decision—all the credit is hers: "She overcomes by her power the natural and ordinary difficulties."[233] One is reminded by this amoral parallel of the Reformation's concept of imputed righteousness: even the goodness in the man who has faith is not his, but Christ's in him; even the success this man wins is not his, but Fortune's gift to him.

I will not run this rather startling parallel into the ground. But even waiving the lesser similarities, if one keeps in mind the agreement of Machiavelli with Calvin and Luther on man's essential badness, it does not seem exaggerated to say that the world ruled by the historian's Fortune and that by the Reformers' God differ only in the absence or presence of the theological premise. Both deny utterly the existence of comprehensible laws governing the universe and directing its course. Both deny the validity of the Christian-humanistic ethical norms. Both oppose almost every one of the various concepts of limit integral to that Christian-humanistic interpretation of life. . . .

Needless to say, most of the Elizabethan passages that develop a world ruled by Chance or Fortune, do not develop the idea as systematically as Machiavelli. Yet Marston's and Chapman's versions are interesting. Andrugio is another of Marston's bitter characters who can in no sense be considered a villain; he is expressing disenchantment, not willful evil, when he says,

> Philosophie maintaines that Natur's wise,
> And formes no uselesse or imperfect thing.
> Did Nature make the earth, or the earth Nature?
> For earthly durt makes all things, makes the man,
> Moulds me up honour; and like a cunning Dutchman,
> Paints me a puppit even with seeming breath,
> And gives a sot appearance of a soule.
> Goe to, goe to; thou liest, Philosophy.
> Nature formes things unperfect, uselesse, vaine.[234]

One cannot attribute the sentiments of Rinaldo, in *All Fools,* to Chapman. But one can testify that Chapman hears current rumors, when we are told that Rinaldo's education has been conducted at Padua, and that the "Machiavel" of the piece likes "his learning well."[235] For Rinaldo's creed is:

> Fortune, the great commandress of the world,
> Hath divers ways to advance her followers:
> To some she gives honour without deserving,
> To other some, deserving without honour;
> Some wit, some wealth, and some wit without wealth;
> Some wealth without wit, some nor wit nor wealth,
> But good smock-faces; or some qualities,
> *By nature without judgment,* with the which
> They live in sensuall acceptation
> And make show only, without touch of substance.[236]

It is a theme which interests Chapman. *Bussy* is full of it. The second scene of the fifth act—entirely a dialogue between Monsieur and Guise—shows how far Chapman's knowledge of the tradition has advanced during the years since *All Fools.* Monsieur declares,

> Now shall we see that Nature hath no end
> In her great works responsive to their worths;
> That she, that makes so many eyes and souls
> To see and foresee, is stark blind herself;

And as illiterate men say Latin prayers
By rote of heart and daily iteration,
Not knowing what they say, so Nature lays
A deal of stuff together, and by use,
Or by the mere necessity of matter,
Ends such a work, fills it, or leaves it empty
Of strength or virtue, error or clear truth,
Not knowing what she does.

All, he maintains, is Fortune. And Guise admits that a worldly man's observation must lead him to agree "that Nature works at random." Monsieur even connects the theme with "cycles of morality"—

As Fortune swings about the restless state
Of virtue, now thrown into all men's hate.[237]

But these negations of purpose and Providence are not exclusively the property of the "villains." Bussy, himself "Fortune's proud mushroom shot up in a night,"[238] opens the play with the categorical statement,

Fortune, not Reason, rules the state of things,
Reward goes backwards, Honour on his head;
Who is not poor, is monstrous; only need
Gives form and worth to every humane seed. . . .[239]

Fortune, Chance, blind Nature vs. God's Providence, purpose, a Nature of law and reason . . .

Machiavelli admitted only two determining forces in the development of history: *fortuna* and *virtù*.[240] Olschki, we have seen, finds a parallel to Leonardo's "necessity and power."[241] Reviewing our discussion to date, we could certainly also substitute "chance" and "efficiency," "fatal necessities and human power."[242] At any rate, he sees a world governed by largely unpredictable forces, and the share that may be predicted is limited to what—by observation of men and events in history and in the present—man can effect by "seconding" Fortune. This calls for exercise of *virtù*—not virtue in the usual sense, but a combination of cunning and courage—which leads, not to happiness or the self-contained reward of virtue or salvation, but *success* (acquisition of power and recognition).

Moreover, in the wholly naturalistic—no, animalistic—world picture that Machiavelli predicates, success is equivalent to preservation, to *self-preservation*. The alternative is ruin: "He who neglects what is done for what ought to be done," Machiavelli writes, "*sooner effects his ruin than his preservation;* for a man who wishes to act entirely up to his professions of virtue soon meets with what destroys him among so much that is evil."[243]

The longer we read and study him, the more we see that he is all of a piece. I have said that this concept of self-preservation is the equivalent of Telesio's similar concept in a naturalistic physics; it is further apparent here that this postulating of ruin and preservation as life's alternatives are another pair of terms to match those Machiavelli uses in his biological concept of the state. For to stay well is to preserve oneself; to become diseased or corrupted, to ruin oneself. And these alternatives he applies (with his usual over-simplifying tendency to regard everything as an organism) to states as well as to individuals. He recognizes only two "motives" in states: self-preservation and expansion. And it is like his recognition of laws and arms as the two means of control. There cannot be good laws without good arms; similarly, that cannot be preservation without aggression and consequent expansion. The world is one of *bellum omnium contra omnia*—and the devil (failure, ruin) take the hindmost. But it is not a case of conscious cynicism, rather a belief (without the benefit of the evolutionary theory) in the popular concept of red-jawed nature.

Including human nature. *Homo homini lupus.* Man is not endowed with any spark of natural reason, or any natural gregariousness. Instead, it is natural to man to have an unlimited desire for acquisition,[244] and once again, self-advancement or self-assertiveness is commensurate with self-preservation.

Such is Machiavelli's world, such is his concept of the nature of men and states. If only students of history and political science like Guicciardini, Bodin and Le Roy seem to have understood even partly the philosophic base of his theory, every one in his time knew him and reacted to him. And the two most prevalent reactions concerned his attitude toward public morality (especially as applied to rulers), and to private morality—in terms of whether or not his advice to "the prince" applied equally to all levels of life.

With regard to the former, we now understand Machiavelli's premises, which lead him to say:

> Hence it is necessary for a prince wishing to hold his own to know how to do wrong, and to make use of it or not according to necessity.

He enumerates a list of virtues, such as mercy, good faith, humaneness, piety and uprightness—and the contrasting vices—before continuing:

And I know that every one will confess that it would be most praiseworthy in a prince to exhibit all the above qualities that are considered good; but because they can neither be entirely possessed nor observed, for human conditions do not permit it, it is necessary for him to be sufficiently prudent that he may know how to avoid the reproach of those vices which would lose him his state, and also to keep himself, if it is possible, from those which would not lose him it; but this not being possible, he may with less hesitation abandon himself to them.[245]

We have already seen (no matter what the philosophic base), that Machiavelli and his more faithful followers do endorse "power politics." Guicciardini says, "in order to preserve power and the State," and Machiavelli himself:

You must know that there are two ways of contesting, the one by the law, the other by force: the first method is proper to men, the second to beasts: but because the first is frequently not sufficient, it is necessary to have recourse to the second. Therefore it is necessary for a prince to understand how to avail himself of the beast and the man.[246]

And he declares on the next page,

A prince, therefore, being compelled knowingly to adopt the beast, ought to choose the fox and the lion . . . a fox to discover the snares and a lion to terrify the wolves.[247]

For man, you will remember, is a wolf to man. . . .

The fox and the lion . . . deceit and force. The fox's characteristics are among those which Innocent Gentillet is to make most famous. It is enough for Machiavelli, he declares indignantly, that the "Prince seems outwardly religious and devout, although he be not so at all . . ."[248] But let us have Machiavelli's own words:

It is necessary . . . to be a great pretender and dissembler; and men are so simple, and so subject to present necessities, that he who seeks to deceive will always find someone who will allow himself to be deceived. . . .

Therefore it is unnecessary for a prince to have all the good qualities I have enumerated, but it is very necessary to appear to have them. And I shall dare to say this also, that to have them and always to observe them is injurious, and that to appear to have them is useful. . . .[249]

These two doctrines of "the fox" are great storm centers: (1) the idea that the prince must deceive; (2) the idea that he must rather simulate virtues than possess them.

Yet it is interesting to note that these doctrines are common to the moral empiricists of antiquity and of the Middle Ages and the Renaissance alike; Machiavelli's contribution, like that of Bacon in another field, is primarily that of publicizing them—his reward, the somewhat dubious one of having his name appended to them thereafter.

For there are passages in Aristotle's *Politics* susceptible to similar interpretations.[250] Carneades, whose views on law and justice are familiar to us, had advocated an out-and-out doctrine of expediency for a state, on an eat-or-be-eaten basis; had declared that it is better to seem to be good, than to be good; and had even applied the practice of exclusive self-interest to private life.[251] And Panaetius, that eclectic Roman Stoic who was influenced by Carneades, and in his turn influenced Cicero, agreed that a double moral system was necessary—one ideal for wise men and a more practical system for the common people.[252]

Averroës believed that it was necessary to deceive a certain class of men about the reality of an after-life;[253] Pomponazzi cites his authority in elaborating the theme:

> Therefore they have posited for the virtuous eternal reward in another life, but for the sinful eternal punishments, which frighten them very greatly. And the greater part of men, if they do good, do it more from fear of eternal punishment than hope of eternal good, since the punishments are more known to us than those eternal goods. And since this last device can benefit all men, of whatever class they are, the legislator, *seeing the proneness of men to evil,* intending the common good, has decreed that the soul is immortal, not caring for truth, but only for righteousness, so that he may bring men to virtue.[254]

Nowhere in Renaissance writings is there implicit a more complete denial of the ideas of natural reason and the natural impulsion toward good. And Pomponazzi continues,

> Nor ought the statesman to be reproached. For just as a physician invents many things to restore a sick man to health, so a statesman makes fables to keep citizens to the right path. But in these fables, as Averroës says in the prologue of the third book of *Physics*, there is properly neither truth nor falsity. . . . If all men were in that class first enumerated [of ability and of a nature well formed by God] . . . they would be upright. But almost none are of that nature. Wherefore one must proceed by other devices.[255]

This idea that most people must be misled by a statesman for their own good is also to be found in Plato's *Laws* and *Statesman*.[256] Again, according to Longarine (in the *Heptameron*), Jean de Meun had held a point of view similar to Machiavelli's about the propriety of a prince's employing deceit. She declares that princes

> are forced to falsehood, hypocrisy, and reigning, which, according to Maître Jean de Meun, are means for vanquishing enemies. Since conduct of this nature is laudable in a prince, though it be censurable in all other men, I will recount to you the device employed by a young prince. . . .[257]

Discussions of the tactics of the Fox appear everywhere in Renaissance literature; it would be tedious to trace down reference after reference. Yet there are endorsements of Machiavelli's and similar points of view which it might be well to note. Guicciardini, for example, assents to the importance of seeming good. Yet—with a greater realism than Machiavelli—he sees difficulties in sustaining this appearance, if it is only feigned:

> Do everything to seem good; that always serves. But, since false ideas do not last, it will be difficult for you to seem so for long if you are not really.[258]

Bodin simply admits that it is necessary "to lie sometime . . . for the advantage of the state";[259] but Bacon deals with all these related points—in the essay "Of Simulation and Dissimulation" and in his *De sapientia veterum*. In the former, his argument is as completely disingenuous as any one may find in the Renaissance. He admits that the "ablest Men"

> have had all an Opennesse, and Francknesse of dealing; And a name of Certainty, and Veracity; But then they were like Horses, well managed; For they could tell passing well, when to stop or turne: And at such times, when they thought the Case indeed, required Dissimulation, if then they used it, it came to passe, that the former Opinion, spread abroad of their good Faith, and Clearnesse of dealing, made them almost Invisible.

He classifies three kinds of "this Hiding, and Vailing of a Mans Selfe": (1) "Closenesse, Reservation, and Secrecy"; (2) "Dissimulation, in the Negative"; (3) "Simulation, in the Affirmative."[260]

The first of these he approves—"therefore set it downe: That an Habit of Secrecy, is both Politick, and Morall." The second is almost inevitable to a small degree if one pursue the first:

> So that no man can be secret, except to give himself a little

Scope of Dissimulation; which is, as it were, but the Skirts or Traine of Secrecy.

After all, he concludes, others insist upon our showing an "inclination" of some sort.[261]

It is only when he comes to treat the third kind that he makes the distinction between "private" and "public" morality:

Simulation, and false Profession; That I hold more culpable, and lesse politicke; except it be in great and rare Matters.

And he finally concludes:

The best Composition, and Temperature is, to have Opennesse in Fame and Opinion; Secrecy in Habit; Dissimulation in seasonable use; And a Power to faigne, if there be no Remedy.[262]

In the essay on Pan in *De sapientia veterum,* discussing the "metaphor" of the "sheep-hook," he says,

So also in all the wiser kinds of human government, they who sit at the helm can introduce and insinuate what they desire for the good of the people more successfully by pretexts and indirect ways than directly, so that every rod or staff of empire is truly crooked at the top.[263]

Yet, after all these passages, he has the effrontery to speak of Machiavelli's advice about seeking the appearance of good, and Lysander's precept, "that children are to be deceived with comfits and men with oaths—and the like evil and corrupt positions!"[264]

Harvey seems adolescent after Bacon:

Satius est, sequi mendacium, quam, verum perniciosam. Ulisseum et Machiavellicum.[265]

In a longer passage he declaims with gusto:

A right fellow to practice in yᵉ world: on, that knowith fasshions: & prettely spiced with yᵉ powder of experience & meetly well-tempered with yᵉ powder of Experience. Machiavel, & Aretine knew fasshions, and were acquainted with yᵉ cunning of yᵉ world. Mach. and Aretine were not to lerne how to play their partes, but were prettely beaten to yᵉ doings of yᵉ world. Mach. & Aretine knew yᵉ lessons by hart & were not to seeke how to use yᵉ wicked world, yᵉ flesh, & yᵉ Divel. They had lernid cunning enough: and had seen fasshions enough: and could & woold use both, with advantage enough. Two curtisan politiques. Schollars, & common youthes, even amongst yᵉ lustiest, and bravist courtiers; ar yet to lerne yʳ lesson jn yᵉ world. Vita, militia: vel Togata, vel Armata.[266]

If, however, the Christian humanists were outraged at the way in which the Machiavellians discussed with calmness and disingenuousness a ruler's denial of the limit to which ideally he should be subjected—that of the laws of God and nature and natural justice —and even their outright adherence to power politics, they were even more alarmed by the denial of limit in the sacred sense of *degree* in society that was apparent in Machiavelli's writings and in those of his followers. A bad ruler, ignoring the universal laws, was a catastrophe; an upstart who threatened the sanctity of class stratification, constituted a threat to the very cornerstones of society and civilization.

And again, however much scholars, writing before Hardin Craig discovered the Elizabethan English translation of the *Prince,* have tried to discount the direct influence of Machiavelli on the Elizabethans,[267] "the Secretarie of Florence" did discuss, most imperturbably, the rise of a private citizen of any rank to political power and authority. It was not, to be sure, a matter of much concern to him to distinguish between this rise of a private man to political authority, and the exercise of Machiavellian principles in private life. Here is where the Elizabethan dramatists, in some cases, went astray in their interpretations. But the point is that Machiavelli saw success, even life itself, entirely in political terms; I suspect that if the nicety of these differences had been put up to him, he would have shrugged his shoulders, with contempt for the man who could content himself with applying sound rules of behavior in so trivial a scene as that of private life.

At any rate then, however crude Christopher Marlowe's "Machiavellian" characters are (and they are not so crude as some scholars have made them out[268]), they are not wild distortions of Machiavelli's own doctrine, but rather a romanticist's version of a naturalist's point of view. This holds for all of them—from Faustus and Tamburlaine to Barabas, Guise and Mortimer.

Where does Machiavelli treat the denial of limit (degree) by a description of, or even an expression of approval for, the man who climbs to power from a lowly status? In the *Prince,* yes—but, as usual, most fully in the *Discourses:*

> And it is impossible that these who have lived as private citizens in a republic, or those who by fortune or courage have risen to be princes of the same . . .[269]

and

> I believe it to be most true that it seldom happens that men rise from low condition to high rank without employing either

> force or fraud [the Lion and the Fox]. . . . Nor do I believe
> that force alone will ever be found to suffice, whilst it will
> often be the case that cunning alone serves the purpose . . .[270]

and

> Nor do I believe that there was ever a man who from obscure
> condition arrived at great power by merely employing open
> force, but there are many who have succeeded by fraud
> alone . . .[271]

and

> In the conduct of the plot the danger is very slight, for a citizen
> may aspire to supreme power without manifesting his inten-
> tions to anyone; and if nothing interferes with his plans, he
> may carry them through successfully, or if they are thwarted
> by some law, he may await a more favorable moment, and
> attempt it by another way. . . . Citizens of a republic, then,
> may by a variety of ways and means aspire to sovereign au-
> thority without incurring great risks.[272]

And finally,

> To usurp supreme and absolute authority, then, in a free state,
> and subject it to tyranny, the people must have already be-
> come corrupt by gradual steps from generation to generation.[273]

Notice that Machiavelli rates the Fox higher than the Lion in
the *ascent* to power. Yet the passages in which he tells how the bold
court Fortune best, he brings the matter to a balance, and it is
certain that he believes the *combination* most effective. Certainly
once the goal has been achieved, he would thoroughly endorse the
following from Guicciardini:

> Fortune is glad to favor him who takes risks. Histories abound
> with examples of persons who have been freed from desperate
> conditions by spirit and frank entrance into perils, which should
> not be feared by a man pressed by necessity.[274]

It should be superfluous to linger over the various Elizabethan
writers who described or presented "Machiavellian climbers": their
number is legion. But perhaps no other one of them gave such certain evidence of his infatuation with Machiavelli's program for self-
preservation and self-advancement as did Gabriel Harvey. Here
are a few of the "pithier" maxims:

> He is not wise, that is not wise for himself.[275]

> Wealth and honour . . . Prompt action . . . Boldness, elo-
> quence, and winning manners lead to success . . . The power

of gold . . . Self-confidence . . . Be serpent and dove, lamb and wolf (The Lion and the Fox) . . . Lose not time.[276]

First cast to shoot right; then be sure to shoot home. Lett not short shooting loose yor game. aime straight, draw home. risoluto per tutto.

Quicquid est in Deo, est Deus; Quicquid est jn Viro, sit Virtus, et vis.

> Quicquid cogitat, Vigor:
> quicquid loquitur, Emphasis;
> quicquid agit, Dynamis:
> quicquid patitur, Alacritas.[277]

The only brave way to lerne al things with no study, & much pleasure.
Robin Goodfellow's Table Philosophy, good sociable Lessons.

> fier will owt; & feates will shew his cunning. . . .
> Mihi solus Caesar plusquam
> Omnes Libri.[278]

Gallant Audacity, is never owt of countenance: But hath ever A Tongue, & A Hand at will.
Begin with resolution: & follow it thorowly for life.[279]

Idle Heddes ar allway in yr transcendentibus & in nubibus: politique Witts, evermore jn concreto activo. . . . omnis theoria puerilis, sine virili praxi.

Regula Regularum. To seeke & enforce all possible advantage.[280]

It is almost incredible, but these are only a few of his gems. And then, suddenly, at the end of a note praising all "fiery natures" from "Richard I Cor Leonis" down, one finds this pathetic little item, so prophetic of the long obscurity which overtook him:

At nihil tali feci. Vae misero mihi, dum fecero etiam singulare et admirabile aliquid in utroque genere tam effectivo quam expressivo. Ut nemo mundo magis famosus.[281]

From Cesare Borgia to Gabriel Harvey—it is a strange progression. . . .

"In the school of the moral empiricists," writes Laurence Stapleton, "there was . . . one principle that enclosed all the others like an envelope: Suit every action to circumstance and occasion."[282]

It is an accurate statement. And at first glance it suggests that these "moral empiricists" were a rather ignoble lot. Expediency, nothing more.

But what have the humanists to say about expediency? Let us turn to Cicero:

> For whether moral goodness is the only good, as the Stoics believe, or whether, as your Peripatetics think, moral goodness is in so far the highest good that everything else gathered together into the opposing scale would have scarcely the slightest weight, it is beyond question that expediency can never conflict with moral rectitude. And so, we have heard, Socrates used to pronounce a curse upon those who first drew a conceptual distinction between things naturally inseparable. With this doctrine the Stoics are in agreement in so far as they maintain that if anything is morally right, it is expedient, and if anything is not morally right, it is not expedient.[283]

This is the great eclectic, the father of the Renaissance Christian humanists, with all the great sources at his disposal. And what he is really saying amounts to this: in a universe ruled by reason and moral law, if a man is to conform to the "main sway of the universe" it is expedient that he live in conformity with reason and moral law. Hence expediency can never conflict with moral right.

But Machiavelli and the Machiavellians did not live in such a world, but in one subject to chance, rocked by Fortune, and inhabited by wolves. Hence expedience and moral right do conflict —and on the subject Machiavelli lays down several rules: (1) Try to conform to the times in which you live; (2) Follow the natural bent of your nature, which will inevitably give you a better chance for success (here he joins hands with the other "natural bent" or "humour" school of individualistic ethics); (3) Recognize necessity as a determining factor in the pursuit of virtue, and impose that necessity upon others to keep them good (i.e., harmless)—hence emphasizing his moral determinism.

As to the first point:

> . . . men in their conduct, and especially in their most prominent actions, should well consider and conform to the times in which they live. And those who, from an evil choice or from natural inclination, do not conform to the times in which they live, will in most instances live *unhappily*, and their undertakings will come to a bad end; whilst, *on the contrary, success* attends those who conform to the times.[284]

Or, for both the first and second points:

> He errs least and will be most favored by Fortune who suits his proceedings to the times, as I have said above, and always follows the impulses of his nature.[285]

In other words, suit your actions to the temper of the times. Also, follow your own natural bent. *Then,* if your *natural* bent does suit the times, Fortune really smiles upon you. Guicciardini says it in a slightly different way:

> Those same ones who attribute everything to wisdom and virtue, and deny with all their strength the power of Fortune, must at least recognize that it is very important to fall, or to be born, in an epoch where the virtues and the qualities which distinguish you will be appreciated. . . .[286]

The third point concerns Machiavelli's moral determinism. He speaks outright of "the impossibility of resisting the natural bent of our characters,"[287] and links this statement with the difficulty of changing a method of approach to problems, once we have been successful with one approach, as the two evidences for a man's inability to change at will.[288] Since times change, these two factors may well cause a man's downfall.

Yet his moral determinism, with its proviso that men are virtuous mostly from necessity, provides the wise man with an implement by which to handle other people:

> And as men work either from necessity or from choice, and as it has been observed that virtue has more sway where labor is the result of necessity rather than of choice, it is a matter of consideration whether it might not be better to select for the establishment of a city a sterile region, where the people, compelled by necessity to be industrious, and therefore less given to idleness, would be more united, and less exposed by the poverty of the country to occasions for discord. . . .[289]

Disenchantment, indeed. And small wonder that the Elizabethans so often exhibit the dichotomy which led me to make this study of their intellectual background. For they were confronted, on the one hand, by that "mirror of perfection," the world of the Scholastics and then the Christian humanists—a world in which "is" and "ought to be" were in substantial accord, a world in which all was ticketed, ordered, limited, to bring about a maximum of harmony and co-operation, order and purpose, everything with its established due place in the hierarchy. The failures were failures, awful examples; they did not challenge the reality or value of the picture.

But on the other hand, there were the rebels, the deniers of this perfection and limit, who said that the image in the mirror was only a show of the truth, and a sadly distorted one—even that the mirror itself was cracked and blurred, and gave no indication of reality, and hence none of practical values. For there were many more than Machiavelli, even on this question of an ethic of expediency. There were even some who turned their backs on the image of perfection and recanted—or defected, in accordance with your point of view.

Such a man was Guillaume Du Vair, whom we have come to know as one of the harmonizers of Christianity and humanism—as one of the two men of the period who formally fitted together Christian and Stoic dogma. Yet in the third book of his *Constancy*, a later piece of work than the *Morall Philosophy of the Stoicks* and the *Sainte Philosophie,* he writes that political government consists of "une prudence particulière": that it cannot be reduced to "une science universelle."[290]

Heresy, of course, yet perhaps it is only a slip. But, no—on the next page there is another:

> Le bon citoyen doit bien avoir pour son but le salut public, et la justice, dont il dépend. Mais quand le chemin ordinaire ne l'y peut amener, si faut-il qu'il s'y conduira par celuy qui reste le plus commode . . .

because

> les affaires et les conseils se mesurent principalement par la fin.[291]

Then there is that other strange man, Erasmus, also a citizen—and a very much respected one—of Utopia. Strange, however, because he would take trips over into Chaos now and then. At least so I understand the ironic ambiguity of the *Praise of Folly.* So I understand his jester: as someone (one of the "selves" within Erasmus) who found the guise of Folly primarily useful to unburden himself, and not simply as a vehicle to ridicule those who upheld these opinions seriously. For example,

> For as nothing is more foolish than preposterous Wisdome, so nothing is more unadvised than a froward unseasonable Prudence. And such is his that does not comply with the present time "and order himself as the Market goes. . . ."[292]

A double-barreled ambiguity that, under the name of Folly, at once presents safely an "ignoble" ideal, and gets off his own chest the weight of its partial truth. . . .

Yet of all the group who "speak truth—not their bellyful, but as much as they dare," there are three whose voices are always most particularly worth listening for.

The first one isn't a very pleasant looking person—rather sinister, in fact. And yet he speaks with an incongruous precision—almost with prim fastidiousness:

> I believe also that he will be successful who directs his actions according to the spirit of the times, and that he whose actions do not accord with the times will not be successful.[293]

A mere careerist. Yet somebody has told a story about him—that when he is in the country, he dresses up ceremoniously in the evening, simply to sit and read the old authors.

The second man seems no livelier at first. Another cold man. Yet it is clear that he can be excited—but it all happens in his head. No heart to him. Yet his eyes light up. He must be saying something impressive.

> To passe from Theologicall, and Philosophical Truth, to the Truth of civill Businesse . . .[294]

A disappointing group.

And the third one, loitering along, just as though he had no intention of keeping up with the others—or with anybody. Sluggish, incurious. And an odd, blunt way of talking:

> We must live by the World, and such as we finde it, so make use of it.[295]

Machiavelli, Bacon and Montaigne . . . In his introduction to the Modern Library edition of the *Prince* and the *Discourses*, Max Lerner has written,

> Machiavelli sought to distinguish the realm of what ought to be and the realm of what is. He rejected the first for the second. But there is a third realm: the realm of what can be. It is in that realm that what one might call a humanist realism can lie.[296]

This is a first-rate statement of where Machiavelli and Bacon failed. In their repudiation of the current too-exclusive emphasis upon the intellectual and moral ideals of the great tradition of Western civilization, they fell into the trap at the other side of the pit. Only Montaigne, of the three, grew eventually into a sort of naturalistic humanism that avoided both pitfalls. Emerson knew what he was talking about when he expressed his famous preference for Montaigne over Cicero. But Emersons are rare, and we have never stood in greater need of a new Montaigne than now.

CHAPTER 7
FOOTNOTES

1.

1. Febvre, *Luther*, 200. For the qualifications and extenuations of this crucial point, cf. *ibid.*, 86–87, and *passim*.
2. Norman Nelson, "Individualism as a Criterion of the Renaissance," *Journal of English and Germanic Philology*, Vol. XXXII (1933), 319. I am indebted throughout this discussion to Mr. Nelson's lucid article.
3. *Ibid.*, 320.
4. *Ibid.*, 332.
5. Cf. *ibid.*, 319.
6. *Ibid.*, 322.
7. Machiavelli, I, 208, 274.
8. Nelson, *ibid.*, 332.
9. Cf. Fletcher, *Italian Renaissance*, 272.
10. Thomas Nashe, *The Unfortunate Traveller*, 61.
11. Harvey, *Marginalia*, 156. My italics.
12. Ben Jonson, *Every Man in his Humour* (1598; in the Quarto of 1601). III, i, 156 ff.
13. Folio Text of 1616: III, iiii, 20 ff.
14. Quarto of 1601, V, iii, 344–345.
15. *Every Man Out of His Humour*, ll. 109–114.
16. Quoted by Fletcher, *Italian Renaissance*, 271.
17. *Volpone*, I, i, 70–72.
18. Chapman, *Bussy D'Ambois*, II, ii, 140–141, 185–190.
19. Greville, *An Inquisition upon Fame and Honour*, st. 12.
20. Cf. Villey, *Essais de Montaigne*, 75–76.
21. Montaigne, II, 418.
22. *Ibid.*, II, 435.
23. *Ibid.*, II, 438. My italics.
24. *Ibid.*, III, 21.
25. *Ibid.*, III, 7–8.

2.

26. John Donne, *LXXX Sermons* (London, Printed by Richard Royston, 1640), 74, p. 755.
27. Ralegh, *Works*, VIII, 571.
28. Cf. Lily B. Campbell, *Shakespeare's Tragic Heroes* (Cambridge, 1930), 66. Miss Campbell's excellent chapter on the Renaissance anatomy of the soul has clarified several confusing points for me.
29. Cf. Ralegh, *Works*, VIII, 585 ff.
30. Du Vair, *Morall Philosophy*, 18–20. These two powers obviously derive ultimately from Plato's "desire" and "passion," although the Renaissance approximation is not exact.
31. Hooker, I, vii, 2. Cf. Aristotle, *Ethics*, III, 1, 3; VI, 2.
32. *Ibid.*, I, viii, 6. Cf. Aristotle, *Politics*, I, v, 5–6.
33. *Ibid.*, I, vii, 3; viii, 6.
34. *Ibid.*, I, vii, 3–4.
35. *Ibid.*, I, vii, 6.
36. *Paradise Lost*, IX, 1123 ff.
37. Davies, *Poems*, 114: *Nosce Teipsum*, Part I.

38. Du Vâir, *Morall Philosophy*, 15.
39. *Ibid.*, 15–21. Du Vair's account of "mutiny" varies from the majority most in its failure to relate how these "upstart passions" subjugate the *Will*. The result is the same—a revolt against Reason—but such an account usually tells how "the Will heard not [Reason's] lore."
40. Cf. Robb, *Neoplatonism*, 25.
41. Sidney, *Arcadia*, II, 339.
42. Appetite, passion, affection. Sometimes specifically the "irascible appetite," sometimes the "concupiscible."
43. Fulke Greville, *Chorus Sacerdotum from Mustapha*, 1609; *Poetry Eng. Renaissance*, 126–127.
44. Erasmus, *Praise of Folly*, 30–32.
45. Harvey, *Letter Book*, 93–94.
46. Bodin, *Théâtre*, 636–637.
47. Da Vinci, *Notebooks*, I, 634.
48. Rabelais, V, 3.
49. Montaigne, II, 276–277.
50. Sidney, *Arcadia*, I, 12, 5.
51. *Ibid.*, I, 18, 3.
52. Greswell, *Memoirs*, 68.
53. Bacon, *Essayes*, 113 ("Of Friendship").
54. Bacon, *Works*, 133.
55. *Ibid.*
56. *Ibid.*, 143.
57. *Ibid.*, 144. My italics.
58. Cf. Zanta, *Renaissance du Stoïcisme*, 37–38.
59. Valla, *De Voluptate*, 29. My italics.
60. Montaigne, III, 60.
61. *Ibid.*, III, 192.
62. Cf. *Hypotyposes*, I, 60–78.
63. Ralegh, *Works*, VIII, 551.
64. Pomponazzi, *De Immortalitate*, 48.
65. Montaigne, II, 174–180.
66. Bonaventure Des Périers, *Cymbalum Mundi or, Satyrical Dialogues Upon several Subjects*, Done into English from the French (London, 1712), 58–59. My italics.
67. *Ibid.*, 60.
68. Chapman, *All Fools*, II, i, 73–76.
69. Bodin, *Théâtre*, 630–631.
70. *Ibid.*, 701. My italics.
71. Montaigne, II, 345.
72. *Ibid.*, 348.
73. Quoted by Villey, *Essais de Montaigne*, 158.
74. Machiavelli, *Discourses*, I, 93.
75. Montaigne, III, 270.
76. *Ibid.*, III, 24. My italics.
77. Bacon, *Essayes*, 2 ("Of Truth").
78. *Ibid.*, 1.
79. Marston, *Antonio's Revenge*, Prologue (ed. cit.).
80. Machiavelli, *Discourses*, I, 2.
81. Machiavelli, *Prince*, 121.
82. Montaigne, II, 440.
83. *Ibid.*, III, 270–271. My italics.
84. Du Vair, *Morall Philosophy*, 2, 4.

85. Pomponazzi, *De Immortalitate*, 49.
86. *Ibid.*, 46.
87. *Ibid.*, 46–47.
88. Guicciardini, *Thoughts and Portraits*, 140.
89. Montaigne, III, 438, 439.
90. *Ibid.*, III, 440.
91. *Ibid.*
92. Erasmus, *Praise of Folly*, 24.
93. Montaigne, III, 267.

3.

94. Machiavelli, *Prince*, 64 (Modern Library edition).
95. John Dee, *A True Relation*, k 2 verso.
96. Cf. Bush, *Renaissance and English Humanism*, 96–97.
97. Sidney, *Arcadia*, I, the "First Eclogues," 134.
98. Donne, *LXXX Sermons*, 74, p. 755.
99. *Republic*, 661.
100. Sir John Davies, *Nosce Teipsum*, 120: Part I.
101. Cicero, *De Officiis*, I, 4.
102. *Ibid.*, III, vi.
103. *Ibid.*
104. Cf. Brierly, *Law of Nations*, 10–18.
105. Cicero, *De Officiis*, III, vi.
106. Montaigne, II, 454, 135.
107. Louis Le Roy, *De la Vicissitude ou variété des choses en l'univers* (Paris, 1575), 6; Atkinson, 372–373.
108. Le Roy, *Des Troubles et différends . . . entre les hommes par diversité des Religions* (Paris, 1573), 29: Atkinson, 373.
109. Le Roy, *Vicissitude*, 8–9; I say "new," because Le Roy acknowledges his debt to Aristotle (11–12) : Atkinson, 406. My italics.
110. Machiavelli, *Discourses*, II, 195–196. My italics.
111. Machiavelli, *Prince*, 25.
112. Du Vair, *Morall Philosophy*, 36.
113. Lipsius, *Constancie*, II, xxv.
114. Erasmus, *Praise of Folly*, 88.
115. Pomponazzi, *De Immortalitate*, 50.
116. *Ibid.*, 50–51. My italics.
117. Machiavelli, *Prince*, 142. My italics.
118. *Ibid.*, 99.
119. Guicciardini, *Thoughts and Portraits*, 14. My italics.
120. Bodin, *Republic*, 661: Atkinson, 374.
121. Ben Jonson, *Discoveries*, ed. by Maurice Castelain (London, n.d.), (from the edition of 1641), 76.
122. Cf. Laurence Stapleton, "Halifax and Raleigh," *JHI* (April, 1941), Vol. II, No. 2, 213.
123. Ralegh, *Works*, VIII, 94.
124. *Ibid.*, 95.
125. Bacon, *Essayes*, 49–50 ("Of Goodnesse and Goodnesse of Nature").
126. Aristotle, *Politics* (Loeb Library edition, edited by H. Rackham), I, i, 12.
127. Harvey, *Letter Book*, 68, 80.
128. John Calvin, *Com. Gen.*, 162.
129. Perkins, *Workes*, I, 558.
130. Calvin, *Institutions*, II, 19.

131. *Ibid.,* II, 2. My italics.
132. Perkins, *Workes,* I, 729.
133. Calvin, *Institutes,* II, ii, 22–24, 26. My italics.
134. *Ibid.,* II, ii, 26. My italics.
135. *Ibid.*
136. Jacques Maritain, *Three Reformers* (New York, 1929), 26.
137. *Ibid.,* 28.
138. *Ibid.,* 30.
139. *Ibid.,* 184–185.
140. Hulme, *Ren. and Ref.,* 365.
141. Febvre, *Luther,* 160.
142. Montaigne, III, 220.
143. *Ibid.,* I, 121; III, 377. My italics.
144. Ralegh, *History of the World,* Preface. My italics.
145. Michael Baudier, *Histoire de la Religion des Turcs* (Paris, 1625), 122: Atkinson, 356. My italics.
146. Montaigne, III, 170–171.
147. *Ibid.,* II, 276.
148. John [Jean] Bodin, *Method for the Easy Comprehension of History,* translated by Beatrice Reynolds (New York, 1945), x.
149. *The Six Bookes of a Commonweale [Republic]* (*ed. cit.*), II, iii, p. 205.
150. Valla, *Donation of Constantine,* 31.
151. Agrippa, *De incertitudine,* II, 654–655.
152. Machiavelli, *Prince,* 141.
153. Guicciardini, *Thoughts and Portraits,* 58–59.
154. Rabelais, I, 28. My italics.
155. *Ibid.,* I, 33. My italics.
156. Machiavelli, *Prince,* 115.
157. Aristotle, *Politics,* V, vii, 15.
158. Guicciardini, *Thoughts,* 65.
159. Machiavelli, *Prince,* 127.
160. Bodin, *Republic,* 217.
161. *Ibid.*
162. Cf. L. A. Weissburger, "Machiavelli and Tudor England," *Political Science Quarterly* (XLII, 1927), 589–607, and especially 607.
163. Cf. Brown, *The Methodus of Jean Bodin,* xix.
164. Machiavelli, *Discourses,* I, 41.
165. Machiavelli, *Prince,* 122. My italics.
166. *Ibid.,* 216.
167. Wilde, "Machiavelli," 223.
168. Chapman, *Revenge of Bussy,* II, i, 29–56. Cf. IV, i, 48 ff., and Guise's verdict (IV, iv, 49): "These are your Machiavellian villains."

4.

169. Machiavelli, *Discourses,* I, 72.
170. *Ibid.,* I, 41–42.
171. *Ibid.,* I, 74.
172. *Ibid.,* III, 338.
173. *Ibid.,* II, 193–194.
174. Cf. Leonardo Olschki, *Machiavelli the Scientist* (Berkeley, 1945), 39. The other scholar is O. Tommasini, cited in this connection by Olschki in a footnote on this same page.
175. Olschki, *ibid.,* 5.
176. *Ibid.,* 10, 22, 25, 26, and *passim.*

177. Machiavelli, *Discourses*, II, 298.
178. *Ibid.*, III, 397–398. This is the first chapter in Part III. The reason he uses the word "religions" in this ambiguous way (ambiguous when the passage is read out of its context) is that later in this chapter, in addition to his discussion of republics and monarchies, he is going to deal with religious bodies. In the latter respect, his most notable example is the return to first principles (of Christianity) led by Francis and Dominic, who so instituted their orders.
179. Olschki, *ibid.*, 39–40. Cf. Leonardo, *Notebooks*, I, 556.
180. Olschki, *ibid.*, 41.
181. *Ibid.*, 40.
182. *Ibid.*, 30.
183. *Ibid.*, 31.
184. *Ibid.*
185. Loys Le Roy, *De la Vicissitude ou Variété des Choses en l'Univers*, selections with an introduction by Blanchard W. Bates (Princeton, 1944: Number One, Princeton Texts in Literature and the History of Thought), xi. My italics.
186. Machiavelli, *Discourses*, I, 114.
187. *Ibid.*, I, 114–115. Bodin sharply disagrees with Machiavelli and others who hold this opinion: Bodin, *Meth. . . . Hist.*, 178.
188. *Ibid.*, III, 494. My italics.
189. Guicciardini, *Thoughts and Portraits*, 29.
190. Marguerite, *Heptameron*, II, 145 (Fifth Day). My italics.
191. Agrippa, *De incertitudine*, I, 226.
192. Bacon, *Essayes*, 241.
193. Greville, *Treatie of Warres* (*ed. cit.*), st. 38.
194. *Ibid.*, st. 39.
195. *Ibid.*, stanzas 41 and 42.
196. Hakewill, *Apologie*, IV, i, 1, 2.
197. Edmund Spenser, *Shepheards Calendar*, edited by C. H. Herford (London, 1907), 17 (February Eclogue).
198. *Ibid.*, 38 (May Eclogue).
199. Le Roy, *De la Vicissitude*, xiii.
200. *Ibid.*, xiv.
201. *Ibid.*
202. *Ibid.*
203. *Ibid.*, xv.
204. Cf. especially Bodin, *Meth. Hist.*, 301–302.
205. *Ibid.*, 302.
206. *Ibid.*, 291.
207. *Ibid.*, 291–292.
208. *Ibid.*, 293–294.
209. *Ibid.*, 294–295.
210. *Ibid.*, 296. My italics.
211. Patrick, *The Greek Skeptics*, 167. Cf. Bury, *Idea of Progress*, 16.
212. See Jaeger, *Aristotle*, 389–390. For a Renaissance exposition of, and attack on, Aristotle's position, see Bodin, *Meth. Hist.*, 304–309.
213. Quoted by Zanta, *Renaissance du Stoïcisme*, 33–34. My own translation and italics.
214. See Farnham's Chapter VII, in his *Med. Her.*, 271 ff.
215. Marston, *Malcontent*, IV, v, 198.
216. Farnham, *ibid.*, 85, and *passim*.
217. Gilson, 370.

218. See, for example, Don Cameron Allen's *The Star-Crossed Renaissance* (*passim*). For particular points just made, see Vossler, I, 141, and Gilson, 366–367.

219. Greswell, *Memoirs*, 18.

220. Sidney, *Arcadia*, III, 10.

221. *Ibid.*

222. *Ibid.*

223. *Ibid.*

224. Spenser, *Faerie Queene*, VII, iii.

225. Des Periers, *Cymbalum Mundi*, III, 53.

226. Machiavelli, *Prince*, 203.

227. Olschki, *Machiavelli*, 38.

228. Compare Olschki, *ibid.*, where in a narrower, more specific context he speaks of it as "the unpredictable circumstances which hamper or favor the free expansion of political will power."

229. Machiavelli, *Discourses*, III, 500–503.

230. *Ibid.*, II, 382.

231. *Ibid.*, II, 383.

232. Machiavelli, *Prince*, 94 (Mod. Lib.).

233. Machiavelli, *Discourses*, III, 518.

234. Marston, *Antonio and Mellida*, III, p. 32.

235. Chapman, *All Fools* (Parrott edition: *The Comedies*), I, i, 316–317; II, i, 201.

236. *Ibid.*, V, i, 1–10. My italics.

237. Chapman, *Bussy*, V, ii, 1–12, 24, 52–53.

238. *Ibid.*, III, i, 117.

239. *Ibid.*, I, i, 1–4.

240. Olschki, *Machiavelli*, 35.

241. *Ibid.*

242. *Ibid.*, 49.

243. Machiavelli, *Prince*, 121.

244. Machiavelli, *Discourses*, I, 208, 274.

245. Machiavelli, *Prince*, 122.

246. *Ibid.*, 141.

247. *Ibid.*, 142.

248. Gentillet, *Contra-Machiavel*, II, 92.

249. Machiavelli, *Prince*, 143.

250. Gilbert, *Machiavelli's Prince*, 81–83.

251. Cicero, *De Re Publica*, III, especially xvii and xviii.

252. Patrick, *Greek Skeptics*, 185–186.

253. Gilson, *Reason and Revelation*, 43.

254. Pomponazzi, *De Immortalitate*, 50. My italics.

255. *Ibid.*

256. Cf. Lemmi, *Classic Deities*, 169; and Brown, *Methodus of Bodin*, 13.

257. Marguerite of Navarre, *Heptameron*, II, xxiv (Third Day), p. 9.

258. Guicciardini, *Thoughts*, 35.

259. In the *Heptaplomeres* and the *Methodus*; cf. Brown, *Meth. Bodin*, 13.

260. Bacon, *Essayes*, 19–20.

261. *Ibid.*, 20–21.

262. *Ibid.*, 21, 23.

263. Quoted by Lemmi, *Classic Deities*, 169.

264. *Ibid.*, 171.

265. Harvey, *Marginalia*, 118.

266. *Ibid.*, 147.

267. Cf. Mario Praz, "Machiavelli and the Elizabethans," *Proceedings of the British Academy*, 14 (1928), 49–97, for an account of Cinthio's influence, and the prominence of Senecan and medieval elements in this kind of "Machiavellianism."

268. See Battenhouse's previously mentioned book on Marlowe and *Tamburlaine* for good evidence.

269. Machiavelli, *Discourses*, I, 142.

270. *Ibid.*, II, 318.

271. *Ibid.*, 319.

272. *Ibid.*, III, 431.

273. *Ibid.*, III, 440.

274. Guicciardini, *Discorsi politici*, 14; quoted by Gilbert, *Machiavelli's Prince*, 216.

275. Harvey, *Marginalia*, 105.

276. *Ibid.*, 107–108.

277. *Ibid.*, 147–148.

278. *Ibid.*, 151.

279. *Ibid.*, 157.

280. *Ibid.*, 199–200.

281. *Ibid.*, 156.

282. Stapleton, "Halifax and Raleigh," 215.

283. Cicero, *De Officiis*, III, iii.

284. Machiavelli, *Discourses*, III, 439. My italics.

285. *Ibid.*, 441.

286. Guicciardini, *Thoughts*, 33.

287. Machiavelli, *Discourses*, III, 443.

288. *Ibid.*, 442–443.

289. *Ibid.*, I, 107.

290. Du Vair, *Constancie*, III, 400; cf. Zanta, *Stoïcisme*, 326.

291. Du Vair, *ibid.*, III, 401–402; cf. Zanta, *ibid.*, 327.

292. Erasmus, *Praise of Folly*, 54–55.

293. Machiavelli, *Prince*, 205.

294. Bacon, *Essayes*, 3 ("Of Truth").

295. Montaigne, III, 298.

296. *The Prince; The Discourses* (Mod. Lib. ed.), xlvi.

CHAPTER
8

THE COUNTER–RENAISSANCE AND THE NATURE
OF NATURE

I. WORLD-VIEWS OF THE COUNTER-RENAISSANCE

WHEN John Donne wrote,

> This terme the law of Nature, is so vari-
> ously and unconstantly deliver'd, as I con-
> fesse I read it a hundred times before I
> understand it once, or can conclude it to
> signifie that which the author should at that time meane . . .[1]

he might well have added that the same situation existed with
regard to the word "Nature" when it was used alone. The exhaustive
work done by Messrs. Lovejoy, Chinard, Boas and Crane in the
first volume (*Primitivism and Related Ideas in Antiquity*) of their
massively planned *A Documentary History of Primitivism and Related Ideas,* reveals the extraordinary number of usages and the
diversity of meanings of the word "Nature" in ancient and classical
times. By the time of the Renaissance, the word's susceptibility to
variant and even conflicting definitions had greatly increased the
confusion.

In a work of this sort, it is not appropriate (or possible, in view
of the book's total scope) to go into the detailed textual study that
Mr. Lovejoy and his colleagues have undertaken. Yet it is highly
pertinent to investigate the most common meanings of "Nature"
during the Renaissance, and to discover the ways in which the
thinkers of the Counter-Renaissance deviated from the attitude of
the traditionalists toward Nature. Since it is also not within my
province to deal with any thoroughness with the final large movement of the Renaissance period—that which I have called the
Scientific Reformation (key figure Galileo, out of the Paduan back-

ground)—I shall say only that with *it* began the more exact modern scientific usages of the term "Nature."

But with the Renaissance Christian-classical humanists and with the various "schools" of the Counter-Renaissance, it is necessary to deal at greater length. Indeed, it is no exaggeration to say that when one understands what each of these various groups meant when they spoke of "Nature," one is close to an understanding of their respective world-views.

There are five such groups to be examined: the Christian humanists; the fideists of occultism and those of the early Reformation; the naturalists of Montaigne's sort; the romanticists like Pico and Bruno; and the materialists or animalists of the Machiavelli-Guicciardini brand. In accordance with the definitions we have already established, the first of these five groups is the classicists; the second and fourth romanticists; the third and fifth naturalists. To reach a comprehension of their world-views, we need to know

1. Their estimate of nature.
2. Their interpretation of original and present *human* nature.
3. Their idea of man's proper ethical goal or his "destination."
4. Their concept of the governing force in the universe.

To the Christian humanists, who "carried on," in however altered a form, that effort to reconcile philosophy with theology, nature with grace, reason with faith, which had characterized the synthesis of the Scholastic philosophers—to them, Reason most frequently was either equivalent or supplementary to Nature. The two terms were used either interchangeably or in mutual support, to designate divine guidance manifested in the created universe; the norm of the virtuous life; the regulative and purposeful concept of law, divinely and wisely originated, in all departments of life. Such an attitude is variously but consistently evident in the thought of Marsilio Ficino, of Sir Thomas More, of Philip Melanchthon, of Justus Lipsius, of Richard Hooker. Primarily optimistic and confident both of the existence of ultimate purpose in the world and of man's capacity to understand much of that purpose and to fulfill his share, these humanists bolstered their Christian faith with the philosophy of the Academicians, the Peripatetics and the Stoics.

They mostly believed that man was originally inclined naturally to good, that this inclination had been weakened by Adam's sin, but that he was still capable, having been redeemed through Christ, of guiding his life to virtue, his proper ethical goal, through the exercise of right reason. They were rarely primitivists—whether chronological (philosophy of history), cultural, technological, or any other sort—save in the sense that they conceived of pre-lapsarian man as essentially good. They did not look backward nostalgically, but this does not mean that they advocated the modern idea of "progress." Rather, over and above man's ethical goal of virtue in private and public life, was his ultimate destination, salvation in and with God—and in a universe ruled by God's rational and comprehensible laws, the order of his divine providence, it was entirely possible for man to achieve virtue in this life and salvation in the next. More, to a large extent it was within his power whether or not he reached his established earthly and heavenly destinations. Man alone was granted by God this creative participation in his own destiny. But the road was set, and road signs abounded.

Finally, these men were for the most part genuine classicists, and, in addition to their Christian heritage, well rooted in the concept of normative Nature advanced by Aristotle and approved by Cicero. Aristotle's most characteristic interpretation of the nature of anything was "its end, since that which each thing is when its development is completed we call its nature, e.g. of a man, a horse, a house. And, furthermore, that for the sake of which a thing is, and its end, is its chief good."[2] Similarly, in Cicero's (followed by Pliny and Augustine, among others) concept of man's unique "perfectibility," the idea is further developed.[3] Add to these major influences the dominant elements of the Christian world-view, and you have a universe saturated in purposiveness. And hence "Nature," whether used in a general or particular sense, shares that purposiveness.

The world-pictures of the various schools contained in the Counter-Renaissance sharply dissent from this optimistic and comprehensibly purposive view. Their protagonists are either skeptical of the existence of any such beneficent and purposeful universal order, or convinced of man's incapability to fathom it.

To the fideists of the Early Reformation (Luther, Calvin), Nature is irremediably corrupted by Adam's sin and hence blighted and decadent. She holds no value in herself, save evil. Like men, she was once good, but no longer contains any good—all of which is now stored up in Heaven, exclusively God's. Man's salvation is to be achieved through faith (the presence of Christ in him) alone, and he cannot even achieve this faith through his own efforts. Predestination settles these matters, says Calvin. Man is powerless since the Fall, and to speak of natural morality is meaningless. All men are sinners, therefore "pecca fortiter," Luther advises, and have faith (if you are lucky). Thrift, success, etc., Calvin admits, may indicate that you are one of the elect, but as for all this talk about virtue and right reason—forget it; it is irrelevant to your only goal: salvation. Finally, this universe is ruled by an inscrutable God, whose will does not bear impious examination, and will not yield its intent or entertain the speculation of men.

I call such men as Agrippa and Paracelsus "occult fideists" because they too stress the exclusive value of faith in salvation, and repudiate the validity of the humanists' ethical norms and goals. But they conceive of Nature as "hidden," rather than bad. She is informed with spiritual presences and concealed virtues, withdrawn since the Fall from the knowledge of men. "True Nature" has, as it were, disappeared, and men know not how to appraise her. Or, as the alchemists put it, she is "sick" since the Fall: their dream is to renovate her and restore her to her pristine vigor. In either case, only the occult seer, the initiate magician, may learn Nature's mysteries through his absorption of secret traditional knowledge. It is not a question of his intellectual powers *discovering* her laws, but rather of the *magus interpreting* her secrets. And he scorns the man who associates nature with reason.

For these occult philosophers, the Fall had deprived man of his goodness; his corruption had rendered him as incapable of virtue as of a true insight into Nature. Yet the true initiate may still function. In Paracelsus, indeed, there is frequently more than a hint that he believes himself to be (or so pretends) Adam Cadmon, or even the reincarnation of Jesus—the naturally or specially good man who has returned to this corrupt world to reinstate the ancient goodness and to bring man again directly in touch with true Nature and God. And in accordance with these other views, the occult fideists hold that God directs the universe as he sees fit, but only the initiate-elect can know his purpose and his decrees.

It should be immediately apparent that a strong parallel exists between the views of the Protestant fideists and those of the occult fideists—once again demonstrating how inadequate is that view of the Reformation which isolates it from these other intellectual currents. Yet if the occult fideists hold out one hand to the Lutherans and Calvinists, they extend the other to the romanticists of the Counter-Renaissance, such as Pico and Bruno—although sharply differing from them in certain respects.

The first significant difference is that Pico and Bruno (I treat here the romantic side of his philosophy)—anti-antiquarian and anti-primitivist—find Nature good, uncorrupted. Yet their "symbolic" and "animistic" views of Nature share the occult philosophers' repudiation of rational laws of nature and their conviction of the existence throughout Nature of spiritual essences. To Pico, these are the "symbols of God," and through them we may know God and God's purpose. Bruno is less explicit.

Both of these romanticists believe that man's ultimate goal is assimilation with God, yet they repudiate the usual fixed ethical norms and limits for man's conduct on earth. Pico asserts the complete autonomy of man's will; self-realization becomes man's goal. Their attitude toward Nature explains their concept of God's government of the universe; indeed, God is immanent in Nature. But neither ever speaks of the *laws* of Nature, in the usual sense.

Where Pico's stress on the unlimited, or infinite, deals with the nature of man, Bruno's is concerned with Nature and God—the one infinite, the other also infinite and hence contradicting the incompatibility of opposites and denying to Him any limitations, even self-imposed.

Such a naturalist as Montaigne shares this view of Nature as infinite, and believes that we know nothing of God's intent or functioning principles. But his Nature is not pantheistic; it is rather "neutralized." She is the indifferent mother of an infinite diversity and mutability, and her works are all equally good, all the children of her fertility in a world innocent of comprehensive systematizing and universal regulative principles of degree, vocation, etc. She is, if you will, Venus Genatrix, mother of instincts and senses, of biological motivation and uninhibited fertility. In addition to Montaigne, Lorenzo Valla and Rabelais had sung her praises; she is also celebrated in the primitivistic poetry of Ronsard and the young John Donne.

For the naturalist of Montaigne's sort is a thorough-going primitivist. There is plenty of evidence of Montaigne's cultural (discontent of the civilized with civilization) and technological (disapproval of man's "art," as opposed to nature) primitivism; and in his enthusiastic picture of the natives of the New World, in such essays as "Of the Cannibals" and "Of Coaches," he even espouses the cause of primitivism of various sorts—economic (primitive communism), marital (the common possession of wives), dietetic (vegetarianism), juristic (no government), and ethical (no "moral" rules or sense of sin).[4] Throughout, he is an advocate of chronological primitivism (attitude toward philosophy of history), who believes that man has so confounded Nature's traces with his artificial rational "rules and laws of nature" that he has lost almost all contact with her and left the best part of his heritage to the other animals:

> The care to increase in wisdome and knowledge was the first overthrow of man-kinde: it is the way whereby man hath headlong cast himselfe downe into eternall damnation. Pride is his losse and corruption: it is pride that misleadeth him from common waies; that makes him to embrace all new fangles. . . .[5]

He finds man to have little or no comprehension of the way in which God works; in this respect he joins hands with the fideists:

> Man is a thing of nothing. So far are our faculties from conceiving that high Deitie, that of our Creators works, those beare his marke best, and are most his owne, which we understand least.[6]

He even invokes the spirit and letter of Tertullian's "credo quia impossibile";

> It is an occasion to induce Christians to believe, when they chance to meet with any incredible thing, that it is so much the more according unto reason, by how much more it is against humane reason. . . .[7]

He differs sharply from most other thinkers of the Counter-Renaissance, however, in his ideas of man's *summum bonum:*

> That part of natures favours which we impart unto beasts, is by our owne confession much more advantageous unto them. We assume unto our selves imaginarie and fantasticall goods, future and absent goods, which humane capacitie can no way warrant unto her selfe; or some other, which by the overweening of our owne opinion we falsely ascribe unto our selves; as reason, honour, and knowledge; and to them as their proper share we leave the essentiall, the manageable, and palpable goods, as peace, rest, securitie, innocencie, and health: Health, I say, which is the goodliest and richest present nature can impart unto us.[8]

This ethic of health, a thoroughly consistent naturalistic position, he maintains in various forms throughout the second half of his *Essayes,* and equates with happiness; as he further develops his "culte de moi-même," it comes increasingly to mean self-adjustment —in the sense of each unique individual's getting to know himself, his potentialities and limitations, and coming to terms with that self. No one else in the period worked out so consistent a philosophically naturalistic position, but many endorsed and developed particular aspects of it. . . .

Finally, there is the world-view of the materialists or "animalists," which can be treated briefly, since we have already developed it at length in studying Machiavelli. It differs quite sharply from Montaigne's naturalistic view (although certainly also naturalistic); indeed, it may best be described as the "profane" twin of the Lutheran-Calvinistic world-view. It is equally pessimistic about human nature, equally certain of man's inability to discern the guiding principles in the universe—but it holds these views without benefit of theology.

Nature, on the other hand, is as neutralized as in Montaigne— the only link that binds such thinkers as Machiavelli and Guicciardini to him. But despite very occasional laconic or conventionally pious references to God and Heaven, the two Italian historians see nature, human events and, indeed, all of the universe to which they refer, as ruled over by fortune or chance. Hence, one may say that they conceive of Nature as "accidental" or "blind"—the atheist Cecropia's point of view. In Guicciardini, this concept is completely neutralized; but in Machiavelli (as we have seen), it is occasionally personified as the goddess Fortuna, who acts with the inscrutability and unpredictability of the Calvinistic God's predestination —seems at times, ironically, to be the lay counterpart of this concept.

Both Machiavelli and Guicciardini find men "always the same," consistently bad. They ignore the Fall; and, strongly anti-primitivistic, picture an original "state of nature" in which men were brutes, almost wild animals.[9] This does not, however, mean that they entertain the idea of progress; on the contrary, they find history, events, always the same. They are obsessed with the cyclical concept of history;[10] while tendencies change from state to state, they are sure that a careful study of past civilizations and conditions gives one a fair opportunity to act in an informed way in the present, and even to predict coming events with some success. In this respect, we may remember Machiavelli's "biological theory of society and the state"—hence the predictions are those of an empirical "scientist," rather than of a seer, or even a philosopher.

In this world-view of a nature ever the same, wholly divorced from metaphysics and theology, and ruled over by a Fortune largely equivalent to chance (if not caprice) and only partially circumventable through prudence and foresight[11]—what is man's good and how is he to act effectively? Here Machiavelli and Guicciardini, with no interest in theology, depart from the pessimism they otherwise share with Luther and Calvin. They preach a vigorous, if amoral, ethic of success, to be attained through the proper exercise of *virtù*. Since all their interest is in politics, this amounts to the individual exercise of power politics. In a world where every one is motivated by self-preservation, self-interest, the furthest advancement of self, or "success," is the only logical goal. Energy and efficiency of operation to this end constitute man's true virtues, however the word may be spelled—and in a world of animal warfare, populated by wolves, this means that one must learn to play both the fox and the lion. *Vae victis!*

2. THE COUNTER-RENAISSANCE AND NATURE VERSUS ART

The world-views of the various schools of the Counter-Renaissance contain one important constant in their attitude toward Nature. However much they otherwise vary, and even contradict each other, they share a disbelief in the identity of, or complementary cooperation between, Nature and Reason. Whether an individual thinker or a given group within the Counter-Renaissance finds Nature "good" or "bad," he gives the lie to the traditional humanistic concept of the close and intimate relationship between Nature and Reason.

The humanist, the classicist, the traditionalist—saw law and reason operative everywhere in the universe, and particularly in the individual and collective life of man on earth. As we have seen, the Counter-Renaissance figures did not. This difference constituted one of the major ideological oppositions of the whole period of the historical Renaissance, and the terms in which the opposition was most often stated were those of Nature and Art.

The opposition—and even in these terms—was a very old one. Most characteristically, the terms have meant simply primitivism vs. civilization, that which is not man-made vs. what is man-made, "natural" or "healthy" vs. "artificial" and "unhealthy." In such connotations, either term may be neutral with regard to value, or one (or the other) may be disparaging. It depends, of course, upon who is speaking. But the division and opposition make a constant that persists.[12]

Yet inevitably, in that persistence lay the seeds for numerous shoots off the main trunk of the controversy; and other eventual Nature-Art oppositions have developed other meanings—among them, practice vs. theory, fact vs. logic, simplicity vs. complexity, untutoredness vs. learning, intuition vs. speculation, passion vs.

reason, and a host of others, many of which we have already re-
viewed (although with different nomenclature from the Nature-Art
sort) in considering the opposition of the Counter-Renaissance to
the traditional humanistic Renaissance.

It would be almost impossible, within the scope of the present
volume, to consider at length all the varieties of ways in which this
conflict manifested itself in the Renaissance; that should occupy a
separate volume, and a long one at that. The best we can do here
is to suggest some of the basic and most representative forms that
the conflict took.

Most of the Christian humanists of the Renaissance held the
position taken by the great central classical philosophical tradition
of the West, which Aquinas, with special reference to Aristotle, had
officially Christianized. Most of them, that is, agreed with Plato
(in the *Laws*) that the antithesis between Nature and Art was
spurious—that "law and also art exist by nature, or by that which
is not inferior to nature" (890d).[13] Art (that is, "the control of life
by the conscious exercise of reason"[14]) is no less a product of universal nature than the non-rational elements in man's constitution;

> since man has been made capable of it, it is an essential part
> of the cosmic scene, and therefore cannot be "contrary to
> nature." To say that positive and moral laws restrictive of the
> uncontrolled play of the other forces in individual and social
> life are artificial (889a) is true; but this does not mean that
> they are unnatural in any sense which implies that they ought
> not to exist, or that "art," of which they are the manifestations,
> produces "lesser works" than does the rest of nature.[15]

So Plato, in his final position. And Aristotle's concept of the
nature of anything as its end is wholly consonant:

> Art in general, though sometimes contrasted unfavorably with
> nature [*Eth. Nic.* 1106 b 14], in the end ceases for Aristotle
> to be antithetic to it. . . . [Until man's capacity for art is uti-
> lized,] the specific nature of man remains unresolved; and art
> as the manifestation of reason, is therefore "nature" in what
> Aristotle considers the most appropriate meaning of the word
> (*Pol.* VII 1334 b 15 ff.). . . . But even when art is said to
> complement nature, it is in reality completing itself. . . .
> [*Phys.* 199 b 30][16]

And finally—not to elaborate at too great length the classical heritage—there was Cicero, the eclectic synthesizer, who adds the
Stoic element to the Academic and Peripatetic:

> In his favorite conception of the originally merely germinal

rationality of man Cicero found what seemed to him a way of resolving the traditional antithesis of nature and art. From the Peripatetics, the Old Academy and the Stoics he had learned to distinguish the *prima naturae* or *prima naturalia* [*De finibus,* II, 34, 35, 38; III, 17, 21, 22, 30; IV, 18, 25, 39; V, 17, 18, 19, 24, 45, 58], the primitive impulses of nature in the individual, from those which are later unfolded; and the latter, being expressive of man's latent reason and of the special kind of sociability which is connected with this, manifest themselves in the arts. These are thus a necessary supplement to nature, i.e. to the *prima naturae,* but are also themselves "natural," in the senses that (a) their development is a part of the purpose of cosmic "nature," and that (b) it is also inherent in the specific "nature" of man, as distinguished from that of other animals by the potentiality of wisdom, or intelligence (*sapientia*). . . . Man [is] the one animal left by nature at birth with powers peculiarly undeveloped, requiring to be completed by his own conscious art.[17]

Nature and Art, harmonious, divisible yet one. And Cicero dealt similarly with Nature and Reason, with particular reference to man:

While sometimes . . . *natura* is distinguished from *ratio,* or is a name for the mere rudiments of the latter, the two are sometimes equivalent, or "nature" is the source of reason; it is "nature which through the force of reason reconciles man with man."[18]

Even Seneca, another popular favorite in the Renaissance, while he seems clearly a primitivist in many respects, does not believe that the *true Stoic* virtue may be attained by nature alone, but that it needs the conscious reflection and discipline of "art": "Primitive men are, so to say, Stoics *sans le savoir;* but the *savoir* is essential. The virtue which comes through insight and inner conflict is both more complete, and of greater intrinsic moral value, than the innocence of man in his natural state."[19]

Such was, in brief, the Renaissance humanists' heritage on the Nature-Art controversy. Drawing on Plato, Aristotle, Cicero and the Stoics, they endorsed the efficacy of art (or "knowledge" or "doctrine" or "education") to complete the work of nature. When Justus Lipsius held that God had given the first elements of the task of right living to man in his possession of his spark of the Divine Reason, *but that education completed the task,* he was indeed following his master Seneca, whom he cites as saying that Nature does

not *give* virtue; the *art* is to become good. But more than that—
he was expounding the central doctrine of most Renaissance middle-
path Christian humanists.

George Chapman echoes this conviction without so peculiarly
Stoic an emphasis:

> Learning, the Art is of good life: they then
> That leade not good lives, are not learned men.[20]

Not only does he agree with Lipsius that this is God's decree, but
he envisions a similar two steps:

> For, virtuous knowledge hath two waies to plant;
> By Powre infus'd, and Acquisition. . . .[21]

Man's goal is virtuous action; he is incited to it by God-given
"natural reason"; and it is the task of "education" to see to it that
the value of this first impetus is not lost or misdirected. Nature *and*
Art: coworkers towards the common end, in accordance with God's
purpose. . . .

Among the various groups of the Counter-Renaissance which we
have considered, it was primarily the naturalists who took direct
issue with this humanistic interpretation of the relation of Nature
and Art. Lutherans and Calvinists necessarily turned their backs on
both nature and art; the occult thinkers and the romanticists of
the Platonist-animist sort, while repudiating the traditional reason-
nature and art-nature alliances, held to the validity of their own
"art," in their several senses, usually claiming that it alone was in
the true sequence from nature; the materialists—aside from con-
fronting and opposing the hypothetical "art" of Scholastic intel-
lectuals and humanistic moralists (which dealt with the way things
ought to be) with their own empirical investigation of nature (the
way things *are*)—were not much interested in the controversy.

Indeed, it was to be expected that it would be the naturalists
who would take issue with the humanists' nature-art alignment,
since they were the only genuine and thoroughgoing primitivists
among these Counter-Renaissance groups. And it is a primitivist
position to refuse to admit the refining and completing process that
art (whether civilization, culture, technology or "reason") adds to
nature, and to insist rather upon the essential opposition of nature
to art, while endorsing the former.

Furthermore, we have contemporary evidence of an awareness
of the battle-lines being drawn in this way—with especial reference
to the ethical conduct of life. Bear in mind, reading the following
discussion, that it was an essentially Stoic interpretation of the rela-

tion of nature and art that Cicero and Seneca expounded in classical times, although, of course, one perfectly consonant with the conceptions of Plato and Aristotle on the subject. . . .

When Guillaume du Vair wrote that his contemporaries must choose between the two irreconcilable philosophies of Nature and Stoicism,[22] he was, then, making an accurate, although generalized, summary of the basic ethical positions of the Counter-Renaissance naturalists and the Christian humanists. How persistent this opposition had been may be perceived from a chapter heading in Valla's *De Voluptate* (1433): *Antonius pro Epicureis, & pro natura contra Stoicos.*[23]

Yet the conflict was not, of course, confined to the Renaissance. For these two—"Nature" or "Epicureanism," and "Stoicism"—had been adversaries long before. They are at least as ancient (when taken in their loose, inclusive Renaissance meaning) as civilization. For, despite hundreds of variations and modifications, there have always been two fundamental ways of looking at man's central moral problem—at that problem of the adjustment of the respective claims of liberty and of discipline, of independence and of duty, of his instinctive self-interest and of his obligations to others. And these two may be called "Epicureanism" and "Stoicism" or Nature and Art, whether one is discussing Epicurus and Zeno or Jean Jacques Rousseau and Irving Babbitt.

In such a treatise as that of Valla, of course, a nominally closer adherence to the positions of the Greek Epicurean and Stoic schools is maintained. The major quarrel between these schools (in ethics) had risen over their interpretations of the highest good for man. The Stoics held that this good lay in virtue, the Epicureans in pleasure. And Valla follows the central distinction faithfully: "Aut voluptatem, aut honestatem bonum esse."[24]

Yet his Epicurean spokesman, Beccadelli, advocates a kind of Epicureanism that Lucretius and Epicurus would not have recognized: his defiant and extreme exaltation of the senses bears little resemblance to the disciplined, dignified, and moderate program set forth in *De Rerum Natura.*[25] Nor is this difference peculiar to Valla; one finds little of the classical Epicurean ideal in the Renaissance.

There is, to be sure, Hedonius' defense of it in the *Colloquies*, with his claim that "none are greater Epicureans than those Christians that live a pious life . . . in that they have a clear Conscience, and Peace with God."[26] Erasmus and (following him?) More, finding nothing incompatible in godliness and "that pleasure that is good and honest,"[27] suggest a sober Epicureanism which places the pleasures of the mind above those of the body. But they are lone voices in the period. To the Renaissance-at-large, ethical Epicureanism means quite definitely an emphasis upon the life of the senses, self-indulgence, and freedom from restraint.

We have already seen how considerable a modification of rigorous doctrinal Stoicism that of the Renaissance humanistic moralists represented.[28] Therefore, when Du Vair opposes "Nature" and "Stoicism" as two irreconcilable philosophies, he is speaking, on the one hand, of those who believe that the life of the senses has as just a claim upon man as that of the mind, those to whom the repression of natural instincts is vicious, those who resent the artificial restraints which society has placed upon them; on the other hand, of that eclectic Stoicism, variously compounded of Academic, Peripatetic, Christian and Stoic ideals, and holding as its central ethical principle the government of life by reason in the pursuit of virtue.

Cicero had been a master welder of the three major Greek ethical schools, maintaining that the "teaching of ethics is the peculiar right of the Stoics, the Academicians, and the Peripatetics," since they alone believed in moral goodness—without which belief there was nothing to be said about duty.[29] He had accounted himself a "followerer of Socrates and Plato"; he had identified the Stoic Law of Nature with the four Platonic cardinal virtues.[30]

Again, he had pointed out the debt of the Stoics (in one of their interpretations of their ubiquitous maxim "to live in accordance with nature") to Aristotle's doctrine of "Ends"[31]—an identification which is so thoroughly established for Renaissance propounders of humanistic ethics that it amounts to a complete assimilation. Du Vair himself writes, in *The Morall Philosophy of the Stoicks:*

> There is nothing in the world that tends not to some End. . . .
> Now the End of Man, and all his thoughts and Inclinations,
> is Good. . . . I think, that, properly to define Good, a man
> may say that it is nothing but the Essence and operation ac-
> cording to Nature; who is so wise a Mistress, as that she hath
> disposed all things to their best Estate; hath given them their
> first inclination to Good, and the End they ought to seek; so
> that who will follow, cannot fail to obtain it. . . . The Good,
> then, of Man consists in his healthful Reason, that is to say,
> his Virtue. . . .[32]

Renaissance or orthodox "Stoic" morality, then, is a compound, and one in which the pure Stoic elements are frequently not predominant. Many specifically Stoic concepts are rejected. Even Du Vair does not follow the Stoic indivisibility of the soul; and one can find no Christian-humanist moralist who advocates the extreme Stoic-Cynic position that all passions or appetites are bad. The Aristotelian doctrine of the mean (the avoidance of both excess and defect) and the Platonic injunction to temperance under the guidance of reason are consistently preferred.

Yet what is central to all three schools and to Christian ethics is the establishing of virtue as man's goal on earth, and the acknowledgment of reason as the guide to virtue. It is therefore quite appropriate to speak of those who held this "philosophy" as "Stoics," for the single concept most basic to this ideal is a Stoic one—that of the rational Law of Nature. "Law rational," writes Richard Hooker,

> which men commonly use to call the Law of Nature, meaning thereby the Law which human Nature knoweth itself in reason universally bound unto, which also for that cause may be termed most fitly the Law of Reason.[33]

The law of man's nature is Reason, which leads to virtue, or—in Hooker's words, "Man's observation of the Law of his Nature is Righteousness."

This, in Cicero's famous words, "Est quidem vera lux, recta ratio, naturae congruens, diffusa in omnes, constans, sempiterna."[34] The line of men who have invoked, in variant forms, this "vera lux" as the guiding principle of human life extends back far before Cicero, and forward well into the nineteenth century. Whether the specific term is "vivere secundum naturam," "the Law of Nature," "synderesis," "the Law of Reason," "the Light of Nature," "law rational," "conscience" or "recta ratio"—the primary significance is retained: there is within man an innate moral imperative. Nature gives him his "first inclination to Good"; reason is the guide which leads him on the way; to follow reason is to follow God's will and to attain to virtue.

It is all in Cicero and Seneca:

> Law is transcendent reason, implanted in nature, commanding what should be done, and forbidding what should not be done.[35]

> Reason is an imitation of nature. . . . What does it demand of us? A very easy thing: that we live in accordance with our nature.[36]

To follow Nature, the best of guides, that is as if one followed God.[37]

Perfect reason is called virtue.[38]

It is also in all the Christian-humanistic reconcilers of reason and faith, from Aquinas to Milton. St. Thomas declares that the rational creature

> has a share of the Eternal Reason, whereby it has a natural inclination to its proper act and end: and this participation of the eternal law in the rational creature is called the natural law.[39]

Sir Thomas More's Utopians

> define virtue to be a life ordered according to nature; and we be hereunto ordained of God; and that he doth follow the course of nature, which in desiring and refusing things is ruled by reason. . . .[40]

For Hooker it is "law rational" or "the Law of Reason;" Lipsius identifies "the voyce of nature" with God's law, and is "carelesse of all cares save one . . . that I may bring in subiection this broken and distressed mind of mine to RIGHT REASON and GOD. . . ."[41]

For Milton it is

> . . . rational liberty . . .
> true liberty
> . . . which always with right reason dwells
> Twinned, and from her hath no dividual being.

Or, as he puts it earlier in *Paradise Lost*,

> God left free the Will; for what obeys
> Reason is free, and Reason he made right.[42]

Among the variations on the details of this theme is a not infrequent disagreement as to the exact nature of man's innate impulse to good. Some expounders of the Law of Nature hold that since there is a spark of the Divine Reason inherent in man, it is proper to speak of that initial capacity to distinguish between good and evil as reason; others do not admit that natural reason, although latent, is exercised until a maturity sufficient to permit of its proper functioning has been reached. Such terms as "the light of nature" and "conscience" remain indeterminate in this respect.

Yet there is a common denominator for all of the orthodox humanists' treatment of "natural reason." All of them hold reason to be the distinctive property of man, *his nature;* all of them speak of it as a congenital gift of God or nature; all of them believe that although impaired by the Fall, it is still capable of adequate functioning for many purposes; finally all of them believe that the innate natural reason, or "light of nature," affords the first impetus to the virtuous conduct of life, but that it must be made and kept effective by training and by constant exercise—by *art.*

Etienne de la Boétie, in his *Discours sur la servitude volontaire,* presents a standard Renaissance exposition of the cooperation of the original gift of reason and its education in the attaining of virtue:

> I think I do not err in stating that there is in our souls some native seed of reason, which, if nourished by good counsel and training, flowers into virtue, but which, on the other hand, if unable to resist the vices surrounding it, is stifled and blighted.[43]

It is the now familiar combination of Nature and Art, coworkers toward the goal of virtuous action.

It is significant that very few of these pre-Renaissance and Renaissance prophets of the Law of Nature acknowledge the primitive Stoic concept of that first impulse to good as a purely instinctive act.[44] Significant, but hardly surprising—for in just this distinction between the Law of Nature as innate reason and the Law of Nature as instinct we have one of the skirmish lines drawn up between the Renaissance "Stoics" and "Epicureans," the Christian humanists and the Counter-Renaissance naturalists.

There was indeed in the very words of Cicero the basis for a distortion of the representative Stoic position on this subject to a naturalistic position:

> To the phraseology in which nature is directed as guide or model or standard, Cicero probably did more than any other Latin author to give currency and sanctity; e.g. *in hoc sumus sapientes, quod naturam optimam ducem tamquam deum sequimur eique paremus. . . . Quid est enim aliud Gigantum modo bellare cum dis nisi naturae repugnare?* (*De Sen.* II, 5); "the first thing that wisdom will look to when she undertakes any action is that it be *naturae accommodatum*" (*Ac.* II, 24); the true conception of good and bad is "that all the things which Nature rejects are among the evils, all that she approves are to be reckoned goods," *omnia, quae natura aspernetur in malis esse, quae asciscat in bonis* (*Tusc. disp.* II, xiii, 30). For Cicero himself such phrases did not ordinarily carry either

primitivistic or ethically "naturalistic" implications; but they easily lent themselves to such interpretations.[45]

Cicero himself saw the danger of these interpretations—the possibility of justifying an inclination by the sanction of such a Law of Nature—and strongly rejected them, as did the Renaissance eclectic Christian Stoics.[46]

But this second version of the Law of Nature found allies, and gained in strength. It was close to the Epicurean emphasis in some respects, notably in its implication of a pleasure-pain basis for values —and influential skeptics of the New Academy like Carneades had held a similar position.

Moreover, there was another orthodox interpretation of the Law of Nature which contained moral dynamite and required careful handling. In addition to the *universal* Law of Nature which concerns man, there is also an *individual* Law of Nature. Cicero writes in *De Officiis:*

> We must realize that we are invested by Nature with two characters, as it were: one of these is universal, arising from the fact of our being all alike endowed with reason and with that superiority which lifts us above the brute. From this all morality and propriety are derived, and upon it depends the rational method of ascertaining our duty. The other character is the one that is assigned to individuals in particular. . . .
>
> Everybody . . . must resolutely hold fast to *his own peculiar gifts, in so far as they are peculiar only and not vicious.* . . . For we must so act as not to oppose the universal laws of human nature, but, while safeguarding those, *to follow the bent of our own particular nature.* For it is of no avail to fight against one's nature or to aim at what is impossible of attainment. . . . Nothing is proper . . . if it is in direct opposition to one's natural genius.[47]

It should be immediately apparent, after the discussion in the preceding chapter of the ethical *individualistic* naturalism of the Counter-Renaissance, the new interpretation of "humour," and the individualists' finding of value in singularity, that the Counter-Renaissance's interpretation of *sequere naturam* as following the bent of one's own nature would be a subversive individualistic-naturalistic one.

Cicero, to be sure, is very careful to qualify this second law of nature—"to follow the bent of our own particular nature." He warns us specifically that this "particular" law is not to be opposed to the "universal" one, and that one must "hold fast to his own peculiar gifts" only "in so far as they are peculiar"—"and not vicious." In its context, this second Law of Nature is supplementary to and harmonious with the first, universal one.

But there are few pastimes that men prefer to that of arbitrarily removing something from its context to serve their own purposes. The consequences of isolating such statements as "it is of no avail to fight against one's nature or to aim at what is impossible of attainment" are immediately apparent. Employed as Cicero used it, the sentence offers an incentive to the pursuit of duty in obedience to the laws of God and nature, and an admonition against disproportionate ambition. But Sidney's Cecropia, for example, can isolate this statement and use it as an argument for giving full play to the life of the senses:

> As it is manifest inough, that all things follow but the course of their own nature, saving only Man, who while by the pregnancie of his imagination he strives to things supernaturall, meane-while he looseth his owne naturall felicitie. Be wise, and that wisedome shalbe a God unto thee. . . .[48]

Inevitably, then, these two concepts—the interpretation of following nature as following one's instincts or inclination, without regard for reason, and the idea of following "the bent of our own particular nature"—produced a kind of bastard Stoicism which was to prove in the Renaissance the strongest opponent to traditional and humanistic eclectic Stoicism. Just as "the most daring departures from Aristotelian science were carried on within the Aristotelian framework, and by means of a critical reflection on the Aristotelian texts . . ."[49] so the most radical opposition to the rational Stoic Law of Nature flaunted an instinctive and individualistic "Stoic" Law of Nature, and a variant reading of the humanists' favorite text (follow Nature) provided the Counter-Renaissance naturalists with their most effective slogan.

Du Vair's two irreconcilable philosophies of "Nature" and "Stoicism" emerge into clear light with an understanding of the two kinds of Stoicism. For Christian-humanistic orthodoxy the Law of Nature is the law of natural reason; for those who represent the "philosophy of nature," it is the law of instinct or the law of one's "own peculiar nature." And whatever the contribution of Epicurean and other elements to the solution of the "Nature" philosophy, its most basic concepts rest upon this variant and antagonistic reading of the Stoic Law of Nature.

Again, it should by now be clear that—*in terms of ethical view-points*—"Nature" and "Stoicism," or the two kinds of Stoicism, are the equivalent of "Nature" and "Art," if one means by "Art" (as did Plato in the *Laws*, for example) "the control of life by the conscious exercise of reason." And almost all of these Renaissance thinkers (on both sides of the fence) did mean just that by "Art" —when speaking in an ethical context.

Moreover, an understanding of the two versions of the Stoic Law of Nature clarifies the ethical positions of otherwise ambiguous or generally misunderstood figures of the period. It becomes possible, for example, to see quite clearly how Montaigne can reject the sovereignty of reason, and at the same time strengthen his exhortations "to follow nature." And, in the light of "the bent of our own particular nature," we gain a new perspective on his pursuit of "son Moi."

His scorn for those who uphold the "rational" Stoic Law of Nature is familiar to us:

> For us to go according to Nature, is but to follow according to our understanding, as far as it can follow, and as much as we can perceive in it. Whatsoever is beyond it, is monstrous and disordered. *By this accompt all shall then be monstrous,* to the wisest and most sufficient; for even to such humane reason hath perswaded that she had neither ground nor footing, no not so much as to warrant snow to be white. . . .[50]

This is the *Apologie;* at this point, he still refers to following nature as following reason, although he denies the efficacy of such a course. Yet even in the same essay, after disposing of "reason" as "an instrument of lead and wax, stretching, pliable, and that may be fitted to all byases and squared to all measures," he goes on to speak of the power of

> *this innated and casual instinct* which makes us to favor one thing more than another, and, without any leave or reason, giveth us the choice in two like subjects. . . .[51]

In this passage he allots to "instinct" the most sacred traditional function of reason. Moreover, he is on the way to the propounding of the "instinctive" Law of Nature, when he declares,

> It is credible that there be naturall lawes, *as may be seene in other creatures,* but in us they are lost; this goodly humane reason engrafting it self among all men, to sway and command, confounding and topsi-turving the visage of all things according to her inconstant vanitie and vaine inconstancy.[52]

Reason, then, is *not natural*.

Montaigne never recants. One is tempted to retrace his slow course through the *Essayes,* ever more outspoken, ever more concerned with nature (and especially his own), ever more contemptuous of reason. But a few passages from the late essays must suffice. In "How One Ought to Governe His Will," he speaks again of the "lawes of nature," but it is now immediately evident that these have nothing to do with the orthodox rational Law of Nature:

> The lawes of nature teach us what is fit and just for us. . . . Wise-men . . . distinguish subtilly *the desires proceeding from nature,* from such as grow from the disorders of our fantasie.[53]

Here is an obvious reference to the instinctive law of nature, and a distinguishing between natural desires, which should be satisfied, and "acquired" ones, presumably harmful. But already, in the previous essay, he had gone further. He had said outright:

> I therefore hate this trouble-feast reason, and these extravagant projects, which so much molest man's life, and these so subtle opinions; if they have any truth, I deeme it over-deare, and find it too incommodious. . . . And without so nicely controlling them, *I follow mine owne naturall inclinations.* . . .[54]

As we move into the very last essays, we find him making reference after hostile reference to reason. One of these passages seems to be a direct answer to Cicero, who had written:

> Man—because he is endowed with reason, by which he comprehends the causes of consequences, perceives the causes of things, understands the relation of cause to effect and effect to cause, draws analogies, and connects and associates the present and future—easily surveys the course of his whole life and makes the necessary preparations for its conduct.[55]

Pierre Villey tells us that Montaigne at last read Cicero's moral tracts before his final revision of the *Essayes,*[56] and the following passage might well have been produced in reaction to that reading:

> I was even now plodding (as often I doe) upon this, what a free and gadding instrument humane reason is. . . . The knowledge of causes doth onely concern him [God] who hath the conduct of things; Not us that have but the sufferance. And who according to our neede, without entering into their beginning and essence, have perfectly the full and absolute use of them. Nor is wine more pleasant unto him that knowes the first faculties of it. . . . The effects concerne us, but the meanes nothing at all.[57]

Several of the Counter-Renaissance creeds meet in this single passage: the antagonism to Nature's secretaries (who pry into God's secrets), the invocation to utility, the disparagement of reason. All that remains is to make the Nature vs. Art conflict explicit, and this Montaigne later does—in a definitive statement of what he means by following nature. He opposes his law of nature, the following of his instincts and natural inclination, to the orthodox humanist doctrine of reason leading to virtue. And although it means sacrificing his beloved Socrates this once, he identifies his own code with Nature and the humanists' with Art.

> I have (as elsewhere I noted) taken for my regard this ancient precept, very rawly and simply: That We cannot erre in following Nature; and that the soveraigne document is for a man to conforme himselfe to her. I have not (as Socrates), by the power and vertue of reason, corrected my natural complexions, nor by Art hindered mine inclination. Looke how I came into the World, soe I goe-on: I strive with nothing.[58]

Montaigne is the arch-philosopher of "Nature." With him we reach the culmination of a long and vociferous protest against the confining of the meaning of life to terms conceived within "the narrow cells of the human understanding." This protest, submerged but often eloquently articulate in the Middle Ages—as with many of the romances and the Provençal tradition of courtly love, with the Goliards, with Jean de Meun and Chaucer—had found full voice with some Italian humanists of the fifteenth century, and a belligerent champion in Lorenzo Valla. Erasmus and Rabelais lent their Lucianic laughters to the cause; Petrarch was strongly attracted to it by temperament; Ariosto, Ronsard and Tasso paid it various and intermittent tribute. It became the central concern of Montaigne's life and work; it received a final exuberant treatment from the Elizabethans; it dwindled away to a degenerate end in the French libertines, Jacobean and Caroline tragedy, and Restoration comedy.

A protest against the confining of the meaning of life to terms conceived within "the narrow cells of the human understanding. . . ." I refer, of course, to that extraordinarily extensive and prolonged reassertion of the rights of the senses, of the value of pleasure, of the excellence of this life on earth in and for itself, of the validity of the passions—that gusto for living which expressed itself both in romantic and naturalistic terms in the fifteenth and sixteenth centuries.

That the observation of this protracted outcry of the natural rights of the flesh has led to many overly picturesque and even grotesque accounts of the "hedonistic" or "pagan" or "libertine" Renaissance revolt against the ascetic Middle Ages, is certainly true. The actuality, as it is represented in the written words of the time, was partly a revolt against asceticism. But asceticism, in the sense of a rigorous Christian monastic ideal, was not the central authority against which the rebellion was directed. At most, its circle was that on the periphery of the target. The bull's-eye was "Reason" —"Art"—excessive moralism and intellectualism—excessive faith in a prescribed and exclusive education, ethic, philosophical orientation on the nature of man and his good. Hence the Counter-Renaissance and its revolt of Nature against Art.

In the camp of the "philosophy of Nature," there were extreme hedonists—advocates of the exclusively sensual life. But these were as rare as the ascetics among their opponents. What the majority of the naturalists were revolting against was, first of all, the humanists' preoccupation with rules for living which were allegedly "natural," but which the naturalists believed to have been made up by that "stretching" and "pliable" instrument, the human reason. The rational Law of Nature, they maintained, might be rational, but it was not natural. It did not take into account man's honest *feelings;* it ignored or suppressed his *instincts;* it did not represent him *as he was.* The "universal Laws of Nature" were simply an artificial body of arbitrary dicta, drawn from opinion, custom and tradition. They had little relation to the *facts* of human nature; they cramped and distorted man's true nature. They were the very apotheosis of Art. . . .

The protest of Nature against Art in the Counter-Renaissance was not, of course, limited to this central ethical dilemma of man's true nature and true good. It expressed itself in all sorts of primitivistic concepts that took issue with the refinements, civilities and established customs of European civilization. It took the form of cultural, technological and communistic primitivism, exalting those societies in which the "disease" of technological and scientific progress, the complexity of manners, and the sense of property were most negligible. As one result, the natives of the New World were regarded with a particular curiosity, beyond the general one of interest in the unfamiliar.

The cosmographers, with or without a naturalistic bent, were much taken with the absence of clothing in the New World. Those of them who did demonstrate a primitivist bias were quick to see the possibilities of another form of the Nature-Art controversy in this question of clothing. Jean de Léry, for instance, contrasts the "nudité ordinaire" (or Nature) of Brazilian women with the extreme costuming (or Art) of European women—to the detriment of the latter.[59] As Jodelle puts it in his title-page verses for André Thevet's *Les Singularités de la France Antartique* (1557):

> Ces barbares marchent tous nus,
> Et nous, nous marchons inconnus,
> Fardés, masqués. . . .[60]

Montaigne, as might be expected, has a good deal to say on the subject—particularly in the essay "On Apparell":

> But as those who by an artificiall light extinguish the brightnesse of the day, we have quenched our proper means by such as we have borrowed. And wee may easily discerne that only custome makes that seeme impossible unto us which is not so.[61]

People go naked in climates as cold as ours, he points out.

> Had we been borne needing petti-coats and breeches, there is no doubt but Nature would have armed that which she hath left to the batteries of seasons and furie of wethers with some thicker skin or hide, as she hath done our finger ends and the soales of our feet.[62]

Pierre Charron was to echo him:

> It seems very probable that the fashion of going entirely naked, still observed by a great part of the world, is the original fashion for men; and the other, of being clothed, artificial and invented to extinguish nature, like those who wish by artificial light to extinguish that of day. For it is not likely that nature, having everywhere sufficiently provided covering for all the other creatures, has treated man less well. . . .[63]

It is perhaps with a somewhat different concept of "Nature" that Valla merges his twin ideals of Nature and Beauty in his preference for having women go very lightly dressed in the summer. Yet Valla, for all of his Shavian joy in shocking the average man, was a serious advocate (and the most notable early Renaissance one) of the "Philosophy of Nature." He is at one with the naturalists who came after him on many of "Nature's rights." For example, he declares frankly that monogamy has engendered jealousy and aggravated the possessive instinct in man, without providing adequate compensatory benefit.[64]

This is an early and variant version of "ce mot Tien & Mien" (the curse of possessiveness and the sense of private property; we shall hear more of the phrase)—and one maintained at some length by Montaigne, who says of himself and his wife:

> of mine own disposition, would wisdome it selfe have had me, I should have refused to wed her. But we may say our pleasure; the custome and use of common life overbeareth us. Most of my actions are guided by example, and not by election. . . .[65]

"A good marriage (if any there be) refuseth the company and conditions of love," he asserts; "it endevoreth to present those of amity."[66] Most marriages produce more jealousy and envy than anything else; he contrasts the attitude of "our wives" with that of the primitive women among his "Cannibales," who

> endevour and apply all their industrie, to have as many rivals as possibly, they can, forasmuch as it is a testimonie of their husbands vertue.

"Our women," he concludes, "would count it a wonder, but it is not so. It is a vertue properly Matrimoniall."[67]

Valla and Montaigne are equally emphatic about chastity—and in much the same tone. "Would that man had fifty senses," says Valla defiantly, "since five can give such delight!" And again,

> I say what I feel. Courtesans and street-women deserve better of the human race than nuns and virgins.[68]

Montaigne praises the vow of virginity because it is the hardest of all vows. Yet to him, as to Rabelais, "Antiphysis" is abhorrent, and he declares, "It is then folly to go about to bridle women of a desire so fervent and so naturall in them."[69]

He, too, is "resolved to dare speake whatsoever I dare do: And . . . displeased with thoughts not to be published." For "few I know will snarle at the liberty of my writings, that have not more cause to snarle at their thoughts-loosenes."[70] He finds in this fact another opportunity for a Nature-Art comparison.

> Shame is matter of some consequence. Concealing, reservation and circumspection are parts of estimation. That sensuality under the maske of Vertu did very ingeniously procure not to be prostituted in the midst of highwaies, not trodden upon and seen by the common sort, alledging the dignity and commodity of her wonted Cabinets.[71]

Most men, he finds, would rather be thieves and have wives who are murderers and heretics, than to find their wives not more chaste than themselves. "Oh impious estimation of vices!" he exclaims:

Both wee [men] and they [women] are capable of a thousand
more hurtful corruptions then is lust and lasciviousness. But
we frame vices and waigh sinnes, *not according to their nature,
but according to our interest. . . .*[72]

This is the substance of the argument of many other contemporary
advocates of nature, who find in "pleasure" one "of the chiefest
kinds of profit."[73] So Nashe's Jack Wilton comes to like his master,
the Earl of Surrey,

because he had discarded those nice tearmes of chastitie and
continencie. Now I beseech God love me so well as I love a
plaine dealing man, earth is earth, flesh is flesh, earth wil to
earth, and flesh unto flesh, fraile earth, fraile flesh, who can
keepe you from the worke of your creation.[74]

These are not lofty sentiments, but Jack himself is not lofty. Montaigne would have approved him before "that sensuality under the
maske of Vertu"; and so, I think, would most of us. He is the sturdy
progenitor of the eighteenth-century Tom Jones, and there is a kind
of amoral health to his "philosophy of Nature" and contempt for
"Art." There was indeed a sufficient number of unhealthy hedonists
in the Renaissance, yet their kind of "libertinism" has been given
too exclusive an emphasis. Nor have we always looked in the right
directions for immorality. Surely Luther's declaration:

If an adultery could be committed in the faith, it would no
longer be a sin[75]

is more unhealthy than the sensuality of the naturalists.

Health, for that matter, is specifically the good which Montaigne
sets up for man in the *Apologie* (in a passage already quoted in
another context), in defiance of orthodoxy:

That part of natures favours which we impart unto beasts, is
by our owne confession much more advantageous unto them.
We assume unto our selves imaginarie and fantasticall goods,
future and absent goods, which humane capacity can no way
warrant unto her selfe; or some other, which by the overweening of our owne opinion we falsely ascribe unto our selves; as
reason, honour, and knowledge; and to them as their proper
share we leave the essentiall, the manageable, and palpable
goods, as peace, rest, securitie, innocencie, and health: Health
I say, which is the goodliest and richest present nature can
impart unto us.[76]

A hundred variations on a single theme, and Montaigne crowds
many of them into this passage. On the one hand, nature: "the

essentiall, the manageable, and palpable goods"; "peace, rest, securitie, innocencie, and health." On the other, art: the "imaginarie
and fantasticall goods" of "opinion"; "reason, honour, and knowledge." And indeed, to secure and retain health, nature is all that
is needed; he has no more use for the art of physicians than for
any other kind:

> Let nature worke; let hir have hir will; She knoweth what she
> hath to doe, and understands hir selfe better than we do. But
> such a one died of it, wil you say; so shal you doubtlesse; if
> not of that, yet of some other disease. And how many have
> wee seene die when they have had a whole Colledge of Physi-
> tians round about their bed, and looking in their excrements?[77]

"Let nature worke; let hir have hir will": it is a rallying cry of
the naturalists. One has only to compare Du Vair's admonition that

> neither Health, nor Body are the Good of Man, seeing they
> are not his End: for he possesses them not, *but to serve him to
> a further Use:* and the most part of his Age, he is miserable
> with all this: unless we shall approve them for happy, to
> whom wealth and strong Constitutions serve only (as to very
> many) to nourish their vices, and foment their Passions . . .[78]

with Valla's definitive

> Voluptas igitur est bonum undecunque quaesitum, in animi
> & corporis oblectatione positum . . .[79]

or Gabriel Harvey's

> The wiser man, y[e] more he cherisheth, & tenderith his animal
> powers[80]—

to see how different the Stoics' position on the subject of health
and the body is from that of the naturalists. To Du Vair man possesses his body only "to serve him to a further use"; to Harvey, it
is an important possession for its own sake, to be cherished for
itself. For DuVair, pleasures of the body are likely to lead to vice;
for Valla, pleasure—of body and soul—is the true good. And just
as Du Vair would preach temperance for virtue's sake, so Montaigne
does, in Epicurean style, for pleasure's sake. Invoking Socrates, he
declares:

> For him temperance is a moderatrix, and not an adversary of
> sensualities. Nature is a gentle guide, yet not more gentle than
> prudent and just. . . . I quest after her track: *we have con-
> founded her with artificiall traces.* And that Academicall and
> Peripateticall *summum bonum* or soveraigne felicity, which is

to live according to her rules: by this reason becommeth difficult to be limited, and hard to be expounded. And that of the Stoicks, cousin germane to the other, which is to yeeld unto nature. Is it not an errour to esteeme some actions lesse worthy forasmuch as they are necessary? Yet shall they never remove out of my head that it is not a most convenient marriage to wedde Pleasure unto Necessity.[81]

Here Montaigne aligns himself (and Socrates) against the three great classical ethical schools; nature against art; pleasure against "soveraigne felicity" or reason's road to virtue. It is putting the same opposition another way to say, as he does elsewhere, that the body has claims equal to the mind's. "For, as they say, 'tis good reason, that the body follow not his appetites to the mindes prejudice or dammage." And why, he demands indignantly, is it not equally right "that the minde should not follow hers to the bodies danger and hurt?"[82] And he contrasts nature's true laws, which are equally concerned with the body, with the ones man has invented for her —to his "own vexation":

Alas, poore silly man, thou hast but too-too many necessary and unavoidable incommodities, without increasing them *by thine owne invention,* and are sufficiently wretched of condition *without any arte.* . . . Findest thou to have supplied or discharged al necessary offices wherto nature engageth thee, and that she is idle in thee, if thou binde not thy selfe unto new offices? *Thou fearest not to offend hir universall and undoubted lawes, and are mooved at thine owne partiall and fantasticall ones.*[83]

This is the burden of Pantagruel's apologue about Physis and Antiphysis:

Physis (that is to say Nature) at her first burthen begat Beauty and Harmony, without carnal copulation, being of herself very fruitful and prolific. Antiphysis, who ever was the counterpart of nature, immediately, out of a malicious spight against her for beautiful and honourable productions, in opposition begot Amodunt and Dissonance, by copulation with Tellumon.[84]

But it is not simply asceticism that Rabelais is inveighing against; the description of Amodunt and Dissonance in the next few paragraphs, and Antiphysis' defense of their appearance, show clearly that, like Montaigne, he is ridiculing men's unconcern with nature's "universall and undoubted lawes," and their satisfaction with their own "partiall and fantasticall ones": Nature vs. Art.

Yet the other side is there, too; Rabelais is concerned with all "deformed and ill-favoured monsters, made in spite of nature." At any rate, it all comes to the same thing in the end; Pomponazzi had very neatly established the two parallels, in defiance of "the Divine Thomas":

> . . . by nature man exists more sensuous than intellective, more mortal than immortal. . . .[85]

A chorus of contemporary voices shouts approval.

> "I am as much convinced as they ["the philosophers of past times"] that it is good to vanquish a vicious passion," said Saffredent, "but to vanquish a natural passion, which has no evil tendency, seems to me a useless victory."[86]

"A thousand natures in my time," declares Montaigne, with a pre-Freudian accent, "have a thwart, a contrary discipline escaped toward vertue or toward vice."[87]

Most often, perhaps, this "protest of nature" is couched in terms of the unending conflict between passion (and appetite) and reason —with the accompanying conviction of the unnatural tyranny of reason. In a preceding chapter, we considered the romanticists' version of this conflict—usually a suffering, protesting one. The naturalists tend rather to assert the material goods of this life, and to present some positive alternative to reason as man's distinctive property.

For Valla, for example, it is laughter that is the gift of nature, not "discourse of reason":

> Loqui enim ipsa natura non possumus, ridere possumus.

Even mutes can indulge in laughter, "quod genus gaudij natura nobis velut muneri dedit."[88]

Among the many others who held a similar point of view is Rabelais:

> For laughter is man's property alone.[89]

Friar John, who in many ways deserves to be considered Rabelais' version of a natural man, is "the gladdest man in the world," one whose creed is that "while we are taking a cup, we do nothing but praise God."[90] And indeed Rabelais' own creed (if one may assume his definition of "Pantagruelism" to indicate its nature) is harmonious with these concepts:

> to be good Pantagruelists, that is to say, to live in peace, joy, health, making yourselves always merry.[91]

And in that other famous definition, he uses "jollity of mind" in exactly the context where a good orthodox Stoic would use reason:

Pantagruelism (which you know is a certain jollity of mind, pickled in the scorn of fortune)[92]

It is in the same spirit that Montaigne declares, "This is my humour, that I love as much to be happy as wise. . . ."[93] And again,

Who forsaketh to live healthy and merrily himselfe, therewith to serve another, in mine opinion taketh a bad and *unnatural* course.[94]

Perhaps we may even sum up the greater part of this "protest of Nature" movement by saying that it was to its adherents the reassertion of man as man—not as angel on the one side, or beast on the other. These last two (as the ingredients of the "compositum mixtum") were favorite alternatives for the Christian humanists, and Montaigne rejects them flatly:

Excuse wee here what I often say, that I seldome repent my selfe, and that my conscience is contented with it selfe; not of an Angels or a horses conscience, but as of a mans conscience. Adding ever this clause, *not of ceremonie,* but of true and essentiall submission. . . . There is truely I wot not what kinde or congratulation of well doing which rejoyceth in ourselves, and a generous jollitie that accompanieth a good conscience.[95]

"Not of an Angels or a horses conscience, but as of a mans conscience. . . ." It is in this sense that I have asserted that Montaigne's final philosophical outlook is a naturalistic humanism. And it is a part of that outlook to reject the Christian humanists' final emphasis on "the other world" and salvation—just as much as his emphasis on right reason and virtue in this one.

Thus he objects to those

wise men who thinke to have no better account of their life then to passe it over and escape it . . . as a thing of an yrkesome, tedious, and to bee disdained quality. But I know it to bee otherwise, and finde it to be priseable and commodious, yea in her last declination, where I hold it.[96]

"There is nothing," he maintains, "so goodly, so faire, and so lawfull, as to play the man well and duely. . . ." It might have been said by one of the humanists, but we know our Montaigne by now —for him this means the Nature of a "common feeling of Humanity," not the Art of the prescribed pursuit of virtue. And indeed he goes on to make his profession of faith:

I cheerefully and thankefully, and with a good heart, accept what nature hath created for me, and am there with well pleased and am proud of it. . . . Of philosophers opinions I more willingly embrace those which are the most solide, *and that is to say such as are most humane and most ours.* . . .[97]

It is not new, not abrupt. It has been coming for a long time, since the beginning of the Renaissance—and before. Dante's "gentle man" does not turn to "meditative repose and pious devotion" until old age.[98] Petrarch finds it difficult to accept Augustine's quotation from Cicero:

A wise man's life is all one preparation for death.

He declares,

I do not think to become as God, or to inhabit eternity, or to embrace heaven and earth. Such glory as belongs to man is enough for me. . . . Mortal myself, it is but mortal blessings I desire.

When Augustine expresses his horror, Petrarch explains that he intended to say

that my wish was to use mortal things for what they are worth, to do no violence to nature by bringing to its good things a limitless desire, and so to follow after human fame as knowing that both myself and it will perish.[99]

The dialogue in the *Secretum* ends inconclusively, but the procession marches on. Castiglione (or Bembo) does not expect the young man to be a true Platonic lover; the Courtier, who *is* expected to attain to this ideal, is explicitly to be an older man, with the heyday in the blood well tamed. Always *humanitas* first, *divinitas* afterward.[100] All of us, as Rabelais puts it, dream of being able

to compass what . . . all men naturally covet so much; and so few, or (to speak more properly) none can enjoy together; I mean a paradise in this life, and another in the next.[101]

Yet the naturalists' dream is exclusively of a paradise in *this* life. Their coat of arms might bear Leonardo's words: "To enjoy—to love a thing for its own sake and for no other reason."[102]

This is a very different philosophy from that incorporated in Thomas Lodge's foreword to his translation of Seneca:

That to be truely virtuous is to be happy, to subdue passion is to be truly a man, to contemne fortune is to conquer her, to foresee and unmaske miseries is to lessen them, to love well is to be vertuous, and to die well is the way to eternitie.[103]

It is only just to give Montaigne both the rebuttal and the benediction. He, too, like Dante, Petrarch, Castiglione, sees each part of life as having a propriety of its own:

> It is one of the chiefest points wherein I am beholden to fortune, that in the course of my bodies estate, each thing hath beene carried in season. I have seene the leaves, the blossomes, and the fruit; and now see the drooping and withering of it. Happily, because naturally.[104]

But is it his "bodies estate" that he is writing about, and he has "happily" fulfilled Petrarch's hope of doing "no violence to nature." Moreover, it is not the ordered progression of the *art* of life, but the natural progression of life. The distinction is not tenuous or arbitrary. For he says,

> There is no course of life so weake and sottish as that which is managed by Order, Methode, and Discipline. . . . A man should apply himselfe to the best rules, but not subject himselfe unto them.

He even recommends that a young man

> often give him selfe to all manner of excesse; otherwise the least disorder wil utterly overthrow him. . . .[105]

We are reminded of Housman's "Mithridates, he died old."

Such advice is necessary, for too often, "we are taught to live when our life is well nigh spent . . ." and "if we have not known how to live, it is injustice to teach us how to die, and deforme the end from all the rest. . . ."[106]

Not that he cares for any lesson in how to die. "Such transcending humours affright me as much as steepy, high, and inaccessible places," and "super-celestiall opinions and under-terrestrial manners are things amongst us I have ever seene to bee of singular accord."[107]

He flares out in the last pages that he wrote:

> We seeke for other conditions because we understand not the use of ours, and goe out of our selves forasmuch as we know not what abiding there is. Wee long enough get upon stilts, for be wee upon them, yet must we goe with our owne legges. And sit we upon the highest throne of the World, yet sit we upon our owne taile.[108]

Inevitably he returns to a "common feeling of Humanity," to "the common mould and humane model," fashioned "without wonder or extravagancy."[109]

His concern is not with death; death will take care of itself, and *naturally*. If there is something beyond, it is not *human life*, and he would certainly exclaim with Erasmus, "As if there were any difference between perishing, and being another thing!"[110]

"Life," says Montaigne as dogmatically as he has ever spoken,

> is a materiall and corporal motion, an action imperfect and disordered by its owne essence; I employ or apply my selfe to serve it according to it selfe.[111]

He quotes from Cicero: "We must so worke as we endeavour nothing against nature in generall, yet so observe it as we follow our owne in speciall,"[112] and he demands scornfully,

> To what purpose are these heaven-looking and nice points of Philosophie, on which no humane being can establish and ground it selfe? And to what end serve these rules that exceed our use and excell our strength?[113]

"Neither the proposer nor the Auditors have any hope at all to follow" these rules, he asserts; the whole process is merely a salaam to the God Reason.

> Thus goes the world, and so goe men. We let the lawes and precepts follow their way, but wee keepe another course; Not only by disorder of manners, but often by opinion and contrary judgement.[114]

However much given the stamp of his own distinctive cast of thought and expression, Montaigne's philosophy of nature and his scorn of "Stoicism" (after having early been a disciple of doctrinal classical Stoicism) illuminate fully the Nature-Art controversy in the Renaissance—and with especial relevance to the ethical conflict engendered by variant readings of the injunction to follow nature. It is tempting to say that Montaigne covers the ground so well that it is superfluous to continue the discussion of this point.

Perhaps this is the case. But no discussion is as effective a presentation of a conflict as that conflict's concrete embodiment in dramatic form. For that reason, I should like to present the Nature-Stoicism opposition briefly as it seems to me to be set forth in George Chapman's companion plays—*Bussy D'Ambois* and *The Revenge of Bussy*. These plays, between them, not only present sympathetically each of the two ideals; they serve handsomely to demonstrate the way in which the conflict permeated Elizabethan thought and literature.

In the former play, Bussy seems to be the explicit representative of the naturalists' or "bastard Stoics'" concept of the Golden Age, miraculously set down (in somewhat the way that Paracelsus considered himself to be) in a *milieu* corrupt and rotten with the institutions forged by "custom" and "opinion." Here is a man "qui ne cognoist les noms de vertu ny de vice," who is "porté de l'appetit de son premier desir,"[115] and yet is respected by the "best" characters in the play. Only in the light of the twofold naturalist interpretation of following nature as following instinct and following the bent of one's own particular nature, can Bussy's violent career be made fully intelligible.

Early in the play, after the king has pardoned him for slaying his opponent in a duel, Bussy expresses the hope that he may be able to double his life—

> That I may so make good what God and nature
> Have given me for my good; since I am free,
> (Offending no just law), let no law make
> By any wrong it does, my life her slave:
> When I am wrong'd, and that law fails to right me,
> Let me be king myself (as man was made),
> And do a justice that exceeds the law. . . .[116]

Not only is "Soymesmes . . . sa loy, son Senat & son Roy";[117] Bussy also repudiates the association of free love with sin. When Tamara expresses remorse after Bussy has had her, he replies,

> Sweet mistress, cease, your conscience is too nice,
> And bites too hotly of the Puritan spice.

When she refuses to be consoled, he declaims,

> Sin is a coward, madam, and insults
> But on our weakness, in his truest valour:
> And so our ignorance tames us, that we let
> His shadows fright us: and like empty clouds,
> In which our faulty apprehensions forge
> The forms of dragons, lions, elephants.
> When they hold no proportion, the sly charms
> Of the witch Policy makes him like a monster
> Kept only to show men for servile money:
> That false hag often paints him in her cloth
> Ten times more monstrous than he is in troth. . . .[118]

In short, "sin" is more often the "shadow" of opinion or custom than a real evil.

Tamara indicates that she has understood, if not accepted, his philosophy, when she exclaims a short time afterward:

> What shall weak dames do, when th'whole work of nature
> Hath a strong finger in each one of us?[119]

Bussy is constantly being extolled as that "great heart," that "great spirit." Chapman builds up his concept of Bussy as a "child of nature" more skillfully than many of his later characters, because more gradually. It is not until the third act that the king makes the final identification of Bussy with the free man of the Golden Age, in a speech that includes a reference to "ce mot Tien et Mien":

> A man so good, that only would uphold
> *Man in his native noblesse,* from whose fall
> All our dissensions rise; that in himself
> (Without the outward patches of our frailty,
> Riches and honour) knows he comprehends
> Worth with the greatest: Kings had never borne
> Such boundless empire over other men,
> Had all maintained the spirit and state of D'Ambois;
> Nor had the full impartial hand of Nature
> That all things gave in her original,
> Without these definite terms of Mine and Thine,
> Being turn'd unjustly to the hand of Fortune,
> *Had all preserv'd her in her prime, like D'Ambois;*
> No envy, no disjunction had dissolved,
> Or pluck'd one stick of the *golden faggot*
> In which *the world of Saturn* bound our lives,
> Had all been held together with the nerves,
> The genius, and th'ingenuous soul of D'Ambois.[120]

And at Bussy's death the Umbra pronounces an appropriate benediction:

> Farewell, brave relics of a complete man.[121]

The villains of the piece, Guise (who is to become an admirable character in *The Revenge of Bussy*) and Monsieur, indicate by their estimates of D'Ambois that they understand the tradition that he embodies. Guise qualifies his willingness to accept Bussy's proffer of friendship—

> I seal to that, and so the manly freedom
> That you so much profess, hereafter prove not
> A bold and glorious licence to deprave[122]

—and Monsieur asserts to Bussy his belief

> That in thy valour th'art like other *naturals*
> *That have strange gifts in nature,* but no soul

> Diffus'd quite through, to make them of a piece,
> But stop at humours. . . .[123]

If Bussy seems at times to belong to that other tradition, to be professing the humanistic faith in natural reason, it is because the reading is incomplete. When he says, for instance,

> Should not my powers obey when she commands,
> My motion must be rebel to my will,
> My will to life . . .[124]

he seems to be subordinating his own nature to universal nature, as Cicero had enjoined. Yet since "she" is Tamara, it is obvious that his will, if it obeys "life," will be obeying *instinct* or *inclination,* not reason.

Again, when he says

> Who to himself is law, no law doth need,
> Offends no law, and is a king indeed . . .[125]

he comes close to speaking the language of the Golden Age man who follows a law within himself—that of natural reason. Yet Spenser's representative account is that in that time before the Fall of Man,

> . . . each unto his lust did make a lawe,
> From all forbidden things his liking to withdrawe,[126]

and Bussy's affair with Tamara makes it quite clear that he, on the other hand, "did make . . . his lust . . . a lawe."

If any final proof is needed to show Bussy's allegiance to the bastard Stoic tradition, it is provided in *The Revenge of Bussy.* For Clermont, Bussy's brother and avenger, is called the perfect "Senecal man . . . rightly to virtue fram'd, in very nature."[127] So Guise describes him, and indeed Clermont is the consistent advocate and follower of reason. He, in contrast to Bussy, makes the law of man's natural bent or individual nature plainly subservient to the universal Law of Nature, in a long speech which contains an elaboration on a passage in Epictetus' *Discourses.*[128]

Clermont expounds doctrinal Stoicism throughout; as the play goes on, he appeals more and more the "the right way of our reason."[129] To Bussy's "native noblesse" he adds Cicero's "humanitas" or "humanity"—or, one might say, while Bussy follows exclusively his own *Nature,* in the sense of instinct and individual nature, Clermont strengthens his *Nature* with the Art of reason, in the manner of the middle-path humanist tradition. He says:

> . . . for as when only Nature
> Moves men to meat, as far as her power rules,
> She doth it with a temperate appetite,
> The too much men devour abhorring Nature;
> And in our most health is our most disease;
> So, when humanity rules men and women,
> 'Tis for society confined in reason.[130]

This is an emphasis totally foreign to Bussy, and it is at once ludicrous and appropriate when Bussy's shade takes on a fideistic tone and chides Clermont for his excessive devotion to reason. Revenge, he urges, is a holy task when the cause is just, but Clermont has deserted "the body of felicity, religion,

> And all her laws, whose observation
> Stands upon faith, above the power of reason.

Bussy accuses him further in the terms in which all the religious anti-humanists warn against the dangers of Stoic ethics:

> You respect not
> (With all your holinesse of life and learning)
> More than the present, like illiterate vulgars;
> Your mind (you say) kept in your flesh's bounds,
> Shows that man's will must rul'd be by his power:
> When (by true doctrine) you are taught to live
> Rather without the body than within,
> And rather to your God still than yourself. . . .[131]

Appropriate—because Bussy, moving from the naturalist creed to the fideistic, remains the child of the Counter-Renaissance. The ghost of the child of nature preaches the gospel of exclusive reliance on faith with almost Calvinistic harshness. In his life a proponent of instinct and individualism, in revolt against the rational Law of Nature—as a shade Bussy attacks the humanists' allegiance to reason from a different angle. The Counter-Renaissance, as we have seen before, fostered strange alliances.

But it is the contrast between Bussy and Clermont that stands out most clearly, dramatizing the conflict between the legitimate and bastard Stoic traditions, between "Stoicism" and "Nature." That Chapman consciously intended to draw just this contrasting picture, revealing the merits of each kind of man, yet distinguishing between them, is increasingly convincing if one remembers how well he knew Seneca's work. The following passage, indeed, might almost have been in Chapman's mind. It displays the same imaginative sympathy for the "natural man" (Bussy), the same intellectual preference for the "Senecal man . . . rightly to virtue fram'd, in very nature" (Clermont).

> But however excellent and guileless their life, the men of that time [the Golden Age] were not wise men, since that name is reserved for the highest of man's achievements. Yet I would not deny that they were men of lofty spirit and—if I may put it so—fresh from the gods. For there is no doubt that the world brought forth better things when it was not yet worn out. But while the native powers of all of them were greater than ours and more fitted for labors, nevertheless those powers had not in all of them been brought to their highest development. For virtue is not bestowed by nature; it is an art to become good. . . . What follows then? They were innocent through ignorance. But it makes a great difference whether a man is unwilling to sin or does not know how to sin. Justice was still unknown to them, and prudence, and self-control, and fortitude. Their rude life had in it certain qualities resembling all these virtues; but virtue itself is attained by the soul only when it has been taught and trained, and by unremitting practice has been brought to perfection. For this, but without it, we were born; and even in the best of men, without instruction, there is but the stuff of virtue, not virtue itself.[132]

Here are the "natural man" and the "Stoic man." If Seneca prefers the one, he is at least sympathetic to the other—and so, too, Chapman. But such was not usually the case, as we have seen; more often, the two ideals are opposed—with one attacked, the other defended. In no way can this be made clearer than through an examination of the opposing traditions' conceptions of the Golden Age, of man's nature in its pristine innocence before the Fall or the intrusion of civilization. Bussy and Clermont are the heirs, the sons, the representatives of two different accounts of the Golden Age. It would be well, then, to turn next to various Renaissance and Counter-Renaissance concepts of that fabulous time of peace and plenty in the innocency of the world—and as well to those discordant versions that denied there had ever been such a time or state of things. For in these differing concepts, we see something of the various prevalent philosophies of history, and hence gain another salient perspective on the intellectual conflicts of the period.

3. THE GOLDEN AGE AND THE STATE OF NATURE

Chronological primitivism is a philosophy of history directly opposed to the idea of a general and necessary law of progress. It is frequently, although not necessarily, antithetic to the idea of progress in general. In any case, it is a nostalgic philosophy of history, one that looks back to the prototype of all "the good old days" before men became contaminated or "lessened" or unhappily complex.[133]

This position was often combined with a concept of four ages— Golden, Silver, Bronze and Iron—that marked a descending order of excellence.[134] In fact, the ideal of the Golden Age is the oldest known manifestation of the concept of chronological primitivism in Western thought, and almost certainly antedates the earliest known literary expression.[135] Assuredly, as simple myth or legend, it is pre-Hesiodic, and there is even evidence of the concept as a time of universal peace and plenty in the pre-Egyptian Sumerian literature. An epic tale of Sumer contains these lines:

> In those days there was no snake, there was no scorpion,
>   there was no *hyena,*
> There was no lion, there was no *wild dog,* no wolf,
> There was no fear, no terror,
> Man had no rival.

> In those days the land Shubur [East], the place of
>   plenty, of righteous decrees,
> *Harmony-tongued* Sumer [South], the great land of the
>   "decrees of princeship,"
> Uri [North], the land having all this is *needful,*
> The land Martu [West], resting in security,
> The whole universe, the people *in unison,*
> To Enlil in one tongue *gave praise.*[136]

Most often in Greek myth and thought, the Golden Age is equivalent to the reign of Cronos (Saturn), and ends with the triumph of Zeus.[137] This Age of Cronos or Saturn, from Hesiod's *Works and Days* down, usually is represented as an age of peace, plenty and freedom, although there are many variants. At any rate, most of the great Greek and Roman writers refer to it in one way or another—among them Plato, Aristotle, Vergil, Ovid, Horace, Seneca and Cicero. Equated with Eden, in terms of a time when obedient and innocent man did not know sin, the concept fitted harmoniously into the Christian story, and was appropriated and reinterpreted by patristic and medieval writers. And so it came down, altered yet basically unchanged, to the Renaissance, during which it enjoyed great popularity.

The traditionalist-humanistic version in the Renaissance sees the

Golden Age as the time when man, in accordance with his "natural reason," is universally impelled toward good, toward virtue. Since the Fall, his "native seed of reason" may be insufficient to resist "the vices surrounding it" and be "stifled and blighted." The "seed" is still there, the innate impulsion to good remains; but— since Eve listened not wisely but too well—it is no longer universally certain that man will follow reason and attain virtue. But before the Fall, the rule was infallible. As Spenser puts it,

> But antique age yet in the infancie
> Of time, did live then like an innocent,
> In simple truth and blamelesse chastitie,
> Ne then of guile had made experiment,
> But voide of vile and treacherous intent,
> Helde virtue for it self in soveraine awe:
> *Then loyall love had royall regiment,*
> *And each unto his lust did make a lawe,*
> *From all forbidden things his liking to withdraw.*[138]

Spenser, to be sure, displays a quasi-Calvinistic pessimism about the possibility of true "beautie" (and hence, in his Platonic terms, by implication, virtue) since that time when "faire grew foule, and foule grew faire in sight"[139]—rather than the moderate optimism of the middle-path humanists. Yet his emphasis in his picture of the Golden Age is identical to theirs:

> Then loyall love had royall regiment,
> And each unto his lust did make a lawe,
> From all forbidden things his liking to withdraw.

It is an exactly opposite emphasis, of course, which we encounter in the Counter-Renaissance naturalistic primitivists' descriptions of the Golden Age. Theirs is a picture of a time when love had no "regiment" at all—when nothing was "forbidden" and "each . . . did make . . . his lust a lawe." In short, man was free to follow all his natural inclinations, which did not necessarily lead to "virtue."

Yet the naturalists do not mean that it was a lawless age in all the senses of "lawless." Without laws, it was—for the naturalists, unlike the humanists, do not invoke the inner "lawe" of reason. However, because man was free to follow his own instincts, his own nature, the Golden Age was an idyllic time, without strife; for to most of these thinkers, too, man was naturally *good*. The distinction between these two Golden Ages rests upon the difference between being naturally good because of "natural reason," and being naturally good because of instinct. And the "goods" differ accordingly: in the one case, virtue; in the other, all the goods of an untrammeled life.

For the outstanding feature of the naturalists' Golden Age was man's freedom from restraint. Perhaps the distinction can best be clarified by a comparison of those two famous Golden Age choruses: the one in Guarini's *Pastor Fido,* the other and earlier one in Tasso's *Aminta.* Guarini concludes,

> Cura d'onor felice,
> Cui dettava Onesta: *Piaccia se lice.* . . .

But Tasso had written,

> . . . legge aurea e felice
> Che Natura scolpi: *S'ei piace, ei lice.*

To Guarini, "what was proper pleased"; to Tasso, "what pleased was proper."[140]

A full treatment of the way in which this inversion of the "virtuous" traditionalist-humanistic account of the Golden Age developed would be a long and complicated task. Professor Bredvold has plausibly suggested Seneca's influence, pointing out the latter's contention that, since men were ignorant in the earliest age, "their happiness was due merely to innocence and natural goodness, not to virtue, which is only achieved by effort and discipline."[141]

"In their perfect innocence," Professor Bredvold continues, "they had no need of institutions; no government guarded private property, for they had all things in common." But—and herein lay the paradox of Seneca's theory—

> as human nature *deteriorated and developed* . . . institutions had to be devised and laws enacted to coerce mankind back to order and regularity though it is never possible to secure by these means the harmony which existed without force in the Golden Age.[142]

Thus Seneca held at once that "in time to come man will know much that is unknown to us" and that "human wickedness has not yet fully developed."[143] Progress in knowledge is matched by deterioration from the original natural goodness, except for the true Stoic philosophers.

This point of view, of course, involves the traditional Stoic distinction between the "man of nature," good but not truly *virtuous,* and the Stoic man of disciplined virtue. Hence Bussy and Clermont most nearly correspond—and perhaps did in Chapman's mind—to

these two concepts. At the same time, Seneca's picture of the original man of nature is one of a man more purely instinctual (like
Bussy) than is that of most rigidly doctrinal Stoics, inherited from
the Cynics. The latter two groups, in contradistinction to the naturalists, or bastard individualistic Stoic tradition, picture the Golden
Age as a time of righteousness and rugged simplicity, not of individualistic self-indulgence. Hence my claim of Bussy's belonging
to the naturalistic tradition (no matter what Chapman's debt to
Seneca), rather than to the orthodox Stoic and Cynic tradition.

The difference is really that which Lovejoy, Boas, et al., describe
as the difference between *hard* and *soft* primitivism. The Golden
Age of the former sort depicts a simple, rigorous life of natural
righteousness; the latter often an age of ease and indulgence—even
sometimes of unbridled individualistic license, though more often
one of "soft" contentment and plenty without strife. It should also
be clear now that the traditionalist humanists of the Renaissance
tended toward hard primitivism, although not often of the strictly
rigorous sort endorsed by the old doctrinal Cynics and Stoics.[144]

Despite Seneca's Stoic allegiance, however, the Counter-Renaissance naturalists' point of view was similar to his in two important
particulars: (1) they, too, distinguished between natural goodness
and rational virtue; (2) they, too, believed that the growth of social
and civil institutions had paralleled a corrupting process in man.

There were, of course, other precedents besides Seneca. Ovid's
picture of the Golden Age was also harmonious with the naturalists',
and Jean de Meun had invoked a "dream of ease and unlimited
freedom and indulgence" in the *Roman de la Rose*.[145] Moreover,
"the protest of Nature" raised by Valla and other Italian humanists
had a related significance. Poliziano's description of the reign of
Venus in his *Stanze per la Giostra* reveals an amorous world that
inevitably suggests the naturalists' Golden Age.

All of nature is animated by love:

> . . . light amorous breezes make
> The little tender grasses gently shake . . .

and

> . . . the tree that so delighted Hercules
> Sports with the plane along the watery leas.

Even the fishes feel love's power,

> nor can chill waters quench the precious flame.

Natural enmities are forgotten:

> The gentle hares, in number hastening
> To amorous sport, fear not that hounds will chase.
> Thus Love where'er he wills in every breast
> Old hate and natural fear can lull to rest.[146]

Yet the very mention of "old hate and natural fear" (*l'odio antico e 'l natural timore*) indicates that this is not the pure naturalists' tradition, for which such terms would be contradictory. The invocation of love in Poliziano's idyll is in some ways closer to the Neoplatonist concept of its functions than the naturalists'. However differently, it "holds the world together" by reconciling naturally warring elements.

When Lorenzo de' Medici prays in his *Selve* for a return of the Golden Age, he identifies it with the rapturous beginnings of his love for his lady:

> To those dear haunts in that departed time
> Oh Love, restore me with my lady fair,
> In those unsullied years, that tender prime,
> Of neither jealousy nor hope aware.
> Let not our days to ripe fulfilment climb
> But let our love become eternal there.
> No other fire in us, nor other grace
> In her; but only that sweet time and place.[147]

This blending of a Golden Age of love with a pre-eminently courtly tradition of love suggests a romantic, rather than the naturalistic, tradition. Nevertheless, in its nostalgic dream of an "eternal" love, unaware of "jealousy" and "hope," it conjures up a similar vision; and it is interesting to note how often overtones of a carefree Golden Age are apparent in the courtly and Petrarchan "eternal love" traditions. Ronsard, for example, writing to his Cassandre of reunion in heaven, suggests a Golden Age in the Elysian Fields that bears little resemblance either to Christian or Neoplatonic versions of heavenly love:

> Parmy le grand espace
> De ce verger heureux,
> Nous aurons tous deux place
> Entre les amoureux,
> Et comme eux sans soucy
> Nous aimerons aussi.[148]

It is one more statement in that "protest of Nature" tradition that includes Aucassin's expression of his preference for Hell and the company of Nicolette, Launcelot's unsanctioned passion for Guinevere, the unrepentance of Paolo and Francesca, the tone of Petrarch's sonnets after the death of Laura, and—as we have already set forth—the magnificent infatuation of Antony and Cleopatra. It is, in short, an assertion of the absolute primacy of human sexual love.

Ronsard, however, also makes some of the strongest naturalist protests of the Renaissance against the inroads of reason and civilization upon the simplicity and freedom of the Golden Age. In *Les Armes, à Jean Brinon,* he pictures "les siecles dorez" as a time when "le peuple oisif" enjoyed a complete simplicity and freedom.

> Alors on n'attachoit (pour les rendre plus seures)
> Des portes aux maisons, aux portes des serrures:
> Et lors on n'oyoit point ce mot de Tien ne Mien:
> Tous vivoient en commun, car tous n'avoient qu'un bien:
> De ce que l'un vouloit, l'autre en avoit envie,
> Et tous d'accord passoient heureusement la vie.[149]

But is is in the *Discours contre Fortune* that he expresses an unqualified allegiance to all the doctrines of the naturalists, in his attack upon Villegagnon's colony in Brazil. There is no more eloquent or impassioned defense of the free Golden Age in Renaissance literature:

> Docte Villegagnon, tu fais une grand faute
> De vouloir rendre fine une gent si peu cante,
> Comme ton Amerique, ou le peuple incognu
> Erre innocentement tout farouche & tout nu,
> D'habit tout aussi nu qu'il est nu de malice,
> Qui ne cognoist les noms de vertu ny de vice,
> De Senat ny de Roy, qui vit a son plaisir
> Porté de l'appetit de son premier desir,
> Et qui n'a dedans l'ame ainsi que nous emprainte
> La frayeur de la loy qui nous fait vivre en crainte:
> Mais suivant sa nature est seul maistre de soy,
> Soymesmes est sa loy, son Senat & son Roy. . . .[150]

Here all the important concepts of the bastard Stoic tradition are to be found, in this picture of a people "qui ne cognoist les noms de vertu ny de vice"; "qui vit a son plaisir, porté de l'appetit de son premier desir"; qui, "suivant sa nature, est seul maistre de soy" —"soymesmes . . . sa loy, son Senat & son Roy." (Here, incidentally, is a moral lexicon for Bussy d'Ambois.) And Ronsard goes on to contrast the miserable lot of his contemporaries with these people

> Qui de coutres trenchans la terre n'importune,
> Laquelle comme l'air à chacun est commune,
> Et comme l'eau d'une fleuve, est commun tout leur bien,
> Sans procez engendrer de ce mot Tien & Mien.[151]

This is the second time we have found Ronsard inveighing against "ce mot Tien & Mien"; he enlarges upon the theme in the following lines, which express a frank economic primitivism, endorsing the communal life and eschewing private property:

> Pource laisse-les là, ne romps plus (je te prie)
> Le tranquille repos de leur premiere vie:
> Laisse-les ie te pri', si pitié te remord,
> Ne les tourmente plus & t'enfuy de leur bord.
> Las! si tu leur apprens à limiter la terre,
> Pour agrandir leurs champs ils se feront la guerre,
> Les procez auront lieu, l'amitié defaudra
> Et l'aspre ambition tourmenter les viendra
> Comme elle fait ici nous autres pauvres hommes,
> Qui par trop de raison trop miserables sommes:
> Ils vivent maintenent en leur âge doré.[152]

Montaigne himself has not laid a heavier charge against "reason." The whole sorry story of the progression (or retrogression) from "le tranquille repos de leur premiere vie," through the birth of "ce mot Tien & Mien" and the inevitable succession of "la guerre," "les procez," and "l'aspre ambition," to the state of "nous autres pauvres hommes"—all laid at the door of "trop de raison!"

And Ronsard repeats the accusation a little later, in terms of himself, and for a moment entertains the dream that he too might share the life of the Golden Age:

> Vivez heureuse gent sans peine & sans souci,
> Vivez joyeusement: ie voudrois vivre ainsi.
> L'Iliade des maux que ma raison travaille,
> Et ceux que le malheur en se iovant me baille
> En rompant mes desseins, ne m'auroit arresté,
> Et gaillard ie vivrois en toute liberté.[153]

"Sans peine & sans souci. . . ." It is the old dream, and perhaps the eternal antithesis of that similar and yet so dissimilar motto of Sir Galahad. But if the accent is on "dream," and the words "ie voudrois vivre ainsi" are almost a sigh, the voice of the final line is still a vigorous masculine one. One has only to compare "Et gaillard ie vivrois en toute liberté" with the tone of the invitation extended by the nymph of Armida's lake in *Jerusalem Delivered:*

> This is the place wherein you may assuage
> Your sorrows past, here is that joy and bliss
> That flourished in the antique golden age,
> Here needs no law, here none doth aught amiss:
> Put off those arms and fear not Mars his rage,

> Your sword, your shield, your helmet needless is;
> Then consecrate them here to endless rest,
> You shall love's champions be, and soldiers blest.
>
> The fields for combat here are beds of down,
> Or heapèd lilies under shady brakes. . . .[154]

It is with considerable accuracy that Ubaldo describes Rinaldo, held captive on this island by his infatuation for Armida, as "a carpet champion for a wanton dame."[155]

It is high time to make a further distinction about kinds of primitivism in the Renaissance and Counter-Renaissance—a distinction at which I have only hinted, in discussing Lorenzo de' Medici's gallant vision of the Golden Age. The distinction between the Classicists' (whether the extreme rigorous ideal of the doctrinal Cynics and Stoics, or the more moderate but highly righteous one of the traditionalist humanists) Golden Age and that of the Naturalists should be clear. But all those who espouse unbridled freedom, or even ease and indolence, do not support the genuine naturalistic position.

What Lorenzo, Tasso, and Ronsard (in a few limited passages) are almost exclusively interested in is the picture of a courtly paradise, close to Spenser's Bower of Bliss in its emphasis upon an ideal of unending (I almost said "unrelieved") sensual love and beauty. That these passages are in a highly developed courtly romanticist tradition we shall see more clearly in the following chapter (IX). Whenever we come across the "Elysian Fields," "Isles of the Blest" or other courtly "Golden Age" pictures of heavily scented fields and bowers of love, we are dealing with this tradition of romantic "soft primitivism." "Soft" it is, but not *really* primitivistic any more than Sidney's Arcadia is *really* pastoral. This tradition is susceptible to a "primitivistic sentiment," but that is as far as it goes.

Genuine naturalistic primitivism of the Counter-Renaissance is quite another matter. It is seriously concerned with presenting arguments for, and examples of, cultural, technological, economic, marital, juristic and ethical primitivism (all briefly defined earlier in this chapter). Among the passages we've read so far, the longer serious ones from Ronsard best illustrate this approach. While, under several of these headings, the naturalists shared the courtly romantics' interest in free love, their treatment of it is much more forthright and assertive, and sometimes even touched by humor. It represents an egoistic hedonism, not a courtly religion of beauty and love. And its concept of this part of the Golden Age was one of contentment and plenty and freedom, not one of beauty and love.

The freedom to follow one's instincts is given by the naturalists an accent like that to be found in one of Machiavelli's rare references to the subject: "a return of the Golden Age, where everyone may keep and defend what reputation he pleases. . . ."[156] It is perhaps most exuberantly stated by John Donne in his seventeenth elegy:

> How happy were our Syres in ancient times,
> Who held plurality of loves no crime!
> With them it was accounted charity
> To stirre up race of all indifferently;
> Kindreds were not exempted from the bands:
> Which with the Persian still in usage stands.
> Women were then no sooner asked then won,
> And what they did was honest and well done,
> But since this title honour hath been us'd,
> Our weake credulity hath been abus'd;
> The golden laws of nature are repeald,
> Which our first Fathers in such reverence held;
> Our liberty's revers'd, our Charter's gone,
> And we're made servants to opinion,
> A monster in no certain shape attir'd,
> And whose originall is much desir'd,
> Formlesse at first, but growing on it fashions,
> And doth prescribe manners and laws to nations.
> Here love receiv'd immedicable harmes,
> And was dispoiled of his daring armes.
> A great want than is his daring eyes,
> He lost those awfull wings with which he flies;
> His sinewy bow, and those immortall darts
> Wherewith he'is wont to bruise resisting hearts.
> Onely some few strong in themselves and free
> Retain the seeds of antient liberty,
> Following that part of Love although deprest,
> And make a throne for him within their brest,
> In spight of modern censures him avowing
> Their Soveraigne, all service him allowing.
> Amongst which troop although I am the least
> Yet equall in perfection with the best,
> I glory in subjection of his hand,
> Nor ever did decline his least command:
> For in whatever forme the message came
> My heart did open and receive the same.[157]

For these naturalists, as for Panurge, the Golden Age ended with "a notable pregnant invention made up and composed of fig-tree leaves. . . ."[158]

However, the eminently masculine idea of "plurality of loves" did not, of course, constitute the whole naturalistic picture. Marriage and family life formed but one of the institutions brought in by "opinion" and "custom" and "tradition"; as Ronsard's version suggests, there were other freedoms that had been lost.

Montaigne, who stated definitively, "I am a duteous servant unto plainnesse, simplicity and liberty,"[159] and suggested his personal version of a Golden Age in his declaration, "My most favoured qualities [are] lethall sloathfulnesse, and a genuine liberty"[160]—Montaigne, in a way similar to Ronsard, sets forth in his famous essay "On Cannibales" a list of the freedoms in his primitivistic "commonwealth" that have been lost with the advent of civilization:

> It is a nation . . . that hath no kinde of traffike, no knowledge of Letters, no intelligence of numbers, no name of magistrate, nor of political superioritie; no use of service, of riches or of povertie; no contracts, no successions, no partitions, no occupations but idle; no respect of kindred, but common, no apparell but naturall, no manuring of lands, no use of wine, corne, or mettel.[161]

He takes the occasion to drive home one of his favorite morals, while discussing the peoples of the New World:

> Those nations seeme therefore so barbarous to me because they have received very little fashion from humaine wit, and are yet neere *their originall naturalitie.* . . .[162]

Having expressed the wish that Plato and Lycurgus might have had a knowledge of these people, he continues, making it clear with his reference to the poets that he had no interest in a romanticist's "Golden Age"—

> for me seemeth that what in those nations we see by experience, doth not only exceed all the pictures wherewith licentious Poesie hath proudly imbellished the golden age, and all her quaint inventions to faine a happy condition of man, but also the conception and desire of Philosophy. They could not imagine a genuitie so pure and simple, as we see it by experience; nor ever beleeve our societie might be maintained with so little art and humane combination.[163]

Nature and Art: here is a passage saturated in the solution of the conflict. The Nature of the "Cannibales" contrasted with the rational "art" of "humane combination"—and the Nature of "experience" to *demonstrate* a Golden Age contrasted with the "inventions" of one by the Art of "Poesie" and "Philosophy." Yet there is justice in the distinction. One has but to turn back to Tasso. Ronsard had utilized an account of a colony in Brazil as a starting-point for his most extended reference to the Golden Age; Montaigne's debt to explorations in the New World in describing a Golden Age is even more solid.

And it is a debt.[164] Those same cosmographers who had held aloft their findings through personal experience had not missed their opportunity to exploit the most ancient of dreams. In a book attributed to Vespucci we find:

> They have no wool cloth, nor linen, nor cotton, because they do not need any. Also they have no private goods; all things are common. They live together without King, without Emperor, and each one is Lord of himself. They have as many wives as they want. . . . Beyond that, they have no churches and keep no law, and yet they are not idolatrous. What more shall I say, except they live according to nature? They should rather be called *epicureans than stoics.*[165]

With the final distinction, we return, surprisingly enough, to Du Vair's opposition of Nature and Stoicism. The passage is of real importance to the subject of this and the preceding section.

Peter Martyr's savages are not explicitly "epicureans" ("wives" are not mentioned), but they have

> land as common amongst them as the sun, air, and water. "This is mine and that is yours" (which is the cause of all discord) is not to be found with them. . . . They have the golden age. . . .[166]

He deals with the whole subject even more interestingly in another passage:

> The inhabitants of these Ilandes have byn ever soo used to live at libertie, in playe and pastyme, that they can hardely away with the yoke of servitude which they attempte to shake of by all meanes they maye. And surely if they had receaved owre religion, I wolde thinke their life most happye of all men, if they might therwith enioye their aunciente libertie. A fewe thinges contente them, having no delite in suche superfluities, for the which in other places men take infinite peynes and commit mainie unlawfull actes, and yet are never satisfied, wheras many have to muche, and none inough. But emonge

these simple sowles, a fewe clothes serve the naked: weightes and measures are not needeful to such as can not skyll of crafte and deceyte and have not the use of pestiferous monye, the seede of innumerable myscheves. So that if we shall not be ashamed to confesse the truthe, they seeme to lyve in that goulden worlde of the whiche owlde wryters speake so much: wherein men lyved simplye and innocentlye without inforcement of lawes, without quarrellinge Iudges and libelles, contente onely to satisfie nature, without further vexation for knowledge of things to come. Yet these naked people also are tormented with ambition for the desyre they have to enlarge their dominions: by reason wherof they kepe warre and destroy one an other: from the which plage I suppose the golden world was not free.[167]

It is quite evident from the context in which J. Macer invokes "le droit de nature" in his *Histoire des Indes* (1555) that he is not referring to the rational Law of Nature, but invoking economic primitivism:

They have no private or particular possessions; but, following natural right, everything there is common to all. They recognize no King or superior at all, and do not wish to subject themselves to the command of anyone. Each one is King, master, and Lord there.[168]

Jean Léon's account of the customs of the inhabitants of Brazil is a direct refutation of the humanists' picture of the Golden Age:

They have neither King, nor Prince, nor Lord. Each is master of himself. . . . They live *without law, without faith and without reason,* having neither temple, nor ceremonies, nor religion. . . .[169]

The ubiquitous "Mien et Tien" is cast once more as a villain in Marc Lescarbot's *Histoire de la Nouvelle France* (1609).[170] Lescarbot, moreover, like Ronsard, contrasts the unhappy lot of the average person in Europe with the felicity of American savages, adding that the savages "are truly noble, performing no action which is not generous. . . ." But, he goes on,

here one should consider that the greater part of the world lived thus at the beginning, and little by little men became civilized, when they came together and formed commonwealths in order to live under certain laws, rules, and polity.[171]

The irrepressible Jean de Léry contrasts, too, "l'humanité de ces gens, lesquels néanmoins nous appelons des barbares," with "les réceptions hypocrites de ceux de l'Europe, qui n'usent que du plat de la langue pour la consolation des affligés. . . ." And he does not fail to point out that the latter have the "advantage" of "les lois divines et humaines," while the savages are "seulement conduits par leur naturel, *quelque corrumpu qu'il soit!*"[172]

There were, of course, many more orthodox cosmographers, who found the rational Law of Nature amply substantiated in the lives of the natives of the Americas. There were even more who described the savages as living "according to nature," but were either too discreet or indifferent to define "nature." In Amadas' and Barlow's account of the first voyage to Virginia is the statement, "We found the people most gentle, loving and faithfull, voide of all guile and treason, and such as live after the maner of the golden age."[173] There is no elaboration of this description, which would have satisfied Spenser and Montaigne equally. Nor in Michael Drayton's ode to "Virginia, Earth's only paradise," is there anything less equivocal than

> To whose the golden age
> Still nature's laws doth give
> No other cares that tend,
> But them to defend
> From winter's age,
> That long there doth not live.[174]

In these lines, however, there is a hint—an echo, perhaps—that harks back to something even more famous than Drayton's ode. It has often enough been remarked that Shakespeare's *As You Like It* is a criticism of the pastoral sentiment. I have never seen it cited as a discourse on the "Golden Age" idea, or as a significant treatment of the Nature-Art theme. Yet it is not much of an exaggeration to say that the entire play is a theme with variations—and one on that very subject.

From Orlando's opening speech, containing a nature-art contrast between his own and his brother Jaques' training, as arranged by the oldest brother Oliver,[175] the play is filled with the general opposition of art and nature—civilization versus primitivism, the manmade versus the natural. And in this first scene, references to the Golden Age begin with Charles's description to Oliver of the old Duke's new existence in the Forest of Arden:

> They say that many young gentlemen flock to him every day, and fleet the time carelessly as they did in the golden world.[176]

To be sure, Shakespeare as usual refuses to divulge his own philosophical position on the general question—even, indeed, any very

marked predilection. On the one hand, there is the admirable picture of Nature represented by Corin and Adam. Corin is simple,
direct, the epitome of the good shepherd of olden times, who has
fallen upon sufficiently evil days to have to tend the sheep of a
churlish master.[177] He sets forth his creed plainly, despite Touchstone's sallies:

> Sir, I am a true laborer; I earn that I eat, get that I wear,
> owe no man hate, envy no man's happiness; glad of other men's
> good, content with my harm; and the greatest of my pride
> is to see my ewes graze and my lambs suck.[178]

If Corin suggests the simple natural man of a true Golden Age
of hard primitivism, Adam (however ambiguously, since he is a
servant) is explicitly linked with such a time, when Orlando praises
him—

> O good old man, how well in thee appears
> The constant service of the antique world,
> When service sweat for duty, not for meed!
> Thou art not for the fashion of these times,
> Where none will sweat but for promotion,
> And having that, do choke their service up
> Even with the having. It is not so with thee . . .

concluding with the assertion

> We'll light upon some settled low content.[179]

Here the problem of "Mien et Tien" re-emerges in a play that is
preoccupied with contrasting the falseness of fashionable standards
with the solid decency of "settled low content":

> Who doth ambition shun
> And loves to live i' th' sun,
> Seeking the food he eats,
> And pleas'd with what he gets,
> Come hither, come hither, come hither!
> Here shall he see
> No enemy
> But winter and rough weather.[180]

Yet, on the other hand, there is the most unpalatable picture of
Nature that the uncouth William and Audrey make—the other and
equally valid side of the coin. There is the genuine danger of a forest
in which wild animals and hunger make a sojourn hazardous. And to
match his first lyric verse, Jaques has "invented" another that paints
a vastly different picture of the old Duke's experiment in living like
"the golden world":

> If it do come to pass
> That any man turn ass,
> Leaving his wealth and ease
> A stubborn will to please,
> Ducdame, ducdame, ducdame!
> Here shall he see
> Gross fools as he,
> An if he will come to me.[181]

Again, if one assesses favorably the way Touchstone's "nature" disposes of Le Beau's "art" in their early exchange,[182] one must also recognize that the very celebration of Nature is open to the most false and artificial of treatments and attitudes. Phebe and Silvius, it is true, are not so much genuine shepherds as Art's interpretation of Nature—yet, in the idiom of the times, they represent one ridiculous extreme to which the idolatry of Nature may lead.

Art fares similarly at Shakespeare's hands. If the old Duke expounds the artificiality and vices of civilization—"painted pomp" and "the envious court"—to which he prefers "the penalty of Adam, the seasons' difference," where one may find "sermons in stones, and good in everything,"[183] he himself is, of course, nevertheless the product of *true* art, a gently civilized character. And if Le Beau, a minor Osric, presents a silly and affected "Art," Rosalind's wit is the true evidence of what Art may add to Nature.

Indeed, one is tempted to accept as a summary of the play the remark Corin makes to Touchstone:

> Those that are good manners at the court are as ridiculous in the country as the behavior of the country is most mockable at the court.[184]

True Art, yes, as true Nature. But the false "art" of affecting Nature deserves as much ridicule as that which plain Nature would get at the redoubt of Art.

Yet the impression of Orlando so much stressed early in the play by Oliver:

> Yet he's gentle; never school'd and yet learned; full of noble device; of all sorts enchantingly beloved, and indeed so much in the heart of the world, and especially of my own people, who best know him, that I am altogether misprised.[185]

—remains so constant and important throughout, that the final scales are tipped in favor of Nature.

But of course one's "final" impression with Shakespeare will always be reversed, or at least balanced, as one reads farther in him.

The lesson Polixenes gives to Perdita in *A Winter's Tale* affirms Shakespeare's approval of Cicero's reconciling position:

> So, over that art
> Which you say adds to nature, is an art
> That nature makes.[186]

Yet, once again, before accepting this as his ultimate position, one must take into account in the same play (and even the same scene) Camillo's estimate of Perdita, the child of Nature:

> I cannot say 'tis pity
> She lacks instructions, for she seems a mistress
> To most that teach.[187]

And similarly, if Gonzalo's famous presentation of Montaigne's primitivistic commonwealth in *The Tempest*[188] does not do the original much honor, Caliban's terse and awful indictment of "Art" evens the balance:

> You taught me language, and my profit on't
> Is, I know how to curse. The red plague rid you
> For learning me your language.[189]

In this matter, as in so many others, Shakespeare plays the great commentator, but his own point of view remains indeterminate. . . .[190]

Thus far, we have dealt fairly extensively with the attitudes of the traditionalist humanists and the Counter-Renaissance naturalists and courtly romanticists toward primitivism and the Golden Age. The attitudes of the other schools of the Counter-Renaissance differ considerably. The two kinds of fideists (those of the Reformation and those of the occult traditions) shared a low estimate of nature and human nature since the Fall, but disagreed in the extent of their interest in the pre-lapsarian period or Golden Age. Man broke his covenant with God, Luther and Calvin reason, and since then being in harmony with Nature is wrong and perilous for man.[191] As for what happened prior to Adam's Fall, they manifest relatively little interest.

Not so the occult fideists. Almost all of them hark back to a Golden Age of Wisdom, whether Jewish or Greek or Persian or Egyptian, and to prophets who made no claims for themselves, but all for God—men who were not inventors or discoverers, or speculative philosophers, but the chosen vessels or illumined priests of God. The individual versions might vary all the way from those which cited Pythagoras' divine origin to those which were content with

relating God's wisdom displayed in Abraham. The constant remained: "C'est Lui qui l'a dit" suggested always that the ultimate
source of the wisdom or truth was God.

Among the Paracelsans, the "Nature" of the Golden Age often
took on a specifically Christian terminology. Thus Oswald Croll, in
his *Basilica chymica* (1609), was not referring to natural reason
when he maintained that "Adam in a state of nature had perfect
knowledge of signatures and named everything aright,"[192] but rather
to Adam's intimate rapport with God. For Croll, as for most alchemists and Hermetic philosophers, that Golden Age of Wisdom when
God revealed the true significance of Nature's symbols was the Age
of Innocence in Eden; the "illumined priest" was pre-lapsarian Adam.

That central concern of the Hermetic philosophers with the "rejuvenation and renovation of men and things,"[193] then, is a logical
sequitur. When Paracelsus declares, "This, therefore, is the most
excellent foundation of a true physician, the regeneration of nature, and the restoration of youth,"[194] he is writing in this tradition. Before the Fall, man understood the symbols of Nature, for
God had revealed them to him. After the Fall, this secret knowledge, this infused capacity to interpret their meanings, was gradually lost—until the words of the interpretations became cryptic and
even unintelligible. It was the task and the dream of the alchemist
to be able to effect a return to the purity of the youth of the world,
to men who once more might understand "God's images," and to
a renewed Nature, whose hidden virtues need no longer be hidden.

One is reminded of Pico's "rediscovery" of the lost Pythagorean
science of numbers and the magical theorems known to Democritus
and Plato, of his readiness to clear up the "darkness" of the poems
of Orpheus and Zoroaster. Whether or not the "Fall" terminology
is used, the analogy is evident; once more the essential consistency
of occult lore is demonstrated.

But how are the "rejuvenation and renovation" to take place, if
not through the individual investigation and the ratiocination of
men? Quite possibly, to the twentieth-century point of view, in no
other way. But this was not the attitude of the initiates. They did
not regard turning back to the hidden wisdom of the ancients as
individual investigation in the scientific sense, but as a return to the
record of revelation. Study, to be sure, was requisite, but it was a
very different process from that of the Schoolmen, for instance—
with a different starting point and different results. Some evade the
full challenge of the question; some profess illumination; a few,
like Paracelsus, claim the miracle—God has chosen them, as he did

his priests of ancient times: the Light of Nature shines unblemished in them.

As for those whose *métiers* are rather the practicings of occult arts than the expounding of the "devout philosophy" (many, of course, combine the two)—to a man they distinguish between *their art* and that "Art" which stands for logical cogitation, for *independent* ratiocination and investigation. *Their art* is a second nature, yet in a sense at once similar and dissimilar to that in which most Renaissance writers of poetics used these words. Similar—so long as a Minturno or a Du Bellay or a Sidney is expounding "furor poeticus"; dissimilar, as soon as he begins saying, as Sidney did, that the poet is "lifted up with the vigor of his own invention."

When Paracelsus says, therefore, that "Art is a second Nature and a universe of its own," and that Nature "brings nothing to the light that is at once perfect in itself, but leaves it to be perfected by man," he hastens to add that "this method of perfection is called Alchemy."[195] True Art for him is Alchemy, which is a second Nature, obedient to and imitative of Nature, finishing and fulfilling Nature's course. In the words of Bacon,

> The Alchemists do . . . much inculcate, that Vulcan is a second nature, and imitateth that dexterously and compendiously which nature worketh by ambages and length of time.[196]

And since we must bear in mind that Nature is simply the manifestation of God, it is clear that the alchemist is the prophet or priest of God, proceeding by means of God's revelation. . . .

Consistently, however, the exponents of all kinds of occult traditions reject any interpretation of their Art as independent thought. Indeed, they attack this sort of "rational art" with as much vehemence as the other Counter-Renaissance rebels.

To Ralegh, for example, "natural magic" is "the wisdom of nature" or "the whole philosophy of nature"—"*not the brabblings of the Aristotelians*, but that which bringeth to light the inmost virtues, and draweth them out of nature's hidden bosom. . . ."[197] He is still more explicit about the Schoolmen elsewhere:

> Most of the schoolmen were rather curious in the nature of terms, and more subtile in the distinguishing upon the parts of doctrine already laid down, than discoverers of any thing hidden, either in philosophy or divinity: of whom it may be truly said, *Nihil sapientiae odiosius acumine nimio;* "Nothing is more odious to true wisdom, than too acute sharpness."[198]

The final emphasis of the quotation which Ralegh employs, as well as his use of "hidden," is in the regular tone of the initiates. But the rest of the passage, either because he himself is not a "true initiate," or because he has involved himself in a not infrequent confusion of mind, fails completely to attain that tone. In fact, he rather "gives the game away."

For his attack upon the Schoolmen is in exactly those terms in which the initiates might be (and often were) attacked. Any uncharitable account of their doctrines of "revelation" and "interpretation," their search for the hidden mysteries of philosophy and divinity and magic, would (and did) emphasize their activity as "distinguishing upon the parts of doctrine already laid down." Here are the best weapons for any direct attack upon them. . . .

No other single occult philosopher of the Renaissance asserts so clearly and defiantly the cleavage between the initiate traditions and the speculative philosophers as does Paracelsus. No other propounder of esoteric dogma so consistently parades his anti-Scholastic bias in terms of the conflict of Art and Nature; no other so definitively presents himself as the chosen vessel of God.

Paracelsus rejects the "philosophical wisdom of the Greeks as being *a mere speculation,* utterly distinct and separate from other true arts and sciences."[199] He attacks Thomas Aquinas with charges of blasphemy against the "secret fire of the philosophers."[200] In a key passage, he professes nothing but scorn for

> Aristotle, Hippocrates, Avicenna, Galen, and the rest, who based all their arts simply upon their own opinions. Even if, at any time, they learnt anything from Nature, they destroyed it again with their own fantasies, dreams, and inventions, before they came to the final issue. . . . For man is assuredly born in ignorance, so that he cannot know or understand anything of himself, but only that which he receives from God, and understands from Nature.[201]

Here is the alchemist version of the Fall, with the consequence that man "cannot know or understand anything of himself." The parallel of the alchemists and the Calvinists emerges once again. To both, man's reason is incapable of any real knowledge since the Fall; to one, God's grace is alone of any force—to the other, "only that which he receives from God, and understands from Nature." But this is only a slight deviation, for Paracelsus is not speaking of "rational nature." This is that Nature which is the manifestation of God, made up of God's symbols and containing his secrets. And the offenders whom Paracelsus cites have "forsaken Nature" and "based all their arts simply upon their own opinions." It is the old charge against "God's spies" (Donne is to warn us specifically against using the "spectacles" of Aristotle and Galen), and Paracelsus has explicitly joined the chorus elsewhere:

> Nor do we care for the vain talk of those *who say more about God than He has revealed to them*, and pretend to understand Him so thoroughly as if they had been in his counsels. . . . Yet we, by custom imitating them, easily learn, together with them, to bend the word of our Teacher and Creator to our own pride.[202]

Here the alchemists' traditional protest against "the forcing of nature" is combined with the conventional anti-intellectualist attack against those who claim to have been in God's counsel. And here the further parallel between Paracelsanism and Calvinism develops, in their common stand against Scholastic and humanistic philosophers, who have tried "to bend the word of our Teacher and Creator to [their] . . . own pride." Against Art of this sort, the initiates and the Elect (the phrasing is not accidental) present an allied front. And finally, both demand a return to *first principles*, the one to the God manifest in the Gospel and in the Apostolic Church, the other to the God manifest in Nature itself. So, in his conclusion to *The Economy of Minerals*, Paracelsus admonishes the reader, "Let him who investigates this difficult and abstruse matter be not so much the disciple of Art as of Nature."[203]

Again, and much more emphatically, after a passage in which he has been sniping at Galen and Avicenna, he points out:

> Not that I praise myself: Nature praises me. Of her I am born; her I follow. She knows me, and I know her. The light which is in her I have beheld in her. . . .[204]

"The light which is in her" is of course God's light. It will perhaps be wise to quote again (and at greater length) that preface to the *Book Concerning the Tincture of the Philosophers* in which Paracelsus formally "introduces" himself as God's prophet:

> From the middle of this age the Monarchy of all the Arts has been at length derived and conferred on me, Theophrastus Paracelsus, Prince of Philosophy and of Medicine. For this purpose I have been chosen of God to extinguish and blot out all the phantasies of elaborate and false works, of delusive and presumptuous words, be they the words of Aristotle, Galen, Avicenna, Mesva, or the dogmas of any among their followers. My theory, proceeding as it does from the light of Nature, can never, through its consistency, pass away. . . .[205]

This passage contains a definitive assertion of Nature against Art in many of the senses in which we have been considering this conflict. Here is the opposition of the true *simplicity* of Nature to "elaborate and false works" of Art; here is the appeal to Nature which expresses the need for direct contact with the source of truth, opposed to the Art of "delusive and presumptuous words"; here, lastly, we find the concept of Nature as a return to *first principles*—indeed, to the pre-Fall first principles, when God revealed freely to man his mysteries and secrets of nature, for the preface is explicitly

> written against those sophists born since the deluge, in the age of our Lord Jesus Christ, the Son of God.[206]

If Paracelsus is here clearly invoking the Golden Age of true and ancient wisdom against the sophistical Art upon which man in his ignorance has depended since the Deluge (here, and often, in like contexts, substituted for the Fall), there is at least a suggestion that he is asserting more than this—that, having "been chosen by God," the true "light of Nature" is within him; that he is, by God's grace, not only a vessel of revelation, but *the Natural Man*, untouched by original sin, and possessing the pre-Deluge revealed wisdom.

"I, Theophrastus Paracelsus, Prince of Philosophy and of Medicine. . . . My theory . . . can never, through its consistency, pass away. . . ." This is a lofty attitude; however skeptical one may be, these are surmises that have always fascinated the human imagination. It is quite comforting to discover on the next page a vindictive piece of billingsgate:

> So then, you wormy and lousy Sophist, since you deem the monarch of arcana a mere ignorant, fatuous, and prodigal quack . . .[207]

Yet this strange and often ridiculous man did leave an unmistakably strong imprint upon his time—an imprint, moreover, belligerently "anti-Art." The whole significance of the initiate traditions in general, and of Paracelsus in particular, for the Counter-Renaissance revolt against "reason," can perhaps best be summarized in Professor Thorndike's account of the message of Gerard Dorn, a follower of Paracelsus. For this passage cites both of the major opponents of the rebels—Scholasticism and humanism. And in its insistence upon "a more Christian way of thinking" in philosophy and "the arts," which would constitute a reform analogous to that which the Church had already experienced, it points the parallel between the early and extreme leaders of the Reformation and the representatives of the initiate traditions. Finally, in its combination of "love" with "nature," its advocacy of "a mystic and spiritual method," it suggests the essential unity of purpose of the Neoplatonists and the occultists. In short, it knits together the diverse evangelistic expressions of the Counter-Renaissance romanticists through their common anti-Scholastic and anti-humanistic cause:

> In this iron and final age nothing but dregs of the arts remained. . . . Learning required a reform analogous to that which religion had undergone earlier in the [sixteenth] century. He [Dorn] affirmed that he had found a better philosophy in Paracelsus and those who followed nature, and a more Christian way of thinking than scholastic Aristotelianism or classical humanism. Paracelsus had impugned worldly and Gentile writers by sacred authorities. Love divine called us to another form of thought than the empty philosophy of Aristotle and other sages of this world. . . . A mystic and spiritual method, a philosophy of love, was needed. . . .[208]

The fideists, of whatever sort, held to the conviction that men had been naturally good but were perverted by the Fall. The materialists or animalists of the Machiavelli-Guicciardini school, however, ignored the Fall, and yet insisted that men were bad—had been, were, and would be. But what, then, one asks, becomes of the Golden Age—if men are *naturally bad?*

The answer is simple and brief: there never was a Golden Age. Man began as an animal, savage and wild; his acquisitive and cruel instincts suffered no restraint—except when he encountered another man who was stronger than he. Instead of the Golden Age, there had been only a State of Nature, ruled by the principle of tooth and claw. And the only reason that man ever sought his fellows in friendship, and desired social institutions and civil government, was for his own protection. For tooth-and-claw came to be too strenuous a law for all but the strongest. Fear and self-preservation replace man's natural gregariousness and brotherliness as motives behind the origin of civil society. *Homo homini lupus* . . .

What such a statement meant to the traditionalists may be surmised by a reconsideration of Cicero's statements on the origin of society, or by listening to the version of so representative a figure as Richard Hooker:

> Forasmuch as we are not by ourselves sufficient to furnish ourselves with competent store of things needful for such a life as our nature doth desire, a life fit for the dignity of man . . .

we are naturally induced to seek communion and fellowship with others. This was the cause of men's uniting themselves at the first in politic Societies. . . .[209]

"That they might be able better to defend themselves," replies Machiavelli,[210] and he is not alone.

Nor is it a new idea, of course. It troubled Glaucon when it was propounded by Thrasymachus and others, and had to be refuted by Socrates.[211] It troubled Rome when propounded by Carneades, and had to be refuted by Cicero (through the person of Laelius).[212] It troubled almost everyone when propounded by Lucretius in the *De Rerum Natura,* and almost everyone had a hand in refuting him. Nor was it difficult to interpret passages in Aristotle's *Politics* as favoring the State of Nature thesis.[213]

No, it was an old idea, but one which attacked the very central citadel of orthodoxy's natural laws and the whole structure of the "very and true commonweale" founded upon the precepts of God and rational Nature. For if man had not followed his natural reason and natural inclination to justice in the first days; if he had really been only a savage animal and had been forced to seek the protection of numbers for mean and selfish reasons—what became of that central tenet upon which all law was built, the hypothesis that

> True law is right reason in agreement with nature; it is of universal application, unchanging and everlasting . . .?[214]

The answer, to the Epicureans, was that it disappeared. The world, they held, had been mechanically formed from atoms, without any intervention of a deity; and man, the chance and barbaric child of nature, had worked his slow way up to his present state of civilization.[215]

Here is Machiavelli's version of the State of Nature and of the origin of society:

> The Inhabitants being dispersed in many and small numbers, find they can not live safe, each one not having strength apart, as well by reason of their situation, as their small number, to resist the violence of those that would force them. . . . Wherefore to escape these dangers, either of themselves, or upon the motion of some one of authority among them, they confine themselves to dwell together, in a place chosen as well for their better commodity of living, as more facility of defence. . . .[216]

The motives are utility and expedience—familiar ones to come from Machiavelli. And in a second, supplementary passage in the *Dis-*

courses, he strikes even harder at humanistic orthodoxy, for he strikes at the rational Law of Nature itself.

> In the beginning of the World, when the Inhabitants were thin, they were scattered abroad for a time like wild beasts; afterwards mankind increasing, they gathered together, and that they might be able better to defend themselves, they began to cast their eyes upon him who had the most strength and courage among them, and made him their head and obeyed him. *Hereupon* began the discerning of things good and honest from bad and hurtful.[217]

Louis Le Roy does not explicitly make this last "sinister" statement, yet the rest of what he has to say certainly implies it:

> In the beginning, men were very simple and rude, in all things little different from beasts.

There is no Golden Age depicted—simply a matter-of-fact account of primitive life, and the gradual progress of men from cave life to pastoral, finally to the point where they began

> to build, gathering together in companies in order to live in greater safety and comfort. In such a way were they brought from the brutal life which they led, into this gentleness and this civility. . . .

Next

> they applied themselves to the study of letters. Because all, naturally, desire to know new, strange, wonderful, beautiful things and to understand the causes of them: cherishing principally, among the senses, sight and hearing, which aid them to have a knowledge of these things. . . . In this progress in knowledge, *they came to know some things through natural instinct without teaching, other things with observation, usage, and experience. . . .*[218]

And where, one inevitably asks with Montaigne, are the accounts of "all those goodly prerogatives"?

Jean Bodin takes a similar approach in the *Methodus.* There was no Golden Age, and in the periods which we have called the "gold" and "silver" ages, men really lived like beasts. Since then there has been a gradual ascent to the civilization that now prevails. Pointing proudly to the inventions of his own time, he declares, "If that so-called golden age could be revoked and compared with our own, we should consider it iron."[219]

Bodin is Harvey's authority for the denial of any Golden Age at the beginning of history—in his famous letter to Spenser:

> You suppose the first age was the goulde age. It is nothing
> soe. Bodin defendeth the goulde age to flourish nowe, and our
> first grandfathers to have rubbid thorowghe in the iron and
> brasen age at the beginninge when all things were rude and
> unperfitt in comparison of the exquisite finesse and delicacye,
> that we are growen unto at these dayes.[220]

He has already invoked the "homo homini lupus" angle of the
State of Nature thesis:

> there be infinite thousands of examples to proove that the first
> men in ye worlde were as well ower masters in villenye as our
> predecessours in tyme or fathers in consanguinitye. . . .[221]

In his *Discourse of War in General,* Ralegh also pictures "men
out of community" as "masters in villanye." Although he admits
the existence of natural reason ("natural conscience"), he declares
that it is insufficient to curb men's passions when there is no law
to restrain them. He has been discussing civil war:

> . . . flying to arms is a state of war, which is *the mere state
> of nature,* of men out of community, where all have an equal
> right to all things; and I shall enjoy my life, my substance, or
> what is dear to me, no longer than he that has more cunning,
> or is stronger than I, will give me leave: for natural conscience
> is not a sufficient curb to the violent passions of men out of
> the laws of society.[222]

The nature of man has undergone a considerable depreciation
in value by the time these gentlemen have finished with it. Etienne
de la Boétie may write,

> If in distributing her gifts nature has favored some more than
> others with respect to body or spirit, she has nevertheless not
> planned to place us within this world as if it were a field of
> battle, and has not endowed the stronger or the cleverer in
> order that they may act like armed brigands in a forest and
> attack the weaker,

and concludes that nature has rather arranged this inequality

> to give occasion for brotherly love to become manifest, some
> of us having the strength to give help to others who are in
> need of it.[223]

But La Boétie is an idealistic humanist, who believes that "in
a world governed by a nature, which is reasonable, there is nothing
so contrary" to that nature "as an injustice":[224] and there have
arisen plenty of men in his own time who will assure him that men

indeed "act like armed brigands in a forest and attack the weaker" —more, that they have always acted so, and that they are that way *by nature*.

Nor do they stop there. If man is not naturally reasonable or just, if he left the state of nature only through fear and the instinct of self-preservation, then how can the state and monarch claim the divine and natural sanction (always provided they obey God's and Nature's laws) which the orthodox acknowledge them to have?

They cannot, replies Guicciardini, pointing out that "if one examines their origin, governments are nothing except a violence. . . ." If you want to live according to God, leave society, he advises— which is another way of saying that you are safer with a few wolves than with many. And he explains in conclusion that he would not make such statements publicly, but that now he is speaking "as the true nature of things demands."[225]

For the whole "homo homini lupus" movement is another revolt of Nature against Art. Invoking experience, observation, and fact against "reason" and theory, these Counter-Renaissance thinkers, like their *confrères* in other fields, are demanding that we look the whole question in the eye—and decide what the nature of man really is, not what the "nature" that man's mind *has made up about him* is.

So when Jean Bodin wants to find out how the first governments were formed, he does not allow his semi-orthodox allegiance to the Laws of Nature to stand in the way of reporting "facts." Describing how "les peuples de Gaoga, en Afrique" happened first to have a king, he relates that one of them visited a neighboring kingdom, and—realizing that it was pleasant to possess such power—enlisted the help of relatives and friends to make himself king "par force et par violence." Bodin concludes,

> Voilà l'origine des Républiques, qui peut eclaircir la définition de Citoyen, qui n'est autre chose que le franc sujet, tenant la souveraineté d'autrui.[226]

We may not be impressed with Bodin's choice of "facts" on this occasion (he usually does much better), but his conclusion—and its purpose—makes his position very clear. Montaigne is equally outspoken:

> Necessitie composeth and assembleth men together. *This casuall combining is afterward framed into lawes. . . . And to say true, all these descriptions of policie, fained by Art and supposition, are found ridiculous and foolish to bee put into practise.* These great and long continuing altercations about the

best forms of societie and most commodious rules to unite us together, are altercations onely proper for the exercise of our wit: As in *arte* divers subjects are found that have no essence but in agitation and disputing, *without which they have no life at all.* Such an Idea of policie, or picture of government, were to be established in a new world; but we take a world already made and formed to certaine customs. . . . Not to speake by opinion, but the most excellent and best policie for any nation to observe, is that under which it hath maintained it selfe.[227]

But with this quotation from Montaigne we leave the Machiavellian materialists. Share their opinion of the hypothetical "Art" of those who uphold the traditionalist concept of the origin of the state, he does. But he does not share their anti-primitivism. And that is what their theory of the "State of Nature" amounts to. I have just said that their *homo homini lupus* theory constitutes another revolt of Nature against Art. And that is so, in the sense of the context as explained. But at all times they are definitely anti-primitivistic.

And so, as has been the case time and again, the adherents of the various schools of the Counter-Renaissance flank the traditional humanists on either side—both in terms of the general Nature-Art controversy and the one about the concept of the Golden Age. The Christian humanists, as usual, occupy a middle position. They formally recognize the existence of a Golden Age (either equated, of course—dependent upon the degree of emphasis on "Christian" —with Eden before the Fall, or accepted as a poetic symbol of original man's natural goodness), but they do not look back to it nostalgically. They find Nature good, but the addition of Art (in its various most prominent meanings) neither antipathetic nor unnatural.

On the other hand, all the protagonists of the Counter-Renaissance revile Art, although with varying interpretations of its meaning. They endorse the opposition of Art and Nature. And finally they either invoke the Golden Age with exclusive enthusiasm and nostalgia, or they deny its existence at all. In the one case they are incorrigibly optimistic about human nature, although not in the traditional humanistic terms; in the other they are emphatically pessimistic.

In this section, we have largely been concerned with the optimists. In the following and last section of this chapter, we shall turn to an examination of some favorite ideas of the pessimists.

4. PESSIMISM AND THE "DISAPPEARANCE" OR SENESCENCE OF NATURE

In Chapter VII, we dealt at some length with the cyclic view of history, inherited ultimately from the Greeks—and in particular considered Renaissance and Counter-Renaissance applications of the cyclic theory to the rise and fall of civilizations, states, cultures. More briefly, we considered cycles in terms of nature, especially as indications of the constancy-in-mutability of all her works. But although we referred (as in the quotation from Spenser about "the Sabaoth Day") to various Christian concepts of the end of the world on Judgment Day, we had no opportunity to investigate the sixteenth century's rather startling preoccupation with the age of the world and perceptible evidences of the "decay of nature."

Perhaps the strongest source for this preoccupation lay in the traditional "hexaemeral literature" or esoteric commentaries on Genesis, which combined the learning of various occult schools with the body of Jewish and Christian dogma. Ficino, for example, we have already seen, called upon Orpheus, Hesiod, Dionysius the Areopagite, Porphyry, Zoroaster and Apollonius "to illustrate and confirm Plato,"[228] while aiming at producing "an image of Plato most similar to the Christian truth"—and still seems to have retained a sincere conviction of the truth of the Christian revelation. But some of his contemporaries were not so successful in keeping this rather fine balance—at least not in the eyes of the Church, or the general public.

Pico, who wrote to Lorenzo (in the dedicatory letter of his *Heptaplus*) that there should be an element of mystery in all true wisdom, was the most persistent offender among the Florentines who tried to establish direct relationships between various occult traditions and Christian dogma. For example, he defends his interpretations of the *Genesis* creation story in his *Heptaplus*[229] by an appeal to Moses' "sources." For Moses, like the Greeks (including Plato, whom he and Ficino called "the Attic Moses") had derived his wisdom from that of Egypt.[230]

Moreover, in his oration *Of the Dignity of Man*, which was drawn up in the form of an address to the learned audience he anticipated for his projected public disputations (he had devised nine hundred theses or "Conclusiones," which he was prepared to defend against all opponents), he asserts that the "institutions" of Moses shadow forth the "sublime course of progressive discipline" necessary for the initiate into esoteric mysteries. This course of discipline is also to be found, he says, in the three celebrated Delphic sentences, in the precepts of Pythagoras, the parables of Zoroaster and the Chaldees, and in the *dogmata* of Moorish and Cabalistic philosophers.

Finally, he was ready, in his "Conclusiones," to illustrate and confirm from the Jewish Cabala the principal truths of the Christian faith and doctrine. Pico's explanation of the validity of this project was that when God had given the written law to Moses on the Mount, he had also favored him with its secret interpretation. This interpretive wisdom had been handed down by oral tradition only, until Esdras had persuaded the Jewish wise men to let him commit it to writing.[231]

To be sure, organized Christianity had been acquainted with much of this or similar material from its earliest days, via Alexandria. The Hexaemera, or interpretive commentaries on *Genesis*, were a mixture of sacred text and philosophy, into which had flowed currents of all sorts. Philo Judaeus and other writers of Jewish Hexaemera or "Wisdom literature" had utilized the noncanonical Hebrew books, and Philo had drawn as well from Plato and Platonizing neo-Pythagoreans, which may in part explain Reuchlin's claim that Pythagoras was the father of Cabalistic philosophy.[232]

At any rate, the Christian hexaemeral tradition, markedly influenced by Plato, the Neoplatonists, and the Hebrews, extended from the early fathers of the Church all the way to Tasso's *Le sette giornate del mondo creato*, Donne's *Essays in Devotion*, Du Bartas' *Première Semaine*, and the early chapters of Ralegh's *History of the World*[233]—and beyond. And for our present purposes, their most interesting characteristic was the way in which they assumed the symbolic significance, for cosmic time, of the days of creation or the first week.

For example, most of the Jewish hexaemera held that each day of the original week represented a thousand years "in the testimony of the heavens." The world, then, was to last 6000 years after the creation, before Judgment Day and a millennium of rest—which equaled the "seventh day."[234] Philo Judaeus also extolled, in this connection, the numerological concept of six as the perfect number, since it is the sum of its factors.[235]

Augustine, in his *De Genesi contra Manichaeos* (I, 23), related the seven ages of the world, by elaborate analogies, to the days of the creation and the famous concept of the seven ages of man.[236] As J. B. Bury puts it,

In Augustine's system the Christian era introduced the last period of history, the old age of humanity, which would endure only so long as to enable the Deity to gather in the predestined number of saved people.[237]

Here we are clearly dealing with the Christian (as before, Jewish) equivalent of the classical concept, already presented, of four or five successive ages. One major difference is that the Græco-Roman theory of cycles meant that, at the end of the last (and worst) age, the destruction of the world (usually by fire)[238] would be followed by its renewing and the beginning of an identical cycle. This could not of course be true for those who followed the Christian revelation or the Jewish interpretation; for them, history was a unique process, enacted only once.

Hence the most importunate corollary, for thinkers of the sixteenth century, was that they were living in the old age of the world—that constantly recurring argument for the futility of achievement, against which Francis Bacon inveighed so eloquently.

Small wonder, one must grant, that the exact age of the world became a matter of serious moment, and that otherwise sober thinkers and writers cited authorities with a sense of urgency. If one accepted the central premise behind such calculations, he was bound to be concerned about the niceties of arithmetic. Exactly how much of the "Great Year" (as Plato's terminology, often borrowed, went) remained? Would the end come during the lifetime of the calculator?

As far back as 1300, Dante had generously calculated that there were five hundred of his postulated 7000 years left. Yet he said, "We have come to the last age of the world,"[239] and the more popular concept allowed only 6000 years in all. How much more reason for a sixteenth-century man to pore over the figures. Pico,[240] Campanella,[241] Le Roy, Bodin—all sorts of solid thinkers of the Counter-Renaissance (and even some of the traditional humanists) cast their estimates.

There was no general agreement about the exact age of the world. Kepler believed that the world began in 3992 B.C., Joseph Scaliger in 3949, Walter Ralegh in 4032; the usual Jewish date given was 3761.[242] All these gave a safe margin to contemporaries; but it was clearly time to think about one's ultimate destination, for all that. Justus Lipsius asserted in 1584 that 5500 years had passed since the habitation of the world, which was "at length come to his dotage."[243] Louis Le Roy, in a slightly different version, cited authorities who believed "that there have already been seven Great

Years in the space of five thousand, five hundred and thirty years
. . . and that the eighth shall be in the year of Christ 1604."[244]

This last prediction, appearing in English in 1594, was hardly
comforting to credulous Elizabethans—for if these "Great Years"
were to be equated with the familiar seven ages, who had ever
heard of an eighth? What could the eighth be but the end?

To be sure, there were those like Jean Bodin, who discussed the
problem at length and almost endlessly cited conflicting authorities,[245] yet emerged with happier conclusions. "When its fall will
take place," he finally asserts, "not even the angels know. . . ."[246]

Nevertheless, and understandably, no group was more concerned
about the matter than the Elizabethans. John Norden, in his *Vicissitudo Rerum* (probably 1599 or 1600), follows the figures quoted
by Le Roy with unmistakably real alarm:

> Of such, some count seven since the world began
> (Five thousand, five hundred, sixty two years),
> The Eighth shall be when four years more are come,
> By testy of the best Astrologers,
>   Presaged thus, it may well summon tears,
>   That he that rules may moderate his ire,
>   Lest World consume with fearful gusts of fire.[247]

Fulke Greville, in *A Treatie of Warres* (stanzas 42–48), rings many
of the changes of Counter-Renaissance doctrine (the Reformation's
view of man's nature since the Fall, the *homo homini lupus* theme,
and others) as argument for both the inevitability and the imminence of the Great Event. And there are others, too numerous to
mention. Even after the passing of the fateful year of 1604, it is
still a matter for lively discussion—even the exclusive concern of
a huge volume of controversy which went into its third edition
in 1635![248]

I said that the Elizabethans were *understandably* concerned—to
a greater degree than their predecessors. By this I meant particularly that there had been an extraordinary convergence of factors
to increase their degree of apprehensiveness over that shown by
earlier generations. A theory of cosmic senescence had usually accompanied the hexaemeral view of cosmic time. It was

> that form of the theory of progressive decline which is based
> upon the analogy of human senescence. The world is like a
> human being who grows old and weak, only to die.[249]

It had usually accompanied it, and for proof there would be cited a range of phenomena from the dwindling stature of men[250] to the appearance of strange portents in the heavens.

But in the Elizabethan period, as we have already suggested,[251] there were a sufficient number of genuine "upheavals" in the heavens to warrant alarm even in the very astronomers who observed them with the greatest meticulousness. It did not require an absurdly superstitious man to wonder, then, if there might be something after all, in the old predictions.

And in the new ones—for all sorts of astrologers, numerologists, and other occult "specialists" took advantage of the psychological climate, intentionally or unintentionally. There are an extraordinary number of documents from the last two decades of the sixteenth century and the first one of the seventeenth to demonstrate the mélange of dire prophecies of the imminent dissolution of "this great frame." Not a few of them, up to the death of Elizabeth, hinted or declared outright that the passing of the great queen might well coincide with the final end of everything.

As a matter of fact, however, the continental picture throughout the preceding century had once again set an emotional tone for the Elizabethans' viewpoint. Rather than explore many of the variant forms in which the "decay of nature" theme had been developed by sixteenth-century continental writers, let us consider one long passage from Justus Lipsius' *De Constantia,* a popular favorite during the Stoic revival in Elizabethan England. It contains most of the important elements of the others.

It is an eternall decree, pronounced of the worlde from the beginning, and of all things Herein, to be borne & to die; to begin and end. That supreame Iudge of all things, would have nothing firme and stable but himself alone. . . .

All these things which thou beholdest and admirest, either shall perish in their due time, or at least bee altered and changed: Seest thou the Sun? He fainteth. The Moone? She laboureth and languisheth. The Starres? They faile and fall. And howsoever the wit of man cloaketh and excuseth these matters, yet there have happened and daily do in that celestiall bodie such things as confound both the rules and the wittes of the Mathematicians. I omit Cometes strange in forme, scituation and motion, which al the universities shal never perswade me to be in the aire, or of the aire. But beholde our Astrologers were sore troubled of late with strange motions, and new starres. This very yeare there arose a star whose encreasing and decreasing was plainly marked, and we saw (a matter hardly to

be credited) even in the heaven itself, a thing to have beginning and end againe. . . . Next unto the heaven, behold the
Aire, it is altered daylie and passeth into windes, cloudes, and
showers. Goe to the waters. Those flouds and fountaines which
we affirme to be perpetuall, doe sometimes faile altogether,
and otherwhiles change their channel and ordinarie course.
The huge Ocean (a great and secrete part of nature) is ever
tossed and troubled with tempests: and if they be wanting,
yet hath it his flowing and ebbing of waters, & that we may
perceive it to be subject to decay, it swelleth and swayeth
daily in his parts.

Behold also the earth which is taken to be immoveable, and
to stand steddy of her owne force: it fainteth and is stricken
with an inward secrete blast that maketh it tremble: Some
where it is corrupted by the water, other where by fire, For
these same things doe strive among themselves: Neither grudge
thou to see warre among men, there is likewise between the
Elements. What great lands have bene wasted, yea wholly
swallowed up by suddaine deluges, and violent overflowings
of the sea? . . .

And if these great bodies which to us seeme everlasting, bee
subject to mutabilitie and alteration, why much more shoulde
not townes, commonwealthes, and kingdomes; which must
needes be mortall, as they that doe compose them? As ech
particular man hath his youth, his strength, olde age, and death.
So fareth it with other bodies. They begin, they increase, they
stand and flourish, and all to this ende, that they may decay. . . .

I have spoken yet of townes and cities: Countries likewise
and kingdomes runne the verie same race. Once the East flourished: *Assyria, Egypt* and *Jewrie* excelled in warre and peace.
That glorie was transferred into *Europe,* which now (like a
diseased bodie) seemeth unto me to be shaken, and to have
a feeling of her great confusion nigh at hande. Yea, and that
which is more (and never ynough) to bee marvelled at, this
world having now bene inhabited these five thousand and five
hundred yeeres, is at length come to his dotage: And that we
may now approove againe the fables of *Anaxarchus* in old time
hissed at, behold now there ariseth els wher new people, &
a new world: O the law of NECESSITY, wonderfull, and not
to be comprehended: All things run into this fatall whirlepoole
of ebbing and flowing: And some things in this world are long
lasting, but not everlasting.

Lift up thine eyes and looke about with mee . . . and beholde the alterations of all humaine affaires: and the swelling
and swaying of them as of the sea: Arise thou: fal thou: rule

thou: obey thou: hide thou thy head: lift thou up thine head
and let this wheel of changeable things run round, so long as
this round world remayneth. Have you Germanes in time past
bene fierce? Be ye now milder than most people of *Europe*.
Have you Brittaines bene uncivill heretofore? Now exceed you
the Egyptians and people of Sybaris in delights and riches. . . .
    Am I deceived? or els do I see the sunne of another new
Empire arising in the West?[252]

There are features, details, in this passage which do not fit the
usual sixteenth-century "decay of nature" treatment—such as the
"new Empire arising in the West." There are suggestions of a cyclical, rather than a straight "decay" point of view—in keeping with
Lipsius' Stoic predilections. But the body of the passage serves sufficiently well, I think, to illustrate the gloomy temper of these
treatises, and the wealth of detail used to elaborate the central point.

Another feature that varies in the case of Lipsius is that he is
predominantly (despite independent tendencies) a representative
of the traditional humanist point of view. As a rule—as I have
already suggested—the decay of nature theory is maintained by
writers and thinkers with a Counter-Renaissance leaning. This is
not an infallible rule, but it makes good sense that this would be
the case with both the Reformers and the Machiavellian materialists, the two genuinely pessimistic schools of the Counter-Renaissance. The former, in hell-and-damnation style, usually predicate
absolute decay and imminent dissolution; the latter, "limited decay"
—limited in the sense of an adherence to cyclical recurrence.

The Christian humanists, moderate as usual, take a middle position, finding in what others call evidence of decay, only aberrant
happenings and mutability in the course of a nature that remains
constant under God's continued direction. The passage from Hooker
quoted near the end of Chapter III admirably illustrates this position.

On the other hand, and consistently, those optimists who oppose
the theory of the decay of nature with at least an elementary idea
of progress are also Counter-Renaissance figures—as a rule, the naturalists. We have already mentioned here and there the cases of
Bodin and Cardan and Bacon; a similar point of view is evident in
Rabelais[253] (who has great satirical sport with the concept of the
decay of nature[254]), Ramus [255] and Le Roy[256]—who, to be sure, treats
with seriousness and some signs of acquiescence the possibility of
a final decline and even death of the world in his time, but whose
dominant note is concerned with the accomplishments of his age.

Montaigne's consideration of the whole question is one of the most interesting, as might be expected:

> Few vessels sinke with their owne weight, and without some extraordinary violence. Cast we our eyes about us, and in a generall survay, consider all the world; all is tottering, all is out of frame. . . . Astrologers may sport themselves with warning us, as they doe, of imminent alterations and succeeding revolutions; their divinations are present and palpable; wee need not prie into the heavens to finde them out. Wee are not only to draw comfort from this universall aggregation of evill and threats, but also some hope for the continuance of our state; forasmuch as naturally nothing falleth where all things fall; a generall disease is a particular health: Conformitie is a qualitie enemie to dissolution.
>
> That which grieveth me most is, that, counting the symptomes or affects of our evill, I see as many merely proceeding of nature, and such as the heavens send us, and which may properly be termed theirs, as of those that our owne surfet, or excesse, or misse-diet, or humane indiscretion confer upon us. The very Planets seeme orderly to declare unto us that we have continued long enough, yea and beyond our ordinary limits. This also grieves me, that the neerest evill threatening us is not a distemper or alteration in the whole and solide masse, but a dissipation and divulsion of it—the extreamest of our feares. And even in these fantasticall humors or dotings of mine, I feare the treason of my memory, least unwarily it have made me to register something twise. I hate to correct and agnize my selfe, and can never endure but grudgingly to review and repolish what hath once escaped my pen. I heere set downe nothing that is new or lately found out. They are vulgar imaginations, and which peradventure having been conceived a hundred times, I feare to have already enrolled them.[257]

He does, and he doesn't. In his most genially skeptical mood, he can see as many arguments against these old wives' tales as his peers do; he laughs at himself for being so credulous. Yet he does not pretend to resolve all his fears, however superstitious, with any positive certainty. . . .

But to return to the Elizabethans. The expositions of the decay of nature (the most famous of which, Donne's *First Anniversary*, we have already partially examined in Chapter III) are literally legion. Let it suffice for present purposes to refer the reader to the section in my *Elizabethan Reader* called "Portents in the Sky," containing pertinent selections from Ashley's translation of Le Roy,

from Norden, Greville, Donne, and Gloucester's and Edmund's soliloquies on the matter in *Lear*—"these late eclipses," etc.—together
with the various optimistic rejoinders of Thomas Nashe (to Gabriel
Harvey's brother's *Astrological Discourse*) and Richard Hooker.[258]
Add for good measure the *Nosce Teipsum* of Sir John Davies,[259]
Spenser's questions and doubts in the *Mutability Cantos,* and further passages from Greville[260]—and you have a more than adequate
cross-section of Elizabethan treatments of the subject. The elements
we have already seen in Lipsius' version reappear again and again
in the accounts of the decay of nature: Sun, moon, planets (strange
conjunctions, for example), comets, and other heavenly bodies and
phenomena behaving aberrantly; the four elements of fire, air, water
and earth distraught and misbehaving; men shrunken in stature and
unnatural in attitudes; states troubled by wars and civil strife; pes-
tilence, famine, floods and conflagrations rampant everywhere, etc.,
etc.

Behind all these treatments of the decay of nature theme, however ingenuously or disingenuously intended, lie several strategic
Counter-Renaissance lines of attack upon traditionalism. If the great
system of universal law is faltering, faulty or decaying, this is good
evidence that it never has existed in the full majesty with which
its adherents invested it—for *then* it could not fail. Furthermore,
the decay of nature was substantial evidence of that general corruption predicated by Calvin and Luther. And under whatever Counter-
Renaissance terms the case might be put, it was a telling argument
for the absence of that mighty and sustaining regulative principle
that the humanists, like the Scholastics before them, maintained ran
like the blood of life through God's entire universe, according to law.

This is perhaps best seen in an idea correlative to that of the
decay and senescence of nature—the idea of the "disappearance"
of Nature, in the sense of the regulative principle or pattern of
nature. It is perhaps wisest to present this idea first in an interesting
semi-occult formula in popular favor during the sixteenth century.

We have already encountered one of these formulæ in the Her-
metic-Pythagorean-Neoplatonic concept of God as a sphere or circle
whose center is everywhere and circumference nowhere. Another,
even more ubiquitous in the Renaissance, is the at once obvious
and cryptic saying to be found in the fragments attributed to Democritus: "Verily we know nothing. Truth is buried deep."[261]

It is no exaggeration to say that this formula, employed in various
ways, was second in popularity during the Renaissance only to the
proverbial "Know thyself." Even a superficial demonstration of its

extensive and varied use requires going well outside the initiate traditions, in any exact sense.

An attempt to pin Renaissance indebtedness for Democritus' axiom to a particular source would probably prove futile, for there were many classical channels through which it could have reached a given individual. As likely a candidate as any is Diogenes Laërtius, who quotes it in his popular *Lives of Eminent Philosophers,* in a passage in which he is describing the arguments which the Greek skeptics employed to establish Democritus, among others, as a forerunner of their school.[262] There were unquestionably other sources, and probably ones which introduced it in somewhat different contexts, but this reference should suffice for our purpose.

Francis Bacon implies the formula's adaptability when he quotes it shortly after his statement (in *The Advancement of Learning*) that there is something artificial about dividing the realms of philosophy (or knowledge) too neatly into distinct categories. For this reason, in addition to his three regular divisions of "Divine philosophy [or "Natural theology"], Natural philosophy, and Human philosophy or Humanity," he designates a loose, general classification which he calls *Philosophia Prima.* This he defines as

> a receptacle for all such profitable observations and axioms as fall not within the compass of any of special parts of philosophy or sciences, but are more common and of a higher stage.[263]

In short, there are certain "observations and axioms" so generally applicable that they may be used profitably in many or all fields of learning. That "Verily we know nothing. Truth is buried deep," was an axiom "of a higher stage" to the Renaissance at large is immediately obvious when one compares and contrasts even a few of its appearances in the literature of the period.

Sir John Davies, for instance, links it with that favorite citation of Socrates which we have already encountered:

> For this the wisest of all Mortall men
> *Said he knew nought, but that he nought did know:*
> And the great mocking Maister mockt not then,
> When he said, *Truth was buried deepe below.*[264]

This passage, of course, invokes Socrates and Democritus in the identical way in which the Greek skeptics invoked them—as skeptical philosophers who maintained the futility of human learning and the ineffectiveness of human reason. Here the axiom is applied to the division of knowledge which Bacon called "Human philosophy" and (although Davies goes on in the second part of *Nosce*

Teipsum to establish a kind of knowledge he does believe possible) is used as a skeptical argument in the "vanity of learning" tradition.

Bacon himself, however, associates the axiom primarily with "Natural philosophy," even inserting the words "of nature" into his quotation, to make it read:

> If then it be true that [which] Democritus said, *That the truth of nature lieth in certain deep mines and caves* . . .

and at least by implication associates it with the "hidden virtues" of alchemy, when he adds

> and if it be true likewise that [again in the sense of "that which"] the Alchemists do so much inculcate, that Vulcan is a second nature, and imitateth that dexterously and compendiously which nature worketh by ambages and length of time. . . .[265]

Ralegh, although he does not quote the Democritan fragment, develops this same theme in terms of natural magic, and then quotes the alchemists' parallel axiom:

> The third kind of magic . . . [is] that which bringeth to light the inmost virtues, and draweth them out of nature's hidden bosom to human use, *virtutes in centro centri latentes;* "virtues hidden in the centre of the centre," according to the chymists.[266]

The idea that nature has hidden her most precious riches deepest is probably as old as human experience; its classical exploitation (as in Pliny's *Natural History*) was echoed in the Renaissance, of course, and used by Erasmus and Chapman to point the morals of study and "secret learning," respectively.[267] But the specific alchemical thesis to which Ralegh refers is based on the belief that the hidden virtues which Nature keeps secret lie "buried deep," and that it is the alchemist's task to "draw" or "lead" them out— to "reveal" them. As Paracelsus puts it,

> Nature, indeed, herself does not bring forth any thing into the light which is advanced to its highest perfection. . . . But a man ought by Spagyric preparations to lead it thither where it was ordained by Nature.[268]

But if Bacon suggests the identification of the fragment of Democritus with the alchemists' "virtues hidden in the centre of the centre,"[269] there are also those who associate it with the ancient wisdom of the oracles, the beginnings of that "certain devout philosophy."

In Rabelais' third book, the learned Epistemon discusses the cessation of the oracles, who "are all of them become as dumb as so many fishes since the advent of that Savior King whose coming to this world hath made all oracles and prophecies to cease. . . ." But Panurge, when filled with the sacred wine which the "trismegistian" Holy Bottle has ordered him to drink, rhymes a different account "in his rapture":

> From Pythian Tripos ne'er were heard
> More truths, nor more to be revered.
> I think from Delphos to this spring
> Some wizard brought that conjuring thing.
> Had honest Plutarch here been toping,
> He then so long had ne'er been groping
> To find, according to his wishes,
> Why oracles are mute as fishes
> At Delphos. Now the reason's clear;
> No more at Delphos they're, but here.
> Here is the tripos, out of which
> Is spoke the doom of poor and rich.
> For Athenaeus does relate
> This Bottle is the womb of Fate;
> Prolific of mysterious wine,
> And big with prescience divine,
> It brings the truth with pleasure forth.

Although we may not be inclined to take the authority of Panurge very seriously when he asserts that

> This oracle is full of troth;
> Intelligible truth it bears . . .

such a judgment does not affect the fact that a particular series of associations (there are more to follow) is made. Nor need we rely on Panurge's "Bacchic enthusiasm" alone. For Pantagruel (whose authority and dignity I think we may trust) has spoken of Bacbuc as "this true priestess," and she it is who calls the temple "these circumcentral regions." Moreover, at the conclusion of the benediction containing the "spherical" definition of God, she exhorts them:

> When you come into your world, do not fail to affirm and witness that the greatest treasures and most admirable things are hidden underground. . . .

And she further declares,

> Your philosophers who complain that the ancients have left them nothing to write of or to invent, are very much mistaken. Those phenomena which you see in the sky, whatever the surface of the earth affords you, and the sea, and every river

contain, is not to be compared with what is hid within the
bowels of the earth.

For this reason the subterranean ruler has justly gained in
almost every language the epithet of rich. . . .[270]

The exact words of the Democritan formula do not, it is true,
appear. Yet truth is found, at the end of a long pilgrimage, in "these
circumcentral regions"—and this truth is associated with the Delphic Oracle. Moreover, that variant version, of "the greatest treasures and most admirable things" being "hidden underground," is
also employed, and attention is called to the name of "the subterranean ruler" in the manner of almost all Renaissance mythographers.[271]

Davies' use of the formula emphasizes skepticism; that of those
who associate it with the alchemists, revelation and "interpretation."
Rabelais takes the second course, although the truth revealed is
that of the ancient "Platonic" tradition, rather than the alchemical.
As the Priestess tells Panurge,

> For you must know, my beloved, that by wine we become
> divine; neither can there be a surer argument or a less deceit-
> ful divine divination. Your academics assert the same when
> they make the etymology of wine, which the Greeks call
> OINOE, to be from *vis*, strength, virtue, and power; *for 'tis
> in its power to fill the soul with all truth, learning and phi-
> losophy.*
>
> If you observe what is written in Ionic letters on the temple
> gate, you may have understood that truth is in wine. The God-
> dess-Bottle therefore directs you to that divine liquour; be
> yourself the expounder of your understanding.

In short, Panurge has become a vessel of truth; when he himself
expounds the answer he has so long sought to the momentous question of whether or not to marry, he is making no rational, independent judgment. As Pantagruel puts it to Friar John:

> Bold monk, forbear! this, I'll assure ye,
> Proceeds all from poetic fury;
> Warmed by the god, inspired with wine,
> His human soul is made divine. . . .[272]

Rabelais connects the "divinity of wine" theme with the "academics." Moreover, there are many Pythagorean-Platonic features
about the temple. The "numerical" steps that lead to the temple-
gate are devised according to the "Pythagorical tetrad": the lantern
observes, "This is the true psychogony of Plato, so celebrated by the

Academics, yet so little understood; one moiey of which consists of the first numbers full of two square and two cubic numbers." The fountain itself, replete with geometrical intricacies, is "more admirable than anything Plato ever dreamt of in limbo." Finally Bacbuc expounds the science of numbers:

> Your philosophers will not allow that motion is begot by the power of figures; look here, and see the contrary. By that single snail-like motion, equally divided as you see, and a five-fold infoliature, moveable at every inward meeting, such as is the vena cava where it enters into the right ventricle of the heart; just so is the flowing of this fountain, and by it a harmony ascends as high as your world's ocean.[273]

Yet Rabelais is Rabelais, and it is in a passing reference by Edmund Spenser that we find what appears to be the most thoroughgoing adaptation of a pure Platonic concept to the axiom of Democritus. In *An Hymne in Honour of Beautie,* he writes:

> WHAT TIME THIS WORLDS GREAT WORK-
> > MAISTER DID CAST
> To make al things such as we now behold
> It seems that he before his eyes had plast
> A goodly Paterne, to whose perfect mould
> He fashioned them as comely as he could. . . .
>
> .   .   .   .
>
> .   .   .   .
>
> .   .   .   .
>
> That wondrous Paterne, *wheresoere it bee,*
> *Whether in earth layd up in secret store,*
> Or else in heaven, that no man may it see
> With sinfull eyes, for feare it to deflore,
> Is perfect Beautie, which all men adore. . . .[274]

Here is the implicit equation of that independently existing "Idea" which served as the model for the created universe with Democritus' "truth . . . buried deep," to serve in combination as the regulating principle, the motivating force, and the harmonious realization of Nature. Agrippa had found the basis for the "theory of occult virtues" in the Platonic "ideas" and "celestial pattern,"[275] but—so far as I know—Spenser is the only writer of the period to have worked out explicitly this exact identification.

Yet is it an exact identification, after all? I say "pure Platonic concept," but I doubt if there is such a thing—in any exclusive sense. Probably Spenser has Plato or a Neoplatonist in mind when he speaks of "that wondrous Paterne," but the pattern itself is pre-Platonic. As M. Brunschvicq has written,

> pour les Pythagoriciens, le nombre n'était pas seulement ce qu'il est pour nous, le résultat d'une opération arithmétique; il était aussi quelque chose qui existe en soi, indépendamment de tout exercice de la pensée . . .

and for many Platonizing Pythagoreans since, as for "le plus curieux peut-être des Pythagoriciens platonisants au 1er siècle l'ère Chrétienne . . . Nicomaque de Gérasa,"

> le nombre est le modèle préexistant à la création dans l'esprit Divin et suivant lequel toutes choses sont construites par Dieu.[276]

Perhaps Spenser did not know that Democritus was popularly held to be an admirer of Pythagoras and probably the pupil of a Pythagorean. Yet this "information" was available in Diogenes Laërtius' *Lives* (ix, 38). At any rate, this Pythagorean concept of the Creation was known and held in the Renaissance—by Kepler, for instance, who professed the belief that

> God created the world in accordance with the principle of perfect numbers, hence the mathematical harmonies in the mind of the creator furnish the cause why "the number, the size, and the motions of the orbits are as they are and not otherwise."[277]

Or, as M. Brunschvicq puts it,

> Entre les nombres, les dix premiers ont une situation privilégiée et ils dérivent d'eux-mêmes d'un dualité, d'une unité primitive, qui sont en Dieu.[278]

Perhaps, again, Spenser was not familiar with Pico's statement that Pythagoras had founded his secret doctrine of numbers on the model of Orphic theology. Yet, whether at first or second hand, he must have had some acquaintance with the Orphic fragments, for, as Professor Fletcher has pointed out, "The term 'Hymne' is used by Spenser, in the sense of the Greek ὕμνος,— a song or pæan in honor of a god or hero, especially as colored philosophically in the so-called 'Orphic Hymns,' or τελεταί, hymns of initiation into the Hellenic religion."[279]

I am not indulging simply in arbitrary mystification—trying to make a complicated matter still more complicated. Indeed, it would be difficult to increase the actual complexity. What we end with is, of course, the possibility that Spenser did not even know the

Democritan axiom, or at least did not have it in mind when he wrote these lines. Perhaps the author of the axiom and the author of the *Hymne* utilized the same source, perhaps related ones, perhaps totally dissimilar ones. M. Saurat has shown many similarities between concepts in the *Faerie Queene* and ones in the cabalistic books. And it has been while rereading *Literature and Occult Tradition* that I have had recalled to mind such lines from the *Mutability Cantos* as

> This great grandmother of all creatures bred,
> Great Nature, ever young, yet full of eld;
> Still moving, yet unmoved from her sted;
> *Unseene of any, yet of all beheld* . . .

and

> Then was that whole assembly quite dismist,
> *And Natur's selfe did vanish, whither no man wist*[280]

—lines which suggest immediately

> That wondrous Paterne, wheresoere it bee,
> Whether in earth layd up in secret store,
> Or else in heaven. . . .

Whether or not Spenser's concept of Nature, as M. Saurat suggests, is indebted largely to the *Zohar* seems to me as finally difficult of demonstration as the other points we have been considering. Yet clearly it is Nature, the "Paterne," the "Idea," which is "unseene of any, yet of all beheld [in the created world]." Moreover, if things equal to the same thing are equal to each other:

"That wondrous Paterne" = "perfect Beautie"
"That wondrous Paterne" = "Natur's selfe"
"Natur's selfe"   = the "perfect Beautie"

And in another *Hymne,* Sapience, whether Wisdom, the Holy Spirit, the Shekinah, or the Virgin Mary, is specifically the "perfect Beautie" again.

I leave the final conclusion to that austere body, the Spenserians, with the reminder that the Garden of Adonis, too, is "layd up in secret store," that "the union of Venus and Adonis results in creation"—and with the lines:

> There is the first seminary
> Of all things that are borne to live and dye
> *According to their kynds.* . . .[281]

If we seem to have wandered from the primary subject of applications of the axiom of Democritus (since it cannot be certainly ascertained that Spenser had it in mind when he wrote the *Hymne* in question), I believe it is only a seeming wandering. There are few lines, even in Renaissance poetry, for which the claim may be made that they *could* have been written with *any one* of the occult traditions in mind. Yet this claim has been established for these lines of Spenser's, I think. All that remains to complete the occult circle is alchemy, and surely Paracelsus' "Perhaps on account of their sins God willed that the Magnalia of Nature should be hidden from many men . . ."[282] comes very close to

> That wondrous Paterne, wheresoere it bee,
> Whether in earth layd up in secret store,
> Or else in heaven, that no man may it see
> With sinfull eyes. . . .

Whatever tradition (occult, or semi-occult, or even non-occult) may be linked in a particular case with a particular interpretation, the basic concept of the "disappearance" of *Nature* should by now be clear as one related to the decay of *nature*. Given the disappearance or departure of *Nature* ("That wondrous Paterne" or "perfect Beautie" or "Natur's selfe" or the Shekinah or Plato's "Child of the Good" or "number as the pre-existed model" or "the celestial pattern" or "the Magnalia of Nature" or "the hidden virtues" or "the truth of nature" or "buried truth")—usually, in Christian terminology, coincident with the Fall of Adam—only *nature*, the created universe, remains, and minus its soul or regulative principle, keeps on a sort of half-existence, while obviously disintegrating and decaying.

Yet another, pre-Christian version of the disappearance of "Nature" should be added to our collection. In one classical version, Justice ruled in the Golden Age, stayed on with indignation in the Silver, left the scene in the Bronze, and never returned.[283] Vergil also brought Justice into his account of the Golden Age under Saturn's rule in his *Fourth Eclogue*—Justice in the traditional form of the Virgin Astraea.[284]

And Astraea is so celebrated again poetically in the Renaissance, and particularly among the Elizabethans. Ronsard links her with the Golden Age of Saturn in one of his lyrics. Sir John Davies, who refers to "Gods handmayde Nature,"[285] explicitly links her, the pattern or model or soul or idea of all nature, with Astraea, throughout a whole poem relating her disappearance.[286] So too, Spenser's Knight of Justice, Artegal, is to dispense justice throughout the world, "bringing back in principle the reign of Saturn when Astraea, goddess of Justice and Artegal's own foster-mother, abode on earth."[287]

Beauty, Harmony, Justice, even Law—all these are really variant ways of describing "This great grandmother of all creatures bred, great Nature. . . ." And she, in turn, the soul of the world, is—or has been—the regulative principle of all nature. She is Nature—hence in less poetic terms, the Law of Nature.

Thinking back now to the third chapter, on "The Repeal of Universal Law," it should not be difficult to see that John Donne's *First Anniversary* is more exactly cast in the tradition we have just been following than in the "legalistic" terms of that study. Since one is the poetic counterpart of the other, it was not invalid to treat the crucial passages in the poem as I did there. Yet the terms are far more exactly the poetic ones of the "disappearance of Nature" than they are those of its intellectualized parallel, "the repeal of universal law."

Some eight years ago, working at Columbia, I discovered a quite regular, although "hidden" framework to the *First Anniversary,* that places the poem unmistakably in the "disappearance" tradition, while also extending considerably and with some certainty its philosophical content. First of all, every time the spelling "Shee" appears, instead of "She," Donne is referring directly to the regulative principle now missing in nature—in other words, to the "Wondrous Paterne," the soul of nature, "Natur's selfe," Astraea, or whatever name one prefers. And whenever "She" with one "e" is used, Donne is paying proper and undistorted tribute to Mistress Elizabeth Drury, the ostensible subject of the poem. (The diligent reader will find Donne's definition of "Shee," although in more theological terms, quoted in Evelyn Simpson's study of his prose works.)[288]

That the *First Anniversary* is a "decay of nature" poem is common enough knowledge. But this discovery makes it possible to see the "decay of nature" developed as the logical result of the "disappearance of Nature" since the Fall—hence, in a single poem, the whole genealogy of the concepts we have been following.

But there is more to it even than that. In Chapter III, I quoted and commented on some of the "decay of nature" passages in the poem, and related the examples cited as proof of Donne's indebtedness to various Counter-Renaissance thinkers and currents. But, as I have just stated, there is also a hidden framework or "plan" to the poem that throws further light upon Donne's meaning. Each of the main sections ends with the refrain "Shee, shee is dead; shee's dead"[289] —followed in each by "when thou knowest this, thou knowest":

how poore a trifling thing man is.[290]

how lame a cripple this world is.[291]

how ugly a maister this world is.[292]

how wan a Ghost this our world is.[293]

how drie a Cinder this world is.[294]

The subject mainly dealt with between the first two refrains is "all cohærance gone; all just supply, and all Relation."[295] If one compares Donne's elaboration of this with Plato's definition of *Justice* in the *Republic*,[296] one finds their meaning almost identical. The subject between the second and third refrains is "Beauty, that's colour, and proportion."[297] "Proportion," we find, corresponds to Plato's definition of *Wisdom* in the *Republic*[298]—"colour" is related to his definition of *Courage*.[299] Furthermore, Donne's subdivision of "proportion" into "symmetree" and "Harmony"[300] corresponds to Plato's relation of *Wisdom's* rule to "gymnastic" and "music."[301] Again, the subject between the third and fourth refrains in the poem—"correspondence of heaven and earth"[302]— bears a clear connection with Plato's definition of *Temperance*.[303] Finally, recognizing the section of the poem before the first refrain as an introduction to the nature of man, his Fall, and the general state of things, and that between the fourth and last refrains as a summary of the whole significance of the loss of Nature, we have the following tentative chart:

    I. State of Man.
    II. Justice.
    III. Wisdom and Courage.
    IV. Temperance.
    V. Summary: state of nature.

I say "tentative," for—despite superficial appearances to the contrary—I am not interested in trying to prove Donne's direct indebtedness to Plato. I even doubt that it existed. As I shall show in a moment, there were too many alternative sources, intermediate between him and Plato, for this to have been likely. Moreover, the framework I have outlined is incomplete; it leaves ragged edges and unsatisfied details.

Yet I think the identification with the four cardinal virtues of those qualities whose passing from the world Donne mourned is clearly significant. As innumerable sources indicate, the four cardinal virtues were literally the pillars of the humanistic ethic, and intimately connected with the reign of natural law and man's "proper" ethical program.[304] What Donne, true and versatile son of the Counter-Renaissance, is saying, then, is that the traditional humanistic view holds no more validity for him. He pays his tribute to Mistress Elizabeth Drury on one level of the poem; on a second, I suspect that he relates the passing of Elizabeth the Queen to the disappearance of *Shee;* but on the third and truly philosophical level, he celebrates the passing of a world order, a philosophical world-view—with the devices of the decay of nature, the disappearance of Nature, and the hidden framework. Hence what more appropriate than that the *Second Anniversary* should be (as is generally conceded) the flight of the soul from this half-world of disintegrating nature to God—through faith alone, and grace? If so, it represents his "positive" interest in the Counter-Renaissance (the Reformation), as the first poem does his "negative."

I suspect that there is a hidden framework here, too, but I cannot make even a tentative guess at its origin and detailed nature. As for the *First Anniversary,* the most probable sources seem to me Augustine's *City of God,*[305] Pico's *"Platonick"* commentary on Benivieni's *Canzona;* one of the hexaemeral works;[306] some combination of occult works;[307] or Macrobius' commentary on the *Somnium Scipionis.*[308] All of these, in varying ways, show Platonic influence. Perhaps he used a combination of them, perhaps one or more of them combined with something else, perhaps a totally different intermediate source.

Whatever the case in this respect, his total intention, I think, is clear. And clear, too—if one compares this analysis with that in Chapter III—is the fact that no other Elizabethan was so widely conversant with the various aspects of the Counter-Renaissance. The Reformation, the Machiavellian materialists, the empirical scientists, the ethical naturalists, the occult philosophers—he knew them all and used them all to express the full extent of his skepticism of the continuing validity of the Scholastic and humanistic traditions, and to persuade himself of the sole efficacy of faith.

FOOTNOTES

CHAPTER 8

I.

1. John Donne, *Biathanatos,* 36. Arthur O. Lovejoy and his colleagues have made an exhaustive and illuminating survey of the many concepts of "Nature" as "Norm." Cf. "Genesis of the Conception of 'Nature' as Norm," *A Documentary History of Primitivism and Related Ideas,* I, 103–117; and " 'Nature' as Æsthetic Norm," *Modern Language Notes,* XLII (1927), 444–450. For a related study with exclusive reference to the Renaissance, see Harold S. Wilson, "Some Meanings of 'Nature' in Renaissance Literary Theory," *JHI* (Oct., 1941), Vol. II, No. 4, pp. 430–438.

2. Lovejoy and Boas, etc., *Prim. and Rel. Ideas,* 188.

3. *Ibid.,* 244. See also Appendix, "Some Meanings of Nature," meanings 40 and 41, pp. 451–452.

4. For all the various sorts of primitivism discussed in this paragraph, see Lovejoy and Boas, *Prim. and Rel. Ideas,* 1–11.

5. Montaigne, II, 222–223.

6. *Ibid.,* 223.

7. *Ibid.,* 223–224.

8. *Ibid.,* 204.

9. Cf. Lovejoy and Boas, *Prim. and Rel. Ideas,* 5; also 130–131, for Lucretius' treatment of this concept.

10. See *ibid.,* 78 and 121–126, for Aristotle and Polybius respectively, and compare, to consider ways in which they may have influenced Machiavelli. For Aristotle and cycles, see 71–74, 75–76; for other cyclical concepts, 24, 26.

11. Machiavelli, *Discourses,* I, 112; II, 380–383, 388; III, 441, 518; *et passim; Prince,* Chap. XXV.

2.

12. For this paragraph, see Lovejoy and Boas, *Prim. and Rel. Ideas,* 111–112.

13. *Ibid.,* 166.

14. *Ibid.*

15. *Ibid.*

16. *Ibid.,* 189–190.

17. *Ibid.,* 246–248.

18. *Ibid.,* 252. For a detailed treatment of this distinction and its variations, see Hicks, *Stoic and Epicurean,* 66–68, 77. See also Lovejoy and Boas, *ibid.,* Appendix, meaning 39, p. 451: "light of nature" and "natural reason."

19. Lovejoy and Boas, *ibid.,* 263.

20. Chapman, *Poems* (ed. cit.), 248.

21. *Ibid.,* 177–178: "The Teares of Peace," ll. 392–393.

22. *Les Œuvres Politiques et Morales* (Geneva, 1621), 899; cf. Villey, *Les Essais de Montaigne,* 104, and Louis I. Bredvold, "The Naturalism of Donne in Relation to Some Renaissance Traditions," *Journal of English and Germanic Philology* (1923), Vol. 22, 493.

23. Laurentius Valla, *De Voluptate ac Vero Bono Libri III* (Basle, 1519). I have used the photostat copy in the Columbia University Library (p. 11).

24. *Ibid.,* 18.

25. Which was in many important respects not at odds with the Stoic program.

26. Erasmus, *Colloquies*, 326–327 ("The Epicurean").
27. More, *Utopia*, 122.
28. In Chapter II, we have discussed the presence of the stricter sort of doctrinal Stoicism and Cynicism in Renaissance thinking, and we shall have occasion to take it up again. But the main tradition is this other, more eclectic one.
29. Cicero, *De Officiis* (Loeb Library), I, ii.
30. *Ibid.*, I, i; I, xxviii.
31. *De Finibus*, IV, vi.
32. Du Vair, *Morall Philosophy*, 1, 2, 4.
33. Hooker, *Of the Laws*, I, viii, 9.
34. Cicero, *De Re Publica*, III, xxii.
35. Cicero, *De Legibus*, I, vi.
36. Seneca, *Epistolae*, quoted by Lipsius, *Manuductio*, II, xvii.
37. Cicero, *De Senectute*, quoted by Zanta, *Stoïcisme*, 200.
38. Seneca, quoted *ibid.*, 202.
39. Aquinas, *Sum. Theol.*, II, I, Question XCI, art. 2.
40. More, *Utopia*, 122.
41. Lipsius, *Constancie*, I, xii; II, iii.
42. John Milton, *Paradise Lost*, XII, 81–85; IX, 351–352.
43. *Anti-Dictator*, The *Discours sur la servitude volontaire* of Etienne de la Boétie, Rendered into English by Harry Kurz (New York, 1942), 13.
44. Cf. Zanta, *Stoïcisme*, 300.
45. Lovejoy and Boas, *Prim. and Rel. Ideas*, 252–253. For the two opposed concepts of "following nature" as found in Seneca, see *ibid.*, 281–282.
46. Zanta, *ibid.*
47. Cicero, *De Officiis*, I, xxx, xxxi. My italics. Refer to Chapter V for the relation of this passage to the traditional medieval and Renaissance concept of "vocation."
48. Sidney, *Arcadia*, III, 10. Observe the similarity (without this "evil" connotation) of some of Montaigne's statements.
49. Randall, "Scientific Method in the School of Padua," 203.
50. Montaigne, II, 260. My italics.
51. *Ibid.*, II, 314–315. My italics.
52. *Ibid.*, II, 336. My italics.
53. *Ibid.*, III, 294. My italics.
54. *Ibid.*, III, 278. My italics.
55. Cicero, *De Officiis*, I, iv.
56. Villey, *Essais de Montaigne*, 102–103.
57. Montaigne, III, 316.
58. *Ibid.*, III, 359.
59. Cf. Atkinson, *Nouveaux Horizons*, 71.
60. André Thevet, *Singularités de la France Antartique* (Paris, 1557) : Atkinson, 314.
61. Montaigne, I, 269–270.
62. *Ibid.*, I, 270.
63. Pierre Charron, *De la Sagesse* (Paris, 1601), I, 14: Atkinson, 330.
64. For a good brief discussion of Valla (on which I have drawn here) see Fletcher, *Italian Renaissance*, 97–102. I accept Beccadelli as Valla's spokesman in the dialogues.
65. Montaigne, III, 81.
66. *Ibid.*, III, 80.
67. *Ibid.*, I, 222.
68. Valla, *De Voluptate*: translation by Fletcher, *Italian Renaissance*, 99.

69. Montaigne, III, 94, 101.
70. *Ibid.*, III, 72.
71. *Ibid.*, II, 341.
72. *Ibid.*, III, 93. My italics.
73. *Ibid.*, III, 400.
74. Nashe, *Unfortunate Traveller*, 42.
75. Quoted by Zanta, *Renaissance du Stoïcisme*, 55.
76. Montaigne, II, 204.
77. *Ibid.*, III, 400.
78. Du Vair, *Morall Philosophy*, 5. My italics.
79. Valla, *De Voluptate*, 18.
80. Harvey, *Marginalia*, 101.
81. Montaigne, III, 436. My italics.
82. *Ibid.*, III, 136.
83. *Ibid.*, III, 118. My italics.
84. Rabelais, IV, 32.
85. Pomponazzi, *De Immortalitate*, 15.
86. Marguerite of Navarre, *Heptameron*, XXXIV (Fourth Day), 59.
87. Montaigne, III, 27. For a "Freudian" statement on dreams, see III, 414.
88. Valla, *De Voluptate*, 14.
89. Rabelais, *To the Readers* (before the Author's Prologue to the First Book).
90. Rabelais, I, 29; V, 8.
91. *Ibid.*, II, 35.
92. *Ibid.*, IV, Author's Prologue.
93. Montaigne, III, 314.
94. *Ibid.*, III, 292. My italics.
95. *Ibid.*, III, 22. My italics.
96. *Ibid.*, III, 432–433.
97. *Ibid.*, 436. My italics.
98. Fletcher, *Italian Renaissance*, 33.
99. *Petrarch's Secret*, translated by W. H. Drapper (London, 1911), 172–173, 189.
100. Cf. Fletcher, *Italian Renaissance*, 33.
101. Rabelais, V, 6.
102. Da Vinci, *Notebooks*, I, 73.
103. Thomas Lodge, "To the Courteous Reader": *The Workes of Lucius Annaeus Seneca. Both Morall and Naturall . . .*, translated by Thomas Lodge (London, 1614); cf. Lipsius, *Constancie*, 29–30.
104. Montaigne, III, 35.
105. *Ibid.*, III, 392, 393, 395.
106. *Ibid.*, I, 187; II, 349.
107. *Ibid.*, III, 438, 439.
108. *Ibid.*, III, 440.
109. *Ibid.*
110. Erasmus, *Praise of Folly*, 24.
111. Montaigne, III, 267.
112. Cicero, *De Officiis*, I, i.
113. Montaigne, III, 268.
114. *Ibid.*
115. Quoted from Ronsard's primitivistic "Discours contre Fortune"; see Section 3 of this same chapter.
116. George Chapman, *Bussy D'Ambois*, II, i, 193–199 (*Tragedies, ed. cit.*). Compare Laertes' attitude in the discussion on *Hamlet* in Chapter X, 1 (*infra*). There, of course, "honor" is specifically invoked, as it is not here.

117. Ronsard, *ibid.*
118. Chapman, *ibid.*, III, i, 1–2; 20 ff.
119. *Ibid.*, III, i, 66–67.
120. *Ibid.*, III, i, 91–107. My italics.
121. *Ibid.*, V, iv, 147.
122. *Ibid.*, III, i, 114–116.
123. *Ibid.*, 435–438. My italics.
124. *Ibid.*, V, iii, 72–74.
125. *Ibid.*, II, i, 203–204.
126. See Section 3 of this chapter.
127. *Revenge of Bussy,* IV, iv, 42.
128. *Ibid.*, III, iv, 48–75.
129. *Ibid.*, V, i, 193; cf. III, ii, 97–117.
130. *Ibid.*, V, i, 177–183.
131. *Ibid.*, V, i, 18, 22–23, 74–81.
132. Quoted by Lovejoy and Boas, *Prim. and Rel. Ideas,* 274.

3.

133. Lovejoy and Boas, *Prim. and Rel. Ideas,* 6, 8.
134. *Ibid.*, 1, 25. Some versions included a fifth age—The Age of Heroes (between the Bronze and the Iron). Hesiod did, for one. See *ibid.*, 25–31. The descending order of excellence was not always followed exactly, either, but the Golden Age was always the best.
135. *Ibid.*, 24.
136. Quoted (and translated) by Samuel Noah Kramer, "Immortal Clay: The Literature of Sumer," *American Scholar,* XV, 3 (Summer, 1946), 319. (Italicized words represent doubtful translations.)
137. Lovejoy and Boas, *ibid.*, 24–25.
138. Edmund Spenser, *Poetical Works,* edited by J. C. Smith (Oxford, 1919), Vol. II, 100. *Faerie Queene,* IV, viii, 30. My italics. Needless to say, I have not, throughout my discussion, used my regular term "Christian humanists," but rather "traditionalist-humanists." The Golden Age is not properly a Christian concept at all—yet many of those whom I call (I think accurately) Christian humanists refer to it regularly. When they take the trouble to explain at all, they equate the Golden Age with Eden before the Fall. On other occasions, they use it in terms of poetic symbolism. At any rate, they seldom feel called upon to explain themselves.
139. *Faerie Queene,* IV, viii, 32.
140. Professor Fletcher called my attention to this peculiarly effective and summarizing comparison.
141. Bredvold, "The Naturalism of Donne," 487.
142. *Ibid.*, cf. Seneca, *Epistolae,* XIV, 2. My italics.
143. Quoted by J. B. Bury, *Idea of Progress,* 14.
144. For the idea of hard moral primitivism, see Lovejoy and Boas, *ibid.*, 34–47, 165–175. In addition to the Cynics and Stoics, some of the Epicureans (contrary to the popular misconceptions about them) held to this point of view, too. For a good discussion of Seneca and primitivism, see *ibid.*, 170–175.
145. Cf. Bredvold, "Naturalism of Donne," 488–491.
146. Angelo Poliziano, *Le Stanze, Orfeo, Le Rime,* ed. Carducci, 2nd ed. (Bologna, 1911); Stanza V, 118, 79, 80, 83, translations by Nesca Robb.
147. Lorenzo de' Medici, *Poesie,* ed. Ross and Hutton, Vol. I, *Selve d'Amore,* Stanza 115, 36, translation by Robb.

148. Pierre Ronsard, *Le Recueil des Odes, A Cassandre* (1550) : Wyndham, *Ronsard and La Pléiade*, 120.

149. *Œuvres Complètes de P. de Ronsard*, Nouvelle Édition revisée, augmentée et annotée par Paul Laumonier (Paris, 1914–1919), Vol. V, 30–31.

150. *Ibid.*, V, 154. For concepts of "the noble savage" in classical antiquity, see Lovejoy and Boas, *ibid.*, 185–187.

151. *Ibid.*

152. *Ibid.*, V, 154–155.

153. *Ibid.*, V, 155. It must be admitted that, although this mood is a highly characteristic one, there are places where Ronsard invokes the orthodox Law of Nature. Cf., for example, V, 420 and 366–367. See also V, 376, where the mood is close to that of the present passages, yet he uses the words "la loi de nature." Yet he also refers to "le bel âge doré, où florissait Saturne avec Astrée" in *Les Sirènes* (III, 476), and declares elsewhere that, were it not for "une certaine foi que Dieu par son esprit de grâce a mise en moi . . . comme les premiers je deviendrois Païen" (V, 367).

154. Torquato Tasso, *Jerusalem Delivered*, translated by Edward Fairfax (1600) edited by Henry Morley (London, 1890), p. 320: XV, 63. Armida's abode is reminiscent of the Classical linking of the Isles of the Blessed with the legend of the Golden Age. See Lovejoy and Boas, *ibid.*, 185, 188.

155. Tasso, *ibid.*, p. 327; XVI, 32.

156. Machiavelli, *Discourses*, I, 47.

157. John Donne, Elegie XVII, ll. 38–73: *Poems*, 102–103.

158. Rabelais, III, 8.

159. Montaigne, III, 102.

160. *Ibid.*, III, 240.

161. *Ibid.*, I, 222.

162. *Ibid.* My italics.

163. *Ibid.*

164. See the sections on Montaigne in Atkinson's *Nouveaux Horizons*.

165. Vespucci (?), *Sensuit le Nouveau Monde*, 74; Atkinson, 142. My italics.

166. Martyr, *Extrait . . . des Iles trouvées*, 33; Atkinson, 142–143.

167. Peter Martyr, *First Decade, Second Booke*, translated by Eden. I am indebted for this passage to Franklyn McCann's as yet unpublished *England Discovers America* (Columbia University Ph.D. dissertation, ms. p. 154).

168. J. Macer, *Les Trois Livres . . . Histoire des Indes* (Paris, 1555), 78; Atkinson, 143.

169. Léon, *Description de l'Afrique*, I, 470–471; Atkinson, 144. My italics.

170. Cf. Atkinson, *Nouveaux Horizons*, 145.

171. Marc Lescarbot, *Histoire de la Nouvelle France* (Paris, 1609), 820; Atkinson, 185.

172. Léry, *Histoire d'un Voyage*, 303; Atkinson, 156. My italics.

173. From Richard Hakluyt, *The Principal Navigations Voyages Traffiques and Discoveries of the English Nation, 1589: Explorations in Living*, edited by Winfield H. Rogers, Ruby V. Redinger and Hiram C. Haydn II (New York, 1941), II, 553.

174. Michael Drayton, *To the Virginian Voyage*, ll. 37–42: *Poet. Eng. Ren.*, 297.

175. Shakespeare, *As You Like It*, I, i, 1–27 (*ed. cit.*).

176. *Ibid.*, 123–125.

177. *Ibid.*, II, iv.

178. *Ibid.*, III, ii, 77–81.

179. *Ibid.*, II, iii, 56–62, 68.

180. *Ibid.*, II, v, 40–47.

181. *Ibid.*, 52–59.

182. *Ibid.,* I, ii, 106–155.
183. *Ibid.,* II, i, 1–18.
184. *Ibid.,* III, ii, 46–49.
185. *Ibid.,* I, ii, 172–177.
186. *Winter's Tale,* IV, iv, 90–92.
187. *Ibid.,* 592–594.
188. *The Tempest,* II, i, 147–168.
189. *Ibid.,* I, ii, 363–365.
190. For other references in Shakespeare to Nature and Art, to the Golden Age and to the State of Nature, see *ed. cit.* (Kittredge), pp. 275, 371, 411, 416, 423, 444, 457, 462, 1021, 1039, 1048, 1049, 1050–1054, 1068, 1069, 1070, 1071, 1073, 1075, 1076, 1106, 1131, 1149, 1160, 1168, 1169, 1210, 1243.
191. This point of view was rare before the advent of Christian other-worldliness, but is occasionally evident in antiquity. See Lovejoy and Boas, *Prim. and Rel. Ideas,* 22.
192. Cf. Thorndike, *Magic and Science,* V, 651.
193. Lemmi, *Classical Deities,* 98.
194. Paracelsus, *Works,* I, 30.
195. *Ibid.,* I, 26; II, 148.
196. Bacon, *Works,* 92.
197. Ralegh, *Works,* II, 391, 384–385; *History of the World,* I, xi, 3, 2. My italics.
198. *Ibid.,* II, 16–17: *History of the World,* I, i, 7.
199. Paracelsus, *Works,* I, 51. My italics.
200. *Ibid.,* 69.
201. *Ibid.,* 73, 72.
202. *Ibid.,* II, 5. My italics.
203. *Ibid.,* I, 113.
204. *Ibid.,* 39.
205. *Ibid.,* 19–20.
206. *Ibid.,* 19.
207. *Ibid.,* 20.
208. Thorndike, *Magic and Science,* V, 631.
209. Hooker, I, x, 1.
210. Machiavelli, *Discourses,* I, 11.
211. Cf. Plato, *Republic,* II, 357 ff.
212. Cf. Cicero, *De Re Publica,* Book III.
213. For anti-primitivistic elements in the thought of Plato, Aristotle and Lucretius, see Lovejoy and Boas, *Prim. and Rel. Ideas,* 168, 177–180, and 239–242, respectively.
214. Cicero, *ibid.,* xxii; cf. Lactantius, *Inst. Div.,* VI, 8, 6–9.
215. Lucretius, *De Rerum Natura,* V, 1448 ff.; cf. Bury, *Idea of Progress,* 15–17.
216. Machiavelli, *Discourses,* I, 4.
217. *Ibid.,* 11. My italics.
218. Le Roy, *Vicissitude,* 25–27; Atkinson, 347–348. My italics. See Atkinson, 393–394, for variant reading. See also Le Roy, *De la Vicissitude (ed. cit.),* 18–19.
219. Bodin, *Methodus,* VII, esp. 353, 356. Cf. Bury, *Idea of Progress,* 38–39.
220. Harvey, *Letter Book,* 86.
221. *Ibid.,* 83.
222. Ralegh, *Works,* VIII, 279. My italics.
223. La Boétie, *Anti-Dictator,* 14.
224. *Ibid.,* 15.
225. Guicciardini, *Thoughts and Portraits,* 67–68.

226. Bodin, *Republic,* 48; Atkinson, 373.
227. Montaigne, III, 221. My italics.

4.

228. Frank L. Schoell, *Études sur l'Humanisme Continental en Angleterre à la Fin de la Renaissance* (Paris, 1926), 10.
229. The reason that some commentaries on Genesis are referred to as *hexaemeral* literature, and others as *heptaemeral,* is that the particular writer may have preferred to refer to the six days of creation, or to include the final day of rest in the first week, making the number seven.
230. Cf. Rigg, *Giovanni Pico della Mirandola,* xiv–xvi.
231. Cf. Greswell, *Memoirs of Angelus Politianus, etc.,* 245, 250, 260.
232. Cf. Thorndike, *Magic and Experimental Science,* VI, 444, for Reuchlin's *De arte cabalistica libri tres Leoni X dedicati,* 1517.
233. For a thorough study of the Hexaemera, see Frank E. Robbins, *The Hexaemeral Literature* (Chicago, 1912).
234. Robbins, *ibid.,* 27.
235. *Ibid.,* 29.
236. *Ibid.,* 72.
237. Bury, *Idea of Progress,* 21.
238. For various Greek treatments of cycles and final conflagration, see Lovejoy and Boas, *Prim. and Rel. Ideas,* 79–84, and 170–173; for Roman versions, *ibid.,* 222–228, 237–239, 285–286.
239. Randall, *Mod. Mind,* 33.
240. Allen, *Star-Crossed Ren.,* 30.
241. Bury, *Idea of Progress,* 62–63.
242. See Preserved Smith, *History of Modern Culture* (New York, 1930), I, 289 ff.
243. Lipsius, *Two Bookes of Constancie,* 110.
244. Haydn (ed.), *Eliz. Reader,* 125 (*Of the Interchangeable Course or Variety of Things in the Whole World,* by Louis Le Roy, translated by Robert Ashley, 1594).
245. Bodin, *Method,* Chapter VIII: "A System of Universal Time," especially 315 ff. For his own conclusions, see 324, 326 ff., and 333.
246. *Ibid.,* 333.
247. Norden, *Vicissitudo Rerum,* st. 33.
248. George Hakewill, *An Apologie or Declaration of the Power and Providence of God in the Government of the World* (*ed. cit.*).
249. Lovejoy and Boas, *Prim. and Rel. Ideas,* 99.
250. For a sixteenth-century discussion of this point, see Bodin, *Method,* 318.
251. Cf. *supra,* p. 204.
252. Lipsius, *Two Bookes,* 107–111.
253. Rabelais (*ed. cit.*), pp. 144–145.
254. *Ibid.,* pp. 114–116, 235–240, 537.
255. Bury, *Idea of Prog.,* 35.
256. *Ibid.,* 46–48, and Le Roy, *De la Vicissitude,* xiv.
257. Montaigne, III, 228.
258. Haydn (ed.), *Eliz. Reader,* 125–139. See also the introduction, 9–13, for comments on these selections and their relation to contemporary astronomical findings.
259. Especially p. 180 (*ed. cit.*).
260. Especially "Caelica," st. XLIV, and "A Treatie of Humane Learning," st. 54 (*ed. cit.*).

261. Charles M. Bakewell, *Source Book in Ancient Philosophy* (New York, 1909: after Diels' text, fragment 117), 59.

262. Diogenes Laertius, *Lives of Eminent Philosophers,* ix, 72. The translation in the Loeb Library edition reads, "Of a truth we know nothing, for truth is in a well."

263. Bacon, *Works,* 89–90 (*Adv. of Learning,* Book II).

264. Sir John Davies, *Poems,* 116 (*Nosce Teipsum,* Part I).

265. Bacon, *Works,* 92 (*ibid.*).

266. Ralegh, *Works,* II, 384–385 (*History of the World,* I, xi, 2).

267. Erasmus, *Paraboles,* and Chapman, Preface to *Ovid's Banquet;* cf. Schoell, *L'Humanisme,* 59–60.

268. Paracelsus, *Works,* I, 28.

269. See Lemmi, *The Classical Deities in Bacon,* for a study of Bacon's interest in and debt to the alchemists, Neoplatonists, and such "mythographers" as Natalis Comes.

270. Rabelais, III, 24; V, 45, 46, 47.

271. Cf., for Comes' version, Lemmi, *Classical Deities,* 90. See Lemmi, 67, for Bacon's and Comes' versions of the belief that the Fates lived in "a huge subterranean cave" since "the fates of individuals are secret." The appositeness of this concept to Panurge's mission is obvious.

272. Rabelais, V, 45, 46. My italics.

273. *Ibid.,* V, 36, 42. Making full allowance for the extremity of specious seriousness to which Rabelais may carry the elaboration of some idea, there is reason to consider this development in Rabelais without too settled a preconception.

It is, first of all, at least suggestive that the tone deepens perceptibly in the Third Book, impressively in the Fourth and Fifth. Anyone who reads all five consecutively and without *a priori* convictions cannot miss the essential changes in the temper of the three leading characters and their relationships. Pantagruel is increasingly intolerant of Panurge; he is sometimes impatient with Friar John. The pilgrimage to the Holy Bottle retains many of the boisterous features of the first two books, but Pantagruel himself is clearly seeking something more than the solution of Panurge's problem. It would take a book to develop in convincing detail the nature of this search; it must suffice here to say that it is characterized by a growing dissatisfaction with the power of reason, and by an increasing evidence of the desire for an inward religion. (See A. F. Chappell, *The Enigma of Rabelais,* Cambridge, 1924, especially 65 and 183.)

Finally, Bacbuc herself (especially when contrasted with Queen of Quintessence) is presented sympathetically. The dignity of her tone matches that of the other serious passages in the whole work. And for all the discords which Panurge and Friar John strike, there is nothing in her "secret" philosophy which we have reason to find incongruous with Rabelais' own point of view. Indeed, he gives it a characteristic tone by his inclusion of features of the rites of Dionysus.

There are many similar indications of this development; I have cited a good many which suggest that the specific form it took was an increasing, though still light-hearted, interest in the tradition of a "certain devout philosophy." If this supposition is correct, there is a final appropriateness to the concluding passage of Book V, where references to some of the familiar names of the tradition are combined with Bacbuc's last and definitive exposition of the search for truth:

Now when your sages shall wholly apply their minds to a diligent and studious search after truth, humbly begging the assistance of the sovereign God, whom formerly the Egyptians in their language called the Hidden and Concealed, and invoking him by that name, beseech him *to reveal and make himself known to them,* that Almighty Being will, out of his infinite goodness, not only make his creatures, but even himself known to them.

Thus will they be guided by good lanterns. For all the ancient philosophers and sages have held two things necessary safely and pleasantly to arrive at the knowledge of God and true wisdom; first, *God's gracious guidance,* then *man's assistance.*

So, among the philosophers, Zoroaster took Arimaspes for the companion of his travels; Æsculapius, Mercury [Hermes Trismegistus]; Orpheus, Musæus; Pythagoras, Aglaophemus; and, among princes and warriors, Hercules in his most difficult achievements had his singular friend Theseus; Ulysses, Diomedes; Æneas, Achates. You followed their examples, and came under the conduct of an illustrious lantern. Now, in God's name depart, and may he go along with you! (Rabelais, V, 47. My italics.)

274. Spenser, *An Hymne in Honour of Beautie,* ll. 29–33, 36–40. My italics.
275. Cf. Morley, *Agrippa,* I, 123.
276. Brunschvicq, *Pythagorisme,* 5, 18.
277. Edwin Arthur Burtt, *The Metaphysical Foundations of Modern Physical Science* (New York, 1925), 54 (Kepler, *Opera,* ed. Frisch, I, 10). There can, of course, be no doubt that Spenser was familiar with at least popular Pythagoreanism. Cf. Vincent Foster Hopper, "Spenser's 'House of Temperance,'" *PMLA,* Vol. LV, No. 4 (December, 1940), 958–967; and *Faerie Queene,* II, ix, 22.
278. Brunschvicq, *ibid.,* 18.
279. Fletcher, *Religion of Beauty,* 117.
280. *Faerie Queene, Mutability Cantos,* vii, 13, 59; Saurat, *Literature and Occult Tradition,* 10–11. My italics.
281. My italics. Cf. Saurat, *ibid.,* 186, 233. There are further significant parallels to be considered in Comes' and Bacon's interpretation of the earth-spirit Proserpine; cf. Lemmi, *Classical Deities,* 90, and then reread Bacbuc's words about "what is hid within the bowels of the earth" (Rabelais, V, 47).
282. Paracelsus, *Alchemical Writings,* I, 29.
283. Lovejoy and Boas, *Prim. and Rel. Ideas,* 34–35.
284. *Ibid.,* 85.
285. Davies, *Poems,* 139.
286. *Ibid.,* especially 195, 197, 247.
287. Fletcher, "The Continental Background of Edmund Spenser" (unpublished manuscript), I, 14–15. See also, for the version concerning the celestial Lady Concord and her earthly handmaid, Cambria, H. G. Lotspeich's *Classical Mythology in the Poetry of Edmund Spenser* (Princeton, 1932), 31.
288. See bibliography for Evelyn Simpson's book. It is appropriate at this point to acknowledge my indebtedness to Marjorie Nicolson for help and advice on this study of Donne's poem. She tells me, incidentally, that more recent students of hers have gone on to further discoveries.
289. *Ibid.,* 213, 214, 217, 218, 220: *ibid.,* ll. 183, 237, 325, 369, 427.
290. *Ibid.,* 213: *ibid.,* l. 184.
291. *Ibid.,* 214: *ibid.,* l. 238.
292. *Ibid.,* 217: *ibid.,* l. 326.

293. *Ibid.*, 218: *ibid.*, l. 370.
294. *Ibid.*, 220: *ibid.*, l. 428.
295. *Ibid.*, 214: *ibid.*, ll. 213–214.
296. Plato, *The Republic*, with an Introduction by Charles M. Bakewell (New York, 1928: The Modern Students' Library), 160–161 (IV, 433, A–E). This is the third edition of the Jowett translation.
297. Donne, *Poems*, 215: *First Ann.*, l. 250.
298. Plato, *Republic*, 152–153 (IV, 428, B–429 A).
299. *Ibid.*, 154–155 (IV, 429 D–430 B).
300. Donne, *Poems*, 216: *First Ann.*, ll. 305–313.
301. Plato, *Republic*, 173 (IV, 441 E–442 A).
302. Donne, *Poems*, 218 (marginal note); also 219: *ibid.*, ll. 396–397.
303. Plato, *Republic*, 158 (IV, 432 A).
304. For the identification of the Stoic law of nature with the four Platonic cardinal virtues, see again Cicero, *De Officiis*, I, i; I, xxviii.
305. See Bodin, *Method*, 316; Dawson, *Prog. and Rel.*, 164–165; De Wulf's *Phil. and Civil.*, for suggestive comments on the *City of God*.
306. See Robbins, *Hex. Lit.*, 6, 8–10, 14–15, 34, 36, 86–87, for pertinent passages. Pico's commentary is to be found in Thomas Stanley's *History of Philosophy* (London, 1743); Professor Fletcher believes this to have given Spenser the plan for his *Fowre Hymnes* ("Spenser," paper cited above, II, 5).
307. See Saurat, *Lit. and Occ. Trad.*, 8, 84–86, for relevant passages.
308. See De Wulf, *Hist. Med. Phil.*, I, 85–86, on this commentary.

CHAPTER
9

THE COURTLY TRADITIONS OF LOVE AND
HONOR

I. THE ROMANTICISTS AND THE NATURALISTS ON LOVE AND
HONOR

ANGER and Lust, Erasmus' jester had called them. . . . The irascible and the concupiscible powers of the sensitive soul, said the orthodox anatomies of the soul. . . . Yet under the names of Honor and Love, two related and essentially courtly ethical codes (or codes of conduct) sprang up in the Counter-Renaissance to challenge the supremacy of the traditionalist-humanists' allegiance to Virtue and Reason. But—once again—"Anger and Lust," said the disillusioned, snorting at the euphemisms. . . .

It was not quite so simple as that, of course. In fact, tracking down just what was meant by Love and Honor at various times in various places by various writers of the period is arduous detective work. Yet the results yield a significance beyond the establishment of merely literary ideological patterns, for they reveal some interesting social phenomena.

Professor Fletcher has written,

> Never perhaps so much as in the Italian Renaissance have human institutions, the state and society itself, been regarded as works of self-conscious art.[1]

With the gradual dying of the absolutism of the traditions of nobility of blood and family, *Quattrocento* court society was compelled, in the words of Burckhardt, "to find its worth and charm in itself. The demeanour of individuals, and all the higher forms of social intercourse, became ends pursued with a deliberate and artistic purpose."[2]

In time, a spokesman for this new but not gauche society appeared in the person of the Conte Baldassare Castiglione, who eventually indeed (with the spread in popularity of his book on the ideal courtier, *Il Cortigiano*) became "*the arbiter elegantiarum* for all Renaissance Europe."[3] The people who appear in *Il Cortigiano*, says Professor Fletcher,

> are consummate artists; they possessed what is declared to be the essence of social refinement—grace, *grazia*, the trained instinct which can do or say difficult things with apparent ease.[4]

"In the Courtier—the *gentleman* of the Renaissance—" he continues, "Cicero's *humanitas* is almost perfectly revived, even to the courtier's supreme virtue as adviser of the State." Yet two differences are readily apparent: (1) the new tradition is one of aristocratic chivalry; (2) the chief influence upon the courtier, the ennobling and refining influence, is that of a beautiful woman.[5]

"The faith of Castiglione's courtier is in the Beautiful," writes Professor Fletcher—

> one might say in Fine Art, in the divine art which made the world beautiful, and all things in it, and more especially beautiful women. But his attitude towards these last is that we have heard prescribed by the Platonist Benivieni. Approach to perfection is by the "ladder of love." But to get started, the courtier must be in love. And here is where the court-lady comes in. Dante's angelic lady descends to earth to become a social force, an agent of spiritual development in the courtier, a refiner of the brutal sex.[6]

Hence it becomes her task to keep a fine balance between "platonic and profane love"—to maintain "una certa mediocrità difficile" ("a certain golden mean of reserve"). If the courtier, in turn, must be "something more than a friend" to her, he "must also be less than a lover."[7]

Out of these delicate adjustments and distinctions, that "religion of beauty in woman" deriving from such assorted predecessors as the Provençal courtly tradition, the medieval cult of the Virgin, the philosophy of the *dolce stil* of Guinizelli and Dante, and the sonnets of Petrarch, took new form. And with the extensive vogue of *Il Cortigiano*, this new version of "Platonic" love and Castiglione's ideal of the Renaissance gentleman and court lady attained eventually such strength that from them sprang an ethical code of love and honor which in certain influential circles challenged the supremacy of the humanistic one.

The statement requires immediate qualification. For, at least as Bembo and Castiglione propounded it, this new code was in no sense a rival to orthodox humanistic ethics. Its ideals of love and honor were not antipathetic to those others of reason and virtue —but rather supplementary. For the love they advocated was eminently "rational" (although there were doubtless those to whom this unphysical devotion to a lady seemed highly irrational); true honor was both consistent with, and (in another sense) the reward of, true virtue. The most serious complaint that orthodox Christians could (and did) make about any feature of the "Platonic system" —that the progress up the ladder of love to the love of God left little for the Church to do, in terms of salvation—was not a question of ethics.

The ethical code of love and honor expounded by Bembo and Castiglione, then, was essentially compatible with that of orthodox humanism; it simply took on a special flavor, a special vocabulary, and a special emphasis appropriate to its aristocratic province—the specialized confines of its application. Furthermore, it was no revolt of Nature against Art. As Professor Fletcher has pointed out, this "institution" was indeed a "work of self-conscious art."

And so it was widely proclaimed before the Renaissance came to an end. Not merely the philosophical naturalists, but all "plain men" of the time, denounced its whole program as artifice of the worst sort; against its "Art," "Nature" drew up as bitter an opposition as that it presented to the Scholastics and humanists.

The most prominent Renaissance ethical code of love and honor, then, begins as an indubitable work of "rational Art," harmonious with and supplementary to the main precepts and arguments of the great orthodox humanist ethical program. Yet its very idealism made it a course difficult to follow with sincerity and fidelity, and we do not get very far beyond Castiglione before the "Nature" in its own proponents begins to rebel. Moreover, elements from other and not strictly compatible courtly ideals of love and honor merge with it, to alter it still more, until—from strong (if somewhat suspect) allies of Reason and Virtue—Love and Honor come to assert their own priority.

This is the progress that we have to trace, and—for the sake of clarity—it will be wise to pursue the tracks of these eventual rivals of the humanistic code separately (insofar as that is possible). Since those of Love are plainer, we had best follow them first.

"Love," says Pietro Bembo to the gallant company assembled at Urbino, is nothing else but a certaine coveting to enjoy beautie: and for somuch as coveting longeth for nothing, but for things known, it is requisite that knowledge goe evermore before coveting, which of his own nature willeth the good, but of himselfe is blind, and knoweth it not.[8]

This priority of the act of knowing to that of loving, and the parallelism between reason (or understanding) and love (or will) in Bembo's description of the progress of the soul to God, we are already familiar with. The emphasis upon reason's relation to love in terms of the courtier and his lady is equally apparent in the fourth book of the *Courtier*.

First of all, the true courtier is "l'amante razionale." When he kisses his lady, it is "non per moversi a desiderio alcuno dionesto," but rather to "open up" a passage for their souls:

> e un aprir l'adito alle anime.

It is indeed for this reason that "the divinely enamoured Plato says that in his kissing his soul came to his lips that it might go forth from the body":

> e pero il divinamente inamorato
> Platone dice che basciando vennegli
> l'anima ai labri per uscir del corpo.[9]

This is the sort of kiss permitted the "Platonic" lover, and it is the utmost physical favor that he may either solicit or receive—if his love and her "honor" are to retain the character of true love and honor. The ideal is fundamentally that of "the marriage of true minds"; the lady refines and inspires the gentleman, and he is her respectful, if witty "servant."

Castiglione entrusts the exposition of this "courtier's religion" to Bembo, its arch-priest, and many of the comments of his other characters suggest that he is fully aware of the openness of the thesis to ridicule. In the *Courtier*, the tone remains highly plausible; this relationship between courtier and lady, if basically artificial, is at least invested with a combination of gallantry and dignity. Although at times it seems only a game in *savoir faire*, there is a seriously idealistic undercurrent which bears the accent of sincerity.

Much the same might be said of the variant but derivative versions of Parlamente (in Marguerite's *Heptameron*), of Spenser, and of Sidney. Yet even with Bembo, there are times when gallantry and the "human" aspects of love seem to supersede the "rational" and less "human" ideal; in the cases of Marguerite and Sidney and Spenser, one can often observe a definite deviation from the consideration of love under the guidance of reason to the direct opposition of love to reason.

With Marguerite, of course, it is less a deviation than a consistent tendency. We have seen how little sympathy she had with the "cause of reason" in general, and how insignificant (if not non-existent) a role it played in her account of the progress of the soul. We have also followed her later tendency to dwell upon love as the exclusive power and meaning of the world and of life—with her evident interest in the "Libertins Spirituels." Among the selections in the *Dernières Poésies* is one which contains a definitive and perhaps defiant statement that love (rather than reason) is the distinguishing mark of man:

> Amour, le vray moyen
> Que l' homme est homme et sans lequel n'est rien. . . .[10]

Throughout the *Hymnes* (and more especially the "Heavenly" ones) Spenser's ideal of love is the true Platonic one of a gradually deepening process of understanding whereby each successive object of love is a higher and worthier one:

> Such is the powre of that sweet passion,
> That it all sordid basenesse doth expell,
> And the refynd mind doth newly fashion
> Unto a fairer forme, which now doth dwell
> In his high thought. . . .[11]

Yet it is "that sweet passion" that has "the powre" to "expell . . . all sordid basenesse" and to "refyne" the "mind." And earlier in the same poem, he has granted an absolute sovereignty to Love which may have been one of the causes of his later apologetic uneasiness over this "Hymne." For he has apostrophized Love as

> GREAT GOD OF MIGHT, that reignest in the mynd,
> And all the bodie to thy hest dost frame. . . .[12]

Here is not only sedition in the soul, but in the whole man.

Again, in the prologue to the fourth book of the *Faerie Queene*, he defends a purely earthly ideal of love, answering those who have reproved him for treating of it so extensively. They ought not, he declares, a

> . . . naturall affection faultlesse blame
> For fault of few that have abused the same.
> For it of honor and all vertue is
> The roote, and brings forth glorious floures of fame.

Moreover, he defies "these Stoicke censours"—implicitly opposing love to reason. For support he calls upon Plato,

> the father of Philosophie,
> Which to his *Critias*, shaded oft from sunne,
> Of love full manie lessons did apply,
> The which these Stoicke censours cannot well deny.[13]

It may be objected, however, that here Spenser is attacking that extreme doctrinal Stoic (and Cynic) stand—the "annihilation" of the passions by reason—rather than specifically preferring Love to Reason as helmsman of the soul and life. This interpretation is tenable, particularly since he invokes Plato in this cause. Yet there is certainly sufficient evidence scattered through the *Faerie Queene* to show that Spenser was not always able to wed even "true" love to reason.

In the writings of the man whom Spenser called "the president of Noblesse and of chivalree"[14] there is indication of a much more violent struggle between an ethical code which placed Reason first and one which acknowledged the primacy of Love. Sidney's description of the "court of Helen, Queene of Corinth," in the second book of the *Arcadia*, is perhaps his most serene picture of the wedding of the two ideals. "So as it seemed," he writes, "that court, to have beene the mariage place of Love and Vertue":

> For never (I thinke) was there any woman, that with more unmoveable determination gave her self to the councell of Love . . . & yet nether her wisedome doubted of, nor honour blemished.[15]

So too in the "Love divining dreame of Amphialus," the ideals of Diana and Venus (significant rivals) finally are merged in one woman, Philoclea. Diana has urged,

> Let us a perfect peace between us two resolve:
> Which lest the ruinous want of government dissolve;
> Let one the Princesse be, to her the other yeeld:
> For vaine equalitie is but contentious field.[16]

But Sidney cannot desert the "contentious field"; he thought and lived, as he died, on it. He allows the "vaine equalitie" to stand in Philoclea, certainly with the implication that he cannot forsake either Diana or Venus totally. And indeed, although both Philoclea and Pamela are all "virtue" and "chastity" and "reason" in their "set piece" speeches, love unguided by reason is evident enough both in their actions and in their private conversations.

Indeed, one might say not unjustly that the *Arcadia's* leit-motif is "the sudden occasion called Love, & that never staid to aske Reasons leave. . . ."[17] It is the central subject of that early dialogue between Musidorus and Pyrocles. Musidorus urges:

> Remember (for I know you know it) that if we wil be men, the reasonable parte of our soule, is to have absolute commandement. . . .[18]

The argument is an extended one, but Musidorus does not win his point. Pyrocles' final answer is:

> Have you all the reason of the world, and with me remaine all the imperfections; yet such as I can no more lay from me, than the crow can be persuaded by the swanne to cast of all his black fethers.[19]

A variant, in short, of "true, and yet true that I must Stella love."

It has been suggested that this is simply a courtly pose on Sidney's part—that he was writing what his fashionable audience demanded of him. Perhaps, but this is just another way of saying that this ethical code which placed love first *was* fashionable. And the theme recurs too often, I think, and in too convincing a tone, to warrant the charge of insincerity. Even Musidorus, we must remember, recants:

> I find indeed, that all is but lip-wisdome, which wants experience. I now (woe is me) do try what love can doo. O *Zelmane*, who will resist it, must have either no witte, or put out his eyes? Can any man resist his creation? Certainly by love we are made, and to love we are made. Beasts onely cannot discerne beauty, and let them be in the role of Beasts that do not honor it. . . .

But Zelmane (Pyrocles' pseudonym) will not let him forget his earlier arguments:

> Remember that love is a passion; and that a worthie mans reason must ever have the masterhood. I recant, I recant (cryed *Musidorus*,) and withall falling downe prostrate, O thou celestiall, or infernall spirit of Love, or what other heavenly or hellish title thou list to have . . .[20]

One could go on and on. Among the "First Eclogues" is that one in which Lalus and Dorus compete in extolling the fairness of their mistresses. Again we encounter a duel between Love and Reason, who advises Love,

> Looke to thy selfe; reach not beyond humanitie:

> Her minde, beames, state farre from thy weake wings
> banished:
> And Love, which lover hurts is inhumanitie.
> Thus Reason said: but she came, Reason vanished. . . .

and Lolus and Dorus chant in unison:

> Such force hath Love above poore Natures power.[21]

Yes, Sidney wrote "Thou blind man's mark" and "Leave me, o love which reachest but to dust," but it is a rather facile and overworked conclusion to predicate a recantation on these grounds. The very violence of the first phrase betrays it; and if one compares the formal beauty of the second with the following lines, it should not be difficult to tell which carries the more passionate conviction:

> No more, my dear, no more these counsels try;
>   Oh, give my passions leave to run their race;
>   Let fortune lay on me her worst disgrace;
>   Let folk *o'ercharged with brain* against me cry;
> Let clouds bedim my face, break in mine eye;
>   Let me no steps but of lost labor trace;
>   Let all the earth with scorn recount my case,
>   But do not will me from my love to fly.
> I do not envy Aristotle's wit,
>   Nor do aspire to Caesar's bleeding fame;
>   Nor aught do care though some above me sit;
> Nor hope nor wish another course to frame,
>   But that which once may win thy cruel heart;
>   *Thou are my wit, and thou my virtue art.*[22]

Here surely is nature protesting against the framework of art within which it is consigned to work; more simply, here is the heart and the honest if wrong-headed human passion crying out against reason and its coercive discipline.

Yet if we see Nature rebelling spontaneously within those who profess the lore of "Platonic" love, we also can find it perfectly frankly confessed, even exalted, in a different courtly tradition. It is a haughtily aristocratic ideal that Ariosto's Rinaldo expounds—and a boldly physical one:

> If like desire, and if an equal flame
>   Moves one and the other . . .

That is sufficient sanction for Rinaldo—a mutual physical attraction, "which to the witless crowd seems rank excess." And he further fulminates against the law which has condemned Geneura to death for following such a course—particularly because it exposes once

more that double standard (so hateful to Montaigne) which says
that women must not do as men.[23]

This frank espousal of the flesh clearly has an aristocratic bias.
Those of the court have privileges which might be misused by the
"witless crowd." If the same qualification is not made by Henry
VIII, history permits us the inference:

> Many one saith that love is ill,
> But those be they which can no skill.
>
> Or else because they may not obtain,
> They would that other should it disdain.
> But love is a thing given by God,
> In that therefore can be none odd;
> But perfect indeed and between two,
> Wherefore then should we eschew?[24]

There were ladies who could have answered him, but they are not
our present concern.

The point of view which reduced the problem to its lowest common denominator—that of desire being sufficient unto itself—is
often presented in direct opposition to the "Platonic" ideal, or to the
dominance of Reason. The voice of Nature, while pleading its own
cause, decries the *dicta* of Art. Thus Tasso speaks of the "sacred
laws of Love and of Nature," and his chorus intones:

> Love, thou alone art a worthy teacher of thyself, and thou art
> expressed only by thyself. . . . Love, let others con the books
> of Socrates. . . .[25]

and Longarine (in the *Heptameron*) disallows the alliance of love
and reason:

> Indeed, that arrogant god disdains all that is common, and de-
> lights only in working miracles every day; such as weakening
> the strong, strengthening the weak, making fools of the wise,
> and knowing persons of the ignorant, favoring the passions,
> destroying reason, and in a word, turning everything topsy-
> turvy.[26]

George Turberville demands outright:

> Shall reason rule where reason hath no right
> Nor never had? Shall Cupid lose his lands?
> His claim? his crown? his kingdom? name of might?
> And yield himself to be in reason's bands?
> No, friend, thy ring doth will me thus in vain.
> *Reason and love have ever yet been twain.*
> They are by kind of such contrary mould

> As one mislikes the other's lewd device;
> What reason wills, Cupido never would;
> *Love never yet thought reason to be wise.*
> To Cupid I my homage erst have done,
> Let reason rule the hearts that she hath won.[27]

Fulke Greville asks,

> Why how now Reason, are you amazed?
> Is worth in Beauty, shrin'd up to be lothed?
> Shall Natures riches by your selfe be razed?

and chides Reason, who prides herself on *her* natural origin, inquiring,

> In what but these can you be finely clothed?[28]

Elsewhere in *Caelica* he asserts,

> Love teares Reasons law in sunder,
> Love, is God, let Reason wonder,

yet concludes

> Here my silly song is ended. . . .[29]

It is high time to distinguish briefly among the creeds of these various champions of Love's supremacy. The aristocratic "Platonic" code of love most prominently endorsed by Bembo and Castiglione is, we have found, in no basic sense antagonistic to the Christian-humanistic ethical program. Rather, it is essentially the courtly complement to the latter, laying different and less sober emphases, but at one with the great central ethical tradition in its acknowledgment of the claims of reason and virtue and the traditional Christian values—consonant, also, with the traditionalist concepts of limit: moderation, degree, balance, etc.

Among those whom I have quoted as expressing a more absolute allegiance to love, however, we have been dealing with the Romantic temper, with an explicit denial of due limit and moderation. Some of these romanticists suggest, however, that curious blend of romanticism and naturalism that we examined at some length in the discussion of *Antony and Cleopatra*. In all cases, the romanticists express a voluntarism, an individualism, a defiant "upward" aspiration that refuses to set limits to the authority of love.

As usual, when such a Counter-Renaissance group stands to one side of the moderate traditionalists (here the Castiglione "Platonic" school), there is a balancing group of naturalists on the other side. Naturalists—with their "downward" point of view—who direct considerable ridicule at the pretentious "art" of "Platonic" love, in the course of insisting upon reducing "love" to natural appetite.

Ridicule is for them an even more effective weapon than literal invective—and is often linked with a profession of faith in Nature, whether the "Nature" of plain, simple, honest human love, or simply appetite. In some of these passages there is also the sly assumption, or even the blunt assertion, that "Platonic" lovers are "Platonic" in name only.

The court scenes in Marston's *Malcontent* contain many obvious caricatures of "Platonic" love. There is also a very vigorous and ribald old disciple of Nature in Maquerelle, who replies, when asked by Emilia, "How many servants[30] thinkst thou I have, Maquerelle?"

> The more the merrier: 'twas well saide, use your servants as you do your smockes; have many, use one and change often, for thats most sweete and courtlike.[31]

Indeed, Marston seems particularly anxious to ridicule Castiglione and the *Courtier*. One of the Venetian courtiers (and an especially foppish and ridiculous one) in *Antonio and Mellida* is named Castilio;[32] and when Malevole (in the *Malcontent*) has finished playing a rather crude Hamlet to Bilioso's Osric, in parting he calls Bilioso "my deare Castilio." That Marston has the Nature-Art combination on his mind is suggested by Malevole's description of Equato in the preceding scene:

> So excellent a Scholler by Art . . .
> So ridiculous a foole by Nature. . . .[33]

Marston's satirical depiction of a court under the dominance of "Platonic" love, as being essentially rotten underneath, is matched by Chapman's picture of the French court in *Bussy D'Ambois*. The Friar feels it his duty to instruct Bussy, Nature's child, on how to proceed in such a world of Art. He tells him that he must act

> . . . with another colour, which my art
> Shall teach you to lay on,

and describes the court as

> this our set and cunning world of love.

Bussy, however, has ample confidence in the capacity of natural cunning, or instinct, to bear its part:

> Give me the colour, my most honour'd Father,
> And trust my cunning then to lay it on.[34]

In the second scene of the play, the Duchess of Guise turns a

cynical parody on the Neoplatonic "ladder of love," describing the
lover's progress from (1) a common lady, or knight's wife, to (2)
a lord's wife, to (3) a countess, to (4) a duchess, "and then turn
the ladder."[35]

Again, Thomas Nashe has Jack Wilton sum up his master's, Surrey's, wooing of the magnifico's wife as a state of being "more in
love with his owne curious forming of fancie than her face." We
can dispense with Jack's full version of the poem which Surrey is
supposed to have written. Suffice it to say that, after a very non-
Platonic flavor indeed, it ends abruptly with this couplet:

> Into heavens ioyes none can profoundly see,
> Except that first they meditate on thee.[36]

T. S. Eliot's sudden shift from Apeneck Sweeney and "Rachel née
Rabinovitch" to his last lyric stanza about Agamemnon's death[37] is
not more startling—or more carefully planned. For Jack continues,

> Sadly and verily, if my master sayde true, I shoulde if I were
> a wench make many men quickly immortall. What ist, what
> ist for a maide fayre and fresh to spend a little lip-salve on an
> hungrie lover. My master beate the bush and kept a coyle
> and a prating, but I caught the birde, simplicitie and plain-
> nesse shall carrie it away in another world.[38]

"Simplicitie and plainnesse shall carrie it away" in this world,
most of these critics of "Platonic" love maintain.

> "I believe," said Parlamente, "that no one ever perfectly loved
> God who did not perfectly love some of his creatures in this
> world."

> "And what do you call loving perfectly?" said Saffredent. "Do
> you believe that those enamoured cataleptics who worship
> ladies at a hundred paces' distance, without daring to speak
> out, love perfectly?"[39]

Indeed, almost every one of the interludes between Marguerite's
tales contains a discussion on some aspect of love, or honor, or both.
And many of these align Nature, whether in terms of physical love,
or simplicity, or experience, against the Art of "Platonic" love.

> "In good faith, Dagoucin," said Simontault, "I do not believe
> you have ever been really in love. Had you known what it is
> to be so, like other men, you would not now be picturing to
> us Plato's Republic, founded on fine phrases, and on little or
> no experience."[40]

Parlamente is clearly the "porte-parole" of Marguerite; Marguerite herself was certainly a sincere "Platonist," but unless she let Des Périers or another courtier write some of these dialogues for her, she permits the anti-"Platonic" characters an extraordinary latitude of telling ridicule.

> "I thought you were quite a different sort of man," said Geburon, "and imagined that virtue was more agreeable to you than pleasure."
>
> "Why," said Saffredent, "is there any greater virtue than to love in the way God has ordained? To me it seems much better to love a woman as a woman, than to make her one's idol, as many do. For my part, I am convinced that it is better to use than to abuse."[41]

Such, for that matter, was even the opinion of one of the characters in Castiglione's own book—"Maister Morello," a plain man whose faith was also in use and in Nature.

> Here maister Morello. The engendring (quoth he) of beautie in beautie aright, were the engendring of a beautifull childe in a beautifull woman, and I woulde thinke it a more manifest token a great deale that shee loved her lover, if she pleased him with this, than with the sweetnesse of language that you speake of. . . .[42]

The most scurrilous and cynical of all the satires on Castiglione's ideal society is Aretino's *La Cortigiana*. The story of how Messer Maco is groomed to become a courtier is as complete a travesty of Castiglione's course of training as could be devised.

But the high (or low) point of cynicism is not reached until Parabolano "makes peace all around" in Act V. Several of his injunctions to the other characters are distortions of some phase of the Law of Nature, or distinctly personal applications of the "follow your bent" philosophy. Thus he himself pardons Alvigia, the brothel keeper, because she was only following her profession! Rosso must be forgiven because he had simply acted with the "astuteness" of the Greek that he was. Hence Valerio must pardon Rosso, for he must admit that Rosso had been exercising his "genius." And (shades of Machiavelli!) the fisherman must be contented with having been swindled, since he had shown himself so little of a Florentine in permitting himself to be duped.[43]

The advice most pertinent to our immediate subject is that given by Parabolano to the baker. The baker must, he says, take back and forgive his wife, for all wives today are whores, and looked upon as more chaste then they are.[44]

"Tell love it is but lust," wrote Ralegh—and Aretino had done so, effectively. We have finished the course with Aretino and his Elizabethan successors, come all the way with the Renaissance courtly tradition of love, from the highly intricate and rational art which it was to Bembo and Castiglione and their followers, to its ultimate deflowering at the hands of the naturalistic satirists of the Counter-Renaissance.

Yet the naturalists were also capable of affirmation on the subject, although an affirmation of a very different sort from Bembo's or Castiglione's—that of Nature as opposed to that of Art, of naturalism as opposed to "Platonism." "Farewell, Bembo and Equicola," calls Montaigne gaily; and if Hircan's question "Do you know that nature is a frisky jade?"[45] is simply a vulgar euphemism for Ralegh's line, the statement which the Lord of Montaigne makes (I would remind you that he was a lord) is not.

He has been discussing (to the horror of his audience, he suspects and hopes) virility and sexual potency. He says,

> Each of my pieces are equally mine, one as another: and *no other doth more properly make me a man than this.*

It is a sentiment whose supporters have probably numbered among the millions, yet comparatively few of them have written essays about it. He goes on,

> The wisedome and reach of my lesson is all in truth, in liberty, in essence: disdaining in the catalogue of my true duties, *these easie, faint, ordinary, and provinciall rules.* All naturall; constant and generall; whereof *civility and ceremonie* are daughters, but bastards. . . . For there is danger that we devise new offices, to excuse our negligence toward naturall offices, and to confound them.[46]

This, at last, is a worthy opponent for the Count Baldassare Castiglione; for although he speaks bluntly, he does not speak scurrilously. He presents the case for Nature with as much dignity, if not as much grace, as his noble adversary does the one for Art. A man (or a true courtier), to Castiglione, is one who acts according to reason and *grazia*, and fulfills his duties to his king, his lady and himself. A man, to Montaigne, is a sexually potent male, who acts according to nature and instinct, and fulfills very different "true duties" to Nature, his ladies and himself. For Castiglione, the rules of living are laid out by Art—in fact, he has had a hand in their making himself. For Montaigne, the rules of living are set down in

Nature's "catalogue"; he has nothing but scorn for "these easie, faint, ordinary and provinciall rules" of Reason and Art. For Castiglione, civility and ceremony are inherent in *noblesse oblige*—at the very core of living. For Montaigne, they are indeed "daughters" of Nature's duties, but "bastards. . . ."

"For there is danger that we devise new offices, to excuse our negligence toward naturall offices, and to confound them." What Montaigne is saying would not apply to Castiglione himself; we may even be confident that he would have realized that. But many a follower in the "Platonic" band was only "a carpet champion for a wanton dame"; most of the satire directed at them had some justification.

Yet for Montaigne it is not simply impotence or effeminacy which causes us to neglect "naturall offices"; it is mostly *shame*. The fundamental dignity of his position emerges when it becomes clear that it is furtiveness and slyness and shame about the natural that he is fighting. For him the unnatural "new offices" that we have built up are, most of all, caused by this perverted sense of shame. So

> each one avoideth to see a man borne, but all run hastily to see him dye. To destroy him we seeke a spacious field and a full light, but to construct him we hide our selves in some darke corner and worke as close as we may.

And, after other parallel examples, he blazes out,

> What monstrous beast is this that makes himselfe a horror to himselfe, whom his delights displease, who tyes himself unto misfortune.[47]

Not long after, his partial disciple, Pierre Charron, was to write in his famous *De l'Amour Charnel:*

> On the one hand nature pushes us violently to this action. . . . [Yet] we call it shameful, and the parts which are used shameful. But why shameful, since so natural, and (kept within limits) so proper, legitimate, necessary, and since the beasts are exempt from this shame? . . . The action is not at all in itself and by nature shameful; it is truly natural, and not shameful—witness the beasts. What am I saying, the beasts! Human nature, says Theology, maintaining itself in its original state, would not have felt any shame in it. . . .
>
> This action then, taken simply and in itself, is neither at all shameful nor vicious, since natural and corporal. . . .[48]

I quote this passage at length, because in it the naturalist points

of view on love and honor meet. Shame is Charron's word—"honte"
—but Honor is Tasso's—"onor"—and we shall see that the two concepts are related. Before the reign of "Honor," Tasso says, was the
Golden Age, happy not simply because naturally abundant and
kindly and joyous and peaceful—

> Ma sol perchè quel vano
> Nome senza soggeto,
> Quell'idolo d'errori, idol d'inganno,
> Quel che dal volgo in sano
> Onor poscia fu detto,
> (Che di nostra natura 'l feo tiranno)
> Non michiava il suo affanno
> Fra la liete dolcezze
> Dell' amoroso gregge;
> Nè fu sua dura legge
> Note a quell'alme in libertate avvezzo:
> Ma legge aurea e felice,
> Che Natura scolpì *Sei piace, ei lice.*[49]

(But only because that empty name without meaning, that
idol of error, idol of falsehood, which hath since been called
by senseless folk, "Honour" (which they made the tyrant of
our nature), did not with its anxieties suffuse the gay pleasures
of the amorous crowd, nor was its hard law known to those
spirits steeped in liberty; but a law golden and happy which
Nature grav'd, "Whate'er pleases is allowed.")[50]

He blames "Honor" specifically for the development of shame and
prudish restraint:

Thou, first, Honour, veiled the fountains of delight, denying
the wave to the amorous thirst, thou taughtest fair eyes to
restrain themselves and to keep their beauty secret from
others. Thou didst gather in a net the locks tossed to the
breeze, thou didst make sweet acts *wanton, shy, ashamed,* thou
gavest to speech a curb, to steps an *art.* It is thy work alone,
Honour, that what was erst a gift of Love is now a theft.[51]

"Opra è tua sola, Onore, Che furto sia quell che fu don d'Amore."
It is the same story as that which Montaigne and Charron have to
tell—but stamped with the courtly idiom of Tasso's environment.

Yet another version is that of the young John Donne:

> But since this title honour hath been us'd,
> Our weake credulity hath been abus'd;
> The golden laws of nature are repeald,

> Which our first Fathers in such reverence held;
> Our liberty's revers'd, our Charter's gone,
> And we're made servants to opinion,
> A monster in no certain shape attir'd,
> And whose originall is much desir'd,
> Formlesse at first, but growing on it fashions,
> And doth prescribe manners and laws to nations.[52]

The story of the Fall (and the symbol of the fig leaf) provides an almost inaudible counterpoint to this essentially non-theological theme of the naturalists. Together with the emphasis on shame, it is stressed that the code of art, of Honor, has ended "the gay pleasures of the amorous crowd," and made known "its hard law . . . to those spirits steeped in liberty."

It is a parallel, again, to Betussi's "Nature has made us free, but reason has placed us under a law, that is, under her own restraint." The Art of Honor is the counterpart in the aristocratic ethical tradition deriving from the new "Platonists," against which the "libertines" rebel, to the Art of Reason in the general humanistic tradition, against which all naturalists rebel. And not only is Honor's tyranny responsible for shame, "Honor" is really only an euphemism for guile, hypocrisy, deceitfulness:

> "Put that out of your head," said Saffredent, "and learn what was the origin of that phrase *honor*, which prudes make such a fuss about. Perhaps those who talk so much about it do not know what it means. In the time when men were not over-crafty—the golden age, if you will—love was so frank, simple and strong, that no one knew what it was to dissemble, and he who loved most was the most esteemed. But malignity, avarice, and sin, having taken possession of men's hearts, drove out from them God and love, and put there, instead of them, self-love, hypocrisy, and feigning. The ladies seeing that they had not the virtue of true and genuine love, and that hypocrisy was very odious amongst mankind, gave it the name of honor. Those, then, who could not compass that true love, said that they were forbidden by honor. This practice they erected into so cruel a law, that even those of their sex who love perfectly dissemble, and think that this virtue is a vice. . . ."[53]

"Many one saith that love is ill," writes Henry VIII bluntly, "but those be they which can no skill."

The two camps, that of the naturalists' and that of "Honor," are at war throughout the *Heptameron*.

"The best thing," said Simontault, "is, that everyone should follow the bent of his nature, and love or not, as he pleases, but always without dissimulation."

"Would to God," exclaimed Saffredent, "that the observance of this law were as productive of honor as it would be of pleasure!"[54]

It is time for a recapitulation. "True Honour," for humanistic orthodoxy, "is the report of a good and vertuous Action, issuing from the Conscience into the Discovery of the People with whom we live. . . ."[55] In short, "Honour," is the deserved reputation accompanying a virtuous action, and is dependent upon "Conscience." It is *not*, however, to be the director of our lives and actions: "the luster of Honour" must "dazle not our Reason,"[56] for the guiding principle is Reason. Hence the humanist ideal of Honor is, like the humanist ideal of Love, supplementary to that of Reason.[57]

Yet one primarily aristocratic code, probably not new in the Renaissance,[58] lays almost exclusive stress on Honor. Honor becomes not only "the report" of virtue, but a set standard by which one achieves virtue. Hence Honor replaces Reason. So the widow in the sixteenth tale of the *Heptameron* tells Bonnivet,

> It is true that honor, which has always been *the ruling principle of my conduct,* would not suffer love to make me do anything which might blemish my reputation.[59]

This code, which puts Honor first, can, of course, be merged harmoniously with the system of "Platonic" love. Dagoucin, for example, is scrupulously loyal to such a concept of honor; at the same time he is the "Platonic" lover *par excellence,* "faithful and loving to perfection."[60]

Finally, there is even a tendency to think of "honor" as an innate quality—similar to the "natural reason" of the humanists. Such, we have seen, is Guarini's concept—in direct contrast to Tasso's position on honor—and it is upon this principle that Gargantua establishes the rules of the famous Abbey of Thélème.

At first it seems that the Thelemites are to be permitted a life analogous to that led in the naturalists' Golden Age. For

> all their life was spent not in laws, statutes, or rules, but according to their own free will and pleasure. They rose out of their beds when they thought good; they did eat, drink, labour, sleep, when they had a mind to it, and were disposed for it. None did awake them, none did offer to constrain them to eat, drink, nor to do any other thing; for so had Gargantua estab-

lished it. In all their rule and strictest tie of their order there was but this one clause to be observed,

DO WHAT THOU WILT.[61]

It would seem, then, certainly, that Rabelais' group is composed of "spirits steeped in liberty." But he has not yet done:

> Because men *that are free, well-born, well-bred,* and conversant in honest companies, have naturally an *instinct* and spur that prompteth them into virtuous actions, and withdraws them from vice, which is called *honour.*[62]

It it indeed an *instinct* which usurps the function of natural reason, and prompts men to virtue. But it must not be confused with the *instinct* of the naturalists or libertines, which does not prompt men to virtue at all, but to pleasure. This instinct is just as much an inner check or law to one's lusts as is the humanists' natural reason —but its name is Honor. The last and most basic prerogative of *reason* is taken from it, and handed to *honor.*

Finally, it must be noted that this too is an exclusively aristocratic code. It is for men (and ladies, the following passage clearly shows) "that are free, well-born, well-bred, and conversant in honest companies." They (and they alone, by implication) possess that "instinct and spur . . . called honour."

And here, of course, Rabelais' debt becomes apparent—if not specifically to the society portrayed by Castiglione, at least to the ideal for which he was the spokesman.[63] For Rabelais' description is almost exactly the equivalent of that combination of Nature and Art—the *trained instinct* required by Castiglione.

To summarize, then: the ethical code of Honor is fundamentally a courtly one, which raises honor from its subordinate position for the humanists (that of meaning a deservedly virtuous reputation) to the highest seat of all—that reserved by traditional orthodoxy for reason. Honor becomes "the ruling principle of . . . conduct," instead of reason; it replaces reason as the guide to virtue; and it becomes the natural "spur" that leads man away from vice—usurping natural reason's prerogative.

The parallel to the three general positions on Love is immediately apparent. For the moment, let us postpone a close consideration of the romanticist position that exalts Honor excessively or even exclusively—and move to the other side of that middle position which is perfectly compatible with the humanistic view, in fact its aristocratic counterpart. To the other side—and the naturalists. To them, as passages from Tasso and the *Heptameron* have demonstrated, the worship of honor is as artificial and arbitrary a concoction of man's rational Art as is the worship of reason. The naturalists attack practically all the aspects and variants of the code of Honor; and for the sake of clarity, we must take up these attacks according to their particular targets—examine the revolt of Nature, first against one specific aspect of "Honor," and then against another.

The most fundamental division of both favorable and unfavorable considerations of Honor as an ethical principle is that which separates this principle's application to women from that to men. The naturalists blame women for naming hypocrisy "honor," and the major concern of both sides in dealing with women's "honor" is of course in terms of the barrier she raises against "free love."

This is all pretense, the naturalists claim—hypocrisy and guile. What "the ladies" are really thinking of, when they refuse their favors to honest men, is their reputations. That is all "honor" means to them; it has no connection with virtue or conscience—and if one of them feels sure that her "fair name" will not suffer, all her scruples disappear. "Art" of the worst sort.

Marguerite of Navarre's tale about the lady named Jambicque is a case in point. Bonnivet's widow had held that "honor" was "the ruling principle" of her "conduct,"—but she had added that therefore she had not allowed "love to make me do any thing which might blemish my reputation."[64] Jambicque's "ideal" is identical, and she carries it to a logical, if not particularly admirable, extreme. For she would meet her lover in a dark gallery each night, but she would never permit him to see her or to know who she was. And when by a trick he discovered her identity and accosted her openly, she not only refused to acknowledge what she had done, but displayed so convincing a semblance of outraged chastity that he suffered for his effrontery.[65]

Geburan tells her story, and he says outright that her ideal of honor merely means that she "preferred the world's respect to her own conscience." She was "a woman who was more afraid of offending men than God, her honor, and love."[66] That is to say, her "honor" was in no sense really honor.

Many of the villains and knaves in Elizabethan drama propound the naturalists' interpretation of a woman's "honor." Thus, when Tamara declares,

> Mine honour's in mine own hands, spite of kings,

Monsieur replies scornfully:

> Honour, what's that: your second maidenhead?

> And what is that? a word: the word is gone,
> The thing remains: the rose is pluck'd, the stalk
> Abides; an easy loss where no lack's found.

And he keeps repeating a cynical satiric refrain:

> my honour? husband?
> Honour and husband![67]

Yet this is not simply a villain expounding evil ideas, for Monsieur's point is that Tamara is really refusing his advances because she doesn't like him; and her seduction of Bussy (for that is what is amounts to, although he is not, of course, unwilling) does indicate that her "honor" is not proof against a strong physical attraction.

Indeed, Chapman's attitude toward women in general is such as to make us believe that while he cannot endorse Monsieur's speeches, he can at least derive satisfaction from the opportunity to deride woman's honor. And it is probably significant that the king himself—a "good" character despite the fact that his court is a "set and cunning world of love"—speaks of "the outward patches of our frailty" as riches and honour."[68]

Such theories as Monsieur's about the real nature of woman's honor have been held by some men in all ages, of course; and in saying that the naturalistic point of view satirized a courtly ideal, I have not meant to imply that all the cynical remarks on woman's honor in Elizabethan plays are confined to aristocratic scenes. Applied to "honor" or "conscience," they appear in many different settings. For instance, there is that unpleasant scene in *Volpone* in which Corvino tries to persuade his wife Celia to give herself to Volpone in order that he may be sure of getting the estate. He says, "Respect my venture," and she replies, "Before your honour?"

> Corvino: Honour? tut, a breath;
> There's no such thing, in nature: a meere terme
> Invented to awe fooles.[69]

This is the husband's, the man's honor—in a related context. And when Volpone is importuning Celia, she makes a similar appeal to him. His answer, in turn, advises her what she should make of "conscience." For, when she says,

> I cannot be taken with these sensuall baits,
> If you have conscience—

he replies,

> 'Tis but the beggar's vertue,
> If *thou* hast *wisdome*, heare me. . . .[70]

It is the advice of Cecropia to Pamela in the *Arcadia:* "Be wise, and that wisedome shalbe a God unto thee. . . ."[71] And this advice, of course, is not "pure" naturalism, for there is a note of expediency in it; one might say that the doctrines of the naturalists and of the "Machiavellian" advocates of fitting your ethical code to the temper of your surroundings meet and merge in such counsel.

Indeed, one might even say Machiavellian without the quotation marks, for the already considered contention that Machiavelli's advice was intended only for a public emergency, and was "pirated" for private ethics, does not wholly hold in this context. In the *Mandragola,* the priest Timotheo, in advising Lucrezia to practice adultery that she may have a child, says to her:

> For the sake of your conscience, you must go on the general principle: Where there is a certain good and an uncertain evil, we must not forsake that good for fear of that evil.[72]

This is exactly Machiavelli's advice to "the Prince"; and while we cannot, of course, affirm categorically (in fact, would be inclined to deny) that he endorses statements made by this repulsive character, we at least must admit that he has himself here specifically applied his theory of realistic political ethics to private life. Indeed, the song at the end of Act III goes further, and definitely links the naturalist creed of following one's desire with the Machiavellian justification of deceit practiced for a "good" end:

> So sweet is deceit
> Toward some desired, dear end,
> That everything is stripped of pain,
> And every bitter taste is made sweet.[73]

And in the letter to two friends which closes the *Discourses,* he writes:

> Enjoy therefore that good *or* that evil which you your selves have desired. . . .[74]

Yet it would be difficult to prove that there is any conscious merging of the naturalistic and Machiavellian currents in such speeches as those of Volpone and Cecropia. For the advice to follow "wisdome" is really implicit in Saffredent's (and others') theory that "honor" is only "hypocrisy." Nor, of course, is the honor-hypocrisy equation Machiavellian in origin.

Hence there is no real evidence of any Machiavellianism in such a speech on woman's honor, or "honesty," as that of old Maquerelle's in the *Malcontent:*

Pish, honesty is but an art to seeme so: pray yee whats honesty? whats constancy? but fables fained, odde old fooles chat, devisde by jealous fooles, to wrong our liberty.[75]

Here, again, with beautiful clarity, the essential opposition is invoked. "Honor" vs. "liberty"; Art vs. Nature. . . .

2. THE SYSTEMATIZATION OF HONOR

"Tell honor how it alters," wrote Walter Ralegh in *The Lie,* with at least one kind of pertinence which may not have been intentional. For just as a new importance and a modified meaning came to be attached to the "honor" of a woman in the Renaissance, so it did to the "honor" of a man. The former trend may be traced with some exactitude to the ideal of "una certa mediocrità difficile" of the courtier's lady—if not specifically to the ladies Elizabetta Gonzaga and Emilia Pia in Castiglione's book, at least certainly to the ideal they represent, one not significantly altered by Castiglione's imitators.

The outstanding courtly code of masculine honor in the Renaissance is not so easy to trace. There are, of course, the general outlines of the code of a Renaissance gentleman in the *Courtier* and in Rabelais' liberal rules (applicable to both ladies and gentlemen) for the inhabitants of Thélème. There are the numerous and largely consistent orthodox Renaissance tracts on the "specialty of rule," the typical books "de Regimine Principium"—notable among them Erasmus' *Education of a Christian Prince* and Sir Thomas Elyot's *The Boke of the Governour*—which stem from a classical and medieval tradition. But the latter, really books of advice to princes, can only in the most general sense be considered as dealing with *honor;* their principal emphasis is laid upon how a good king becomes a good king, and what he does to remain one—with a sideglance at those sempiternal laws of natural justice and order and degree which make up the "true commonweale." One may say quite fairly that the political ethics set forth in them are primarily concerned with virtue and reason—by which the good king, the good citizens (each in his degree), and the good commonwealth are guided.

Again, of course, there are vestigial remains of the Age of Chivalry apparent, in modified forms, in almost any treatise which deals with the behavior of the gentleman or courtier. But when all this has been said, the nearest thing to an actual ethical system founded upon a concept of honor, within the confines just described, is to be found in Castiglione's *Courtier*. There the ideal of the "trained instinct" and "the master of the ready word" sets forth in a general way such a system. Such a courtier will above all be a good adviser to his prince; he will be a devoted "lover" to his lady (and a devout one, for herein lies his "religion of beauty"); he will be a soldier of parts. In short, it is a versatile ideal.

Yet not at all one subversive to "reason." The specialized Art of the courtier fits into the general Art of the state at large—a state founded upon the rational laws of nature, and according to natural justice. The love of true honor will never conflict with the exercise of reason or with the pursuit of the cardinal virtues.[76]

So far, so good. But there arose in the Renaissance a new and rather specialized code of honor, stemming on the one hand from an intellectual tradition, on the other from a popular one. And this code held within it the seeds of still another revolt against traditional Christian-humanistic values.

It would be difficult to say just where it began. But, although there are traces of it in the *Orlando Furioso*, its first notable and extended exposition is to be found in the allegory which Tasso attached a year after publication—in belated obedience to classical authority—to his *Jerusalem Delivered*. He writes,

> The army compounded of divers princes, and of other Christian soldiers, signifieth Man, compounded of soul and body, and of a soul not simple, but divided into many and diverse powers. Jerusalem the strong city placed in a rough and hilly country, whereunto as to the last end are directed all the enterprises of the faithful army, doth here signify the civil happiness which may come to a Christian Man . . . which is a good very difficult to attain unto, and situated upon the top of the Alpine and wearisome hill of Virtue; and unto this are turned, as unto the last mark, all the actions of the Politic Man.

He now proceeds with a largely orthodox anatomy of the soul:

> Godfrey, which of all the assembly is chosen chieftain, stands for Understanding, and particularly for that understanding, which considereth not the things necessary, but the mutable and which may diversely happen, and those by the will of God. And of princes he is chosen Captain of this enterprise, because Understanding is of God, and of nature made lord over the other virtues of the soul and body, and commands these, one with civil power, the other with royal command.

Having established the rule of reason, he continues:

Rinaldo, Tancredi, and the other princes are in lieu of the other powers of the Soul, and the Body here becomes notified by the soldiers less noble.[77]

The microcosm is established, but he has only begun his use of analogy;

And because that, through the imperfection of human nature and by the deceits of his enemy, Man attains not this felicity without many inward difficulties, and without finding by the way outward impediments, all these are noted unto us by poetical figures.

After dealing with the "outward impediments," he turns to the "inward difficulties":

love, which maketh Tancredi and the other worthies to dote, and disjoins them from Godfrey, and the disdain which enticeth Rinaldo from the enterprise, do signify the conflict and rebellion which the concupiscent and ireful powers do make with the reasonable.[78]

Having established the force of these two powers of the sensitive soul, Tasso continues with illustrations of the other pitfalls on the road to virtue. In turn, completing his exposition of these, he recounts "the inward and outward helps, with which the civil man, overcoming all difficulty, is brought to this desired happiness."[79]

That Tasso's position thus far is that of the middle-path reconciler of reason and faith, of philosophy and religion, is made ultimately clear in the course of this description of man's "helps." For the Hermit "doth show unto us the supernatural knowledge received by God's grace, as the Wise Man doth human wisdom."[80] These two guides are reminiscent of Dante's Beatrice and Vergil.

"It is feigned," Tasso goes on, completing his identification with the middle-path tradition of orthodoxy,

that this Wise Man was by birth a Pagan, but being by the Hermit converted to the true faith, becometh a Christian. . . . Albeit that philosophy be born and nourished amongst the Gentiles in Egypt and Greece, and from thence hath passed over unto us, presumptuous of herself, a miscreant bold and proud above measure: yet of St. Thomas and the other holy doctors she is made the disciple and handmaid of divinity. . . .[81]

At last Tasso turns to the passage which is for our purpose most significant.

Godfrey and Rinaldo being two persons which in our poem do

hold the principal place, it cannot be but pleasing to the reader that I, repeating some of the already spoken things, do particularly lay open the allegorical sense, which under the veil of their actions, lies hidden.

He treats of Godfrey first:

Godfrey, which holdeth the principal place in this story, is no other in the allegory but the Understanding, which is signified in many places of the poem as in that verse,

"By thee the counsel given is, by thee the sceptre ruled."

And more plainly in that other:

"Thy soul is of the camp both mind and life."

And life is added, because in the powers more noble the less noble are contained: therefore Rinaldo, which in Action is in the second degree of honour, ought also to be placed in the Allegory in the answerable degree. But what this power of the mind, holding the second degree of dignity, is, shall be now manifested. *The Ireful Virtue is that, which amongst all the powers of the mind, is less estranged from the nobility of the soul, insomuch that Plato, doubting, seeketh whether it be different from reason or no.*[82]

It is at last apparent that Tasso's "anatomy" is not, after all, identical with the representative orthodox one of the Renaissance, although close to it. For this "Ireful Virtue" which Rinaldo symbolizes, while corresponding to the Renaissance variant of the "irascible power," is clearly held in more esteem by Tasso than the other by the orthodox humanists. But he has given us his authority, and accurately. It will therefore be necessary to make a side-expedition into Plato's *Republic,* if we are to understand clearly what follows:

Must we not acknowledge, I [Socrates] said, that in each of us there are the same principles and habits which there are in the State; and that from the individual they pass into the State?—how else can they come there?[83]

Socrates proceeds to take up "the quality of passion or spirit," "the love of knowledge," and "the love of money," explaining how they are found in states because the individuals of particular nations possess these qualities. He continues:

But the question is not quite so easy when we proceed to ask whether these principles are three or one; whether, that is to say, we *learn* with one part of our nature, *are angry* with another, and with a third part *desire* the satisfaction of our natural appetites; or whether the whole soul comes into play in each sort of action. . . .[84]

He first establishes a clear distinction between the first and the third of these principles, concluding,

Then we may fairly assume that they are two, and that they differ from one another; the one with which a man reasons. we may call *the rational principle* of the soul, the other with which he loves and hungers and feels the flutterings of any other desire, may be termed *the irrational or appetitive*. . . .[85]

His audience having agreed, he goes on,

Then let us finally determine that there are two principles existing in the soul. And what of passion, or spirit? Is it a third, or akin to one of the preceding?

And the reply is, "I should be inclined to say—akin to desire."[86]

But Socrates disproves this, with a story which shows that "anger at times goes to war with desire." "Passion" or "spirit" is nobler than it at first seems to be. He concludes,

passion or spirit appeared at first to be a kind of desire, but now we should say quite the contrary; for in the conflict of the soul spirit is arrayed on the side of the rational principle.[87]

And now "a further question arises," to which Tasso has referred:

Is passion different from reason also, or only a kind of reason; in which latter case, instead of three principles in the soul, there will be only two, the rational and the concupiscent; or rather, as the State was composed of three classes, *traders, auxiliaries, counsellors,* so may there not be in the individual soul a third element which is passion or spirit, and *when not corrupted* by bad education is *the natural auxiliary of reason?*[88]

The analogy is beautifully lucid. The counsellors (or "guardians" of the ruling class) correspond to reason; the auxiliaries (or "soldiers") to passion or spirit; the traders (or "merchants") to desire. And Socrates' hearers assenting, he concludes,

We . . . are fairly agreed that the same principles which exist in the State exist also in the individual, and that they are three in number[89]

—and further, that

the rational principle, which is wise, and has the care of the whole soul . . . [should] rule, and the passionate or spirited principle . . . be the subject and ally. . . .[90]

We may return to Godfrey and Rinaldo with more confidence. Godfrey, or "Understanding," is the "rational principle" of man's soul, the "guardian" or "counsellor" of the "state." Rinaldo, or the "Ireful Virtue," is the subordinate but allied "passionate or spirited principle" of man's soul, the "auxiliary" or soldier of the "state." And we may finally align them in terms of reason and honor if we turn once more to Socrates' account.

> It seems to me that to these three principles [of the soul or the state] three pleasures correspond; also three desires and governing powers. . . . There is one principle with which, as we were saying, a man learns, another with which he is angry; the third . . . is denoted by the general term "appetitive". . . . We . . . might truly and intelligibly describe this part of the soul as loving gain or money. . . . Again, *is not the passionate element wholly set on ruling and conquering and getting fame?* . . . Suppose we call it the contentious or ambitious—
> On the other hand, every one sees that the principle of knowledge is wholly directed to the truth. . . . "Lover of wisdom," "lover of knowledge," are titles which we may fitly apply to that part of the soul? . . . One principle prevails in the souls of one class of men, another in others, as may happen?
> Then we may begin by assuming that there are three classes of men—lovers of wisdom, *lovers of honour,* lovers of gain?[91]

We should expect, then, to find in Godfrey a "lover of wisdom," in Rinaldo a "a lover of honour."

This is exactly the case. Although Tasso does not make this precise identification in his allegorical exposition, it is evident in several scenes in the poem proper. In the discussion as to who shall lead the group of knights which is to help Armida, Eustace addresses Rinaldo as

> Thou star of knighthood, flower of chivalry.

and speaks of "the spreading wings" of his "immortal fame." Rinaldo is stirred by this tribute:

> . . . the knight's sweet words and praises soft
> *To his due honour did him fitly call,*
> And made his heart rejoice, for well he knew,
> Though much he praised him, all his words were true.[92]

Again, when, near the end of the poem, Rinaldo apologizes to Godfrey for his conduct in the Gernando affair, he is careful to explain that what he is sorry about is that he has offended Godfrey, not that he has killed Gernando—for *that* had been necessary to keep his honor immaculate:

"My soveraign lord," Rinaldo meekly said,
"To venge my wrongs against Gernando proud
My honour's care provoked my wrath unstayed;
But that I you displeased, my chieftain good,
My thought yet grieve, my heart is still dismayed. . . ."[93]

Here Tasso quite clearly identifies the ideal of "honor" with
"wrath" (or the "ireful power"). And in the body of the allegory,
he makes all those other identifications of Socrates. For instance,
he compares the "Ireful Virtue" to the soldier-auxiliary:

And such it is in the mind, as the chieftain in an assembly of
soldiers; for as of these the office is to obey their princes, which
do give directions and commandments to fight against their
enemies; so is it the duty of the ireful, warlike, and soveraign
part of the mind, to be armed with reason against concupiscence, and with that vehemency and fierceness which is proper
unto it, to resist and drive away whatsoever impediment to
felicity.[94]

The comparison is a little confused, and what confusion there is,
is all to the advantage of the Ireful Virtue. For whereas the soldiers, including their chieftain, obey their princes, the ireful part of
the mind is called "soveraign" and merely arms itself with reason.

Yet if the details are cloudy, Tasso goes on to follow Plato dutifully. For, he says, when the Ireful Virtue

doth not obey reason, but suffers itself to be carried of her own
violence, it falleth out, that it fighteth not against concupiscence but by concupiscence, like a dog that biteth, not the
thieves, but the cattle committed to his keeping.

Moreover,

this violent, fierce, and unbridled fury, as it cannot be fully
noted by one man of war, is nevertheless principally signified
by Rinaldo, where it is said of him, that being

"A right warlike knight
Did scorn by reason's rule to fight."

And he notes particular occasions on which Rinaldo represents
"anger not governed by reason," while when "he disenchanteth
the wood, entereth the city, breaketh the enemy's array," he is
"anger directed by reason."[95]

He next deals with Rinaldo's "return and reconciliation to Godfrey," which he says "noteth obedience, causing the ireful virtue to
yield to the reasonable." He points out that "in these reconciliations
two things are signified"—and these are important—

> first, Godfrey, with civil moderation, is acknowledged to be
> superior to Rinaldo, teaching us that reason commandeth anger,
> *not imperiously, but courteously and civilly. . . .*[96]

Once again, he is careful to make it clear that, although "reason"
is undisputed chief, the secondary virtue of "anger" *is* a virtue—
and worthy of respect.

> Secondly, that as the reasonable part ought not,—for herein
> the Stoics were very much deceived,—to exclude the ireful
> from actions, nor usurp the offices thereof, for this usurpation
> should be against nature and justice, but it ought to make
> her her companion and handmaid, so ought not Godfrey to
> attempt the adventure of the wood himself, thereby arrogating
> to himself the other offices belonging to Rinaldo.[97]

In this passage Tasso is, of course, referring to the extreme doctrinal Stoic position that all the passions are bad, yet it is pertinent
to note that most of the writers who speak of the Stoics in these
terms are those who show some affiliation with one of the courtly
ethical traditions. It was in defense of Love that Spenser was to
write:

> The which those Stoicke censours cannot well deny.

Still, Tasso does in this passage affirm his allegiance to the temperate middle-path tradition, which he invokes as "nature and
justice." And in his listing of the "offices belonging to Rinaldo" or
to the "ireful power," he is completely at one with orthodoxy's interpretation of the functions of the irascible power. For it is "the
moving power by which the soul . . . effects its purposes";[98] to
this extent, its superiority to the concupiscible power (which, stirred
by the senses, merely begins the whole process of reaction and
election) is as clear in orthodox anatomies as in Socrates' or Tasso's
expositions.

"Finally," declares Tasso, "to come to the conclusion,"

> the Army wherein Rinaldo and the other worthies by the grace
> of God and advice of Man, are returned to their Chieftain, sig-
> nifieth Man brought again into the state of natural justice and
> heavenly obedience: where the superior powers do command,
> as they ought, and the inferior do obey, as they should. Then
> the wood is easily disenchanted, the city vanquished, the en-
> emy's army discomfited; that is, all external impediments being
> easily overcome, man attaineth the politic happiness.[99]

Yet, again, when he brings man "into the state of natural justice
and heavenly obedience," it is the "superior *powers*" that "do com-

mand, as they ought." Thereby, "man attaineth the politic happiness." And to Tasso, this is the next highest aim "of a Christian man" to that final one of "everlasting felicity."

Orthodox enough, at first glance. Yet not quite—not even quite faithful to Plato and Socrates. For Socrates' version reads:

> And do you not say that he is temperate who keeps these same elements in friendly harmony, in whom the *one ruling* principle of reason, and the *two subject* ones of spirit and desire are equally agreed that reason ought to rule, and do not rebel?
>
> Certainly, he said, that is the true account of temperance, *whether in the State or individual.*[100]

And this is exactly the nature of the division in the orthodox Christian-humanist anatomies: "the one ruling principle of reason," and the "two subject" powers of the sensitive soul—the irascible and the concupiscible. To be sure, the rules of the "very and true commonweale" demand order and degree; the "superior powers" should indeed command the "inferior." But "degree" postulates only one supreme power, only "one ruling principle": the rest is a graded scale, from courtier to artisan and farmer.

And this is not merely quibbling. For although Tasso frequently affirms the final authority of reason, these careless allusions in the plural keep sliding in. They may be justified in terms of "passion" being an ally of "reason" against "desire," yet the tone and the wording are not quite Plato's—as the last quotation from the *Republic* shows. It is possible, again, that the absence of any specific treatment of the "will" in Tasso's account may mean that he delegates its (relative) dignity and authority to his "Ireful Virtue." Or he may be remembering Aristotle's version:

> There remains then a kind of active life of the Rational Nature: and of this Nature there are *two parts* denominated Rational, the one as being obedient to Reason, the other as having and as exercising it.[101]

Be that as it may, both in Tasso's occasional, almost imperceptible, advancing of the importance and dignity of the Ireful Virtue, and in his frequent allusions throughout the poem to "wrath" and "honour," a new ethical code—later to lay almost exclusive stress upon honor—is emergent. Tasso never goes the whole way, never explicitly rejects the final authority of reason, but he does elevate honor and wrath to a new eminence.

The positions of orthodox eclectic humanists, from Cicero to Du Vair, on the subject of anger or wrath or the irascible part of the soul, vary somewhat. Yet it is mostly a question of variation in terms of how severely and rigidly they envision reason's government. None of them anywhere gives to anger a worth equivalent to that which Tasso accords it.

Du Vair expresses his distrust of anger, even when it is correcting a vice:

> Reason (which should govern) will admit no such officers as execute at their own license without her authority: to her violence is improper, who will (like Nature) do all by the Compass. . . .

And he declares categorically,

> Whilst we are transported, we do nothing to purpose: Reason is of no more use to us in our passions, than wings to a bird that is caught by the feet. . . .[102]

To be sure, Du Vair is more a systematic Stoic than most of the middle-path "reconcilers"; as such, he would oppose apathy or forbearance to violence. Yet an examination of the words of Cicero, of Aquinas, of Erasmus or More or Hooker, of Robert Ashley in *Of Honour*, will reveal not dissimilar positions. Anger or wrath as the instrument by which the soul effects its purposes is one thing; anger which is close to violent rage is another. And none of these men, of course, was concerned with a courtly code of honor.

But Sidney, that "president of Noblesse and of chivalree," was—and in his very careful distinction between honor as rational valor and honor as mere wrath is a clear indication of the growth of a tradition of honor which he sees as a threat to the "authentic" one. (A threat, despite his own frequent tendencies to exalt honor to a perilous eminence.) He describes Prince Anaxius as a representative of this menace:

> No man, that in his owne actions could worse distinguish between Valour and Violence: So proud, as he could not abstain from a *Thraso*-like boasting, and yet (so unluckie a lodging his vertues had gotten) he would never boast more than he would accomplish: falsely accounting an unflexible anger, a couragious constancie: esteeming feare, and astonishment, right causes of admiration, then Love and Honour.[103]

And when Amphialus, accepting Phalantus' challenge, writes

> Prepare therefore your armes to fight, but not your hart to malice; since true valure needes no other whetstone, then desire of honour,[104]

here is another knight whose "vertues had gotten" an "unluckie lodging" clearly advocating a disproportionate devotion to "desire of honour." For "true valure" would make a more modest evaluation of "honour," if it were expressed by the ideal Renaissance knight—whose allegiance to honor would not supersede or be antagonistic to his allegiance to God and reason, his prince or king, his lady.

Incongruously enough, these varying attitudes toward honor are beautifully illustrated by Pantagruel and Friar John. When Pantagruel, for instance, declares,

> Nay, I will engage mine honour, which is the most precious pawn I could have in my possession although I were sole and peaceable dominator over all Europe, Asia, and Africa . . .[105]

we know, both from the context and his character, that "true honour" is to him (if with a somewhat more courtly accent), as to Du Vair,

> the report of a good and vertuous Action, issuing from the Conscience into the Discovery of the People with whom we live. . . .[106]

But when Friar John storms out,

> Is it not better and more honourable to perish in fighting valiantly than to live in disgrace by a cowardly running away?[107]

when he cries,

> Ods-belly, 'tisn't in my nature to lie idle; I mortally hate it. Unless I am doing some heroic feat every foot, I can't sleep one wink o'nights. Damn it, did you then take me along with you for your chaplain, to sing mass and shrive you?—

when he demands,

> What made Hercules such a famous fellow, d'ye think? Nothing but that while he travelled he still made it his business to rid the world of tyrannies, errors, dangers, and drudgeries; he still put to death all robbers, all monsters, all venomous serpents and hurtful creatures. Why then we do not follow his examples, doing as he did in the countries through which we pass?—

and concludes,

> Come, he that would be thought a *gentleman*, let him storm a town; well, then, shall we go?[108]

we have a beautiful illustration of the "Ireful Virtue" concept of honor. Indeed, as the good Friar says, "I am no clericus, those that are such tell me so."[109] And the attitudes toward honor which one might expect from representatives of Plato's tri-partite division of the soul are made complete by Panurge (surely the concupiscent power incarnate), who both reveals his own code and defines Friar John's during the argument about whether or not to land on the Isle of Ganabim:

> Believe me, sir, said Friar John, let's rather land; we will rid the world of that vermin, and inn there for nothing. Old Nick go with thee for me, quoth Panurge. This rash hardbrained devil of a friar fears nothing, but ventures and runs on like a mad devil as he is, and cares not a rush what becomes of the others; as if everyone were a monk, like his friarship. A pox on grinning honour, say I.[110]

If (at least until near the end of the fifth book) Pantagruel is tolerant of Friar John's passionate pursuit of honor, Godfrey is no less so of the knights who wish to aid Armida. For he says to "the worthies," after urging them to refrain from the expedition,

> But if to shun these perils, sought so far,
> May seem disgraceful to the *place you hold;*
>   If grave advice and prudent counsel are
>   *Esteemed detractors from your courage bold:*
> Then know, I none against his will debar,
> Nor what I granted erst I now withhold;
>   But be my empire, *as it ought of right,*
>   Sweet, easy, pleasant, gentle, meek, and light.[111]

He is the good prince, but he is equally—if we accept Tasso's own interpretation—"reason" commanding "anger, not imperiously, but courteously and civilly." Moreover, he acknowledges that for "the place" they "hold," it is possible that his advice may seem inappropriate: reason, while "esteemed," may be a "detractor" from the "courage bold," or ideal of honor, of these knights.

There are two important distinctions here, and in the answer which his brother makes: (1) that just as "grave advice and prudent counsel" are the proper characteristics of the ruler, so "courage bold" is that of the auxiliary-knights—or, as reason is *his* province, so honor is *theirs;* (2) that the pursuit of honor is as appropriate to the young as that of wisdom to the old—the former's virtue being perfect honor, as the latter's is perfect wisdom or reason. This second distinction is analogous to Castiglione's reservation of "Platonic" love for the older man, who is also the counsellor; it is not dissimilar to the whole "first, *humanitas;* then *divinitas*" tradition.

Both distinctions appear with some exactness in Eustace's reply to his brother, Godfrey, with still a third—that between the function of the reasoning power as counsel, and that of the irascible as action:

> My lord, as well it fitteth thee to make
> *These wise delays* and cast these doubts and fears,
> So 'tis our part at first to *undertake;*
> Courage and haste beseems *our might and years;*
> And this proceeding with so grave advice,
> *Wisdom, in you, in us were cowardice.*[112]

Tasso repudiates this attitude in this particular context, but *only* because Eustace's words are a subterfuge, an appeal to honor when he is really motivated by his desire for Armida:

> . . . thus devised the knight,
> To make men think the sun of honour shone
> There where the lamp of Cupid gave the light:
> The rest perceive his guile, and it approve,
> And call that knighthood which was childish love.[113]

All of these three distinctions played some part in the development of a code based on honor, rather than reason—(1) the sanctioning of a greater emphasis upon honor than upon reason for those who are "auxiliaries," rather than "guardians"; (2) the positing of their proper functioning or "vocation" as being tied to an ideal of honor; (3) the conviction that honor is as satisfactory an ideal for youth as wisdom or reason for age. But the first was perhaps the most influential, and it is interesting to note that it is this one which Edmund Spenser emphasizes in his letter to Ralegh, telling of his own allegorical purpose in the *Faerie Queene,* and referring to Tasso's. Whether or not intentionally, Spenser further distorts Tasso's distinction between "auxiliaries" and "guardians."

For, having defined his own purpose as the fashioning of "a gentleman or noble person in vertuous and gentle discipline," he lists the precedents given him by the great poets of the past:

> First Homere, who in the Persons of Agamemnon and Ulysses hath ensampled *a good governour* and *a vertuous man,* the one in his Ilias, the other in his Odysseis: then Virgil, whose like intention was to doe in the person of Aeneas: after him Ariosto comprised them both in his Orlando: and lately Tasso *dissevered* them againe, and formed both parts in two persons, namely that part which they in Philosophy call Ethice, or vertues of a private man, coloured in his Rinaldo: The other named Politice in his Godfredo.[114]

This is, of course, a very imperfect rendering of Tasso's distinction, although a variant whose origin can easily be traced. But then the description of Ariosto's Orlando is almost ludicrously inaccurate, too, and Spenser's next words make it clear why he is trying to press the purposes of these other epic poets into a standard mould —simply to justify and lend prestige to his own procedure.

> By ensample of which excellente Poets, I labour to pourtraict in Arthure, before he was king, *the image of a brave knight*, perfected in the twelve private morall vertues, as Aristotle hath devised, the which is the purpose of these first twelve bookes: which if I finde to be well accepted, I may be perhaps encoraged, to frame the other part of polliticke vertues in his person, after that hee came to be king.[115]

Now this is all very well for Spenser's purposes; the meaning, to a reader of average intelligence, is that Spenser equates with the "vertuous man," Arthur as "a brave knight"; with the "good governour," Arthur as a "king." To the first two, "private morall vertues" are appropriate; to the latter two, "polliticke vertues." And his convenient classifying of Rinaldo and Godfrey makes the same distinction—"Ethice, or vertues of a private man," are "coloured in his Rinaldo: The other named Politice in his Godfredo."

This is not quite what Tasso said, but it is a justifiable interpretation. Yet, what it must have meant to the fashionable aristocratic audience of the *Faerie Queene* was that Rinaldo was a man to model on. And it would be interesting to know just what effect this passage had upon the development of a literary and courtly code of honor. For some cantos of the *Jerusalem Delivered* were already available in translation, and Edward Fairfax completed the task in 1600—four years after the date of Spenser's letter. And—for here is the snare—while Spenser's development of "private vertues" is largely orthodox, Rinaldo's personification of them is not.

It is true that he returns rather meekly to Godfrey's supervision in the eighteenth of the twenty cantos—but throughout the greater part of the poem he has been far more concerned with his "honour's care" which frequently provoked his "wrath unstayed," than with following the guidance of reason. Yet Tasso, too, in the allegory, while pointing out his occasional failures to keep his warlike wrath within bounds, has for the most part approved of him.

There is no need to press the point further, except to make one more distinction. For Tasso, Rinaldo is a knight, the contemporary equivalent of Plato's auxiliary-soldier class. For Spenser, Rinaldo may represent a knight (if considered as a parallel to "Arthure,

before he was king")—but what he certainly and explicitly does
"colour" is the "vertues of a private man." And it is interesting to
see that the growing recognition in Elizabethan literature of a code
of honor which is represented as placing honor above reason, and
wrath above reason, is extended beyond courtly circles. Perhaps it
was inevitable, with the familiar psychological concepts of the
irascible part of the soul as identical with "Passions more powerful,
and more difficult to tame"; with Elizabethan theories of "blood"
and of the four "humours." Yet none of these explains the identification of honor with wrath; none of these can account for the
development of an ethical code based on honor which matches the
progress of the similar one based on love.

For such a development, such a progress, is evident. From honor
the subsidiary ideal, corresponding to passion or spirit as the ally
of reason, there emerges the ideal of honor without regard to reason
—a code which postulates honor as the exclusive virtue of the courtier or knight or gentleman, as reason or wisdom is for the king
or public person. And finally, just as there came those who cried,
"Tell 'love' it is but lust," so there were also those who said, "Tell
'honor' it is but wrath."

The "rebellion of honor" and its relation to wrath is apparent,
for example, in Chapman's *Conspiracy of Byron.* Henry, the good
orthodox king, refuses to grant Byron's favor, saying,

> I have no power, more than yourself, in things
> That are beyond my reason.[116]

Byron, rebuffed, storms away, declaring,

> But I will be mine own king . . .

and, when he finds he has created amusement:

> What's grave in earth, what awful, what abhorr'd,
> If my rage be ridiculous? I will make it
> *The law and rule* of all things serious.[117]

"Hybris," the Senecan critics say,[118] and of course it is. But more
specifically, it is the exposition of a code of honor which places
wrath or anger or "passion" or "spirit" first. It is what Sidney referred to in the words:

> falsely accounting an inflexible anger, a couragious constancie:
> esteeming feare, and astonishment, right causes of admira-
> tion, then Love and [true] Honour—

and it is implicit in Byron's statement of his philosophy:

> Give me a spirit that on this life's rough sea
> Loves t'have his sails fill'd with a lusty wind,
> Even till his sail-yards tremble, his masts crack,
> And his rapt ship run on her side so low
> That she drinks water, and her keel plows air.[119]

"Cette fine fleur de folie" invades private life in Ben Jonson's
Every Man in his Humour. Hesperida says to Giuliano,

> Brother indeede you are to violent
> To sudden in your courses, and you know
> My brother *Prosperos* temper will not beare
> Any reproofe, chiefly in such a presence,
> Where every slight disgrace he should receive,
> Would wound him in opinion and respect.

"Respect?" Giuliano demands—

> what talke you of respect mongst such as ha' neyther spearke
> of manhood nor good manners, by God I am ashamed to
> heare you: respect?[120]

Giuliano is "violent," but it is Prospero who carries the banner
of anger:

> No harme done brother. I warrant you: Since there is no harm
> done, anger costs a man nothing: and *a tall man is never his
> owne man til he be angry:* to keep his valure in obscuritie is
> to keepe himselfe as it were in a cloke-bag; whats a musition
> unlesse he play? whats a tall man unlesse he fight? for indeed
> all this my brother [Giuliano] stands upon absolutely, and that
> made me fall in with him so resolutely.[121]

The Elizabethan expositions of the honor-wrath theme are legion.
Indeed, all the proponents of individualistic ethics—whether of force
in political ethics, of honor in courtly ethics, or of instinct or inclination in naturalistic ethics—do have a common denominator in
a certain assertive violence. They are all children of the "Ireful
Virtue" rather than of Reason; they all profess some kind of *virtù*,
rather than virtue.
    Listen to Bacon:

> Wonderfull like is the Case of Boldnesse in Civill Businesse;
> What first? Boldnesse; what Second, and Third? Boldnesse.
> *And yet Boldnesse is a Childe of Ignorance, and Basenesse,
> farre inferiour to other Parts.* But nevertheless, it doth fas-
> cinate, and binde hande and foot, those, that are either shallow
> in Judgment or weake in Courage, which are the greatest Part;
> Yea and prevaileth with wise men, at weake times. . . .[122]

What was it that Sidney has written of Prince Anaxius?

> esteeming feare, and astonishment, right causes of admiration . . .[123]

And Bacon concludes his essay by saying that bold people should be second in command:

> For in Counsell, it is good to see dangers; and in *Execution*, not to see them, except they be very great.[124]

In a letter to Spenser, Harvey proclaims an age of "braverye." He has just been describing the universality of mutability, and he declares,

> So it standith with mens opinions and iudgmentes in matters of doctrine and religion. On fortye yeares the knowledge in the tunges and eloquence karrieth the creddite and flauntith it owte in her satin dobletts and velvet hoses. Then exspirith the date of her bravery, and everye man havinge enoughe of her, philosophy and knowledge in divers naturall morall matters, must give her the Camisade and beare ye swaye an other while. Every man seith what she can doe. At last comith braverye and iointith them both.

In the same letter, he speaks out for the following of one's own nature or appetite:

> Untill a mans fansye be satisfied, he wantith his most soveraigne contentment, and cannot be at quiet in himselfe. You suppose most of these bodily and sensual pleasures are to be abondonid as unlawfull and the inward contemplative delightes of the mind more zealously to be imbracid as most commendable. Good Lord, you a gentleman, a courtier, an yuthe, and go aboute to revive so owlde and stale a bookish opinion, deade and buried many hundrid yeares before you or I knewe whether there were any worlde or noe!

One begins to see, after this tirade, why Harvey takes such a delight in running over the list of innovators. And now he moves on to attack Reason by name:

> To be shorte . . . your greatist and most erronious suppose is that Reason should be mistrisse and Appetite attend on her ladiships person and a pore servante and hand mayden of hers. Nowe that had bene a probable defence and plausible speache a thousande yeares since. . . .[125]

But it is in the *Marginalia* that we get the clearest idea of which "Appetite" is Harvey's "mistresse." For there we find him a true servant of the "Ireful Virtue"—propounding action, force, self-interest, with the most astounding frequency. He builds a veritable burlesque religion of Energy—only to make the whole bombastic pretence a little pitiful through his eventual cry of self-disillusionment.[126]

Even Ben Jonson's Celia, trying to repulse Volpone, makes a qualified salute to "a tall man":

> Yet feed your wrath, sir, rather than your lust;
> (It is a vice, comes neerer to manlinesse)
> And punish that unhappy crime of nature,
> Which you miscal my beauty.[127]

Yet these two powers of the sensitive soul—wrath and lust—are almost necessarily allies when wrath rebels against reason. Following Plato, Tasso declares that when anger "does not obey reason, but suffers itself to be carried of her own violence, it falleth out, that it fighteth not against concupiscence but by concupiscence," and thus "whilst he served Armida" Rinaldo "may be noted unto us anger not governed by reason."[128]

So Ariosto had written,

> 'Tis seldom Reason's bit will serve to steer
> Desire, or turn him from his *furious* course,
> When pleasure is in reach . . .[129]

and indeed most of the satirists of the "honor-wrath" code also ridiculed the "love-lust" one. . . .

With the Elizabethans, still another element is prominent as a vital part of the code of honor—revenge.[130] F. T. Bowers has traced, in his *Elizabethan Revenge Tragedy,* the rise of the private duel and of a new code of honor in the late years of Elizabeth's reign and especially after the accession of James I.[131] Monsieur's defense of dueling in *Bussy* suggests a trend in this tradition parallel to that we have followed in the honor-wrath one. He speaks of the

> law of reputation, which to men
> Exceeds all positive law. . . .[132]

Now, "positive law," according to Hooker, although not "natural law" (since it is peculiar to any given nation, rather than universal in application), is "the very soul of a politic body."[133] Therefore, the subversive tendency of this "law of reputation" toward those laws which men, acting according to natural reason and justice, had seen fit to apply to their particular commonwealth, matched the general insubordination of Honor toward Reason.

Similarly, a clear line of demarcation may be drawn up between the sober Christian-humanist point of view on revenge, and the courtly one. To the former, revenge is a matter for God; it is both impious and irrational for man to attempt to take its execution upon himself.[134] Yet the courtly tradition held that there was a *right* revenge, not only just, but obligatory and above all authority of positive law. In keeping with its concept of honor as the "private moral virtue," it placed the avenging of a father or sister or wife *first,* but with this proviso—that the act of revenge be carried out in a spirit of just anger, controlled by reason.

Thus Tasso says that Rinaldo, "whilst fighting against Germando . . . did pass the bounds of civil revenge"[135]—because the slight he had suffered was not grave enough to warrant the killing of the offender, and because he did it "in his desperate wrath."[136] This is the view which Godfrey heard first, at least, from observers who favored Gernando. And although Rinaldo's uncle pleads that he did it "with reason," Rinaldo's hasty departure forces Godfrey to the former conclusion.[137]

Yet once again Tasso's position is ambiguous, for his description of the actual scene presents Rinaldo favorably:

> But not for this the wrongèd warrior stayed
> His just displeasure and incensed ire,
> He cared not what the vulgar did or said,
> To vengeance did his courage fierce aspire. . . .[138]

Similarly, Bussy asserts,

> . . . let no law make
> By any wrong it does, my life her slave:
> When I am wrong'd, and that law fails to right me,
> Let me be king myself (as man was made)
> And do a justice that exceeds the law. . . .[139]

Here the naturalist code of individualism and the revenge code of honor meet.

And, indeed, it is over-simplification to call the "revenge code of honor" simply an aristocratic one. As portrayed in Elizabethan drama, it is a compound of many simples, including Senecan tragedy and a more popular Italian tradition, stemming from the *novelle* and the unacademic tragedies. Roger Ascham's famous "Inglese Italianato è un diablo incarnato" was directed at the influx of all sorts of "Machiavellian" and "Aretinish" vice, supposedly imported from Italy, and including the popular ideas of Italianate revenge. It is such a tradition that Nashe is invoking when his Cutwolfe says on the scaffold:

This is the falt that hath called me hether, no true Italian but will honor me for it. Revenge is the glory of armes, & the highest performance of valure, revenge is whatsoever we call law or iustice. The farther we wade in revenge the nearer we come to ye throne of the almightie. To his scepter it is properly ascribed, his scepter he lends unto man, when he lets one man scourge an other. All true Italians imitate me in revenging constantly and dying valiantly: Hangman to thy taske, for I am readie for the utmost of thy rigor. . . .[140]

But this crude interpretation of the laws of revenge would hardly please the follower of honor's code more than the orthodox Christian-humanist. The aristocratic tradition is not difficult to distinguish from the plebeian one; it unfailingly asks if the act of revenge was done according to the "rules"—whether those rules follow honor and reason, or honor alone. It is on the former grounds that Sidney, for instance, indicts Anaxius' thirst for revenge after the death of Amphialus: he is carried away by rage. . . .[141]

There is one final and inevitable identification to be briefly cited—that of such an independent code of honor as the one we have followed, with ambition. Says Guillaume Du Vair,

Ixion's wheel is the motion of desires, which turn and return continually from above to below, allowing no repose to the mind. Let us then fix our Souls against this troublesome motion, that so disturbs our peace; and so moderate our affections, that the luster of Honour dazle not our Reason; and plant our minds with good resolutions for a breast-work against the assaults of Ambition: Let us first satisfie ourselves that there is no true honour in the world, but that of Vertue; and that Vertue desires no larger, nor more eminent Theater to present her self to mens Eyes upon, than her own Conscience. . . .[142]

It was an inevitable identification, because if wrath deserts her subordinate position to reason, asserts her independence, her ideal of Honor is no longer subordinate to that larger one in which it occupied only a special province. Inevitable, because with the desertion of reason, there is no bridle on the "moving" power of the soul; the exclusive appeal to "Honour" must end in "o'er-vaulting ambition."

So Byron's determination to make his "rage . . . the law and rule of all things serious" becomes "the fatal thirst of his ambition."[143] So Fulke Greville, in his *Inquisition upon Fame and Honour,* declares

Wee shall discerne the roote of this Ambition

> To be conceipt, that glory doth containe
> Some supernaturall sparke, or apparition,
> More than the common humour can attaine . . .[144]

in a passage which merges concepts of ambition, *hybris,* and honor or "glory."

Thomas Nashe is less exalted, more exact:

> Why cal I him Ambition, when he hath changed his name unto honor? I meane not the honour of the fielde (Ambitions onely enemy), which I could wish might be ever and onely honourable, but Brokerly blowne up honour, honour by antick fawning bridled up, honour bestowed for damned deserts.

Honor has deserted its rightful province under the guidance of reason—"the fielde," where it may rightly be first—to become "Brokerly blowne up honour" or "Ambition." More, it (or wrath) has rebelled against reason, its rightful monarch in the soul, as it has rebelled against its rightful monarch in the land in which it lives. Nashe concludes,

> Over and over I repeate it double and treble, that the spyrite of monarchizing in pryvate men is the spyrite of *Lucifer.*[145]

Rinaldo, we remember, is to Spenser "Ethice, or vertues of a private man." To Nashe he would be "the spyrite of monarchizing in private men," which is "the spyrite of Lucifer." The Ireful Virtue sometimes goes under the name of the Ireful Vice.

Marguerite of Navarre puts it less euphemistically. For when Parlamente says to her husband Hircan that it may be true that women are

> by nature disposed to sin; but it must be owned, nevertheless, that our temptations are not similar to yours: and if we sin through pride, no one suffers for it, and neither our body nor our hands receive any stain. *But your pleasure consists in dishonoring women, and your glory in killing men in war;* which are two things absolutely opposed to the law of God—[146]

she is answering with some effectiveness woman's detractors throughout the Renaissance, from Ariosto to George Chapman. . . .

Anger and Lust, Erasmus had called them. . . . The irascible and the concupiscible powers of the sensitive soul, said the orthodox anatomies of the soul. . . . Yet under the names of Honor and Love, two related and essentially courtly ethical codes sprang up in the Renaissance to challenge the supremacy of the traditional humanistic one. But—once again—"Anger and Lust," said the disillusioned, snorting at the euphemisms.

And among·those who said it scornfully and bitterly was William Shakespeare.

3. VARIATIONS ON THE THEME OF HONOR IN SHAKESPEARE'S PLAYS

Not at first. Shakespeare's treatment of the theme of honor in the early plays is largely orthodox. But from the turn of the century on, it is continually evident that he is aware of the trends we have been considering in this chapter. More—before long it is clear that he is sufficiently exercised about them to treat them extensively, and even with some heat.

It is true, however, that throughout his career, he does not maintain any consistent philosophical position on the subject, any more than he does on other currently debated themes and concepts. And throughout, his always apparent sense of nicety (despite the strictures of Ben Jonson and others) protects him from incongruities that would mar the effectiveness of a given play. For example, in all the Roman plays—whether concerned with a discussion of the conduct of Brutus, of Coriolanus, or of Antony—he appropriately confines his consideration of *honor* to the traditional humanist interpretation.

Yet he manages to consider the meaning of the word in all the senses that made it so hotly contested a subject during the years of the attack upon the citadel of tradition by the various forces of the Counter-Renaissance. He deals extensively, for example— and with variant verdicts—with the meaning of *honor* in terms of woman's nature and the relation of her honor to her reputation. A study of this subject's treatment in Shakespeare—from *All's Well That Ends Well,* through *Measure for Measure* and *Othello,* all the way to *Cymbeline,* would be rewarding. It would be rewarding both in terms of its content for historians of ideas and its demonstration of the versatility of Shakespeare's genius—the extraordinary gift he had for playing variations on a single theme without ever indicating (for longer than the duration of a single play) a personal predilection, and without being trapped into a position which must be maintained.

Shakespeare also dealt at length with the ramifications of the concept of honor (and of love) that constituted the courtly rebellion against the traditional humanistic ethic. For example, we have already observed how regular the establishment of a central opposition between the proponents of honor and the naturalists who derided it as trivial "art" was, on the one hand—and on the other, that between the same courtly tradition and the doctrinal Stoics and Cynics. The first of these oppositions is well illustrated in the scene in *Othello* between Iago and Cassio, when Cassio is hurt "past all surgery":

> *Cassio.* Reputation, reputation, reputation! O, I have lost my reputation! I have lost the immortal part of myself, and what remains is bestial. My reputation, Iago, my reputation!
>
> *Iago.* As I am an honest man, I thought you had receiv'd some bodily wound. There is more sense in that than in reputation. Reputation is an idle and most false imposition; oft got without merit and lost without deserving. You have lost no reputation at all unless you repute yourself such a loser.[147]

As for the opposition between the adherents of *honor* and the Stoic-Cynic philosophers, the encounter between Alcibiades and the Senators in *Timon of Athens* (a key passage for an understanding of Hamlet's conflict, as we shall see in the final chapter) affords a beautifully lucid exposition. Here, in miniature, is a full development of that opposition: "honor" vs. Stoicism; art vs. nature. "In miniature," because it affords a short but epitomizing parallel to the struggle throughout the play between the forces of the court and those best represented by Apemantus the Cynic—a struggle which is resolved (for the purposes of the play) when Timon himself is won over to the side of "nature" and Stoicism:

> My long sickness
> Of health and living now begins to mend,
> And *nothing* brings me all things.[148]

The burden of the scene in the Senate House is that Alcibiades, an Athenian captain, is pleading the cause of a friend of his, "who in hot blood hath stepp'd into the law."[149] He pleads for mercy, attesting that his friend has killed in an honorable way:

> Nor did he soil the fact with cowardice
> (An honour in him which buys out his fault)
> But with *a noble fury* and fair spirit,
> Seeing his *reputation* touch'd to death.
> He did oppose his foe. . . .[150]

In vain. The Senators reply with a true Stoic contempt for such courtier-like protestations:

> He's truly valiant that can wisely suffer

The worst that man can breathe, and make his wrongs
His outsides, to wear them like his raiment, carelessly,
And ne'er prefer his injuries to his heart,
To bring it into danger.[151]

And in the face of Alcibiades' further plea of the soldier's proper devotion to honor, the Senators remain adamant. There is no reconciliation.

But our major concern in this section is Shakespeare's treatment of the masculine code of honor, and especially of that courtly code of honor and love which we have traced in such detail. We find that his earliest full-dress treatment of it, in *Henry IV, Part I*, bears an interesting resemblance to Rabelais' tripartite interpretation and use of Pantagruel, Friar John and Panurge.

Indeed, the roles assigned to Prince Hal, Harry Hotspur and Falstaff correspond so exactly that the unwary might try to establish a direct debt. But it is far more likely that both writers were simply adhering to the conventional tripartite division of Plato (reason, passion or the ireful virtue, and desire or the concupiscible) or the familiar Aristotelian doctrine of the golden mean (excess, proper balance and moderation, and defect—of whatever virtue is in question: here, that of honor). It is probably no exaggeration to add that both writers in actuality were almost certainly not consciously following one of these patterns, but rather giving expression to so generally accepted a concept that they never questioned its validity.

The play, then, has a theme-with-variation treatment of *honor* as extensive as Shakespeare's handling of art and nature in *As You Like It*. But if Hal logically carries away the honors, after his reformation into a man of responsibility to whom honor has the just, traditional meaning—it is, nevertheless, of course Hotspur, the offender, the fiery and unrepentant champion of honor, who dominates the scene—even in defeat and death—and lingers in the mind.

So far as I can see, his only predecessor (and that only a partial ancestor) is Mercutio in *Romeo and Juliet*. Without expressly declaring his exclusive devotion to honor, Mercutio in several scenes portrays the same unbridled, violent allegiance and spurns the reign of "soft reason."[152]

From the very outset, Hotspur and honor are clearly practically synonymous. In the first scene of the play, King Henry speaks enviously of him (in explicit contrast to Hal) in these terms:

In envy that my Lord Northumberland
Should be the father to so blest a son—

A son who is the theme of honour's tongue,
Amongst a grove the very straightest plant;
Who is sweet Fortune's minion and her pride;
Whilst I, by looking on the praise of him,
See riot and dishonour stain the brow
Of my young Harry.[153]

So he is praised again and again—by the King,[154] by Hal himself,[155] by Douglas.[156] Yet there are ample occasions when even his own kinsfolk recognize that his devotion to honor is unbalanced—the ireful virtue in revolt—and sure to end in catastrophe, rather than success. His father[157] and his uncle Worcester[158] chide him for this fault, and Prince Hal's caricature of him is not without basis in fact:

I am not yet of Percy's mind, the Hotspur of the North; he that kills me some six or seven dozen of Scots at breakfast, washes his hands, and says to his wife, "Fie upon this quiet life! I want work."[159]

Hotspur himself, over and over again, expresses his willfulness, or his inability to curb his wrath with reason. For example:

An if the devil come and roar for them,
I will not send them. I will after straight
And tell him [the King] so; for I will ease my heart,
Albeit I make a hazard of my head.[160]

Nay, I will! That's flat![161]

Whither I must, I must. . . .[162]

I'll have it so. A little charge will do it.[163]

I cannot choose.[164]

I rather of his absence make this use:
It lends a lustre and more great opinion,
A larger dare to our great enterprise. . . .[165]

He is blunt and contentious at all points; his utter inability to show the slightest tact about the vagaries or even mere differences of others leads him to quarrel savagely with Glendower and Mortimer in that marvelous scene that opens Act III, and to come perilously close to insulting all his comrades as well as his foes. Only his charming and shrewd wife, who loves him, "mad ape" though he be, is any sort of match for him.

And nowhere does he demonstrate more thoroughly his wrongheadedness than in his obstinate embracing of battle against over-

whelming odds, and in his unendingly impatient desire to fight
even before the drop of a hat:

> O let the hours be short
> Till fields and blows and groans applaud our sport![166]

> O, I could divide myself and 'go to buffets for moving such a
> dish of skim milk with so honourable an action![167]

> This is no world
> To play with mammets and to tilt with lips.
> We must have bloody noses and crack'd crowns,
> And pass them current too. Gods me, my horse![168]

> Doomsday is near. Die all, die merrily.[169]

There is real justification for Worcester's rebuke:

> In faith, my lord, you are too wilful-blame,
> And since your coming hither have done enough
> To put him quite besides his patience.
> You must needs learn, lord, to amend this fault.
> Though sometimes it shows greatness, courage, blood—
> And that's the dearest grace it renders you—
> Yet oftentimes it doth present harsh rage,
> Defect of manners, want of government.
> Pride, haughtiness, opinion, and disdain;
> The least of which haunting a nobleman
> Loseth men's hearts, and leaves behind a stain
> Upon the beauty of all parts besides,
> Beguiling them of commendation.[170]

"True, and yet true that I must Stella love"—Hotspur transcends
all this criticism. In him the romantic temper that places honor
above reason and makes a fetish—or an ethical code, as you will—
of the precedence of passion or the ireful virtue, joins with that
other romantic temper of the metaphysical ache, to which I have
already referred. From the magnificent

> By heaven, methinks it were an easy leap
> To pluck bright honor from the pale-fac'd moon,
> Or dive into the bottom of the deep,
> Where fadom line could never touch the ground,
> And pluck drowned honour by the locks,
> So he that doth redeem her thence might wear
> Without corrival all her dignities . . .[171]

and the handsome call to battle,

> O gentlemen, the time of life is short!
> To spend that shortness basely were too long
> If life did ride upon a dial's point,
> Still ending at the arrival of an hour.
> An if we live, we live to tread on kings;
> If die, brave death, when princes die with us![172]

to the final tribute of his widow,

> For his [honor], it stuck upon him as the sun
> In the grey vault of heaven, and by his light
> Did all the chivalry of England move
> To do brave acts. He was indeed the glass
> Wherein the noble youth did dress themselves.
> He had no legs that practis'd not his gait;
> And speaking thick (which nature made his blemish)
> Became the accents of the valiant;
> For those that could speak low and tardily
> Would turn their own perfection to abuse
> To seem like him; so that in speech, in gait,
> In diet, in affections of delight,
> In military rules, humours of blood,
> He was the mark and glass, copy and book,
> That fashion'd others. And him—O wondrous him!
> O miracle of men![173]

—throughout his career, and even after it, Hotspur transcends, not only his own faults, but those of the whole school of the idolatry of honor, whose model and preceptor he was. He belongs to that rare company of characters (among others, Falstaff and Cleopatra) whom Shakespeare so abundantly loved that he lavished upon them all the prodigal richness of mingled faults and attributes—so great a richness that their wasteful superfluities exceed in vitality and human stature the careful and conscious virtues toward which the rest of us strive.

Hal may, as he reforms, represent that true honor which is never overweening, always compatible with the governance of reason—but he never stirs our imagination in this way. He says the right things, as before he said the wrong ones; he comes to full life only when he is with Falstaff. Yet, with Hotspur on one side of him and Falstaff on the other, we must accept him as the personification of honor in due measure, remembering that the conventionally good are seldom moving—and in Shakespeare even less often than usual.

Yet this does not mean that we need linger over him. Once resolved, he behaves very well. He asserts his purpose to his father with confidence, but without arrogance.[174] His invitation to Hotspur to join in single combat, is courteous, modest and courageous,[175] and it is so reported to Hotspur by Vernon.[176] When he kills Hotspur, his attitude is again chivalrous; he pays him just tribute.[177] And he displays a final magnanimity in freeing Douglas at the end of the play.[178]

If Hotspur is the excess of honor, Falstaff is as surely the defect. If Hotspur is the irascible appetite incarnate, Falstaff is the concupiscible. And if Hotspur displays, as does no other single figure, the romantic temper of the adherents of honor in an upward metaphysical assertion—Falstaff as surely epitomizes the "downward" materialistic emphasis of the naturalistic deprecators of the romantic temper.

It takes no straining to complete a pattern to make this declaration. Shakespeare never presents variant and contradictory attitudes toward one theme in several characters in a single play unless he desires us to consider that theme closely. And he has made Falstaff, too, highly articulate on the subject of honor.

Falstaff sets the tone of his attitude as soon as the news of imminent war reaches him:

> Rare words! brave world! Hostess, my breakfast, come.
> O, I could wish this tavern were my drum![179]

His famous catechism on honor is definitive:

> Well, 'tis no matter; honour pricks me on. Yea, but how if honour prick me off when I come on? How then? Can honour set to a leg? No. Or an arm? No. Or take away the grief of a wound? No. Honour hath no skill in surgery then? No. What is honour? A word. What is that word honour? Air. A trim reckoning! Who hath it? He that died a Wednesday. Doth he feel it? No. Doth he hear it? No. 'Tis insensible then? Yea, to the dead. But will it not live with the living? No. Why? Detraction will not suffer it. Therefore I'll none of it. Honour is a mere scutcheon—and so ends my cathechism.[180]

And on the field, coming upon Sir Walter Blunt lying dead, he finds confirmation for the catechism: "There's honour for you!"[181]

His action throughout is consonant with his words. His method of conscription for the war, his counterfeiting of death on the field, his stabbing of the dead Hotspur and attempt to claim him as his own victim—these provide ample evidence that Sir John has not been speaking idly. Ignoble he may be; he is equally consistent in the allegiance of word and deed to forthright condemnation of the fantastic "art of honor."

In no other Shakespearian play are the various points of view on honor so clearly set forth, so neatly balanced. Later treatments are more subtle, more complex. They are also more concerned with the specific courtly code. Hotspur's *élan* has other elements than those of this tradition; his is a less restricted and elaborately conscious concept of honor; moreover, he makes his own code. He seems not so much a devotee of the Ireful Virtue as its very personification.

It is quite another matter when we come to *Hamlet*, and the allegiance to honor of Fortinbras, and especially of Laertes. But this approach, tied in with one of the sources of Hamlet's internal conflict, must wait our treatment of that conflict in the next, and final, chapter. Suffice it to say that in *Henry IV, Part I*, Shakespeare's attitude toward *honor* as personified by Hotspur, is at least imaginatively sympathetic. The serious treatment in *Hamlet* is more discriminatingly critical—less balanced and symmetrical, more shaded and qualified and thoughtful.

In *Troilus and Cressida*, on the other hand, his treatment of the courtly codes of honor and love is sharply satirical—scornful and even bitterly antagonistic. O. J. Campbell has long since proved conclusively to my satisfaction that *Troilus and Cressida* was presented at the Inns of Court, and I would go a step further to proclaim my conviction that its audience was largely a courtly one —that it was even written with such an audience specifically in mind. However strongly antagonistic Shakespeare felt toward the courtly codes of honor and love, he would hardly have gone to such elaborate trouble to lampoon them unless he was sure of a knowing audience, from whom the allusions and satirical sallies would bring an instant and perhaps even malicious response.

Moreover, I do not think it far-fetched to keep in mind the current interest in the whole courtly honor-wrath-passion tradition that Spenser and others found in Tasso and developed. Fairfax completed the translation of *Jerusalem Delivered* in 1600; the date that Kittredge finds most reasonable for *Troilus and Cressida* is 1602.[182]

Moreover, there are textual similarities between these two works, which, if accidental, constitute an unusual coincidence. For example, Nestor's offering to fight Hector if no other Greek champion will,[183] immediately brings to mind old Raymond's shaming of the younger champions among the Crusaders in a similar situation.[184] Again, the way in which Pandarus and Cressida "review" the Trojan troops from the wall[185] parallels almost exactly the similar scene between the Saracen king and Erminia.[186] I believe that a close textual study of the two works will disclose other similarities.

But enough of sources. The play throughout illustrates copiously, and with scant sympathy, the revolt of the new courtly traditions against the main-line Christian-humanistic one. When Ulysses, for example, in his famous speech early in the play, describes the unsatisfactory situation in the Greek camp by pointing out how "the specialty of rule has been neglected"; "Degree . . . vizarded"; and the various related concepts of limit slighted[187]—it is the ireful virtue that he finds responsible. Achilles he calls scornfully, "Sir Valour,"[188] and of the sulky and overbearing pair, Ajax and Achilles, he remarks:

> They tax our policy and call it cowardice,
> Count wisdom as no member of the war,
> Forestall prescience, and esteem no act
> But that of hand. The still and mental parts,
> That do contrive how many hands shall strike
> When fitness calls them on, and know by measure
> Of their observant toil the enemies' weight—
> They call this bedwork, mapp'ry, closet war;
> So that the ram that batters down the wall,
> For the great swinge and rudeness of his poise,
> They place before his hand that made the engine
> Or those that with the fineness of their souls
> By reason guide his execution.[189]

If this is not a clear case of the revolt of Plato's military and passionate class against the governing class whose particular forte is reason or wisdom, I do not know what it is. The ireful virtue, attempting to rule without help, is suborning "the specialty of rule."

To put it in different but equally accurate terms, those whose lives are guided by a concept of honor are totally rebellious against the traditional view of this concept—that it must be congruous with the still more important one of reason-and-virtue. . . . But it is at a meeting within the Trojan camp that this rebellion against the humanistic precepts is made most unmistakably explicit.

In this scene, Priam consults with his sons—Hector, Troilus, Paris and Helenus. Early in the discussion Hector, the perfect knight to the Elizabethans (whose allegiance to the Trojans is well-known), points out how many of their own people have been sacrificed to the keeping of Helen, and demands,

> What's merit in that reason which denies
> The yielding of her up?[190]

Troilus immediately picks up the implicit gauge, reproving Hector for weighing "the worth and *honour* of a king so great as our dread father in a scale of common ounces,"[191] and for his arguing on the basis of "fears and reasons."[192]

Helenus, the priestly son, responds sharply,

> No marvel though you bite so sharp at reasons,
> You are so empty of them. Should not our father
> Bear the great sway of his affairs with reason,
> Because your speech hath none to tell him so?[193]

To the devotee of the humanist faith, the king traditionally is under a moral imperative greater than himself; to the champion of honor, his power is limitless, so that it adheres to the code of honor:

> You are for dreams and slumbers, brother priest;
> You fur your gloves with reason. Here are your reasons:
> You know an enemy intends you harm,
> You know a sword employ'd is perilous,
> And reason flies the object of all harm. . . .[194]

Reason vs. honor, and again Troilus links reason with the opposite of honor's valor: fear. He continues,

> Nay, if we talk of reason,
> Let's shut our gates and sleep. Manhood and honour
> Should have hare hearts, would they but fat their thoughts
> With this cramm'd reason. Reason and respect
> Make livers pale and lustihood deject.[195]

This is the very problem that is so to agonize Hamlet. But here Hector replies forthrightly, "Brother, she is not worth what she doth cost the holding."[196]

And when Troilus advances the relativistic argument of the Counter-Renaissance, "What is aught but as 'tis valu'd?"[197] Hector replies with the traditional argument that "value dwells not in particular will. . . ."[198]

But Troilus is not convinced. Once a man (here Paris) has chosen his wife, even if he later regrets what he has done, it is done: "There can be no evasion to blench from this and to stand firm by honour."[199] The fact that Paris has not chosen a wife, but stolen another man's, is to him, as the exponent of honor, justified by the fact that "it was thought meet Paris should do some *vengeance* on the Greeks."[200]

After an interruption by Cassandra, who prophesies the doom of Troy unless Helen is returned, Hector resumes his argument with an appeal to Troilus to heed the prophecy, concluding,

> Or is your blood
> So madly hot that no discourse of reason,

> Nor fear of bad success in a bad cause,
> Can qualify the same?[201]

But Troilus scornfully rejects losing "the *courage of our minds* because Cassandra's mad."[202] He asserts,

> Her brainsick raptures
> Cannot distaste the goodness of a quarrel
> Which hath over several honours all engag'd
> To make it gracious.[203]

Paris now takes up Troilus' argument, despite a rebuke from his father, and propounds a similar code of honor-and-love. Whereupon Hector launches into a longish dissertation, traditionally humanistic, to show both Troilus and Paris their mistakes. He says in part,

> The reasons you allege do more conduce
> To the *hot passion of distemp'red blood*
> Than to make up a *free determination*
> 'Twixt right and wrong; for *pleasure* and *revenge*
> Have ears more deaf than adders to the voice
> Of any *true decision. Nature* craves
> All dues be rend'red to their owners. Now
> What nearer debt in all humanity
> Than wife is to the husband? If this *law*
> Of *nature* be corrupted through *affection,*
> And that great minds, of partial indulgence
> To their *benumbed wills,* resist the same,
> There is a *law* in each well-ord'red nation
> To curb those *raging appetites* that are
> Most *disobedient and refractory.*
> If Helen then be the wife to Sparta's king
> (As it is known she is), these *moral laws*
> *Of nature and of nations* speak aloud
> To have her back return'd. Thus to persist
> In doing wrong extenuates not wrong,
> But makes it much more heavy. Hector's opinion
> Is this in way of *truth.*[204]

A definitive statement of the traditional humanistic view, and an excoriation of the code of honor. On the one hand—"free determination"; "true decision"; "the law of nature"; the "moral laws of nature and of nations"; determined "truth." On the other—"hot passion"; "distemp'red blood"; "pleasure and revenge"; "corrupted through affection"; "benumbed wills"; "raging appetites"; "disobedient and refractory." How astounding then, when Hector concludes without a pause,

Hector's opinion
Is this *in way of truth*. Yet ne'ertheless,
My sprightly brethren, I propound to you
In resolution to keep Helen still;
For 'tis a cause that hath no mean dependence
Upon our joint and several dignities.[205]

Beside the cynicism of this—from the great champion of champion—Troilus and Paris seem inoffensive. Truth may have it so and so, Hector explains, but resolution has it thus—and I abide by resolution! Reason is true, but honor is the star I follow anyway. Can there be any doubt as to Shakespeare's intention after this speech?

And now Troilus summarizes the position. It is not a question of angry self-indulgence, unmitigated wrath, but of the pursuit of glory and renown:

Why, there you touch'd the life of our design.
Were it not glory that we more affected
Than the performance of our heaving spleens,
I would not wish a drop of Troyan blood
Spent more in her defence. But, worthy Hector,
She is a theme of honour and renown,
A spur to valiant and magnanimous deeds,
Whose present courage may beat down our foes,
And fame in time to come canonize us.[206]

And Hector responds in kind, even indulging in fatuous boasting.[207] And while his later conduct and speeches in the play[208] expound a much nobler concept of honor, it is impossible to forget this important and decisive scene. And it is instructive to contrast Troilus' theme of "glory" and Helen's spur "to honour and renown" with the heaving of his spleen over Cressida. Yet his ultimate disillusionment suggests that he, at least, believed the validity of the courtly tradition he extols until he found it nearer to "wrath and lechery" than to "honor and love."

We cannot linger over the numerous lesser variations Shakespeare plays upon the Trojans' and Greeks' blind and fatuous devotion to the religion of honor. Æneas, with his high-sounding palaver, is its "Osric"[209]—and Shakespeare enjoys the encounter between him and the bluntly naturalistic, or even materialistic, Diomed.[210] Ajax and Achilles provide excellent examples of the unheeding revolt of the ireful virtue; both lose their value to the Greek cause when they refuse to be led by passion's rightful guide, the reason that Agamemnon, Nestor and Ulysses can provide.[211] The whole play is shot through with satirical variations on the revolt and rule of "blood," "passion," "revenge," "honor," "glory," etc.

But it also combines the theme of the courtly code of love with that of honor. Agamemnon links the two expressly.[212] Paris, Helen and Pandarus juggle the two themes throughout a whole scene.[213] And it is the story of Troilus and Cressida themselves that best illustrates the combination of themes, and Shakespeare's view of them.

Despite Troilus' insistently articulate high-mindedness, it is Pandarus who, from the start, sets the tone of the affair to come with his leering, titillating, elbow-nudging talk and insinuations.[214] When the two lovers finally come together, Troilus vacillates between awkward, high-sounding phrases and almost touchingly naïve directness; Cressida between an experienced forthrightness and an eloquent swearing of faithfulness.[215] Then they proceed to bed.

The next time we see them, it is on the verge of the trading of Cressida to Diomed for Antenor the Trojan. There is already a subtle change in mood, appropriate to affairs that are exclusively carnal: Troilus laughs at a double meaning;[216] Cressida regrets having given herself to him, since, like all other men, he now will not "tarry."[217] And although she swears she will not leave him, exchange or no exchange, we know that she will. It all ends, as we know it will, with her yielding to Diomed, and Troilus' unhappy witnessing of the yielding.[218]

It has been customary for Shakespearian scholars to find both Troilus and Cressida repulsive characters. I do not think this was Shakespeare's chief concern, or even his intent. Troilus is, it seems to me, a not very experienced man of real potential stature, infatuated with the current creed of honor-and-love. He is frequently foolish, sometimes boorish—but not beyond the expectations of his years and greenness. Through him, we see how the "art" of such a code may take in a susceptible young man—but he is never guilty of the selfishness, stupidity and cynicism of Achilles, Ajax and (even) Hector, respectively. He is never fatuous in either Æneas' or Paris' manner; he never goes beyond the venal excesses of his itch for Cressida and his hot-headedness.

As for Cressida, she is warm and weak and willing. That is the worst one may say of her. And at her best, when she is all too aware of her own frailty, there is something genuinely touching in her not very effective struggle to rise above the limitations of her nature.

Why, then, do I say that Shakespeare satirizes the honor-love ethical code through them? What is he trying to show, if he does not regard them as repulsively animalistic and dishonorable? Simply, I think, that whereas the protestations of the courtiers and ladies of the time bespeak a noble and high-minded aristocratic ethical code, here—in these two imperfect young people, caught in an environment full of such lip-service and very contrary practice —here is the truth of the matter; here is the actual motivation—not at all noble and hifalutin', but very frail and faulty.

He is not so gentle with the others—with Paris and Helen, Achilles and Patroclus, Æneas and the rest—not even with Hector. And thus the middle ground which Troilus and Cressida do seem to me to represent does not in any way invalidate my premise of the satirical purpose of the play. The advocates of honor-and-love on the whole are a sad collection of bullies, braggarts and perverts.

Is this ever explicit—or only satirically implicit? Quite explicit. As he has elsewhere, Shakespeare uses in *Troilus and Cressida* the device of the two satiric commentators—the sturdy moral teacher and the buffoon or depreciating scurrilous railer[219]—to drive home the bitter things he has to say. Ulysses largely performs the first function, Thersites the second.[220]

The former passes his major judgments in the famous speech in Act I, Scene iii, and in his treatment of Ajax (II, iii) and Achilles (III, iii),[221] although he contributes some plain-speaking throughout. As a sort of supplementary plain-speaker, Diomed may be associated with him, although not in any other way. Ulysses passes traditional moral judgment as a ruler; Diomed is the rough-and-ready naturalist who either satirizes or debunks the honor-and-love code in the very teeth of its adherents.[222]

As for Thersites, he reduces the code to its lowest possible terms on every occasion. Ajax is "Mars, his idiot."[223] Of Helen and Menelaus, he says, "All the argument is a whore and a cuckold."[224] Achilles is "a valiant ignorance"[225]; he and Ajax "may run mad" with "too much blood and too little brain."[226] Most of these allegations are too close to the truth to be dismissed as mere ugly ranting.

Yet does this mean that Shakespeare chooses these men as the champions of truth and virtue? Not at all. Ulysses is sometimes pompous, and sometimes misses the point; Diomed is far from admirable. Thersites' avowed estimate of himself is accurate: "I am a rascal, a scurvy railing knave, a very filthy rogue."[227] It is not necessarily the nature of the traditional satirical commentator to be the positive opposite to the negative he berates, and Thersites' unpleasant character does not invalidate his contribution to the naturalistic interpretation of the courtly tradition of love and honor:

> Lechery, lechery! still wars and lechery! Nothing else holds fashion.[228]

"Anger and lust." . . . "Wars and lechery." It is fine, appropriate irony for Thersites to summarize, and for Pandarus to speak the epilogue.

Thersites' character, I say, does not invalidate his estimate of the courtly tradition. And Shakespeare's use of moral "railers" and re-bukers of the fleshly or the falsely aristocratic does not, of course, mean that he endorses the ascetic ideal—whether in so grotesque a form or in the more dignified one of the doctrinal Stoic or Cynic observer. Except for special, crucial situations, he holds to a middle, humane position, tolerant and generous. Always the observer, the balancer, however, he is quick to see the dramatic conflict possible in the exploitations of opposing points of view, positions, systems. And as we move, at the last, into a brief study of his great tragedies, we find him seriously interested in the opposition discussed so often, in passing, in this chapter—that between the proponents of honor and those of Stoicism.

CHAPTER 9
FOOTNOTES

I.

1. Fletcher, *Italian Renaissance*, 194. Professor Fletcher points out that this is the main thesis of Burckhardt's famous book on the Italian Renaissance.
2. *Ibid.*, 194–195.
3. *Ibid.*, 194.
4. *Ibid.*, 195.
5. *Ibid.*, 196–197.
6. *Ibid.*, 197.
7. *Ibid.*, 198.
8. Castiglione, *Courtier*, 303.
9. Baldassare Castiglione, *Il Cortigiano*, ed. V. Cian (Florence, 1908), 424. Translation by Robb.
10. Marguerite, *Dernières Poésies*, 216.
11. Spenser, *Hymne in Honour of Love*, ll. 190–194.
12. *Ibid.*, ll. 43–44.
13. Spenser, *Faerie Queene*, IV, Prologue, 2, 3.
14. Spenser, *Shepheards Calendar*, "To His Booke," ll. 3–4.
15. Sidney, *Arcadia*, II, 21.
16. *Ibid.*, III, 9.
17. *Ibid.*, III, 1.
18. *Ibid.*, I, 12.
19. *Ibid.*
20. *Ibid.*, I, 18.
21. *Ibid.*, I, "The First Eclogues," pp. 129, 131.
22. *Poetry Eng. Ren.*, 115–116. My italics.
23. Ariosto, *Orlando Furioso*, IV, lxiii–lxvii.
24. Henry VIII, *Whoso that will* (from Additional Ms. 31922): *Poet. Eng. Ren.*, 9.
25. Torquato Tasso, *Aminta*, Act II, Chorus and Entr'act: Louis E. Lord, *A Translation of the Orpheus of Angelo Politian and the Aminta of Torquato Tasso* (London, 1931), 150, 149.
26. Marguerite, *Heptameron*, II, xxiv (Third Day), 9.
27. George Turberville, *To His Love, That sent him a ring wherein was graved, "Let reason rule"* (from *Epitaphs, Epigrams, Songs and Sonnets,* 1567): *Poet. Eng. Ren.*, 75. My italics.
28. Fulke Greville, *Caelica*, XIV, ll. 1–4.
29. *Ibid.*, LXXV, ll. 211–212, 219.
30. "Platonic" lovers.
31. John Marston, *The Malcontent*, IV, i, p. 187.
32. Cf. Oscar James Campbell, *Comicall Satyre and Shakespeare's Troilus and Cressida* (San Marino, California, 1938), 143–146. Professor Campbell points out that Marston gives Castilio's full name as Signor Castilio Balthazar, making the identification certain.
33. Marston, *ibid.*, I, iv, p. 153; I, iii, p. 146.
34. Chapman, *Bussy*, II, ii, ll. 146–147, 149, 150–151.
35. *Ibid.*, I, ii, ll. 94–97.
36. Nashe, *Unfortunate Traveller*, 58–59.
37. T. S. Eliot, "Sweeney Among the Nightingales": *Collected Poems (1909–1935)* (New York, 1936), 66.

38. Nashe, *ibid.,* 59.
39. Marguerite, *Heptameron,* I, xix (Second Day), p. 142.
40. *Ibid.,* I, viii (First Day), p. 47.
41. *Ibid.,* I, xii (Second Day), p. 94.
42. Castiglione, *Courtier,* 314.
43. Pietro Aretino, *Works,* translated into English from the original Italian . . . privately printed for the Rarity Press, Inc. (New York, 1931), 277–278.
44. *Ibid.,* 277.
45. Marguerite, *Heptameron,* II, xliv (Fifth Day), p. 117.
46. Montaigne, III, 129. My italics.
47. *Ibid.,* III, 117–118.
48. Charron, *De la Sagesse,* I, 24; Atkinson, 330.
49. Torquato Tasso, *Opere* (Pisa, 1821), II, 37; cf. Bredvold, "The Naturalism of Donne," 492.
50. Translation by Lord, pp. 129–130.
51. Lord, p. 130. My italics. Cf. Greville, *Caelica,* XLIV.
52. Donne, Elegie XVII, ll. 46–55: *Poems,* p. 102.
53. Marguerite, *Heptameron,* II, xlii (Fifth Day), p. 101.
54. *Ibid.,* I, xiv (Second Day), p. 110.
55. Du Vair, *Morall Philosophy,* 40.
56. *Ibid.,* 42.
57. For a thoroughly conventional Elizabethan humanist attitude on the subject, see Robert Ashley, *Of Honour,* edited with introduction and commentary by Virgil B. Heltzel (The Huntington Library: San Marino, California, 1947), especially 29, 34, 37, 38, 40, 45, 47.
58. It is not within the scope of my task to deal at any length with the question of concepts of "honor" in the Middle Ages. Undoubtedly, there are roots for this particular interpretation there, but with different emphases. How the medieval chivalric tradition eventually acquired a specifically Christian tinge is discussed by De Wulf, *Phil. and Civ.,* 24–30.
59. Marguerite, *Heptameron,* I, xvi (Second Day), p. 125. My italics.
60. *Ibid.,* I, xviii (Second Day), p. 136.
61. Rabelais, I, 57. For classical versions of "innate honor" see Lovejoy and Boas, *Prim. and Rel. Ideas,* 195–196.
62. *Ibid.* My italics.
63. Cf. Clement, "The Eclecticism of Rabelais," 368.
64. Cf. fn. 59 (*supra*).
65. Marguerite, II, xliii (Fifth Day).
66. *Ibid.,* pp. 107, 102.
67. Chapman, *Bussy,* II, ii, ll. 9–13 ff.
68. *Ibid.,* III, i, 94–95.
69. Jonson, *Volpone,* III, vii, ll. 38 ff.
70. *Ibid.,* ll. 210 ff. My italics.
71. Sidney, *Arcadia,* III, 10.
72. Machiavelli, *La Mandragola,* translated by Stark Young (New York, 1927), 153 (III, xi).
73. *Ibid.,* 157.
74. Machiavelli, *Discourses,* III, 508. My italics.
75. Marston, *Malcontent,* V, ii, p. 203.

2.

76. Yet even Castiglione has been suspect in this connection to some scholars, among them the famous Burckhardt. See his distinction between "duty"

and "honor": Jacob Burckhardt, *The Civilization of the Renaissance in Italy* (Middlemore's translation), London, 1944, 235.

77. Tasso, *Jerusalem Delivered*, 438 (The Allegory of the Poem).
78. *Ibid.*, 438–439.
79. *Ibid.*, 439–440.
80. *Ibid.*, 440.
81. *Ibid.*
82. *Ibid.* My italics.
83. Plato, *The Republic* (third edition of the Jowett translation), (New York, 1928), IV, 435, D.
84. *Ibid.*, 436, A, B. My italics.
85. *Ibid.*, 439, D. My italics.
86. *Ibid.*, E.
87. *Ibid.*, 440, A, E.
88. *Ibid.*, 440, E; 441, A. My italics.
89. *Ibid.*, 441, C.
90. *Ibid.*, 441, E.
91. *Ibid.*, IX, 580, D. E; 581, A, B, C. My italics.
92. Tasso, *Jerusalem Delivered*, V, 9, 11, 13. My italics.
93. *Ibid.*, XVIII, 1.
94. *Ibid.*, Allegory, 441.
95. *Ibid.*, 441–442.
96. *Ibid.*, 442. My italics.
97. *Ibid.*
98. See diagram—anatomy of the soul, *supra.*
99. Tasso, *ibid.*, 442–443.
100. Plato, *Republic*, IV, 442, C–D. My italics.
101. Aristotle, *Nichomachean Ethics*, I, v. (Camelot series: Chase's translation, newly revised, London, Walter Scott, Ltd., n.d.), 16.
102. Du Vair, *Morall Philosophy*, 81, 85.
103. Sidney, *Arcadia*, III, 15.
104. *Ibid.*, III, 11.
105. Rabelais, III; 46.
106. Du Vair, *Mor. Phil.*, 40.
107. Rabelais, I, 39.
108. *Ibid.*, V, 15. My italics.
109. *Ibid.*
110. *Ibid.*, IV, 46.
111. Tasso, *Jerusalem Delivered*, V, 4. My italics.
112. *Ibid.*, V, 6. My italics.
113. *Ibid.*, V, 7.
114. Spenser, *Works*, II, 485. My italics.
115. *Ibid.* My italics. This whole theme is well developed in Professor Fletcher's unpublished paper, "The Continental Background of Edmund Spenser," II, 2, 3–5, 8.
116. Chapman, *Conspiracy of Byron*, V, i, 83–84.
117. *Ibid.*, V, i, 138; V, ii, 2–4. My italics.
118. Yet, for Seneca's linking of wrath, courage and freedom, see Lovejoy and Boas, *Prim. and Rel. Ideas*, 365.
119. Chapman, *Conspiracy of Byron*, III, iii, 135–139.
120. Jonson, *Every Man in his Humour*, III, iv, 177–185 (First Quarto).
121. *Ibid.*, IV, iii, 7–14. My italics.
122. Bacon, *Essayes*, 45 ("Of Boldnesse"). My italics.
123. Sidney, *Arcadia*, III, 15.

124. Bacon, *ibid.*, 46. My italics.
125. Harvey, *Letter Book*, 86–88.
126. For these passages, turn back to the ones quoted in Chapter VIII (*supra*).
127. Jonson, *Volpone*, III, vii, 249–252.
128. Tasso, *Jer. Del.*, 441–442.
129. Ariosto, *Orlando Furioso*, XI, i. My italics.
130. This does not, of course, originate with the Elizabethans. Spanish and Italian codes of honor stress an elaborate system of "honorable revenge." For the Spanish tradition's origin and nature, see George Ticknor, *History of Spanish Literature* (4th edition, Boston, 1891), especially II, 447–473.
131. F. T. Bowers, *Elizabethan Revenge Tragedy* (Princeton, N. J., 1940), especially 30–33.
132. Chapman, *Bussy*, II, i, 155–156.
133. Hooker, I, x, 10.
134. Cf. Bowers, *Revenge Tragedy*, 184–216.
135. Tasso, *Jer. Del.*, 442.
136. *Ibid.*, V, 33.
137. *Ibid.*, 59.
138. *Ibid.*, 29. Notice similarity to Ariosto's scorn of the vulgar (fn. 23, *supra*).
139. Chapman, *Bussy*, II, i, 195–199.
140. Nashe, *Unfortunate Traveller*, 121.
141. Sidney, *Arcadia*, III, 25.
142. Du Vair, *Morall Philosophy*, 42.
143. Chapman, *Tragedy of Byron*, I, i, 21.
144. Greville, *Inquisition upon Fame and Honour*, st. 38.
145. Nashe, *Works*, II, 81, 82, 91 (*Christs Teares over Ierusalem*).
146. Marguerite, *Heptameron*, II, xxvi (Third Day), p. 27.

3.

147. *Othello*, II, iii, 262–272.
148. *Timon of Athens*, V, i, 189–191.
149. *Ibid.*, III, v, 11–12.
150. *Ibid.*, 16–20. My italics.
151. *Ibid.*, 31–35.
152. See *Romeo and Juliet*—especially II, iv, 29–37, and III, i, 76–77 and 104–108.
153. *Henry IV, Part I*, I, i, 79–86.
154. *Ibid.*, III, ii, 112–117.
155. *Ibid.*, III, ii, 139–140; and V, iv, 86–101.
156. *Ibid.*, IV, i, 10.
157. *Ibid.*, I, iii, 129 and 236–238.
158. *Ibid.*, III, ii, 177–189; V, ii, 16–21.
159. *Ibid.*, II, iv, 114–118.
160. *Ibid.*, I, iii, 125–128.
161. *Ibid.*, 218.
162. *Ibid.*, II, iii, 108.
163. *Ibid.*, III, i, 115.
164. *Ibid.*, 148.
165. *Ibid.*, IV, i, 76–78.
166. *Ibid.*, I, iii, 301–302.
167. *Ibid.*, II, iii, 34–36.
168. *Ibid.*, 94–97.
169. *Ibid.*, IV, i, 134.
170. *Ibid.*, III, i, 177–189.

171. *Ibid.,* I, iii, 201–207.
172. *Ibid.,* V, ii, 82–87. Observe the conventional conclusion (lines 88–89), appended as a dry or impatient afterthought:

> Now for our consciences, the arms are fair,
> When the intent of bearing them is just.

The "now" is a wonderful illustration of Shakespeare's capacity for characterization in a single short word.

173. *Henry IV, Part II,* II, iii, 18–33.
174. *Henry IV, Part I,* III, ii, 129–159.
175. *Ibid.,* V, i, 83–100.
176. *Ibid.,* V, ii, 52–69.
177. *Ibid.,* V, iv, 86–101.
178. *Ibid.,* V, v, 27–31.
179. *Ibid.,* III, iii, 228–229.
180. *Ibid.,* V, i, 130–144.
181. *Ibid.,* V, iii, 33.
182. Kittredge, *Complete Works of Shakespeare,* 879.
183. *Troilus and Cressida,* I, iii, 291–301.
184. Tasso, *Jer. Del.,* VII, 61–66.
185. *Troil. and Cr.,* I, ii, 192–296.
186. Tasso, *Jer. Del.,* III, 12, 17–20, 37–40, 58–63.
187. *Tr. and Cr.,* I, iii, 78–134.
188. *Ibid.,* 176.
189. *Ibid.,* 197–210.
190. *Ibid.,* II, ii, 23–24.
191. *Ibid.,* 26–28. My italics.
192. *Ibid.,* 32.
193. *Ibid.,* 33–36.
194. *Ibid.,* 37–41.
195. *Ibid.,* 46–50.
196. *Ibid.,* 51–52.
197. *Ibid.,* 52.
198. *Ibid.,* 53.
199. *Ibid.,* 67–68.
200. *Ibid.,* 72–73. My italics.
201. *Ibid.,* 115–118.
202. *Ibid.,* 121–122. My italics.
203. *Ibid.,* 122–125.
204. *Ibid.,* 168–189. My italics.
205. *Ibid.,* 188–193. My italics.
206. *Ibid.,* 194–202.
207. *Ibid.,* 207–213.
208. See especially V, iii, 26–28.
209. *Ibid.,* I, iii, 215–309.
210. *Ibid.,* IV, i, 1–34.
211. *Ibid.,* I, iii; III, iii; V, i, 52–55.
212. *Ibid.,* I, iii, 284–288.
213. *Ibid.,* III, i.
214. *Ibid.,* I, i, 1–107; I, ii, 38–321.
215. *Ibid.,* III, iii.
216. *Ibid.,* IV, ii, 37–38.
217. *Ibid.,* 15–18.
218. *Ibid.,* V, iii.

219. Cf. Campbell's *Shakespeare's Satire,* 105–106, and my discussion in Chapter II, Section 4 *(supra)*.

220. See Campbell, *ibid.,* and more especially his *Comicall Satyre and Shakespeare's Troilus and Cressida,* passim.

221. It is my conviction that the oft-noted book Ulysses carries and refers to in this scene is Montaigne's *Essays,* and that he has it open to the famous "Apology."

222. See *Tr. and Cr.,* IV, i; IV, iv; V, ii. This is not to say that Diomed is especially admirable in his own right, or any more trustworthy because of his plain-spokenness than is "honest Iago," another "forthright" man.

223. *Ibid.,* II, i, 58.

224. *Ibid.,* II, iii, 77–78.

225. *Ibid.,* III, iii, 314–315.

226. *Ibid.,* V, i, 52–53.

227. *Ibid.,* V, iv, 31–32.

228. *Ibid.,* V, ii, 195–196.

CHAPTER
10

SHAKESPEARE AND THE COUNTER–RENAISSANCE

I. HAMLET: HONOR VS. STOICISM

THROUGHOUT the literature of the Counter-Renaissance, from Ariosto and Tasso, through Rabelais and Marguerite of Navarre, to Elizabethan court writers like Sidney and Spenser, there are frequent references to the opposition between the courtly tradition of love and honor and the severe Stoic ethical code. It is essentially the conflict between an aristocratic ideal of gracious and sophisticated living (which could degenerate into a soft and decadent caricature of the original ideal) and a philosophical ideal of inner serenity (which could wither into a harsh and self-righteous condemnation of every one who took pleasure in the external goods of this world). In accordance with the prejudices of the writer or the exigencies of the particular story, one or the other ideal might be treated satirically or contemptuously, portrayed in misapplied excess.

We have already seen (in *Troilus and Cressida*) how devastatingly Shakespeare could deal with the insincerity of the romantic courtly ideal. He was not less interested in, or more gentle with, the extreme "Stoicke censour." As usual, his range of variation in treatment was wide. Jaques (in *As You Like it*), Malvolio, Antonio and the Old Duke (in *Measure for Measure*), Ulysses, Iago, Kent, Apemantus and even Enobarbus—all in quite different ways, ranging from genuine if austere virtue, through melancholy, sentimentality and cynicism, to total hypocrisy—belong at least partly to the "spying into abuses" or "plain-speaking righteous commentator" traditions. Occasionally there is explicit indebtedness to the Cynic-Stoic lineage which I have already described; more often it is clear that the figure in case has his chief significance in being representative of a tendency in Shakespeare's own times. Hence the ideological quarrel between the courtly tradition and the Stoic-Cynics (later, the Puritans) paralleled a less intellectualized opposition between the advocates of a worldly "art of living" and the proponents of an austere adherence to God's and nature's path of virtue.[1]

Finally, of course, there was the middle position—at least formally upheld by a majority of Elizabethans: the Christian-humanistic attitude toward life, with its emphasis upon moderation and harmony and balance. It had its admixture of Stoicism, to be sure, but it frowned upon the extreme doctrinal variety. It found the Castiglione courtly ideal compatible with its own tenets, but disapproved of the excessive exaltation of the ireful virtue to which that ideal, in its later variations, was likely to lead in practice. All three of these attitudes are apparent in *Hamlet*. . . .

Any consideration of honor and Stoicism in *Hamlet* must take into account the fact that Hamlet himself acts, a fair share of the time, in the "Stoicke censour" tradition. His bitter comments on the "fatness of these pursy times"—not alone in speaking to his mother, but in his whole estimate of the court, Denmark and the world ("an unweeded garden")—are couched in the savage terms of the tradition, and at times he even rails like an Apemantus.

Yet this is not his true nature. We have more evidence than that of Ophelia,[2] that he has been endowed with a rich abundance of talents, and educated to be the perfect courtier—"the glass of fashion and the mould of form." He has been as "observ'd" as Hotspur, but free of Hotspur's excesses. He has been that mixture of "scholar" and "soldier" that makes the Castiglione ideal so balanced and admirable.

And all this, indeed, we see briefly, in concrete action, at the beginning of the play. If his "Unhand me, gentlemen, By heaven, I'll make a ghost of him that lets me,"[3] displays the violent passion of which he is capable (making Maurice Evans' hysterical interpretation downright ludicrous); his courteous reception of Horatio and the guards[4] early shows us that the ireful virtue is ordinarily a virtue in Hamlet—an obedient or cooperative, not a ruling passion.

Here is a man, then, trained to the precepts of true, not excessive honor, suddenly so overwhelmed by the destruction of the very foundations of his world that he repudiates that world altogether. The honor and decency of mothers, the justice and moral responsibility of kings, the chastity and pure beauty of maidens, the faithfulness of counselors, the integrity of princes and sons—all these, in their various manifestations or in his feverish imaginings, are false and repulsively hypocritical. In his revulsion, he swings to the extreme Stoic-Cynic repudiation of the goods of the world and reviles it, constantly spying into its abuses, finding them ugly and it spiritually bankrupt.

Yet his training, his whole previous experience, has led him to the belief that it is good, and he is not spiritually or intellectually at home in this new orientation. "Stoicke censour" he may be, but he finds in himself no capacity for the positive side of this philosophical position. His blood is too hot, his allegiance to honorable positive action too ingrained, for him to find peace in an ideal of endurance, patience, passive fortitude—the Stoic "apathy." Hence, as we shall see in examining the great soliloquies, he expresses mostly contempt for the Stoic ideal, and is far more tolerant, even, of the excesses of the advocates of honor. On the level of external action, he is seeking honorable, just revenge; on the level of philosophical orientation, he is searching for *integration—a condition in which word and action may become one, with a mind at peace*. And because, until he attains this condition, *just and honorable* revenge is impossible, the resolution of the action must await the philosophical solution.

But before we examine this process bubbling in Hamlet's mind, it would be well to introduce the other figures in the play who represent concretely the option of choices, of attitudes open to him. In terms of an allegiance to the code of honor, Fortinbras and Laertes are the important characters. Fortinbras, in Horatio's words,

> Of *unimproved mettle hot and full,*
> Hath in the skirts of Norway, here and there,
> Shark'd up a list of *lawless resolutes,*
> For food and diet, to some enterprise
> That hath a stomach in't; which is no other,
> As it doth well appear unto our state,
> But to recover of us, *by strong hand*
> *And terms compulsatory,* these foresaid lands
> So by his father lost. . . .[5]

This "delicate and tender prince" whose spirit, as Hamlet later says, is "puff'd" with "divine ambition," is never associated with the fashionable courtly code of honor. He is honor's devotee in the much more general sense of the pursuer of glory, the hot-headed man of courage and action. His attempted revenge of his father's defeat and loss of lands at the hands of Hamlet's father is—though based on force and violence—an open and not dishonorable attempt So, by some standards, in his later invasion of Poland. Yet in the latter venture, there is a flaw (the flaw that persists in all codes which place individual honor—in the sense of glory and fame—first), and Hamlet, as we shall see, detects it.

In the last analysis, Polonius' words to Reynaldo about Laertes cover the situation of Fortinbras adequately, and his place in the intellectual texture of the play. Fortinbras' ambition and irresponsibility, we are allowed to believe, are

> the taints of liberty,
> The flash and outbreak of a fiery mind,
> A savageness in unreclaimed blood,
> Of general assault.[6]

In short, they are the faults of the unrestrained ireful virtue, appropriate enough—or at least forgivable and even promising—in a youth and soldier, although reprehensible in an older man and ruler. And since one may apply these words of Polonius to Fortinbras only in a general public way, as he conducts himself in terms of war, not of personal private conduct, one may assume that Fortinbras (even more than Prince Hal, for instance) will grow into a reliable and able king, to whom wisdom will then mean not individual honor, but the welfare of his people. Hence the satisfactoriness, in this respect, of the ending of the play, with Fortinbras succeeding to the throne.

Laertes is another matter. He is directly associated with the elaborate courtly code; in fact, he explicitly states his allegiance to it in the final dueling scene. Polonius' cynical delegation of Reynaldo to spy on Laertes, shortly after he has dispatched his son with the pretentious nobility of the "to thine own self" speech, reveals that very combination of an idealistic lip service to the honor code and a cynical acquaintance with its baser manifestations, with which we became familiar in *Troilus and Cressida*. It is, moreover, abundantly clear that for all his precautions, Polonius is not unduly alarmed over the prospects of Laertes' "unreclaimed blood." He wants to "have the goods" on him, to know just what the situation is, but he would rather have him a devotee of honor, renowned for "courtly" exploits, than a less "fiery mind." Success is virtue; in his own somewhat pitiful way (as compared with Claudius, for example) Polonius is a Machiavellian.

Laertes, like Hamlet, eventually faces the problem of revenge. But there is never any danger of conscience making a coward of him: in the established courtly tradition, he immediately recognizes revenge as rightful, above all authority of positive law. But unlike

Hamlet, who throughout remembers (even when he damns himself for it) that such a revenge must be executed in a spirit of just anger, controlled by reason, Laertes is carried away by "hot blood":

> That drop of blood that's calm proclaims me bastard . . .[7]

and

> To hell, allegiance! vows, to the blackest devil!
> Conscience and grace, to the profoundest pit!
> I dare damnation.[8]

When the king asks him,

> Who shall stay you?

he replies,

> My will, not all the world![9]

His will, directed only by his passion, rules all his actions. So, for example, when the priest explains why Ophelia, after her suicide, may not have the full rites of the church, he blurts out,

> I tell thee, churlish priest,
> A minist'ring angel shall my sister be
> When thou liest howling.[10]

He is ruled by passion—not ungenerous passion, to be sure, but unbridled. The only authority that he recognizes beyond that of his own impulses and will is that of the courtly code of honor—the formal articulated expression of his natural temperament. Hence, when Hamlet, in one of the most generous and moving speeches of the play, asks his forgiveness before they duel, Laertes replies,

> I am satisfied in nature,
> Whose motive in this case should stir me most
> To my revenge. But in my terms of honour
> I stand aloof, and will no reconcilement
> Till by some elder masters of known honour
> I have a voice and precedent of peace
> To keep my name ungor'd. But till that time
> I do receive your offer'd love like love,
> And will not wrong it.[11]

In short, Laertes accepts, in the spirit in which it is offered, Hamlet's apology—in nature (in terms of his feeling as a son) and in love. Yet he is skittish about accepting it in terms of honor, and thereby clearly shows that the "law of reputation" is more important to him than any other. Moreover, he entrusts to "some elder masters of known honour" the authority for a decision as to whether or not he may, *in terms of reputation*, safely forgive Hamlet. Thus the elaborate *code of honor*—when all the time he finds nothing dishonorable in reassuring Hamlet, while planning to run him through with a poisoned foil! Shakespeare's attitude toward the courtly code is not very different here from what it is in *Troilus and Cressida*. . . .

It has often been observed that Horatio is a Stoic, or at least that he possesses many attributes generally considered Stoic. When Hamlet is dying, and has entrusted to Horatio the task of reporting his cause aright, Horatio replies,

> Never believe it.
> I am more an antique Roman than a Dane.
> Here's yet some liquor left.[12]

Thus he explicitly makes the connection himself, and, like a true Roman Stoic, proposes to die at his own hands, once his "mission" in this world so full of "the storms of fate" is complete.[13]

Beyond this identification, however, there are the very terms in which Hamlet describes Horatio to his face, after telling him that he is the most just man he has ever known:

> For thou hast been
> As one, in suff'ring all, that suffers nothing;
> A man that Fortune's buffets and rewards
> Hast ta'en with equal thanks; and blest are those
> Whose blood and judgement are so well commingled
> That they are not a pipe for Fortune's finger
> To sound what stop she please. Give me that man
> That is not passion's slave, and I will wear him
> In my heart's core, ay, in my heart of heart,
> As I do thee.[14]

There are other relevant passages, but this one is so direct and explicit that it suffices by itself. Horatio, says Hamlet (to all intents and purposes), is the perfect Stoic. He is so completely the master of his soul that he has attained indifference to the goods and ills that Fortune, or the chance external events of this world, may bring to him. His state of grace as a Stoic is complete, for he relies only upon the inner goods of his own soul—he cannot be driven this way and that, as are most men, either by Fortune or by his own passions.

Once again, however, it is important to distinguish between the extreme ascetic position of the harsh Stoic-Cynic reformer and the milder, more balanced position of the sort of Stoicism advocated at times by Cicero (and by him equated with the ethical programs of Plato and Aristotle), the sort readily assimilated into the eventual Christian-humanistic position. Horatio, as we see in the final scene, is definitely, not vaguely, a Stoic—yet it is equally clear that he belongs to the more humane tradition and would advocate and practice not the extermination of the passions, but their control and direction.

In fact, Hamlet makes much of this point, stresses how *"well commingled"* are Horatio's "blood and judgement." And this, of course, is the nexus of his own problem. He has "blood" aplenty— his sudden passionate rages and abrupt sallies into violent action tell us this. When he acts, through most of the play, he acts with all the violence of the excessive proponents of the ireful virtue. When he thinks and delays and ponders the niceties of conscience and judgment, he also does this to excess, and his will to action is paralyzed. His "Stoicke censour" vituperations, again, demonstrate both "blood" (in their very passionate excesses, as with his mother) and "judgement" (in their excoriation and repudiation of the passions, as with his advice to Ophelia—"get thee to a nunnery")—but never "well commingled." To achieve such a state, to approximate the integration of an Horatio—*this* is his self-appointed task. Until he can achieve it, he is too finely tuned morally to permit himself to move to revenge, for it will be an ill-consummated revenge, accomplished in the hot blood of the extreme "honor" tradition. And meanwhile he must rest in the "patience and endurance" tradition of Stoicism. Yet this yoke chafes and binds him, rather than directs him—for it is a forced patience and endurance, not the true and positive variety practiced by Horatio. Hamlet knows the words of the Stoic litany; he does not feel them or wholly believe them.

But let us follow him more closely, and watch the cumulative process of this conflict and its eventual resolution. Let him speak for himself.

We should first note that early in the play Hamlet is ready for revenge. When his father's ghost appears and urges him to the act (before disclosing the murderer's identity), Hamlet's reply is prompt:

> Haste me to know't, that I, with wings as swift
> As meditation or the thoughts of love,
> May sweep to my revenge.[15]

Then he learns that it has been Claudius, and for the first time fully realizes the role his mother has played in relation to the two kings. Hamlet's first reaction is one of horror; his second, in accordance with his peculiarly generalizing intellectual nature (which makes so admirably for the intertwining of the philosophical and plot levels of the play), is to identify the falseness of Claudius and Gertrude with that of the whole pattern of the world he has known—and to repudiate the pattern, as well as the individuals, in his concentration upon revenge:

> Yea, from the table of my memory
> I'll wipe away *all trivial fond records,*
> *All saws of books, all forms, all pressures past*
> *That youth and observation copied there,*
> And thy commandment all alone shall live
> Within the book and volume of my brain,
> Unmix'd with baser matter.[16]

Here are two significant points: he will not only expunge from his memory all the personal devotions of his childhood and youth, but also all the "records" and injunctions and convictions he has learned from study and observation. This is the first point—his sweeping indictment of all that has hitherto seemed right and good, and his determination to find a new orientation, of which so far he knows nothing except that it must include obedience to the imperative for revenge. And the second, related point is that this marks a conscious end to his youthful immaturity. The apprenticeship to life is over; with this violent traumatic experience, he must accept maturity and find a mature orientation, or he is lost.

A few lines later, speaking to Horatio, he is so full of his discovery that things are not as they have seemed to be, that he bursts out grimly,

> There are more things in heaven and earth, Horatio,
> Then are dreamt of in your philosophy.[17]

But he has made a promise to his father, and this is not the time for words or philosophizing. So he goes on to explain that he is going to put on an "antic disposition." It seems clear that in deciding this so promptly (aside from the dramatic exigencies that demand getting on with the action, and first laying the ground) Hamlet knows only that henceforth he is a stranger in a strange land —and with that quick intuitive gift for ironic appropriateness that led him to the identification of the funeral and marriage meats, has decided only that he must act mad in so mad a world, if he is to retain his sanity. At this moment he is brisk, all for action; yet as the scene closes, the apprehensive shadows of the future are already closing over him, and he is cursing the fate that has set him the task of righting this wrong.[18] The dichotomy is established.

For he is not ready for such a task. He has resolutely cast off "all saws of books, all forms," and he has as yet no new orientation.

His dilemma is underlined for him by his session with the players, and the first of the three famous soliloquies on his plight is the direct consequence of observing the passion the first player has put into his speech about Hecuba. What appalls him is that an actor, feigning passion, could give so convincing a portrayal of grief: "What's Hecuba to him, or he to Hecuba, That he should weep for her? What would he do, Had he the motive and the cue for *passion* That I have?"[19]

Passion is the power of the soul that can properly deal with matters of revenge. Passion he has and shows—yet uses it only, he declares,

> (like a whore) [to] unpack my heart with words
> And fall a-cursing like a very drab,
> A scullion![20]

What has not usually been noticed about this passage is that at first, given the example of the actor, he reproaches himself for being a "John-a-dreams," who "can *say* nothing!"[21] Then, after repudiating the self-charge of cowardice,[22] and then in bewilderment accepting it, since he has *done* nothing in way of revenge,[23] he catches himself in the act of mouthing "vengeance" like a Senecan tragic hero or (as he says) "a whore." Immediately he reprimands himself for lack of direction—"About, my brain!"—and sets to work on a plan.

The players are to hand, and he conceives "The play within a play." Thus he'll "have grounds more relative than this"[24]—that is, more certain evidence than his father's ghost, which may not have been his father's real spirit, but the devil assuming that form,[25] has provided him. The scene ends with Hamlet for the first time resolute and purposeful.

It is not much to our present purpose to argue the pros and cons of the validity of his doubts about the "honesty" of his father's ghost. Whether Shakespeare intended us to take Hamlet's statement here literally, or wanted us to accept it as rationalization that would enable Hamlet to defend to himself his delay, is not so important to the course of this argument as the fact that Hamlet is at this point aware of a state of irresoluteness and bewilderment, with a resultant paralysis, and that he *temporarily* resolves his dilemma by planning a course of action which will determine the validity of Claudius' guilt. In either case, all his instincts and training have made him a man who shrinks from acting unjustly. But, more, he is too highly conscious a man to be willing to proceed

without being convinced of an ultimate meaning and pattern of
human life into which this single act can fit coherently and con-
gruously. The philosophical issue is not joined as yet.

But it is joined in the very next scene, when the two basic alternatives of action—both in general and in his specific situation—are
presented in his most famous soliloquy.

> To be, or not to be—that is the question:
> Whether 'tis nobler in the mind to suffer
> The slings and arrows of outrageous fortune
> Or to take arms against a sea of troubles,
> And by opposing end them.[26]

The words merit a close examination, "To be"—that is, to endure;
for Hamlet goes on to present the parallel construction: "Whether
'tis nobler in the mind to suffer The slings and arrows of outrageous
fortune. . . ." Then "Or not to be," which is paralleled by "Or to
take arms against a sea of troubles, And by opposing end them."

The first alternative is the patience and endurance of the Stoic,
who suffers with equanimity all that fortune brings, strong in his
inner serenity. The second is the position of honor, which seeks a
just revenge, and with it an unsullied reputation, no matter what
the other consequences to himself. We have already seen Shakespeare considering these alternatives in a later play, *Timon of
Athens,* so exactly that it would be wise to requote the speeches of
Alcibiades and the Senator. Here the captain upholds honor's right:

> Nor did he soil the fact with cowardice
> (An honour in him which buys out his fault)
> But with a noble fury and fair spirit,
> Seeing his reputation touched to death,
> He did oppose his foe. . . .[27]

To this the Senator, maintaining the Stoic attitude, replies:

> He's truly valiant that can wisely suffer
> The worst that man can breathe, and make his wrongs
> His outsides, to wear them like his raiment, carelessly,
> And ne'er prefer his injuries to his heart,
> To bring it into danger.[28]

Stoic, I say, for while Christian sufferance and patience may bear
a like mien,[29] the references to Horatio the Stoic and the repetition
of allusions to the buffetings of Fortune in *Hamlet,* and the classical
background and explicit Cynic pedigree of Apemantus in *Timon,*
make it clear that Shakespeare intends the point of view to be Stoic.

The opposition of the two points of view is more briefly set forth in the opening lines of the "To be or not to be" soliloquy. And, since the odds against Hamlet, if he does "take arms against a sea of troubles," are great enough to make it likely that he will end those troubles by his own death, he moves on to the question of death:

> To die—to sleep—
> No more; and by a sleep to say we end
> The heartache, and the thousand natural shocks
> That flesh is heir to. 'Tis a consummation
> Devoutly to be wish'd.[30]

This is precisely the Stoic view of death—a man's task done, death is the release from storm-tossed life. But Hamlet, musing, is caught on a repetition of the words "to die—to sleep."

> To sleep—perchance to dream: ay, there's the rub!
> For in that sleep of death what dreams may come
> When we have shuffled off this mortal coil
> Must give us pause.[31]

Since he is not *ready,* since he has not yet come to a satisfactory conclusion about the nature of man, and of life and death, he cannot accept the Stoic concept of death as release, and sleep. Indeed, he goes on to say that uncertainty is the only reason that anyone accepts the Stoic doctrine of passive endurance: "There's the respect That makes calamity of so long life":

> For who would bear the whips and scorns of time,
> Th' oppressor's wrong, the proud man's contumely,
> The pangs of despis'd love, the law's delay,
> The insolence of office, and the spurns
> That patient merit of th' unworthy takes,
> When he himself might his quietus make
> With a bare bodkin? Who would these fardels bear,
> To grunt and sweat under a weary life,
> But that the dread of something after death—
> The undiscover'd country, from whose bourn
> No traveller returns—puzzles the will,
> And makes us rather bear those ills we have
> Than fly to others that we know not of?[32]

This passage shows how far as yet Hamlet is from an acceptance of the Stoic conception of either life or death. He has no confidence in the concept of death as release when "the day's work is done"; he is almost contemptuous in his description of the ideal of patient endurance. Indeed, he sees the whole process of the life of submission as rationalization for cowardice:

> Thus conscience does make cowards of us all,
> And thus the native hue of resolution
> Is sicklied o'er with the pale cast of thought,
> And enterprises of great pith and moment
> With this regard their currents turn awry
> And lose the name of action.[33]

Conscience vs. resolution; the pale cast of thought vs. the name of action. Here all his training, his traditional background bursts out again: he is honor's child, supporting the revolt of the ireful virtue, and as scornful of the Stoic's patient appeal to reason and "apathy" as Troilus was when he said in not dissimilar words:

> Nay, if we talk of reason
> Let's shut our gates and sleep. Manhood and honour
> Should have hare hearts, would they but fat their thoughts
> With this regard their currents turn awry
> Make livers pale and lustihood deject.[34]

Once again Hamlet is in a state of passionate paralysis. The rival codes of honor and Stoicism, with their attitudes toward the good life and toward death, have been considered. The former he feels incapable of; the latter he dismisses with contempt. He leaves this session with himself, ripe to overwhelm Ophelia with his railings against the discrepancy between the ideals we profess and the practices we pursue.

Yet the brew is fermenting. That he can appreciate the relevance of the Stoic virtues to other people and situations than his own is apparent in the very next scene, when he pays his tribute to Horatio. It seems as though, whenever he soliloquizes, the introspective passage ends in a negative picture of himself; yet each time he moves on to a consolidation of either a further course of action, or a closer approximation of an understanding of which way integration may be found. Here, having given the lie to the Stoic's doctrine of patient imperturbability—as being only the cowardly choice of the lesser (since the better known) of two evils—he refers to it with respect, in designating Horatio as its living example.

Then the playlet, and the king's obvious guiltiness. Hamlet's nervous exultation borders on the hysterical, yet he retains enough of this growing confidence and purpose to dispose of Rosencrantz and Guildenstern with point and ease—and it is interesting to note that he uses the "pipe" imagery. To Horatio he has praised men who "are not a pipe for Fortune's finger To sound what stop she please." Now he accuses Guildenstern of trying to play on him in just this fashion:

Why, look you now, how unworthy a thing you make of me! You would play upon me; you would seem to know my stops; you would pluck out the heart of my mystery; you would sound me from my lowest note to the top of my compass; and there is much music, excellent voice, in this little organ [the recorder], yet cannot you make it speak. 'Sblood, do you think I am easier to be play'd on than a pipe? Call me what instrument you will, though you can fret me, you cannot play upon me.[35]

Here, clearly, is a growing sense of command of himself, and purpose and direction for both his specific and general errands in life. That he uses this imagery (if we keep its former employment in our minds, as he evidently has in his) is of further significance. He is on his way—his opponents may still "fret" him, but they can no longer play upon him.

And so it proves—through the scene of Claudius at prayer, that with his mother, the stabbing of Polonius, and the dismissal to England. He is far from clear as yet about the particulars of the route he must follow, but there is a sense of savage urgency, of movement and purposiveness, about him, that has been missing until now.

Then comes the third important soliloquy ("How all occasions do inform against me"), which occurs on his way to take ship to England. He questions Fortinbras' captain about the expedition against Poland. As with the case of the player mourning Hecuba, Hamlet finds in Fortinbras a reproach to himself for his "dull revenge." He considers again why he has not consummated the revenge. Is it "bestial oblivion, or some craven scruple Of thinking too precisely on th'event"? For he knows that he has—and too many Shakespearian scholar-detectives forget this—"cause, and *will,* and *strength,* and *means* To do't."[36] The player can weep for a queen in a play; Fortinbras can consider it a matter of his honor to battle over "a little patch of ground That hath in it no profit but the name"[37]:

> Examples gross as earth exhort me.
> Witness this army of such mass and charge,
> Led by a delicate and tender prince,
> Whose spirit, with divine ambition puff'd,
> Makes mouths at the invisible event,
> Exposing what is mortal and unsure
> To all that fortune, death, and danger dare,
> Even for an eggshell.[38]

Even though the text indicates no pause here, there is one, if we know Hamlet's habit of mind. So far he has considered the "grossest" example of all—in this devotee of honor who dares all without question, "even for an eggshell." A pause—for a Hamlet cannot, beyond his moment's envy for a man so full of "great enterprises" and so faithful to "the name of action," accept this immoderate and indiscriminate interpretation of honor. No, he stops—a full stop—and when he takes up again, it is to define true honor and true greatness:

> Rightly to be great
> Is not to stir without great argument,
> But greatly to find quarrel in a straw
> When honour's at the stake.[39]

This is to repudiate Fortinbras' conception of honor; it is also to reaffirm, to consolidate anew the task before Hamlet. The lesson to be found in this expedition is no less valid than before, but it is not the same as before:

> How stand I then,
> That have a father kill'd, a mother stain'd,
> Excitements of *my reason and my blood,*
> And let all sleep, while to my shame I see
> The imminent death of twenty thousand men
> That for a fantasy and trick of fame
> Go to their graves like beds, fight for a plot
> Whereon the numbers cannot try the cause,
> Which is not tomb enough and continent
> To hide the slain? O, from this time forth,
> My thoughts be bloody, or be nothing worth![40]

It is, as it has always been taken, a summons to resolution after seeing twenty thousand men, who have no such cause as his, go unprotestingly to probable death. But if they shame him in this sense, it is not because he finds what they are doing good—still less that he approves the arrogant ambition of Fortinbras, who casually sentences them to death "for a fantasy and trick of fame." No, now that Hamlet has formally defined honor to himself—has, through this meeting, defined it emotionally as well as intellectually, so that he is not merely reciting a definition, but stamping it upon his soul—he recognizes "excitements of *my reason and my blood,*" and seems for the first time to feel that "commingling" which he has so admired in Horatio. He has the "great argument"; hence his true honor really is at stake. He has established convincing evidence of guilt; hence he should be ready to find "quarrel in a straw."

But—"greatly." It is too easy to forget the "greatly." First, "Rightly to be great"; then, "great argument"; finally, "*greatly* to find quarrel in a straw." Not just to kill in turn, not just to incite in order to bring about the chance for revenge—but to do it "greatly," magnanimously, justly, as befits a man whose reason and blood are allies, not opponents. As befits a man who is *whole*, not divided—a man capable of greatness because in full command of himself.

What is finally hinted here, then, is Hamlet's beginning to feel, as well as to understand, that the opposition between honor and Stoicism, between blood and reason, between action and thought, is unnecessary to *him*. In Horatio, he has long since understood this, but his discovery of its possibilities for himself has remained an almost abstract concept. He finally believes, now, that he is capable of it—and while his thoughts will be bloody, his actions will be purposeful and, given the situation, reasonable. Integration is imminent.

We do not see him again until near the end. The mad Ophelia, the revenge-bound Laertes, and the shaken Claudius hold the stage. Yet as always Shakespeare is playing ironic variations on his theme: Claudius, whom Hamlet has spared at prayer, says to Laertes that "No place indeed should murther sanctuarize," and (on the heels of Hamlet's coming to a decision of when and how revenge is honorable) remarks that "Revenge should have no bounds."[41]

When Hamlet returns (we first see him in the graveyard with Horatio), he is sad and contemplative, but there is a marked difference, all the same. True, his thoughts, even before he picks up Yorick's skull, are all of death, and the humor that considers Alexander's and Cæsar's dust is grim. But not morbid. When Horatio thinks that he is considering "too curiously," he denies the charge, with a "catechism" that suggests a new imperturbability toward death and a loss of his fears about the dreams that may follow it:

> No, faith, not a jot; but to follow him thither with modesty enough, and likelihood to lead it; as thus: Alexander dies, Alexander was buried, Alexander returneth into dust; the dust is earth; of earth we make loam; and why of that loam (whereto he was converted) might they not stop a beer barrel?[42]

It is the calmer, more considered version of "a king may go a progress through the guts of a beggar."[43]

True, he grapples with Laertes in Ophelia's grave. He is enraged at what he feels is "mouthing" and "ranting"—and with some justice, since Laertes has struck a posture in the open grave and told the attendants to pile the dirt upon "the quick and the dead"; all that we know of him suggests that this is a wildly exaggerated display of his love for his sister.

Moreover, Hamlet is well in control of himself in this scene. When Laertes, crying "The devil take thy soul," grasps him by the throat, Hamlet's speech shows a restraint that suggests all the more effectively the strength held back:

> Thou pray'st not well.
> I prithee take thy fingers from my throat;
> For, though I am not splenitive and rash,
> Yet have I in me something dangerous,
> Which let thy wisdom fear. Hold off thy hand![44]

It is not, I think, pressing the point to assume that Hamlet is explicitly thinking of Laertes as "splenitive and rash," and implicitly camparing his kind of "ireful virtue" honor with Hamlet's own hard-won kind. And while he appeals to Laertes at the end of the scene to tell him why he feels so antagonistic when he (Hamlet) has ever "lov'd" him, he ends on a note, not of indifference, but of acceptance that things will be as they will be.[45]

The note is sustained and developed in the next scene, to become a forthright profession of faith—a profession containing many Stoic elements. This is in the conversation between Hamlet and Horatio in which Hamlet relates what has happened to him during his absence from Denmark. What has "happened" (externally) is interesting to Horatio; what has happened to Hamlet's nature interests him and us more. And it has been considerable; it emerges in short, epigrammatic judgments.

The first of these Hamlet sums up in the discovery that "There's a divinity that shapes our ends, Rough-hew them how we will—" a discovery that comes from the way in which his "rashness" and "indiscretion" aboard ship, in hunting out Guildenstern's and Rosencrantz' packet, has served him better than all his "deep plots"; and a discovery to which Horatio replies quietly, "That is most certain."[46]

This acceptance of destiny, of *pronoia* or the Stoic *fatum*, means a real change in Hamlet—as it prepares him for a readiness to fit himself to "the main sway of the universe." True liberty and purpose, for the Stoic, lie in the inner strength and calm to which I have referred, and they in turn come only to the man who has accepted "the course of things": *the gods lead those who are willing.* . . .

Hamlet's new strength and confidence in the rightness of his actions in letting "Guildenstern and Rosencrantz go to't" draws from Horatio an exclamation over the change that has taken place in him: "Why, what a king is this!"[47] And when Hamlet, pursuing the subject, is able to say, "is't not perfect conscience . . ."[48] we know that what has been apparent to the rest of us all the time is now finally squared in Hamlet's own mind—that the seeds planted in the soliloquy after talking to Fortinbras' captain have come to full fruition.

The change is so complete that Hamlet can confess his regret about having challenged Laertes in the grave without self-recrimination, to which he has been so prone in the past. As for Horatio's concern about what will happen when Claudius learns of Rosencrantz' and Guildenstern's death, Hamlet answers briefly and calmly,

> It will be short; the interim is mine,
> And a man's life's no more than to say "one."[49]

And after the nonsense with Osric (who plays the caricature of the honor tradition even more grotesquely than did Æneas in *Troilus and Cressida*), and despite the uneasiness he feels "about my heart," his presentiment of what's to come, Hamlet enlarges upon the theme:

> Not a whit, we defy augury; there's a special providence in the fall of a sparrow. If it be now, 'tis not to come; if it be not to come, it will be now; if it be not now, yet it will come; the readiness is all. Since no man knoweth aught of what he leaves, what is't to leave betimes? Let be.[50]

The readiness is all. The struggle toward integration and consequent resolution is complete. His house is in order, its owner in possession. He has made his peace with himself, and hence with the order of things in general, and with the eventualities of life and death. He has become that man he would wear in his heart of heart—"that man that is not passion's slave."

In what happens thereafter, he acts with justice, with confidence and power, with purpose and honor. He is not only in control of himself, but (with all the odds against him) of the whole situation. When he asks Laertes for forgiveness, when he towers over the cowering king, when he forbids Horatio to follow him into death until he has reported things aright—he dominates the scene. His task done, he is "absolute for death" as no one in *Measure for Measure* ever is. And he accepts the Stoic's view of death when he says to Horatio,

> Absent thee from felicity awhile,
> And in this harsh world draw thy breath in pain,
> To tell my story.[51]

He accepts the Stoic's view of death—and of life ("the readiness is all")—yet in so doing he finds that he is acquitting himself in the truest tradition of honor. He reconciles the opposites, which he finds at the last not inevitable opponents—but only so when "held in the extreme." And so he comes to that conciliatory, positive position of the great central Christian-humanistic tradtion. Indeed, there are (as notably in Horatio's farewell: "Goodnight, sweet prince, And flights of angels sing thee to thy rest!"[52]) explicit Christian overtones in this, alone of the tragedies.

Yet when all is said, it is not useful to try to pin Shakespeare down to the exact lines of any one of these intellectual traditions we have been following. As we shall shortly see, his treatment of Stoicism in *Lear* is related, yet quite different. Our purpose in these studies is to show his awareness of these currents, rather than his alignment with any particular one. What does seem to me to emerge again and again in his plays, whether stated negatively or positively, bitterly or joyfully, is "Nothing too much—and nothing too little." The excess of devotion to honor may catch his imagination in a Hotspur; but any excess is out of proportion and false and bad —the excess of harsh dogmatic Stoicism equally so. There is room for the positive features of both of these attitudes, and more, many more. What there should never be room for is either stern prohibition or wanton extravagance—though he can deal indulgently or even sympathetically with both. But that is because he was a great creative spirit, not because he holds to so indiscriminate a philosophical view.

When one has finished the story of Hamlet's struggle for solution, integration and resolution, as when one has finished so much else of Shakespeare, one could do worse than return to Hamlet's advice to the players—advice that he eventually was able to follow himself:

> Nor do not saw the air too much with your hand, thus, but use all gently; for in the very torrent, tempest, and (as I may say) whirlwind of your passion, you must acquire and beget a temperance that may give it smoothness. . . . Be not too tame neither; but let your discretion be your tutor. Suit the action to the word, the word to the action; with this special observance, that you o'erstep not the modesty of nature. . . .[53]

This is not relevant alone to actors' techniques.

2. LEAR: NATURE VS. STOICISM

When we turn to *Lear,* and reconsider it in the light of the ideological currents of the Renaissance and Counter-Renaissance, we are immediately confronted again with Guillaume du Vair's two great general opponents: "Nature" or "Epicureanism" and "Stoicism." These two, Du Vair had proclaimed, were the only two philosophies still tenable, and Shakespeare presents the world of *Lear* as though he had used this statement for a foreword.

Du Vair, we have seen, probably employed his two terms in the sense of the rival ethical positions of "bastard Stoicism" and eclectic humanistic "Stoicism." The latter, the traditional Christian-humanistic program, he propounds in the books of his early and middle period. The former substitutes the "law" of individualistic naturalism for the rational law of nature, instinct for reason, the particular for the universal, the motive of self-preservation for that of virtue and justice. We have further considered this opposition in terms of Nature vs. Art; we have followed its personification in Bussy and Clermont D'Ambois.

But the opposition reaches out to cover a still larger stage—one that is wheeled into sight every time a state, a world, a way of life is threatened with disintegration. It is not an accident that the Epicureans and Stoics dominated the philosophical scene in the days when Rome was decaying and dying. For in the face of imminent catastrophe and the almost certain extinction of the familiar order of things, there are only two points of view that seem valid and pertinent to most people: the one, to operate on a pleasure-pain principle, and squeeze the best that remains out of life for oneself; the other, to find an inner contentment and security that constitute a reward in themselves, and a bulwark against all "the slings and arrows of outrageous fortune."

These are very imperfect renderings of the points of view of Roman Epicureanism and Stoicism, yet they will do for our purposes, if we retain the wider perspective of "Epicureanism" and "Stoicism" in the large generalized senses in which I have used them. Both points of view are withdrawals from the active arena of public life, although their proponents would seldom admit this. They are withdrawals, because they concede defeat in the given social context, and concentrate on some sort of inner victory to be achieved through escape or transference of "the battle" from the public social and political stage to the private one of the individual soul.

Ironically enough, both philosophies would maintain that they are concerned with the relation of the individual human soul to the *whole* general order of things, rather than to the *particular* order of things in a given society or civilization. Ironically—since

this is a valid point. Yet, both in motive and result, the retreat from
the particular and immediate to the "eternal" defeats the application of the "eternal" principles in that particular immediate. And
since the universal may become effective only through particulars,
the very end sought is likely to be lost through the "search." Between the individual and the "eternal," then, lies a gap which might
be filled by the individual's working toward the realization of the
"eternal" ideals *in* the particular social context in which he finds
himself. Without this intermediate step, the relation is apt to take
on a "vacuum" character.

"Something too much of this." What we have propounded is that,
in times of the breaking up of an old order (whether a political,
social or ideological order), the dominant philosophies are apt to
be philosophies of desperation, even of despair. And such (despite
the qualifications made above) were Epicureanism and Stoicism
in Roman times, and—for a modern example—Existentialism today.
There may be nobility of a sort in these positions, and usually they
are motivated by a desire for substantial positive values. But through
their rejection of the intermediate world of their socio-political or
philosophical environment, which is disintegrating (or, at the best,
changing drastically), and through their attempt to consider the
individual exclusively *sub specie aeternitatis,* they may justly be
called philosophies of desperation or despair.

That Du Vair had something of the sort in mind, when he spoke
of "Nature" and "Stoicism" as alone *tenable* in his time, seems to
me probable—especially since, in his later writings, he underwent
so radical a change in his own point of view, moving from a traditional humanistic (and explicitly Stoic) position to a semi-cynical,
wholly disillusioned Machiavellian one.[54] And certainly the picture
of the complete reorientation necessary to those aware of the implications of the Counter-Renaissance—whether concerning an acceptance of those implications or an attempt at the renovating of
traditional views to meet the new challenges—justifies his concern,
if not the exact terms of his statement.

Lear presents the same picture in dramatic form. The whole play
is unmistakably concerned with a dying order, in which the protagonists of Nature and Stoicism fight for supremacy. This general
conclusion is not at all original. It has been treated at length by
numerous scholars, using various approaches and orientations. The
most recent of these (at this writing) is perhaps the most comprehensive, balanced and informed—Robert B. Heilman's *This Great
Stage.*[55] Mr. Heilman recognizes the same central opposition that

I do, although he does not use the same terms. And he deals with this opposition at much greater length than I can in the scope of this chapter. The contribution of my interpretation must remain that of setting the opposition in the intellectual context of the times, and against the backdrop of the Counter-Renaissance.

Let us turn first to the protagonists of the philosophy of "Nature" in *Lear*. The tone for their part in the drama is set almost immediately by Gloucester, as he describes Edmund, his illegitimate son, to Kent in the first scene:

> . . . Though this knave came somewhat saucily into the world
> before he was sent for, yet was his mother fair, there was good
> sport at his making, and the whoreson must be acknowledged.[56]

"The whoreson must be acknowledged. . . ." Without immediate comment, let us turn next to the statement of Edmund himself, not long thereafter:

> Thou, Nature, art my goddess; to thy law
> My services are bound. Wherefore should I
> Stand in the plague of custom, and permit
> The curiosity of nations to deprive me,
> For that I am some twelve or fourteen moonshines
> Lag of a brother? Why bastard? wherefore base?
> When my dimensions are as well compact,
> My mind as generous, and my shape as true,
> As honest madam's issue? Why brand they us
> With base? With baseness? bastardy? base, base?
> Who, in the lusty stealth of nature, take
> More composition and fierce quality
> Than doth, within a dull, stale, tired bed,
> Go to th' creating a whole tribe of fops
> Got 'tween a sleep and wake? Well then,
> Legitimate Edgar, I must have your land.
> Our father's love is to the bastard Edmund
> As to th' legitimate. Fine word—"legitimate"!
> Well, my legitimate, if this letter speed,
> And my invention thrive, Edmund the base
> Shall top th' legitimate. I grow, I prosper.
> Now, gods, stand up for bastards![57]

Here, in two speeches early in the play, is contained the core of the naturalists' *raison d'être* and ethical program in *Lear*. Gloucester's description of Edmund's origin is soaked in the "bastard Stoic" (the pun is unintentional) attitude toward the imperative needs of the flesh, the debunking of exclusively idealistic and noble mo-

tives—in short, to the acknowledgment of "the whoreson." Edmund
professes defiantly and openly his devotion to the Goddess Nature,
which means to him Venus Genatrix. His references to "the plague
of custom," and "the curiosity of nations," his assertion that his
natural attributes should outweigh the niceties of that "custom" and
"law," his contempt for the word "legitimate" and its meaning—all
are reminiscent of the tradition of individualistic naturalism. His
"Nature" is uninhibited by established concepts of "law" and
"reason"; fertile, amoral, she recognizes none of these man-made
hypotheses about her. Nor does he.

In his origin, then, and in his justification for his point of view,
he presents in fact and in speech the naturalistic position—the protest of nature. Yet two lines in his speech which should not be overlooked are

> Who, in the lusty stealth of nature, take
> More composition and fierce quality. . . .

They should not be overlooked, for they suggest that "religion of
energy," of *virtù*, which belongs more closely to the materialistic-
animalistic school of naturalism that I have identified with Machiavelli and Guicciardini, than to the blander primitivistic-naturalistic
school that Montaigne most ably represents. And indeed, as we
watch Edmund move on through the play, we see that whatever
his origin and formal profession may be, his practical philosophy
is Machiavellian—a debased Machiavellianism, to be sure, but recognizable.

To take only one example, consider the implications of the instructions and advice he tenders a captain late in the play:

> Come hither, Captain; hark.
> Take thou this note [*gives a paper*]. Go follow them
>   [*Cordelia and Lear*] to prison.
> One step I have advanc'd thee. If thou dost
> As this instructs thee, thou dost make thy way
> To noble fortunes. Know thou this, that men
> Are as the time is. To be tender-minded
> Does not become a sword. Thy great employment
> Will not bear question. Either say thou'lt do't,
> Or thrive by other means.[58]

Here is the ethical philosophy of *success* in as neat a nutshell as
one could find, replete with such explicit Machiavellianisms as
"men are as the time is" and "To be tender-minded does not become a sword."

More than that, Goneril and Regan, the other two important practitioners of the "philosophy of Nature" in *Lear,* demonstrate the same blend of the naturalistic recognition of the primacy of appetite and the Machiavellian-materialistic dedication to success.

Nor does this indicate any confusion in Shakespeare's mind. It should be remembered that to maintain consistently the philosophic naturalism of a Montaigne, and—granted the central premise of naturalism—to see life sanely and whole, and finally from that vision to produce a naturalistic humanism, requires a *philosopher,* however informal and unsystematic a one. I have already pointed out that many of the Elizabethan literary protagonists of naturalism had in common with Montaigne only the central principles of naturalism, and were apt to be "villains" propounding both "individualistic-naturalistic" and "materialistic" (as I have defined these) values.

Moreover, in practice, these points of view could easily blend and merge. The differences among the conscious proponents of "bastard Stoicism," Machiavellian materialism, the "follow your bent" school, and the fashionable "humour" school, lie mostly in their philosophical origins. What they all share, once the technical niceties are disposed of, is their contempt for the traditional humanistic values of "justice" and "law" and "right reason" and "virtue," which they find (in the consistent manner of the Counter-Renaissance) simply to be man-made custom, opinion, prejudice—hypothetical "art" that is not in any sense established, as the humanists claimed, in the very nature of things.

And what they share, by way of a positive program, is the determination to get ahead, to preserve themselves and forward their own ambitions, to recognize only the "law of their own natures" and follow their own inclinations. There being to them no perceptible ultimate purpose and moral order in the nature of things (or, as we shall see, in nature itself), these "naturalists" substitute *virtù* for virtue in the traditional sense. The ends (success, advancement) justify the means in a jungle world that is truly animalistic.

For it is no accident that there are so many references to beasts in *Lear.* Machiavelli's fox, lion and wolves are implicit throughout in the actions and points of view of Edmund, Goneril, Regan, Cornwall; this disintegrating world is explicitly peopled by sub-human species, half or wholly animal. Lear continually dwells on the subject in his "reasoned madness"; Albany refers to it in an important speech. The "beast" images, indeed, recur again and again.[59] And no better description of the two evil sisters exists than "the gilded serpent" and "the tigress."

So much, briefly, then, for the proponents of "Nature." Those of Stoicism are dealt with in much more detail. What was of importance in *Hamlet*, in *Lear* is of still greater importance, and is treated with an obviously extensive knowledge of dogmatic Stoicism.

It was Professor Marjorie Nicolson who first suggested to me that *Lear* was a "Stoic play" and pointed out many of the Stoic qualities in the career and speeches of Kent and the ordeal of Lear. Following up her lead, I have found confirmation of her conviction in the characters of Cordelia and Edgar and the "juxtaposition" of Kent and the Fool, as well as in the points of view of many of the characters toward the "nature of nature" and the moral order of the universe, and in the "hard primitivism" advocated by various characters in the best Stoic-Cynic manner.

Let us begin with Kent. We have already noted (in Chapter II) that Lear's fool is the wise "buffoon" type of satirical commentator, and that Kent is the other sort of commentator, the sturdy Stoic wise man, who deals in "plain speaking." That is, he imitates Cynic behavior as "the expression of the right and duty of the truly virtuous man to rebuke evil in others."[60] We have already noted, too, the scene in which Cornwall, coming to the rescue of Oswald, makes this identification of Kent with the traditional "plain man"—commenting satirically, to be sure, but without effectiveness to the audience, since he is already established as an evil character.[61] The final confirmation of this role of Kent's will be apparent if we turn to the first scene in the whole play, and especially to the lines

> To plainness honour's bound
> Where majesty falls to folly.[62]

But Kent is a Stoic in a much more comprehensive and exact sense than simply as a "plain man" commentator. Indeed, he is an almost perfect doctrinal Stoic, endures the stocks and all of fortune's ills with true "apathy," and leaves the stage at the end of the play to commit suicide—now that his task's done. For, as Hicks says in his *Stoic and Epicurean,*

> Virtue [to the Stoic] does not consist in doing the greatest possible number of good actions, but in an uninterrupted series of such acts. Temporal prolongation can add no whit to happiness. . . .[63]

This uninterrupted series Kent has performed in the service of the old King and truth. But there is another reason why "the doctrine of suicide was indeed the culminating point of Roman Stoicism."

The proud, self-reliant, unbending character of the philosopher could only be sustained when he felt that he had a sure refuge against the extreme forms of suffering and despair. . . . Stoicism taught men to hope little, but to fear nothing. It did not array death in brilliant colors, as the path to positive felicity, but it endeavoured to divest it, as the end of suffering, of every terror. Life lost much of its bitterness when men had found a refuge from the storms of fate, a speedy deliverance from dotage and pain. Death ceased to be terrible when it was regarded rather as a remedy than as a sentence.[64]

This passage reads almost as though it were a description of the death of Lear and the conclusion of the play. Death is indeed "the end of suffering, of every terror" for Lear—"a refuge from the storms of fate, a speedy deliverance from dotage and pain" and "a remedy rather than a sentence. . . ." And it is inevitably Kent who realizes and expresses this Stoic idea:

> Break, heart; I prithee break[65]

and

> Vex not his ghost. Oh, let him pass! He hates him
> That would upon the rack of this tough world
> Stretch him out longer.[66]

But we were talking about suicide. Since "death and the time of death are neither morally good nor morally evil, but things indifferent"[67] the Stoic believed that there were times when it was not only proper, but imperative to take death into one's own hands.[68] Such an occasion had arrived for Kent, who had served Lear faithfully and honestly and uninterruptedly—who had completed his task, so to speak, and who himself had merited "a refuge from the storms of Fate." So he refuses to share the throne with Edgar, declaring,

> I have a journey, sir, shortly to go;
> My master calls me, I must not say no.[69]

Kent is the most fully developed Stoic in the play. Yet there are others whose "rightness" is set forth in quite exact and explicit Stoic terms. There is Cordelia, whose refusal at the outset of the play to heave her heart into her mouth and match her sisters' extravagant professions of love for Lear stamps her as a model of virtuous plain-spokenness and truth. When Lear demands, "So young, and so untender?" she replies, "So young, my lord, and true" —a speech so apt and fair that it sets off Kent's first protest: "Think'st thou that duty shall have dread to speak When power to flattery bows? To plainness honour's bound When majesty falls to folly."[70]

And the picture of Cordelia is completed by an exchange between
Kent and a gentleman of the French court:

> Gent: . . . It seem'd she was a queen
> 　　　　Over her passion, who, most rebel-like
> 　　　　Sought to be king o'er her.
> Kent:　　　　O, then it mov'd her?
> Gent: Not to a rage. Patience and sorrow strove
> 　　　　Who should express her goodliest.[71]

Compact of feeling, she is yet the very epitome of *patience* throughout all the tribulations she undergoes.

Then there is Edgar. Although in very different terms, with quite
different emphases and shadings, he and Edmund make as strong
a contrast in brothers as Clermont and Bussy. Nor, I think, can
there be any doubt of Shakespeare's intent in having the legitimate
brother the dutiful son of Stoicism, and the illegitimate one the
representative of "the philosophy of Nature."

Edgar's journey through the play parallels on a smaller scale the
passage of Lear through the storms of fortune. But Edgar from the
beginning has been at least somewhat the master of himself. He,
like Cordelia, is full of patience and resoluteness. The dogmatic
Stoics held that until a man was stripped down to his bare and elemental self, with no external comforts, no props of civilization to
support him—and yet was patient, calm, untroubled—he had not
been put to the test. This test Edgar faces:

> 　　　　. . . My face I'll grime with filth.
> Blanket my loins, elf all my hair in knots,
> And with presented nakedness outface
> The winds and persecutions of the sky.[72]

And after he has observed how Lear has been treated by his children, his load seems lighter to him: he is all humility and fortitude.[73] And still later he declares,

> Yet better thus, and known to be contemn'd,
> Then still contemn'd and flatter'd. To be worst,
> The lowest and most dejected thing of fortune,
> Stands still in esperance, lives not in fear.
> The lamentable change is from the best;
> The worst returns to laughter. Welcome, then,
> Thou unsubstantial air that I embrace!
> The wretch that thou hast blown unto the worst
> Owes nothing to thy blasts.[74]

And toward the end of the play, he makes his most resolute of all statements in two short pieces of Stoic advice to his unfortunate father:

> Bear free and patient thoughts[75]

and

> What, in ill thoughts again? Men must endure
> Their going hence, even as their coming hither;
> Ripeness is all.[76]

Reading through the speeches of Edgar in chronological order, one can make an excellent case for his development from a largely good but as yet untried young man to a conscious Stoic philosopher, a man of proved virtue and endurance. At first he is unafraid, but inclined to complain of the ill-treatment he has received. Then he is the more ready to endure bad fortune because he realizes that others, of greater estate, are also undergoing it. Finally, after helping his blinded father, and thus returning good for ill, he is so sure of himself and his place in the scheme of things that he even turns didactic and instructs his father. He has successfully undergone the Stoic ordeal of fortune's storms and is his own man.

But Edgar's ordeal is on a small scale, as the play moves—it amounts only to a minor variation on the gigantic theme of Lear's ordeal. The virtuous son's mistreatment, reconciliation with, and forgiveness of, his father, has none of the dramatic power of the unruly old man's mistreatment of, reconciliation with, and forgiveness by, his daughter. Edgar at his best is still a little prissy and self-righteous. Lear at his worst is still magnificent, and matches in stature the physical and spiritual storms of this disintegrating world.

It is a long road the old man must travel. Even Regan recognizes from the beginning that "he hath ever but slenderly known himself."[77] Lear himself early professes his conviction that the mind cannot endure the sufferings of the body without being affected by them:

> . . . We are not ourselves
> When nature, being oppress'd, commands the mind
> To suffer with the body[78]—

and his long accustomedness to having, for the asking, the gratification of his whims and physical desires for comforts, leads him to burst out to Regan:

> O, reason not the need! Our basest beggars
> Are in the poorest thing superfluous.
> Allow not nature more than nature needs,
> Man's life is cheap as beasts'.[79]

And at this point, turned off by both the daughters to whom he has bequeathed his kingdom, he for the first time prays to the gods for patience:

> You heavens, give me that patience, patience I need!

Yet he adds that if the gods have indeed stirred his daughters' hearts against him,

> . . . fool me not so much
> To bear it tamely; touch me with noble anger. . . .[80]

He feels like weeping, but declares that first he will go mad.

Here is, then, a man who values everything that is counter to the Stoic point of view—external goods, comforts, the indulgence of his whims and passions. Imperious, violent, self-indulgent, he is to be, in keeping with his unconscious prophecy, broken on Fortune's wheel and made ready for the profession of that very humility, patience and endurance which he despises.

So he is exposed alike to the terrific physical storms of the play, and to those of fortune. He seems to be aware that his destination is Stoic patience; he keeps repeating "No, I will be the pattern of all patience; I will say nothing"[81]; yet he will the next moment outrage the elements.

And so he is left shelterless in the tempest, accompanied only by the faithful Fool and the disguised Kent. When "Poor Tom" (Edgar) is added to the company, it is complete. And it is no accident that Lear addresses him (superficially because of his own genuine madness) as "noble philosopher."[82] Lear is by now stripped down to the company of a fool, a madman and a Stoic philosopher—from the point of view of the man he has been, the last extremity of company; from the point of view of what he is working toward, the aristocracy of Stoic-Cynic primitivism.[83] The values of the one world reverse those of the other. And just as Edgar takes comfort in the realization of Lear's tribulation, so does Lear come to a first realization of the suffering of "poor naked wretches" everywhere, and to a first feeling of pity for them:

> . . . O, I have ta'en
> Too little care of this! Take physic, pomp;
> Expose thyself to feel what wretches feel,
> That thou mayst shake the superflux to them
> And show the heavens more just.[84]

And now the "stripping" is completed—the physical act symbolizes the sloughing off of the last of the false values by which he has lived, the pitiful last of the external comforts he has enjoyed, and the reaching of the final Stoic extremity of facing the storms of life naked:

> Why, thou wert better in thy grave than to answer with thy uncover'd body this extremity of the skies. Is man no more than this? Consider him well. Thou ow'st the worm no silk, the beast no hide, the sheep no wool, the cat no perfume. Ha! Here's three on's are sophisticated! *Thou art the thing itself; unaccommodated man is no more but such a poor, bare, forked animal as thou art.* Off, off, you lendings! Come, unbutton here.[85]

This last reduction to "unaccommodated man" is the end of the old life, the necessary preliminary to the new. From this final exposure, this ultimate stripping down to bare essential man, one may move forward to the building of the man aright. But for Lear the ordeal has been too much; he has no strength left with which to begin the new slow climb to patience and fortitude. He cracks, and enters into his madness.

Yet this, too, is a part of the purging ordeal, and when he wins through its long nightmare to a serene if broken peace, the doctor's verdict is that "The great rage . . . is kill'd in him. . . ."[86] He accepts the ill fortunes of battle; he accepts his and Cordelia's capture as though it were a blessing. Cordelia declares

> We are not the first
> Who with best meaning have incurr'd the worst.
> For thee, oppressed king, am I cast down;
> Myself could else outfrown false Fortune's frown.[87]

But when she follows this Stoic declaration with the question, "Shall we not see these daughters and these sisters?" Lear outdoes her with the gladness with which he accepts the idea of prison shared with her:

> No, no, no, no! Come, let's away to prison.
> We two alone will sing like birds i' th' cage.
> When thou dost ask me blessing, I'll kneel down
> And ask of thee forgiveness. So we'll live,
> And pray, and sing, and tell old tales, and laugh
> At gilded butterflies, and hear poor rogues
> Talk of court news; and we'll talk with them too—
> Who loses and who wins; who's in, who's out—
> And takes upon's the mystery of things,
> As if we were God's spies; *and we'll wear out,*
> *In a wall'd prison, packs and sects of great ones*
> *That ebb and flow by th' moon.*[88]

Gone is all value placed on external goods; he gladly accepts the physical prison; since thus imprisoned with Cordelia, he feels that he will be more spiritually free than ever before. He has shaken off the real bondage—that of his passions—and prison walls have no more meaning for him. Secure within himself, and with her, he can "wear out . . . packs and sects of great ones"; for their "greatness" is spurious: it ebbs and flows "by th' moon."

Yet one reservation about Lear's arrival at Stoic patience must be made. Consider the words *with her*. The Stoic ideal is one that admits of no need outside of oneself. Yet throughout the play, the idea that misery loves company has been stressed. Edgar takes heart because Lear, *too*, is suffering; Lear comments on it in his miserable company during the storm; here it shows up again. In its nobler expressions, moreover, it conveys the idea of tempering Stoic fortitude with love, and it seems to me to indicate again Shakespeare's lack of sympathy for the complete austerity of the dogmatic Stoic ideal. "Nothing too much" recurs in the reader's mind.

However, the tempering of endurance with love and the need of others' love, is not matched by any tempering of justice with mercy in the views of the characters in the play about the nature of the universe and the way in which it is administered. The divergent points of view toward nature and the gods are sharply drawn, with the proponents of "Nature" and of Stoicism radically differing. On the one hand, blind nature, controlled only by fortune and chance; on the other, a nature governed by gods who represent a law of retributive justice. There is "a providence that shapes our ends," equivalent to the Stoic *fatum*, and there is a moral order not unlike the retributive justice in Greek tragedy, which overtakes any man who disobeys the law of *moira* or proper limit, and is thus guilty of *hybris*. But this justice is not tempered with mercy, and no Christian love softens the harsh equity of this moral order.

The battle line is drawn early, in the famous speeches of Gloucester and Edmund on the strange phenomena in the heavens. Gloucester is worried and afraid, in a speech that is in the "decay and dissolution of nature" tradition:

> These late eclipses in the sun and moon portend no good to
> us. Though the wisdom of nature can reason it thus and thus,
> yet nature finds itself scourg'd by the sequent effects. Love
> cools, friendship falls off, brothers divide. In cities, mutinies;
> in countries, discord; in palaces, treason; and the bond crack'd
> 'twixt son and father. This villain of mine comes under the
> prediction; there's son against father: the King falls from bias

of nature; there's father against child. We have seen the best of our time. Machinations, hollowness, treachery, and all ruinous disorders follow us disquietly to our graves.[89]

Consider this speech in the light of, say, Donne's "First Anniversary," and you will see that it is the same sort of "decay of nature" passage. Gloucester does not question the existence of a moral order and of law in nature, but he believes that that order is cracking up, and being accompanied by a similar disintegration in the world of human affairs. Edmund, complete naturalist, reasons (as does Iago) like the standard Elizabethan atheist who believes only in a "blind" Nature:

> This is the excellent foppery of the world, that, when we are sick in fortune, often the surfeit of our own behaviour, we make guilty of our disasters the sun, the moon, and the stars; as if we were villains on necessity; fools by heavenly compulsion; knaves, thieves, and treachers by spherical predominance; drunkards, liars, and adulterers by an enforc'd obedience of planetary influence; and all that we are evil in, by a divine thrusting on. An admirable evasion of whoremaster man, to lay his goatish disposition to the charge of a star! My father compounded with my mother under the Dragon's Tail, and my nativity was under Ursa Major, so that it follows I am rough and lecherous. Fut! I should have been that I am, had the maidenliest star in the firmament twinkled on my bastardizing.[90]

It has been said frequently that this is an eloquent and intelligent defense of free will. But such a conviction shows a lack of understanding of contemporary philosophical positions. The last of Edmund's speech explicitly accepts a sort of naturalistic determinism: he was *bound* to be what he is, he believes, because he believes that he is motivated by appetites and passions unaffected by the influence of the stars. But according to the humanists, this is not free will, Edmund is not in command of himself; he is the slave, or at the least the victim, of his appetites. Moreover, the true Christian humanist—as the true Stoic—does not believe that the stars inevitably control what happens to man. They (or *fatum*) do control many of the outward events of his life, but what really happens to the Stoic wise man, happens within him—and this he may and must control. Hence, in the Stoic context of this play, Edmund is knocking down a straw man, to further his own naturalistic arguments.

Gloucester's concern sets the tone for the expression of many

doubts and even downright denials that follow in the play. In the
extremity of his misery, before Edgar re-educates him, he bursts out

> As flies to wanton boys are we to th' gods.
> They kill us for their sport[91]—

an outright declaration of a conviction that there is no moral order,
no justice and reign of law through the universe.

In the very next scene, Albany, Goneril's husband, implies a
doubt about the governance of cosmic justice when he hears that
Gloucester's eyes have been put out. More, if no retributive justice
is forthcoming, if there is no such moral order in the nature of things,
he envisions a wholly bestial order to come in the world of men:

> If that the heavens do not their visible spirits
> Send quickly down to tame these vile offences,
> It will come,
> Humanity must perforce prey on itself,
> Like monsters of the deep.[92]

And this world is described in further animalistic terms by Lear,
in the terrible speeches of his not unreasoned madness[93] about
men's motives as they really are—a world filled with animal lust,
ruthless ambition, lying, greed, cheating and murder: Machiavelli's
jungle world.

But Albany sees in the news that Gloucester's torturer has been
killed an evidence of the presence of the gods:

> This shows you are above,
> You justicers, that these our nether crimes
> So speedily can venge![94]

And Kent and Edgar, of course, proclaim with ardor the same
proposition. Kent declares, with reference to Cordelia's being sister
to such as Goneril and Regan,

> It is the stars,
> The stars above us, govern our conditions,[95]

and Edgar, speaking of his father's sin and punishment,

> The gods are just, and of our pleasant vices
> Make instruments to scourge us.[96]

Yet men such as these must have felt uneasiness in their faith,
to find it necessary to make use of every shred of evidence available to state what should have been a matter of course to them.
They, too, have felt Gloucester's uneasiness—an uneasiness apparent
throughout in all the images of disintegration and imminent dis-

solution, and in the constant reiteration of such phrases as Albany's "this great decay."[97]

In the end, it is a true Stoic world, and justice has been dispensed. But it is also a dying world, as is reflected in Albany's concluding speech:

> The oldest have borne most; we that are young
> Shall never see so much, *nor live so long*.[98]

These lines may be accepted only as psychological truth, but in view of the trouble Shakespeare has taken to establish the picture of a dying order, it seems fair to me to accept them literally as well, within the terms of the play.

In the end, I said, it is a true Stoic world, in which retributive justice is enacted. But it is not a world in which love and mercy play a positive and effective part, and there is no final benediction like Horatio's over Hamlet. Justice, moral law, is as stark as Albany paints it—

> This judgment of the heavens, that makes us tremble,
> Touches us not with pity.[99]

He is speaking of the death of Goneril and Regan, but it might as well be said of the attitude of the gods in their judgment on Gloucester, and especially on Lear. These two are allowed to undergo purgation by fire and to reach the promised land of Stoic patience, but not to enjoy it. The almost gratuitous deaths of the Fool and Cordelia establish only the grim unpredictability of *fatum,* and the fact that man's only refuge is the acquisition of his unconquerable soul. Thus it is kindness, as Kent proclaims, to permit poor broken and twice-robbed Lear to die. There is no other answer to the old man's pitiful "And thou no breath at all?"[100]

3. THE COUNTER-RENAISSANCE AND SHAKESPEARE'S TRAGIC WORLDS

By now it should be clear that I am making no attempt to "claim" Shakespeare for what I call the Counter-Renaissance. That is, I am not in any sense trying to establish him as a conscious adherent of any of the central points of view characteristic of the movement. Indeed, that has not been my intention with many of the Elizabethans we have considered. Almost alone among them, John Donne and Francis Bacon seem to me to have taken consistently Counter-Renaissance positions of one sort or another. But the scope of the movement is so wide that many Elizabethans did endorse one or another premise of it, without necessarily accepting all, or even most, of the major premises. It has, of course, been convenient, in discussing a particular view of Spenser or Chapman or Marston, not to trouble to repeat qualifying phrases to the effect that the point in question does not make him a true son of the Counter-Renaissance. Actually—aside from Donne and Bacon—Marlowe, Ralegh, Greville, Harvey and Marston show the most consistent adherence to Counter-Renaissance views; Chapman, Spenser, Sidney and Nashe a genuine interest but divided allegiance; men like Jonson, Hooker, Daniel and Sir John Davies almost always a traditional humanist attitude, in repudiation of all sorts of Counter-Renaissance doctrine.

In very fact, it is those divided allegiances that produced especially the dichotomy in the Elizabethans that I stressed at the beginning of the book. Whether the holding to certain traditionalist beliefs and the abandoning of others split a man's philosophical position in a particular case, or whether the intellectual conflict between the traditional humanists and the rebels of the Counter-Renaissance left him perplexed, is not so important, as a rule, as the fact of the split.

As for Shakespeare, what I have primarily been trying to demonstrate is the way in which he *made use* of these conflicts for dramatic purposes. What I think has already been made clear, in this chapter and in earlier ones, is that he was actually aware of the conflicts—that the Counter-Renaissance (not, of course, under that name, or even in the sense of his being aware of a comprehensive intellectual revolution, coherently related in its apparently dissimilar parts) did have an impact upon him.

The substantial evidence offered should do much, I think, to dispel further doubts about his "literacy" and his philosophical acumen and awareness of intellectual trends in his time. It should do more to substantiate the already formidable reputation he has as a great creative artist. To take the tragedies alone, the way in which he employed these current ideological controversies to buttress and give added scope and meaning to the familiar stories he retold, is perhaps the greatest literary achievement in history.

Consider the difference between his treatment of these themes, and those of other Elizabethans. The intellectual and philosophical material often sticks out, undigested, in Marlowe—even more in Marston. Poets like Daniel and Davies are downright literal and didactic. Chapman, Spenser, Sidney assimilate such matter better, but they, too, are apt to stop and moralize. The extraordinary thing about Shakespeare's use of it (as in the case of all the really great masters) is the way in which he makes it his own—and the play's own—the way in which he uses it at once as a broader backdrop and a generalized parallel to the concrete individual problem; as an occasion for the playing of many variations on a single dominant theme; and as an opportunity to increase the stature and significance of his characters.

He translates the raw material of thought, controversy and ideology into genuine literary terms—and this is the largest single reason for students' insufficient recognition of his use of that material.

So far, I have skirted the edge of any decisive comment as to where he stood in the midst of these ideological battles. Rather, perhaps, I have pointed out over and over again the difficulty, even the stupidity, of trying to pin down so versatile and many-sided a genius to a single consistent point of view. Yet it is tempting to go at least a little way on this journey, and to attempt an approximation of that point of view. We have already seen in detail his approach to these controversies in his individual plays, and suggested his solutions, or perhaps better, resolutions. Can we go further and find a philosophical constant running through, say, the four major tragedies?

In the cases of *Hamlet* and *Lear,* we have had one such constant —the Stoic goal and resolution. We know already that Cicero's eclectic Stoicism was a strong ingredient in the traditional humanistic point of view, but we also know that in the Elizabethan period the great revival of interest in Seneca, and the lesser but sufficient one in extreme dogmatic Stoicism and Cynicism, produced another and different popular Stoic attitude. The latter, in its excessive austerity, was in many respects closer to the spirit of the early Reformation and of the Puritans, than to that of Christian humanism. Just as the excessive and extreme "honor" tradition really "belongs" to the Counter-Renaissance, although the original Castiglione ideal was largely compatible with the traditional humanistic position —so the extreme dogmatic Cynic-Stoic position "belongs" to certain aspects of the Counter-Renaissance, although the eclectic Stoic ideal is thoroughly consistent with the humanistic part of the traditionalist viewpoint. In both cases, the more moderate attitude is congruent with the concept of "limit" that dominated the humanistic point of view, but the more extreme attitude denies it.

Moreover, that tendency of the traditionalists to harmonize and balance various elements that had often been in conflict (reason and faith, nature and supernature) could apply as well to special concepts like "honor" and "Stoicism" as to the more general ones it had historically reconciled. But the Counter-Renaissance had the opposite tendency—to *split* these realms, or elements, or concepts; to develop their opposition rather than their reconciliation; and to support one at the expense of the other. It should be obvious how this tendency applied to the extreme dogmatic variety of Stoicism, while not at all to the more moderate eclectic sort.

But before we attempt to appraise the exact nature of the "Stoic" resolutions in *Hamlet* and *Lear*, it would be well to consider the four tragedies in the most general way—ascertain more exactly the qualities of the tragic worlds Shakespeare develops in them. And this approach, it is interesting to note, brings about a different alignment, one separating *Hamlet* and *Lear*, and surprisingly obedient to the laws of growth—for it follows the chronological order of the tragedies, dividing them into two periods. The first is that of *Hamlet* (1600 or 1601) and *Othello* (1604); the second that of *Lear* (1605 or 1606) and *Macbeth* (1606).[101] This division, arrived at solely on the basis of the philosophical approaches in the plays, thus happens to fit the approach of those scholars who emphasize the biographical element.

At any rate, it seems to me clear that the tragic worlds of *Hamlet* and *Othello* differ greatly from those of *Lear* and *Macbeth;* and that there is an evident kinship between the worlds of the first two plays, and between those of the latter two. In *Hamlet* and *Othello,* we find a corrupt and decadent world which does not deny the existence of the traditionalists' moral order of the universe, but which shows the wide discrepancy between the theoretical operation of that order and what actually goes on in human affairs—the discrepancy between profession and practice. In *Lear* and *Macbeth,* we find a world close to disintegration and extinction, in which sober men can express grave doubts as to the very existence of that moral order; in which the discrepancy noted in *Hamlet* and *Othello* no longer shocks, but is taken for granted; and which, while still evidently governed by a grim moral law of retributive justice, has lost all sense of the creative and benevolent administration that observes even "the fall of a sparrow."

In *Hamlet* we find constant references to the discrepancy between the humanistic concepts of the nature of the state and of man, and the actualities in human affairs. We have already seen how this view in Hamlet himself is a result of the shock he suffers in his personal relations. Yet, characteristically, he extends the particular to the general, and while pursuing and elaborating on the differences between what he has thought of his mother, Claudius, Ophelia and himself, and what he now finds (or believes he finds) to be true about them, he also develops parallel differences in the general professed and actual nature of men.

Take his famous expression of his disillusionment in Act II:

> . . . Indeed, it goes so heavily with my disposition that this goodly frame, the earth, seems to me a sterile promontory; this most excellent canopy, the air, look you, this brave o'erhanging firmament, this majestical roof fretted with golden fire— why, it appeareth no other thing to me than a foul and pestilent congregation of vapours. What a piece of work is a man! how noble in reason! how infinite in faculties! in form and moving! how express and admirable in action! how like an angel in apprehension! how like a god! the beauty of the world, the paragon of animals! And yet to me what is this quintessence of dust? Man delights me not—no, nor woman either, though by your smiling you seem to say so.[102]

As I said early in the book, this is no conventional humanistic *mixtum compositum* picture of man, part a god and part a beast. Hamlet first presents the resplendent array of the humanists' perfectly ordered universe, macrocosm and microcosm, beautiful and complete; then he contrasts it with what he actually finds in the world and in man. The difference is as drastic as that between the two kings, his father and his uncle, when he confronts his mother with their pictures.[103] What should be (his father), "assurance of a man," is opposed to what now is (Claudius), "a mildew'd ear."[104] It is as though he were thus symbolizing the world and man as we claim them to be, and the world and man as they really are. Small wonder, then, that "something is rotten in the state of Denmark";[105] that "the time is out of joint";[106] that the world seems to Hamlet "an unweeded garden that grows to seed";[107] that virtue must beg pardon of vice "in the fatness of these pursy times";[108] and that, hence, "To be honest, as this world goes, is to be one man pick'd out of ten thousand."[109] "Use every man after his desert, and who should scape whipping?"[110] Hamlet demands.

We may put it this way. The world of his idealistic youth conformed (or seemed to) in every respect with the traditional optimistic humanistic picture. "This goodly frame . . . this most excellent canopy . . . this brave o'erhanging firmament . . . this majestical roof . . ."—all were (or seemed to be) as they were proclaimed. Denmark was a goodly realm; the elder Hamlet a king in the traditional sense of what a king should be; Gertrude and

Ophelia the models of virtuous wife and mother, and virtuous and lovely maid.

Then the catastrophe, and the discovery that "all these goodly prerogatives" were seldom exercised—so seldom that they seemed to exist only in fairy tales. And since there is no one more bitter, cynical and pessimistic than a disillusioned idealist, Hamlet stresses throughout most of the play the revolting discrepancy between the world of his youth and that of his maturity. Nor is his account entirely subjective. There are the facts of Claudius' Machiavellian ruthlessness and guile, his mother's easy faithlessness and duplicity. There are sycophants and rogues like Polonius, Rosencrantz and Guildenstern, Osric. There are ambitious and intemperate pursuers of glory and honor like Fortinbras and Laertes.

Yet there are also innocents like Ophelia and whole men like Horatio. And when Hamlet attains his hard-won "readiness" at the end, he has found out that reality lies somewhere between what ought to be and the sordid world of "a foul and pestilent congregation of vapours"—rather, that it is compounded of both these and many other elements. Perhaps, although this is never explicit, he has even come to realize that the ideal world in which he grew up was also partly subjective.

But to catch the peculiar quality of the given tragic world, one must not linger over the resolution of the tragedy. *Hamlet* is soaked in the solution of the discrepancy between what ought to be and what is, a recurring Counter-Renaissance *motif*; between the professed humanistic ideal and the gross "naturalistic" actuality which Hamlet comes to perceive. When he declares, "O God, I could be bounded in a nutshell and count myself a king of infinite space, were it not that I have bad dreams,"[111] he expresses first the humanistic ideal of fullness-in-limit in the nature of man the microcosm, the "little king" whose "mind a kingdom is," and whose liberty lies in his freedom to do right—and then repudiates it. And his philosophical "bad dreams" are all of the Counter-Renaissance variety.

There is a similar discrepancy at the heart of *Othello,* but not an identical one. Here it is a question of the discrepancy between what seems to be and what is.[112] This too (see Chapter IV) is a favorite Counter-Renaissance theme, and it is no accident that Iago, the key character in this as in other respects, is one of Shakespeare's most thoroughgoing Counter-Renaissance men.

More, he is a thoroughgoing pragmatic Machiavellian, in a fairly exact sense. He displays his credentials to Roderigo in the very first scene:

> Whip me such honest knaves! Others there are
> Who, trimm'd in forms and visages of duty,
> Keep yet their hearts attending on themselves;
> And, throwing but shows of service on their lords,
> Do well thrive by them, and when they have lin'd their coats,
> Do themselves homage. These fellows have some soul;
> And such a one I do profess myself. For, sir,
> It is as sure as you are Roderigo,
> Were I the Moor, I would not be Iago.
> In following him, I follow but myself;
> Heaven is my judge, not I for love and duty,
> *But seeming so,* for my peculiar end;
> For when my outward action doth demonstrate
> The native act and figure of my heart
> In compliment extern, 'tis not long after
> But I will wear my heart upon my sleeve
> For daws to peck at. *I am not what I am.*[113]

Here is the express statement that the key figure in the play bases his actions on the principle of deliberate dissimulation. In this one speech, moreover, Iago announces his allegiance to the Machiavellian principles of self-preservation, success, playing "the fox," and following the bent of one's peculiar nature. Even earlier, in discussing Cassio's promotion over himself, he has applied the nature-art conflict in the Machiavellian terms of practice vs. theory, experience vs. hypothesis:

> And what was he?
> Forsooth, *a great arithmetician,*
> One Michael Cassio, a Florentine
> (A fellow almost damn'd in a fair wife),
> *That never set a squadron in the field,*
> *Nor the division of a battle knows*
> *More than a spinster; unless the bookish theoric*
> Wherein the toged consuls can propose
> As masterly as he. *Mere prattle, without practice,*
> Is all his soldiership. But he, sir, had th' election;
> And I (of whom *his eyes had seen the proof*
> *At Rhodes, at Cyprus, and on other grounds*
> *Christian and heathen*) . . .[114]

Iago also belongs, then, to the hand-in-the-wound (*C'est moi qui l'ai vu*) school; he is a devotee of the "science of the particular."

Finally, it must be recognized that he posits his philosophy of action on his estimate of human nature. That estimate has the "downward" Machiavellian tendency, and also the general natural-

istic scorn for idealistic emotions, especially for love—which he calls
"merely a lust of the blood and a permission of the will."[115] In
his famous "Virtue, a fig! 'Tis in ourselves that we are thus or
thus . . ."[116] speech (part of which Edmund is to echo), it is true
that he speaks conventionally of "reason" and its ability "to cool
our raging motions, our carnal stings, our unbitted lusts."[117] But
he is mostly quoting conventional attitudes to get the effects he
wants from Roderigo; that he is not thinking of that "right reason"
which is implanted in man to guide him to virtue, is evident when
we read his estimate of the extent of men's baseness: "If the balance of our lives had not one scale of reason to balance another
of sensuality, the blood and baseness of our natures would conduct
us to most prepost'rous conclusions."[118]

And there are frequent evidences, as in the scene where Iago
watches Cassio talking to Desdemona,[119] that he views all love as
lust, with or without adequate provocation in a given instance. In
this very scene, he later uses the grossest language about Desdemona
to Roderigo, in terms of the lust he is convinced stirs her: "Her eye
must be fed . . . again to inflame it and to give satiety a fresh
appetite. . . . Very nature will instruct her in it . . ." etc., etc.[120]
And when Roderigo protests, saying that "she's full of most blessed
condition," Iago bursts out with his estimate of all human nature,
"Blessed fig's end! The wine she drinks is made of grapes."[121]

In itself, this is a healthy enough naturalism. But there is nothing
healthy about Iago, who seems to find his only sexual satisfaction
in expressing his abhorrence of the sexual activities of others, placing the lowest possible interpretations on them, and even inventing
them where they don't exist. And here he continues, in a cross between the manner of Thersites and that of the Antonio of *Measure
for Measure*:

> Lechery, by this hand! an index and obscure prologue to the
> history of lust and foul thoughts.[122]

To Iago, the air is thick with lust wherever he turns. And whatever the terms in which Shakespeare conceived of his motives (aside
from the stagy and unconvincing ones expressed in the soliloquies[123])
it is certain that his malignancy (definitely not motiveless) is that
of the impotent (whether or not literally) and sexually frustrated
man who is envious of healthy men and women, and hence, in his
perverted hatred of normal sex, attributes the gross connotations
within his own mind to other people, and takes delight in punish-
ing them for their "sins."

But all this is related to the "Counter-Renaissance side" of Iago's nature only in its and his relation to the "downward" naturalistic evaluation of such ideals as love and honor. What is most pertinent is that Iago, believing all love to be lust and lechery, disposing of "virtue" with "A fig!" and of nobility and delicacy of feeling with the coarse matter-of-factness of "The wine she drinks is made of grapes"—Iago here, too, is a true Counter-Renaissance naturalist. And, like Machiavelli, he says, "This is the world as I see and know. Since people are as they are . . ."

But to pursue too curiously all of the ways in which Iago is authentically Counter-Renaissance, or even Machiavellian, is beyond the scope of the immediate study. On the latter (Machiavellian) score, it should be noted, however, that although the emphasis in Iago and in the play is on deceit and craft (the Fox), not on boldness and force (the Lion), Iago is aware of the importance of using both. Hence, at a crucial point in his plotting, he concludes in truly Machiavellian words:

Dull not device by coldness and delay.[124]

To return to the central point. Hamlet had said of Claudius that "one may smile, and smile, and be a villain . . ."[125] and Iago, of course, is the very embodiment of this precept. As the conscious and consistent advocate of the philosophy of exploiting for one's own gain the discrepancy between what seems to be and what is, he is glad to be known to everyone as "honest Iago." Whether Desdemona says, "O, that's an honest fellow,"[126] or Cassio, with unconscious irony, remarks, "I never knew A Florentine more kind and honest,"[127] or Othello declares, "I know thou'rt full of love and honesty"[128]—it is all grist to his mill.

More than that, he plays up his role as a rough, sturdy fellow, devoted by nature and practice to plain-speaking. Here is another of those infinite variations that Shakespeare can juggle. What Cornwall, in Lear, accuses Kent of being—a plain-speaker of a specious sort—Iago actually is. The very familiarity of the "virtuous man's right to rebuke vice" to all those characters who know Iago lends a greater authenticity to his seeming "honesty." Thus, in the opening scene at Cyprus, when Iago and Cassio stage a duel of words about the nature of woman (a favorite Renaissance controversy), Iago can be as blunt as he chooses without offending either Desdemona or Emilia, and can win from Cassio the tribute: "He speaks home, madam. You may relish him more in the soldier than in the scholar."[129]

So Iago plays the spyer into abuses with Othello. He declares outright,

> (As I confess it is my nature's plague
> To spy into abuses, and oft my jealousy
> Shapes faults that are not)—[130]

thereby, in "discrediting" in advance what he has to say about Cassio and Desdemona, seeming all the more disarming and honest and responsible.

In direct opposition to Iago is Othello—"of a free and open nature That thinks men honest that but seem to be so"[131]—a man "great of heart" but who "being wrought" is "perplex'd in the extreme."[132] Othello, Desdemona, Cassio, Roderigo, even the shrewd Emilia— all these are victims of Iago's exploitation of their inability to distinguish between what seems to be and what is. The range is from people of nobility and stature to obvious simple gulls; yet all are deceived by Iago. And even when Iago's real nature is disclosed and he is stabbed by Othello, his last word (except to say later that he will say nothing, a further indication of continued defiance) is a proud and defiant "I bleed, sir, but not kill'd."[133]

It is easy enough to see and say that in this play, too, there is retributive justice of a sort—in the final price Othello pays, for it was his permitting his passions and blood to rule his judgment (in the sense that the pictures Iago created in his mind's eye outweighed in urgency his sense of Desdemona's true nature) that brought on the tragedy. Yet he was largely passive, and in the hands of the most diabolically clever man Shakespeare ever portrayed. Indeed, throughout the play, Iago towers over the rest, including the great figure of Othello himself, like a marionette master pulling the strings of his puppets.

Moreover, one leaves *Othello* with a greater sense of needless waste than in the case of any of the other tragedies. Waste of beauty, love, vigor, happiness, life itself—and all needless. And the great malevolent figure of Iago is unbowed. No tortures to come, we feel sure, will break his sense of triumph.

What, then, is Shakespeare trying to say to us, beyond pointing to the old discrepancy between the ideal humanistic world in which virtue is truly its own reward and vice its own hell, and the world of "actuality," where things go quite differently? Before we attempt the answer, and a final consideration of the four tragedies as a group, we must move on to a brief consideration of the tragic worlds of *Lear* and *Macbeth*.

In the very last scene of *Othello*, Othello declares,

> . . . But O vain boast!
> Who can control his fate?[134]

and there is no answer. In *Lear* and *Macbeth*, the question is asked
again, and answered, but in different ways. The answer in Lear we
have already discussed. Only the Stoic, learning that "ripeness is
all," and living accordingly, has the inner strength and patience
to endure all the storms of fortune and control his fate in the larger
sense by becoming master of himself.

But at the end of *Lear*, when the long battle between *humanus*
and *homo ferus* is over, order restored, and all of the leading characters dead or about to die, there is another question asked, to
which there is no reply except the relief of death—Lear's words
over the body of Cordelia, "And thou no breath at all?"

Once again we will postpone an attempt to answer. The thing
to note for the moment, as we move from the world of *Othello* to
that of *Lear*, is that we leave a superficially placid but narrow and
decadent world where the old values are professed but infrequently
followed, and where those who do follow them seem utterly exposed and at the mercy of those who are prepared to exploit the
discrepancy—leave it to enter a dark, storm-ridden world where the
camps are clearly drawn, the battle is on, and the imminence of
the dissolution of "this great stage" hangs as threateningly over the
whole scene as the great clouds of the central storm in the play.

In *Lear*, only Lear himself is even for a moment in doubt about
the forces at work. The play is an angry one from the beginning,
and there never seems to be any doubt in Kent's or Cordelia's mind
as to the nature of the struggle before them. It is a devastated
world, even before the battle begins, and if it also is decadent, it
is in a stage of decadence far beyond the soft sort in *Othello*. Man
has advanced, or regressed, in decadence to a primitive state, on
the verge of the condition Albany foresees when he says,

> It will come,
> Humanity must perforce prey on itself,
> Like monsters of the deep.[135]

Macbeth relates the story of another front in this war, a lesser
part of this world. Its scope is not so comprehensive as that of
Lear, but its terror, its sense of unrelieved bleakness, is even more
intense. Here, as in *Lear*, mankind's animal nature is displayed
everywhere. Here, as in *Lear*, there is evident a world ruled by a
fate equivalent to retributive justice—this time personified by the
witches or Weird Sisters, who approximate the Norns of Scandi-

navian mythology—"great powers of destiny, great ministers of fate."[136] And here, as in *Lear*, the existence of that governing fate —the proof of a moral order, however grim and stark, in the universe—is not clearly evident to many of the characters throughout much of the play, during which time they fear that there is no cosmic government save fortune or chance, and that they live in a Machiavellian jungle world, where only *virtù* guarantees survival.

Thus Macbeth himself compares his deed and his world with "the state of nature" in primitive times (clearly the Machiavellian-materialist's concept, and not any Golden Age one):

> Blood hath been shed ere now, i' th' olden time,
> Ere humane statute purg'd the gentle weal . . .[137]

and Ross warns Lady Macduff,

> . . . cruel are the times, when we are traitors
> And do not know ourselves; when we hold rumour
> From what we fear, yet know not what we fear,
> But float upon a wild and violent sea
> Each way and none.[138]

The following exchange between Lady Macduff and her son, just before they are both murdered, eloquently reveals the quality of this world, in which a boy can conclude,

> Then the liars and swearers are fools; for there are liars and
> swearers enow to beat the honest men and hang them up.[139]

And when a final messenger warns Lady Macduff that the murderers are approaching, she cries out,

> Whither should I fly?
> I have done no harm. But I remember now
> I am in *this earthly world, where to do harm*
> *Is often laudable, to do good sometime*
> *Accounted dangerous folly*. Why then, alas,
> Do I put up that womanly defence
> To say I have done no harm?[140]

a very exact rendering of Machiavellian dogma.

There is this difference between the world of *Lear* and that of *Macbeth*—in the latter there is no character at once virtuous and of sufficient strength to endure with equanimity the worst fortune might bring him. Macduff, the nearest to it, is unimpressive alongside Kent and Cordelia. In this world, Machiavellian power tactics meet little opposition until the end, and jungle evaluations are rife. Macbeth, hiring the murderers of Banquo, finds it natural to turn to the animal world for an analogy:

> Ay, in the catalogue ye go for men,
> As hounds and greyhounds, mongrels, spaniels, curs,
> Shoughs, water-rugs and demi-wolves are clipt
> All by the name of dogs. The valued file
> Distinguishes the swift, the slow, the subtle. . . .[141]

And woe to the slow! There is a softness, hence a weakness (as this world goes), in Macbeth himself; and his formidable lady stresses it:

> . . . Thou wouldst be great;
> Art not without ambition, but without
> The illness should attend it. What thou wouldst highly,
> That wouldst thou holily; wouldst not play false,
> And yet wouldst wrongly win.[142]

He is "too full o' th' milk of human kindness To catch the nearest way."[143]

Not she, however:

> . . . Come, you spirits
> That tend on mortal thoughts, unsex me here,
> And fill me, from the crown to the toe, top-full
> Of direst cruelty! Make thick my blood;
> Stop up th' access and passage to remorse,
> That no compunctious visitings of nature
> Shake my fell purpose nor keep peace between
> Th' effect and it![144]

She admonishes Macbeth in true Machiavellian style:

> . . . To beguile the time,
> Look like the time; bear welcome in your eye,
> Your hand, your tongue; look like the innocent flower,
> But be the serpent under't.[145]

And when Macbeth declares, in the next scene, his determination not to go through with the murder of Duncan, saying in self-justification,

> I dare do all that may become a man.
> Who dares do more is none—[146]

she replies scornfully,

> What beast was't then
> That made you break this enterprise to me?
> When you durst do it, then you were a man;

And to be more than what you were, you would
Be so much more the man.[147]

This is reminiscent of Goneril haranguing Albany, and indeed Lady
Macbeth is made of some of the same stuff as Goneril and Regan.
But she is a more impressive tragic figure than they, since less un-
relievedly black, more complex, a woman of more dimensions.

There are other Machiavellian elements and references in *Macbeth*—notably in the pathetic subterfuge which Malcolm feels it
necessary to employ with Macduff in England, to test him out.[148]
But the general tone should be sufficiently clear by now. This is the
world in which these people live—a world inhabited by the ruthless
and predatory, or the weak and insecure—and in which they fear
they must always live, since, like Lady Macduff, they see no evidence of any end to this order. But, as in *Lear*, though in very
different terms, retributive justice is on the march. The Weird Sisters' prophecy is fulfilled; Birnam Wood does remove to Dunsinane;
and the moral order of things is restored.

Yet here, one last time, it is an imperfect order that is restored.
Malcolm and the rest (except possibly Macduff) are the mere au-
tomatons of peace and order, not impressive and positive characters. The great figures in *Macbeth*, unlike the other three tragedies
(with the exception of Iago and possibly Claudius), are the evil
ones. One has little satisfaction or confidence in the triumph of
Malcolm; the "gor'd state" may finally be at peace, but neither
author nor reader is much interested. In this case, however, there
is no tormenting unanswered question like that involving the waste
of life in *Othello* and *Lear*.

It is time to recapitulate. *Hamlet* and *Othello* are tragedies of
character, acted out in imperfect worlds, where the traditional moral
order of the universe is not denied, but is insufficiently evident—
and, in terms of men, insufficiently practiced. *Lear* and *Macbeth*
are tragedies of destiny and fate, acted out in grim, bleak worlds
of elemental forces, in which the moral order of things is harsher
and more formidable than in the two earlier plays. By this I do
not mean that providence, destiny, retributive justice, play no part
in the first two plays, or that the tragic flaw in character is not
important and even decisive in the latter two. (Any consideration
of the characters of Lear and Macbeth would make the latter concept ridiculous.)

What I do mean is that the worlds of *Hamlet* and *Othello* are
relatively soft and sophisticated worlds, in which some men are
complex and troubled by new concepts and attitudes, and others

pay lip service to traditional values, while cynically acknowledging in practice a wholly different set of values. The lines are blurred.

In the worlds of *Lear* and *Macbeth*, there is no blurring. The issues are sharply drawn, the moral oppositions sternly clear-cut. Macbeth does evil, but knows it is evil; Lear and Gloucester move through purgation from self-indulgence to endurance and patience, to a Stoic acceptance of the moral order of *fatum*. All the other important characters in the two plays consciously endorse and follow a Machiavellian naturalism, on the one hand, or a Stoic virtue, on the other. (There is, of course, no stress on the latter in *Macbeth*, yet the only character with any perceptible virtuous strength, Macduff, receives the news of the murder of his family with a restrained grief that is reminiscent of the description of Cordelia's receipt of the letters about Lear's misfortune.[149]) There is never, in either of these plays, a character as really perplexed, as uncertain, as consciously searching for tenable values and moral answers as is Hamlet, or even Othello.

Another way of stating the difference is to say that *Hamlet* and *Othello* are played out in sick worlds, where the answer is still to be found in traditional values, but where those values have been sufficiently challenged to make for uncertainty and complication —and where they are being insufficiently practiced to make the discrepancy between profession and practice a cause for alarm or even skepticism. On the other hand, *Lear* and *Macbeth* are enacted in a predatory world of impending doom—a world so early or so late in time (state of nature or the last decay of nature; the human values of these two are practically identical) that there are no blurred edges or complications possible. Only the endurance of Stoicism or the self-preservation and self-indulgence of "the philosophy of nature" are possible programs for action.

And the answers? Shakespeare's own answers? There is a perceptible continuous progression here, too. The Stoicism exemplified by Horatio and eventually achieved by Hamlet is substantially the moderate eclectic variety of Christian humanism. Indeed, the play contains specific Christian allusions that are important to the whole meaning.[150] Justice is fulfilled, but touched with mercy and a sense of peace at the end. Hamlet's death carries no connotation of waste; he has fulfilled his moral and his literal missions, finding himself in the process; those he has loved best (except Horatio) are dead; given the beginning circumstances, there is no reason to think, "If only this or that had not happened!"

This is not true of *Othello*. If the true tragedy is one of a noble nature's falling victim to its flaw, it is proper material for a tragedy and in keeping with traditional values. Yet actually Othello's flaw is not immoderate and extreme jealousy. To borrow Hamlet's terminology, he is played upon—and by an expert in human nature, and it is his very openness and credulity that bring about his downfall, not his jealousy in any mean sense. The man who says early with such notable restraint and control of himself and the situation, "Keep up your bright swords, for the dew will rust them,"[151] has no hysterical fear of cuckoldry, no inordinate feeling of insecurity. He has the violent depths of his nature well in control.

Yet he falls victim to Iago, and all he can say is, "Who can control his fate?" The confidence in the ultimate rightness of things, and the certainty of there being a purposeful moral condition to reach, that one finds in *Hamlet*, seem quite gone. The tone is closer to that of the dark comedies, and an Iago, triumphant "Spartan dog," can say defiantly, "I bleed, sir, but not kill'd."

We must wait for *Lear* to have the answer to Othello's question. In *Lear*, the skies are always black—lighted only by occasional flashes of lightning. One cannot imagine the sun shining in *Lear*. Yet a man *can* control his fate. Kent and Cordelia prove it.

But now a new question arises. Hamlet's semi- (or wholly) Christian-Stoic providence is gone, and replaced by the inscrutable *fatum* which dispenses retributive justice. There is a moral order, but not one in which man creatively participates. The victory lies in endurance; the reward is not in heaven, but in release from the strenuous vicissitudes of fortune. Stern justice is dispensed, without mercy.[152]

Macbeth, the most conventional tragedy, changes little in the picture, and so, as before, we are left with Lear bending over Cordelia: "And thou no breath at all?"

Doctrinally, we must then be satisfied with Lear's subsequent death. There is nothing left for him to live for, and as Kent says, "He hates him that would upon the rack of this tough world stretch him out longer." Yet we are not satisfied, either in terms of Cordelia or of Lear. Why must she die? Why must he suffer this, too? The answer, to the Stoic, is because this is the way things happen, and all that matters is to be able to face them, unbeaten, or to win the sweet oblivion of death. Yet we have been conscious of Shakespeare's dissatisfaction with the austerity of the Stoic dogma, evinced by the need for others, for sharing, for some sort of love, displayed by many of the characters suffering adversity.

And so it seems clear to me that Shakespeare's final position, as seen through the tragedies, is that indeed "The readiness is all," and the Stoic is substantially right—but that he could not stomach the harsh comprehensive demands of Stoicism for "being absolute for death." The man who depicts with such brilliant imaginative understanding a Falstaff, a Hotspur, a Cleopatra, a Lear, and a Hamlet, had a range of sympathy that went beyond forgiveness of faults and frailties to a realization of the arrogance implicit in forgiveness. "Be absolute for death," yes; be absolute, too, for resoluteness—"the better for the embittered hour." But absolute absoluteness is too much to ask; the Stoic readiness should be tempered by love and understanding and even, sometimes, a faulty warmth.

If then, his final position is unquestionably humanistic, it is not so in any prescribed narrow sense. If it is Christian humanism, it is his own loose variety. If it is naturalistic humanism, the same is true. Clearly he did not embrace many of the positions of the Counter-Renaissance; most of its proponents whom he depicts are "villains." Yet there is an admixture of their points of view in his essential philosophical conservatism, and perhaps in temper and outlook he comes closer to Montaigne than to any other individual we have studied. But he had a much wider range, a much greater versatility, and a deeper reservoir of passion.

Finally, then, I am admitting the traditional defeat. I can establish Shakespeare's awareness of the intellectual conflicts of his time, his use of Counter-Renaissance ideas and themes. And I can indicate the consistent elements in his point of view as he expressed it in the major tragedies. Yet, when that is done, it is little enough. The man escapes me, as he escapes every one else. There are all the other plays to contradict me; other scholars' material findings to suggest other influences than those I have cited, and other directions. Most of all, there is the man's insistent interest in life as spectacle, rather than argument, and the incredible range of his creative sympathies.

What is there left to say? Only that the intellectual world which has been the subject of this book was his world.

FOOTNOTES

CHAPTER 10

I.

1. Consider the hubbub over Marston's, Jonson's, Donne's and other writers' satires, particularly in the 1590's. These were strong condemnations, primarily, of current looseness of living.
2. *Hamlet,* III, i, 158–169.
3. *Ibid.,* I, iv, 84–85.
4. *Ibid.,* I, ii, 160–168.
5. *Ibid.,* I, i, 96–103. My italics.
6. *Ibid.,* II, i, 32–35.
7. *Ibid.,* IV, v, 117.
8. *Ibid.,* 131–133.
9. *Ibid.,* 136–137.
10. *Ibid.,* V, i, 263–265.
11. *Ibid.,* V, ii, 255–263.
12. *Ibid.,* 351–353.
13. See W. E. H. Lecky, *A History of European Morals* (New York, 1897), I, 217–218, 222–223, and Seneca, *Epistles,* lxx, for this point of Stoic doctrine.
14. *Hamlet,* III, ii, 70–79.
15. *Ibid.,* I, v, 29–31.
16. *Ibid.,* 98–104. My italics.
17. *Ibid.,* 166–167. It seems to me clear that "your" is used in the loose Elizabethan fashion here—not to mean Horatio's (Stoic) philosophy.
18. *Ibid.,* 189–191.
19. *Ibid.,* II, ii, 585–588. My italics.
20. *Ibid.,* 613–615.
21. *Ibid.,* 595–596. My italics.
22. *Ibid.,* 598–602.
23. *Ibid.,* 603–609.
24. *Ibid.,* 631–632.
25. *Ibid.,* 626–631.
26. *Ibid.,* III, i, 56–60.
27. *Timon of Athens,* III, v, 16–20.
28. *Ibid.,* 31–35.
29. Compare Machiavelli's discussion of the problem, where he comments on how the Christian virtues of forbearance and submission have destroyed *l'antico valore* (*Discourses,* II, 284–286) .
30. *Hamlet,* III, i, 60–64.
31. *Ibid.,* 65–68.
32. *Ibid.,* 68–82.
33. *Ibid.,* 83–88.
34. *Troilus and Cressida,* II, ii, 46–50.
35. *Hamlet,* III, ii, 379–389.
36. *Ibid.,* IV, iv, 45–46.
37. *Ibid.,* 18–19.
38. *Ibid.,* 46–53.
39. *Ibid.,* 53–56.
40. *Ibid.,* 56–66. My italics.
41. *Ibid.,* IV, vii, 128–129.

42. *Ibid.*, V, i, 228–235.

43. *Ibid.*, IV, iii, 32–33.

44. *Ibid.*, V, i, 282–285.

45. *Ibid.*, 312–315.

46. *Ibid.*, V, ii, 6–11.

47. *Ibid.*, 63.

48. *Ibid.*, 67.

49. *Ibid.*, 73–74.

50. *Ibid.*, 230–235.

51. *Ibid.*, 358–360.

52. *Ibid.*, 370–371.

53. *Ibid.*, III, ii, 5–9, 18–22.

2.

54. See last few pages of Chapter VII (*supra*).

55. Published by Louisiana State Press, 1948. See especially Chapter V, 115–130, which is called "The Nature of Nature." I did not see a copy of this book until after I had titled my own eighth chapter.

56. *Lear*, I, i, 20–24.

57. *Ibid.*, I, ii, 1–22.

58. *Ibid.*, V, 26–34.

59. Heilman's book, *This Great Stage,* treats the matter in detail.

60. Epictetus, *Discourses*, III, 22, 13. It is worth remembering, too, how close the dates of *Timon* (with the professional Cynic character, Apemantus) and *Lear* are, each to the other.

61. *Lear*, II, ii, 98–120.

62. *Ibid.*, I, i, 150–151.

63. Hicks, *Stoic and Epicurean*, 98.

64. Lecky, *Hist. Eur. Morals*, I, 222–223.

65. *Lear*, V, iii, 312.

66. *Ibid.*, 313–315. Compare Horatio's and Hamlet's exchange at the end of *Hamlet,* and the similarity of the *roles* of Horatio and Kent.

67. Hicks, *ibid.*, 98–99.

68. Cf. Lecky, *ibid.*, 217–218, 222; Seneca, *Epistles*, lxx.

69. *Lear*, V, iii, 321–322. There is no space here to discuss further Shakespeare's *general* interest in Stoicism and Cynicism, but I find it extensive in plays which I have not even mentioned. Consider, for example, how, in *Measure for Measure,* the old Duke, who advises Claudio to "Be absolute for death" in Stoic terms (cf. Seneca, Epistle lxxvii), disguises himself as a friar. It is at least interesting, in view of the way in which the Duke plays the part of a "satiric commentator," to observe that the Cynics have been called "the monks of Stoicism" and "missionary friars." (Cf. Lecky, *ibid.*, 309–310.) I am convinced that a great deal about the relation of Shakespeare to Stoicism and this Stoic-Cynic tradition remains to be explored.

70. *Lear*, I, i, 108, 109, 149–151.

71. *Ibid.*, IV, iii, 15–19.

72. *Ibid.*, II, iii, 9–12.

73. *Ibid.*, III, vi, 108–116.

74. *Ibd.*, IV, i, 1–9.

75. *Ibid.*, IV, vi, 80.

76. *Ibid.*, V, ii, 9–11. Compare Hamlet's "the readiness is all" (V, ii, 234).

77. *Ibid.*, I, i, 296–297.

78. *Ibid.*, II, iv, 108–110.

79. *Ibid.*, 267–270.
80. *Ibid.*, 277–279.
81. *Ibid.*, III, ii, 37–38.
82. *Ibid.*, III, iv, 177.
83. See Heilman, *This Great Stage*, 221, where the author finds in this combination a Christian transubstantiation of the values of Lear's pagan world. For the similarity between Stoic and Christian values in this respect, and the tendency, in Renaissance times, to equate the Stoic wise man and the "lowly" Christian reformer, see Chapter II (*supra*).
84. *Lear*, III, iv, 32–36.
85. *Ibid.*, 105–114. My italics.
86. *Ibid.*, IV, vii, 78–79.
87. *Ibid.*, V, iii, 3–6.
88. *Ibid.*, V, iii, 7–19. My italics.
89. *Ibid.*, I, ii, 112–125.
90. *Ibid.*, 129–145.
91. *Ibid.*, IV, i, 36–37.
92. *Ibid.*, IV, ii, 46–50.
93. *Ibid.*, IV, vi, 109–134, 153–159, 161–177.
94. *Ibid.*, IV, ii, 78–80.
95. *Ibid.*, IV, iii, 34–35.
96. *Ibid.*, V, iii, 170–171.
97. *Ibid.*, 297.
98. *Ibid.*, 325–326. My italics.
99. *Ibid.*, 231–232.
100. *Ibid.*, 307.

3.

101. I have followed the dates used by Kittredge in his introductions to the plays in his *Complete Works of Shakespeare*.
102. *Hamlet*, II, ii, 309–322. My division of words and punctuation in the series of exclamatory "how like . . ." follows the conviction of many scholars that this reading adheres more closely to the traditional expression of the traditional concept of man's nature than does the variant "in form and moving how express and admirable! in action how like an angel," etc.
103. *Ibid.*, III, iv, 53–88.
104. *Ibid.*, 62, 64.
105. *Ibid.*, I, iv, 90.
106. *Ibid.*, I, v, 189.
107. *Ibid.*, I, ii, 135–136.
108. *Ibid.*, III, iv, 153–154.
109. *Ibid.*, II, ii, 178–179.
110. *Ibid.*, 554–555.
111. *Ibid.*, 260–262.
112. Theodore Spencer, in his *Shakespeare and the Nature of Man,* has applied himself to these discrepancies in almost all of Shakespeare's plays, with many excellent insights. But I think he weakened his case by lumping all of them under the too general head of appearance *vs.* reality.
113. *Othello*, I, i, 49–65. My italics.
114. *Ibid.*, 18–30. My italics.
115. *Ibid.*, I, iii, 339–340.
116. *Ibid.*, 322–323.
117. *Ibid.*, 334–337.
118. *Ibid.*, 330–334.

119. *Ibid.*, II, i, 168–180.
120. *Ibid.*, 223–253.
121. *Ibid.*, 256–257.
122. *Ibid.*, 263–265.
123. *Ibid.*, I, iii, 389–410; II, i, 295–321.
124. *Ibid.*, II, iii, 394.
125. *Hamlet*, I, v, 108.
126. *Othello*, III, iii, 5.
127. *Ibid.*, III, i, 42–43.
128. *Ibid.*, III, iii, 118.
129. *Ibid.*, II, i, 166–167.
130. *Ibid.*, III, iii, 146–148.
131. *Ibid.*, I, iii, 405–406.
132. *Ibid.*, V, ii, 361, 345–346.
133. *Ibid.*, 288.
134. *Ibid.*, 264–265.
135. *Lear*, IV, ii, 48–50.
136. Kittredge, *Complete Works of Shakespeare*, 1114.
137. *Macbeth*, III, iv, 75–76.
138. *Ibid.*, IV, ii, 18–22.
139. *Ibid.*, 56–58.
140. *Ibid.*, 73–79. My italics.
141. *Ibid.*, III, i, 93–96.
142. *Ibid.*, I, v, 19–23.
143. *Ibid.*, 18–19.
144. *Ibid.*, 41–48.
145. *Ibid.*, 64–67.
146. *Ibid.*, I, vii, 46–47.
147. *Ibid.*, 48–51.
148. *Ibid.*, IV, iii, especially 19–24 and 117–120.
149. *Ibid.*, 174–235; *Lear*, IV, iii, 11–33.
150. *Hamlet*, I, i, 158–165; V, ii, 370–371.
151. *Othello*, I, ii, 59.
152. Of course the historical (or legendary) setting of these plays required the use of now one philosophy, now another. I have not bothered to explain that a Christian approach would be incongruous as well as anachronistic in *Lear*, etc. I have not bothered because, even though this is true, there remains the fact that Shakespeare chose his subjects when he did for his own reasons—and his philosophical approach in a given play cannot be attributed wholly to the dramatic and logical exigencies of that subject matter. Moreover, the consistencies, the constants, suggest that there is ample justification for the ideas expressed in relation to his philosophical development.

BIBLIOGRAPHY

AGRIPPA, HENRY CORNELIUS VON NETTESHEIM, De incertitudine & Vanitate scientiarum, 1537. (Also French edition, edited by Sr. M. de Guendeville, 1726).
Of the Vanitie and Uncertaintie of Artes & Sciences, Englished by Ja[mes] San[ford], Gent. London, 1569. (photostat)

ALBRIGHT, EVELYN MAY, "Spenser's Connections with the Letters in Gabriel Harvey's 'Letter-Book,' " Modern Philology, XXIX, No. 4 (May, 1932), pp. 411–436.

ALLEN, DON CAMERON, "John Donne's Knowledge of Renaissance Medicine," Journal of English and Germanic Philology, XLII, 3 (July, 1943), pp. 323–326.
The Star-Crossed Renaissance, Durham, N. C., 1941.

ANDERS, H. R. D., Shakespeare's Books, Berlin, 1940.

ANDERSON, RUTH L., Elizabethan Psychology and Shakespeare's Plays, Iowa City, Iowa, 1927.

AQUINAS, THOMAS, Summa contra Gentiles, literally translated by the English Dominican Fathers from the latest Leonine edition, London, 1924–28.
Summa Theologica, literally translated by the Fathers of the Engl. Dom. Prov., London, 1922.
Summa Theologica, Editio Altera Romana, Rome, 1894, VI (Indices: Lexicon: Documenta).

ARETINO, PIETRO, Works, translated into English from the original Italian . . . privately printed for the Rarity Press, Inc., N. Y., 1931.

ARIOSTO, LUDOVICO, Orlando Furioso, translated by William Stewart Rose, London, 1915.

ARISTOTLE, The Nicomachean Ethics, Chase's translation, newly revised, with an introductory essay by George Henry Lewes, Walter Scott, Ltd. (Camelot Series), London, n.d.
Politics, translated by H. Rackham (Loeb Library).

ASHLEY, ROBERT, Of Honour, edited, with introduction and commentary, by Virgil P. Heltzel, The Huntington Library, San Marino, Calif., 1947.

ASHTON, J. W., "The Fall of Icarus," Philological Quarterly, Vol. 20 (July, 1941), pp. 345–351.

ATKINSON, GEOFFROY, Les Nouveaux Horizons de la Renassance Française, Paris, 1935.

AUGUSTINE, ST., City of God, translated by Marcus Dods (A Select Library of the Nicene and Post-Nicene Fathers of the Christian Church, edited by Philip Schaff, Vol. II), New York, 1907.
Confessions (Everyman edition).
De Libero Arbitrio Voluntatis (On The Freedom of the Will), translated by Carroll Mason Sparrow, Charlottesville, Va., 1947.

BABB, LAURENCE, "The Physiological Conception of Love in the Elizabethan and Early Stuart Drama," Publication of the Modern Language Association, Vol. LVI, No. 4, Part 1 (Dec., 1941), pp. 1020–1035.

BACON, FRANCIS, Essayes or Counsels, New York, 1901 (based on the 1625 edition).
New Atlantis, World's Classics, Oxford University Press, London, n.d.
Novum Organum, translated by Ellis and Spedding (New University Library), London, n.d.
Philosophical Works, reprinted from the texts and translations of Ellis and Spedding, edited by John M. Robertson, London, 1905.

BAKELESS, JOHN, Tragic History of Christopher Marlowe, Cambridge, Mass., 1942.

BAKEWELL, CHARLES M., Source Book in Ancient Philosophy, New York, 1909.

BARON, HANS, "Toward a More Positive Evaluation of the Fifteenth Century Renaissance," Journal of the History of Ideas, Vol. IV, No. 1 (January, 1943), pp. 21–49.

BARTAS, GUILLAUME DU, The Divine Weeks, translated (and supplemented) by Joshua Sylvester, edited by Theron Haight, Waukesha, Wis., 1908.

BASKERVILL, CHARLES READ; HELTZEL, VIRGIL B.; AND NETHERCOT, ARTHUR H. (editors), Elizabethan and Stuart Plays, New York, 1934.

BATTENHOUSE, ROY W., Marlowe's Tamburlaine, Nashville, Tenn., 1941.

BECKER, CARL, The Heavenly City of the Eighteenth Century Philosophers, New Haven, 1932.

BENNETT, JOSEPHINE W., "Spenser and Gabriel Harvey's Letter-Book," Modern Philology, XXIX (1931), pp. 163–186.

BLAU, JOSEPH LEON, The Christian Interpretation of the Cabala in the Renaissance, New York, 1944.

BOAS, FREDERICK S., Christopher Marlowe, a Biographical and Critical Study, Oxford, 1940.
Marlowe and his Circle, London, 1931.

BODIN, JEAN, Method for the Easy Comprehension of History, translated by Beatrice Reynolds, New York, 1945.
Methodus ad Facilium Historiarum . . . 1566, and Les six livres de la République, 1576 (The Six Bookes of a Commonweale [Republic]), out of the French and Latine Copies, done into English, by Richard Knolles, London, Impensis C. Bishop, 1606.
Le Theatre de la Nature Universelle, Traduict du Latin par M. Francois de Fougerolles Bourbonnais Docteur aux Arts & en Medecine, A Lyon, par Jean Pillehotte, a l'enseigne du nom de Jesus, 1597.

BOETHIUS, DE CONSOLATIONE, (Loeb Library edition).

BOÉTIE, ETIENNE DE LA, Anti-Dictator (Discours sur la servitude volontaire), rendered into English by Harry Kurz, New York, 1942.

BOWERS, F. T., Elizabethan Revenge Tragedy, Princeton, N. J., 1940.

BOYER, C. V., The Villain as Hero in Elizabethan Tragedy, New York, 1914.

BRADBROOK, M. C., The School of Night, Cambridge, 1936.

BREDVOLD, LOUIS I., Intellectual Milieu of John Dryden, Ann Arbor, Michigan, 1934.
"The Naturalism of Donne in Relation to Some Renaissance Traditions," Journal of English and Germanic Philology, 1923, Vol. 22, pp. 471–502.
"The Religious Thought of Donne in Relation to Medieval and Later Traditions," Studies in Shakespeare, Milton, and Donne, New York, 1925.

BRIERLY, J. L., The Law of Nations, Oxford, 1938.

BROOKE, C. F. TUCKER, "Sir Walter Ralegh as Poet and Philosopher," ELH, Vol. 5, No. 2 (June, 1948), pp. 93–112.

BROWN, BEATRICE DAW, "Marlowe, Faustus, and Simon Magus," PMLA, LIV (1939), pp. 82–121.

BROWN, HUNTINGTON, Rabelais in English Literature, Cambridge, Mass., 1933.

BROWN, JOHN L., The Methodus ad Facilem Historiarum Cognitionem of Jean Bodin: a Critical Study, Washington, D. C., 1939.

BROWNE, SIR THOMAS, Religio Medici, Little, Brown and Co., Boston, n.d.

BRUNO, GIORDANO, Concerning the Cause, the Principle, and the One, translated by Royce, Josiah and Katherine, Modern Classical Philosophers, edited by Benjamin Rand, Boston, 1908.

BRUNSCHVICQ, Le Rôle de Pythagorisme dans l'Évolution des Idées, Paris, 1937.

BUCKLEY, GEORGE T., Atheism in the English Renaissance, Chicago, 1932.

BULLOUGH, GEOFFREY, "Bacon and the Defense of Learning," Seventeenth Century Studies, Oxford, 1938.

BUNDY, MURRAY W., "Bacon's True Opinion of Poetry," Studies in Philology, Vol. XXVII, No. 2 (April, 1930), pp. 215–219.

BURCKHARDT, JACOB, The Civilization of the Renaissance in Italy (Middlemore's translation), London, 1944.

BURNET, JOHN, Greek Philosophy, London, 1924.

BURTT, EDWIN ARTHUR, The Metaphysical Foundations of Modern Physical Science, New York, 1925.

BURY, J. B., The Idea of Progress, New York, 1932.

BUSH, DOUGLAS, The Renaissance and English Humanism, London, 1939.

CALVIN, JOHN, Institutes of the Christian Religion, translated by John Allen, Philadelphia, 1928.

CAMPANELLA, TOMMASO, Sonnets, translated by John Addington Symonds, London, 1878.

CAMPBELL, LILY B., Shakespeare's Tragic Heroes, Cambridge, 1930.

CAMPBELL, OSCAR JAMES, Comicall Satyre and Shakespeare's Troilus and Cressida, San Marino, Calif., 1938.

"Jacques," Huntington Library Bulletin, No. 8 (Oct., 1935), pp. 71–102.
Shakespeare's Satire, New York and London, 1943.

CAPELLANUS, ANDREAS, Art of Courtly Love, New York, 1941.

CARDAN, JEROME, The First Book of De Subtilitate, translated by Myrtle Marguerite Cass, The Bayard Press, Williamsport, Pa., 1934.

CARLYLE, R. W., and A. J., A History of Medieval Political Theory in the West, Vol. V, London, 1928.

CASADY, EDWIN, "The Neo-Platonic Ladder in Spenser's Amoretti," Philological Quarterly, Vol. 20 (July, 1941), pp. 284–295.

CASSIRER, ERNST, "Giovanni Pico della Mirandola" (I), Journal of the History of Ideas, April, 1942, Vol. III, No. 2, pp. 123–144, (II), June, 1942, Vol. III, No. 3, pp. 335 ff.
"Some Remarks on the Question of the Originality of the Renaissance," JHI, Vol. IV, No. 1 (Jan., 1943), pp. 49–56.
"The Place of Vesalius in the Culture of the Renaissance," Yale Journal of Biology and Medicine, Vol. 16, No. 2 (Dec., 1943).

CASTIGLIONE, COUNT BALDASSARE, The Book of the Courtier, Done into English by Sir Thomas Hoby, 1561 (Everyman edition).

CAWLEY, ROBERT RALSTON, Unpathed Waters, Princeton, N. J., 1940.

CELLINI, BENVENUTO, Autobiography, translated by John Addington Symonds (Modern Library edition).

CERVANTES, MIGUEL DE, Don Quixote (Modern Library edition).

CHAMBERS, R. W., Thomas More, New York, 1935.

CHAPMAN, GEORGE, Plays and Poems, edited by Thomas Marc Parrott, London, 1914.
Poems, edited by Phyllis Brooks Bartlett, New York, 1941.

CHAPPELL, A. F., The Enigma of Rabelais, Cambridge, 1924.

CHEW, SAMUEL C., The Crescent and the Rose: Islam and England during the Renaissance, New York, 1937.
"Time and Fortune," ELH, VI (1939), pp. 83–113.

CICERO, DE FINIBUS, translated by Walter Miller (Loeb Library).
De Natura Deorum, translated by H. Rackham (Loeb Library).
De Officiis, translated by Walter Miller (Loeb Library).
De Re Publica, translated by Clinton Walker Keyes (Loeb Library).

CLARK, ELEANOR, Ralegh and Marlowe, New York, 1941.

CLARK, ROBERT T., Sr., "Herder's Conception of 'Kraft,'" PMLA, Vol. LVII, No. 4, Part 1 (Dec., 1942), pp. 737–52.

CLEMENT, N. H., "The Eclecticism of Rabelais," PMLA, XLII (1927), pp. 339–84.
"The Influence of the Arthurian Romances on the Five Books of Rabelais," University of California Publications in Modern Philology, Vol. 12, No. 3 (1926), pp. 147–257.

COFFIN, CHARLES M., John Donne and the New Philosophy, New York, 1937.

COLLINS, JOSEPH B., Christian Mysticism in the Elizabethan Age, Baltimore, 1940.

CRAIG, HARDIN, The Enchanted Glass: the Elizabethan Mind in Literature, New York, 1936.

CURRY, WALTER CLYDE, Shakespeare's Philosophical Patterns, Baton Rouge, Louisiana, 1937.

DANTE, ALIGHIERI, Divine Comedy, translated by Jefferson Butler Fletcher, New York, 1931.

DAVIES, SIR JOHN, Poems, with an introduction and notes by Clare Howard, New York, 1941.

DAWSON, CHRISTOPHER, Progress and Religion, London, 1929.

DEAN, LEONARD F., "Literary Problems in More's Richard III," PMLA, Vol. LVIII, No. 2 (June, 1943), pp. 22–41.

DEE, JOHN, A True & Faithfull Relation of What passed for many Yeers Betweene Dr. John Dee and some Spirits . . . with a Preface by Meric Causabon, London, 1659.

DE WULF, MAURICE, History of Mediaeval Philosophy, translated by E. C. Messinger, London, 1926.
Philosophy and Civilization in the Middle Ages, London and Princeton, N. J., 1922.

DIOGENES LAËRTIUS, Lives of Eminent Philosophers (Loeb Library edition).

DONNE, JOHN, Biathanatos, reproduced from the first edition, with a bibliographical note by J. William Hebel, New York (The Facsimile Text Society), 1930.
Complete Poetry and Selected Prose, edited by John Hayward, Bloomsbury, 1929.
The Courtier's Library, or Catalogus Librorum Aulicorum incomparabilium et non vendibilium, edited by Evelyn Mary Simpson, London, 1930.
Essays in Divinity, edited by Augustus Jessopp, London, 1855.
Ignatius his Conclave, New York, 1941.
Paradoxes and Problemes, London, 1923.
Poems, edited by H. J. C. Grierson, London, 1933.
LXXX Sermons, preached by that learned and reverend divine, John Donne, London, printed for Richard Roylston, 1640.
Works, edited, with a Memoir of his Life, by Henry Alford, London, 1839, 6 volumes.

DORAN, MADELEINE, "On Elizabethan Credulity," Journal of the History of Ideas, Vol. I, No. 2 (April, 1940), pp. 151–176.

DULLES, AVERY, Princeps Concordiae, Cambridge, Mass., 1941.

DURAND, DANA B., "Nicole Oresme and the Medieval Origins of Modern Science," Speculum, XVI, 2 (April, 1941), pp. 167–185.
"Tradition and Innovation in Fifteenth Century Italy," Journal of the History of Ideas, Vol. IV, No. 1 (Jan., 1943), pp. 1–20.

ELIOT, SIR JOHN, The Monarchie of Man, edited by Alexander B. Grosart, London, 1879.

ELIOT, T. S., Collected Poems, New York, 1936.

ELLIS-FERMOR, UNA, Christopher Marlowe, London, 1927.

ELTON, OLIVER, "Giordano Bruno in England," Modern Studies, London, 1907, pp. 1–36.

ELYOT, SIR THOMAS, The Boke Named the Governour, edited by Foster Watson (Everyman edition).

ERASMUS, DESIDERIUS, Colloquies, translated by N. Bailey, edited by the Rev. E. Johnson, M.A., London, 1878.
The Education of a Christian Prince, translated with an introduction by L. K. Born, New York, 1936.
Epistles, with translation and commentary by Francis Morgan Nichols, London, 1904.
Praise of Folly, translated by John Wilson in 1668, edited by Mrs. P. S. Allen, Oxford, 1913.

FARNHAM, WILLARD, The Medieval Heritage of Elizabethan Tragedy, Berkeley, California, 1936.

FEBVRE, LUCIEN, Martin Luther: A Destiny, translated by Roberts Tapley, New York, 1929.

FIGGIS, JOHN NEVILLE, Studies of Political Thought from Gerson to Grotius, Cambridge, 1927.

FIRENZVOLA, AGNOLO, Of the Beauty of Women, translated by Clara Bell, with an introduction by Theodore Child, London, 1892.

FLETCHER, GILES AND PHINEAS, Poetical Works, edited by Frederick S. Boas, Cambridge, 1908.
FLETCHER, JEFFERSON BUTLER, "Continental Background of Edmund Spenser," unpublished article.
Literature of the Italian Renaissance, New York, 1934.
Religion of Beauty in Women, New York, 1911.
"Spenser the Puritan," unpublished article.
"A Study in Renaissance Mysticism: Spenser's 'Fowre Hymnes,'" PMLA, XXVI, pp. 452–475.
Symbolism of the Divine Comedy, New York, 1921.
"The 'True Meaning' of Dante's Vita Nuova," Romanic Review, XI (1920), pp. 133–136.

FOSS, MARTIN, The Idea of Perfection in the Western World, Princeton, N. J., 1946.

FRICK, Z. S., "The Theory of the Mixed State and the Development of Milton's Political Thought," PMLA, Vol. LVII, No. 3 (Sept., 1942), pp. 705–736.

FROMM, ERICH, Escape from Freedom, New York, 1941.

GENTILLET, INNOCENT, A Discourse upon the Meanes of Wel Governing and Maintaining in Good Peace, a Kingdome, or other principalitie, Against Nicholas Machiavel the Florentine, translated into English by Simon Patericke, London, 1608.

GIERKE, OTTO, Natural Law and Theory of Society, translated by Ernest Barker, Cambridge, 1934, Vol. I.

GILBERT, ALLEN H., "Fortune in the Tragedies of Giraldi Cintio," Philological Quarterly, Vol. XX, No. 3 (July, 1941), pp. 224–235.
Machiavelli's Prince and its Forerunners: The Prince as a Typical Book de Regimine Principium, Durham, North Carolina, 1938.

GILSON, ETIENNE, Reason and Revelation in the Middle Ages, New York, 1938.
Spirit of Mediaeval Philosophy, translated by A. H. C. Downes, New York, 1936.

GREENLAW, EDWIN, Studies in Spenser's Historical Allegory, Baltimore, 1932.

GRESWELL, W. PARR, Memoirs of Angelus Politianus, Johannes Picus of Mirandula . . .: Translations from their Poetical Works: and Notes & Observations concerning other Literary Characters of the Fifteenth and Sixteenth Centuries, Second Edition, London, 1805.

GREVILLE, FULKE, The Poems and Dramas, edited by Geoffrey Bullough, Edinburgh, 1939.

GRIERSON, H. J. C., The Background of English Literature, and other collected essays and addresses, New York, 1926.
Cross-Currents in English Literature of the Seventeenth Century, London, 1929.

GUARINI, BATTISTA, Il Pastor Fido, Paris, 1766.

GUICCIARDINI, FRANCISCO, Guichardin: Pensées et Portraits, translated by Juliette Bertrand, with an introductory study by Jacques Bainville, Paris, 1933.

HAKEWILL, GEORGE, An Apologie or Declaration of the Power and Providence of God in the Government of the World, 3d ed., London, 1635.

HAKLUYT, RICHARD, The Principal navigations, voyages, traffiques & discoveries of the English nation. . . . London and New York, 1907.

HANFORD, JAMES HOLLY, A Milton Handbook, 3d edition, New York, 1939.
"A Platonic Passage in Troilus and Cressida," Studies in Philology, Vol. 13 (1916), pp. 100–109.

HANKINS, J. E., The Character of Hamlet and Other Essays, Chapel Hill, North Carolina, 1941.

HARINGTON, SIR JOHN, The Metamorphosis of Ajax, edited by Peter Warlock and Jack Lindsay, London, 1927.

HARMAN, ALICE, "How Great was Shakespeare's Debt to Montaigne?" PMLA, Vol. LVII, No. 4, Part I (Dec., 1942), pp. 988–1008.

HARMAN, EDWARD GEORGE, Gabriel Harvey and Thomas Nashe, London, 1923.

HARVEY, GABRIEL, Letter Book, edited by E. J. L. Scott, London, 1884.
Marginalia, collected and edited by G. C. Moore Smith, Stratford-on-Avon, 1913.
Works, edited by A. B. Grosart, London, 1884–85.

HAYDN, HIRAM (editor), Portable Elizabethan Reader, New York, 1946.

HEARNSHAW, F. T. C. (editor), The Social and Political Ideas of Some Great Thinkers of the Sixteenth and Seventeenth Centuries, London, 1926.

HEBEL, J. WILLIAM, AND HUDSON, HOYT H. (editors), Poetry of the English Renaissance (1509–1660), New York, 1938.

HEILMAN, ROBERT, This Great Stage, Baton Rouge, 1948.

HELLMAN, C. DORIS, The Comet of 1577: Its Place in the History of Astronomy, New York, 1944.

HICKS, R. D., Stoic and Epicurean, New York, 1910.

HÖFFDING, HARALD, A History of Modern Philosophy, translated from the German edition by B. E. Meyer, London, 1924.

HOOKER, ELIZABETH ROBINS, "The Relation of Shakespeare to Montaigne," PMLA, Vol. XVII (ns. x), 1902, pp. 312–366.

HOOKER, RICHARD, Of the Laws of Ecclesiastical Polity, edited by Ronald Bayne (Everyman edition).

HOPPER, VINCENT FOSTER, "Spenser's 'House of Temperance,' " PMLA, Vol. LV, No. 4 (Dec., 1940), pp. 958–967.

HUGHES, MERRITT Y., "Spenser's Palmer," ELH, II (1935), pp. 151–164.

HULME, EDWARD M., The Renaissance, the Reformation and the Catholic Reformation in Continental Europe, New York, 1915.

JAEGER, WERNER, Aristotle, Fundamentals of the History of His Development, translated by Richard Robinson, Oxford, 1934.

JOHNSON, FRANCIS H., Astronomical Thought in Renaissance England, Baltimore, 1937.
"Preparation and Innovation in the Progress of Science," Journal of the History of Ideas, Vol. IV, No. 1 (Jan., 1943), pp. 56–58.
and LARKEY, SANFORD V., Thomas Digges, the Copernican System, and the Idea of the Infinity of the Universe in 1576, Cambridge, Mass., 1934 (reprinted from the Huntington Library Bulletin, No. 5, April, 1934).

JONES, RICHARD FOSTER, Ancients and Moderns (Washington University Studies, New Series, Language and Literature, No. 6), St. Louis, 1936.

JONSON, BEN, Discoveries, a Critical Edition by Maurice Castelain, London, n.d.
Works, edited by C. H. Herford and Percy Simpson, Oxford, 1937.

KEMPIS, THOMAS À, Imitation of Christ, preface by H. P. Liddon, New York, 1889.

KOCHER, PAUL H., "Backgrounds for Marlowe's Atheist Lecture," Philological Quarterly, Vol. 20 (July, 1941), pp. 304–324.
Christopher Marlowe: A Study of His Thought, Learning and Character, Chapel Hill, N. C., 1946.

KOYRÉ, ALEXANDER, "Galileo and Plato," Journal of the History of Ideas, Vol. IV, 3 (October, 1943), pp. 400–428.

KRAMER, SAMUEL N., "Immortal Clay: The Literature of Sumer," American Scholar, XV, 3 (Summer, 1946), pp. 319 ff.

KRISTELLER, PAUL O., "Augustine and the Renaissance," International Science, May, 1941, p. 7 (reprint pagination).

"Florentine Platonism and Its Relation with Humanism and Scholasticism," Church History, VIII (1939).

Philosophy of Marsilio Ficino, translated by Virginia Conant, New York, 1943.

"The Place of Classical Humanism in Renaissance Thought," Journal of the History of Ideas, Vol. IV, No. 1 (Jan., 1943), pp. 59–62.

"The Theory of Immortality in Marsilio Ficino," Journal of the History of Ideas, Vol. I, No. 3 (June, 1940), pp. 299–319.

and RANDALL, JOHN HERMAN, JR., "The Study of the Philosophies of the Renaissance," Journal of the History of Ideas, Vol. II, No. 4 (October, 1941), pp. 449–496.

LANGDALE, ABRAM BARNETT, Phineas Fletcher, Man of Letters, Science, and Divinity, New York, 1937.

LECKY, W. E. H., A History of European Morals, New York, 1897.

LEFRANC, ABEL, Grands Ecrivains Français de la Renaissance, Paris, 1914.

LEIGH, OLIVER H. G., English Belles Lettres, London, 1901.

LEMMI, CHARLES W., The Classical Deities in Bacon, Baltimore, 1933.

LE ROY, LOYS, De La Vicissitude ou Variété des Choses en l'Univers, selections with an introduction by Blanchard W. Bates (Princeton, 1944: No. 1, Princeton Texts in Literature and the History of Thought), xi.

LIPSIUS, JUSTUS, Two Bookes of Constancie, Englished by Sir John Stradling, edited by Rudolf Kirk, notes by Clayton Morris Hall, New Brunswick, N. J., 1939.

LOCKWOOD, DEAN P., "It is Time to Recognize a New 'Modern Age'," Journal of the History of Ideas, Vol. IV, No. 1 (Jan., 1943), pp. 63–64.

LOTSPEICH, H. G., Classical Mythology in the Poetry of Edmund Spenser, Princeton, 1932.

LOVEJOY, ARTHUR O., "The Dialectic of Bruno and Spinoza," The University of California Publications, Vol. I, pp. 141–176, Berkeley, California, 1904.

"Genesis of the Conception of 'Nature' as Norm," A Documentary History of Primitivism and Related Ideas, Baltimore, 1935, I, 103–117.

The Great Chain of Being, Cambridge, Mass., 1936.

"The Meaning of Romanticism for the Historian of Ideas," Journal of the History of Ideas, Vol. II, No. 3 (June, 1941), pp. 257–276.

"'Nature' as Æsthetic Norm," Modern Language Notes, XLII (1927), 444–450.

and BOAS, GEORGE; CHINARD, GILBERT; CRANCE, RONALD S. (general editors), A Documentary History of Primitivism and Related Ideas, Vol. I, Primitivism and Related Ideas in Antiquity, Baltimore, 1934.

LOWES, J. L., Geoffrey Chaucer, Boston and New York, 1934.

LUPTON, J. H., A Life of John Colet, D.D., London, 1887.

MacCURDY, EDWARD, The Mind of Leonardo da Vinci, New York, 1928.

MACHIAVELLI, NICCOLÒ, Discourses upon the First Decade of T. Livius, translated by E[dward] D[acres], London, 1674.

Discourses on the first ten books of Titus Livius, translated by Christian E. Detmold (Modern Library edition), New York, 1940.

Mandragola, translated by Stark Young, New York, 1927.
The Prince, translated by W. H. Marriott (Everyman ed.)

MARGUERITE OF NAVARRE, The Heptameron of the Tales, newly translated from the authentic text, with an essay upon the Heptameron, by George Saintsbury, London (Aldus Classics), 1903.
Les dernières poésies, edited by Abel Lefranc, Paris, 1896.

MARITAIN, JACQUES, "The Conflict of Methods at the End of the Middle Ages," The Thomist, Vol. III, No. 4 (October, 1941), pp. 527–538.
Three Reformers, New York, 1929.

MARLOWE, CHRISTOPHER, Works, edited by C. F. Tucker Brooke, Oxford, 1910, 1929.

MARSTON, JOHN, Plays, edited by H. Harvey Wood, London, 1934.
The Scourge of Villaine (1589), The Bodley Head Quartos, edited by G. B. Harrison, M.A., London and New York, 1925.

McCANN, FRANKLYN, England Discovers America, unpublished article (Columbia University Ph.D. dissertation).

MENUT, ALBERT D., "Castiglione and the Nicomachean Ethics," PMLA, Vol. LVIII, No. 2 (June, 1943), pp. 309–321.

MERRILL, ROBERT VALENTINE, The Platonism of Joachim Du Bellay, Chicago, 1925.

METZ, RUDOLPH, "Bacon's Part in the Intellectual Movement of His Time," translated by Joan Drever, Seventeenth Century Studies, Oxford, 1938.

MEYER, EDWARD, Machiavelli and the Elizabethan Drama, Weimar, 1897.

MICHELANGELO BUONARROTI, Sonnets, translated by John Addington Symonds, London, 1878.

MILTON, JOHN, Works, edited by Frank Allen Patterson, New York, 1931.
Complete Poetical Works, edited by W. V. Moody (Student's Cambridge Edition), Boston, 1924.

MIRANDOLA, GIANFRANCESCO PICO DELLA, On the Imagination, translated by Harry Caplan, London, 1930.

MIZWA, STEPHEN P., Nicholas Copernicus (1543–1943), New York, 1943.

MONTAIGNE, MICHAEL, LORD OF, Essayes, translated by John Florio (1603) (The World's Classics), New York, 1920–24.

MORE, SIR THOMAS, Utopia, ed. H. Goitrin from the 1551 translation of Ralph Robinson, London, n.d.
English Works, edited by W. F. Campbell, London, 1931.
Giovanni Pico della Mirandola, translated from the Latin by Sir Thomas More, edited with introduction and notes by J. M. Rigg, Esq. (London, 1890).

MORLEY, HENRY, The Life of Henry Cornelius Agrippa von Nettesheim, London, 1856.
(editor), Medieval Tales, London, 1884.

MUELLER, GUSTAV E., "Calvin's Institute of the Christian Religion, as an illustration of Christian Thinking," Journal of the History of Ideas, Vol. IV, No. 1 (January, 1943), pp. 287–300.

NASHE, THOMAS, The Unfortunate Traveller, or the Life of Jack Wilton, edited by H. F. B. Brett Smith (The Percy Reprints, No. 1), Oxford, 1920. Works, edited by R. B. McKerrow, London, 1904.

NASSH, L., AND WITKOWSKI, G. J., Le Nu au Théâtre depuis l'Antiquité, Paris, 1914.

NELSON, NORMAN, "Individualism as a Criterion of the Renaissance," Journal of English and Germanic Philology, Vol. XXXII, 1933.

NELSON, WILLIAM, "Thomas More, Grammarian and Orator," PMLA, Vol. LVIII, No. 2 (June, 1943), pp. 337–352.

NICOLSON, MARJORIE, "Kepler, the Somnium, and John Donne," Journal of the History of Ideas, Vol. I, No. 3 (June, 1940), pp. 259–280.
"Milton and the Telescope," ELH, Vol. 2, No. 1 (April, 1935), pp. 1–32.
"'The New Astronomy,' and English Literary Imagination," Studies in Philology, XXXII (July, 1935), pp. 449–462.
"The Telescope and Imagination," Modern Philology, XXXII (1935), pp. 233–260.

NORDEN, JOHN, Vicissitudo Rerum (1600), Shakespeare Association Facsimiles, No. 4, London, 1931.

NUGENT, ELIZABETH M., "Sources of Rastell's Four Elements," PMLA, Vol. LVII, No. 1, Part 1 (March, 1942), pp. 74–88.

OLSCHKI, LEONARDO, Machiavelli the Scientist, Berkeley, California, 1945.

PADELFORD, FREDERICK M., "Spenser's Fowre Hymnes, a Resurvey," Studies in Philology, Vol. XXIX, 1932, pp. 225–230.

PALINGENIUS, MARCELLUS (STELLATUS), The Zodiake of life, translated out of Latine into English by Barnabie Googe, London, 1588.

PARACELSUS (AUREOLUS PHILIPPUS THEOPHRASTUS BOMBAST, OF HOHENHEIM), The Hermetic and Alchemical Works, translated and edited by A. E. Waite, London, 1894.

PATRICK, MARY MILLS, The Greek Skeptics, New York, 1939.

PATRIZI, FRANCESCO, "On Physical Man" ('De Spacio'), translated by Benjamin Brickman, Journal of the History of Ideas, Vol. IV, No. 2 (April, 1943), pp. 224–245.

PERIERS, BONAVENTURE DES, Cymbalum Mundi or, Satyrical Dialogues upon several Subjects, Done into English from the French, London, 1712.

PERKINS, WILLIAM, Workes, Printed at London by John Legatt, Printer to the Universitie of Cambridge, 1612. (I am indebted to Prof. French Fogle, of Barnard College, for the use of his notes on Perkins' Workes—notes taken at the Henry E. Huntington Library.)

PETRARCH, FRANCIS, Secret, translated by W. H. Drapper, London, 1911.
The Sonnets, translated by Joseph Auslander, New York, 1932.

PHILLIPS, JAMES EMERSON, The State in Shakespeare's Greek and Roman Plays, New York, 1940.

Pico (Giovanni) della Mirandola, [Selected Works] translated from the Latin by Sir Thomas More, edited by J. M. Rigg, London, 1890.
A Platonick Discourse in Explication of a Sonnet by Hieronimo Benivieni, in Thomas Stanley, History of Philosophy, London, 1743.
Of the Dignity of Man, translated by Elizabeth L. Forbes, Journal of the History of Ideas, Vol. III, No. 3 (June, 1942), pp. 351–352.

Plato, Republic (third edition of the Jowett translation), with an introduction by Charles H. Bakewell, New York, 1928.
Symposium or Supper, newly translated into English, with an introduction by Shane Leslie, The Fortune Press, London, n.d.

Plotinus, Les Ennéades, translated by M. H. Bouillet, Paris, 1861.

Plutarch, Morals, translated from the Greek by several hands, corrected and revised by W. W. Goodwin, Boston, 1883.

Poliziano, Angelo, The Tale of Orpheus, translated by Louis E. Lord, London, 1931.

Pomponazzi, Petrus, Tractatus de Immortalitate Animae, translated by William Henry Hay II, Haverford College, 1938.

Praz, Mario, "Machiavelli and the Elizabethans," Proceedings of the British Academy, 14 (1928), pp. 49–97.

Rabelais, François, Works, completely translated into English by Urquhart and Motteux (Åldus Classics), London, 1903.

Ralegh, Sir Walter, Poems, edited by Agnes H. Latham, London, 1929.
Selections, edited by G. E. Hadow, Oxford, 1917.
Works, edited by Oldys and Birch, Oxford, 1829.

Rand, E. K., "The Humanism of Cicero," Proceedings of the American Philological Society, Vol. LXXI, No. 4 (1932).

Randall, John Herman, Jr., "The Development of Scientific Method in the School of Padua," Journal of the History of Ideas, Vol. I, No. 2 (April, 1940), pp. 177–206.
Making of the Modern Mind, New York, 1940.

Richards, I. A., Science and Poetry, London, 1935.

Robb, Nesca, Neoplatonism of the Italian Renaissance, London, 1935.

Robbins, Frank E., The Hexaemeral Literature, Chicago, 1912.

Roberts, Michael (editor), Elizabethan Prose, London, 1933.

Robertson, John MacKennon, Montaigne and Shakespeare, London, 1909; Oxford, 1897.

Rogers, W. H.; Redinger, Ruby V.; and Haydn, Hiram (editors) Explorations in Living, second edition, New York, 1942.

Ronsard, Pierre de, Œuvres Complètes, Nouvelle Édition revisée, augmentée et annotée par Paul Laumonnier, Paris, 1914–19.

Rosen, Edward, "The Ramus-Rheticus Correspondence," under "Notes and Documents," The Journal of the History of Ideas, Vol. I, No. 3 (June, 1940), pp. 363–368.

RUGOFF, MILTON A., Donne's Imagery: a Study in Creative Sources, New York, 1939.

RYAN, LOUIS A. O. P., "Of Charity and the Social Order," The Thomist, Vol. III, No. 4 (October, 1941).

SAURAT, DENIS, Literature and Occult Tradition, translated by Dorothy Bolton, New York, 1930.

SCÈVE, MAURICE (and others), Les Poëtes Lyonnais, Introduction et Notes de Joseph Aynard, Paris, 1924.

SCHOELL, FRANCK L., Études sur l'humanisme Continental en Angleterre à la Fin de la Renaissance, Paris, 1926.

SEESHOLTZ, ANNA, The Friends of God, New York, 1934.

SENECA, Epistulae Morales, translated by R. H. Gummere (Loeb Library).
Moral Essays, translated by John W. Basore (Loeb Library).
The Works of Lucius Annaes Seneca Both Morall and Naturall, translated by Thomas Lodge, London, 1614.

SEXTUS EMPIRICUS, Hypotyposes, with an English translation by the Rev. R. G. Bury (Loeb Library), 1933.

SHAKESPEARE, WILLIAM, Complete Works, edited by George Lyman Kittredge, Boston and New York, 1936.

SHOREY, PAUL, Platonism, Ancient and Modern, Berkeley, California, 1938.

SIDNEY, SIR PHILIP, An Apologie for Poetrie, in English Belles Lettres, ed. by Oliver H. C. Leigh, London, 1901.
Astrophel and Stella, ed. by Alfred Pollard, London, 1888.
The Countesse of Pembrokes Arcadia, ed. by Albert Feuillerat, Cambridge, 1912.

SIMPSON, EVELYN M., A Study of the Prose Works of John Donne, Oxford, 1924.

SINGER, DOROTHEA WALEY, "The Cosmology of Giordano Bruno (1548–1600)," Isis, XXXIII, Part 2, 88 (June, 1941), pp. 187–196.

SMITH, G. GREGORY (editor), Elizabethan Critical Essays, London, 1904.

SMITH, PRESERVED, A History of Modern Culture, Vol. I, New York, 1930.

SMITH, SIR THOMAS, De Republica Anglorum: A Discourse on the Commonwealth of England, edited by L. Alston, Cambridge, 1906.

SPENCE, LEWIS, Cornelius Agrippa, Occult Philosopher, London, 1921.

SPENCER, THEODORE, Death and Elizabethan Tragedy, Cambridge, Mass., 1936.
A Garland for John Donne (editor), Cambridge, Mass., 1931.
"Hamlet and the Nature of Reality," ELH, V (1938), pp. 253–277.
Shakespeare and the Nature of Man, New York, 1942.

SPENSER, EDMUND, The Faerie Queene, edited by J. C. Smith, Oxford, 1909.
The Fowre Hymnes, ed. by Lilian Winstanley, Cambridge, 1930.
Poetical Works, ed. by J. C. Smith, Oxford, 1919.
Shepheards Calendar, ed. by G. H. Herford, London, 1907.

STANLEY, THOMAS, The History of Philosophy, London, 1743.

STAPLETON, LAURENCE, Justice and World Society, Chapel Hill, N. C., 1944.
"Halifax and Raleigh," Journal of the History of Ideas, Vol. II, No. 2
(April, 1941), pp. 211–224.

STEINER, ARPAD, "The Faust Legend and the Christian Tradition," PMLA, LIV
(1931), pp. 391–404.

STEVENS, HENRY, OF VERMONT, Thomas Hariot: the Mathematician, the Philosopher, and the Scholar, London, 1900.

STEWARD, JANE SEMPLE, Giordano Bruno in England (unpublished Master's
essay, Smith College, 1932).

STOKES, ELLA HARRISON, The Conception of a Kingdom of Ends in Augustine,
Aquinas, and Leibniz, Chicago, n.d.

STRONG, EDWARD W., Procedures and Metaphysics, Berkeley, Calif., 1936.

SYKES, NORMAN, "Richard Hooker," in Social and Political Ideas, ed. Hearnshaw.

SYMONDS, JOHN ADDINGTON, Renaissance in Italy, New York, 1881

TAPPER, BONNO, "Aristotle's 'Sweet Analutikes' in Marlowe's 'Doctor Faustus,' "
Studies in Philology, Vol. XXVII, No. 2 (April, 1930), pp. 215–219.

TASSO, TORQUATO, Aminta, translated by Louis E. Lord, London, 1931.
Jerusalem Delivered, translated by Edward Fairfax (1600), edited by Henry
Morley, London, 1890.

TAWNEY, R. H., Religion and the Rise of Capitalism, New York, 1926.

TAYLOR, A. E., Aristotle, London and Edinburgh, 1919.

TAYLOR, GEORGE C., Shakespeare's Debt to Montaigne, Cambridge, 1925.
"Two Notes on Shakespeare," Philological Quarterly, Vol. 20 (July, 1941),
pp. 371–376.

TAYLOR, HENRY OSBORN, Thought and Expression in the Sixteenth Century,
Vol. I, New York, 1920.

THALER, ALVIN, "Franklin and Fulke Greville," PMLA, Vol. LVI, No. 4, Part 1,
(Dec., 1941), pp. 1059–1064.

THOMPSON, EDWARD JOHN, Sir Walter Ralegh; the Last of the Elizabethans, London, 1935.

THORNDIKE, LYNN, A History of Magic and Experimental Science, New York,
Vols. V, VI, 1941.
"Renaissance or Prerenaissance?" Journal of the History of Ideas, Vol. IV,
No. 1 (Jan., 1943), pp. 65–74.

TICKNOR, GEORGE, History of Spanish Literature, 4th ed., Boston, 1891.

TILLEY, ARTHUR, Francis Rabelais, London, 1907.

TILLYARD, E. W., The Elizabethan World Picture, New York, 1944.

TRINKAUS, C. E., Adversity's Noblemen, the Italian Humanists on Happiness, New York, 1940.

TROLTSCH, E., The Social Teachings of the Christian Churches, translated by Olive Wyon, 2 vols., London, 1931.

TUVE, ROSAMOND, "Spenser and the 'Zodiake of Life,' " Journal of English and Germanic Philology, XXXIV (1935), pp. 1–19.

UPHAM, A. H., The French Influence in English Literature, New York, 1911.

VAIR, GUILLAUME DU, The Morall Philosophy of the Stoicks, Englished by Charles Cotton, Esq., London, 1664.
Les Œuvres Politiques et Morales, Geneva, 1621.

VALLA, LAURENTIUS, The Treatise on the Donation of Constantine, text and translation into English by Christopher B. Coleman, New Haven, Conn., 1922.
De Voluptate ac Vero Bono Libri III, Basle, 1519 (photostat).

VILLEY, PIERRE, Les Essais de Michel de Montaigne, Paris, 1932.

VINCI, LEONARDO DA, Notebooks, arranged and rendered into English and introduced by Edward MacCurdy, New York, 1936.

VIVES, JUAN LUIS, On Education (De Tradendis Disciplinis), translated by Foster Watson, Cambridge, 1913.

VOSSLER, KARL, Medieval Culture, an introduction to Dante and His Times, translated by William C. Lawton, New York, 1929.

WEBER, ALFRED, History of Philosophy, authorized translation by Frank Tilly, New York, 1899.

WEBER, MAX, The Protestant Ethic and the Spirit of Capitalism, translated by Talcott Parsons, London, 1930.

WEISSBURGER, L. A., "Machiavelli and Tudor England," Political Science Quarterly, XLII, 1927, pp. 589–607.

WELLS, HENRY W., "The Philosophy of Piers Plowman," PMLA, Vol. LIII, No. 2 (June, 1938), pp. 339–349.

WHITEHEAD, ALFRED NORTH, Science and the Modern World, New York, 1925.

WILDE, NORMAN, "Machiavelli," The International Journal of Ethics, Vol. XXXVIII, No. 2 (January, 1928), pp. 212–225.

WILKINS, ELIZA G., The Delphic Maxims in Literature, Chicago, 1929.

WILLEY, BASIL, The Seventeenth Century Background, London, 1934.

WILLIAMSON, GEORGE, "Mutability, Decay, and 17th Century Melancholy," ELH, II (1935), pp. 121–150.

WILSON, HAROLD S., "Some Meanings of 'Nature' in Renaissance Literary Theory," Journal of the History of Ideas, Vol. II, No. 4 (Oct., 1941), pp. 430–448.

WILSON, J. DOVER, The Essential Shakespeare, Cambridge, 1932.

WOLF, A. J., A History of Science, Technology, and Philosophy in the 16th and 17th Centuries, London, 1935.

WRIGHT, ERNEST H., The Meaning of Rousseau, Oxford, 1929.

WRIGHT, LOUIS B., "The Significance of Religious Writings in the English Renaissance," Journal of the History of Ideas, Vol. I, No. 1 (January, 1940), pp. 59–68.

WYNDHAM, GEORGE, Ronsard et la Pléiade, with Selections from their Poetry, London, 1906.

YATES, FRANCES A., A Study of Love's Labour's Lost, Cambridge, 1936.

ZANTA, LÉONTINE, La Renaissance du Stoïcisme au XVIᵉ Siècle, Paris, 1914.

ZILSEL, EDGAR, "The Origins of William Gilbert's Scientific Method," Journal of the History of Ideas, Vol. II, No. 1 (January, 1941), pp. 1–32.

ZWEIG, STEFAN, Right to Heresy: Castellio against Calvin, translated by Eden and Cedar Paul, New York, 1936.

INDEX

This is an index of names which appear in the text.
Variations are listed separately, but where it seems necessary, the reader is referred to the alternative names. Names
appearing only in the footnotes after the chapters are
not listed. Quotations are marked: q.

Abelard, 48
Abraham, 514
Academicians, 462, 473
Academicism, 329
Academics, 538
Academy, New, 101, 477
Academy, Old, 470
Achilles, 305, 606, 609, 610, 611
Adam, 33, 62, 113, 151, 160, 162, 300,
   320, 349, 390, 416, 511, 513, 514, 541
Addison, 1, 15
Adonis, 540
Advancement of Learning, Bacon, q.,
   257, 259, 260, 261 f., 265 f., 534
Adversity's Noblemen, Trinkaus, q., 55
Advice of Man to His Soul, Benivieni,
   q., 346
Ægidius, 45
Æneas, 372, 589, 609, 610, 611, 635
Æschylus, 15
Africa, 218, 523, 587
Agamemnon, 297, 566, 589, 610
Age of Reason, 116
Aglaophemus, 43, 213
Agrippa, Cornelius, 4, 14, 21, 84, 149,
   150, 151, 152, 154, 159, 160, 161, 165,
   176, 179, 184, 185, 220, 228, 255, 341,
   342, 381, 434, 464, 538; q., 77, 79 f.,
   118 f., 120, 140 f., 145 f., 147 f., 225,
   420
———, De Incertitudine, 430; q., 213 f.
———, Of the Vanitie and Uncertaintie
   of Artes and Sciences, 90, 146
Ajax, 606, 609, 610, 611
Albany, 641, 664; q., 650, 661
Albertus Magnus, 45, 77, 99, 178, 180,
   181, 189, 192
Alchemists, 264, 535
Alcibiades, 600; q., 599, 628
Alexander, 189, 420, 633
——— of Aphrodias, 61, 100, 435
——— VI, Pope, 404
Alexandria, 526
Alexandrians, 326, 435
Alexandrists, 50, 62, 100
Alfarabi, 99

All Fools, Chapman, q., 400, 440
All's Well, Shakespeare, 229, 598
Altercazione, Lorenzo de' Medici, q.,
   351
Alvigia, 567
Amadas, q., 510
Americas, 510
Aminta, Tasso, q., 500
Amour Charnel, De l', Pierre Charron,
   q., 569
Amphialus, 560, 596; q., 586
Amyras, 369
Anatomie of the World, An, Donne,
   13, 21. See "First Anniversary"
Anaxagoras, 309
Anaximander, 308; q., 309
Anaxius, Prince, 586, 593, 596
Androgyno, q., 110
Anglican church, 38
Anglicans, 49
Anima et Vita, De, Vives, 198, 216
Animadversiones Aristotelicae, Ramus,
   328
Anselm, q., 31
Antenor, 610
Antipodes, 218, 219
Antonio, 619, 658
Antonio and Mellida, Marston, q., 565
Antonio's Revenge, Marston, q., 93, 402
Antony, 373, 503, 598; q., 317, 369, 370
   f., 372
Antony and Cleopatra, 373, 564
Apemantus, 107, 599, 619, 628
Apollonius, 525
Apologie for Poetrie, An, 7; q., 8
Apologie of Raymond Sebond, Mon-
   taigne, 90, 119; q., 80, 140, 141 f., 236,
   479, 485 f.
Apostolic Church, 121
Aquinas, Thomas, 3, 14, 17, 28, 30, 31,
   36, 37, 39, 41, 44, 50, 51, 52, 54, 60,
   61, 67, 77, 86, 88, 94, 98, 99, 102, 116,
   135, 136, 137, 146, 185, 192, 215, 274,
   298, 313, 315, 326, 329, 333, 345, 346,
   357, 366, 435, 469, 516, 586; q., 32,
   42, 43, 65, 66, 131, 132, 133, 295 f.,

300, 475. *See also* St. Thomas and *Summa Theologica*
Arabians, 99
Arabs, 434
Arcadia, 505
Arcadia, Sidney, 7; q., 8, 392 f., 396, 406, 437, 560, 561
Archimedes, 201, 249
Arden, Forest of, 510
Aretino, Pietro, 67, 385, 446, 568; q., 384
——, *La Cortigiana*, 567
Ariosto, 481, 589, 590, 597, 619; q., 562, 594
——, *Orlando Furioso*, 228
Aristotelianism, 37, 99, 100, 357, 435, 519; Renaissance, 329
Aristotelians, 195, 202, 515
Aristotle, 31, 35, 51, 53, 54, 61, 64, 67, 77, 79, 81, 88, 91, 99, 114, 119, 134, 135, 185, 186, 200, 207, 209, 215, 216, 228, 232, 250, 260, 275, 294, 295, 298, 301, 302, 309, 312, 326, 328, 329, 398, 408, 434, 435, 463, 469, 470, 472, 473, 498, 516, 517, 562, 590, 624; q., 422, 469, 585
——, *De Caelo*, 156
——, *Politics*, 133, 415, 444, 520; q., 414
Armes, Les, à Jean Brinon, Ronsard, q., 503
Armida, 504, 505, 582, 588, 594
"Ars Magna," Lully, 181
arte cabalistica, De, Reuchlin, 182, 340
arte dubitandi, De, Sebastian Castellio, q., 104
Artegal, 541, 542
Arthur, 590
As You Like It, Shakespeare, 619; q., 510
ascensione mentis in Deum per scalas creaturarum, De, Cardinal Bellarmino, 343
Ascham, Roger, 2, 3, 57; q., 595
Asclepius, Hermes, 181
Ashley, Robert, 532
——, *Of Honour*, 586
Asia, 218, 587
Asper, q., 385
Assyria, 530
Assyrians, 433
Astraea, 541, 542
Astrological Discourse, 533
Astronomia Nova, Kepler, 253
Astrophel, 362
Astrophel and Stella, q., 7 f.
Athenaeus, 536
Athens, 213
Atkinson, Geoffroy, q., 209
——, *Nouveaux Horizons de la Renaissance Française*, 207 f., 218

Aucassin, 95, 371, 502
Audrey, 511
Augustan Age, 1
Augustine, 36, 45, 52, 100, 106, 120, 294, 308, 343, 347, 415, 463, 490, 527
——, *City of God*, 544
——, *De Genesi contre Manichaeos*, 526
Augustinism, 114
Autobiography, Jerome Cardan, q., 192
Averroës, 61, 99, 100, 114, 399, 400, 434
——, *Physics*, 444
Averroism, 99, 100; "Latin," 99
Averroistic Aristotelianism, 99, 100
Averroists, 50, 62, 100, 414, 435
Avicenna, 99, 185, 516, 517

Babbitt, Irving, 472
Babel, 222
Babylon, 49, 433
Bacbuc, q., 536 f.
Bacchus, 182
Bacon, Francis, 2, 4, 12, 21, 86, 197, 198, 199, 202, 203, 228, 238, 250, 251, 258, 269, 270, 276, 367, 453, 527, 531, 651, 652; q., 10 f., 15, 26, 115 f., 166, 178, 207, 222, 225 f., 229, 254, 255, 256, 261 f., 272 f., 273, 274, 397, 398, 401 f., 414, 430 f., 445 f., 515, 535, 593
——, *Advancement of Learning*, q., 257, 259, 260, 261 f., 265 f., 534
——, *De sapientia veterum*, q., 446
——, *Great Instauration*, q., 243 f.
——, *History of the Reign of Henry VII*, 255
——, *Instauratio Magna*, q., 253
——, *Novum Organum*, 30, 240; q., 267 f.
Bacon, Roger, 178, 180, 181, 189, 195
Baconians, 257
Baker, Mathew, 212
Banquo, 663
Barabas, 368, 447
Barlow, q., 510
Baron, Hans, q., 154
Bartolus, 81
Basilica chymica, Oswald Croll, q., 514
Bates, q., 433
Baudier, Michael, q., 419
Baxter, 105
Beatrice, 36, 579
Beccadelli, 472
Becker, Carl, q., 32
Bellarmino, Cardinal, *De ascensione mentis in Deum per scalas creaturarum*, 343
Bellay, Joachim du, 84, 327, 515
Bembo, Pietro (Cardinal), 66, 327, 490, 564, 568; q., 343, 353, 557 f.

——, in *Courtier*, q., 333, 345, 352
——, *Gli Asolani*, q., 344
Bemboism, 355
Benedetti, 200
Benivieni, 55, 327, 344, 346, 347, 556; q., 342, 352, 353
——, *Advice of Man to His Soul*, q., 346
——, *Canzona dello Amore celeste et divino*, 327, 544
——, *Ode of Love*, 343, 345; q., 311, 332 f.
Bernard of Chartres, 35
—— of Clairvaux, 43
Bessarion, 36, 326
Betussi, q., 571
Bèze, Théodore de, q., 104
Bible, 214
Bilioso, 565
Billingsley, Henry, 194
Birnam Wood, 664
Biron, 303
Blagrave, John, 211
Blunt, Sir Walter, 604
Boas, George, 461, 501
Boccaccio, 67
——, *De Casibus*, 435
Bodin, Jean, 6, 21, 84, 154, 159, 165, 196, 252, 255, 273, 381, 415, 442, 522, 523, 527, 531; q., 394 f., 400, 407, 413, 422 f., 433 f., 528
——, *Colloquium heptaplomeres*, q., 47 f.
——, *Démonomanie des Sorciers*, q., 197
——, *Methodus*, 223 f., 419, 420; q., 521
——, *Republic*, 423; q., 223 f., 237, 343 f., 420
——, *Le Théâtre de la Nature Universelle*, 197; q., 225, 339
Boethius, 310
Boétie, Etienne de la, q., 522
——, *Discours sur la servitude volontaire*, q., 476
Boke Named the Governour, The, Sir Thomas Elyot, 3, 137, 577
Bologna, University of, 339
Bonaventura, 44, 94, 335, 343
Bonnivet, 572, 574
Book Concerning the Tincture of the Philosophers, Paracelsus, q., 215, 517
Book of the Courtier, The, Castiglione, 7
Borgias, 404
Borough, William, *A Discours of the Variation of the Cumpas*, 211; q., 208
Bossuet, q., 401
Bourne, William, 211, 212
Bowers, F. T., *Elizabethan Revenge Tragedy*, 594
Brahe, Tycho, 21, 157, 200, 251; q., 203

Brazil, 410, 503, 508, 509
Bredvold, Louis I., 112; q., 500
Bref Récit et succincte narration, Jacques Cartier, 208
Bridlegoose, 92
Britons, 531
Broadway, 12
Bronze Age, 541
Browne, Sir Thomas, q., 115
Bruni, Leonardo, *Isagogicon of Moral Discipline*, 53
Bruno, Giordano, 14, 20, 21, 145, 154 ff., 157, 158, 159, 160, 165, 240, 252, 263, 267, 337, 338, 359, 360, 366, 462, 464, 465; q., 155, 162, 341, 381, 428
——, *Gl'Eroici Furori*, 354
Brunschvicq, M., q., 214 f., 539
Brutus, 317, 598
Budé, Guillaume, 17
——, *De Transitu Hellenismi ad Christianismum*, 45
Bunyan, 105
Buondelmonte, Zanobi, 223
Burckhardt, Jacob, 2, 30, 383; q., 555
Burtt, E. A., 248
Bury, J. B., q., 526 f.
Bush, Douglas, 3, 4, 8
——, *The Renaissance and English Humanism*, 2
Bussy. See D'Ambois, Bussy
Bussy d'Ambois, Chapman, 594; q., 386, 440, f., 492 ff., 565 f.
Byron, 1, 15, 596; q., 21 f., 591 f.

Cabala, 37, 177, 179, 180, 181, 188, 189, 213, 214
Cabinet-Council, Ralegh, 6; q., 413
Cadmon, Adam, 464
Caelica, Fulke Greville, q., 564
Caelo, De, Aristotle, 156
Caesar, 371, 449, 562, 633
Caliban, q., 513
Calvin, John, 4, 14, 19, 24, 38, 47, 50, 84, 85, 102, 103, 105, 111, 245, 247, 334, 350, 356, 357, 418, 435, 436, 438, 439, 463, 468, 513, 533; q., 120, 415 f.
——, *Institutes of the Christian Religion*, 83, 104, 109
Calvinism, 109, 120, 186, 246, 355, 434, 517
Calvinists, 110, 415, 464, 471, 516
Camillo, q., 513
Campanella, Tomasso, q., 204, 273, 527; q., 338
Campbell, Oscar James, 12, 605; q., 107
Campion, Thomas, 367; q., 363 f.
Canterbury, Archbishop of, 315 f.
Canzona dello Amore celeste et divino, Benivieni, 327, 544
Cardan, Jerome, 177, 197, 198, 252, 263, 341, 381, 531

——, *Autobiography,* q., 192
——, *De Subtilitate,* q., 192 f.
Carlisle, Lady, 327
Carlyle, Thomas, 16
Carneades, 89, 101, 415, 444, 477, 520
Cartier, Jacques, *Bref Récit et succincte narration,* 208
Cartwright, Thomas, 19, 110, 121
Casibus, De, Boccaccio, 368, 435
Cassandre, 372, 502
Cassio, Michael, 607, 608, 657, 658; q., 599, 659, 660
Cassiopeia, 204
Cassirer, Ernst, 348; q., 37, 182, 213, 340, 341, 349, 383
Castellio, Sebastian, *De arte dubitandi,* q., 104
Castiglione, Baldassare, 327, 345, 352, 490, 491, 557, 564, 568, 569, 573, 588, 620, 653; q., 567
——, *The Book of the Courtier,* 7, 66, 344, 558, 565, 577, 578
——, *Il Cortigiano,* 556
Castilio, 565
Catherine of Aragon, 198
Cato, 46
Cavalcanti, Guido, q., 355
Cecropia, 437, 438, 467, 576; q., 478
Celia, q., 575, 594
Cervantes, *Don Quixote,* 228
Cesare Borgia, 449
Chaldeans, 45, 434
Chaldees, 213, 526
Champier, Symphorien, 45
Chapman, George, 3, 12, 67, 328, 332, 367, 497, 500, 501, 535, 597, 652; q., 58, 59, 106, 303, 348, 361, 371, 471, 493 ff., 495 f., 575
——, *All Fools,* q., 400, 440
——, *Bussy d'Ambois,* 492; q., 386, 440 f., 565 f.
——, *Conspiracy of Byron,* q., 591 f.
——, *Eugenia,* q., 331
——, *The Revenge of Bussy,* 55, 492; q., 82, 424
——, *Tragedy of Byron,* q., 21 f.
Charles, q., 510
Charron, Pierre, 66, 570; q., 483
——, *De l'Amour Charnel,* q., 569
Chaucer, Geoffrey, 35, 93, 229, 481
Cheke, Sir John, 2, 19, 57
Chew, Samuel, 435
Chinard, Gilbert, 461
Chivalry, Age of, 577
Christ, 24, 37, 38, 41, 46, 48, 56, 57, 58, 59, 60, 62, 65, 79, 94, 96, 97, 98, 102, 103, 113, 114, 120, 121, 220, 331, 347, 358, 380, 439, 462, 463, 518
Christendom, 133, 136, 315, 409
Christian humanism, 30 ff., *passim*

Christiana Religione, De, Ficino, q., 37, 327
Christianity, 3, 31, 32, 37, 38, 43, 45, 46, 47, 48, 50, 53, 55, 56, 59, 62, 96, 114, 120, 133, 212, 245, 320, 329, 432, 436, 526
Christians, 44, 56, 120, 176, 466, 472, 557
Christs Teares, Thomas Nashe, 6
Chrysostom, 221
Cicero, 3, 35, 36, 37, 38, 46, 55, 64, 89, 107, 109, 137, 216, 232, 305, 315, 326, 329, 415, 453, 463, 469, 470, 472, 476, 495, 498, 513, 519, 520, 556, 585, 586, 624, 653; q., 63, 408, 409, 411, 450, 473, 474, 480, 490, 492
——, *De Finibus,* 53
——, *De Officiis,* 53; q., 54, 477 f.
——, *Tusculan Disputations,* q., 53
City of God, Augustine, 544
Classicists, 15 ff., *passim*
Claudio, 622, 625, 627, 631, 635, 655, 656, 659; q., 633
Clement, q., 385
Clementia, De, Seneca, 109
Cleopatra, 372, 373, 503, 603, 667; q., 369 f., 372
Cole, Humfrey, 212
Colet, John, 37, 60, 331; q., 57, 97, 120
Collins, Joseph B., q., 347
Colloquies, Hedonius, q., 472
Colloquium heptaplomeres, Jean Bodin, q., 47 f.
Colonna, Vittoria, 327, 344
Conclusiones, Pico, q., 338
Conspiracy of Byron, Chapman, q., 591 f.
Constancy, Guillaume du Vair, q., 452
Constantia, De, Justus Lipsius, q., 529 ff.
Constantine, Donation of, 159
Convivio, 35
Coornhert, 47
Copernicanism, 164, 196
Copernicus, 14, 87, 155, 203, 204, 220, 221, 248, 338, 342; q., 339
——, *De Revolutionibus Orbium Celestium,* 21, 154; q., 196
Cordelia, 640, 642, 650, 651, 661, 662, 665, 666; q., 643, 644, 647, 648
Corin, q., 511, 512
Corinna, 364
Coriolanus, 598
Coriolanus, q., 317
Cornelius, 187, 214; q., 188, 189
Cornwall, 641, 642, 659; q., 107
Cortigiana, La, Aretino, 567
Cortigiano, Il, Conte Baldassare Castiglione, 556
Corvino, q., 575
Counter-Renaissance, 14 ff., *passim*

Courtier, Bembo (in), q., 333, 345, 352, 327
Courtier, Castiglione, 344, 558, 565, 577, 578
Craig, Hardin, 447
Crane, 461
Cressida, 605, 609, 610, 611
Croll, Oswald, *Basilica chymica,* q., 514
Cronos, 498
Crusaders, 605
Cupid, 563, 564, 589
Cusanus, Nicholas, 155, 181, 195, 356
——, *De docta ignorantia,* q., 335
——, *De Ludo globi,* q., 335
Cutwolfe, q., 595 f.
Cydnus, 371
Cymbalum Mundi, Des Périers, q., 400, 438
Cymbeline, Shakespeare, 598
Cynicism, 653
Cynics, 81, 82, 107, 118, 501, 505, 599
Cynthia's Revels, Jonson, q., 386
Cyprus, 657, 659

Daedalus, 265
Dagoucin, 566, 572
D'Ambois, Bussy, 82, 373, 386, 494, 497, 500, 501, 503, 565, 575, 637, 644; q., 361, 441, 493, 494, 495 f., 595
——, Clermont, 82, 497, 500, 637, 644; q., 495 f.
Daniel, 433, 434
——, Samuel, 2, 3; q., 81, 233 f.
Dante, 14, 15, 46, 50, 52, 106, 117, 133, 134, 136, 491, 556, 579, 652; q., 33, 35 f., 58, 490, 527
——, *Divine Comedy,* 29, 36, 327
——, *Paradiso,* 345
Davies, Sir John, 2, 3, 537, 652; q., 24, 111, 407, 534, 541
——, *Nosce Teipsum,* 11, 533, 534 f.
——, *Orchestra,* 11
Dawson, Christopher, q., 32
De Wulf, Maurice, 383; q., 239, 303
Dee, John, 177, 184, 193, 194, 195, 196, 198, 210, 220, 248, 340; q., 406
——, *Scientia Experimentalis,* q., 194
Deism, 46, 47, 48
Delphic Oracle, 537
Delphos, 536
Democritus, 272, 514, 534, 535, 538, 539, 540; q., 533
Démonomanie des Sorciers, Jean Bodin, q., 197
Denmark, 620, 634, 655
Dernières Poésies, Marguerite of Navarre, q., 559
Descartes, 28, 76, 267; q., 339 f.
Desdemona, 658; q., 659, 660
Dialogue of the Two Chief Systems, Galileo, 30

Diana, q., 560
Dido, 368
Digges, Thomas, 21, 193, 200, 210, 248, 273; q., 196, 204, 220
Dignity of Man, On the, Pico, 213; q., 182, 525 f.
Diogenes, 107
Diogenes Laërtius, *Lives of Eminent Philosophers,* 89, 534, 539
Diomed, 609, 610, 611
Dionysius, 300
—— Areopagita, 334
—— the Areopagite, 525
——, Pseudo-, 294, 295, 335 f.
Diotima, q., 312, 336
Discorsi e Demonstrazioni, Galileo, q., 253
Discours contre Fortune, Ronsard, q., 503
Discours sur la servitude volontaire, Etienne de la Boétie, q., 476
Discours of the Variation of the Cumpas, A, William Borough, 211; q., 208
Discourse of War in General, Ralegh, q., 522
Discourses, Epictetus, 495
Discourses on the First Ten Books of Titus Livius, Machiavelli, 152, 422, 439, 453; q., 149, 153, 216, 223, 234, 243, 253, 402, 411, 425 f., 429, 438, 447 f., 520 f., 576
Divine Comedy, Dante, 29, 36, 327; q., 49
docta ignorantia, De, Cusanus, q., 335
Doctor Faustus, Marlowe, q., 189, 367
Documentary History of Primitivism and Related Ideas, A, 461
Don Quixote, Cervantes, 228
Donne, John, 2, 4, 12, 22 f., 67, 78, 112, 115, 160 ff., 163, 165, 166, 273, 361, 365, 367, 465, 517, 533, 651, 652; q., 15, 23, 111, 113, 114, 142, 164, 366, 388, 461, 506, 570 f.
——, *An Anatomie of the World,* 13, 21
——, *Elegies,* 10
——, *Essays in Devotion,* 526
——, *First Anniversary,* 532, 544, 649; q., 312, 542 f.
——, *Ignatius, his Conclave,* q., 221 f., 252
——, *Litanie,* q., 113
——, *Second Anniversary,* 544
Dorn, Gerard, 518, 519
Dorus, 561; q., 562
Douglas, 601, 604
Drayton, Michael, q., 510
Drury, Elizabeth, 13, 23, 165, 542, 544
Du Bartas, *Première Semaine,* 526
Du Bellay, *see* Bellay
Du Vair, Guillaume, 41, 55, 358, 436,

472, 474, 478, 508, 585, 587, 637, 638; q., 40 f., 390 ff., 403 f., 411, 486, 586, 596
——, *Constancy*, q., 452
——, *Morall Philosphy of the Stoicks*, 452; q., 9, 473
——, *Sainte Philosophie*, 452
Duncan, 663
Duns Scotus, 44, 45, 77, 81, 99, 192, 346
Dunsinane, 664

Eckhart, Meister, 94
Economy of Minerals, The, Paracelsus, q., 517
Eden, 514, 524
Edgar, 639, 642, 648, 650; q., 644, 645, 646
Edmund, 533, 641, 644, 648, 658; q., 639, 640, 649
Education, Of, Montaigne, q., 89
Education of a Christian Prince, Erasmus, 137, 577; q., 46
Edward II, 368
——— VI, 217
Egypt, 181, 525, 530, 579
Egyptians, 213, 531
Einstein, 276
Electra, 339
Elegies, Donne, 10
Eliot, Sir John, *The Monarchie of Man*, 3
——, T. S., 566
Elizabeth, Queen, 208, 211, 217, 256, 273, 529, 544, 594
Elizabethan Reader, The Portable, 532
Elizabethan Revenge Tragedy, F. T. Bowers, 594
Elizabethan World Picture, The, E. M. Tillyard, 3
Elizabethans, 1, 2, 3, 4, 9, 11, 12, 14, 15, 17, 18, 21, 22, 82, 107, 165, 233, 246, 250, 359, 360, 361, 363, 365, 369, 386, 387, 431, 434, 447, 451, 481, 528, 529, 532, 541, 594, 606, 620, 651, 652
Elyot, Sir Thomas, 19, 57; q., 296, 306, 315, 326
——, *The Boke Named the Governour*, 3, 137, 577
Elysian Fields, 502, 505
Emerson, 299, 453
Emilia, 659, 660; q., 565
Empedocles, 309, 335
England, 30, 66, 100, 193, 198, 209, 210, 217, 259, 273, 327, 344, 603, 631, 664; Caroline, 327; Elizabethan, 110, 121, 211, 529; Puritan, 58; Tudor, 57
English literature, 1, 2
Enneads, Ficino (trs.), q., 435
Enneads, Plotinus, 327
Enobarbus, 619; q., 370

Ente et Uno, De, Pico, 37; q., 346, 351 f.
Epernon, q., 24 f.
Epictetus, 107, 328; q., 108
——, *Discourses*, 495
Epicureanism, 472, 473, 637, 638
Epicureans, 434, 472, 476, 508, 520, 637
Epicurus, 53, 434, 472
Epistemon, q., 535 f.
Epistles, Ficino, q., 44
Epistles, Plato, 328
Equato, 565
Equicola, 568
Erasmus, 3, 17, 37 f., 41, 42, 45, 53, 58, 60, 65, 81, 97, 103, 118, 326, 331, 332, 351, 361, 472, 481, 535, 555, 586, 597; q., 38, 46, 56, 77, 411, 492
——, *Education of a Christian Prince*, 577; q., 46
——, *The Praise of Folly*, 90; q., 92, 96, 106, 394, 405, 452
Erichthonius, 264
Erminia, 605
Esdras, 213, 526
Essay on Man, Pope, 29
Essayes, Montaigne, 228, 232; q., 91, 206, 236, 480
Essays in Devotion, Donne, 526
Estienne, Henri, 90
Ethiopians, 410
Euclid, 194, 201, 249, 340
Eugenia, Chapman, q., 331
Europe, 53, 66, 87, 218, 433, 509, 530, 531, 587; Renaissance, 556; Western, 136, 320
Eustace, q., 582, 589
Evans, Maurice, 620
Eve, 62, 320, 390
Every Man in his Humour, Jonson, q., 385, 592
Every Man Out of his Humour, Jonson, q., 385
Examen Vanitatis, Gianfrancesco Pico della Mirandola, 101
Exeter, 315
Existentialism, 349, 638
Experience, Of, Montaigne, q., 216

Faerie Queene, Spenser, 10, 540, 589, 590; q., 559 f.
Fairfax, Edward, 590, 605
Falstaff, 372, 600, 603, 667; q., 604
Farnham, Willard, q., 373
Faustus, 15, 189, 214, 362, 368, 369, 373, 447; q., 186, 187 f., 366, 367
Fenton, Geffray, q., 226
Ferrara, Council of, 326
Feste, 106
Ficino, Marsilio, 17, 36, 41, 45, 46, 48, 55, 59, 181, 326, 328, 332, 335, 344,

345, 346, 347, 358, 362; q., 43 f., 50, 62, 100, 212 f., 335, 348, 353, 525
——, *De Christiana Religione,* q., 37, 327
——, *Enneads,* q., 435
——, *Epistles,* q., 44
——, *Laus philosophiae,* q., 44
——, *Theologica Platonica de Immortalita Animae,* 327
Fideism, 98 ff., 105 ff.
Fideists, 98
Finibus, De, Cicero, 53
First Aniversary, Donne, 532, 544, 649; q., 312, 542 f.
Flanders, 41
Fletcher, Jefferson, 110; q., 235, 332, 342, 539, 555, 556, 557
Florence, 55, 412, 447; Council of, 326
Florentine Academy, 36, 37, 43, 50, 55, 56, 58, 66, 181, 326, 327, 339
Florentines, 45, 58, 525
Florio, John, 233; q., 386 f.
Folly, Erasmus, q., 405. *See Praise of Folly, The*
Fool, 642, 646, 651. *See* Lear's Fool
Fortinbras, 605, 621, 622, 631, 632, 635, 656
Fortuna, 435, 439, 467
Fourth Eclogue, Vergil, 432, 541
France, 66, 67, 327, 328, 344, 423
Francesca, 372, 502
Francis I, 214, 423
Francis of Verulam, q., 261 f.
Franciscans, 94
Franciscus, 45
Franck, Sebastian, 47
Frankfurt, 158
Frederick II, 100
Free Will, On, 103
French, 234
French Civil War, 418
Freud, Sigmund, 410
Friar John, 537, 600; q., 488, 587 f.
"Friends of God," 94

Galahad, 9, 504
Galen, 77, 99, 185, 186, 217, 516, 517
Galileo, 28, 86, 87, 116, 157, 200, 201, 236, 239, 329, 428, 461; q., 203 f.
——, *Dialogue of the Two Chief Systems,* 30
——, *Discorsi e Demonstrazioni,* q., 253
——, *Siderius Nuncius,* 163
Ganabim, Isle of, 588
Garden of Adonis, 540
Gargantua, 572
Gargantua, Rabelais, 395
Gascoigne, George, 106
——, *The Steel Glass,* q., 93
Gay, 1

Geburon, q., 567, 574
Gemisthus Pletho, 43. *See* Pletho, Gemisthus
Genesi contre Manichaeos, De, Augustine, 526
Genesis, 180, 525, 526
Geneura, 562
Geneva, 412
Gentiles, 43, 579
Gentillet, Innocent, 443
Germans, 433, 531
Germany, 66, 100, 119
Gernando, 582, 583, 595
Gertrude, 626, 655
Gianfrancesco Pico della Mirandola, 346
Gilbert, William, 197, 210, 263; q., 342
——, *De Magnete,* q., 338 f.
Gilson, Etienne, 383; q., 31, 33, 301, 308, 336
Giuliano, q., 592
Glaucon, 520
Glendower, 601
Gl'Eroici Furori, Bruno, 354
Gli Asolani, Bembo, q., 344
Gloucester, 65, 533, 665; q., 639, 648 ff.
Godfrey, 578, 579, 580, 582, 584, 589, 590, 595; q., 588
Golden Age, 121, 409, 425, 494, 495, 497, 498, 499, 500, 501, 502, 503, 504, 505, 506, 507, 508, 509, 510, 511, 513, 518, 519, 521, 524, 541, 570, 572, 662
Goliards, 481
Goneril, 560, 641, 651, 664
Gonzaga, Elizabetta, 327, 577
Gonzalo, 513
Goodfellow, Robin, 449
Gostanzo, q., 400
Grangousier, q., 421
Great Chain of Being, Arthur O. Lovejoy, 325 f.
Great Instauration, Francis Bacon, q., 243 f.
Greece, 579
Greeks, 45, 46, 185, 213, 433, 516, 525, 607, 609
Greene, Robert, 2, 12
Gresham College, 210
Greville, Fulke, 4, 9, 12, 41, 78, 106, 432, 434, 533, 652; q., 109, 111, 208, 386
——, *Caelica,* q., 564
——, *Inquisition upon Fame and Honour,* q., 596 f.
——, *Mustapha,* q., 364 f., 393
——, *Treatie of Humane Learning,* 90; q., 110, 246 ff.
——, *A Treatie of Warres,* 528; q., 431
Grierson, Sir Herbert, 10, 105
Grocyn, 37
Guarini, 572

——, Pastor Fido, q., 500
Guicciardini, Francisco, 6, 21, 84, 159, 197, 216, 225, 228, 232, 238, 251, 258, 381, 408, 432, 442, 462, 467, 519, 640; q., 226, 227, 404, 413, 420 f., 422, 430, 443, 448, 451, 523
——, History of Italy, 226
Guildenstern, 630, 634, 635, 656
Guinevere, 372, 502
Guinizelli, 556
Guise, 368, 440, 447, 495; q., 441, 494
——, Duchess of, q., 565 f.

Hague, The, 113
Hakewill, George, q., 251, 431
Hal, Prince, 600, 603 f., 632; q., 303 f., 601
Hamlet, 9, 14, 165, 373, 565, 599, 605, 607, 621, 622, 623, 651, 665, 666, 667; q., 25, 26, 620, 624, 625, 626, 627, 628, 629 ff., 631, 632, 633, 634, 635, 636, 654 f., 656, 659
Hamlet, the elder, 655
Hamlet, Shakespeare, 229, 605, 642, 653, 654, 664, 665, 666; q., 620, 627, 628
Harfleur, 208
Hariot, Thomas, 21, 106, 186, 204, 218, 273
Harvey, Gabriel, 4, 7, 12, 67, 106, 384, 533, 652; q., 78, 103, 105, 245, 252, 364, 385, 394, 414 f., 448 f., 486, 521 f., 593
——, Marginalia, 6, 593
——, Pierces Supererogation, q., 212
Hebrews, 45, 214, 526
Hector, 605, 609, 610, 611; q., 606, 607, 608
Hecuba, 627, 631
Hedonius, 472
Heilman, Robert B., This Great Stage, 638
Helen, 362, 560, 606, 607, 609, 610, 611
Helenus, 606; q., 607
Hellenism, 120
Hemmingsen, Niels, 63
——, De lege naturae apodictica methodus, 62
Henrietta Maria, 327
Henry, 45; q., 591
Henry, King, q., 303, 600 f.
Henry VIII, 198, 563; q., 571
Henry VI, Part I, Shakespeare, 605; q., 600 f.
Heptameron, Marguerite of Navarre, 558, 573; q., 80 f., 95, 355 f., 430, 445, 563, 572
Heptaplus, Pico, 180, 213, 525
Heraclitus, 309
Herbert of Cherbury, 47, 48, 50

Hercules, 353, 501, 587
Herder, 19
Hermes Trismegistus, 45, 213, 215, 326, 333, 335
——, Asclepius, 181
——, Pimander, 181
Hesiod, 309, 432, 525
——, Works and Days, 498
Hesperida, q., 592
Hester, John, 212
Hexaemera, 526
Hicks, Stoic and Epicurean, q., 642
Higgins, John, Mirror for Magistrates, q., 316
Hippocrates, 77, 99, 516
Hippothadeus, q., 78
Hircan, 597; q., 568
Histoire des Indes, J. Macer, q., 509
Histoire de la Nouvelle France, Marc Lescarbot, q., 509
History of Italy, Francisco Guicciardini, 226
History of the Reign of Henry VII, Francis Bacon, 255
History of the World, Walter Ralegh, 5, 6, 22, 434, 526
Hobbes, Thomas, 267; q., 409
Hoby, Sir Thomas, q., 352
Höffding, Harald, 155, 192; q., 158
Homer, 309
——, Iliad, 589
——, Odyssey, 589
Hominis Dignitate, De, Pico della Mirandola, q., 44 f.
Honour, Of, Robert Ashley, 586
Hood, Thomas, 210
Hooker, Richard, 3, 17, 18, 19, 60, 111, 137, 160, 161, 312, 328, 332, 333, 366, 392, 408, 462, 531, 533, 586, 652; q., 49, 50, 57, 58, 63, 65, 83, 106, 160 f., 162, 296, 302, 304, 310, 311, 313, 318, 345, 388 f., 474, 475, 519 f., 594
——, Of the Laws of Ecclesiastical Polity, 18, 22; q., 39 f., 138
Horace, 498
Horatio, 25, 620, 625, 626, 628, 630, 632, 633, 634, 635, 651, 656, 665; q., 621, 624
Hotspur, Harry, 9, 373, 600, 604, 605, 620, 636, 667; q., 367, 601, 602 f.
Housman, A. E., q., 491
Huguenots, 328
Hulme, E. M., q., 119, 336, 346, 417 f.
humani corporis fabrica, De, Vesalius, q., 198
Humanism, 27 ff., passim.
Hus, 119
Hutchins, Robert, 3
Hylton, Of Mixed Life, 52
Hymne, An, . . ., Spenser, 540
Hymne of Heavenly Love, Spenser, 357

Hymne in Honour of Beautie, An, Spenser, q., 538
Hymnes, Spenser, q., 559
Hypotyposes, Sextus Empiricus, 90

Iago, 2, 619, 649, 664; q., 599, 656 f., 658, 659, 660, 666
Iamblichus, 181
Idols of the Cave, 263
Idols of the Theatre, 264
Ignatius, his Conclave, Donne, 252; q., 165, 221 f.
Il Principe, 165
Iliad, Homer, 589
Immortalitate Animae, De, Pietro Pomponazzi, q., 61
Incertitudine, De, Agrippa, 430; q., 213 f.
Inns of Court, 10, 605
Inquisition upon Fame and Honour, Fulke Greville, q., 596 f.
Instauratio Magna, Francis Bacon, q., 253
Institutes, Justinian, 186
Institutes of the Christian Religion, Calvin, 83, 104, 109
Isabella d'Este, 327
Isagoicon of Moral Discipline, Leonardo Bruni, 53
Iseult, 372
Isles of the Blest, 505
Italian Renaissance, 2, 35
Italians, 213, 430, 596
Italy, 14, 30, 36, 100, 210, 326, 327, 344, 434

Jambicque, 574
James I, 209, 259, 594
Jaques, 107, 510, 619; q., 511 f.
Jerome, 35, 186, 221
Jerusalem, 578
Jerusalem Delivered, Tasso, 363, 590, 605; q., 504 f., 578 ff.
Jesuits, 49, 221
Jesus, 464
Jew of Malta, The, 368
Jewish Cabala, 526
Jewry, 530
Jews, 120
Jodelle, q., 483
John, Friar. *See* Friar John
John of Jandun, 114; q., 99, 100
Johnson, Francis, *Astronomical Thought in Renaissance England,* q., 193 f., 210
Jones, Tom, 485
Jonson, Ben, 2, 3, 12, 19, 78, 106, 107, 387, 598, 652; q., 18, 110, 316, 594
——, *Cynthia's Revels,* q., 386

——, *Every Man in his Humour,* q., 385, 592
——, *Every Man Out of his Humour,* q., 385
——, *Timber,* q., 413
——, *Volpone,* q., 154, 386
Judaism, 47
Julian the Apostate, q., 409
Juliet, 372
Jupiter, 93, 394, 438; q., 406
Justin, q., 31
Justinian, *Institutes,* 186
Juvenal, 107

Keats, 1, 15, 16
Kelley, Edward, 193
Kent, 619, 639, 642, 646, 651, 659, 661, 662; q., 107, 643, 644, 650, 666
Kepler, 87, 116, 200, 248, 339, 527; q., 203, 204
——, *Astronomia Nova,* 253
——, *Mysterium cosmographicum,* 203
King Lear, Shakespeare, 23 f., 26, 55, 107, 229, 533; q., 108. *See Lear*
King Solamona, 254
Kinsey, 401
Kittredge, G. L., 605
Kristeller, Paul Oskar, 348; q., 44, 347
Kyd, Thomas, 12

Lacedaemonians, 150
Lactantius, 35, 80, 415
Laelius, 520
Laertes, 605, 621, 622, 633, 635, 656; q., 9, 623, 634
Lalus, 561; q., 562
Landino, Christoforo, 57, 327, 347
——, *Quaestiones Camaldulenses,* q., 56, 351
Lara, 16
Lateran Council, 101
Latins, 45
Launcelot, 372, 502
Laura, 503
Laus Philosophiae, Ficino, q., 44
Laws, Plato, 445, 479; q., 469
Laws of Ecclesiastical Polity, Of the, Richard Hooker, 18, 22; q., 138
Le Beau, 512
Le Roy, Louis, 21, 159, 165, 197, 225, 255, 273, 413, 415, 428, 442, 531, 532; q., 237 f., 252, 410 f., 432 f., 521, 527 f.
Lear, 14, 23, 165, 306, 640, 642, 653, 654, 664, 665, 667; q., 643, 644, 645, 646, 647, 648, 651, 661, 666
Lear, 636, 637, 638, 641, 659, 660, 662, 664, 665; q., 639, 640, 642, 661, 666
Lear's Fool, 106. *See* Fool
Lefranc, Abel, 328, 355, 356; q., 80, 337

lege naturae apodictica methodus, De,
Niels Hemmingsen, 62
Leibniz, 267
Léon, Jean, q., 509
Leonardo da Vinci, 193, 200, 427, 441;
q., 395, 490
——, *Notebooks,* q., 205
Lepanto, 47
Lerner, Max, q., 453
Léry, Jean de, q., 208, 483, 509 f.
Lesbia, 363
Lescarbot, Marc, *Histoire de la Nou-
velle France,* q., 509
"Libertins Spirituels," 47, 94, 357, 559
"Lie, The," Walter Ralegh, q., 5 f., 577
Life of St. Francis, P. Sabatier, q., 94
Linacre, 37
Lippmann, Walter, 3
Lipsius, Justus, 17, 55, 61, 65, 351, 358,
413, 436, 462, 470, 471, 531, 533; q.,
411, 527
——, *De Constantia,* q., 529 ff.
——, *Manuductio,* q., 40
——, *Two Bookes of Constancie,* q., 40
Literature and Occult Tradition, 540
Little Brothers of Assisi, 94
Lives of Eminent Philosophers, Dioge-
nes Laërtius, 89, 534, 539
Locke, John, 28, 267
Lodge, Thomas, q., 490
London, 158, 210
Longarine, q., 95, 356, 445, 563
Lorenzo, 385, 525
Loupgarou, 120
Lovejoy, Arthur O., 331, 332, 461, 501;
q., 308, 320, 329 f., 337 f., 343
——, *Great Chain of Being,* 325 f.
Low Countries, 100
Lower, Sir William, 218
Lowlands, 66
Loyola, Ignatius, 105, 221
Lucifer, 186, 221, 597
Lucretius, 472
——, *De Rerum Natura,* 520
Lucrezia, 576
Ludo globi, De, Cusanus, q., 335
Lully, Raymond, 48, 180, 185
——, "Ars Magna," 181
Luther, Martin, 4, 14, 24, 38, 50, 85,
95, 97, 105, 119, 245, 247, 334, 350,
381, 415, 418, 435, 438, 439, 463, 468,
513, 533; q., 19, 102, 103, 104, 120,
417, 485
Lutherans, 57, 464, 471
Lyceum, 37
Lycurgus, 150, 507
Lysander, q., 446

Macbeth, 2, 25, 305, 664, 665; q., 662,
663
——, Lady, q., 663 f.

Macbeth, Shakespeare, 26, 229, 654,
660, 661, 665, 666; q., 662, 663 f.
Macduff, 662, 664
——, Lady, 664; q., 662
Macer, J., *Histoire des Indes,* q., 509
Machiavelli, Niccolò, 4, 6, 14, 21, 23,
84, 85, 145, 154, 159, 160, 164, 197,
221, 222, 225, 226, 232, 238, 240, 251,
255, 256, 257, 258, 266, 271, 381, 382,
383, 384, 404, 408, 421, 430, 431, 432,
434, 440, 444, 446, 450, 452, 462, 467,
506, 519, 520, 567, 640, 641, 650, 659;
q., 20, 116, 148, 149 f., 151 f., 228,
229, 262, 401, 413, 420, 441, 442, 443,
451, 520
——, *Discourses on the First Ten
Books of Titus Livius,* 149, 422, 439,
453; q., 153, 216, 223, 234, 243, 253,
402, 411, 423, 424, 425 f., 427, 428,
429, 438, 447 f., 520 f., 576
——, *The Prince,* 149, 152, 153, 226,
234, 235, 422, 425, 439, 447, 453; q.,
223, 243, 402, 405 f., 411, 423, 424,
438
Machiavellianism, 576, 640
Machiavellians, 397, 423, 424, 447, 450
Maco, 567
Macrobius, 544
Magica Theoremata, Pico, q., 184
Magnete, De, William Gilbert, q., 338 f.
Magnus, Albertus, 3
Mahometans, 421
Malcolm, 664
Malcontent, Marston, q., 565; q., 576 f.
Malevole, q., 565
Malvolio, 305, 619
Mandragola, q., 576
Manuductio, Justus Lipsius, q., 40
Maquerelle, q., 565, 576 f.
Marginalia, Gabriel Harvey, 6, 593
Marguerite of Navarre, 96, 327, 337,
358, 359, 619; q., 94 ff., 120, 335, 336,
357, 566 f., 574, 597. *See* Navarre,
Queen of
——, *Dernières Poésies,* q., 559
——, *Heptameron,* 558; q., 80 f., 355 f.
Maritain, Jacques, 3, 383; q., 417
Marlowe, Christopher, 2, 4, 5, 12, 67,
190, 365, 367, 373, 383, 447, 652; q.,
186, 366, 368, 369
——, *Doctor Faustus,* q., 189, 367
——, *Tamburlaine,* q., 367 f.
Mars, 504, 611
Marston, John, 4, 6, 12, 78, 106, 107,
365, 652; q., 81 f., 118, 435, 440
——, *Antonio and Mellida,* q., 565
——, *Antonio's Revenge,* q., 93
——, *Malcontent,* q., 565
——, *The Scourge of Villanie,* q., 110
Martha, 56
Martu, 498

Martyr, Peter, q., 508 f.
Mary, 56
Massacre at Paris, The, 368
Measure for Measure, Shakespeare, 229, 598, 619, 635, 658
Medes, 434
Medici, Cosmo de', 326
———, Lorenzo de', 67, 347, 397, 505; q., 396
———, *Altercazione,* q., 351
———, *Selve,* q., 502
Melanchthon, Philip, 17, 38, 49, 62, 63, 97, 137, 462
Menelaus, 611
Menenius, q., 317
Mephistopheles, 186, 188; q., 362, 367
Mercutio, 43, 93, 213, 438, 600
Mermaid Tavern, 2
Mesva, 185
Methodus, Jean Bodin, 223 f., 419, 420; q., 521
Metz, Rudolf, q., 267, 274
Meun, Jean de, 35, 208, 229, 445, 481
———, *Roman de la Rose,* q., 501
Michelangelo, 344; q., 352
Michelet, 30
Middle Ages, 2, 14, 31, 32, 33, 35, 36, 42, 44, 48, 51, 55, 60, 65, 88, 103, 132, 133, 134, 136, 149, 156, 190, 200, 229, 252, 307, 308, 310, 326, 409, 430 f., 444, 481, 482
Milton, John, 17, 41, 58, 87, 98; q., 319, 390
———, *Paradise Lost,* q., 475
———, *Paradise Regained,* 57
Minerva, 265
Minturno, 515
Mirror for Magistrates, John Higgins, 435; q., 316
Mithras, 46
Mithridates, 491
Mixed Life, Of, Hylton, 52
Monarchie of Man, The, Sir John Eliot, 3
Montaigne, Michel de, 4, 14, 23, 67, 81, 82, 84, 85, 97, 112, 146, 148, 152, 154, 158, 159, 160, 164, 165, 197, 199, 234, 235, 238, 242, 247, 251, 258, 260, 261, 267, 381, 382, 407, 408, 410, 429, 430, 453, 462, 464, 467, 504, 510, 513, 521, 563, 640, 641, 667; q., 20 f., 76, 77 f., 92, 117, 118, 120, 143 ff., 176, 206, 208, 215 f., 217, 226, 230, 231, 232, 233, 243, 253, 325, 384, 386 f., 387, 395, 398 f., 400 f., 402 f., 404 f., 409, 418, 419, 466, 481, 483, 484 f., 487, 488, 489 f., 491, 492, 507, 508, 523 f., 532, 568, 569
———, *Apologie of Raymond Sebond,* 76, 90, 119; q., 80, 140, 141, 236, 479, 485 f.

———, *Of Education,* q., 89
———, *Essayes,* 228, 232; q., 91, 206, 236, 480
———, *Of Experience,* q., 216
———, *Of Phisiognomy,* q., 91
Morall Philosophy of the Stoicks, Guillaume du Vair, 452; q., 9, 473
More, Sir Thomas, 3, 19, 37, 41, 57, 58, 60, 65, 81, 217, 224, 331, 332, 462, 472, 586; q., 475
———, *Utopia,* q., 38, 46, 56
Morello, q., 567
"Moria," q., 96
Morris, 16
Mortimer, 368, 447, 601
Moses, 182, 213, 215, 353, 525, 526
"Moses, the Attic," 525
Much Ado, Shakespeare, 229
Mulcaster, 2, 57
Muscovy Company, 210
Muses, 265
Musidorus, 8; q., 396, 561
Mustapha, Fulke Greville, q., 364 f., 393
Mutability Cantos, Spenser, 533; q., 540
Mysterium cosmographicum, Kepler, 203

Nashe, Thomas, 4, 7, 12, 78, 533, 652; q., 361, 384, 485, 566, 595 f.; q., 597
———, *Christs Teares,* 6
———, *The Unfortunate Traveller,* 6; q., 362
natura rerum juxta propria principia, De, Bernardino Telesio, 239
Natural History, Pliny, 535
Naturalists, 16 ff., *passim*
"Nature and Montaigne, Inc.," 76
Navarre, Queen of, 95. *See* Marguerite of Navarre
Neoaristotelians, 84
Neoplatonism, 36, 181, 325, 326, 329, 337, 338, 347, 357, 358, 359, 360; Florentine, 352, 354; Italian, 345; Renaissance, 326, 327; Syrian, 181
Neoplatonists, 46, 84, 158, 294, 309, 310, 326, 327, 328, 332, 333, 334, 336, 338, 342, 343, 347, 351, 353, 354, 357, 359, 380, 519, 526; Florentine, 344, 350; Italian, 343; Renaissance, 332, 333, 337, 342, 346, 358
Neopythagoreanism, 181
Neostoics, 84
Nestor, 605, 609
New Academy, 101, 477
New Attractive, Robert Norman, 208; q., 211 f.
New Testament, 31, 41
New World, 47, 207, 209, 218, 410, 465, 482, 507, 508
Newton, 28, 30, 86

——, *Principia Mathematica*, 27
Newtonian Age, 29, 48
Nicholas of Cusa, 36
Nicolette, 371, 502
Nicolson, Marjorie H., 163, 642; q., 164
Nicomaque de Gérasa, 539
Nietzsche, q., 120
Nominalism, 88
Norden, John, 533
——, *Vicissitudo Rerum*, 22; q., 528
Norman, Robert, q., 244
——, *New Attractive*, 208; q., 211 f.
Norns, 661
Northumberland, 186
Norway, 621
Nosce Teipsum, Davies, 11, 533, 534 f.
Notebooks, Leonardo da Vinci, q., 205
Nova, 15
Novara, 234, 339
Novum Organum, Francis Bacon, 30, 240; q., 267 f.
Nouveaux Horizons de la Renaissance Française, Geoffroy Atkinson, 207 f., 218
Numenius, 44

Ockham, 119, 139, 179, 200
Ockhamism, 89, 100
Octavius, 372; q., 371
Ode of Love, Benivieni, 343, 345; q., 311, 332 f.
Odyssey, Homer, 589
Œta, 353
Officiis, De, Cicero, 53; q., 54
Oiselle, 356
Old Duke, 619
Old Testament, 31
Oliver, 510; q., 512
Olschki, Leonardo, 425, 438, 441; q., 427, 428
Ophelia, 620, 623, 625, 630, 633, 655, 656
Orchestra, Davies, 11
Orient, 47, 99, 181, 207, 209, 218
Origen, 221
Orlando, 510, 512, 589, 590; q., 511
Orlando Furioso, Ariosto, 228, 578
Orpheus, 43, 184, 213, 326, 514, 525
Orphism, 184
Osric, 512, 565, 609, 635, 656
Oswald, 107, 642
Othello, 25, 665, 666; q., 660 f.
Othello, Shakespeare, 229, 598, 654, 656, 660, 661, 664, 665; q., 599, 666
Ovid, 498, 501
Oxford, 200
Oxford reformers, 3

Padua, 87, 115, 200, 201, 202, 249, 273, 412, 434, 440; University of, 100

Paduans, 201, 202, 203, 205
Pamela, 560, 576; q., 437
Panaetius, 444
Pandarus, 605, 610, 612
Pannonius, Johannes, 50, 100
Pantagruel, 93, 106, 536, 600; q., 92, 120, 335, 487, 537, 587
Pantagruelism, 488, 489
Pantagruelists, 488
Panurge, 92, 106, 446, 507, 537, 600; q., 536, 588
Paolo, 372, 502
Parabolano, 567
Paracelsan Revival, 191
Paracelsanism, 250, 517
Paracelsans, 514
Paracelsus, Theophrastus, 14, 21, 177, 182, 184, 195, 215, 219, 221, 252, 267, 341, 342, 381, 464, 519; q., 77, 185, 186, 190, 191, 198, 263, 514, 515, 516, 517, 518, 535, 541
——, *Book Concerning the Tincture of the Philosophers*, q., 517
——, *The Economy of Minerals*, q., 517
Paradise Lost, Milton, q., 475
Paradise Regained, Milton, 57
Paradiso, Dante, 345
Paris, 89, 99, 100, 200, 606, 607, 608, 609, 610, 611
Parlamente, 558; q., 80, 355, 356, 566, 597
Parthians, 434
Pascal, 87
"Passionate Man's Pilgrimage," Walter Ralegh, 5
Pastor Fido, Guarini, q., 500
Paul, 38, 101, 120, 139; q., 304, 315
Patrizzi, Francisco, q., 240
Patroclus, 611
Pax Romana, 133
Peasants' Revolt, 119, 211
Percy, 601
Perdita, 513
Périers, Des, 567
——, *Cymbalum Mundi*, q., 400, 438
Peripateticism, 329
Peripatetics, 100, 450, 462, 470, 473
Perkins, William, q., 415, 416
Persians, 433
Peter, 139, 164, 271
Petrarch, 30, 41, 46, 66, 67, 76, 82, 106, 372, 481, 491, 502 f., 556; q., 77, 490
——, *De Remediis Utriusqve Fortuna*, 392
——, *Secretum*, q., 52
Phaedrus, Plato, 335, 343
Phalantus, 586
Phebe, 512
Philo, 44, 526
—— Judæus, 526
Philoclea, 560

Phisiognomy, Of, Montaigne, q., 91
Phlegon, q., 400
Pia, Emilia, 577
Pico della Mirandola, Giovanni, 36, 46, 48, 55, 220, 326, 327, 328, 329, 332, 345, 347, 348, 357, 359, 360, 366, 383, 384, 404, 407, 418, 462, 464, 465, 514, 526, 527, 539, 544; q., 45, 181, 182, 183, 184, 194, 333, 334, 340, 341, 342, 344 f., 346, 349 f., 353, 385
——, *Conclusiones,* q., 338
——, *Of the Dignity of Man,* 213; q., 182, 525 f.
——, *De Ente et Uno,* 37; q., 346, 351 f.
——, *Examen Vanitatis,* 101
——, *Heptaplus,* 180, 213, 525
——, *De Hominis Dignitate,* q., 44 f.
——, *Magica Theoremata,* q., 184
Picrochole, q., 421
Pierces Supererogation, Gabriel Harvey, q., 212
Piers Plowman, 52, 93
Pillars of Hercules, 253, 275
Pimander, Hermes, 181
Plato, 3, 15, 31, 36, 37, 38, 43, 44, 46, 53, 78, 91, 113, 134, 139, 181, 213, 216, 221, 224, 231, 294, 301, 304, 325, 326, 327, 328, 331, 333, 429, 432, 470, 472, 473, 498, 507, 514, 525, 526, 527, 538, 541, 558, 560, 585, 588, 590, 594, 606, 624
——, *Epistles,* 328
——, *Laws,* 445, 479; q., 469
——, *Phaedrus,* 335
——, *Republic,* 329, 543; q., 580 f.
——, *Statesman,* 445
——, *Symposium,* 335
——, *Timaeus,* 309, 329
Platonic Academy, 45
Platonism, 36, 37, 39, 64, 120, 133, 212, 325, 326, 327, 332, 357, 568; Christian, 328, 331; French, 328; Renaissance, 326, 327, 328, 329
Platonists, 17, 44, 326, 328, 334, 335, 571; Cambridge, 48; Pythagorizing, 335
Pletho, Gemisthus, 36, 326. *See* Gemisthus Pletho
Pliny, 77, 192, 463
——, *Natural History,* 535
Plotinus, 36, 44, 181, 182, 213, 307, 330, 332, 333, 334, 335, 353; q., 294
——, *Enneads,* 327
Plutarch, 53, 55, 113, 329, 536
Poland, 621, 631
Politics, Aristotle, 133, 415, 444, 520; q., 414
Polixenes, q., 513
Poliziano, Angelo, 346, 396; q., 37
——, *Stanze per la Giostra,* q., 436, 501 f.

Polonius, 106, 631, 656; q., 622
Polybius, 429
Pomponazzi, Pietro, 62, 66, 100, 114, 398, 403, 413; q., 399, 412, 444, 488
——, *De Immortalitate Animae,* q., 61
Pope, Alexander, 1, 12, 15, 294; q., 295
——, *Essay on Man,* 29
Porette, Marguerite, q., 95
Porphyry, 525
Praise of Folly, The, Erasmus, 77, 90, 92; q., 96, 106, 394, 452 f. *See Folly*
Predestination, On, 103
Première Semaine, Du Bartas, 526
Priam, 606
Primitivism and Related Ideas in Antiquity, 461
Prince, The, Machiavelli, 149, 152, 153, 226, 234, 235, 422, 425, 439, 453; q., 223, 243, 402, 405 f., 411, 423, 424, 438
Proclus, 181
Proserpina, 364
Prospero, q., 592
Protagoras, 139
Protestantism, 38, 47, 89
Protestants, 49, 97, 102
Ptolemy, 77, 99
"Ptolomeus," 220
Puritan Age, 105
Puritanism, 105
Puritans, 19, 39, 49, 110, 620, 653
Pyrocles, 8, 396; q., 561
Pyrrho, 101
—— of Elis, 89
Pythagoras, 43, 181, 184, 213, 215, 309, 325, 513, 526, 539
Pythagoreanism, 179, 214, 339
Pythagoreans, 45, 177, 214, 526

Quaestiones Camaldulenses, Cristoforo Landino, q., 56, 351
Quod Nihil Scitur, Francisco Sanchez, 90; q., 235

Rabelais, 4, 14, 21, 67, 84, 90, 165, 228, 252, 465, 481, 484, 531, 573, 577, 600, 619; q., 78, 92, 335, 395, 421, 487, 488, 490, 535 f., 537 f.
——, *Gargantua,* 395
Racine, 15
Ralegh, Sir Walter, 2, 4, 7, 67, 78, 106, 186, 335, 336, 367, 527, 589, 652; q., 118, 195, 209 f., 310, 362, 419, 515, 535, 399, 438, 568
——, *Cabinet-Council,* 5 f.; q. 413
——, *Discourse of War in General,* q., 522
——, *History of the World,* 5 f., 22, 434, 526

——, "The Lie," q., 577
——, "The Passionate Man's Pilgrimage," 5 f.
——, "School of Night," 12
——, *Treatise of the Soul*, q., 388
Ramus, Peter, 202, 238, 267, 269, 273, 531; q., 79, 186, 204
——, *Animadversiones Aristotelicae*, 328
Rand, E. K., 35
Randall, John Herman, Jr., 200, 249; q., 30, 153, 201 f., 250, 301 f.
Raymond, 605
—— of Sabunde, 48
"R. B.," 252; q., 191 f., 220
Recorde, Robert, 210, 248
——, *Whetstone of Witte*, q., 195 f.
Reformation, 38, 50, 55, 60, 62, 79, 80, 83, 85, 93, 94, 95, 102, 119, 137, 146, 161, 178, 186, 212, 220, 245, 246, 328, 415, 417, 439, 464, 513, 519, 528, 544, 653; Catholic, 105; Early, 463; Lutheran, 97, 120; Scientific, 85, 87, 140, 157, 166, 200, 202, 205, 236, 239, 241, 250, 252 f., 270, 271, 273, 275, 461
Reformed Countries, 62
Reformers, 113, 358, 380, 435, 439, 531
Regan, 641, 650, 651, 664; q., 645
Remediis Utriusque Fortuna, De, Petrarch, 392
Renaissance, 3, 27 ff., 45, 46, 48, 49, 51, 55, 57, 65, 67, 84, 181, 215, 296, 328, 329, 331, 335, 341, 343, 382, 406, 408, 409, 410, 435, 436, 444, 461, 468, 469, 470, 472, 473, 478, 490, 498, 501, 505, 516, 533, 534, 535, 537, 541, 556, 572, 577, 578, 580, 597, 636; English, 46; Italian, 555
Renaissance and English Humanism, The, Douglas Bush, 2
Renaissance-at-large, 395
Republic, Jean Bodin, 423; q., 223 f., 237, 343 f., 420
Republic, Plato, 329, 543; q., 580 f.
Republica Anglorum, De, Sir Thomas Smith, q., 217
Rerum Natura, De, Lucretius, 472, 520
Reuchlin, 45, 47, 81, 97, 181, 526
——, *De arte cabalistica,* 182, 340
——, *De verbo mirifico,* 182, 340
Revenge of Bussy, George Chapman, 55, 492, 494; q., 82, 424, 495 f.
Revolutionibus Orbium Celestium, De, Copernicus, 21, 154; q., 196
Reynaldo, 622
Rheticus, 202, 204
Rhodes, 657
Riccio, Aloisio, 396
Richard I, 449
—— III, 2
Rinaldo, 505, 579, 580, 582, 584, 589, 590, 594, 595, 597; q., 440, 562, 583

Robb, Nesca, q., 354
Roderigo, 656, 657, 658, 660
Roman Catholic Church, 51, 102, 121
Roman Empire, 433
Roman de la Rose, Jean de Meun, 501
Romans, 433
Romantic period, 1
Romanticists, 15 ff., *passim*
Rome, 371, 415, 520, 637
Romeo and Juliet, Shakespeare, 600
Ronsard, 67, 84, 465, 481, 505, 507, 508, 509, 541; q., 372, 502, 504
——, *Les Armes, à Jean Brinon,* q., 503
——, *Discours contre Fortune,* q., 503
Rosalind, 512
Rosencrantz, 630, 634, 635, 656
Ross, q., 662
Rosso, 567
Rousseau, 19, 472
Royal Society, 29
Rucellai, Cosimo, 223

Sabatier, P., *Life of St. Francis,* q., 94
Saffredent, 576; q., 566 f., 571, 572
St. Albans, Lord of, 116
Saint Paul's, 10, 366
St. Thomas, 232, 300. *See* Aquinas
Sainte Philosophie, Guillaume du Vair, 452
Salomon's House, 254
Salutati, Coluccio, *The World and Religion,* 55
Sanchez, Francisco, 238, 269
——, *Quod Nihil Scitur,* 90; q., 235
Sansovino, 413
sapientia veterum, De, Francis Bacon, q., 446
Saracen Empire, 47
Sartre, 349
Saturn, 498, 541
Saurat, Denis, 181, 540; q., 337, 338
Savonarola, 55, 346
Scaliger, Joseph, 527
Scève, Maurice, 327
Scholasticism, 84, 99, 117, 178; Thomistic, 134
Scholastics, 28, 31, 33, 42, 43, 51, 54, 58, 60, 64, 79, 85, 87, 89, 97, 99, 117, 134, 135, 136, 219, 228, 238, 248, 259, 293, 309, 380, 451, 557
"School of Night," Ralegh, 12
Schoolmen, 99, 514, 515, 516
Scientia Experimentalis, John Dee, q., 194
Scott, Sir Walter, 16
Scotus, Duns. *See* Duns Scotus
Scotus Eriugena, 42
Scourge of Villanie, The, John Marston, q., 110
Scripture, 49, 120, 400

Scriptures, 113, 132
Second Anniversary, Donne, 544
Secretum, Petrarch, 106, 490; q., 52
Selve, Lorenzo de' Medici, q., 52
Senamus, 48
Senators, 600; q., 599 f.
Seneca, 11, 46, 53, 64, 82, 107, 113, 137, 329, 472, 474, 490, 496, 500, 501, 653; q., 341 f., 470, 497, 498
——, *De Clementia*, 109
sette giornate del mondo creato, Le, Tasso, 526
Sextus, 91
—— Empiricus, 101, 112, 139, 399
——, *Hypotyposes*, 90
Shakespeare, 2, 4, 11, 12, 67, 228, 361, 364, 367, 372, 627, 628, 633, 636, 637, 641, 648, 651, 652, 653, 654, 658, 659, 660, 665, 666, 667; q., 25, 26, 297, 303 f., 315, 319, 372, 373, 512, 603, 604, 609
——, *All's Well*, 598
——, *Antony and Cleopatra*, q., 369 f.
——, *As You Like It*, 600, 619; q., 510
——, *Cymbeline*, 538
——, *Hamlet*, 605; q., 620
——, *Henry IV, Part I*, 605; q., 600 f.
——, *King Lear*, 23 f., 55, 107; q., 108. *See also Lear*
——, *Measure for Measure*, 598, 619
——, *Othello*, 598
——, *Tempest*, q., 513
——, *Timon of Athens*, 107; q., 628
——, *Troilus and Cressida*, 605, 619; q., 606 ff., 611 f.
——, *Winter's Tale*, q., 513
Shakespeare and the Nature of Man, Theodore Spencer, 4
Shekinah, 540, 541
Shelley, 1, 16
Shenstone, 1
Shepheards Calendar, Spenser, 110; q., 432
Shorey, Paul, 51
Shubur, 498
Shute, John, 212
Sicily, 100
Siderius Nuncius, Galileo, 163
Sidney, Sir Philip, 4, 7 ff., 12, 41, 67, 78, 327, 361, 364, 367, 505, 515, 558, 596, 619, 652; q., 331, 332, 362, 478, 562, 586, 591, 593
——, *Arcadia*, q., 392 f., 396, 406, 437, 560, 561
Siger of Brabant, 99
Silver Age, 541
Silvius, 512
Simontault, q., 566, 573
Simpson, Evelyn, 542
Singularités de la France Antartique, Des, André Thevet, q., 483

Smith, Sir Thomas, *De Republica Anglorum*, q., 217
Socrates, 91, 92, 118, 206, 312, 325, 326, 331, 336, 473, 481, 487, 520, 534, 563, 583, 584; q., 580 f., 585
"Socrates, Saint," 37, 42, 46
Solomon, 101
Somnium Scipionis, 328, 544
Sophocles, 339
Southey, 1
Spain, 99
Spaniards, 219
Spencer, Theodore, *Shakespeare and the Nature of Man*, 4
Spenser, Edmund, 4, 7, 12, 67, 311, 327, 332, 361, 362, 364, 365, 367, 394, 505, 510, 521, 539, 541, 558, 593, 597, 605, 619, 652; q., 121, 437 f., 495, 499, 525, 541 f., 584, 589, 590
——, *Faerie Queene*, 10, 540, 589, 590; q., 559 f.
——, *An Hymne . . .*, 540
——, *Hymne of Heavenly Love*, 357
——, *An Hymne in Honour of Beautie*, q., 538
——, *Hymnes*, q., 559
——, *Mutability Cantos*, 533; q., 540
——, *Shepheardes Calendar*, 110; q., 432
Spenserians, 540
Spinoza, 28, 85, 267, 275
Sprat, Thomas, q., 48
Stanze per la Giostra, Poliziano, q., 436, 501 f.
Stapleton, Laurence, q., 449
Statesman, Plato, 445
Steel Glass, The, George Gascoigne, q., 93
Stella, 362, 602
Stoic-Cynics, 620
Stoic and Epicurean, Hicks, q., 642
Stoicism, 55, 64, 109, 133, 329, 341, 409, 436, 472, 473, 478, 479, 492, 495, 496, 508, 599, 612, 620, 624, 625, 630, 633, 636, 637, 638, 641, 642, 644, 648, 653, 654, 665, 667
Stoics, 81, 107, 118, 301, 328, 432, 450, 462, 470, 472, 473, 476, 486, 487, 501, 505, 508, 584, 599, 637; Christian, 477
Strong, E. W., 249
Studia humanitatis ac litterarum, Cicero, 35
Suarez, 49, 137
Subtilitate, De, Jerome Cardan, q., 192 f.
Sumer, q., 498
Summa Theologica, St. Thomas Aquinas, 18, 27, 39. *See also Aquinas*
Surrey, 566
——, Earl of, 485
Swiss, 234

Sybaris, 531
Symposium, Plato, 335, 343

Tamara, 386, 495, 575; q., 493 f., 574
Tamburlaine, 22, 368, 373, 383, 384, 447; q., 49, 366, 368, 369
Tamburlaine, Marlowe, q., 367 f.
Tancredi, 579
Tansillo, 354
Tartaglia, 200
Tasso, Torquato, 67, 481, 505, 508, 572, 573, 581, 582, 585, 619· q., 570, 583, 584, 589, 590, 594, 595
——, Aminta, q., 500
——, Jerusalem Delivered, 363, 605; q., 578 ff.
——, Le sette giornate del monde creato, 526
Tauler, John, q., 101
Taylor, Henry Osborn, q., 226, 234
Telesio, Bernardino, 21, 197, 202, 240, 251, 254, 255, 256, 267, 270, 383, 442
——, De natura rerum juxta propria principia, 239
Tempest, Shakespeare, 229; q., 513
Tenaud of Mellynays, Abbé, q., 214
Tertullian, 115, 116, 176; q., 466
Théâtre de la Nature Universelle, Jean Bodin, 197; q., 225, 339
Theism, 48
Thélème, 577
——, Abbey of, 572
Thelemites, 572
Themistius, 399
Theologica Platonica de Immortalitate Animae, Ficino, 327
Theresa, 95
Thersites, 107, 658; q., 611 f.
Thevet, André, Les Singularités de la France Antartique, q., 483
This Great Stage, Robert B. Heilman, 638
Thomalin, 110
Thomas, 215, 275, 436, 488. See Aquinas, and St. Thomas
"Thomas, Saint," 81, 579
Thomists, 65, 98, 99, 299, 414
Thorndike, Lynn, 518; q., 178, 250
Thracians, 213
Thrasymachus, 520
Tiber, 371
Tillyard, E. M., 4
——, The Elizabethan World Picture, 3
Timaeus, Plato, 35, 301, 309, 329
Timber, Jonson, q., 413
Timon, q., 599
Timon of Athens, Shakespeare, 107, 229; q., 599 f., 628
Timotheo, q., 576

Todi, Jacopone da, 94
Tom, Poor, 646
Toralba, 48
Torrid Zone, 218
Touchstone, 511, 512
Tradendis Disciplinis, De, Vives, q., 241 f., 245
Tragedy of Byron, Chapman, q., 21 f., 24 f.
Tragedy of Dido, The, 368
Transitu Hellenismi ad Christianismum, De, Guillaume Budé, 45
Treatie of Humane Learning, Fulke Greville, 90; q., 110, 246 ff.
Treatie of Warres, A, Fulke Greville, 528; q., 431
Treatise of the Soul, Ralegh, q., 388
Trebezonde, 421
Trent, Council of, q., 101 f.
Triboulet, 92
Trinkaus, Adversity's Noblemen, q., 55
Trismegistus, 184, 339, 342
Tristan, 372
Trithemius, 185 f.
Troilus, 606, 611, 630; q., 607, 609, 610
Troilus and Cressida, Shakespeare, 228, 605, 619, 622, 624, 635; q., 606 ff., 611 f.
Trojans, 606, 609
Troy, 607
Turberville, George, q., 563 f.
Turkey, 47
Turks, 421
Tusculan Disputations, Cicero, q., 53
Two Bookes of Constancie, Justus Lipsius, 61; q., 40

Ubaldo, 505
Ulysses, 303, 589, 609, 611, 619; q., 297, 606
Unfortunate Traveller, The, Thomas Nashe, 6 f.; q., 362
Urbino, 343, 558
Ursa Major, 649
Utopia, 452
Utopia, Sir Thomas More, 137; q., 46, 56
Utopians, 38, 41, 47, 49, 56, 57, 60, 149, 223, 475

Valdes, 187, 189, 214; q., 188
Valerio, 567
Valla, Lorenzo, 67, 82, 159, 465, 481, 483; q., 398, 420, 484, 486, 488
——, De Voluptate, q., 472
Vanitie and Uncertaintie of Artes and Sciences, Of the, Cornelius Agrippa, 90, 146
Venus, 154, 501, 540, 560

—— Genatrix, 465, 640
verbo mirifico, De, Reuchlin, 182, 340
Vergil, 35 f., 498, 579, 589
——, *Fourth Eclogue*, 432, 541
Verulam, Lord of, q., 273, 274
Vesalius, 14, 21, 197
——, *De humani corporis fabrica*, q., 198
Vespucci, Amerigo, q., 508
Vicissitudo Rerum, John Norden, 22; q., 528
Villegagnon, 503
Villey, Pierre, 480; q., 216
Virgin Mary, 540
Virginia, 510
Vives, Juan Luis, 21, 84, 86, 197, 200, 202, 208, 238, 246, 251, 267; q., 198, 199, 205 ff., 251, 269
——, *De Anima et Vita*, 198, 216
——, *De Tradendis Disciplinis*, q., 241 f., 245
Volpone, 575, 576, 594; q., 386
Volpone, Jonson, q., 154, 386, 575
Voluptate, De, Valla, q., 472
Von Martin, 55
Vulcan, 264, 265, 535
Vulcanus, 265

Wagner, 187
Watson, Foster, 269
Weird Sisters, 661, 664

Whetstone of Witte, Robert Recorde, q., 195 f.
Whitehead, A. N., 134; q., 136, 325
Whitgift, Archbishop, 19
William, 511
—— of Ockham, 86, 88, 99, 100
Wilton, Jack, q., 485, 566
Winter's Tale, A, Shakespeare, q., 513
Worcester, 601; q., 602
Wordsworth, 1, 16, 19, 410
Works and Days, Hesiod, 498
World and Religion, The, Coluccio Salutati, 55
Would-Bee, Sir Politick, q., 154
Wright, Ernest Hunter, q., 54
——, Thomas, 3
Wycliffe, John, 119

Xavier, Francis, 105

Yorick, 633

Zabarella, 201, 202, 249
Zelmane, 8; q., 561
Zeno, 107, 110, 472
Zenocrate, 368
Zeus, 498
Zohar, 181, 540
Zoroaster, 43, 180, 212, 213, 326, 333, 514, 525, 526
Zwingli, 47, 62